A STRUCTURALIST
THEORY
OF
LOGIC

ARNOLD KOSLOW
The Graduate Center of the City University of New York, and Brooklyn College

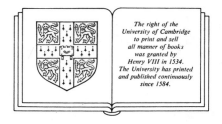

The right of the
University of Cambridge
to print and sell
all manner of books
was granted by
Henry VIII in 1534.
The University has printed
and published continuously
since 1584.

CAMBRIDGE UNIVERSITY PRESS
Cambridge
New York   Port Chester   Melbourne   Sydney

Published by the Press Syndicate of the University of Cambridge
The Pitt Building, Trumpington Street, Cambridge CB2 1RP
40 West 20th Street, New York, NY 10011-4211, USA
10 Stamford Road, Oakleigh, Victoria 3166, Australia

First published 1992

Printed in the United States of America

Library of Congress Cataloging-in-Publication Data
Koslow, Arnold.
A structuralist theory of logic / Arnold Koslow.
p. cm.
Includes bibliographical references and index.
ISBN 0–521–41267–6 (hard)
1. Logic, Symbolic and mathematical. 2. Implication (Logic)
3. Structuralism. I. Title.
BC135.K67 1992
160–dc20   91–23787
                                     CIP

A catalog record for this book is available from the British Library.

ISBN–0–521–41267–6 hardback

For
Richard B. Braithwaite

Hail to Thee
Blithe Spirit,
Dear Teacher, and Lost Friend

Contents

Preface

This study has emerged in much longer form than I had ever intended. In part this happened because I was unsure how familiar or foreign its central ideas might be. I was concerned that enough detail and examples be provided so that the project would come to look more familiar and less foreign than it otherwise might appear initially. That concern, thanks to the encouragement of good friends and patient audiences, now seems to me to have been exaggerated. Still, there is the need to illustrate the power and the range of what are essentially several simple ideas that enable one to provide a uniform picture and some perspective on the enterprise of logic, standard and nonstandard. The work has also taken longer to appear than I would care to quantify. The resources used are far fewer than those normally used in logical studies, and it was not always clear what could be established and what could not. Theorem-proving aside, I must say that it took a long time to gain some understanding of the significance of the results that were obtained. It seems to me that there is still much more that needs to be understood.

Some of these ideas are found in one form or another in the literature, and others are part of the folklore. The intellectual inspiration for much of what follows derives from the seminal writings of G. Gentzen, P. Hertz, and A. Tarski. I have tried to indicate the sources of this project in Part I (Introduction) and to provide some comparison with related ideas. If the ideas seem natural, it is because such authors first gave us fruitful insights and showed how they could be used to shed light on the nature of logical theory. Standing on the shoulders of giants is a precarious perch for anyone, but in this case it is where we find ourselves. It is a happy circumstance, for where would we be without them?

The central idea in this study is the concept of an *implication structure*. These structures consist of a nonempty set, together with an implication relation on it that satisfies certain conditions – essentially those that Gentzen called "structural." The elements of the set are not required to be signs, or to have a syntax or semantics. There is a vast array of examples of such structures. One's favorite syntactic and semantic examples are part of this story, but they are only a part of the story. Part II (Implication Relations) is devoted to explaining and illustrating this abstract or general notion of a structure. Against a background theory of implication structures, Part III (The Logical Operators) is devoted to the problem of characterizing the various logical operators. These operators are taken to be functions that are defined over the implication structures. Each of these operators is described by specifying a condition on the implication relation and requiring the value of the operator to be the set of the weakest members of the structure that satisfy that condition (they will all be equivalent). All the logical operators have this uniform characterization, and each is specified without reference to any of the others. There is an extended discussion of the notion of the extensionality of the logical operators (using results from Part I) that considers the ways in which the extensionality of the various operators are related, and there is also a discussion of the duals of logical operators (using results from Part II). It is shown that classical structures arise exactly when negation and dual negation coincide and that in nonclassical structures the laws of classical negation separate – some hold for negation, and others hold for dual negation. Finally, Part III closes with a type of completeness result in which it is shown, roughly speaking, that those laws that hold in all structures correspond precisely to the theses of intuitionistic logic, whereas those laws that hold in a smaller collection of structures (those called "classical") correspond exactly to those of classical logic. Part IV (The Modal Operators) considers those functions that map an implication structure to itself and proposes a simple condition that specifies when those functions have modal character. We think that most, if not all, of the familiar modal connectives that have been studied in the literature have operators associated with them that have modal character in this sense. Questions of when modals exist on a structure, and their comparative strengths when several exist on a structure, are considered. The nonextensionality of modal operators follows from their characterization. (This is, of course, no news, but it is nice to have it as a result of the characterization of the modal operators.) Moreover, it is shown how a Kripkean-style systematization of the modals can be provided without possible worlds. An accessibility relation is associated with each modal, where that relation is defined over theories of the structure (subsets that are closed under implication). The familiar coordination between types of modal operators and their associated accessibility relations is then recovered. The characterization of modality provides a simple answer to the question of why one should study the modals. Given the centrality of implication in logic, the study of the modal operators is just the study of certain functions under which implication is preserved. Modal theory, in this light, is the continuation of the study of implication itself.

I am grateful for the support and encouragement of many. In that respect I have been truly fortunate. The germ of the idea for this project began in a joint seminar with D. T. Langendoen on the logical operators. We had planned two volumes: one like this volume, and the other to cover the logical particles of English. I continue to learn from him. I owe him much, and I have not given up on that second volume. David Rosenthal attended the first of several seminars, and his critical acumen and enthusiasm have provided constant support. Isaac Levi has, as always, been one on whom I could rely for incisive criticism and a good sense of how broader issues in epistemology and the philosophy of science connect up with this study. Warren Goldfarb read a penultimate draft with the kind of care and attention to lucidity and mathematical elegance that saved me from many errors and infelicities.

My gratitude also to Jody Azzouni, George Boolos, Melvin Fitting, Richard Grandy, Hans Herzberger, Shaughan Lavine, Hugh Mellor, Elliot Mendelson, Rohit Parikh, Charles Parsons, Tim Smiley, Sarah Stebbins, R. S. Tragesser, and the students at the Graduate Center, CUNY, for their unflagging interest in the subject and their enthusiasm.

To the Fellows of Darwin College and King's College, Cambridge, my thanks for providing superb working conditions and for making me feel as if I had never left. Above all, there is my heartfelt indebtedness to Julian and Jennifer. There was, of course, no necessity that this study be written; but they made it possible.

PART I

Background

1

Introduction

This project is an attempt to give an account of the logical operators in a variety of settings, over a broad range of sentential as well as nonsentential items, in a way that does not rely upon any reference to truth conditions, logical form, conditions of assertability, or conditions of a priori knowledge. Furthermore, it does not presuppose that the elements upon which the operators act are distinguished by any special syntactic or semantic features. In short, it is an attempt to explain the character of the logical operators without requiring that the items under consideration be "given" or regimented in some special way, other than that they can enter into certain implication relations with each other. The independence of our account from the thorny questions about the truth conditions of hypotheticals, conjunctions, disjunctions, negations, and the other logical operators can be traced to two sources. Our account of the logical operators is based upon the notion of an *implication structure*. Such a structure consists of a nonempty set together with a finitary relation over it, which we shall call an *implication relation*. As we shall see, implication relations include the usual syntactic and semantic kinds of examples that come to mind. However, implication relations, as we shall describe them, are not restricted to relations of deducibility or logical consequence. In fact, these relations are ubiquitous: Any nonempty set can be provided with an implication relation. Insofar as our account of the logical operators is based upon these structures, no constraints are placed upon the kind of elements on which the operators can act. The second source of independence has to do with the basic question we wish to ask about the logical operators. We shall not be concerned directly with questions about those conditions under which hypotheticals, conjunctions, negations, and the other logical operators are true, or assertable, or those under which they are false or refutable. Instead, we shall focus on a question that appears to be much simpler: What are the conditions under which a certain item is to count as a hypothetical, a conjunction, a negation, or a disjunction, or as existentially or universally quantified? Our question concerns what it is like to be a hypothetical or a conjunction, for example, not what it is for a hypothetical, conjunction, or other logical type of item to be true, false, assertable, or refutable.

In the remainder of this study we shall sharpen this question along the following lines: Suppose that one had an element of some implication structure. What conditions would that element have to satisfy, using only the relevant implication relation of that structure, so that it would count as a hypothetical, a conjunction, a negation, or a disjunction of that structure?[1]

The conditions we shall propose for each of the logical operators do not ensure that there always will be an element of that structure that will meet those conditions, or that there will be only one, if there are any. Thus, for certain implication structures, there may not be a hypothetical with antecedent A and consequent B, for certain elements A and B, of that structure, or there may be several. The conditions describe a class of elements of a structure that count as hypotheticals, or conjunctions, for example, and, in general, it is left open whether these classes, for any given structure, are empty or multiply membered.

The answer we shall give to the question of what it is like for an item to belong to a certain logical category appeals solely to the role that the element plays with respect to the implication relation of the structure under consideration. Because the elements of an implication structure need not be syntactical objects having a special sign design, and they need not have some special semantic value, an explanation of what can count as hypotheticals, disjunctions, negations, and quantified items (existential or universal) can proceed in a way that is free of such restrictions.

On this account, each of the logical operators is characterized relative to an implication relation. The idea is to separate the theory of the operators into two parts or components. The first concerns a theory of implication relations that itself does not rely upon any use of the operators, and the second part develops a theory of each of the operators by describing how each of them acts on implication structures (sets provided with implication relations). The logical operators are then to be thought of as certain types of functions that are defined on each structure and whose values (if they exist) are the hypotheticals, conjunctions, negations, and other logical types of that structure.

Each component of this theory will be studied separately. However, in order to see, in a preliminary way, what the basic ideas are, and to anticipate certain objections, let us turn to a brief description of the conditions that characterize implication relations and a simplified description of one operator: conjunction.

Throughout the remainder of this study, we shall think of an *implication relation* on a set S as any relation "$\Rightarrow$" that satisfies the following conditions:

1. Reflexivity: $A \Rightarrow A$, for all A in S.
2. Projection: $A_1, \ldots, A_n \Rightarrow A_k$, for any $k = 1, \ldots, n$.
3. Simplification: If $A_1, A_1, A_2, \ldots, A_n \Rightarrow B$, then $A_1, \ldots, A_n \Rightarrow B$, for all A_i and B in S.
4. Permutation: If $A_1, A_2, \ldots, A_n \Rightarrow B$, then $A_{f(1)}, A_{f(2)}, \ldots, A_{f(n)} \Rightarrow B$, for any permutation f of $\{1, 2, \ldots, n\}$.
5. Dilution: If $A_1, \ldots, A_n \Rightarrow B$, then $A_1, \ldots, A_n, C \Rightarrow B$, for all A_i, B, and C in S.
6. Cut: If $A_1, \ldots, A_n \Rightarrow B$, and $B, B_1, \ldots, B_m \Rightarrow C$, then $A_1, \ldots, A_n, B_1, \ldots, B_m \Rightarrow C$, for all A_i, B_j, B, and C.

These conditions[2] are closely related to the rules of inference that G. Gentzen and his teacher P. Hertz isolated as a concept worthy of independent study. The historical source and the wide variety of relations that count as implicational will be explored in greater detail in the next chapter. For the present, some brief remarks will have to suffice. Each of these conditions bears a name derived from the corresponding structural rules of inference studied by Gentzen. The first, which usually figures as an axiom in Gentzen's studies, follows from the second condition. Nevertheless, we list it so that the notion of an implication relation will be more perspicuous. The fifth condition is sometimes called "Thinning," but we prefer "Dilution." It follows from Projection, together with Cut.

In a way, these conditions will seem quite familiar, because syntactic notions of deducibility and semantic concepts of logical consequence for a set consisting of the sentences of some first-order language are two natural examples of implication relations. Nevertheless, although there are these familiar, perhaps favorite, examples ready at hand, implication relations are not limited simply to these. In the next chapter we shall see that they are part of the story to be told about implication relations, but they are not the entire story. Perhaps an analogy will clarify the kind of generality that we wish to give to implication relations. Equivalence relations, for example, are singled out from relations in general by the conditions that require them to be binary, symmetric, and transitive. Implication relations are also singled out, only the conditions that do so are different. There are the customary, favorite examples of equivalences, just as there are those for implication. But no one would arbitrarily restrict equivalences to one or two well-known examples, and the situation is similar for implications. Equivalence relations have a generality: There is no restriction on the kinds of sets that can possess equivalence relations; every set has at least one, and generally several. Some of them may be more interesting than others; some may be more worthy of study. Implication relations are no different. They have the same kind of generality:[3] Every nonempty set has at least one such relation, and generally several. And, as with equivalences, some will have greater mathematical, logical, scientific, or philosophical interest than others.

Each of the logical operators will be characterized as a certain kind of function that acts or operates upon each of the implication structures. The conjunction operator, for example, will, given any implication structure, determine the set of those items in that structure that count as conjunctions.

It will be helpful to consider a simplified account of the conjunction operator in order to see how an abstract view of conjunction, in particular, can be based upon the concept of an implication structure. Let us denote by $I = \langle S, \Rightarrow \rangle$ an implication structure with set S and implication relation "$\Rightarrow$". The conjunction operator C acts on the implication structure I in the following way. To any elements A and B that belong to the set S, C assigns a subset $C_{\Rightarrow}(A, B)$ of S whose members (if they exist) satisfy the following conditions [we shall use "$C_{\Rightarrow}(A, B)$" to indicate conjunctions – that is, members of S, as well as the set of such members, since they are all equivalent with respect to "$\Rightarrow$"]:[4]

C_1. $C_{\Rightarrow}(A, B) \Rightarrow A$, and $C_{\Rightarrow}(A, B) \Rightarrow B$, and

C_2. $C_{\Rightarrow}(A, B)$ is the weakest member of S that satisfies the condition C_1. That is, for any T contained in S, if $T \Rightarrow A$, and $T \Rightarrow B$, then $T \Rightarrow C_{\Rightarrow}(A, B)$.

Consequently, a conjunction of A and B in the structure I will imply A, as well as B, and it will be weaker than any member of S that implies A as well as B.

Several things are now evident from this characterization of the conjunction operator. For one, the members of S need not be syntactical objects. We do not assume, for example, that in order for C to be a conjunction of A and B, it must have some special sign – say "&" – embedded in it, either prefixed or infixed. To be a conjunction, C plays a role with respect to implication, but it does not have to have a certain shape or sign-design to do so. More generally, it need not have A and B as parts of it, discriminable or not. As we shall see, the relaxation of the requirement that conjunction and the other logical operators act upon, and yield, syntactical objects is a key difference between this program for the operators and the programs of G. Gentzen and N. Belnap, Jr. The generality of this way of viewing conjunction and the other operators has certain advantagaes. There are cases where it makes no sense to think of a special sign for conjunction as embedded in the item that is a conjunction. For example, there are implication structures in which S is a set of sets, and implication is just set inclusion. In such a setting, the conjunction of two sets A and B is (if it exists) some set $C(A, B)$ such that

1. $C(A, B) \subseteq A$, and $C(A, B) \subseteq B$, and
2. if T is any set of S, then if $T \subseteq A$ and $T \subseteq B$, then $T \subseteq C(A, B)$.

Thus, the conjunction of two sets A and B is the intersection of A and B. This is, of course, well known. But the perspective is different. Set-theoretical intersection usually is thought of as analogous to conjunction. On this account, however, set intersection is not analogous to conjunction; it is conjunction, when the implication structure is the one that was described. It would be incoherent to think that a set that is the conjunction of two others has some conjunction sign embedded in it. Signs, connectives, or any other type of expression are not linguistic parts of abstract items such as sets. Moreover, certain items are thought of as conjunctions, even though a sign for conjunction is absent. The sentence "This is a red square" is plausibly thought of as a conjunction. On our account of conjunction, this is possible if certain implication relations hold between "This is a red square" and some other sentences – perhaps "This is red" and "This is square" – regardless of whether the word "and" or a suitable equivalent occurs in it. Furthermore, there are sentences with "and" in them that are not conjunctions. A good candidate would be "Laugh and the world laughs with you." One moral to be drawn from these kinds of examples is that it is not the occurrence of "and" in the right places that makes the sentence a conjunction. On our account, what is conclusive is the sentence's implicational role with respect to other sentences.

Another advantage of this characterization of the conjunction operator arises from the fact that no consideration of truth values entered into its description. We did not describe the conjunction of A with B as some C that was true if and only if both A and B were true. It is therefore possible to regard certain items as conjoined even if they are not truth-bearers. In fact, we have already done so in the preceding example, where we considered the conjunction of sets. There are other

applications of interest that are possible, once one relaxes the requirement that the logical operators can act only on syntactical objects, or
can act only on items that can be said to have a truth value. It is often
assumed that theories, whether in mathematical logic or in the physical
sciences, can best be construed as systems, or theories in Tarski's sense:
They are sets of sentences that are closed under some consequence
relation. It would be convenient to be able to speak of the conjunction
(or the disjunction) of such theories, but the usual requirement that
conjunction is an operation appropriate only to sentences stands as
an obstacle. On our account, however, the nonsentential character of
Tarskian theories is no impediment to considering their conjunction.[5]

In a similar vein, it would be incoherent to think of certain names as
conjunctions of others, given that names are not truth-bearers. However, in the sentence "John and Mary are friends," the noun phrase
"John and Mary" is conjunctive. The explanation of the conjunctive
character of the noun phrase, for some sentences like "John and Mary
are flautists," consists in noting that it is equivalent to the conjunction of
the sentences "John is a flautist" and "Mary is a flautist." But "friends"
is not like "flautists" in this regard. One could think of the noun phrase
as conjunctive simply because there is an occurrence of the word "and"
in it. But this is no more plausible an explanation here than it is in the
case where "and" occurs between sentences. The occurrence of "and"
does not automatically guarantee that the result is a conjunction, and an
appeal to truth conditions is beside the point. On our account, however,
it makes sense to ask whether there are conjunctions of names, provided
that a set of names is supplied with an implication relation so as to form
an implication structure. Given such a structure, we can inquire into
what the logical operator of conjunction is, in this particular setting. Of
course, it might be objected that it no more makes sense to think of
implication relations between names than to think of the conjunction
of names. However, as we have already noted, there is no need to think
of implication relations as restricted to syntactical objects or truth-
bearers. It is possible, therefore, to inquire into the conditions under
which names can be used to form conjunctions, and whether it is
possible for a name to be a negation of some other name.[6]

Hypothetical interrogatives provide another example of the kind of
application that is available on a general account of the logical operators. The sentence "If you are free, will you marry me?" is not only an
interrogative, but it seems plausible that it is hypothetical as well. If we
were restricted in an account of the hypotheticals to only those items

that are truth-bearers, then there can be no hypothetical with a declarative sentence as the antecedent and an interrogative as consequent. On our account of the hypothetical operator, the fact that interrogatives do not have truth values is no obstacle in accounting for the hypothetical character of this kind of sentence.[7]

Thus far we have sketched an account of the conjunction operator to illustrate how a theory of the logical operators can be based upon a theory of implication relations. The intention is to convey, with the example of conjunction, some rough idea of the more detailed account of conjunction and the other logical operators that follows.

The logical operators can act in a broad variety of settings, sentential and otherwise. In particular, the actions of the operators on structures of sets, names, and interrogatives, to cite just some nonstandard examples, are mentioned because the items in these cases fail in an obvious way to be syntactical or fail to be truth-bearers. However, although our account of the logical operators is not restricted to the objects or expressions that have a special syntax, or have a special semantic value, nevertheless it is applicable to those sorts of items as well, provided that they can be considered as the elements of an implication structure. As we shall see, if one considers a structure consisting of the set of well-formed formulas of, say, some standard first-order language, together with an implication relation – either the usual deducibility relation or some semantic relation of logical consequence – then it is possible to ask whether the operator that assigns "p & q," formed with the aid of the connective "&" (which, for the sake of the example, we assume to be part of the logical vocabulary of the first-order language under consideration), is a conjunction operator in our sense. The answer is that the operator corresponding to the connective "&" is a conjunction operator, provided that the rules governing its use are the standard Gentzen-style "Introduction" and "Elimination" rules for "&." This is, of course, no news. And that is as it should be. Although our concept of conjunction covers many more situations than those that concern "&" in a standard first-order logic, it is important that there be agreement with the standard cases, even though these are only some of the cases that conjunction covers. The case is no different for the operators that correspond to the other connectives, standardly described.

Thus we keep touch with the standard views, but the perspective on the customary cases is very different from the usual one. The logical operators, as we think of them, are applicable to a wide-ranging variety of structures, of which the first-order case is an important example, but an example nonetheless, and not the whole story.

Before we turn to some closing general remarks that relate our account to two well-known studies that develop two-stage theories of the logical connectives (rather than operators), it is worth noting that two questions arise in a natural manner once we think of the operators as special functions that act on implication structures. The first question concerns the *stability* of the logical operators. The stability of an operator can be thought of as a problem raised by the situation in which the same elements may belong to different implication structures. Suppose that in one implication structure, I, it turns out that A is a conjunction of B and C. In another implication structure, I', which contains those three elements, will A still be a conjunction of B and C? There is a simple positive answer to this question about the stability of conjunction, as well as the other logical operators, that gives a guarantee of stability when one passes from one implication structure to another that is a conservative extension of it (where I' is a conservative extension of I if and only if the elements of I stand in an implication relation if and only if they also do so in I'). This is an important assurance, especially for a theory of the operators such as ours, which makes them relative to implication relations. The conjunction of elements in a structure continues to be their conjunction in any conservative extension of it (and similarly for the other logical operators).[8]

The second question that naturally arises for the logical operators might be called the problem of their *distinctness*. In first-order languages, for example, a disjunction of items is syntactically different from, say, their conjunction, even though for certain items they might be logically equivalent. Given the general character of implication structures, we do not have at hand such a device for distinguishing the operators from each other. Let us say that two operators are *distinct* (on an implication structure I) if and only if for some items in the structure the two yield nonequivalent members of the structure. Thus, distinct operators might sometimes yield equivalent results, but they do not always do so. The question of their distinctness arises once we have various descriptions of the operators in place.

Definition 1.1. An implication structure $I = \langle S, \Longrightarrow \rangle$ is *trivial* if and only if its members are equivalent to each other.

Then the following will be shown: Any two logical operators are distinct on an implication structure if and only if the structure is not *trivial*.

Consequently, any two logical operators are distinct in an implication structure if and only if there are at least two nonequivalent members in it. Even though the class of disjunctions and the class of conjunctions may overlap in a given structure, they cannot be identical without the entire structure degenerating into one element and its equivalents.

2

The program and its roots

Thus far we have suggested that our account of the logical operators is, in broad outline, a two-component theory. One component is a theory of implication structures consisting of a number of conditions that, taken together, characterize implication relations. Implication structures, which the first component studies, are sets together with implication relations defined over them. The second component consists in descriptions of the various logical operators with the aid of implication relations. The operators are taken to be functions that to any given implication structure assign members (or sets of members) of that structure.[1]

There are two other programs that may be familiar to the reader, that of G. Gentzen and P. Hertz, on the one hand, and that of N. Belnap, Jr., on the other. Each of them, however, is different in scope and aim from the program described here.

2.1 The Gentzen–Hertz program

The allusion to a functional account of the logical operators, to their roles with respect to implication relations, will strike a familiar note for those who have studied the logical insights of Gentzen and Hertz. It was Gentzen (1933) who developed and extended the work of his teacher Hertz (1922, 1923, 1929) and adumbrated the view that the logical *connectives* were to be understood by their roles in inference (Gentzen, 1934). The Gentzen–Hertz insight, as it developed, isolated those aspects of inference against which the "meanings" of various logical connectives were to be explained or understood: There was a division of labor. Those features of inference that formed the background theory for the connectives should not themselves appeal or refer to any of the connectives. They ought to be sufficiently rich to convey the idea of what could be said about inference alone, without appealing to the structure of the items that were to be related by inference. The theory was to consist, as Gentzen (1934) said, of "structural" rules of inference. Against the background theory of inference, additional rules, called "logical rules," were set forth, explaining each of the connectives. The structural rules provided what could be said about inference in general, and they were distinguished by Gentzen (1934) from the logical rules that jointly involve inference and the various connectives.

The Gentzen–Hertz program is widely shared, and it is one to which this study owes much. This study bears an overall similarity to it that is reflected in our separation of an account of the various logical operators from a general structural theory of implication. Here, each operator is studied independently of the others and is explained relative to the background theory of implication. So we have here a two-tier theory: implication as the basis, against which there is the account of the operators.

Although our program has the same overall shape as that of Gentzen–Hertz, it differs on each of the components. The particular theory of implication structures that we shall use as a basis for the operators has close affinities with the structural rules of Gentzen, although it is more abstract and algebraic. Nevertheless, we hasten to add that the root idea for our more general theory of implication relations can be found in the work of Hertz (1922, 1923, 1929), as well as in Gentzen's first paper (1933), which set out to solve Hertz's problem as it was formulated in Hertz's 1929 paper.[2]

Thus, there is a fairly direct connection between the concept of an implication relation in this study and the early ideas of Gentzen and Hertz. The differences, however, between the Gentzen-style second component concerning the logical connectives and our account of the logical operators are more difficult to compare directly, although here, too, there are strong general affinities.

The earliest paper of Gentzen lays bare the notion of a structural rule of inference (just Dilution and Cut). However, there is no account in it of the logical connectives (and certainly none for the operators). That absence was not an oversight, but simply a reflection of the fact that the paper was designed to solve a problem set by Hertz. The problem was to determine under very general conditions when there is an axiomatization of a system of sentences* (expressions of the form $A_1, \ldots, A_n \to^* B$) by means of an independent subsystem. Hertz intended the inquiry to be very general, and as a result he deliberately treated the sentences* as composed of elements that were not assumed to have any special logical form. The logical complexity of the elements was deliberately omitted, for that would have delimited the scope of generality. Since there was to be no appeal to the logical complexity of the elements of the system, small wonder that no use was made of rules that governed the logical connectives. In his succeeding papers, Gentzen added to those rules that he called "structural," and he also set forth a different class of rules for the logical connectives, which he called "logical rules." As is characteristic of Gentzen's approach, the logical rules come in pairs – two to a connective. Each pair consists of an "Introduction" rule and an "Elimination" rule for the logical connective. Gentzen seems to have thought of the Introduction rules of each pair as providing "as it were" the meaning or "definition" of the connective, though he left these ideas largely unexplained. The Elimination rule in each case was supposed to draw upon, or be a consequence of, what was already understood by means of the corresponding Introduction rule.[3]

Another way of stating the difference is that Gentzen, at least in the 1933 paper, suggested an abstract way of understanding implication. In succeeding papers, when he characterized the various logical connectives, he limited his discussion to those special structures that have linguistic expressions as their elements. Consequently, although the logical connectives were explained with the aid of implication, the abstract or general character of the concept of implication was not brought to bear upon the corresponding theory of the logical operators. The latter were considered only for the special structures whose elements were syntactic. Thus, although the theory of the connectives was based on implication, as is our theory of the logical operators, it was not as abstract or general a theory as the concept of implication upon which it rested. On our theory, parity is restored, and the account of the operators is as abstract as the theory of implication upon which it rests. Implication structures that contain syntactic elements or specially designed signs or connectives embedded in them are special cases for which the question of the meanings of the connective signs may have significance, but in general this will not be so.

Although it is difficult to have a direct comparison between the two accounts, because this account is more general or abstract than the one that Gentzen considered, nevertheless a comparison is still possible, at least over the class of those implication structures that correspond to the first-order theories that Gentzen did consider. The matter is worth considering in a bit more detail, because an interesting difference emerges in this special case over the roles of Introduction and Elimination rules in the two accounts of the operators.

According to Gentzen, the Introduction and Elimination rules for, say, conjunction ("&") convey the meaning of that connective. Indeed, he suggested, it is just the Introduction rule that does this. Gentzen has a pair of rules for "&," and we have a characterization, given earlier, of what sort of items of the structure count as conjunctions. On our account, an element A of a structure is a conjunction of two others, B and C, if it implies each of them and is implied by any element that implies B as well as C.

Now, Gentzen's Introduction and Elimination rules for "&" state, respectively, that

$$I\ \&:\quad \frac{p \qquad q}{p\ \&\ q} \qquad\qquad E\ \&\ (\text{two parts}):\quad \frac{p\ \&\ q}{p} \qquad \frac{p\ \&\ q}{q}$$

If we read these rules as saying that an implication relation "$\Rightarrow$" relates p and q to $p\ \&\ q$ (i.e., $p, q \Rightarrow p\ \&\ q$), and the same implication relation relates $p\ \&\ q$ to p and also to q (i.e., $p\ \&\ q \Rightarrow p$, and $p\ \&\ q \Rightarrow q$), then we might call these the Introduction and Elimination *conditions* for conjunction that correspond to Gentzen's two rules for "&." The Introduction and Elimination conditions give us the following assurances: The two parts of the Elimination condition tell us that there is some member of the implication structure that implies each of p and q – namely, $p\ \&\ q$. But is $p\ \&\ q$ a conjunction of p and q according to our account of that operator? There is an additional condition that must be satisfied: If any element of the structure implies p as well as q, then it implies $p\ \&\ q$. However, the condition that corresponds to Gentzen's Introduction rule for "&" assures us, in this special situation, that $p\ \&\ q$ is implied by any element u of the structure for which $u \Rightarrow p$ and $u \Rightarrow q$, for if the latter two statements are granted, and we have p, $q \Rightarrow p\ \&\ q$, then the Cut condition for implication relations ensures that $u \Rightarrow p\ \&\ q$. Thus, for any p and q in the implication structure, the conditions on implication that correspond to Gentzen's Introduction and Elimination rules guarantee that "$p\ \&\ q$" is a conjunction of p with q according to our account.

If we think of an operator that assigns the sentence "$p\ \&\ q$" to the pair of sentences (p, q), then the preceding argument shows that the operator that corresponds to the logical connective "&" is the conjunction operator on this particular structure.[4]

We have a uniform characterization of all the logical operators in terms of a characteristic condition together with a clause that "minimizes" that condition. In the special case of a first-order language with an appropriate implication relation on it, the characteristic condition for the logical operator corresponds to Gentzen's Elimination rule for the corresponding logical connective, and his Introduction rule for that connective corresponds to the "minimizing" condition for the associated operator. We can therefore regard the two conditions that characterize each of the logical operators as a generalization of Gentzen's Introduction and Elimination rules that is applicable in any implication structure.

Once the descriptions of the familiar logical operators are in place, another interesting feature of this account will become evident: The characteristic condition that is used in the description of each of the operators is not just any condition expressed with the aid of the implication relation. Each of the characteristic conditions is what we shall call a *filter condition*. A condition $C(A)$ is a *filter condition* on an implication structure if and only if whenever $C(A)$ holds, and $B \Rightarrow A$, then $C(B)$ holds as well. Thus, filter conditions are closed "from above." On our account, all of the familiar logical operators "minimize" filter conditions. Indeed, we think that that is no accident and that it is worth pursuing the idea that the logical operators on implications structures are precisely those functions that are specified by two clauses: one that specifies some filter condition, and one that requires that the values of the operator be the weakest members of the structure (if they exist) that satisfy that condition.

It might be helpful to look at the hypotheticals as a second example of how the Gentzen Introduction and Elimination rules for connectives (or their corresponding conditions) guarantee the nonemptiness of certain logical categories. The case for hypotheticals is no different from that for conjunctions or any of the other logical operators. Although a fuller account of the hypothetical as a logical operator is reserved for a later chapter, it will be useful if we anticipate that discussion with a few observations.

Let us suppose that I is an implication structure. On our account, the hypothetical operator H acts on the structure in the following manner: For any elements A and B in the structure, $H(A, B)$ is the hypothetical with antecedent A and consequent B, if and only if the following conditions are satisfied:

H_1. $A, H(A, B) \Rightarrow B$, and
H_2. $H(A, B)$ is the weakest member (implicationally) of the implication structure to satisfy H_1. That is, if T is any member of the implication structure such that $A, T \Rightarrow B$, then $T \Rightarrow H(A, B)$.[5]

Now there is no difficulty in motivating the first condition, since it corresponds to the usual rule of modus ponens, only in a general setting. The second condition corresponds to what is usually known as the deduction theorem, when the context is some standard logical language, and the implication relation is taken to be a deducibility relation. There is no assurance that in general there is a hypothetical with antecedent A and consequent B for arbitrary members of the structure.

Is there any assurance of the existence of hypotheticals on our account in the special case in which the structure is the set of sentences of some formulation of first-order logic, and the implication relation is a deducibility relation? The answer in this case is that the expression "$p \supset q$" is indeed what the hypothetical operator assigns to the pair (p, q). In this special case a positive answer can be given that appeals to Gentzen's Introduction and Elimination rules (or the corresponding conditions) for the connective "$\supset$."[6]

Gentzen's Elimination rule for "$\supset$" $(p, p \supset q / q)$ ensures that "$p \supset q$" satisfies the condition H_1 for hypotheticals, and his Introduction rule ensures that the second condition H_2 is satisfied, since it ensures that if $r, p / q$, then $r / (p \supset q)$.[7] Thus, Gentzen's Introduction and Elimination rules, or the conditions corresponding to them, guarantee that to any p and q in the structure, the hypothetical operator H assigns the value "$p \supset q$."

Gentzen's program uses a pairing of rules, Introduction and Elimination, for each logical connective. When an implication structure consists of the sentences of a first-order language (containing various connectives as part of its logical vocabulary), then the role of these two kinds of rules, taken together, highlights a difference between his program and our program.

On our account of the operators, the Gentzen rules or conditions have an existential character: They guarantee that certain logical categories like conjunctions and hypotheticals are, in this special structure, nonempty. Another way of stating the matter is this: In the structure just considered, let C be a function that assigns the expression "$p \& q$" to every pair (p, q), and let H be the function that assigns "$p \supset q$" to every pair (p, q). We shall say that C and H are the operators that correspond to the connectives "$\&$" and "$\supset$," respectively. The Introduction and Elimination conditions for "$\&$" and "$\supset$," respectively, not only show that the operators C and H that correspond to the connectives "$\&$" and "$\supset$" are just the conjunction and the hypothetical operators over this particular implication structure; they also show that C and H are nonempty. The situation is the same for all the other logical operators as well.

There is certainly no conflict in having the Introduction and Elimination rules play the role that they do in the construction of deductive patterns, with their corresponding conditions guaranteeing that certain logical categories in some implication structures are nonempty. Neither

is there any conflict between our existential claim and Gentzen's claim
that these rules provide a meaning or sense for the various connectives.
The point worth noting is that it is unnecessary to appeal to the thesis
that the rules provide meanings in order to show, for example, that the
logical operator corresponding to the connective "&" is the conjunction
operator in a special setting.

3

Introduction and Elimination conditions
in a general setting*

Although the particular Introduction and Elimination rules for each connective are easily understood, the overall characterization is not easy to comprehend, nor is the general connection that each has to the other. Gentzen thought (1) that the Introduction rules provided a "definition" of the connectives, (2) that they also provided a sense of those connectives, (3) that it should be possible to display the E-inferences as unique functions of their corresponding I-inferences, and (4) that "in the final analysis" the Elimination rules were consequences of the corresponding Introduction rules. What he said about the character of each type of rule and their connections with one another is very much worth quoting in full:

To every logical symbol &, $\vee$, $\forall$, $\exists$, $\supset$, $\neg$, belongs precisely one inference figure which "introduces" the symbol – as the terminal symbol of a formula – and one which 'eliminates' it. The fact that the inference figures &-E and $\vee$-I each have two forms constitutes a trivial, purely external deviation and is of no interest. The introductions represent, as it were, the 'definitions' of the symbols concerned, and the eliminations are no more, in the final analysis, than the consequences of these definitions. This fact may be expressed as follows: in eliminating a symbol we are dealing 'only in the sense afforded it by the introduction of that symbol'. An example may clarify that is meant: We were able to introduce the formula $\mathscr{A} \supset \mathscr{B}$ when there existed a derivation of $\mathscr{B}$ from the assumption formula $\mathscr{A}$. If we then wished to use that formula by eliminating the $\supset$-symbol (we could of course, also use it to form longer formulae, e.g., $\mathscr{A} \supset \mathscr{B} \vee \mathscr{C}$, $\vee$-I), we could do this precisely by inferring $\mathscr{B}$ directly, once $\mathscr{A}$ has been proved, for what $\mathscr{A} \supset \mathscr{B}$ attests is just the existence of a derivation of $\mathscr{B}$ from $\mathscr{A}$. Note that in saying this we need not go into the 'informal sense' of the $\supset$-symbol.

By making these ideas more precise it should be possible to display the E-inferences as unique functions of their corresponding I-inferences, on the basis of certain requirements.[1]

Gentzen seems not to have elaborated upon these ideas, but there have been several studies inspired by his brief remarks.[2] It would seem that our program for the logical operators would not have much to say about these rather intriguing but dark passages from Gentzen. The reason is

---

simply that the logical operators, on our account, are so characterized as to be applicable to arbitrary implication structures and do not seem to have that much to say about any particular implication structure as such. It is an account of the operators that is supposed to hold whether or not there are any connectives present. Thus, how could one expect the conjunction operator, for example, to tell us much about a connective like "&"? In contrast, Gentzen's Introduction and Elimination rules focus on various connectives, and it might appear that what he has to say about their character and the ways in which they relate to one another depends crucially upon the presence of connectives. Indeed, in the form in which Gentzen thought of them, they are rules governing the use of connectives. How could we think of them apart from such logical signs?

Nevertheless, we think that our account of the logical operators does bear upon Gentzen's rules. Just as first-order languages with deducibility relations on them are special cases of implication structures, so, too, the distinction between Gentzen's Introduction and Elimination rules is a special case of a more general distinction. This more general distinction does not concern the use of specific connectives, but it may still be of some interest. In this chapter we shall describe a way in which a generalized notion of Introduction and Elimination conditions for the logical operators can be developed, even in the absence of connectives. Moreover, on this general account, almost all of the relations between the Introduction and Elimination rules at which Gentzen hinted can be directly established without appealing to a special theory of the meanings of the logical connectives.

We have already described the conjunction operator as the operator that, given any A and B of any implication structure, will pick out the set of conjunctions $C(A, B)$ as the weakest members of the structure that imply A as well as B. More schematically, there is a condition $\Phi(A, B, C)$ such that C is a conjunction of A and B in the implication structure $I = \langle S, \Rightarrow \rangle$ if and only if

1. $\Phi(A, B, C)$, and
2. for any T in S, if $\Phi(A, B, T)$, then $T \Rightarrow C$.

Conditions 1 and 2 are just restatements of the first and second conditions on the conjunction operator, where the condition $\Phi(A, B, C)$ is taken as the condition that T implies A and T implies B. Thus, we have a twofold schema consisting of (1) a condition expressed with the aid of implication and (2) a requirement that the operator under discussion yield exactly (the set of) those elements of the structure that are the weakest of those that satisfy the condition.

The schema for conjunction is not special. The same schema holds for all the other logical operators, using an appropriate condition that corresponds to each operator. To any logical operator φ there corresponds a condition Φ such that the operator assigns to each pair (if the operator acts on pairs) the set of all items in the structure that are the weakest members of all those that satisfy the condition. That is (suppressing reference to the arguments of the operator), we have the schema

(G) 1. $\Phi(T)$, and
        2. if $\Phi(A)$, then $A \Rightarrow T$,

and the operator φ has the value T, or, officially, the set of such T's (they are all equivalent).

We shall refer to this general schema as "the way of the weakest," and we shall say more about this schema later. But for the present, let us assume that this is a basic pattern that characterizes each of the logical operators. With one additional modification, the way is now open for a general perspective on the Introduction and Elimination rules for the connectives as an example of a more general phenomenon.

We have noted that the two clauses, when we consider the *connectives*, correspond to the Elimination and Introduction rules, respectively, that Gentzen provided for them. The modification we have in mind concerns the second condition, which tells us that the item that the operator assigns is always the weakest member of a certain set. The first condition, which tells us within which set we take the weakest, will be left unchanged. The reason for the modification of the second condition has to do with the observation by Gentzen that in the Elimination rules, the sign to be eliminated occurs in the antecedent position.

In the particular case of conjunction, for example, the first condition is given by

(I) 1. $C(T)$: $T \Rightarrow A$, and $T \Rightarrow B$, and the second is given by
        2. if $C(E)$, then $E \Rightarrow T$.

Thus, if T^* implies T, and $C(T)$, then, by Cut, we obtain the result that T^* implies A as well as B. Consequently, $C(T^*)$. The first condition is a filter condition, and similarly for the conditions used for the other logical operators.

Now the modification that we have in mind is this: In the second condition, strengthen the "if" to "if and only if," to obtain the strengthened schema (I'):

(I') 1'. $C(T)$ [the same as condition 1 in (I)].
       2'. $C(E)$ if and only if $E \Rightarrow T$.

Note that since $T \Rightarrow T$ in all implication structures, 1' is a consequence of 2'. We shall retain both, in order to keep the parallelism with Gentzen's two types of rules.

   This is a plausible modification for the logical operators once we note that for the logical operators, the condition $C(A)$ is always a filter condition, and that if $C(A)$ is a filter condition, then (I) and (I') are equivalent. The reason is straightforward: Clearly, if (I') holds, then so too does (I), since conditions 1 and 1' are the same, and 2' implies 2. Conversely, suppose conditions 1 and 2, and suppose that $C(A)$ is a filter condition. Conditions 1 and 1' are identical. Moreover, given condition 2, we have only to show that for any E, if $E \Rightarrow T$, then $C(E)$, to obtain 2'. Suppose that $E \Rightarrow T$. Then from $C(T)$, and the assumption that C is a filter condition, $C(E)$.

   Thus, (I) and (I') are equivalent for any filter condition. In fact, it is also true that any condition C that is used in the strengthened schema (I') has to be a filter condition.

   In the remainder of this study we shall use schemata of the form (I). One reason for doing so is that despite the equivalence of the two schemata, it is more readily evident that conditions like 2 correspond to Gentzen's Introduction rules.[3]

   Nevertheless, there is something to be gained by using the biconditional version 2' rather than the conditional version 2. With its aid we can show that much of what Gentzen wanted to say about the differences between Introduction and Elimination rules (or conditions) turns out to be correct, leaving not as dark a series of claims as one might think.

   For a logical operator φ and its characteristic condition Φ, we had the general schema (G). Let us call the equivalent schema, with the second condition as a biconditional, the *generalized Gentzen schema* (GG). We shall need a bit more terminology. Where φ is a logical operator with characteristic condition Φ, let us call the first condition $\Phi(T)$ the *Elimination condition for* φ, and the second condition the *generalized Introduction condition for* φ. That is,

(GG) 1. $\Phi(T)$, and
       2. for all E (in S), $\Phi(E)$ if and only if $E \Rightarrow T$

(where φ is the logical operator under discussion). Assuming, for example, that φ acts on pairs (A, B) of members of S, φ assigns to (A, B) the set of all T's such that

1. $\Phi(A, B, T)$, and
2. $\Phi(A, B, E)$ if and only if $E \Rightarrow T$ for all E.

In addition, we shall say that the condition $\Phi(A, B, T)$ is the *Elimination condition for the operator* φ, and if $\Phi(A, B, R)$ holds for some R [$\Phi(R)$ holds for some R in S], then we shall say that Φ *eliminates the element R.*

Similarly, we shall say that the condition [$\Phi(E)$ if and only if $E \Rightarrow T$] (for all E in S) is the *Introduction condition for the operator* φ, and if [$\Phi(E)$ if and only if $E \Rightarrow R$] (for all E in S) holds for some R in S, then we shall say that *R is introduced by the Introduction condition for the operator* φ.

It is more perspicuous to write (GG) as follows: For any logical operator φ (say, of two variables), there are, for the set of its values T, Elimination conditions E_φ and Introduction conditions I_φ, such that

(GG) 1. $E_\varphi(T)$ (Elimination condition), i.e., $\Phi(A, B, T)$, and
   2. $I_\varphi(T)$ (Introduction condition), i.e.,
      $E_\varphi(R)$ if and only if $R \Rightarrow T$ for all R.

Gentzen remarked that his Introduction rules were "as it were" "definitions," that they provided a sense for the various connectives, that it should be possible to display the E-inferences as unique functions of their corresponding I-inferences, and that "in the final analysis" the Elimination rules are consequences of the corresponding Introduction rules.

These ideas that Gentzen had about the relation between the two kinds of rules seem to hold in a simple manner between the corresponding (generalized) Introduction and Elimination conditions. In this more generalized form, using operators rather than connectives, and conditions on implication relations rather than rules of inference, each of his views has a convincing argument for it. We turn next to those intriguing observations of Gentzen.

3.1 Introduction conditions as "definitions"

Are the Introduction conditions definitional? Well, [$E_\varphi(R)$ if and only if $R \Rightarrow T$ (for all R in S)] does have the form of a generalized biconditional. Moreover, if we think of $I_\varphi(R)$ as introducing the element R of the structure, then if $I_\varphi(R)$ introduces the element R as well as the element

R^*, it follows that R and R^* are equivalent. That is, if $I_\varphi(R)$ and $I_\varphi(R^*)$, then $R \Longleftrightarrow R^*$. Consequently, $I_\varphi(R)$ is like an *implicit definition*. The reason is that if $I_\varphi(R)$ and $I_\varphi(R^*)$, then $E_\varphi(U)$ if and only if $U \Longrightarrow R$, and $E_\varphi(U)$ if and only if $U \Longrightarrow R^*$, for all U in S. Therefore, $U \Longrightarrow R$ if and only if $U \Longrightarrow R^*$, for all U in S. Since $R \Longrightarrow R$ and $R^* \Longrightarrow R^*$, it follows that $R \Longleftrightarrow R^*$.

Gentzen thought that an analysis should show how to display the E-inferences as unique functions of their corresponding I-inferences, and he believed that the Elimination rules were consequences of their corresponding Introduction rules (Gentzen, 1934, pp. 80–1).

3.2 Elimination conditions as uniquely determined by Introduction conditions

The generalized E-conditions are, in the following sense, unique functions of their corresponding I-conditions: The Introduction conditions I_φ have no slack with respect to Elimination conditions E_φ, for if there were another Elimination condition for the operator, say E_φ^*, such that $I_\varphi(R)$ was given by $E_\varphi(U) \leftrightarrow U \Longrightarrow R$ (for all U), as well as by $E_\varphi^*(U) \leftrightarrow U \Longrightarrow R$ (for all U), then it would follow that $E_\varphi(U) \leftrightarrow E_\varphi^*(U)$ for all U in S. Thus, Introduction conditions implicitly define their associated Elimination conditions. The elimination conditions are determined up to coextensionality by their associated Introduction conditions.[4]

We turn now to what is perhaps the most puzzling of Gentzen's observations about Introduction and Elimination rules: "in the final analysis," he says, "the Elimination rules are consequences of the corresponding Introduction rules." When we look at the situation for generalized Introduction and Elimination conditions, the result is obvious:

3.3 Elimination conditions as consequences of their corresponding Introduction conditions

Let φ be a logical operator, and let its Elimination condition be $E_\varphi(T)$ and its Introduction condition be $I_\varphi(T)$; that is, $E_\varphi(U)$ if and only if $U \Longrightarrow T$. Now suppose that I_φ holds of some item, say T. So $I_\varphi(T)$. Therefore, $E_\varphi(U)$ if and only if $U \Longrightarrow T$ for all U in S. Since $T \Longrightarrow T$, we conclude that $E_\varphi(T)$ if and only if $T \Longrightarrow T$. But $T \Longrightarrow T$ holds in any implication structure. Consequently, $E_\varphi(T)$.

Thus, for any T in the implication structure, if $I_\varphi(T)$, then $E_\varphi(T)$. And this shows that E_φ is a consequence of I_φ, for it tells us that T can be eliminated by the E_φ condition, if it is introduced by the I_φ condition.

Therefore, Gentzen's observation that "in eliminating a symbol, we may use the formula with whose terminal symbol we are dealing only in the sense afforded it by the introduction of that symbol" can be taken in two ways, one weaker than the other. The weaker of the two simply requires that in order for an element T to be eliminated by the condition E_φ [i.e., for $E_\varphi(T)$ to hold], it is sufficient that T be introduced by I_φ [i.e., that $I_\varphi(T)$ hold]. No appeal to informal meanings is necessary. Only this much must be understood about T: that $I_\varphi(T)$ holds. The second, stronger way of understanding Gentzen's remark requires that when the Introduction condition is used to introduce T, it provides a meaning or sense for T, and it is this sense that ensures that the corresponding Elimination condition will hold for T. I am inclined toward the weaker version. The immediate context of Gentzen's remarks about the sense that Introduction rules provide makes it clear that his reference to "sense" is a way of expressing the general claim that Elimination rules are "in the final analysis" consequences of the corresponding Introduction rules.

This is not to underestimate the value of trying of capture the difference between Introduction and Elimination rules (or their corresponding conditions) by means of a theory of meaning. We have attempted to draw the difference generally, and given the wide variety of elements that Introduction conditions can cover, it does not seem plausible that what they always convey is a meaning. It might be plausible that in special cases the elements concerned do have meanings. On our account, however, the relations suggested by Gentzen hold in general, without any need to appeal to that fact about them.[5]

4

The Belnap program

Another program for understanding the logical operators is due to N. D. Belnap, Jr. It is similar to that of Gentzen and our own, in that it involves a division of labor: a background theory of implication that is structural, and a theory of the operators characterized against that background.

In a witty and elegant essay, Belnap developed a view about the significance of the logical connectives that stressed the role of the connectives with respect to inference. Belnap's theory clearly has the Gentzen style: A general theory of inference (which he calls "deducibility") is set forth. As he remarked, it makes no difference whether one chooses to use a syntactic notion of deducibility or a semantic concept of logical consequence to represent what he intended by "inference." Against the theory of inference, a theory of the logical *connectives* is developed as an extension of the theory of inference. The meaning of a connective like "and" is, according to Belnap, given by its role in inference. Although the strategy of explanation is Gentzenesque, the resultant theory is somewhat different in detail from Gentzen's, and very different from our own use of the Gentzen framework.

Belnap's remarks were designed to answer a probing challenge by A. N. Prior to the claim that "the complete answer" to the question of what is the meaning or the definition of the logical particle "and" could be given by describing the role that "and" plays in a class of inferences that Prior called "analytic."[1] Thus, the "complete" story about "and" on such a view would be given by indicating the (analytic) inferences in which compound expressions *P*-and-*Q* figure: *P*-and-*Q* implies *P* as well as *Q*, and *P* together with *Q* implies *P*-and-*Q*. This strategy is supposed to yield the meaning or definition of "and" – even if we had no prior understanding of that expression. As for the expression "*P*-and-*Q*," all qualms about whether or not for any sentences *P* and *Q* there is a sentence *R* that satisfies the two rules of inference are supposedly eased by the observation that "*P*-and-*Q*" is introduced to express just such a sentence.

We should say in passing that the question whether "*P*-and-*Q*" is a compound or complex proposition is one that contemporary logical studies have passed over in silence. As Prior (1960) noted, J. S. Mill thought that "Caesar is dead and Brutus is alive" is not a single proposition, but represents a plurality of propositions. It is about as convincing, Mill said, to call it a compound or complex proposition as to call a street a complex house.[2]

Prior's forceful challenge to this account of the meaning of "and" can be summarized as follows – unfortunately, without the delightful irony of the original: There is a connective called "tonk." Here is its meaning: For any P, Q, there is the sentence "P-tonk-Q" whose role in inferences is completely given by two requirements: (1) P implies P-tonk-Q for any P and Q, and (2) P-tonk-Q implies Q for any P and Q. The "complete" story on "tonk" has now been given, since the Introduction and Elimination rules that have been provided tell us how to infer from "tonked" sentences to the sentences that are their parts, and how to infer to "tonked" sentences. Moreover, one should have no qualms about whether or not there is for any sentences P and Q a sentence R that satisfies the rules, since it is precisely by means of "tonk" that we can form such a sentence.

What has gone wrong? The obvious consequence of admitting "tonk" as a connective is that with its aid, any sentence P implies any sentence Q, since P implies P-tonk-Q, and P-tonk-Q implies Q. Is there any way to separate the story of "and" from that of "tonk," or must they stand or fall together? Since this story for "tonk" has a disastrous ending, the moral for "and" is obvious enough.

Belnap located the difference between the proposed definitions of "and" and "tonk": The former is successfully defined; the latter is not. The general methodological observation is that certain requirements must be satisfied whenever a definition is introduced as a supplement to a consistent theory. Otherwise the extended theory may be inconsistent. His view is that the Introduction and Elimination rules provide an adequate definition of "and" when taken as adjunctions to a theory of inference or deducibility. However, the rules that Prior used for "tonk" violate a condition for being a definition – they transform or extend a consistent theory of implication into an inconsistent theory.

The contrast between Belnap's program and our own can be illustrated by what happens with conjunctions on the two accounts. First, a brief look at how Belnap thinks of conjunction. He begins with a set of sentences S, none of which contains the expression "&," the connective to be defined.[3]

The problem is to define "&" against theory of inference that itself does not employ "&." Since the same theory of inference is to be used for the definitions of all of the logical connectives, one cannot use any of those connectives in its formulation. What is needed is a "structural" theory of inference, and a good candidate for such a theory, as noted by Belnap, is the set of structural rules provided by Gentzen.[4]

We suppose, according to Belnap, that we have some set S of sentences, none of which contains any occurrence of "&" in it, and that there is some deducibility relation "⊢" defined over the set. Essentially, then, $\langle S, \vdash \rangle$ is an implication structure consisting of syntactic or semantic objects. The next step in Belnap's construction is the formation of a new set S^* that is the smallest set to include S and contain the sentence "P & Q," if it contains both P and Q.

The final step in Belnap's proposal requires some preliminary definitions.

> **Definition 4.1.** Let "$\Rightarrow$" and "$\Rightarrow'$" be implication relations on the sets S and S', respectively. We shall say that "$\Rightarrow'$" *is an extension of* "$\Rightarrow$" (or "$\Rightarrow'$" *extends* "$\Rightarrow$") if and only if S is a subset of S', and for any $A_1, \ldots, A_n$ and B in S, if $A_1, \ldots, A_n \Rightarrow B$, then $A_1, \ldots, A_n \Rightarrow' B$.

For implication structures $I = \langle S, \Rightarrow \rangle$ and $I' = \langle S', \Rightarrow' \rangle$, we shall say that I' *is an extension of* I if and only if "$\Rightarrow'$" is an extension of "$\Rightarrow$."

> **Definition 4.2.** For implication relations "$\Rightarrow$" (on S) and "$\Rightarrow'$" (on S'), we shall say that "$\Rightarrow'$" *is a conservative extension of* "$\Rightarrow$" if and only if (1) it is an extension of "$\Rightarrow$" and (2) for any $A_1, \ldots, A_n$ and B in S, if $A_1, \ldots, A_n \Rightarrow' B$, then $A_1, \ldots, A_n \Rightarrow B$.

Similarly, one implication structure is a conservative extension of another if and only if its implication relation is a conservative extension of that of the other. Thus, in passing from an implication structure $I = \langle S, \Rightarrow \rangle$ to a conservative extension, the two implication relations will be coextensional on S.

Belnap completes his proposal with the introduction of a new deducibility relation "⊢*," which is an extension of "⊢." Introduction and Elimination rules, using the new deducibility relation, are then provided for "&": P & Q ⊢* P, P & Q ⊢* Q, and P, Q ⊢* P & Q.[5]

Belnap appeals to a methodological constraint on definitions: A necessary condition on definitional extensions is that they be conservative: For all the P_i and Q belonging to S, $P_1, \ldots, P_n \vdash^* Q$ if and only if $P_1, \ldots, P_n \vdash Q$. Thus, the conservative extension "$\vdash^*$" is a deducibility relation whose restriction to the subset S is coextensional with the deducibility relation "$\vdash$" on S.[6]

What, then, is the matter with "tonk"? If the argument for having defined "&" is run through again, only this time using "tonk" rather than "&," together with its Introduction and Elimination rules, then what we have is this: We begin with a set of "tonk"-less sentences S, together with some deducibility relation over S. This structure is then extended to S_{tonk} – so that if P and Q are any sentences of S, then "P-tonk-Q" belongs to S_{tonk}. "P-tonk-Q" does not belong to the starter set S, since all of its sentences are taken to be "tonk"-less. The Introduction and Elimination conditions are those available, by courtesy, from Prior:

$P_1.$ $P \vdash^* P$-tonk-Q, and
$P_2.$ P-tonk-$Q \vdash^* Q$,

where "$\vdash^*$" is a deducibility relation that extends the deducibility relation over the set S.

As Belnap notes, the extension "$\vdash^*$" so defined fails to be a conservative extension of "$\vdash$"; it does not agree with "$\vdash$" over the set of "tonk"-less sentences S. The reason is that for any P, Q in S, we have $P \vdash^* P$-tonk-Q (by P_1), and P-tonk-$Q \vdash^* Q$ (by P_2). Since the deducibility relation "$\vdash^*$" is transitive, we have that $P \vdash^* Q$ for all P and Q in S. Consequently, all the sentences of S are equivalent (using "$\vdash^*$"). If "$\vdash^*$" were conservative, then $P \vdash Q$ for all P and Q in S. That is, all the sentences of S, the starter set, would be equivalent by the deducibility relation "$\vdash$" on it. However, it is assumed by Belnap that there are nonequivalent members of S (using "$\vdash$"). Since the extension for "tonk" fails to be conservative, the conclusion is that "tonk" is not a connective.

This result, as Belnap noted, depends upon two assumptions: that not all members of S are equivalent by the deducibility relation on the structure I, and that the deducibility relation is transitive. The failure of either of these conditions will revise the fate of "tonk." For example, if it were true that $P \vdash Q$ for all P and Q in S, then the extension I^* over I would be conservative, and "tonk" would count as a connective. Belnap's analysis uncovers the natural way in which the existence of a connective depends upon the background theory of inference.

This, then, according to Belnap, is the difference between "&" and "tonk." Given the theory that he constructs for "&," it is a persuasive, clear difference that his theory establishes between the two terms.

Belnap's account is satisfactory for the special case that it covers, but it is only a limited case, for it requires that in order for expressions to be conjunctions, each must have a conjunctive sign like "&" embedded in it. Consider, first, what might be called the case of the missing conjunction. On Belnap's version of conjunction, there is no conjunction of the sentences P and Q unless they flank some special sign – in this case, "&." This is fine if all one wants to do is characterize some syntactically designated set of sentences, called conjunctions, that are distinguished in form by their having the shape of "P & Q", where P and Q are sentences. Consequently, there are no conjunctions in the set S of "&"-less sentences with which Belnap begins his construction. On his account, one obtains conjunctions of the sentences of S only in the extension $S_\&$ of S.

On our view, however, there are situations in which there are conjunctions in S that Belnap's account misses – indeed, that cannot be picked out given his account of conjunction. Suppose that we have a simple implication structure $I = \langle S, \Rightarrow \rangle$

for some sentences P, Q, and R, with the implication relations between them as indicated by the single arrows. In this structure, R is the conjunction of P and Q. The reason is just that R implies P as well as Q (the first condition on conjunctions). Moreover, if any member of the structure implies P as well as Q, then it also implies R. This is so because R is the only element of this structure to imply P as well as Q, and R implies R. Thus, the second condition on conjunctions is satisfied. Consequently, R is the conjunction of P and Q, regardless of whether or not it has some special sign embedded in it. Here, then, we have an example of a structure I in which there is a conjunction of P with Q on our account of conjunction, but there are no conjunctions at all to be found in the structure according to Belnap's theory.

Moreover, on our account, the conjunction R implies each of P, Q for the original deducibility relation ("⊢") on I. However, conjunctions in Belnap's version are never related by "⊢" to their conjuncts. Thus, P & $Q \vdash P$ always fails, for the simple reason that "⊢" is not defined for

sentences such as P & Q. It is only the extended deducibility relation
"⊢*" that is designed to cover such cases.

On our account, there could be structures in which there would be
conjunctions such as R, without "&" being embedded in it. So there is,
on our view, a conjunction in I that not only is overlooked by the Belnap
theory but also is positively discounted by Belnap, because it does not
have the right shape.[7]

Moreover, since "⊢" is an extension of "⊢," and P & Q ⊢* P (as well
as Q), and P, Q ⊢* P & Q, it follows that R is equivalent to P & Q in I^*,
and R has the same inferential role with respect to P and Q in I^* that it
has in I. Thus, conjunctions, on Belnap's theory, are distinguished by
some special syntactic design in addition to their special inferential role.

There is a further difference between the two accounts that is more a
matter of emphasis than of scope. Belnap requires that the definitional
extension from I to I^* be conservative (with respect to I). The use of
conservative extensions is an important and well-motivated concept of
logical theory. We do not want a "mere" definitional extension, either,
to add to or detract from those inferences we had without the definition.
The insistence upon conservative extensions is a strength of Belnap's
analysis; that is what makes "tonk" look so bad by comparison. But
there is another way of seeing the value of conservative extensions. On
our account of the logical operators, the virtue in passing from one
structure to a conservative extension of it is that it is then guaranteed
that the operators are *stable*. That is, for example, an item that is a
conjunction in one structure will continue to be a conjunction in any
conservative extension of it. Both accounts value conservative extensions of structures, though for different reasons. The more acute difference, however, is not whether or not the element R is a conjunction that
continues to be a conjunction in the passage to a conservative extension;
the issue is whether or not R is a conjunction in the first place.

Although the difference between "&" and "tonk" emerges very
clearly on Belnap's analysis, the difference is no less clear on our
account of conjunction, which uses operators rather than connectives.

Let us recast the problem of distinguishing between "&" and "tonk"
as connectives and consider the corresponding operators. What difference is there between the conjunction operator $C(A, B)$ and a "tonk"
operator $T(A, B)$? For the "tonk" operator, we have the following:

T_1. $A \Rightarrow T(A, B)$, and
T_2. $T(A, B) \Rightarrow B$.

Thus, the way in which the "tonking" of A with B is registered notationally is ignored. "Tonking" yields an item that is indicated as the value of the function T, that is, as $T(A, B)$, and that element of the structure is related implicationally to A and to B by T_1 and T_2, respectively.

Any implication structure $I = \langle S, \Rightarrow \rangle$ in which $T(A, B)$ exists for all A and B must be trivial. Its members are equivalent to each other. The reason is that for any A and B, $A \Rightarrow T(A, B)$, and $T(A, B) \Rightarrow B$. By transitivity, $A \Rightarrow B$ for all A and B in the structure.

However, the trivial structures are exactly those in which the distinction between the various logical operators vanishes. The "tonk" operator is empty on all but the trivial structures, and on those it cannot be distinguished from any one of the logical operators – nor can they be distinguished from each other.[8] There is no point to studying the differences between "tonk" and the other logical operators, for there are no differences that can be studied.

PART II

Implication relations

5

The theory of implication relations

5.1 Conditions on implication

In Part I we outlined a program for the logical operators that has two components, one consisting of implication relations, the other consisting of characterizations of the logical operators relative to these implication relations. If we think of an implication structure $I = \langle S, \Rightarrow \rangle$ as a nonempty set S together with an implication relation "$\Rightarrow$" on it, then the logical operators are functions that on each implication structure assign (sets of) elements of it that count as hypotheticals, conjunctions, negations, disjunctions, quantifications, and so forth, of that structure. Thus, the general picture is one in which the logical operators are relativized to implication relations, and each one is specified without recourse to any of the operators to be characterized. Otherwise the program would be circular from the outset.

Our present concern, then, is the study of implication structures, nonempty sets with implication relations on them. We have described implication relations (on a set S) as any finitary *relation* on S (which we write with a double arrow) that satisfies the six conditions specified in Chapter 1. Any relation will count for us as an implication relation if it satisfies these conditions. Some of these conditions follow from the others, but we shall retain the less elegant formulation for the sake of greater perspicuity.

Thus, it should be noted that condition 1 (Reflexivity) follows from condition 2 (Projection). More interestingly, Projection, together with Cut (condition 6), yields Dilution (condition 5). Let us say that a relation that fails to satisfy Dilution is *nonmonotonic*. Those who drop the Dilution condition will also have to give up either the Projection condition or Cut. To my knowledge no one has seriously thought of giving up Cut, with its guarantee of the transitivity of implication.[1] Thus, in nonmonotonic variants of implication relations, Projection does not hold. That is, for some $A_1, \ldots, A_n$ and A_k, $A_1, \ldots, A_n \not\Rightarrow A_k$. This has suggestively been called a "forgetting" notion of implication, although it is, strictly speaking, not an implication relation.

There is an extensive variety of implication relations to be had. Not all of them are of theoretical interest. There are some very familiar and favored examples (syntactic and semantic concepts of logical consequence) that are part of the story that needs to be told, but these familiar examples are not nearly the whole story about implication relations. Before we turn to some examples of the wide variety of relations that qualify as implicational, something should be said about the general features of the conditions that have already been given.

5.2 Implications as relational

We think of implication on a set S as a certain kind of relation on S. Although we indicate that $A_1, \ldots, A_n$ implies B by using a double arrow ("$\Rightarrow$"), it is easy to think that the double arrow is a logical connective – a special sign used to construct complex sentences (if these are the members of S) out of others. However, that is not our use of the double arrow. For us, it is a way of indicating that a certain kind of relation holds among finitely many members of S.

We do not generally have the possibility of multiply embedded expressions like "$A \Rightarrow (B \Rightarrow C)$" on the construal of "$\Rightarrow$" as a relation. Thus, the double arrow, in what follows, is not to be confused with a similar sign used by Ackermann (1956) as a connective, to specify a "strict implication," nor with the single arrow ("$\rightarrow$") used by Anderson and Belnap (1975) for a similar purpose. It also should not be confused with the "fishhook" sign used by Lewis and Langford (1932) as a binary modal connective to express what they call "strict implication."

Another way to see the thrust of the wide variety of implication structures is to notice that if "$\Rightarrow$" were construed as a connective (with the intended reading, for example, "that . . . entails that ---"), the result would be to require that all implication structures have statements among their elements. No set of nonsentential elements could ever qualify as an implication structure. Moreover, we require of the double arrow that $A \Rightarrow A$, $A, B \Rightarrow A$, $A, B, C \Rightarrow A$, and so forth, so that we think of the double arrow as a relation having finite degree, but no fixed degree. Therefore, it cannot be thought of as a connective, for the latter usually are required to have fixed degree – that is, each must be only unary, or binary, or ternary, and so forth.[2]

There is a naturalness in construing the statement "$A, B \Rightarrow C$" as expressing a relation among A, B, and C – if we want to include those cases where the elements of the structure may not be sentential.

The early works of Gentzen and his teacher Hertz are, aside from the work of Tarski, other sources of the relational way of construing implication. This claim about Hertz and Gentzen is somewhat controversial. Both wrote about special "sentences," $A_1, \ldots, A_n \to B$ (sometimes called "sentences*," or "Hertzian sentences"), in a series of papers, in ways that could easily lend themselves to two interpretations of the single arrow that they used. According to one interpretation, the sentence expresses a relation between the A_i's and B; according to the other, the single arrow is a connective.

The question remains whether the Gentzen–Hertz single arrow is to be understood as a relation or as a connective. Before we discuss the matter further, it is worthwhile having before us Gentzen's striking description (1933) of this situation (changing the notation slightly):

A sentence* has the form $A_1, A_2, \ldots, A_n \to B$. The A's and B's are called elements*. We might think of them as events, and the "sentence" then reads: The happening of the events $A_1, \ldots, A_n$ causes the happening of B.

The "sentence" may also be understood thus: A domain of elements containing the elements $A_1, \ldots, A_n$ also contains the element B.

The elements may furthermore be thought of as properties and the "sentence" can then be interpreted thus: An object with the properties $A_1, \ldots, A_n$ also has the property B.

Or we imagine the elements to stand for "propositions," in the sense of the propositional calculus, and the "sentence" then reads: If the propositions $A_1, \ldots, A_n$ are true, then the proposition B is also true.

Our considerations do not depend on any particular kind of informal interpretation of the "sentences", since we are concerned only with their formal structure.

Do these observations of Hertz and Gentzen settle the question of whether they intended the single arrow to be a connective or a type of relation? It seems to me that although something can be said for either construal, on the whole the sign was intended to express a relation between the elements of a domain.[3]

There are other features that seem to support the relational rather than the connective reading. Gentzen (1934) remarked that the single arrow is not a logical symbol;[4] it is not listed along with "&," "∨", "¬," "∀," and "∃." Instead, it is listed as an auxiliary symbol, along with the left and right parentheses. That observation, together with the fact that there are no nestings of "→" in the formulas of the system he developed, and no formation of complex sequents from others, using "→," would tend to the conclusion that the single arrow is not a connective, either for formulas or for sequents of formulas. There is another reason that is relevant: In the 1934 paper, Gentzen provided Introduction and Elimination rules for all of the logical connectives, but none was given for the single arrow that was used to express sequents.

That could hardly have been an oversight. It might be objected that even though the single arrow is not a *logical* connective, it might be a connective nevertheless. But that, too, seems wrong. For whatever else a connective may be, I take it that it is a sign of some kind, say "#," such that for at least some members A and B of the relevant set of objects, $A \# B$ is also a member of that set. However, as we observed earlier, according to Gentzen, the single arrow is not used to derive new formulas from others, and it is not used to form new sequents from other sequents. Thus, "$\rightarrow$" fails to be a connective for formulas as well as for sequents.

In summary, then, we think of the Hertz, (1922, 1923, 1929) and Gentzen (1933) papers as employing sentences* of the Hertzian kind that are constructed with the aid of "$\rightarrow$," but are thought of as relational. That much is clear from all the examples they offered as sentences*. The transition in Gentzen's thought from sentences* to sequents as they are used in his 1934 paper is, on balance, we think, this: Sequents with single succedents or consequents are just the old Hertz–Gentzen sentences* (where the elements of the sentences* are restricted, in the paper, to formulas of some standard formulation of first-order logic). The relational character of sequent $A_1, \ldots, A_n \rightarrow B$, in this case, is brought out by the result proved by Gentzen that the sequent corresponds to the relational statement that B depends upon the assumption formulas $A_1, \ldots, A_n$ in a derivation in a system of natural deduction.

This stresses the continuity between Gentzen's two papers, which were published little more than a year apart. However, if we are mistaken in thinking that Gentzen was still using Hertzian-style sentences* in 1934, and the continuity between the two papers was broken, then what would follow would be this: The antecedents of our account of implication relations can be traced to the 1922 and 1923 papers of Hertz and Gentzen (1933); Gentzen's 1934 paper would then mark a parting of the ways.

We shall, whatever the history of these events may be, keep to the insights of those early papers that set forth a general account of implication relations.

Before we turn to a discussion of the various kinds of implication relations and their uses, there are two points that may have raised the reader's curiosity. One concerns the possibility of emending or varying the six conditions that we have used to characterize implication relations. The other point concerns the status of the conditions that we have adopted (see Chapter 10).

6

Implications: Variations and emendations

Recent studies have suggested ways in which the theory of implication relations might be weakened. There have not, to my knowledge, been any suggestions that would strengthen the theory. We have already referred to the suggestion that the Dilution condition be rejected – or at least not required. The theory of the logical operators that we shall develop in this study uses the full six conditions on implication relations. It is also possible to relativize the operators to nonmonotonic "implication" relations. The behaviors of the operators will, as a consequence, be different. The section later in this study that is devoted to component implication (relevance implication) is a case in point. But the general picture of the logical operators in the nonmonotonic case is largely unexplored, and thus far we have no systematic results to present.

The Cut condition has been included as a part of the characterization of an implication relation. When this condition and the others are taken as rules of inference of a system of logic, it can sometimes be shown that the Cut rule is eliminable – that is, it becomes, for such systems, a derived rule of inference.[1]

One might suspect that the Cut condition is a consequence of the remaining conditions, but it is not. Suppose that the set S consists of the elements $A_1, A_2, \ldots$, and that "$\Rightarrow$" satisfies these conditions: (1) $A_i \Rightarrow A_j$ if and only if j is less than or equal to $i + 1$, and (2) $A_{i_1}, \ldots, A_{i_n} \Rightarrow A_{i_k}$ if and only if $A_{i_r} \Rightarrow A_{i_k}$ for some r belonging to $\{1, \ldots, n\}$. It is easy to see that "$\Rightarrow$" satisfies all the conditions 1–5 in Chapter 1, but that condition 6 (Cut) fails because $A_1 \Rightarrow A_2$, and $A_2 \Rightarrow A_3$, but $A_1 \not\Rightarrow A_3$.

Thus, the Cut condition is not redundant for the characterization of implication relations. We include it because it is a feature of most concepts of inference and therefore is central to the notion of an implication relation – even though there are examples of implication relations that do not correspond to rules of inference.

Thus far we have been considering suggestions for dropping some of the six conditions for implication relations. To my knowledge there have been no suggestions for additions to the list that do not follow from those already given. There is one possible condition, independent of the rest, that seems a natural candidate for addition. It concerns the case in which an implication relation fails to hold.

If we think of the special case of a consequence relation on the set of sentences of a first-order language that has conjunction, then we know that if $A_1, \ldots, A_n \not\Rightarrow B$, then there is an element of the structure that implies each of the A_i's but does not imply B – namely, their conjunction. Thus, we might entertain a "star"-condition as an addition to our theory of implication relations:

(*).   For any $A_1, \ldots, A_n$ and B, if $A_1, \ldots, A_n \not\Rightarrow B$, then there is some
        C that implies all the A_i but does not imply B.

The (*)-condition is easily proved to hold in any structure in which conjunctions of elements always exist. It is easy to see that (*) does not follow from the six conditions for implication relations. However, whether or not one should incorporate it into the theory depends upon the theory that results upon its adoption. On the positive side, there is the consequence that its adoption makes a theory of dual implication relations simpler than it would be otherwise: Given the (*)-condition, it will be shown that any implication relation is identical with its double dual (see Chapter 9, Theorem 9.8). Despite this positive side to the (*)-condition, there is a drawback that we believe to be decisive against taking it as a general condition for implication relations.

Although (*) is a natural condition in the structure we used to motivate it, it does not have the same generality as the other conditions on implication relations. The chief reason for thinking so is that (*) does not hold in some simple structures. Consider, for example, the structure given by

Clearly, $A, B \not\Rightarrow D$ [for if $A, B \Rightarrow D$, then $A \Rightarrow H(B, D)$; since $H(B, D)$ is just D, we would have $A \Rightarrow D$, which does not hold in this structure]. By (*) we would have to conclude that there is some E in the structure such that E implies A as well as B, but does not imply D. However, nothing in the structure implies both A and B.

Now the six conditions on implication relations given thus far hold in this structure. The requirement that for all elements of the structure either $A_1, \ldots, A_n \Rightarrow B$ or else there is some element that implies all the A_i's would narrow the range of structures considerably. The (*)-condition, in our view, is not sufficiently general.

Exercise 6.1. Define an implication relation "$\Rightarrow$" as *minimal* on the set S if and only if it extends every implication relation "$\Rightarrow'$" on S for which (for all A and B in S) $A \Rightarrow B$ if and only if $A \Rightarrow' B$. Show that an implication relation satisfies the (*)-condition if and only if it is minimal.

In the next few chapters we shall study a broad variety of examples of implication structures. These should help to provide a picture of the generality that is involved in thinking of the logical operators as functions defined on structures. The familiar examples of deducibility and logical consequence provide a convenient way to begin.

7

Familiar implication relations: Deducibility and logical consequence

It would be implausible to think of implication relations as not including the familiar notions of deducibility and logical consequence, and it would be misleading to think that implication relations were limited to cases of just these two types. A concept of (syntactic) deducibility is usually introduced over a well-defined set of sentences, according to which $A_1, \ldots, A_n \vdash B$ holds if and only if there is a sequence of sentences $C_1, \ldots, C_m$ such that C_m is B, and every C_i is either an A_j (or an axiom if we are concerned with axiomatic formulations of the theory) or follows from one or more preceding sentences of the sequence by any member of a finite collection of rules R. It is easy to verify that "$\vdash$" satisfies the condition for being an implication relation.[1]

The semantic concept of consequence is also familiar. Starting with a well-defined set of sentences of, say, the propositional calculus, the notion of an interpretation is defined, and for any $A_1, \ldots, A_n$ and B, we say that B is a logical consequence of $A_1, \ldots, A_n$; that is, $A_1, \ldots, A_n \vDash B$ if and only if every interpretation that assigns "true" to all the A_i's also assigns "true" to B.[2] It is easy to see that "$\vDash$" is an implication relation. The details are familiar and need not be reviewed here.

Although these examples qualify as implication relations, some of the details of their construction are misleading in regard to the general picture. For one thing, both examples usually concern systems of sentences (of the propositional, predicate, or some higher-order theories). However, there are implication relations for any set of objects whatever, so the sentential examples just reviewed do not represent the general situation. Moreover, these familiar relations rely in their construction upon the use of certain logical connectives or their associated operators. This is clear from the fact that in defining "deducibility,"certain rules are referred to, and these usually concern logically complex sentences whose complexity is expressed with the aid of certain logical connectives. Similarly, the notion of an interpretation or model usually will take the logical complexity of sentences into account in its definition. Now, this feature of deducibility and logical consequence can be misleading in regard to the general picture of how the logical operators are based upon the notion of implication relations, for the whole project of a two-tiered account of the logical operators could be undermined if implication relations always required reference to some logical operators in their description. Fortunately, there are examples of implication relations that easily correct that impression. They are relations created "from scratch," as it were, making no reference to the general notion of conjunctions, disjunctions, hypotheticals, negations, and so forth, in their construction. Of course, one can, on the account we shall give of the operators, study what happens when some operators are used to describe an implication relation, thus yielding an implication structure to which the operators, in turn, can be applied. This is a compounding that has real interest. But this describes only one possibility, rather than what happens generally. On our account, the logical operators are always relativized to an implication relation, but the converse is not always so.

Syntactic and semantic implication relations have, thanks to A. Tarski and, more recently, D. Scott, been studied in a general way.[3] One of these relations is the *Tarskian consequence relation* "$\vdash_T$," which is an example of an implication relation. Let $Cn(S)$ be the set of all consequences of the set S. The notion of consequence can be taken semantically, though that does not matter in what follows. One can think of A's being a consequence of the set S as a relation ("$\vdash_T$") between S and A. The concept of logical consequence can now be freed from the details of its semantic origin by axiomatizing a small but characteristic theory for the relation "$\vdash_T$" as follows:

1. $\{a\} \vdash_T \{a\}$ for all a (Reflexivity),
2. if $A \vdash_T B$, then $A, A' \vdash_T B$ (Dilution), and
3. if $A, \{c\} \vdash_T B$ and $A \vdash_T \{c\}$, then $A \vdash_T B$ (Cut),

where $a, b, c, \ldots$ range over sentences, $A, B, C, \ldots$ range over finite sets of sentences, the union of the sets A and A' is indicated as in condition 2 by the sequence A, A' on the left-hand side of "$\vdash_T$," and only single-member sets are indicated on the right-hand side of "$\vdash_T$."

Scott (1974) has introduced a family of consequence relations that blend some of Tarski's views with those of Gentzen. A Scott consequence relation is a binary relation $A \Vdash B$, where A and B range over finite sets of sentences. Unlike the Tarskian consequence relations, there is no restriction of B to only single-member sets. This is akin to Gentzen's symmetric sequents $a_1, \ldots, a_n \to b_1, \ldots, b_m$ with multiple consequents (or succedents). A *Scott consequence relation* is any binary relation on finite sets of sentences such that

1. $A \Vdash A$ (where A is nonempty) (Reflexivity),
2. if $A \Vdash B$, then $A, A' \Vdash B, B'$ (Monotonicity or Left-and-Right Dilution), and
3. if $A, \{a\} \Vdash B$, and $A \Vdash B, \{a\}$, then $A \Vdash B$ (Cut).

The Scott consequence relation, in its general form, is not an implication relation in our sense, since we consider only those relations with single consequents. Nevertheless, we shall see that it can be considered as a (relational) product of implication relations in our sense.[4]

The basic result here is due to Scott (1974), who proved that if "$\vdash_T$" is any Tarskian consequence relation, then there are two (Scott) consequence relations "$\Vdash_{T^+}$" and "$\Vdash_{T^-}$" such that (1) if B has exactly one member in it, then $A \Vdash_{T^+} B$ if and only if $A \Vdash_{T^-} B$ if and only if $A \vdash_T B$, and (2) if "$\Vdash$" is any (Scott) consequence relation that is coextensional with "$\vdash_T$," then $\Vdash_{T^-} \subseteq \Vdash \subseteq \Vdash_{T^+}$. If B contains more than one member, then the Tarski and Scott consequence relations cannot be compared, since the Tarski relation is not defined. If B contains exactly one member, then Tarski's and Scott's relations are coextensional.

We have begun with some familiar, though complex, examples, deductive and semantic, of implication relations. Let us now give some very simple examples of implication relations that can be created "from scratch."

8

Implication relations: Direct and derived

8.1 Projective implication

One of the very simplest implication relations can be obtained by regarding an element B of a set S as implied by finitely many members listed as $A_1, \ldots, A_n$, just in case B is A_j for some j in $\{1, \ldots, n\}$. The verification of the conditions for implication relations is straightforward.

8.2 Millean implication

This is a kind of implication relation for which $A_1, \ldots, A_n$ implies B if and only if some A_j implies B for some j in $\{1, \ldots, n\}$ (see Chapter 4, note 2).

> **Exercise 8.1.** Let "#" any reflexive and transitive binary relation on a set S of at least two members. Let "$\Longrightarrow^{\#}$" hold between $A_1, \ldots, A_n$ and B if and only if A_j # B for some j in $\{1, \ldots, n\}$. Show that "$\Longrightarrow^{\#}$" is a Millean implication relation.

8.3 Bisection implication

A much more theoretically interesting example whose properties we shall now study in some detail arises from a consideration of the various ways in which a nonempty set S can be partitioned into two nonempty, mutually exclusive subsets.

> **Definition 8.1.** A *bisection* of a set S is any pair $T = \langle K, L \rangle$ of nonempty subsets of S such that (1) $K \cap L = \varnothing$, and (2) $K \cup L = S$. The bisections of an implication structure $I = \langle S, \Longrightarrow \rangle$ are the bisections of S.

> **Definition 8.2.** Let $T = \langle K, L \rangle$ be a bisection of a set S. We shall say that "$\Longrightarrow^{T}$" is a *bisection implication relation* if and only if for every $A_1, \ldots, A_n$ and B in S,

Closed sets j-σ
L and KUL.

$A_1, \ldots, A_n \Rightarrow^T B$ and only if some A_i is in K or B is in L.[1]

with $n=0$ *as well?*

The theoretical interest in bisections and the implication relations based upon them lies in the result that certain kinds of bisections provide a general concept of a truth-value assignment on arbitrary implication structures, with membership in L corresponding to "truth" [an insight essentially due to Scott (1974)]. With the aid of such bisections, a general concept of the extensionality of logical operators on arbitrary implication structures can be defined (see Chapter 19), and the extensionality or nonextensionality of the logical operators in various implication structures can be studied. Those results will follow the detailed study of the logical operators in Part III. First, however, a review of some of the basic properties of bisection implication is in order.

Theorem 8.1. "$\Rightarrow^T$" *is an implication relation.*

The proof is straightforward and is left to the reader.

Exercise 8.2. Show that every bisection implication relation is Millean.

Definition 8.3. We shall say that a set R is *strongly closed* under an implication relation "$\Rightarrow$" if and only if the following holds: If $A_1, \ldots, A_n \Rightarrow B$, and all the A_i's belong to R, then B is in R. It is *weakly closed* if and only if whenever $A \Rightarrow B$, and A is in R, then so too is B.

Definition 8.4. A bisection $T = \langle K, L \rangle$ of the structure $I = \langle S, \Rightarrow \rangle$ is a *strong (weak) bisection* of I if and only if L is strongly (weakly) closed under "$\Rightarrow$" (parallel usage for strong and weak bisection implication relations).

Theorem 8.2. *Let S be any nonempty set, and let $T = \langle K, L \rangle$ be any bisection of S. Then the set L is strongly closed under the bisection implication relation "$\Rightarrow^T$."*

Proof. Suppose that $A_1, \ldots, A_n \Rightarrow^T B$ and that all the A_i's belong to L. By the definition of "$\Rightarrow^T$," either some A_k is in K or B is in L. But no A_i is in K. Consequently, B is in L.

Thus, there is a certain "ubiquity" of implication relations: Every

We see from the preceding two theorems that there always is a "made-to-order" implication relation that is available on any set: Suppose that we have a set of objects S and that L is a proper subset whose members are regarded with special favor, or as having special interest. Then there is an implication relation on S under which L is strongly closed. Just take the bisection implication relation that corresponds to the bisection $T = \langle K, L \rangle$, where $K = S - L$.

Theorem 8.3. *Let $T = \langle K, L \rangle$ be any bisection on S, and let "$\Rightarrow^T$" be the corresponding implication relation. Then (under "$\Rightarrow^T$") all the members of K are equivalent, all the members of L are equivalent, and every member of K implies every member of L.*

Proof. The proofs are obvious.

Exercise 8.3. If, under an implication relation, a set S splits into two equivalence classes such that every member of the one implies every member of the other (but not conversely), then it is a bisection implication relation.

We can use certain bisection implications on a structure $I = \langle S, \Rightarrow \rangle$ to study the implication relation "$\Rightarrow$" of the structure itself.

Theorem 8.4. *Let $I = \langle S \Rightarrow \rangle$ be an implication structure, and let $T = \langle K, L \rangle$ be any strong bisection of I. Then the bisection implication relation "$\Rightarrow^T$" is an extension of "$\Rightarrow$."*

Proof. Suppose that $A_1, \ldots, A_n \Rightarrow B$. If all the A_i's are in L, then B is in L, since L is strongly closed under "$\Rightarrow$". Thus, either some A_i is not in L or B is in L. However, if A_i is not in L, then it is in K. Consequently, either some A_i is in K or B is in L. Therefore $A_1, \ldots, A_n \Rightarrow^T B$.

Theorem 8.5. *If $\Rightarrow \subseteq \Rightarrow^T$, where $T = \langle K, L \rangle$, then L is strongly closed under "$\Rightarrow$".*

The proof is left as an exercise. Thus, for any implication relation "$\Rightarrow$" on S, and any bisection $T = \langle K, L \rangle$ on S, $\Rightarrow \subseteq \Rightarrow^T$ if and only if L is strongly closed under "$\Rightarrow$."

These results concern conditions under which any implication relation is extended by a bisection implication. Can a bisection implication ever be extended by some implication relation? Not if there are three elements

Theorem 8.6. *Let* $I = \langle S, \Rightarrow \rangle$ *be an implication structure such that there are A, B, and C in S for which* $A \Leftrightarrow B$, $B \Leftrightarrow C$, *and* $A \Leftrightarrow C$. *Then there is no bisection* $T = \langle K, L \rangle$ *for which* $\Rightarrow^T \subseteq \Rightarrow$.

Proof. Suppose that $\Rightarrow^T \subseteq \Rightarrow$. Since none of A, B, and C are equivalent under "$\Rightarrow$", none of them are equivalent under "$\Rightarrow^T$." Consequently, whichever set (K or L) that B belongs to, A must belong to the other, and so too much C. Therefore, A and C belong to either K or L. So they are equivalent under "$\Rightarrow^T$" and, as a result, equivalent under "$\Rightarrow$." But that is impossible.

Thus far we have considered how bisection implications compare with implication relations generally. If we ask how they compare with each other, then there are some things that we can say about two different cases: bisection implications over the same set and over different sets. The first thing to observe is that of any two bisection implication relations over the same set, neither is an extension of the other. That is,

Theorem 8.7. *If* $T = \langle K, L \rangle$ *and* $T^* = \langle K^*, L^* \rangle$ *are two bisections over the set S, then if* $\Rightarrow^T \subseteq \Rightarrow^{T*}$, *then* $\Rightarrow^T = \Rightarrow^{T*}$.

Proof. Assume that $\Rightarrow^T \subseteq \Rightarrow^{T*}$. Let A be any member of L. Then $B \Rightarrow^T A$ for all B in S. Consequently, $B \Rightarrow^{T^*} A$ for all B in S. Take some B in L^*. Since L^* is strongly closed under "$\Rightarrow^{T^*}$," we conclude that A is in L^*. Thus, $L \subseteq L^*$ (and so $K^* \subseteq K$). Similarly, $K \subseteq K^*$ (and so $L^* \subseteq L$). For let A be in K. Then $A \Rightarrow^T B$ for all B in S. Therefore $A \Rightarrow^{T^*} B$ (all B). So A is in K^* (if it were in L^*, then all B would be in L^*, and that is impossible). Consequently, $L = L^*$ and $K = K^*$. So $\Rightarrow^T = \Rightarrow^{T^*}$.

Let us consider what happens if we compare bisection implications over different sets S and S'.

Definition 8.5. Let $T = \langle K, L \rangle$ and $T' = \langle K', L' \rangle$ be bisections on the sets S and S', respectively. T is a *refinement* of T' if and only if $K \subseteq K'$ and $L \subseteq L'$.

Exercise 8.4. If T and T' are bisections on S and S', respectively, and T is a refinement of T', then (1) S is a subset of S', and (2) "$\Rightarrow^{T'}$" is an extension of "$\Rightarrow^T$."

Theorem 8.8. *If* $T = \langle K, L \rangle$ *and* $T' = \langle K', L' \rangle$ *are bisections of* S *and* S', *respectively, and* T *is a refinement of* T', *then* "$\Rightarrow^{T'}$" *is a conservative extension of* "$\Rightarrow^{T}$."

Proof. From the preceding exercise we know that S is a subset of S'. Let $A_1, \ldots, A_n$ and B be in S. Suppose that $A_1, \ldots, A_n \Rightarrow^{T} B$. Then either some A_k is in K or B is in L. Consequently, some A_k is in K' or B is in L (and so in L'). Therefore, $A_1, \ldots, A_n \Rightarrow^{T'} B$. Conversely, suppose that $A_1, \ldots, A_n \Rightarrow^{T'} B$. Then some A_j is in K' or B is in L'. Suppose that $A_j \not\Rightarrow^{T} B$. Then A_j is in L and B is in K. Since K is included in K', B is in K'. Therefore B is not in L'. Since A_j is in K' or B is in L', it follows that A_j is in K'. But A_j is in L, and so it is in L'. That is impossible. Therefore $A_j \Rightarrow^{T} B$, and so $A_1, \ldots, A_n \Rightarrow^{T} B$.

It is interesting to think of what this simple theorem comes to in a special case. Suppose that we think of S as a collection of sentences that have truth values. We can then partition S into two nonempty proper subsets: K, the set of the false sentences of S, and L, the truths of S (we assume that S is such as to contain at least one truth and one falsehood). In this case, $A_1, \ldots, A_n \Rightarrow^{T} B$ if and only if either some A_i is false or B is true.[2] Then Theorem 8.8 states, for this special case, that if we have a set S divided into truths and falsehoods, and a larger set S' similarly divided, so that all the truths of S are among the truths of S', and all the falsehoods of S are among the falsehoods of S', then there is no difference between the two bisection implication relations over the smaller set S. There is a converse to this theorem:

Theorem 8.9. *If* $S \subseteq S'$, *and* $T = \langle K, L \rangle$ *and* $T' = \langle K', L' \rangle$ *are bisections of* S *and* S', *respectively, and* "$\Rightarrow^{T'}$" *is a conservative extension of* "$\Rightarrow^{T}$," *then* T *is a refinement of* T'.

Proof. Since $S' = K' \cup L'$ and $S \subseteq S'$, we know that $S \cap S' = S \neq \varnothing$. Therefore, $S \cap (K' \cup L') \neq \varnothing$. Consequently, either $S \cap K'$ is nonempty or $S \cap L'$ is nonempty. Now assume that A is in K. Then $A \Rightarrow^{T} B$ for all B in S. Therefore, $A \Rightarrow^{T'} B$ for all B in S. Suppose that $S \cap K'$ is nonempty, and let B be in $S \cap K'$. Consequently, B is in K', and since L' is closed under "$\Rightarrow^{T'}$," it follows that A is in K'. So if $S \cap K'$ is nonempty, then $K \subseteq K'$. Similarly, if $S \cap L'$ is nonempty, then $L \subseteq L'$. For let B be in L. Then $A \Rightarrow^{T} B$ for all A in S. Therefore, $A \Rightarrow^{T'} B$ for all A in S. Choose an A in $S \cap L'$. Since A is in L', it follows (since $A \Rightarrow^{T} B$) that B is in L'.

Thus far we know that $S \cap K'$ is nonempty or that $S \cap L'$ is nonempty and, consequently, that either $K \subseteq K'$ or $L \subseteq L'$. Notice, however, that if $K \subseteq K'$, then $L \subseteq L'$. For suppose that $K \subseteq K'$. Let B be any element of K. If A is any element in L, then $A \not\Rightarrow^T B$ (since B is in K). Now if A is in K', then $A \Rightarrow^T B$, but that is impossible. Therefore, A is not in K' – that is, A is in L'. Therefore, if $K \subseteq K'$, then $L \subseteq L'$. Conversely, if $L \subseteq L'$, then $K \subseteq K'$. For suppose that $L \subseteq L'$. Let B be any member of K. Let A be any member of L. Then $A \not\Rightarrow^T B$. Now A is in L and therefore in L'. If B is in L', then $A \Rightarrow^T B$. This is a contradiction. Consequently, B is not in L' – that is, B is in K'. Thus, if $L \subseteq L'$, then $K \subseteq K'$. Since we have shown that either $K \subseteq K'$ or $L \subseteq L'$, we conclude that $K \subseteq K'$ and $L \subseteq L'$.

Combining the two preceding theorems, we have the following:

Theorem 8.10 (conservativeness). *Let* $T = \langle K, L \rangle$ *and* $T' = \langle K', L' \rangle$ *be bisections of S and S', respectively, where* $S \subseteq S'$. *Then "*$\Rightarrow^{T'}$*" is a conservative extension of "*$\Rightarrow^T$*" if and only if T is a refinement of T'.*

The next result tells us that although an implication relation of a structure is at least as strong as any of the strong bisection implications of the structure, it is equivalent to all of them taken together.

Lindenbaum?!

Theorem 8.11 (strong completeness) (Lindenbaum–Scott). *Let I* $= \langle S, \Rightarrow \rangle$ *be any nontrivial implication structure (Definition 1.1 from Chapter 1). Then* $A_1, \ldots, A_n \Rightarrow B$ *holds if and only if* $A_1, \ldots, A_n \Rightarrow^T B$ *holds for all strong bisection implication relations "*$\Rightarrow^T$*" of the structure I.*

Proof. We have already seen (Theorem 8.4) that if $T = \langle K, L \rangle$ is a strong bisection of the structure $I = \langle S, \Rightarrow \rangle$, then "$\Rightarrow^T$" is an extension of "$\Rightarrow$." So that takes care of one half of the theorem. Let us assume that $A_1, \ldots, A_n \Rightarrow^T B$ for all strong bisections $T = \langle K, L \rangle$ of S. We want to show that $A_1, \ldots, A_n \Rightarrow B$. Suppose that $A_1, \ldots, A_n \not\Rightarrow B$. Let U be the set of all members C of S such that $A_1, \ldots, A_n \Rightarrow C$. Clearly, U is nonempty, since all of the A_i's are in it, and clearly U is a proper subset of S, since B is not in U. Consequently, $T = \langle S - U, U \rangle$ is a bisection of S. Furthermore, U is strongly closed under "$\Rightarrow$." For suppose that $B_1, \ldots, B_m \Rightarrow C$, where all the B_j's belong to U. By the definition of U, it follows that $A_1, \ldots, A_n \Rightarrow B_j$ for all the B_j's. By using Cut n times, we conclude that

$A_1, \ldots, A_n \Rightarrow C$. Therefore, C is in U, and hence U is strongly closed under "$\Rightarrow$."

Now, by hypothesis, $A_1, \ldots, A_n \Rightarrow^T B$ for all strong bisections of S. In particular, $A_1, \ldots, A_n \Rightarrow^T B$, where $T = \langle S - U, U \rangle$. However, $A_1, \ldots, A_n \Rightarrow^T B$ holds if and only if some A_i is in $S - U$ or B is in U. But all the A_i's are in U and not in $S - U$. Therefore B is in U. By the definition of U, however, it follows then that $A_1, \ldots, A_n \Rightarrow B$. That is impossible. Consequently, $A_1, \ldots, A_n \Rightarrow B$.

There is a weak version of the preceding theorem that concerns implication when there is just one antecedent, rather than several antecedents:

Theorem 8.12 (weak completeness). *Let $I = \langle S, \Rightarrow \rangle$ be a nontrivial implication structure. Then for all A and B in S, $A \Rightarrow B$ if and only if $A \Rightarrow^T B$ holds for all weak bisections T of I.*

Proof. The proof is simple, and we leave it as an exercise. (Either note that weak completeness is strong completeness when there is one antecedent, or else run through the proof of Theorem 8.11 with $n = 1$.)

These completeness results do not constitute a definition of arbitrary implication relations "$\Rightarrow$" in terms of the simpler bisection implication relations "$\Rightarrow^T$." The reason is that the relevant bisection implications are based on bisections $\langle K, L \rangle$, where the L's are in turn characterized by the implication relation "$\Rightarrow$" (L is required to be either strongly or weakly closed under "$\Rightarrow$"). Although some bisection implications can be constructed from scratch, the ones that figure in these theorems are not from scratch, but depend upon the implication relation "$\Rightarrow$" of the structure for their construction.

Definition 8.6. If $I = \langle S, \Rightarrow \rangle$ is an implication structure, we shall say that *C is a thesis of I* if and only if $A \Rightarrow C$ for all A in S. We shall say that *C is an antithesis of I* if and only if $C \Rightarrow A$ for all A in S.

i.e.
$c \in d(\phi)$
$d(c) = I$.

Definition 8.7. Let $I = \langle S, \Rightarrow \rangle$ be an implication structure. We shall say that "$\Rightarrow$" is *complete* (on S) if and only if every A in S is either a thesis or an antithesis of I (this is the counterpart of the concept of syntactic completeness).[3]

Theorem 8.13. *Let* $I = \langle S, \Rightarrow \rangle$ *be any nontrivial implication structure. Then (a) if "$\Rightarrow$" is a bisection implication relation (on S), then it is complete (on S), and (b) if "$\Rightarrow$" is complete and the structure has theses as well as antitheses, then it is a bisection implication relation.*

Proof. We leave the proof to the reader in the exercise that follows.

Exercise 8.5. Prove Theorem 8.13 by noting (1) that every bisection implication relation is complete, and (2) for any nontrivial complete structure $I = \langle S, \Rightarrow \rangle$, "$\Rightarrow$" is identical with the bisection implication "$\Rightarrow^T$," where L is the set of all theses of I, and K is its set of antitheses (provided that they exist).

Although not every implication relation is complete, we do know the following:

Theorem 8.14. *Let* $I = \langle S, \Rightarrow \rangle$ *be any nontrivial implication structure. Then "$\Rightarrow$" can be extended to a complete implication relation on S.*

Proof. Since I is nontrivial, there are A and B in S such that $A \not\Rightarrow B$. Set $L(A) = \{C \mid A \Rightarrow C\}$, and $K(A) = S - L(A)$. $L(A)$ is easily seen to be strongly closed under "$\Rightarrow$," and therefore "$\Rightarrow$" is a subset of "$\Rightarrow^{T(A)}$," where $T(A) = \langle K(A), L(A) \rangle$. Moreover, "$\Rightarrow^{T(A)}$" is a complete implication relation on S.

With Theorem 8.13(a), the Lindenbaum–Scott theorem (Theorem 8.11) can be stated in a more familiar idiom:

Theorem 8.15. *The implication relation of any nontrivial implication structure* $I = \langle S, \Rightarrow \rangle$ *is the intersection of all the complete implication relations on S that extend it.*[4]

9

Implications from implications

There are examples of implication relations that are not quite "from scratch." One kind of example uses the particular structure that the elements have in order to define an implication relation over them. Thus, there are implication relations that can be defined over sets, taking into account that it is sets over which the relation is to be defined. Another example uses theories or Tarskian systems in order to define an implication relation. A third example studies certain implication relations over individuals (or their names) and uses the fact about these individuals that they have parts that can enter into a whole–part relation. A fourth example defines an implication relation over interrogatives, exploiting the fact that these interrogatives are of a type that have "direct answers" (Chapter 23), and there is an interesting implication relation that can be defined for the integers when they are encoded in binary notation in the programming language called BASIC (see Appendix A). These examples are very different from the simple bisection relations. The latter are genuinely "topic-neutral" in that they are not sensitive to whatever structure the elements may have. These examples exploit the particular nature of the elements in the implication structure.

The second kind of example we shall describe involves the construction of implications on a set, by using an implication that is already in place. The most theoretically interesting of this type is the notion of a dual implication relation, although a second example, component implication, has some theoretical interest as well.

9.1 Implications on sets

Let S be the set of all subsets of some set. For any subsets A and B of S, $A \Rightarrow B$ if and only if A is a subset of B. And for any subsets A_1, A_2, ..., A_n and B of S, $A_1, \ldots, A_n \Rightarrow B$ if and only if $A_1 \cap A_2 \cap \ldots \cap A_n \Rightarrow B$.

> **Exercise 9.1.** Let S be a set as in the preceding paragraph. Show that "$\Rightarrow$" satisfies the (*)-condition (see Chapter 6).

Exercise 9.2. Let S be as before. For any subsets A and B of S, say that $A \Rightarrow^\wedge B$ if and only if B is a subset of A, and say that $A_1, \ldots, A_n \Rightarrow^\wedge B$ if and only if $A_1 \cup A_2 \cup \ldots A_n \Rightarrow^\wedge B$. Show that "$\Rightarrow^\wedge$" is an implication relation on S.

Exercise 9.3. Let S be as before. For every nonempty A in S, define $L(A)$ as the set of all B that have A as a subset, and let $K(A) = S - L(A)$. Then $T(A) = \langle K(A), L(A) \rangle$ is a strong bisection implication relation on S, such that the empty set is not in $L(A)$, and $\cap L(A)$ [the intersection of all members of $L(A)$] belongs to $L(A)$. Show also that if $T = \langle K, L \rangle$ is any weak bisection on S such that $(\cap L)$ is a member of L, then $L = L(A)$ for some nonempty A in S, namely, $(\cap L)$.

Exercise 9.4. Let $I = \langle P(X), \Rightarrow \rangle$ be an implication structure on all the subsets of some set X, where "$\Rightarrow$" holds if and only if the intersection of all the antecedent sets is a subset of the consequent set. Let S^* be a subset of $P(X)$ that contains a set C^*, but not some subset C of C^*. Finally, let $I^* = \langle S^*, \Rightarrow^* \rangle$, where "$\Rightarrow^*$" is the restriction of "$\Rightarrow$" to S^* ($A_1, \ldots, A_n \Rightarrow^* B$ if and only if all the A_i and B are in S^*, and $A_1, \ldots, A_n \Rightarrow B$). Then show that although $C^* \Rightarrow^* C^*$, nevertheless C^*, $C \not\Rightarrow^* C^*$. This is an elementary example of so-called nonmonotonic implication relations. In fact, generally, if $I = \langle T, \Rightarrow \rangle$ is an implication structure, and T^* is a proper subset of T, and "$\Rightarrow^*$" is the restriction of "$\Rightarrow$" to T^*, then "$\Rightarrow^*$" is a nonmonotonic relation on T.

The interest in the preceding example and in those to follow is not merely in illustrating the variety of implication relations that are available, but in seeing what the logical operators of conjunction, negation, disjunction, and the hypothetical yield when they are relativized to such implication relations. We saw in Chapter 1 that the conjunction operator relativized to the subset implication relation yields the result that the conjunction of any two sets is their intersection. The results for the other logical operators will be postponed until the detailed accounts of the other logical operators are in place (Part III). We can anticipate somewhat by noting that the disjunction of two sets will be proved to be their union, the exclusive disjunction (exjunction) of A and B is just the symmetric difference $(A - B \cup B - A)$, and the negation of a set A is the relative complement, $S - A$. These results are, of course, familiar, but the perspective is different. It is not that these algebraic operations on sets are analogous to the logical operators; they are the logical operators when the operators are relativized to the particular implication relation given by the subset relation.[1]

9.2 Implication relations on Tarskian theories

The special sets that Tarski called "systems" or "theories" constitute a powerful tool in mathematical logic.[2] They also play an important role in our provision of a systematic "Kripke-style" systematization of the modal operators without appeal to possible worlds, in which an accessibility relation will be defined on Tarskian theories (Chapter 35). Moreover, the passage from a set to the smallest Tarskian theory that includes it is an example, on our account of modality, of a modal operator. It is possible to use the structure that Tarskian theories (hereafter, "theories") have in order to define an implication relation for them.

Let $I = \langle S, \Rightarrow \rangle$ be an implication structure. Then we have the following:

> **Definition 9.1.** A *consequence operation Cn* on I is any function that maps subsets of S to subsets of S such that (1) $X \subseteq Cn(X)$, (2) if $X \subseteq Y$, then $Cn(X) \subseteq Cn(Y)$, (3) $CnCn(X) \subseteq Cn(X)$, and (4) $Cn(X \cup Y) = Cn(Cn(X) \cup Cn(Y))$ for all subsets X and Y of S.

In the remainder of this study we shall use the specific consequence relation on implication structures for which $Cn(X)$ is the set of all members of S that are implied by finitely many members of X.

> **Definition 9.2.** Let $I = \langle S, \Rightarrow \rangle$ be an implication structure. For any subset X of S we shall say that $Cn(X)$ is the (consequence) *closure* of X and that X is *closed* if and only if $X = Cn(X)$. A *Tarskian theory* (or *system*) of I is any closed subset of I.

We can now define an implication relation $I = \langle T, \Rightarrow_A \rangle$ for the theories of an implication structure I. Let $U, V, W, \ldots$ range over the theories of I, and let T be the set of all the theories of I. For any theories U and V of I, we shall say that $U \Rightarrow_A V$ if and only if $U \subseteq V$, and $U_1, \ldots, U_n \Rightarrow_A V$ if and only if $U_1 \cap U_2 \cap \ldots \cap U_n \Rightarrow_A V$.

This implication relation for theories is like the one we provided in Section 9.1 for the set of all subsets of a given set. However, in this case, the fact that "$\Rightarrow_A$" is an implication relation rests on the result that the intersection of any two theories of I is always a theory of I (otherwise Dilution would fail).

Exercise 9.5. Show that the intersection of any two theories of I is also a theory of I.

There are other implication relations that can be defined for theories:

Exercise 9.6. Let T be the set of all theories of the structure $I = \langle S, \Rightarrow \rangle$. In general, the union of two theories is not a theory, since there may be elements that the union of two theories implies (under "$\Rightarrow$") that are implied by neither theory alone. If U and V are any two theories of I, say that $U \Rightarrow^{\wedge}_A V$ if and only if V is a subset of U, and $U_1, \ldots, U_n \Rightarrow^{\wedge}_A V$ if and only if $V \subseteq Cn(U_1 \cup \ldots \cup U_n)$, then "$\Rightarrow^{\wedge}_A$" is an implication.

It is worth noting that the logical operators on structures of theories do not yield the standard Boolean operations. If the members of the set consist of Tarskian systems or theories, then the logical operators of conjunction, disjunction, and negation on such a structure are just the algebraic operations that Tarski used for the calculus of such systems: set intersection, the closure of the union (which he called "the logical sum"), and the closure of the union of all theories whose intersection with X is the set of theses of the structure $I = \langle S, \Rightarrow \rangle$ for the complement of X (which he called the logical complement of X).

Thus, even if we had not had the genius of Tarski to show us what the appropriate algebraic operations are for his systems or theories, a study of the logical operators on a structure of such theories would have led to those operations, for the logical operators on a structure consisting of Tarskian theories and the set-theoretical implication relation described earlier are just the Tarskian algebraic operations on systems. The algebraic study of Tarski's "calculus of systems" is the study of the logical operators on the particular implication structure $I = \langle T, \Rightarrow_A \rangle$, where T is the set of all theories of the structure $\langle S, \Rightarrow \rangle$.[3]

9.3 Implication relations on individuals

It might be thought that the whole idea of an implication relation holding between individuals is incoherent. On the general view that we have advocated, the fact that individuals are not truth-bearers is no impediment to the development of a theory of the logical operators on them. All that is required, since all the logical operators are relativized to implication relations, is that an implication relation be specified for them.

We shall define an implication relation "$\Rightarrow^i$" on a set of individuals by using the fact that it is *individuals* that are so related. We shall take it as a minimal condition that as individuals they satisfy certain conditions, given by the "calculus of individuals," that involve the "whole–part" (or, alternatively, the "overlap") relation, which will be explained later.[4]

There is the striking but simple result that with the choice of "$\Rightarrow^i$" the key concepts of the calculus of individuals are the logical operators relativized to "$\Rightarrow^i$." Thus, the disjunction operator (relative to "$\Rightarrow^i$") turns out to be the familiar notion of the *sum* of individuals in the calculus of individuals, conjunction is the mereological concept of the *product* of individuals, and the *negate* of an individual is just the negation operator (see Chapter 22 for details). In a sense, then, the calculus of individuals is just the study of the logical operators with respect to a natural notion of implication on individuals.

9.3.1 Calculus of individuals

It is customary to think of the calculus of individuals as a first-order theory that is obtained by adding an additional two-place predicate, together with some additional axioms for it, to first-order quantification theory. Sometimes, "∘," the *overlap relation*, is taken as primitive, and the two-place relation "<," the *part–whole relation*, is defined with its aid. Sometimes the part–whole relation is taken as primitive, and the overlap relation is defined with its aid. We shall not explore this theory in any detail. The theory was introduced by S. Lésniewski and studied in some detail by H. Leonard and N. Goodman, and more recently by W. Hodges, and D. Lewis, and G. Hellman.[5] However, even if we did not have the pioneering work of Lésniewski, Leonard, and Goodman to lead us, the concepts they introduced for the study of individuals could be obtained by seeing what the logical operators are with respect to a certain implication relation.[6]

Let us begin with a nonempty set of *individuals*. By that we mean any nonempty set S together with "<," a binary relation ("A is a part of B") on it, such that the following conditions are satisfied:

1. Reflexivity: For all A in S, $A < A$.
2. Transitivity: For all A, B, and C in S, if $A < B$, and $B < C$, then $A < C$.
3. For any A and B in S, $A < B$ if for every C that is a part of A there is some D that is a part of C as well as a part of B.

Thus, every member of S is a part of itself, and any part of a part of any C in S is a part of C. And if every part of A has a part that is also a part of B, then A is a part of B.

We then can define another binary relation "$\circ$" on S, the *overlap relation* on S, by requiring that A and B overlap ($A \circ B$) if and only if they have some part in common. And we shall say that A and B are *discrete* ($A \# B$) if and only if they have no part in common.

It follows that the overlap relation is reflexive and symmetric and that A is a part of B if and only if every C that overlaps A also overlaps B.

A definition of identity can be provided for individuals: The individuals A and B are identical if and only if every part of A is a part of B, and conversely.

Before we introduce an implication relation for individuals, it is worthwhile completing the basic picture with some of the key definitions of the calculus of individuals.

Definition 9.3. (a) The *sum* of A and B [SUM(A, B)] is that individual such that an individual overlaps it if and only if it either overlaps A or overlaps B.[7] (b) The *product* of A and B [PRO(A, B)] is that individual whose parts are exactly those that are the parts of both A and B. (c) The *negate* of A [NEG(A)] is that individual whose parts are exactly those that are discrete from A.

9.3.2 The whole–part relation as implication on individuals

Let S be any nonempty set with a part–whole relation "$<$" on it that satisfies conditions 1–3 in Section 9.3.1. On these individuals, consider the following implication relation "$\Rightarrow^i$": For any A, A_1, ..., A_n and B and S,

1. $A \Rightarrow^i B$ if and only if $A < B$, and
2. A_1, ..., $A_n \Rightarrow^i B$ if and only if for every C in S, if $C \Rightarrow^i A_i$ for all A_i, then $C \Rightarrow^i B$.

The first condition uses the part–whole relation if it is a question of an implication with only one antecedent. The second condition is a way of using the part–whole relation to cover the cases in which the implication involves several members of S as antecedents.

Exercise 9.7. Show that the foregoing conditions 1 and 2 agree for the case $n = 1$ if and only if "$<$" is reflexive and transitive.

Exercise 9.8. Show that "$\Rightarrow^i$" is an implication relation.

Exercise 9.9. Show that the relation "$\Rightarrow^\wedge$" on individuals is an implication relation where (1) $A \Rightarrow^\wedge B$ if and only if B is a part of A, and (2) $A_1, A_2, \ldots, A_n \Rightarrow^\wedge B$ if and only if B is a part of $\mathrm{SUM}(A_1, \ldots, A_n)$.

Before we turn to a class of implication relations that are defined with the aid of other implication relations, it is worth noting in passing that when integers are suitably encoded, it is possible to define an implication relation for them under which certain numerical operations turn out to be just the logical operators on such a structure. This is so for the numerical functions of the programming language BASIC, where the integers are treated as sequences in binary notation.[8]

9.4 Relativized implication relations (fixed and variable)

9.4.1 Fixed relativization

Let $I = \langle S, \Rightarrow \rangle$ be an implication structure on the nonempty set S, with implication relation "$\Rightarrow$." Let $S^* = \{S_1, S_2, \ldots, S_m\}$ be any *finite* nonempty subset of S, and define a new implication relation "$\Rightarrow^{S^*}$" as follows:

$A_1, \ldots, A_n \Rightarrow^{S^*} B$ if and only if $S_1, \ldots, S_m, A_1, \ldots, A_n \Rightarrow B$.

The following two results are simple consequences: (1) "$\Rightarrow^{S^*}$" is an extension of "$\Rightarrow$," and (2) "$\Rightarrow$" and "$\Rightarrow^{S^*}$" are identical if and only if S^* is a set of theses of I.

9.4.2 Variable relativization

Let $I = \langle S, \Rightarrow \rangle$ be an implication structure, and let M be any nonempty subset of S, finite or possibly infinite. We shall say that

$A_1, \ldots, A_n \Rightarrow^M B$ if and only if $A_1, \ldots, A_n \Rightarrow^{M^*} B$ for some finite (nonempty) subset M^* of M.

Here, in contrast with the fixed relativization, M^* can shift, depending on $A_1, \ldots, A_n$ and B. It follows immediately that (1) "$\Rightarrow^M$" is an implication relation on S if "$\Rightarrow$" is likewise, (2) "$\Rightarrow^M$" is an extension of "$\Rightarrow$," and (3) "$\Rightarrow^M$" and "$\Rightarrow$" are identical if and only if M is the set of all theses of I.

Relativized implication relations are what one would use in a situation in which one wished to consider what was implied with the aid of a select collection of members of S. Thus, for example, sometimes an implication relation is set up using some notion of deducibility from axioms. In addition, one can then introduce a new relation, derivability from premises, in which one considers what is deducible from the axioms together with the premises. The new relation of deducibility from premises is a special case of what we have called relativized implication. There are other situations in which it is helpful to switch from an implication relation on a structure to a relativized version: The explanation of certain kinds of relative modality is a case in point.[9]

Exercise 9.10. Let $I = \langle S, \Rightarrow \rangle$ be an implication relation, and let U and V be two nonempty subsets of S. If $U \subseteq V$, then "$\Rightarrow^V$" is an extension of "$\Rightarrow^U$."

Exercise 9.11. Let $I = \langle S, \Rightarrow \rangle$ be an implication structure, and let U and V be subsets of S that are strongly closed under "$\Rightarrow$." If "$\Rightarrow^V$" is an extension of "$\Rightarrow^U$," then $U \subseteq V$.

9.5 Dual implication relations

Given any implication relation "$\Rightarrow$," we shall now show how one can obtain another, its dual, "$\Rightarrow^\wedge$." The dual of an implication relation is not just one more implication relation of the kind that have other implication relations as their sources. It is a very useful and powerful kind of relation to have, for with its aid one can define the dual of an operator as follows: Let $I = \langle S, \Rightarrow \rangle$ be any implication structure, and let $I^\wedge = \langle S, \Rightarrow^\wedge \rangle$ be the dual implication structure. Let O be an operator on I. Then $O^\wedge$, the dual of the operator O on the structure I, assigns to any elements of S what the operator O assigns to those elements on the dual structure $I^\wedge$.

We shall prove, once the various logical operators have been defined, that in those implication structures that have conjunctions and disjunctions the dual of the conjunction operator is disjunction, and conversely (see Section 13.6 and Theorem 14.6). As for the negation operator, N, it too has its dual, $N^\wedge$. It will be seen (Chapter 17) that, in general, negation and its dual are nonequivalent operators on a structure, but a necessary and sufficient condition for their being equivalent is that the negation operator be classical – that is, for every element A of the structure, $NN(A) \Rightarrow A$. Moreover, when negation on a structure is nonclassical, this definition of duality permits one to prove that N is always stronger than its dual – that is, $N(A) \Rightarrow N^\wedge(A)$ for all A. With the aid of this concept of duality, it follows that when negation is nonclassical on a structure, then N and its dual $N^\wedge$ split the work of classical negation between them, so that although $NN(A)$ does not always imply A (since N is nonclassical), nevertheless $N^\wedge N^\wedge(A)$ always implies A; although the disjunction of any sentence A with its negation $D(A, N(A))$ is not always a thesis of the structure, nevertheless the disjunction of any sentence A with $N^\wedge(A)$ is always a thesis of the structure. It is only when negation is classical, so that $N(A) \Leftrightarrow N^\wedge(A)$, that the separate theses that hold for N, on the one hand, and $N^\wedge$, on the other, become fused together as theses about a single negation operator, classical negation. We can think of classical negation as the coming together, in special circumstances, of a negation operator and its dual; in nonclassical structures they are kept distinct.

In the usual accounts of duality, rules are given for obtaining the dual of an expression F that is constructed from atomic sentences using only negation, disjunction, and conjunction. These involve replacing each atomic sentence by its negation, and each occurrence of conjunction (disjunction) by disjunction (conjunction). The rules rely heavily on the syntax of the expressions, and it is required that negation be classical.

On our account, duality is a much more general concept. It applies to structures that may not have syntactical objects, and it covers the cases in which negation may not be classical. It even covers those cases in which disjunction or conjunction may not be available in the structure under consideration. However, the principal examples of pairs of dual operators are conjunction and disjunction, and, as we shall see, some of the more interesting theorems about duality hold for structures that have disjunctions and conjunctions for their elements.

Let $I = \langle S, \Rightarrow \rangle$ be an implication structure. Then the dual "$\Rightarrow^\wedge$" of "$\Rightarrow$" is the relation on S such that

$A_1, A_2, \ldots, A_n \Rightarrow^\wedge B$ if and only if for every T in S, if $A_1 \Rightarrow T$, and $\ldots$, and $A_n \Rightarrow T$, then $B \Rightarrow T$.

And the implication structure $I^\wedge$, dual to I, is $\langle S, \Rightarrow^\wedge \rangle$.

Exercise 9.12. If "$\Rightarrow$" is an implication relation, then so too is "$\Rightarrow\hat{}$."

We shall write "$\Rightarrow\hat{}\hat{}$" for "$(\Rightarrow\hat{})\hat{}$" (the double dual of "$\Rightarrow$"), and triple duals are the duals of double duals. The following theorems explore some of the basic features of dual implication.

Theorem 9.1. *Single-antecedent case: Let* $I = \langle S, \Rightarrow \rangle$ *be an implication structure. Then for any A and B in S, $A \Rightarrow\hat{} B$ if and only if $B \Rightarrow A$.*

Proof. Suppose that $A \Rightarrow\hat{} B$. Then, according to the definition of the dual, for any T in S, if $A \Rightarrow T$, then $B \Rightarrow T$. But in any structure, $A \Rightarrow A$. Therefore, $B \Rightarrow A$. Conversely, suppose that $B \Rightarrow A$. Then, by Cut, for any T, if $A \Rightarrow T$, then $B \Rightarrow T$. So for all T in S, if $A \Rightarrow T$, then $B \Rightarrow T$. But the latter holds if and only if $A \Rightarrow\hat{} B$.

Thus, when implications involve only single antecedents, the dual of any implication relation is just its converse.

We shall be concerned in the remainder of this section with the properties of dual implication relations that do not require logical operators for their description. But it is worth noting here that it will be proved that if disjunctions are available in an implication structure $I = \langle S, \Rightarrow \rangle$, then $A_1, \ldots, A_n \Rightarrow\hat{} B$ if and only if (under "$\Rightarrow$") B implies the disjunction of the A_i's (see Chapter 14, Theorem 14.8).

There is a feature of the dual of an implication relation that is simple to understand, although somewhat unusual. It serves as a clear example of why there is no automatic connection between an implication relation and the preservation of truth, or an automatic connection between implication relations and arguments. There are some implication relations that hold among items that have truth values, but that fail to be preservers of truth. For example, any relativized implication relation "$\Rightarrow^T$" (where T is a false statement) will not guarantee the truth of B, even if $A_1, \ldots, A_n$ are true and $A_1, \ldots, A_n \Rightarrow^T B$. The dual of a truth-preserving implication relation is a more radical case.

The short story is that if "$\Rightarrow$" is an implication relation that is truth-preserving (if $A_1, \ldots, A_n \Rightarrow B$, and all of the A_i's are true, then so too is B), then the dual implication, "$\Rightarrow\hat{}$," is false-preserving. Moreover, if $A_1, \ldots, A_n \Rightarrow\hat{} B$, and B is true, then at least one of the A_i's is true (a sort of kernel-of-truth doctrine). The question whether or not they are related to arguments is a more subtle issue that we shall not pursue here.[10] However, in the single-antecedent case, note that if "$\Rightarrow$" is truth-preserving, then since $A \Rightarrow\hat{\ } B$ if and only if $B \Rightarrow A$ (Theorem 9.1), it follows that if A is false (not true), so too is B.

One natural question is whether or not an implication relation is ever identical with its dual. We need the notion of an *almost-trivial structure*:

Definition 9.4. An implication structure $I = \langle S, \Rightarrow \rangle$ is *almost trivial* if and only if for every A and B in S, if $A \Rightarrow B$, then $A \Leftrightarrow B$. Thus, an implication structure is almost trivial if and only if it has a number of elements such that none of them implies any of the others, and every member of the structure is equivalent to some one of them.

It is a straightforward matter to show the following:

Theorem 9.2. *If $I\hat{\ }$ is the dual implication structure of I, then $\Rightarrow = \Rightarrow\hat{\ }$ if and only if I is almost trivial and "$\Rightarrow$" satisfies the (*)-condition (see Chapter 6).*

We leave the proof as an exercise. There is a perspicuous way of describing the dual of an implication that picks it out from a family of implication relations:

Theorem 9.3. *If $I = \langle S, \Rightarrow \rangle$, then "$\Rightarrow\hat{\ }$" is that implication relation on S that extends all the implication relations "$\Rightarrow'$" on S such that $A \Rightarrow' B$ if and only if $B \Rightarrow A$.*

Proof. Suppose that $A_1, \ldots, A_n \Rightarrow' B$, and $A \Rightarrow' B$ if and only if $B \Rightarrow A$. By Cut, for all T, if $T \Rightarrow' A_i$ (all A_i), then $T \Rightarrow' B$. Therefore, for all T, if $A_i \Rightarrow T$ (all A_i), then $B \Rightarrow T$. Consequently, $A_1, \ldots, A_n \Rightarrow\hat{\ } B$.

A theorem follows immediately:

Theorem 9.4. *On any implication structure I, $\Rightarrow \subseteq \Rightarrow\hat{\ }\hat{\ }$.*

Proof. By the preceding theorem, "$\Rightarrow\hat{\ }\hat{\ }$" extends any implication relation "$\Rightarrow'$" on S such that $A \Rightarrow' B$ if and only if $B \Rightarrow\hat{\ } A$. By Theorem 9.1, $A \Rightarrow B$ if and only if $B \Rightarrow\hat{\ } A$. Therefore "$\Rightarrow\hat{\ }\hat{\ }$" extends "$\Rightarrow$."

Exercise 9.13. Show that $\Rightarrow^{\wedge} = \Rightarrow^{\wedge\wedge\wedge}$.

Exercise 9.14. If "$\Rightarrow_1$" and "$\Rightarrow_2$" are implication relations on the set S, whose duals are different, then $\Rightarrow_1 \neq \Rightarrow_2$.

It is worthwhile spending some effort on the question of when an implication relation is its own double dual. First, a definition:

Definition 9.5. Let $I = \langle S, \Rightarrow \rangle$ be an implication structure. We shall say that an implication relation "$\Rightarrow^*$" on S is the *(*)-extension* of "$\Rightarrow$" if and only if for all $A_1, \ldots, A_n$ and B in S, $A_1, \ldots, A_n \Rightarrow^* B$ if and only if for every T in S, if $T \Rightarrow A_i$ (for all A_i), then $T \Rightarrow B$.

Exercise 9.15. Show (1) that "$\Rightarrow^*$" is an extension of "$\Rightarrow$," (2) that $A \Rightarrow B$ if and only if $A \Rightarrow^* B$ for all A and B in S, and (3) that "$\Rightarrow^*$" satisfies the (*)-condition (Chapter 6).

We then have this simple but useful result:

Theorem 9.5. *Let $I = \langle S, \Rightarrow \rangle$. Then "$\Rightarrow^*$" extends all those implication relations "$\Rightarrow'$" on S for which $A \Rightarrow' B$ if and only if $A \Rightarrow B$ for all A and B in S.*

Proof. If $A_1, \ldots, A_n \Rightarrow' B$, then by Cut, for all T in S, if $T \Rightarrow' A_i$ (for all A_i), then $T \Rightarrow' B$. Therefore, for all such T, if $T \Rightarrow A_i$ (all A_i), then $T \Rightarrow B$. Consequently, $A_1, \ldots, A_n \Rightarrow^* B$.

We know that "$\Rightarrow^*$" is an extension of "$\Rightarrow$" (Exercise 9.15). The next theorem concerns the extensions of "$\Rightarrow^*$."

Theorem 9.6. *For any implication structure I, $\Rightarrow^* \subseteq \Rightarrow$ if and only if the (*)-condition holds for "$\Rightarrow$."*

Proof. Suppose that the (*)-condition holds for "$\Rightarrow$" and that $A_1, \ldots, A_n \Rightarrow^* B$, but that $A_1, \ldots, A_n \not\Rightarrow B$. From the latter, there is some T in S such that $T \Rightarrow A_i$ (all A_i), but $T \not\Rightarrow B$. Therefore, $A_1, \ldots, A_n \not\Rightarrow^* B$. But that is impossible. So "$\Rightarrow$" is an extension of "$\Rightarrow^*$." Conversely, suppose that $\Rightarrow^* \subseteq \Rightarrow$. If $A_1, \ldots, A_n$ do not imply B (under "$\Rightarrow$"), then they do not imply B (under "$\Rightarrow^*$"). Therefore, by the definition of "$\Rightarrow$*," there is a T such that $T \Rightarrow A_i$ (all A_i), but $T \not\Rightarrow B$. So the (*)-condition holds for "$\Rightarrow$."

Thus, from Exercise 9.15 and the preceding theorem, we know that an implication relation "$\Rightarrow$" is identical with its (*)-extension if and only if the (*)-condition holds for "$\Rightarrow$."

There is a simple connection between (*)-extensions and double duals:

Theorem 9.7. *If $I = \langle S, \Rightarrow \rangle$ is an implication structure, then* $\Rightarrow$* = $\Rightarrow^{\wedge\wedge}$.

Proof. By Theorem 9.3, "$\Rightarrow^{\wedge\wedge}$" is the implication relation that extends all those implication relations "$\Rightarrow'$" for which $A \Rightarrow' B$ if and only if $B \Rightarrow^{\wedge} A$, that is, for which $A \Rightarrow' B$ if and only if $A \Rightarrow B$. But "$\Rightarrow$*" extends all "$\Rightarrow'$" for which $A \Rightarrow' B$ if and only if $A \Rightarrow B$. Therefore they are identical.

Combining Theorems 9.4, 9.6, and 9.7, we obtain a necessary and sufficient condition:

Theorem 9.8. *Let $I = \langle S, \Rightarrow \rangle$. Then $\Rightarrow = \Rightarrow^{\wedge\wedge}$ if and only if "$\Rightarrow$" satisfies the (*)-condition.*

Exercise 9.16 Every implication relation "$\Rightarrow$" can be extended to one that is its own double dual. [Hint: Use the (*)-extension "$\Rightarrow$*" of "$\Rightarrow$," and show that $\Rightarrow$* = $(\Rightarrow$*$)^{\wedge\wedge}$.]

Theorem 9.9. *Let $I = \langle S, \Rightarrow \rangle$. If for every $A_1, \ldots, A_n$ in S there exists some C such that C implies each of the A_i's, and $A_1, \ldots, A_n \Rightarrow C$, then $\Rightarrow = \Rightarrow^{\wedge\wedge}$.*

Proof. Under the condition of this theorem, "$\Rightarrow$" satisfies the (*)-condition. Suppose that $A_1, \ldots, A_n \not\Rightarrow B$. There is some C that implies each of the A_i's and $A_1, \ldots, A_n \Rightarrow C$. Moreover, C fails to imply B (if $C \Rightarrow B$, then $A_1, \ldots, A_n \Rightarrow B$, and that is impossible). The conclusion follows by the preceding theorem.

Finally, there is another necessary and sufficient condition of some interest:

Theorem 9.10. *Let* $I = \langle S, \Rightarrow \rangle$. *Then* $\Rightarrow\ =\ \Rightarrow^{\wedge\wedge}$ *if and only if* "$\Rightarrow$" *is the dual of some implication relation on* I.

Proof. Suppose that "$\Rightarrow$" is the dual of some implication relation "$\Rightarrow°$." Since $\Rightarrow\ =\ (\Rightarrow°)^{\wedge}$, we have $\Rightarrow^{\wedge\wedge}\ =\ (\Rightarrow°)^{\wedge\wedge\wedge}\ =\ (\Rightarrow°)^{\wedge}$ (by Exercise 9.13). So $\Rightarrow^{\wedge\wedge}\ =\ \Rightarrow$. Conversely, of course, if $\Rightarrow\ =\ \Rightarrow^{\wedge\wedge}$, then "$\Rightarrow$" is the dual of an implication relation.

9.6 Symmetric sequents as products of implication relations and their duals

Gentzen (1934) introduced a concept of a *symmetric sequent*, $A_1, \ldots,$ $A_n \Rightarrow B_1, \ldots, B_m$, which contrasts with the sequents we have been considering, in that there can be multiple as well as single consequents.

There is no doubt as to the mathematical power and notational compactness that the use of symmetric sequents yields. But there is some controversy whether or not it has any direct connection with implication, or, to revert to Gentzen and Hertz's original motivation, to some notion of dependence. There may well be some natural use of such a symmetric relation for the expression of certain kinds of inferences. Shoesmith and Smiley (1978), in their account of multiple-conclusion logic, attempt to provide a realistic case. However, without settling the matter, one way or the other, it is worth noting that the Gentzen symmetric sequent, under certain familiar conditions, can be regarded as a combination, a "relational product" of an implication relation and its dual. And, conversely, under certain conditions the relational product of an implication relation and its dual is a Gentzen symmetric relation.

There are three results: (1) If we have a symmetric sequent relation denoted by, say, "$\Rightarrow^G$," then, under certain conditions, there is some implication relation "$\Rightarrow$" such that

$A_1, \ldots, A_n \Rightarrow^G B_1, \ldots, B_m$ if and only if for some member of S, say C, $A_1, \ldots, A_n \Rightarrow C$ and $B_1, \ldots, B_m \Rightarrow^{\wedge} C$.

There is a converse as well: (2) Under certain conditions on an implication structure $I = \langle S, \Rightarrow \rangle$, one can define a relation "$\Rightarrow^g$," which satisfies the conditions for being a symmetric Gentzen relation, by defining $A_1, \ldots, A_n \Rightarrow^g B_1, \ldots, B_m$ as

$$A_1, \ldots, A_n \Rightarrow C \quad \text{and} \quad B_1, \ldots, B_m \Rightarrow^{\wedge} C$$

for some C in the structure.

(3) It is also possible to define the notion of the dual of a Gentzen symmetric relation, essentially along the lines that we used to define the dual of an implication relation, so that under certain conditions the dual of any Gentzen symmetric relation is just its converse: $A_1, \ldots, A_n$ $(\Rightarrow^G)^\wedge B_1, \ldots, B_m$ if and only if $A_1, \ldots, A_n \Rightarrow^G B_1, \ldots, B_m$.

However, all three results are not true for all structures. The conditions referred to amount to the requirement that disjunctions and conjunctions always exist in the structure and, in the case of the second result, that negation also be classical. It is true that the results do hold in those structures associated with the logical systems that Gentzen studied. (For a more detailed description of the basic characteristics of the Gentzen symmetric relation, and a proof of these results, see Appendix B.)

Although the Gentzen symmetric relation is a compact and powerful concept on certain structures, it is not useful if one wants to study those structures that are nonclassical, or those in which disjunctions or conjunctions may not always exist.

9.7 Component implication and relevance

We have been exploring the range of relations that qualify as implicational. In all the examples thus far, we have considered a set S and an implication relation over it that satisfy certain conditions. We have not considered, in any detailed way, the possibilities for deviation from those conditions, nor have we noted the consequent effects upon the logical operators, once they are relativized to those variants. The reason is not lack of interest, but lack of a fund of results in this largely unexplored situation. Let us consider an example of how a more refined structure can be introduced on a set S that has an implication relation "$\Rightarrow$" on it, so that a new relation "$\Rightarrow^c$" can be introduced on S that takes into account a certain amount of structure already imposed by "$\Rightarrow$." This new relation, "$\Rightarrow^c$," we shall call *component implication*, because it takes into account the way in which "$\Rightarrow$" splits the set S into nonempty subsets that we shall call its components. It departs from the conditions we gave for implication relations and is not, strictly speaking, an implication relation.

Consider the structure $I = \langle S, \Rightarrow \rangle$:

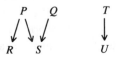

It is natural to think of S as breaking up into two distinct components: C_1, consisting of P, Q, R, and S, and C_2, consisting of just T and U, which are mutually disjoint and together exhaustive of S.

Notice that no member of one component implies or is implied by any member of the other; they are implicationally separated. However, as is obvious from the diagram, there still can be members of a component neither of which implies the other. The problem is to capture the idea that an element of S belongs to a component if it is caught up in a network of implications and that any other member of that component is caught up in precisely the same network. The idea, then, is to start with an item A and indicate its implicational network or component. Before we turn to the details of such a construction, it is worth describing the general notion of a component.

9.7.1 Structural components

Let $I = \langle S, \Longrightarrow \rangle$ be an implication structure. We shall single out certain subsets of S as the components of I. Let E be an equivalence relation (binary, reflexive, symmetric, and transitive) on a set S. The equivalence classes of E are the nonempty subsets T of S such that for some B in S, every A is in T if and only if $E(A, B)$. If E and E^* are equivalence relations on S, then E is said to be finer than E^* if and only if E is a subset of E^*.

> **Definition 9.6.** Let $I = \langle S, \Longrightarrow \rangle$ be an implication relation. Let E_c be the finest equivalence relation on S such that if $A \Longrightarrow B$, then $E_c(A, B)$. The *components* of I are the equivalence classes of E_c.

We shall think of the members of each component as being *relevant* to each other in this sense: When we trace out from any member A of S to all those elements that are related implicationally to A (implying or being implied by A), and then trace those members in turn, and those in turn, continuing on this way, then B will turn up in the process. And if we started with B and ran a similar construction, then A would turn up. "Relevance" may not be the most felicitous choice of terminology, since it suggests a definite family of special logical systems based on a family of entailment relations, and the results we are about to develop overlap but do not coincide with any of the more familiar systems of "relevance logics" that have been proposed.[11]

We shall say that A and B are *relevant* if and only if they belong to some component of the structure. Thus the relevance relation so defined is reflexive, symmetric, and transitive. The latter condition may conflict with certain intuitions that allow A to be relevant to B, and B to C, but not A to C. We think that relevance is a transitive notion and do not attempt to refine the notion further.[12]

What we mean is that any A and B are implicationally relevant to each other if A determines an implicational network to which B belongs, and B does likewise.

It should be noted that if the implication structure has a thesis or an antithesis, then there are no components (i.e., there is only one).

It is now possible to study a new implication relation on S that takes its component structure into account:

9.7.2 Component implication

Let us defer the details of the construction of components based upon the implication relation "$\Rightarrow$," and suppose that the implication structure $I = \langle S, \Rightarrow \rangle$ can be partitioned into a system of components C_i. We can then define a new relation on S, *component implication*, "$\Rightarrow^c$," as follows:

Definition 9.7. Let $I = \langle S, \Rightarrow \rangle$. Then "$\Rightarrow^c$" is a *component implication relation* on S if and only if $A_1, \ldots, A_n \Rightarrow^c B$ holds if and only if (1) $A_1, \ldots, A_n \Rightarrow B$ and (2) all the A_i's belong to the same component as B.

Component implication, strictly speaking, is not an implication relation: The Dilution condition fails. It is not true, in general, that if $A, B \Rightarrow^c C$, then for any $E, A, B, E \Rightarrow^c C$. Simply choose any E that is not in the component of C.[13]

Component implication is a nonmonotonic relation, and there is some question whether this kind of relation has any natural examples that one might find used in some type of reasoning or argument, or indeed whether there are any theoretically interesting examples. It is therefore a little early to explore the general case in which logical operators are relativized to nonmonotonic "implications" rather than implication relations. It is possible, however, to consider the special case of component implication and investigate in a preliminary way how the logical operators can be adjusted when they are relativized to such a relation. For a sketch of how these results align with those already in the literature, the reader is referred to Appendix C.

10

Implication relations and the a priori:
A further condition?

The background theory against which the various logical operators are characterized requires that implications be relations on sets. These implication structures of the theory are at the heart of our account of the logical operators as well as the modal operators (Part IV). It is integral to our theory of the logical operators that any two implication relations that extend each other (are coextensional) will result in logical operators that are equivalent by either implication relation.

Recently, Peacocke (1981) has objected to the extensional treatment of deducibility relations in Hacking's account (1979) of the logical connectives. On Hacking's view, it makes no difference which of two coextensional deducibility relations is used to account for the logical connectives. Hacking's account is the target of Peacocke's objection, and the substance of the objection easily carries over to our own. In substance, Peacocke claims to have produced a case of two coextensional implication relations, such that conjunction relative to one is just the standard "&," whereas conjunction with respect to the other is some nonstandard, partially defined connective.

Peacocke's remedy is this: Not all coextensional implication relations are on a par for a theory of the logical connectives. Instead of requiring that implication relations (he calls them "deducibility relations") satisfy the conditions of Reflexivity, Dilution, and Transitivity, he requires instead that it is a priori that the relation satisfies those conditions (Peacocke, 1976, 1981).

Peacocke assumes that there is an implication relation "$\Rightarrow$" that leads to the standard conjunction operator "&," and he claims to have defined another relation "$\Rightarrow^\$$," coextensional with "$\Rightarrow$," except that it leads to a nonstandard, partially defined connective "$." He denies that the second relation, "$\Rightarrow^\$$," is an implication relation; it is not a priori that it satisfies Reflexivity, Dilution, and Transitivity. Briefly, then, not every relation that is coextensional with an implication relation is an implication relation. To think otherwise is a case of what Peacocke calls "excess extensionality."

The imposition of epistemic conditions for implication relations is, in our opinion, a drastic solution that brings more unclarity with it than it removes. Whether or not there is a problem depends critically upon the cogency of Peacocke's example. However, that example is seriously flawed.

Following Peacocke, let "$\Rightarrow^\$$" be a new relation. Let us call it *Rockefeller implication*, according to which

($\Rightarrow^\$$): $A_1, \ldots, A_n \Rightarrow^\$ B$ if and only if Rockefeller is wealthy, and $A_1, \ldots, A_n \Rightarrow B$.

He claims that if Rockefeller is wealthy, then "$\Rightarrow^\$$" is coextensional with "$\Rightarrow$." Since "$\Rightarrow$" is an implication relation, but "$\Rightarrow^\$$" is not, it follows that coextensionality is not enough.

The problem, as Peacocke sees it, concerns whether or not "$\$$" is a classical logical connective, where "$A \$ B$" is introduced relative to "$\Rightarrow^\$$" in the way in which conjunction is introduced with respect to "$\Rightarrow$." He claims that "$\$$" is not a classical logical connective.

Peacocke draws three conclusions for the operator "$\$$" based upon "$\Rightarrow^\$$." Instead of yielding the usual truth-value entries for conjunction, the use of "$\Rightarrow^\$$" yields (he says)

1. "$A \$ B$" is true if Rockefeller is wealthy and A and B are both true.
2. "$A \$ B$" is false if Rockefeller is wealthy and either A or B is false.
3. The rules determine nothing about the truth value of "$A \$ B$" in the case in which Rockefeller is not wealthy.

He sums it up this way: "So the meaning of '$A \$ B$' is specified by a partial truth function of the truth values of A, B and 'Rockefeller is wealthy'" (Peacocke, 1981, p. 169).

Unfortunately, these are not consequences of using the relation "$\Rightarrow^\$$" in place of "$\Rightarrow$." A straightforward computation shows (provided it is granted that "$\Rightarrow$" is truth- preserving), *pace* Peacocke, that

1'. "$A \$ B$" is true if A and B are true.
2'. "$A \$ B$" is false if either A or B is false.

Here is how the calculation for conclusion 1' goes: According to conjunction-style rules, $A, B \Rightarrow^\$ A \$ B$, which holds if and only if Rockefeller is wealthy, and $A, B \Rightarrow A \$ B$. Consequently, $A, B \Rightarrow A \$ B$. Therefore, if A and B are true, then so too is $A \$ B$.

As for conclusion 2', notice that $A \$ B \Rightarrow^\$ A$, and $A \$ B \Rightarrow^\$ B$. Therefore, Rockefeller is wealthy, and $A \$ B \Rightarrow A$, and also Rockefeller is wealthy, and $A \$ B \Rightarrow B$. Consequently, $A \$ B \Rightarrow A$, and $A \$ B \Rightarrow B$. Thus, if either A or B is false, then $A \$ B$ is false.

Finally, consider conclusion 3. Notice that if Rockefeller is not wealthy, then all the statements $A_1, \ldots, A_n \Rightarrow^\$ B$ are false, since each is the conjunction of R with $A_1, \ldots, A_n \Rightarrow B$. Consequently, "$\Rightarrow^\$$" is not an implication relation: The condition of Reflexivity fails, for $A \Rightarrow^\$ A$ holds if and only if Rockefeller is wealthy, and $A \Rightarrow A$. But this conjunction is false if Rockefeller is not wealthy. Thus, if "Rockefeller is wealthy" is false, then "$\$$" is not a connective introduced with respect to an implication relation. Moreover, we can go further and say that there is not even a statement "$A \$ B$" if Rockefeller fails to be wealthy. The reason is that "$A \$ B$" is supposed to be a statement for which the following are true: $A, B \Rightarrow^\$ A \$ B$, $A \$ B \Rightarrow^\$ A$ and $A \$ B \Rightarrow^\$ B$. But none of these is true if Rockefeller is not wealthy.

Statements 1–3 are not, contrary to Peacocke's claim, consequences of using "$\Rightarrow^\$$" to introduce the connective "$\$$." Instead, they are exactly the consequences one would draw by using a different implication relation, "$\Rightarrow^R$" – the one that consists in relativizing the implication relation "$\Rightarrow$" to the statement that Rockefeller is wealthy ("R").

Let us define another implication relation, R-implication, "$\Rightarrow^R$," using the implication relation "$\Rightarrow$" and the Rockefeller statement R:

$(\Rightarrow^R)$: $A_1, \ldots, A_n \Rightarrow^R B$ if and only if $R, A_1, \ldots, A_n \Rightarrow B$.

Now, "$\Rightarrow^R$" is an implication relation (whether R is true or not) provided that "$\Rightarrow$" is likewise. (It is, in fact, what we have called a relativized implication relation.) However, "$\Rightarrow^R$" is not coextensional with "$\Rightarrow$." For suppose that it is. Then, for all A and B, $A \Rightarrow^R B$ if and only if $A \Rightarrow B$. Now $A \Rightarrow^R R$ for all A, so that $A \Rightarrow R$ for all A. That is, in particular, "Rockefeller is wealthy" is a thesis (with respect to "$\Rightarrow$"), so that $(A \vee \neg A) \Rightarrow R$. And clearly that is not so. Let us use "$\$\$$" for the connective introduced by conjunctive-style rules with respect to "$\Rightarrow^R$." We then obtain the following results:

1″. $A, B \Rightarrow^R (A \$\$ B)$. That is, $R, A, B \Rightarrow (A \$\$ B)$; and
2″. $(A \$\$ B) \Rightarrow^R A$ and $(A \$\$ B) \Rightarrow^R B$. That is, $R, (A \$\$ B) \Rightarrow A$ and $R, (A \$\$ B) \Rightarrow^R B$.

Thus, we see from statement 1″ that if Rockefeller is wealthy and A and B are true, then "$A \$\$ B$" is true. This is just Peacocke's conclusion 1. From statement 2″ we see that if Rockefeller is wealthy and either A or B is false, then "$A \$\$ B$" is false. This is just Peacocke's conclusion 2. Finally, if R is false, then results 1″ and 2″ do not determine any value for "$A \$\$ B$." But this is just Peacocke's conclusion 3. Thus, conclusions 1–3 are not consequences of using "$\Rightarrow^\$$," but of using "$\Rightarrow^R$" instead.

What happens to Peacocke's attempt to construct a maverick implication relation that is coextensional with "$\Rightarrow$"? It was designed to show that not all coextensional deducibility relations are on a par. However, that point cannot be sustained.

In English, the statement "R and A implies B" is ambiguous. It could mean either (1) R, and A implies B ($A \Rightarrow^\$ B$), or (2) ($R$ and A) implies B ($A \Rightarrow^R B$). There is, however, a clear difference between $A \Rightarrow^\$ B$ and $A \Rightarrow^R B$. The former conjoins R to an implication statement, and the latter requires that R be one of the antecedents of an implication statement. The relations fail to be coextensional unless R is a thesis or theorem. However, for his example to work, Peacocke needs R to be a contingent truth.

If Peacocke's example is the Rockefeller implication, "$\Rightarrow^\$$," then it is coextensional with "$\Rightarrow$," but it does not have the damaging consequences 1–3 for the connective "$\$$." On the other hand, "$\Rightarrow^R$" does have the damaging consequences that Peacocke has described, but it is not coextensional with "$\Rightarrow$."

PART III

The logical operators

11

Hypotheticals

It will prove useful in this study to split the operators into two groups: the hypothetical, negation, conjunction, and disjunction in one group; quantification and identity in the other. In studying the features of these operators it will be convenient as well to begin with a simple characterization of each of them. Later (Chapter 15) we shall describe the official, parameterized forms for them. This division into the simple and the parameterized forms segregates the features of the logical operators in a way that makes for a more perspicuous picture, but separates the features in a way that has its own theoretical interest. We begin with the simple, unparameterized story.

11.1 The simple characterization

If $I = \langle S, \Rightarrow \rangle$ is an implication structure, then the hypothetical operator H (on I) is the function $H_{\Rightarrow}$ that assigns to each pair $\langle A, B \rangle$ of members of S a special subset $H(A, B)$ of S. The special character of the subset is given by a condition that characterizes the function H – just as the special characters of the other logical operators are brought out by certain conditions that characterize them in turn. In fact, as we shall see, all the members (if there are any) of $H(A, B)$ are equivalent to each other with respect to the implication relation "$\Rightarrow$" of I, so that often we shall simply refer to the hypothetical $H(A, B)$ as if it were a member of S rather than a subset of S. This is innocent enough provided that there is only one implication relation that is under consideration. If there are two implication relations under study on the same set S, then it is best to keep to the idea of the hypothetical as a set of elements, since it can happen that two members of $H(A, B)$ are equivalent according to one implication relation, but fail to be equivalent with respect to the other.

Definition 11.1. An operator $H_{\Rightarrow}$ is a hypothetical on the implication structure $I = \langle S, \Rightarrow \rangle$ if and only if the following conditions are satisfied:

(H)　H_1. A, $H_\Rightarrow(A, B) \Rightarrow B$, and

　　　H_2. $H_\Rightarrow(A, B)$ is the weakest member of S that satisfies the first condition. That is, for any T in S, if A, $T \Rightarrow B$, then $T \Rightarrow H_\Rightarrow(A, B)$.[1]

We shall say that for any A and B in S, $H_\Rightarrow(A, B)$ is the hypothetical with antecedent A and consequent B. The point of the two conditions on hypotheticals is to provide a way of sorting out what is to count as a hypothetical with antecedent A and consequent B from all the other members of S. Let us, for the sake of convenience, suppress the reference to the implication relation of I and use the simpler expression $H(A, B)$.

The two conditions specify the hypotheticals on a structure in terms of the implication relation of the structure. There is no appeal to truth conditions, assertibility conditions, or any syntactical features or semantic values of the elements of the structure.

We shall soon generalize this characterization of the hypothetical and the other logical operators (Chapter 15) so that the official characterizations of all the logical operators will have what we shall call parameterized form. The parametric form is not just a convenience. It is needed to prove certain features of the hypothetical such as transitivity, exportation, and contraposition.

It is worth calling attention to the obvious fact that the first condition for hypotheticals corresponds to the rule of modus ponens. This might seem controversial, since there have been some objections to the validity of modus ponens.

Most of the objections of which I am aware do not seem to be telling. Harman (1975) has claimed that the conditional corresponding to modus ponens is not a logical truth, that it is not a priori, and not true in virtue of its "logical form." However, our account does not require that the first condition on hypotheticals be known a priori (see Chapter 10). Moreover, given the general account of implication structures, we certainly cannot say that the condition holds in virtue of logical form, since in general, the sets S of implication structures may not have members for which talk of their "logical form" makes any sense. It would make no more sense than to ask if the condition for e being an identity element of a group [for all members a of the group G, $(e \circ a) = (a \circ e) = a$] holds in virtue of logical form.

Adams (1975) has raised serious questions about the patterns of inference that hold for indicative conditionals of, say, English. The problems seem to arise for inferences from A and If A, then B, to B, when B is itself a conditional. However, most, if not all, of those problems concern whether or not it would be rational to believe B if it was rational to believe A and rational to believe the conditional, If A, then B, where the rationality condition is spelled out probabilistically. In a similar vein, McGee (1985) has raised related problems about whether or not one should believe B if one believes A and believes that if A, then B. In both cases it seems to me that these are serious problems about rational acceptance and belief, rather than a challenge to the implication of the consequent of a hypothetical by a hypothetical and its antecedent. Even if we grant the counterexamples offered by Adams and McGee, what we have are cases where $A_1, \ldots, A_n \Rightarrow B$, for which it does not follow that a person's believing A_1, and $\ldots$ and believing A_n implies that the person believes B. In our terminology, set out in Part IV, the belief operator does not distribute over the implication relation "$\Rightarrow$." Consequently, those proposed counterexamples, if accepted, would show that the belief operator is not a modal operator. For the Adams examples, it would follow that the operator "it is rational to accept A" (construed probabilistically) also fails to be a modal operator with respect to the implication relation "$\Rightarrow$." One could, of course, try to frame a new implication relation for which the relevant operator would distribute over it, and thereby restore modality to belief. This is, in fact, what I think Adams does when he introduces the notion of probabilistic implication.[2]

The second condition on hypotheticals (H_2) is the counterpart to a deduction theorem that is available in many logical systems. In the present context, it is a condition that isolates $H(A, B)$ as the weakest (implicationally) of all those elements of the structure that satisfy the first condition. What we are calling a hypothetical with antecedent A and consequent B is very weak. For example, if there were subjunctive conditionals in a particular implication structure, and it was granted that they satisfied the first (modus ponens) condition, then it would follow that for any subjunctive conditional $S(A, B)$ with antecedent A and consequent B, $S(A, B) \Rightarrow H(A, B)$.[3]

Although $H(A, B)$ is the weakest member of the structure that satisfies the first condition, it does not follow that it is a material conditional. One reason why this is so is simply that in general the members of the implication structure may not be truth-bearers, so that the whole notion of a material conditional is inappropriate. More interestingly, even when the implication structure does have truth-bearers as members, it does not follow that $H(A, B)$ will behave as a material conditional. In fact, if we think of a material conditional in a general way as the hypothetical $H_T(A, B)$ when a bisection implication relation is used on a structure, then it is only in very special implication structures that $H(A, B)$ will be equivalent to $H_T(A, B)$.

There may be a whole variety of hypotheticals on a given implication structure. Some may arise by varying the implication relation of the structure, but keeping the set S the same. In such cases we would have a variety of hypotheticals, each relativized to different implication relations. Variation can also arise through modifications of the conditions for being a hypothetical. For example, we might wish to introduce the idea of a first-order hypothetical $H^1(A, B)$ as the weakest member of the implication structure $I = \langle S \Rightarrow \rangle$ that satisfies the first condition for hypotheticals, but is not equivalent to $H(A, B)$ (the weakest of those that are not equivalent to the weakest). Although there are many hypotheticals that can be associated with an implication structure, we have chosen to isolate for study those that are the weakest with respect to the implication relation of the implication structure under study. Here is a bottom line. There is no hypothetical available that is weaker, unless the condition corresponding to modus ponens is violated.

Our characterization of the hypothetical operator leaves open the question whether or not for any A and B in the structure, the hypothetical $H(A, B)$ exists. Here is a simple example: For a finite structure on which the hypothetical may fail to exist, let S be the set $\{A, B, C, D\}$, with an implication relation as follows:

Then the hypothetical $H(A, B)$ does not exist in this structure, even though $A \Rightarrow B$. The reason is that $H(A, B)$ is the weakest member of S such that $A, H(A, B) \Rightarrow B$. Clearly, all the members of S satisfy the condition, since $A \Rightarrow B$. So $H(A, B)$ would have to be the weakest member of the structure, and that is impossible, since S does not have a weakest member.

11.1.1 Hypotheticals: Simple consequences

Before we turn to the full, parameterized characterization of the hypothetical operator, it is worth nothing that some features of the hypothetical can be proved using just the simple unparameterized account, whereas others, such as transitivity, contraposition, and exportation, depend upon full parameterization. Let us begin with a general observation on the way in which implication and the hypothetical are related:

Theorem 11.1. *Let* $I = \langle S \Rightarrow \rangle$ *be an implication structure. For any A and B in S, if H(A, B) exists, then* $A \Rightarrow B$ *if and only if H(A, B) is a thesis of I.*

Proof. Suppose that $H(A, B)$ is a thesis of I. Then $C \Rightarrow H(A, B)$ for all C in S. Therefore, in particular, $A \Rightarrow H(A, B)$. Since $A \Rightarrow A$, and $A, H(A, B) \Rightarrow B$, we have $A \Rightarrow B$, by Cut. Conversely, suppose that $A \Rightarrow B$. By Dilution, $A, C \Rightarrow B$ for any C in S. Therefore, by condition H_2, $C \Rightarrow H(A, B)$ for all C in S. Consequently, $H(A, B)$ is a thesis of I.

Thus, although the implication relation and the hypothetical are very different notions, they are systematically related to each other. The difference between them emerges quite sharply if one considers an implication structure that does not contain any statements in it. In that case, "$A \Rightarrow B$" is a statement (but not in the structure), and $H(A, B)$ is an element of the structure, but not a statement. If there is any chance of confusing the implication relation with the hypothetical, the consideration of structures that do not contain statements makes the difference stand out in high relief.

We have mentioned in several places that the hypothetical is unique, up to implication. That is,

Theorem 11.2. *Let* $I = \langle S, \Rightarrow \rangle$ *be an implication structure. If H(A, B) and H*(A, B) are both hypotheticals with antecedent A and consequent B, then* $H(A, B) \Leftrightarrow H^*(A, B)$.

Proof. Since H and H^* both satisfy the first condition (H_1) for hypotheticals, and each is the weakest to do so, it follows that each implies (under "$\Rightarrow$") the other.

The reader probably will have noticed that the proof of the uniqueness of the hypothetical (up to equivalence under "$\Rightarrow$") did not depend upon the particular content of the first condition on hypotheticals (H_1). The proof rests on the requirement that if an element of the structure is a hypothetical, then it is the weakest member of the structure to satisfy the first condition. Throughout the rest of this study, we shall see that all the logical operators are characterized with the same format: There is a first condition on the elements that is characteristic for the operator, and a second condition that requires that any element that is a value of that operator be the weakest to satisfy the first condition. It follows that *on any implication structure, all of the logical operators in this study (if they exist) are unique up to the implication relation of the structure.*

Here are some features of the hypothetical that follow from its unparameterized characterization (we assume that the relevant hypotheticals exist in the given implication structure):

Theorem 11.3. *If $I = \langle S, \Rightarrow \rangle$ is an implication structure, and A and B are any members of S, then*

(a) $B \Rightarrow H(A, B)$,
(b) $B \Rightarrow H(A, A)$,
(c) $H(H(A, A), B) \Rightarrow B$,
(d) $H(A, H(A, B)) \Rightarrow H(A, B)$.

Proof. (a) We know that $A, B \Rightarrow B$. But $H(A, B)$ is the weakest member of S that together with A implies B. Therefore $B \Rightarrow H(A, B)$.

(b) By Projection, $A, B \Rightarrow A$. But $H(A, A)$ is the weakest member of S that together with A implies A. Consequently, $B \Rightarrow H(A, A)$ for all B in S.

(c) In cases such as these, where there are several hypotheticals involved, it is sometimes helpful to use "$A \to B$" instead of "$H(A, B)$." It should be borne in mind, however, that in general, neither the values of the operators nor what they operate upon need have any special syntactic or semantic character. Thus, in using "$A \to B$" we do not wish the reader to suppose that the hypothetical is a special expression, or even a set of such expressions, consisting of a single arrow, flanked at each end by some special linguistic expression. With this caution, (c) can be expressed as $((A \to A) \to B) \Rightarrow B$. By Theorem 11.3(b), $H(A, A)$ is a thesis, so that $H(H(A, A), B) \Rightarrow H(A, A)$. Since $H(H(A, A), B) \Rightarrow H(H(A, A), B)$, and by condition H_1, $H(A, A), H(H(A, A), B) \Rightarrow B$, we conclude, by Cut, that $H(H(A, A), B) \Rightarrow B$.

(d) We know from condition H_1 that $A, H(A, H(A, B)) \Rightarrow H(A, B)$, and from Projection we have $A, H(A, H(A, B)) \Rightarrow A$. But $A, H(A, B) \Rightarrow B$. Therefore, by Cut, $A, H(A, H(A, B)) \Rightarrow B$. Consequently, by condition H_2, we obtain the result that $H(A, H(A, B)) \Rightarrow H(A, B)$.

The reader may already have noticed that our description of the hypothetical operator on an implication structure involved no reference to any other logical operator on that structure. This "purity" of the characterization of the hypothetical is true also of our account of the other logical operators. It is a theoretically useful feature to have, but we shall not say more about its utility in this study.[4]

11.2 A nonthesis

Given the familiarity of the two conditions on hypotheticals from the study of classical sentential logic, one might have thought that the general features of the hypotheticals, those that they have in all implication structures (in which they exist), would be precisely the ones that they have classically. Here is an example (Peirce's law),[5] involving only the hypothetical, that holds classically, but fails to hold in all implication structures:

Theorem 11.4. *There is a structure $I = \langle S, \Rightarrow \rangle$ in which $H(H(H(A, B), A), A)$ (Peirce's law) $[((A \to B) \to A) \to A]$ is not a thesis.*

Proof. Let S be the set $\{A, B, C\}$, and let the implication relation be as follows, where the single arrows indicate only those implications that hold:

We need first to calculate $H(A, B)$, $H(B, A)$, and $H(C, A)$: (1) $H(A, B)$ is just B. The reason is this: Consider those members of S that together with A imply B. B certainly qualifies. A does not, for if A together with A implied B, then A would imply B, which it does not. And C together with A does not imply B, for in that case, since A implies C, by Cut, A would imply B, and that is impossible. B is therefore the only qualifier, and therefore the weakest. (2) $H(B, A)$ is just C. The reason is that since B implies A, every member of S together with B implies A. Since $H(B, A)$ is the weakest to do so, it is C, the weakest member of S. (3) $H(C, A)$ is A, for C together with A implies A. And C together with B implies A, since B implies A. C, however, does not imply A. Therefore $H(C, A)$ is the weakest of $\{A, B\}$, that is, A. Now, $H(H(H(A, B), A), A)$ is $H(H(B, A), A)$, which is $H(C, A)$, which is A. However, A is not a thesis, since C does not imply it.

These theorems and counterexamples may seem to cloud the picture of what kind of hypothetical it is that emerges once we relativize the hypothetical (and the other logical operators) to implication relations. In fact, however, the picture is relatively clear. It will be seen (Chapter 21) that the features that the hypothetical operator has in all implication structures correspond exactly to those that the hypothetical has in "intuitionistic sentential logic." If the implication structures are narrowed down to just those that we shall call "classical," then the features that the hypothetical operator has in all classical implication structures correspond exactly to those that the hypothetical has in classical sentential logic. Moreover, the situation is the same for all the other logical operators as it is for the hypothetical.

There are several results showing that our relativization of the hypothetical to implication relations is a well-behaved notion. Some of these results (Chapter 19) concern the concept of extensionality in general, and the ways in which the extensionality of the logical operators are related to each other.

One type of result concerns a question that arises in a natural way if the operators are regarded as relativized to implication structures. If an element is a hypothetical in one structure, when will it continue to be one in some other structure? This is a question that can be raised for each of the logical operators, and it has a definite answer in each case. We consider the case for hypotheticals.

11.3 The stability of the hypothetical

Definition 11.2. Let $I = \langle S, \Rightarrow \rangle$ and $I^* = \langle S^*, \Rightarrow^* \rangle$ be any implication structures such that I^* is a conservative extension of I (Chapter 4), and let H and H^* be the hypothetical operator on I and I^*, respectively. We shall say that the hypothetical operator is *stable* if and only if for any A and B in S, $H(A, B) \Leftrightarrow^* H^*(A, B)$.

Definition 11.3. Let $I = \langle S, \Rightarrow \rangle$ be any implication structure, and let $I^* = \langle S^*, \Rightarrow^* \rangle$ be any conservative extension of it. Let H^* be the hypothetical operator on I^*. We shall say that S *is*

closed under the hypothetical operator H^* *if and only if for every*
A *and* B *in* S, *if* $H^*(A, B)$ *exists, then there is some element* C
in S *such that* $C \Longleftrightarrow^* H^*(A, B)$.

One word about the closure condition. On the preceding assumptions, S
is a subset of S^*. If the hypothetical H^* has a value for A and B in S,
then it is an element of S^*. We do not know, nor do we assume, that it
will also be a member of the subset S. The condition that S is closed
under H^* requires only that $H^*(A, B)$ be equivalent (under "$\Longrightarrow^*$") to
some member of S; it does not require that $H^*(A, B)$ itself be a member
of S. We can then prove the following:

Theorem 11.5 (stability). *Let* $I^* = \langle S^*, \Longrightarrow^* \rangle$ *be a conservative*
extension of $I = \langle S, \Longrightarrow \rangle$, *and let* H *and* H^* *be the hypothetical*
operators on I *and* I^*, *respectively. If* S *is closed under* H^*, *then*
for any A *and* B *in* S *[for which* $H(A, B)$ *and* $H^*(A, B)$ *exist]*,
$H(A, B) \Longleftrightarrow^* H^*(A, B)$.

Proof. (1) We first show that for all A and B in S, $H(A, B)$
$\Longrightarrow^* H^*(A, B)$. Since $A, H(A, B) \Longrightarrow B$, and A, B, and $H(A,$
$B)$ are in S, and "$\Longrightarrow^*$" extends "$\Longrightarrow$," we have $A, H(A, B)$
$\Longrightarrow^* B$. However, $H^*(A, B)$ is the weakest member T, of S^*,
such that $A, T \Longrightarrow^* B$. Consequently, $H(A, B) \Longrightarrow^* H^*(A, B)$.
(2) In order to show that $H^*(A, B) \Longrightarrow^* H(A, B)$ we note first
that for any A and B in S (and therefore in S^*), $A, H^*(A, B)$
$\Longrightarrow^* B$. Since S is closed under H^*, there is some C in S such
that $C \Longleftrightarrow^* H^*(A, B)$. Therefore $A, C \Longrightarrow^* B$. But A, B, and
C are in S. Since I^* is a conservative extension of I, it follows
that $A, C \Longrightarrow B$. Therefore $C \Longrightarrow H(A, B)$, and so $C \Longrightarrow^*$
$H(A, B)$. Consequently, $H^*(A, B) \Longrightarrow^* H(A, B)$. And that
concludes the proof.

It is worth noting that given the condition that I^* is a conservative
extension of I, the closure condition on H^* is not only sufficient for the
stability of the hypothetical but also necessary, for if $H(A, B) \Longleftrightarrow^*$
$H^*(A, B)$, there is some C in S such that $H^*(A, B) \Longleftrightarrow^* C$, namely,
$H(A, B)$. So the closure condition is the best result under these
conditions.

Exercise 11.1. Let $I = \langle S, \Longrightarrow \rangle$ be a structure with $S = \{A, C\}$,
and "$\Longrightarrow$" is such that C implies A. Let $I^* = \langle S^*, \Longrightarrow^* \rangle$ be a

structure in which $S = \langle A, B, C \rangle$, and "$\Rightarrow$*" is such that C implies* A as well as B. Show that (1) I^* is a conservative extension of I, (2) $H(A, C)$ is C, a hypothetical in I, but that C fails to be a hypothetical in I^*, and (3) S is not closed under H^* [$H^*(A, C)$ is B and does not belong to S, even though A and C do].

In the preceding theorem, S was a subset of S^*. That theorem can be used to cover the case where S is homomorphic to a subset of S^*:

Definition 11.4. Let $I = \langle S, \Rightarrow \rangle$ and $I^* = \langle S^*, \Rightarrow^* \rangle$ be two implication structures. We shall say that I^* is a *homomorphic conservative extension* of I with respect to a mapping φ of S to S^* if and only if

$A_1, \ldots, A_n \Rightarrow B$ if and only if $\varphi(A_1), \ldots, \varphi(A_n) \Rightarrow^* \varphi(B)$ for all $A_1, \ldots, A_n$ and B in S.

We then have the following result:

Theorem 11.6 (homomorphic stability). *Let I^* be a homomorphic conservative extension of I with respect to the mapping φ of S to S^*. Let H^* be the hypothetical operator on I^*, and let $\varphi[S]$ be the set of all $\varphi(A)$ for A in S. If $\varphi[S]$ is closed under H^*, then $\varphi(H(A, B)) \Leftrightarrow^* H^*(\varphi(A), \varphi(B))$ for all A and B in S.*

Proof. By an application of Theorem 11.5. We leave the proof for the reader. {Form the structure I^+, consisting of $\varphi[S]$ and the restriction of "$\Rightarrow$*" to the set $\varphi[S]$. Note that I^* is a conservative extension of I^+ and that $\varphi[S]$ is closed under H^*. Show that $\varphi(H(A, B))$ is the hypothetical with antecedent $\varphi(A)$ and consequent $\varphi(B)$ in I^+. By Theorem 11.5, $\varphi(H(A, B)) \Leftrightarrow^* H^*(\varphi(A), \varphi(B))$.} Given that I^* is a homomorphic conservative extension of I, the closure of $\varphi[S]$ under H^* is also a necessary condition for the homomorphic stability of the hypothetical operator.

There is a companion result that concerns the stability of failure to be a hypothetical:

Theorem 11.7. *Let $I = \langle S, \Rightarrow \rangle$ be an implication structure. If D is not a hypothetical with antecedent A and consequent B in the structure I, then D also fails to be a hypothetical with*

antecedent A and consequent B in any implication structure I*
that is a conservative extension of I.

Proof. Suppose that $D \Leftrightarrow H(A, B)$, where A, B, and D are in S, and H is the hypothetical operator on I. Let $I^* = \langle S^*, \Rightarrow^* \rangle$ be a conservative extension of I, and let H^* be the hypothetical operator on I^*. We need to show that $D \Leftrightarrow^* H^*(A, B)$.

Since D is not equivalent to $H(A, B)$, it follows that either (1) $A, D \not\Rightarrow B$ or else (2) $A, D \Rightarrow B$, and there is some E in S such that $A, E \Rightarrow B$, and $E \not\Rightarrow D$. That is, either D does not satisfy the first condition on hypotheticals, or it does, but it is not the weakest to do so. In the first case, since I^* is a conservative extension of I, $A, D \not\Rightarrow^* B$. So the first condition on hypotheticals in I^* fails. Consequently, $D \Leftrightarrow^* H^*(A, B)$. As for the second case, we know by conservativeness that $A, D \Rightarrow^* B$ and that for some E in S, $A, E \Rightarrow^* B$ and $E \not\Rightarrow^* D$. Therefore, D is not the weakest member in S^* to satisfy the second condition on hypotheticals. Consequently, $D \Leftrightarrow^* H^*(A, B)$.

11.4 Conditionals in English

Those who have looked to logical theory for significant ways of analyzing natural languages might consider this account of the logical operators for some help with the characterization of hypotheticals or conditionals in English. After all, there is a rich literature on the adequacy of the material conditional as an account of conditionals in English, and there is a matching subtle and complex literature on the futility of such accounts.[6] But the problem is no easier on this account of hypotheticals than it would be if we restricted ourselves to the material conditional. In fact, "matching" up English conditionals with the hypothetical operators on implication structures involves rather subtle theoretical problems, hopefully of some interest, but largely unexplored. On our account of the logical operators, the determination of whether or not an English statement is a conditional requires much more than a simple check of its truth conditions against that of the associated material conditional, and more than a comparison of how the statement is related implicationally to its components.

The first set of problems concerns the simple fact that the English statement would have to be located as a member of some implication structure. What, then, is the appropriate S, and what is the appropriate implication relation on S? S is a set of English statements. But how much of English is to be used for S? All? Of course, if the English conditional involves two statements, A and B, then they have to belong to S as well. But how much more? Is there some background set $S(A, B)$ determined by A and B that is to be included in S, and is this set constant over a range of A's and B's, or does it vary with them?

The second problem concerns the implication relation. What is that supposed to be for English? Even if there are several suitable candidates, how do we determine when something is suitable? For example, if it were thought necessary that modus ponens hold, then we should first have to determine whether or not a conditional together with its antecedent implies its consequent. But that requires, in turn, that we have already identified the conditionals in the structure, and that requires that we have some suitable implication relation for English, and so on.

Suppose that these problems have been settled in some way that is satisfactory, by a judicious choice of structure in which the English statement E is to be evaluated as a conditional. There are two further desiderata: one local, the other global. The first condition on hypotheticals requires that $A, E \Rightarrow B$. And this is a local matter, involving just the three statements. The second condition on hypotheticals is obviously global: It requires that E be the weakest statement T in the structure such that $A, T \Rightarrow B$. In general, E has to be compared with members of the structure that may be other than A and B.

These are difficult problems that have to be faced if the problem is to show a "matchup" of the English statement E with a hypothetical in a structure. There are equally difficult problems in trying to show that there is a "mismatch" of E with a hypothetical. We shall present two examples of what we mean.

Sometimes it is argued that at least some conditionals of English cannot be constructed as material conditionals, because there is a failure of matching truth conditions. Material conditionals are always true if their antecedents are false. But supposedly there are conditionals in English with false antecedents, some of which are true, and others false. This looks bad for the uniform use of material conditionals. Here, too, the case is not as secure as it might seem.[7] But my present interest is not in defending the utility of the material conditional for an analysis of English conditionals. I am more concerned with showing the resourcefulness of our account of the hypotheticals in the face of the "mismatch" argument. The response here is simple.

Consider a simple example of an implication structure that shows that

hypotheticals with false antecedents can sometimes be true, and sometimes false. Let $S = \{A, B, C\}$, with an implication relation as diagrammed:

We assume that these are three statements of English, and that "A" and
"B" are false, while "C" is true. The hypothetical $H(A, B)$ is C. (Since
$A \Rightarrow B$, the weakest member T, such that $A, T \Rightarrow B$, is just the
weakest member of S.) So the hypothetical $H(A, B)$, with false antecedent A, is true. On the other hand, the hypothetical $H(B, A)$ is A (the
only member of S that together with B implies A). Consequently,
$H(B, A)$ is false, even though it has a false antecedent. So we are back
once again to the crucial problem of what structures are to be used in the
evaluation of English conditionals.

There is yet another possibility available. It may be that the English
statement E is a hypothetical, but not the kind that we have characterized. Recall that the hypothetical $H(A, B)$, if it exists, is implied by B.
Suppose that there were English conditionals with antecedent A and
consequent B for which such an implication failed to hold. Even if that
were so, it still might be the case that although E would not be the
weakest kind of hypothetical, it still might be of the type we called
first-order in the early part of this chapter. For first-order hypotheticals
it is not generally true that they are implied by their consequents (nor
are they implied by the negations of their antecedents). They are not the
kind of hypothetical we have been studying in this chapter, but they are
close cousins.

Exercise 11.2. Let $I = \langle S, \Rightarrow \rangle$ be an implication structure,
with $S = \{A, B, C, D\}$, where the implication relation has D
implying A as well as B, and A and B each imply C (and the
implications run only one way). Let H^1 be a first-order hypothetical on I. Show that $H^1(A, B)$ is D, so that $B \not\Rightarrow H^1(A, B)$.

We have noted that the logical operators can act on items that are not
truth-bearers. That feature of our theory can be used to provide an
account of the hypothetical character of such English statements as this:

"If you are free, will you marry me?" Here we have an interrogative with an interrogative in the consequent. Almost all current theories require that both the antecedent and consequent of hypotheticals be truth-bearers. However, our own account of hypotheticals is not blocked by such a constraint. We shall show, assuming a certain theory of interrogatives (Chapter 23), that such interrogatives are hypotheticals; they meet the conditions that we have been exploring in this chapter.

There are subtle theoretical problems that must be settled in any account of conditionals in English, no matter what the logical theory may be. As far as I can see, it is not an easy matter on any theory we have, including the theory presented here.

12

Negations

12.1 The simple characterization

Our aim here, as in the preceding chapter, is to characterize the negation operator as a special kind of function that can act on all implication structures, general and special.

Let $I = \langle S, \Rightarrow \rangle$ be an implication structure. For any A in S, we shall say that $N(A)$ is a negation of A if and only if it satisfies the following two conditions:

N_1. $A, N(A) \Rightarrow B$ for all B in S, and

N_2. $N(A)$ is the weakest member of the structure to satisfy the first condition. That is, if T is any member of S such that $A, T \Rightarrow B$ for all B in S, then $T \Rightarrow N(A)$.

As with the hypotheticals, the negation operator on the structure is supposed to sort out, for any A, those elements in the structure that are the negations of A. Strictly speaking, then, the negation operator assigns to each A of S a set of members of S that will satisfy the preceding conditions. That set may be empty, for there is, as we shall see later, no guarantee that negations always exist. However, if there are several members, then they will be equivalent under the implication relation of the structure. Thus, as long as there is only one implication relation that is being studied on a set S, there will not be any confusion if we treat $N(A)$ as if it were an element of S.[1]

> **Definition 12.1.** Let $I = \langle S, \Rightarrow \rangle$ be an implication structure, and let N be the negation operator on it. We shall say that N is a *classical negation operator* on I if and only if for all A in S, $NN(A) \Rightarrow A$.

The negation operator is not classical on every structure. There are structures on which $NN(A) \Rightarrow A$ holds for every A in the structure, and there are other structures on which it fails. *Classical implication structures* are those for which the negation operator is classical;

otherwise we shall say that the structure is *nonclassical*. We shall say more about these different kinds of structures later. One concept that is helpful in understanding some of the differences between classical and nonclassical structures is the dual of the negation operator (*dual negation*).

When N is the negation operator on a structure I, then its dual, $N^\wedge$, is just the negation operator on the dual implication structure $I^\wedge$ (Section 9.5). It is also a logical operator on I. The dual negation is a very interesting operator, but little known. It will be seen that a negation operator N is classical if and only if $N = N^\wedge$. It also allows us to think of nonclassical negation as "split" into two parts, N and its dual $N^\wedge$: When the negation operator N is not classical on a structure, it will have some classical features, but not others. The dual, $N^\wedge$, picks up the slack. For example, in general, $A \Rightarrow NN(A)$ holds (for all A) in all structures, but the converse fails in those that are nonclassical. On the other hand, $N^\wedge N^\wedge(A) \Rightarrow A$ holds (for all A) in all structures, though the converse fails to hold in some. Of course, if N is classical, then N is equivalent to $N^\wedge$, and we have, as a consequence, the familiar result that $A \Leftrightarrow NN(A)$ for all A.

There is a concept of negation, *partial negation*, that arises in a natural way when the first condition on negations is relaxed. Suppose that instead of requiring that A together with its negation imply all the members of the structure, we require that they imply the members of some subset of the structure. There are numerous partial negation operators that arise in connection with different subsets of the structure. They are systematically related to each other and to the hypotheticals on the structure, and therefore are worth a bit of attention.

We shall now turn to some simple consequences of the negation operator. Before we do so, it is important to note that there is no guarantee that every member or indeed any member of a structure will have a negation.

12.2 The existence and nonexistence of negations: Examples

12.2.1 A structure in which every member has a negation, and negation is classical

Let $I = \langle S, \Rightarrow \rangle$, where S consists of just two members, A and B, and the implication is as follows:

$N(A)$ is B, and $N(B)$ is A: $N(A)$ is the weakest member of S that together with A implies every member of S. But A implies every member of S, so that $N(A)$ is just the weakest member of S, namely, B. $N(B)$ is the weakest member that together with B implies every element. B does not qualify, since B does not imply A. A does qualify and is therefore the only element to do so. Moreover, every member of S is implied by its double negation.

12.2.2 A structure in which negation is everywhere defined, but the negation operator is not classical

Let $I = \langle S, \Longrightarrow \rangle$, where $S = \{A, B, C\}$, and the implication relation is given by

$N(A)$ is C, $N(C)$ is A, and $N(B)$ is A. As in the preceding example, since A implies every member of S, $N(A)$ is the weakest member of S, namely, C. $N(C)$ is the weakest member that together with C implies all of S. It cannot be B, because $C, B \not\Longrightarrow A$ (if $C, B \Longrightarrow A$, then since B implies C, by Cut, $B \Longrightarrow A$, and that is impossible in this structure). Now C together with A does imply everything in S, since A does. Finally, $N(B)$ is A. B does not qualify, since B together with B does not imply every member, and C fails as well since B together with C would imply every member (and so B would imply every member). A qualifies and is the only one that does. Since $NN(B) = N(A) = C$, N is non-classical, because $NN(B) \not\Longrightarrow B$.

Exercise 12.1. Modify the foregoing example to show that for every cardinality greater than 2, there is a nonclassical structure.

Exercise 12.2. Show that there is a denumerably infinite non-classical structure. (Let $S = \{A_1, A_2, \ldots, B\}$, where for all positive integers i and j, $A_i \Rightarrow A_j$ if and only if i is greater than or equal to j, and all $A_i \Rightarrow B$.)

Exercise 12.3. Describe an implication structure in which some member A has a negation $N(A)$, but does not have a double negation $NN(A)$.

Thus far, the examples have been such that every element of the structure has had a negation. The following are several examples of structures in which negation is not everywhere defined.

12.2.3 A structure $I = \langle S, \Rightarrow \rangle$ in which negation is not everywhere defined

Let $S = \{A, B, C\}$, and let the implication relation be as follows:

$N(A)$ is B, $N(B)$ is A, and there is no element in S that is the negation of C. We leave the computation of $N(A)$ and $N(B)$ for the reader. As for $N(C)$, note that it cannot be C, since C does not imply all members of S. And it cannot be A, for if C together with A implies all the members of S, then A implies all those members. And that is impossible. Similarly, $N(C)$ cannot be B. (Readers who may have surmised that C is the disjunction of A and B will have noted that this is a case where two elements have negations, but their disjunction does not.)

Exercise 12.4. Using the notion of the conjunction operator (Chapter 1), give an example of a structure in which two members have negations, but their conjunction does not.

12.2.4 A structure $I = \langle S, \Rightarrow \rangle$ in which the negation operator is nowhere defined

Let S be the set $\{A_i\}$, for all integers i, with the following implication relation:

It is clear that no matter what A_i we consider, there is no A_j in the structure such that $A_i, A_j \Rightarrow B$ for all B in S. The reason is that one of the two will imply the other. Say that A_i implies A_j. Then, by Cut, A_i implies all the members of S. But none of the members of S implies all the rest. Thus, every A_i fails to satisfy even the first condition of negation.

12.2.5 *The intuitionistic sentential calculus and nonclassical negation*

A familiar example of a nonclassical structure can be obtained by using the implication structure associated with the intuitionistic sentential calculus (ISC). If S is the set of sentences of a logical system, and "⊢" is a deducibility relation on S, then the pair $\langle S, \Rightarrow \rangle$ is the implication structure associated with the system, where for any sentences $A_1, \ldots, A_n$ and B of S, $A_1, \ldots, A_n \Rightarrow B$ holds if and only if ⊢(A_1 & ... & $A_n \to B$) (where we assume that the connectives "&" and "→" are present in the system, either primitively or defined). Thus, corresponding to ISC we have the implication structure $I_{\text{ISC}} = \langle S_{\text{ISC}}, \Rightarrow^{\text{ISC}} \rangle$. Let N be the mapping of S_{ISC} to itself, whereby to every sentence A of ISC, $N(A)$ is "$\neg A$," where "$\neg$" is the connective for negation in ISC. N satisfies the conditions for being a nonclassical negation operator on I_{ISC}: Since ⊢$\neg\neg A \to A$ will fail in ISC for some sentence A, it follows that $NN(A) \not\Rightarrow^{\text{ISC}} A$.

12.3 The negation operator: some theorems

Theorem 12.1. *Let* $I = \langle S, \Rightarrow \rangle$ *be an implication structure. Then for every A in S, $A \Rightarrow NN(A)$.*

Proof. From the first condition on negation, $A, N(A) \Rightarrow B$ for all B in S. Consequently, by Permutation, $N(A), A \Rightarrow B$ for all B in S. Now $N(A), NN(A) \Rightarrow B$ for all B in S where $NN(A)$ is the weakest of all those members of S that together with $N(A)$ implies everything in the structure. But A together with $N(A)$ implies all the members of the structure. Consequently, $A \Rightarrow NN(A)$ for all A in S.

This simple result comes with very little cost. Given the characterization of the negation operator, only the Permutation condition on implication relations is needed.

Theorem 12.2. *Let* $I = \langle S, \Rightarrow \rangle$ *be an implication structure. Then for any A and B in S, if $A \Rightarrow B$, then $N(B) \Rightarrow N(A)$.*

Proof. Suppose that $A \Rightarrow B$. By Dilution, $A, N(B) \Rightarrow B$, and by Projection, $A, N(B) \Rightarrow N(B)$. Now, from the first condition on negations, $B, N(B) \Rightarrow C$ for all C in S. Consequently, by Cut, $A, N(B) \Rightarrow C$ for all C in S. By the second condition on negations, therefore, $N(B) \Rightarrow N(A)$.

It follows immediately that iteration of the negation operator any finite number of times will yield either N or NN, depending upon whether the number is odd or even. That is,

Theorem 12.3. *On any implication structure* $I = \langle S, \Rightarrow \rangle$, $N(A) \Leftrightarrow NNN(A)$ *for all A in S.*

Proof. Since $A \Rightarrow NN(A)$ holds for all A in the structure, it holds for $N(A)$ in particular. Therefore $N(A) \Rightarrow NNN(A)$ for all A in S. On the other hand, since $A \Rightarrow NN(A)$, by Theorem 12.2, $NNN(A) \Rightarrow N(A)$ for all A in S.

Theorem 12.4. *Let* $I = \langle S, \Rightarrow \rangle$ *be an implication structure. For all A and B in S, $N(A) \Rightarrow H(A, B)$.*

Proof. $A, N(A) \Rightarrow C$ for all C in S. In particular, $A, N(A) \Rightarrow B$. But $H(A, B)$ (if it exists) is the weakest member that together with A implies B. Therefore $N(A) \Rightarrow H(A, B)$.

Theorem 12.5. *Let* $I = \langle S, \Rightarrow \rangle$ *be an implication structure that has an antithesis F as a member. Then for all A in S,* $N(A) \Leftrightarrow H(A, F)$.

Proof. $A, N(A) \Rightarrow F$, since $A, N(A) \Rightarrow B$ for all B in S. Therefore $N(A) \Rightarrow H(A, F)$ (by H_2). Moreover, since $A, H(A, F) \Rightarrow F$ and $F \Rightarrow B$ for all B in S, it follows that $A, H(A, F) \Rightarrow B$ for all B in S. Therefore $H(A, F) \Rightarrow N(A)$ (by N_2).

12.4 The negation operator: Onto or not onto?

In Section 12.2.2 we had an example of a nonclassical structure where $S = \{A, B, C\}$. Since $N(A)$ is C, $N(B)$ is A, and $N(C)$ is A, the set of all those members of S that are equivalent to the negation of some member of S is just the proper subset $\{A, C\}$ of S. This feature of the example can be generalized:

Let $I = \langle S, \Rightarrow \rangle$ be an implication structure. Since the negation operator N is a mapping, let $N[S]$ be the *image of S under N*: Any C in S is a member of $N[S]$ if and only if it is equivalent to a negation of some A in S. So $N[S]$ is a subset of S. N is a mapping *onto* S (or *surjective*) if and only if $N[S] = S$. Otherwise we shall say that the negation operator is *not onto* S (or *not surjective*).[2] We now have the following result:

Theorem 12.6. *Let* $I = \langle S, \Rightarrow \rangle$ *be an implication structure. The negation operator N is classical on I if and only if N is a mapping of S onto S.*

Proof. $A \Rightarrow NN(A)$ for all A in S. If N is classical, then for every A in S, $A \Leftrightarrow NN(A)$. Therefore, every A in S is equivalent to the negation of some member, namely, $N(A)$. So S is a subset of $N[S]$. Therefore $S = N[S]$, and N is a mapping of S onto S. Conversely, suppose that N is a mapping of S onto S. Since $S = N[S]$, for every A in S there is some A^* in S such that $A \Leftrightarrow N(A^*)$. Therefore $NN(A) \Leftrightarrow NNN(A^*) \Leftrightarrow N(A^*) \Leftrightarrow A$. Consequently, $NN(A) \Rightarrow A$.

12.5 Modifying nonclassical structures

Suppose that $I = \langle S, \Rightarrow \rangle$ is a nonclassical implication structure. Can one obtain a classical implication structure either by shifting on the set S or by shifting the implication relation of the structure? Since I is nonclassical, $N[S]$, the image of S under N, is a proper subset of S. Let $I_N = \langle N[S], \Rightarrow^N \rangle$ be a new implication structure, where the implication relation "$\Rightarrow^N$" is the restriction of "$\Rightarrow$" to $N[S]$. Then we have the following:

Theorem 12.7. *Let* $I = \langle S, \Rightarrow \rangle$ *be a nonclassical implication structure, and let* $I_N = \langle N[S], \Rightarrow^N \rangle$ *be the substructure of* I *described above. Then* I_N *is a classical implication structure.*

Proof. We leave it to the reader to check that on the set $N[S]$, the negation operator on I_N and N, the negation operator on I, are equivalent. But N is a mapping of $N[S]$ onto itself, so that the negation operator of I_N is a mapping of $N[S]$ onto itself. By Theorem 12.6, negation on I_N is classical.

The next observation has to do with obtaining a classical structure from a nonclassical one by extending its implication relation. It is a result that we shall prove in connection with the question of the extensionality of the various logical operators (Chapter 19), but it is worth anticipating the result:

Suppose that $I = \langle S, \Rightarrow \rangle$ is an implication structure and that there is at least one strong bisection $T = \langle K, L \rangle$ of I for which $N(A)$ is in L if and only if A is in K (for all A in S). Then there is an implication relation "$\Rightarrow^\#$" on S such that (1) "$\Rightarrow^\#$" is an extension of "$\Rightarrow$," (2) $N^\#$, the negation operator on $I^\# = \langle S, \Rightarrow^\# \rangle$, is classical, and (3) $N^\#$ is weaker than N (in $I^\#$). That is, for every A in S, $N(A) \Rightarrow^\# N^\#(A)$.

In this situation, it is possible to shift to a weaker implication relation that yields a classical negation operator that is weaker than the nonclassical one. However, it is an open question whether there always is such a strong bisection on every nonclassical implication structure or whether one has to apply the theorem case by case.

The implication structures, as we have described them, come in two varieties: nonclassical and classical. It is only in nonclassical structures that the dual negation operator will be distinct from the negation operator. Since it is not a familiar logical notion, we shall explore some of its more interesting features (those that involve the operators of conjunction and disjunction are deferred to Chapters 13 and 14).

12.6 The dual of the negation operator

If N is a negation operator on the structure $I = \langle S, \Rightarrow \rangle$, then its dual, $N^{\wedge}$, is the negation operator on $I^{\wedge}$, the implication structure that is the dual of I (Section 9.5).

Consequently, $N^{\wedge}$ satisfies the conditions for being a negation operator on the dual structure $I^{\wedge}$. That is,

$N_1^{\wedge}$. $A, N^{\wedge}(A) \Rightarrow^{\wedge} B$ for all B in S, and

$N_2^{\wedge}$. $N^{\wedge}(A)$ is the weakest (by the implication relation "$\Rightarrow^{\wedge}$") to satisfy, $N_1^{\wedge}$. That is, for any T in S, if $A, T \Rightarrow^{\wedge} B$ for all B in S, then $T \Rightarrow^{\wedge} N^{\wedge}(A)$.

Theorem 12.8. *Let* $I = \langle S, \Rightarrow \rangle$ *be an implication structure. Then* $N^{\wedge}N^{\wedge}(A) \Rightarrow A$ *for all* A *in* S.

Proof. Since $N^{\wedge}$ is the negation operator on $I^{\wedge}$, by Theorem 12.1, $A \Rightarrow^{\wedge} N^{\wedge}N^{\wedge}(A)$ for all A in S. Consequently, $N^{\wedge}N^{\wedge}(A) \Rightarrow A$ (Theorem 9.1).

Theorem 12.9 *Let* $I = \langle S, \Rightarrow \rangle$. *For any* A *and* B *in* S, *if* $A \Rightarrow B$, *then* $N^{\wedge}(B) \Rightarrow N^{\wedge}(A)$.

Proof. Suppose that $A \Rightarrow B$. Then $B \Rightarrow^{\wedge} A$. Since $N^{\wedge}$ is the negation operator with respect to "$\Rightarrow^{\wedge}$," $N^{\wedge}(A) \Rightarrow^{\wedge} N^{\wedge}(B)$ (by Theorem 12.2). Consequently, $N^{\wedge}(B) \Rightarrow N^{\wedge}(A)$.

Theorem 12.10. *Let* $I = \langle S, \Rightarrow \rangle$. *Then* $N^{\wedge}N^{\wedge}N^{\wedge}(A) \Leftrightarrow N^{\wedge}(A)$ *for all* A *in* S.

Proof. By Theorem 12.8, (1) $N^{\wedge}N^{\wedge}(A) \Rightarrow A$ for all A in S. *Therefore, for all* $N^{\wedge}(A)$, (2) $N^{\wedge}N^{\wedge}N^{\wedge}(A) \Rightarrow N^{\wedge}(A)$. Moreover, by Theorem 12.9, it also follows that (3) $N^{\wedge}(A) \Rightarrow N^{\wedge}N^{\wedge}N^{\wedge}(A)$.

Exercise 12.5. Show, in the implication structure $I = \langle S, \Rightarrow \rangle$, where $S = \{A, B, C\}$ and A implies B, which in turn implies C, that $C \not\Rightarrow N^{\wedge}N^{\wedge}(C)$.

Exercise 12.6. Using the implication structure of Exercise 12.5, show that $B, N^{\wedge}(B) \not\Rightarrow A$.

There are implication structures in which an element A will have a negation $N(A)$, but the dual negation, $N^{\wedge}(A)$, does not exist. Here is a relatively simple structure of that sort:

$\Longrightarrow$:   and its dual implication $\Longrightarrow$:

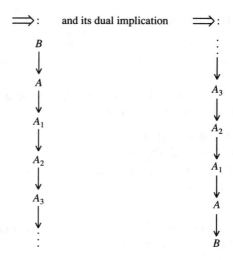

In this structure (on the left), the negation $N(A)$ of A is B, since B together with A implies all the members of the structure and is the only member to do so. On the other hand, there is no negation $N^{\wedge}(A)$ of A in the dual structure, since no element of the structure together with A implies ("$\Longrightarrow^{\wedge}$") all its members: If for some C in the structure, A together with C implies all the members, then since either A implies C or C implies A, either A implies all the members of the structure or else C does. But no member of the dual structure implies all its members.

There is a feature of the dual of the negation operator that runs parallel to those of the duals of the other logical operators. We shall see (Chapters 13 and 14) that the dual of the conjunction operator is disjunction and that the dual of the disjunction operator is conjunction. Although disjunction on the structure I is the conjunction operator on $I^{\wedge}$, it is also a logical operator on the structure I itself. As such it can be given a characterization along the lines uniformly given to all the other logical operators.

The situation is similar for $N^{\wedge}$. Although it is the negation operator on the dual structure $I^{\wedge}$, it is also a logical operator on the structure I itself. To see why this is so, we have to give a characterization of the dual negation that shows it to be a logical operator on I. Here is such a result. The idea is to describe a logical operator N' and show that on I it is equivalent to the dual $N^{\wedge}$ of N.

Let $I = \langle S, \Longrightarrow \rangle$ be an implication structure. Let N' be an operator on I that satisfies the following two conditions: For any A in S, $N'(A)$ is such that

N_1'. for all T, if [for all U in S, if $A \Rightarrow U$ and $T \Rightarrow U$, then $C \Rightarrow U$ for all C], then $N'(A) \Rightarrow T$, and

N_2'. $N'(A)$ is the weakest member of S to satisfy the first condition.

Theorem 12.11. *Let $I = \langle S, \Rightarrow \rangle$ be an implication structure, and let N' be the logical operator on I, described above. Then for all A in S, $N'(A) \Leftrightarrow N^\wedge(A)$.*

Proof. By the second condition on dual negation, for any T, if $A, T \Rightarrow^\wedge C$ for all C in S, then $T \Rightarrow^\wedge N^\wedge(A)$ [i.e., $N^\wedge(A) \Rightarrow T$]. Therefore, $N^\wedge(A)$ satisfies N_1'. Since $N'(A)$ is the weakest to do so, $N^\wedge(A) \Rightarrow N'(A)$. Conversely, if we let T be $N^\wedge(A)$, then the antecedent of N_1' holds. Therefore $N'(A) \Rightarrow N^\wedge(A)$.

Exercise 12.7. Show that N' is a logical operator on I by noting that the first condition is a filter condition (if any member of S satisfies N_1', then so too does any member that implies it).

12.7 Partial negation

There is a variation in the characterization of the negation operator that is of some interest. Recall that the first condition on the negation operator required that in any implication structure $I = \langle S, \Rightarrow \rangle$, A, $N(A) \Rightarrow B$ for all B in S. Suppose now that some nonempty subset S^* of S is singled out, and the requirement on a *partial negation operator* N^* is given by

N_1^*. $A, N^*(A) \Rightarrow B$ for all B in S^*, and

N_2^*. $N^*(A)$ is the weakest member of S such that the first condition holds. That is, for any T in S, if $A, T \Rightarrow B$ for all B in S^*, then $T \Rightarrow N^*(A)$.

N^* is a logical operator on I. Despite the departure from our definition of the negation operator, many of the old features of negation remain, although some have to be qualified. In one case, partial negation fails to connect up with the hypothetical in the way that negation does. Here are a few simple consequences:

Theorem 12.12. *Let $I = \langle S, \Rightarrow \rangle$ be an implication structure. Then for all A and B in S,*

(a) $A \Rightarrow N^*N^*(A)$,

(b) if $A \Rightarrow B$, then $N^*(B) \Rightarrow N^*(A)$.

Proof. (a) The same proof as given for N (Theorem 12.1). (b) $A, N^*(B) \Rightarrow N^*(B)$. Since $A \Rightarrow B$, it follows that $A, N^*(B) \Rightarrow B$. By Cut, then, $A, N^*(B) \Rightarrow C$ for all C in S^*. But $N^*(A)$ is the weakest of all those members of S that together with A imply all the members of S^*. So $N^*(B) \Rightarrow N^*(A)$.

There are counterparts for Theorems 12.4 and 12.5:

Theorem 12.13. *Let $I = \langle S, \Rightarrow \rangle$ be an implication structure, with S^* some nonempty subset of S. Then for any A in S and B in S^*, $N^*(A) \Rightarrow H(A, B)$.*

Proof. Let B be any member of S^*. Then $A, N^*(A) \Rightarrow B$, by N_1^*. Since $H(A, B)$ is the weakest member of S that together with A implies B, $N^*(A) \Rightarrow H(A, B)$.

The chief difference between this result and $N(A) \Rightarrow H(A, B)$ (Theorem 12.4) is that with partial negation, B cannot be any member of S; it has to be a member of the subset S^*.

Exercise 12.8. Describe a structure in which $N^*(B) \not\Rightarrow H(B, A)$ where A is not a member of S^*. [Let $S = \{A, B, C\}$, where A implies B, which implies C, and $S^* = \{B, C\}$. Show that although $N(B)$ is A, $N^*(B)$ is C.]

Theorem 12.14. *Let $I = \langle S, \Rightarrow \rangle$ be an implication, and let S^* be a subset of S such that there is a C in S^* that implies all the members of S^*. Then $N^*(A) \Leftrightarrow H(A, C)$ for all A in S.*

Proof. $A, H(A, C) \Rightarrow B$ for all B in S^*, since $A, H(A, C) \Rightarrow C$. $N^*(A)$ is the weakest to do so. Therefore $H(A, C) \Rightarrow N^*(A)$. Conversely, $A, N^*(A) \Rightarrow C$, since C is in S^*. Therefore $N^*(A) \Rightarrow H(A, C)$.

Exercise 12.9. If S^* is the set $\{B\}$ (or B together with all its equivalents) and N^* is the partial negation with respect to S^*, then $N^*(A) \Leftrightarrow H(A, B)$ for all A in S (an immediate consequence of the preceding theorem).

Simple though this theorem is, it does tell us that the hypothetical with respect to a fixed consequent is an operator that has many of the properties of negation because it is a partial negation operator. In general, the negation operator on an implication structure is always stronger than any of the partial negations on that structure. That is,

Theorem 12.15. *Let $I = \langle S, \Rightarrow \rangle$ be an implication structure, and let N^* be a partial negation operator with respect to some nonempty subset S^* of S. Then $N(A) \Rightarrow N^*(A)$ for all A in S.*

Proof. $A, N(A) \Rightarrow B$ for all B in S^*, since $A, N(A) \Rightarrow B$ for all B in S. However, $N^*(A)$ is the weakest member of S that together with A implies all the members of S^*. Consequently, $N(A) \Rightarrow N^*(A)$.

Exercise 12.10. If there are two partial negations based on two subsets of S, the partial negation corresponding to the more inclusive set is the stronger of the two.

12.8 The stability of the negation operator

As in the case of the hypotheticals, we would like to know what happens to the negation $N(A)$ when one passes from a structure I to a conservative extension I' of it. If the negation $N(A)$ (relative to I) exists, then is it equivalent (in I') to the negation $N'(A)$? Moreover, if a member of I fails to be equivalent to a negation $N(A)$, will it still fail to be equivalent to $N'(A)$ in the conservative extension I'?

Theorem 12.16 (stability). *Let $I = \langle S, \Rightarrow \rangle$ and $I' = \langle S', \Rightarrow \rangle$ be two implication structures such that S is a subset of S', and I' is a conservative extension of I. Let N and N' be the negation operators on I and I', respectively. If S is closed under N', then $N(A) \Leftrightarrow' N'(A)$ for all A in S.*

Proof. (1) $N'(A) \Rightarrow' N(A)$. Since $A, N'(A) \Rightarrow' B$ for all B in S', it follows that $A, N'(A) \Rightarrow' B$ for all B in S (since S is a subset of S'). Suppose that A is in S. There is some C in S for which $N'(A) \Leftrightarrow' C$, since S is closed under N'. Consequently, $A, C \Rightarrow' B$, where A, B, and C all belong to S. Since I' is a conservative extension of I, $A, C \Rightarrow B$ for all B in S, and so $C \Rightarrow N(A)$. But I' extends I, so that $C \Rightarrow' N(A)$. Therefore $N'(A) \Rightarrow N(A)$ for all A in S, since $C \Leftrightarrow' N'(A)$.
    Conversely, (2) $N(A) \Rightarrow N'(A)$ for all A in S. $A, N(A) \Rightarrow B$ for all B in S. Since S is closed under N', there is some C in S

such that $C \Leftrightarrow' N'(A)$. So $A, N(A) \Rightarrow C$. Therefore $A, N(A)$ $\Rightarrow' C$. Consequently, $A, N(A) \Rightarrow' N'(A)$ [and also $A, N(A)$ $\Rightarrow' A$]. But $A, N'(A) \Rightarrow' E$ for all E in S'. By Cut, then, A, $N(A) \Rightarrow' E$ for all E in S'. Consequently, $N(A) \Rightarrow' N'(A)$.

The next simple result tells us when something that fails to be a negation still fails to be a negation as we pass from one structure to a conservative extension of it:

Theorem 12.17. *Under the conditions stated for Theorem 12.16, for any A and B in S, if B fails to be a negation of A in I [that is, $B \not\Leftrightarrow N(A)$], then B also fails to be the negation of A in I' [that is, $B \not\Leftrightarrow' N'(A)$].*

Proof. Suppose that $B \not\Leftrightarrow N(A)$. Since I' is a conservative extension of I, $B \not\Leftrightarrow' N(A)$. By Theorem 12.16, $N(A) \Leftrightarrow'$ $N'(A)$. Consequently, $B \not\Leftrightarrow' N'(A)$.

We now consider a more general situation in which the stability of negation is considered when one passes from an implication structure to another in which it can be embedded by some homomorphism. In this more general situation, there need be no inclusion between the sets of the two structures.

Let $I = \langle S, \Rightarrow \rangle$ and $I' = \langle S', \Rightarrow' \rangle$ be two implication structures such that I' is a homomorphic conservative extension of I with respect to the mapping of S to S' (Definition 11.4). Then we have the following:

Theorem 12.18 (homomorphic stability). *If $\varphi[S]$ is closed under N' (the negation operator with respect to I'), then for all A in S, $\varphi(N(A)) \Leftrightarrow' N'(\varphi(A))$.*

Proof. We leave this proof for the reader. Like the proof for the parallel result for the hypothetical, it applies the preceding theorem by showing that I' is a conservative extension of the structure that consists of the image of S under φ, together with an implication relation that is the restriction of "$\Rightarrow'$" to that image.

Exercise 12.11. Let $I' = \langle S', \Rightarrow' \rangle$ be a conservative extension of $I = \langle S, \Rightarrow \rangle$, S^* be a nonempty subset of S, and N^* be the partial negation operator on I with respect to S^*. In addition, let N' be the partial negation operator on I' with respect to S^*

(which, being a subset of S, is also a subset of S'). Show (a) that
$N^*(A) \Longleftrightarrow' N(A)$ for all A in S and (b) that if N is the negation
operator on I, and $N^\#$ is the partial negation operator on I' with
respect to S, then $N(A) \Longleftrightarrow' N^\#(A)$ for all A in S.

The very generality of our account of the logical operators leads, in the
case of negation, to a consequence that might be regarded as counterintuitive. If we can always ask what negation is like in any implication
structure, then what is negation like in the very special kind of implication structure that in Chapter 1 we called *trivial*?

12.9 Negation and trivial implication structures

Since an implication structure $I = \langle S, \Longrightarrow \rangle$ is *trivial* if and only if any
two members of S are equivalent, every member is equivalent to its own
negation. This result looks counterintuitive, or even worse. Here we
have a case of the simplest implication structure there is. All the
conditions for being an implication structure are satisfied; negation is
everywhere defined, and is even classical.

First, it is worth noting that the existence of an element of a structure
that is equivalent to its own negation is not an isolable or local matter. If
there is any member of a structure that is equivalent to its own negation,
then the entire structure is trivial.

Theorem 12.19. *Let* $I = \langle S, \Longrightarrow \rangle$ *be an implication structure. If
S has a member A such that $A \Longleftrightarrow N(A)$, then I is trivial.*

Proof. Suppose that $A \Longleftrightarrow N(A)$. Since $A, N(A) \Longrightarrow B$ for all
B in S, it follows that $A \Longrightarrow B$ for all B in S. Moreover, for any
B in S, $A, B \Longrightarrow A$ [as well as $N(A)$], so that $A, B \Longrightarrow C$ for all
C in S. Consequently, $B \Longrightarrow N(A)$. So $B \Longrightarrow A$.

Thus, the property of being equivalent to one's own negation is infec-
tious. Other members of the structure, if they have negations, will also
have that property.

It might be thought that there is something radically wrong with the
way that negation operates on trivial structures, since it requires every
element to be equivalent to its own negation. Consider the special case
in which the elements of the structure are sentential or propositional,
and one of the sentences is equivalent to its own negation. Such a
sentence seems paradoxical, and the whole situation incoherent. It

would be an example, so one might think, of a sentence that was both true and false. If our characterization of negation permits such a case, something might seem to be amiss. However, our theory does not imply that the sentence is both true and false. It is simply not true that in all structures a sentence and its negation have to have different truth values (for a general discussion of the necessary and sufficient conditions for an element and its negation to have different truth values, see the discussion of the extensionality of the negation operator, Chapter 19). The following is a simple case in which the structure is not even trivial:

Consider a structure with two members, A and B, for which $A \Rightarrow B$ (though not conversely). In this structure (discussed in Section 12.2.1), negation is classical, and $N(A)$ is B [and $N(B)$ is A]. Suppose that A and B were both true (or both false). In that structure, both a sentence and its negation would be true (or both false). The difference in truth values for a sentence and its negation in a structure depends upon additional assumptions about the structure, beyond the definition of negation and the preservation of truth under the particular implication relation. For example, if it is assumed that there are at least two members of the structure that have different truth values, it will follow that no sentence and its negation will have the same truth value. If it is assumed that the structure has two members that are not equivalent, then no sentence (if it has a negation) will be equivalent to its own negation. These are assumptions that hold for some structures, but not for others. The contrast between an element and its negation (whether it is specified as a difference of truth values or more generally as nonequivalence) will be present in some structures, but absent from others.

Consider a parallel situation from geometry. Normally we do not believe that a given figure can be both a circle and a square. We think that his contrast can be explained by appeal to the definitions of "circle" and "square," and we let the matter rest. But it is possible for some figure to be both a circle and a square without tampering with the characterization of a circle as the set of all points that are equidistant from some one point, or the usual characterization of squares. If we allow the space over which these figures are defined to be finite, then the following figure is a circle whose center is E:

$$A. \qquad\qquad B.$$

$$E.$$

$$D. \qquad\qquad C.$$

All of its points, A, B, C, and D, are equidistant from E. If we think of the lines of this finite geometry as all the two-member sets of points (so that any two points determine a line, and every line has at least two points), then the figure A, B, C, D will also be a square. We leave it for the reader to supply the natural notions of distance, angle, and parallel lines to check that the four-point figure is a square. Thus, a given figure can be a circle and a square, if the space of points is finite. Now the usual situation is one in which the definitions of "circle" and "square" are applied to sets of points that are continua or, at the very least, dense. But there is nothing in the characterization of these notions that precludes their application in sets less richly endowed. In similar fashion, there is nothing in the characterization of the negation operator that precludes its application to trivial structures, in which elements are equivalent to their own negations, or bars its application to those structures in which a sentence and its negation will have the same truth value. Our characterization of negation does not bar us from applying it to all structures, no more than certain basic terms of geometry bar us from considering what happens in the finite case. Just as we can consider the properties of circles, lines, and squares in finite spaces, we can study the properties of negation on special structures (trivial or not) without conceding that in these special cases our concepts have ceased to be well defined.

Exercise 12.12. Negation and the Sheffer stroke: There is an operator version of the Sheffer stroke connective (not both A and B). Let $I = \langle S, \Rightarrow \rangle$ be an implication structure. For any A and B in S, let $V(A, B)$ be characterized by the following two conditions: V_1: $V(A, B), A, B \Rightarrow C$ for all C in S. V_2: $V(A, B)$ is the weakest member of S to satisfy the first condition. That is, for any T in S, if $T, A, B \Rightarrow C$ for all C in S, then $T \Rightarrow V(A, B)$. Show that (1) V_1 is a filter condition, so that V is a logical operator, and (2) for any A in S, $N(A) \Leftrightarrow V(A, A)$. Unlike the case for classical structures, the Sheffer stroke has limited utility in the general case. The conjunction, disjunction, and hypothetical operators cannot be defined in every implication structure using only the Sheffer stroke.

13

Conjunctions

13.1 Conjunctions: the simple characterization

Let $I = \langle S, \Rightarrow \rangle$ be an implication structure. The conjunction operator is a logical operator characterized by the following two conditions: For any A and B in S,

(C) C_1. $C(A, B) \Rightarrow A$, and $C(A, B) \Rightarrow B$, and
    C_2. $C(A, B)$ is the weakest member of S to satisfy the first condition. That is, for any T in S, if $T \Rightarrow A$ and $T \Rightarrow B$, then $T \Rightarrow C(A, B)$.

These two conditions tell us what it is to be a conjunction in any structure, but they do not guarantee that every structure will have conjunctions for every pair of its members. Here are some structures in which conjunctions exist, and some in which they do not:

13.2 Existence and nonexistence

Consider the following three implication structures:

(1)   (2)   (3)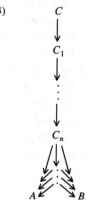

In the first implication structure we have a situation in which C is the conjunction of A with B: C is the only member of the structure that implies A as well as B, so that it is also the weakest to do so. In the second structure there is no conjunction of A with B. The first condition on conjunctions fails: There is no member of the structure that implies A as well as B. In the third structure there are infinitely many members that satisfy the first condition: All the C's imply A as well as B. However, the second condition on conditionals fails: There is no weakest member of all the C's.

There are, therefore, implication structures in which some members may not have a conjunction. That possibility is relevant to an objection that might be lodged against our characterization of conjunction: It is circular to characterize conjunction with respect to implication structures, because the very notion of an implication relation already requires the notion of a conjunction. The supposed reason for the circularity is that $A, B \Rightarrow D$ if and only if $C(A, B) \Rightarrow D$. Therefore, the attempt (on our part) to introduce the notion of conjunction, once an implication structure is in place, is circular. The answer to this objection consists in noticing that the so-called equivalence cited between $A, B \Rightarrow D$ and $C(A, B) \Rightarrow D$ holds in some implication structures, but it does not hold in others[1] (the second structure in the preceding figure, with D taken to be C, is an example).

In one direction, however, we know the following:

Theorem 13.1. *In any implication structure, if $C(A, B)$ exists and $A, B \Rightarrow C(A, B)$, then for any D, if $C(A, B) \Rightarrow D$, then $A, B \Rightarrow D$.*

Proof. By Cut, $A, B \Rightarrow D$, since $C(A, B)$ implies A as well as B.

13.3 Some simple consequences

Although we have used the simple (unparameterized) characterization of conjunction, some consequences are immediate. Others require the parameterized, official characterization of the conjunction operator.

Theorem 13.2 (symmetry). *If $I = \langle S, \Rightarrow \rangle$ is an implication structure, then for any A and B in S, $C(A, B) \Leftrightarrow C(B, A)$.*

Proof. $C(B, A) \Rightarrow A$, and $C(B, A) \Rightarrow B$. Therefore $C(B, A) \Rightarrow C(A, B)$, by C_2. Similarly, $C(A, B) \Rightarrow C(B, A)$.

Theorem 13.3. *If $I = \langle S, \Rightarrow \rangle$ is an implication structure, then for any A in S, $C(A, A) \Leftrightarrow A$.*

Proof. $C(A, A) \Rightarrow A$, by C_1. Since $A \Rightarrow A$, by C_2, $A \Rightarrow C(A, A)$.

Theorem 13.4 (associativity). *If* $I = \langle S, \Rightarrow \rangle$ *is an implication structure, and A, B, and D are any members of S, then* $C(A, C(B, D)) \Leftrightarrow C(C(A, B), D)$.

Proof. $C(A, C(B, D))$ implies A as well as $C(B, D)$, and $C(B, D)$ implies B as well as D. Therefore $C(A, C(B, D))$ implies A as well as B. By C_2, $C(A, C(B, D)) \Rightarrow C(A, B)$. Since it also implies D, by C_2, $C(A, C(B, D)) \Rightarrow C(C(A, B), D)$. The converse is proved similarly.

Exercise 13.1. Show that if $A \Rightarrow A^*$ and $B \Rightarrow B^*$, then $C(A, B) \Rightarrow C(A^*, B^*)$.

The point of the preceding simple results is not to prove the obvious. These results, and those that follow, show how the familiar features of conjunction emerge in a general setting, without any reliance upon syntactic or semantic assumptions about the elements that are conjoined.

There are other ways of characterizing the conjunction operator on implication structures. The following example exploits the feature of conjunction that says that a conjunction adds no additional content to the antecedents of an implication that already includes its conjuncts.

Let $I = \langle S, \Rightarrow \rangle$ be an implication structure. Let $C^\#$ be an operator that assigns (sets of) members of S to pairs of elements of S in accordance with the following scheme:

$C_1^\#$. For all T in S, if $C^\#(A, B), A, B \Rightarrow T$, then $C^\#(A, B) \Rightarrow T$.

$C_2^\#$. $C^\#(A, B)$ is the weakest member of S to satisfy the first condition. That is, for any U, [if for all T in S, if $U, A, B \Rightarrow T$, then $U \Rightarrow T$], then $U \Rightarrow C^\#(A, B)$.

It is then easy to see that for any A and B in the structure, $C^\#(A, B)$ and $C(A, B)$ are equivalent. That is,

Theorem 13.5. *Let* $I = \langle S, \Rightarrow \rangle$ *be an implication structure. Then* $C^\#(A, B) \Leftrightarrow C(A, B)$ *for all A and B in S.*

Proof. Clearly, $C(A, B)$ satisfies $C_1^\#$: Since $C(A, B)$ implies A as well as B, it follows (by Cut) that if $C(A, B), A, B \Rightarrow T$, then $A, B \Rightarrow T$ (for all T in S). Therefore, taking U to be $C(A, B)$, the antecedent of $C_2^\#$ holds. Therefore $C(A, B) \Rightarrow$

$C^{\#}(A, B)$. Conversely, since $C^{\#}(A, B) \Rightarrow A(\text{and } B)$, it follows from C_2 that $C^{\#}(A, B) \Rightarrow C(A, B)$.

Exercise 13.2. Show that $C^{\#}(A, B) \Rightarrow A$ (and B) follows from $C_1^{\#}$.

13.4 Conjunctions in English

If one had a reasonable way of specifying an implication structure with English statements as its members, and an appropriate implication relation on them, then the question whether or not one statement was a conjunction of certain others would have a clear sense.

Consider the seemingly simple problem of whether or not

(1) "He put on his parachute and he jumped"

is a conjunction of

(2) "He put on his parachute"

and

(3) "He jumped."

On one view, fairly popular in elementary expositions of standard logical theory, (1) is not a conjunction of (2) and (3), because (1) neither implies nor is implied by

(4) "He jumped and he put on his parachute."

However, it is noted that conjunctions are symmetric in their conjuncts, so that "and" cannot be construed in either (1) or (4) as the conjunction of standard logical theory (or any theory that requires symmetry of conjunction). On the other hand, it can be argued quite powerfully along Gricean lines that (1) and (2) are equivalent and that appearances to the contrary are due to the fact that generally in conversation or communication there is a presumption that in a narrative the order of the statements reflects the order of the events they describe, or to which they may refer. Information about the temporal order of the events in (1) and (4) is a conversational implicature, not something that is implied by them.

Without any arguments over whether or not "and" is ambiguous, sometimes having the meaning of "and then," the issue for us comes down to whether (1) and (4) are equivalent or neither implies the other. If they are equivalent, then we have this kind of structure:

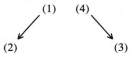

If neither implies the other, then we have this structure:

In the former case, (1) [as well as (4)] is the conjunction of (2) with (3). In the latter structure, neither (1) nor (4) is the conjunction of (2) with (3), for each implies (2) as well as (3). However, since neither (1) nor (4) implies the other in this structure, neither is weaker than the other, and in fact there is no weakest member of the structure to imply (2) as well as (3).

It does not matter whether or not "and" can sometimes mean "and then." An appeal to the ambiguity of "and," even if correct, is an attempt to explain the independence of (1) and (4). Once it is admitted that (1) and (4) are independent, then it follows, on our account, that neither of them can be the conjunction of (2) with (3).

It is the implication relation that settles the matter of what is a conjunction and what is not. But that observation obviously does not settle the matter of which implication relation is the one to be used. It is clear that there is disagreement over whether or not (1) and (4) imply each other. One group attempts to explain the independence by an appeal to the ambiguity of "and," whereas "Griceans" defend the claim that (1) and (4) are equivalent and offer an explanation for why it might be thought (mistakenly) that they are not. The difference remains a fundamental disagreement over the appropriate implication relation for the statements under study. Perhaps one more small example will help make the point clear.

Suppose that it is noted that in the appropriate structure are two other statements whose implicational relations to the others should be noted. One might appeal to

(5) "After he put on his parachute he jumped"

and

(6) "After he jumped he put on his parachute."

It is, I shall assume, uncontroversial that (5) implies (1) as well as (2) and (3). Similarly, (6) implies (4) as well as (2) and (3). This is shared ground. So the structure thus far looks like this:

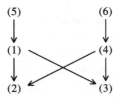

The problem that arises concerns whether or not these are all the implication relations among the six statements. Griceans certainly will not agree that (1) implies (5). "He put on his parachute and he jumped" does not imply "After he put on his parachute he jumped." The latter is something one might come to believe because of a conversational implicature concerning the usual way in which narrative is constructed. But it is not implied. Similarly, they would deny that (4) implies (6). Opponents of that view might try to explain their position by arguing that (1) and (5) have the same meaning [similarly for (4) and (6)], and that explains why the implication goes both ways, not just in the direction from (5) to (1) and from (6) to (4). But, explanations aside, their nonconjunctivist position holds whether or not they push for an equivalence of (1) with (5), for in either case, in our view of conjunctions, there still is no conjunction of (2) with (3) in this structure, since there is no weakest member of the structure of all those that imply (2) as well as (3). The Griceans would, of course, maintain that what is being missed is that (1) and (4) imply each other, so that the structure should go this way:

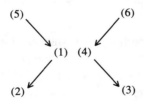

And in this structure, (1) and (4) are the conjunctions of (2) with (3), because they are the weakest members of the structure to imply (2) as well as (3). Both of these structures have an additional nice feature: The negation of (5) is (6), and the negation of (6) is (5). So it comes down to a standoff: some maintaining the equivalence of (1) and (4), others denying it.

The present account of conjunction bypasses issues of whether or not certain statements are ambiguous. What counts for or against the conjunctive status of (1) and (4) is how those statements are related implicationally to the other statements of the structure. Appeals to ambiguity, conversational implicatures, and the like, are attempts to explain various claims about whether or not one specific sentence implies or fails to imply some other. We can adopt those claims, or deny them, in order to see what the claims about conjunctions come to in the structures that result from those adoptions and denials. Reference to different implication structures helps, I think, to facilitate the discussion. But as far as the present theory goes, it will tell us only what happens in one structure, rather than another. Our account can settle what the conjunctions are in an implication structure, but it cannot settle the choice of structure, if the only things specified are some of its members. That is a difficult problem for all theories, not just this one.

13.5 The stability of the conjunction operator

Theorem 13.6 (stability). *Let $I^* = \langle S^*, \Rightarrow^* \rangle$ be a conservative extension of $I = \langle S, \Rightarrow \rangle$, and let C and C^* be the conjunction operators on I and I^*, respectively. If S is closed under C^*, then $C(A, B) \Leftrightarrow^* C^*(A, B)$ for any A and B in S.*[2]

Proof. $C(A, B) \Rightarrow^* A$ (and B), since $C(A, B) \Rightarrow A$ (and B). Consequently, $C(A, B) \Rightarrow^* C^*(A, B)$. Conversely, $C^*(A, B) \Rightarrow^* A$ (and B). Since S is closed under C^*, there is some E in S such that $E \Leftrightarrow^* C^*(A, B)$. Therefore $E \Rightarrow^* A$ (and B). Since I^* is a conservative extension of I, and E, A, and B are in S, it follows that $E \Rightarrow A$ (and B). Therefore $E \Rightarrow C(A, B)$, and so $E \Rightarrow^* C(A, B)$. But $C^*(A, B) \Leftrightarrow^* E$. Consequently, $C^*(A, B) \Rightarrow^* C(A, B)$.

Theorem 13.7 (homomorphic stability). *Let I^* be a homomorphic conservative extension of I with respect to the mapping φ of S to S^*. If $\varphi[S]$ is closed under C^*, then $\varphi(C(A, B)) \Leftrightarrow^* C^*(\varphi(A), \varphi(B))$ for all A and B in S.*

Proof. The proof is essentially along the lines given for the parallel result for the hypothetical, and it is left for the reader.

The stability theorem speaks to the question of when a conjunction of A and B in a structure I continues to be a conjunction of A and B in a structure that is a conservative extension of I. The next simple theorem concerns the question of when some member of I that is *not* a conjunction of members A and B of I still fails to be a conjunction of A and B in an extension of I.

Theorem 13.8. *If D is not a conjunction of A with B in a structure I, then D is not a conjunction of A with B in every conservative extension I* of that structure.*

Proof. Suppose that D is not equivalent to $C(A, B)$ in the implication structure $I = \langle S, \Rightarrow \rangle$. Then (1) $D \not\Rightarrow A$, or (2) $D \not\Rightarrow B$, or (3) D implies A as well as B (under "$\Rightarrow$"), and there is some E in S that implies A as well as B, but $E \not\Rightarrow D$. In case (1), $D \not\Rightarrow^* A$, since I^* is a conservative extension of I. In that case, D is not equivalent to a conjunction in I^* of A with B, for if $D \Leftrightarrow^* C^*(A, B)$, then $D \Rightarrow^* A$. Similar remarks hold for case (2). In case (3), $D \Rightarrow^* A$, $D \Rightarrow^* B$, $E \Rightarrow^* A$, and $E \Rightarrow^* B$, but $E \not\Rightarrow^* D$, since I^* is a conservative extension of I. Therefore, D cannot be the weakest in I^* to imply (under "$\Rightarrow^*$") A as well as B. Consequently, D is not equivalent in I^* to the conjunction of A with B.

It may be more perspicuous to put this simple result differently: Let A, B, and D be members of S, where $I = \langle S, \Rightarrow \rangle$ is an implication structure. If D is a conjunction of A with B in some structure I^* that is a conservative extension of I, then D is a conjunction of A with B in I.

It should be noted in passing that not all programs that relativize the logical operators to implication will yield these stability results. Belnap's program is a case in point (Chapter 4). His account of conjunction permits there to be two structures I and a conservative extension I^* of I, such that there are members of I that have a conjunction in I^*, but do not have any conjunction in I itself.

13.6 The dual of the conjunction operator

It is not difficult to recover, in this general setting, the familiar result that conjunction is the dual of the disjunction operator (and that the dual of disjunction is conjunction). The customary arguments for these claims usually rely upon rules for transforming sequences of syntactic expressions into others, and they use logical systems in which negation is classical. It is possible, however, to see the connection between conjunction and its dual without any reliance upon syntactic considerations and without the assumption that negation on the structure is classical.

Let $I = \langle S, \Rightarrow \rangle$ be an implication structure, and let $I^\wedge$ be the dual of I. Let $O_\Rightarrow$ be the operator O on the structure I, and let $O^\wedge_\Rightarrow$ denote the dual, $O^\wedge$, on the implication structure I. $O^\wedge_\Rightarrow$ is defined as the operator

O on the dual implication structure $I^\wedge$ (i.e., $O_{\Rightarrow^\wedge}$). Thus, the condition on duals of operators is that on any structure I, the two functions are identical. That is, $(O^\wedge)_\Rightarrow = O_{\Rightarrow^\wedge}$.

Exercise 13.3. Let $O^{\wedge\wedge}$ be shorthand for the double dual, $(O^\wedge)^\wedge$. Show that if $\Rightarrow\ =\ \Rightarrow^{\wedge\wedge}$, then $O_{\overset{\wedge\wedge}{\Rightarrow}} = O_\Rightarrow$.

In particular, let C be the conjunction operator on I. Then its dual, $C^\wedge$, is just the conjunction operator on $I^\wedge$. Now we know that the conjunction operator on $I^\wedge$ satisfies these two conditions (just the conditions for conjunction on $I^\wedge$):

1. $C^\wedge(A, B) \Rightarrow^\wedge A$, and $C^\wedge(A, B) \Rightarrow^\wedge B$, and
2. $C^\wedge(A, B)$ is the weakest (under "$\Rightarrow^\wedge$") member in S to satisfy the first condition. That is, for any T in S, if $T \Rightarrow^\wedge A$ and $T \Rightarrow^\wedge B$, then $T \Rightarrow^\wedge C^\wedge(A, B)$.

Since $A \Rightarrow^\wedge B$ holds if and only if $B \Rightarrow A$ (Theorem 9.1), these conditions can be rephrased, using only the implication relation "$\Rightarrow$" of I:

(1) $A \Rightarrow C^\wedge(A, B)$, and $B \Rightarrow C^\wedge(A, B)$, and
(2) for any T in S, if $A \Rightarrow T$ and $B \Rightarrow T$, then $C^\wedge(A, B) \Rightarrow T$.

Now it is apparent that, intuitively, the disjunction of A with B satisfies these two conditions. It is true that the disjunction operator is exactly the operator that satisfies these conditions. In order to see that the dual of the conjunction operator is the disjunction operator, we must first describe disjunction on implication structures.

14

The disjunction operator

14.1 Disjunction: the simple characterization

We saw in preceding chapters how the duals of various logical operators can be defined. In the case of the hypothetical, H, its dual, $H^\smallfrown$, has rarely been studied, if at all.[1] In the case of negation, as we pointed out, the dual $N^\smallfrown$ has an important role to play in the study of generalizations of classical results within nonclassical implication structures. Likewise with conjunctions: The dual of conjunction, $C^\smallfrown$, is just conjunction on the dual structure $I^\smallfrown$ and is, as we noted, a logical operator on I as well. But contemporary logicians think of the dual of conjunction not merely as the dual of an operator, but as an important logical operator in its own right. There is a direct characterization of $C^\smallfrown$ as a logical operator on I, since $C^\smallfrown$ is, as we indicated in the preceding chapter, a well-known logical operator on I in its own right, namely, disjunction on I.

Let $I = \langle S, \Rightarrow \rangle$ be an implication structure. For any A and B in S, the logical operator of disjunction is a function that satisfies the following two conditions:

D_1. For any T in S, if $A \Rightarrow T$ and $B \Rightarrow T$, then $D(A, B) \Rightarrow T$, and

D_2. $D(A, B)$ is the weakest member in S to satisfy the first condition. That is, for any U in S, if [for all T in S, if $A \Rightarrow T$ and $B \Rightarrow T$, then $U \Rightarrow T$], then $U \Rightarrow D(A, B)$.

As with the other logical operators, the characterization is pure, depending upon no other logical operator for its characterization. Moreover, like all the logical operators, it uses a filter condition (D_1) in its characterization. As with the other logical operators, there is no guarantee that each pair of members of an arbitrary structure will have a disjunction. It may be that (the set) $D(A, B)$ is empty. Nevertheless, if $D(A, B)$ has any members at all, then any two of them are equivalent (under "$\Rightarrow$"). Finally, we remind the reader that, strictly speaking, the two conditions on disjunction are a simplified but handy version. The official parameterized version will be described in Chapter 15.

14.2 Existence and nonexistence

It is relatively easy to see that there are structures in which there are disjunctions for every pair of elements. Consider the implication structure diagrammed in Section 13.2; in part (2) there are three elements, A, B, and C, and A and B each imply C. The disjunction of each member with itself exists and, as we shall see, is equivalent to that member. The more interesting case concerns $D(A, B)$. Does it exist? Note that C satisfies the condition D_1. That is, for every T in the structure, if $A \Rightarrow T$ and $B \Rightarrow T$, then $C \Rightarrow T$, for there are only three members in the structure. A and B satisfy the condition vacuously (the antecedent is false), and C also satisfies the condition, since $C \Rightarrow C$. Therefore, $D(A, B)$ is C, since C is the weakest to satisfy D_1. Here is an example where $D(A, B)$ fails to exist:

Consider the implication structure consisting of three members A, B, and C, diagrammed in Section 13.2; in part (1), C implies each of A and B, but neither A nor B implies the other. There is no disjunction $D(A, B)$. Every element satisfies the first condition: If $A \Rightarrow T$ and $B \Rightarrow T$, then $D(A, B) \Rightarrow T$. For whether T is A, B, or C, the antecedent condition fails. $D(A, B)$, if it exists, is the weakest of A, B, C. But there is no weakest of the three.

14.3 Simple consequences

Theorem 14.1. *Let $I = \langle S, \Rightarrow \rangle$ be an implication structure, and let A and B be any members of S. Then $A \Rightarrow D(A, B)$, and $B \Rightarrow D(A, B)$.*

Proof. Clearly, for any T in S, if $A \Rightarrow T$ and $B \Rightarrow T$, then $A \Rightarrow T$. Thus, A satisfies D_1. Since $D(A, B)$ is the weakest to do so, $A \Rightarrow D(A, B)$. Similarly, $B \Rightarrow D(A, B)$.

Theorem 14.2. *If $I = \langle S, \Rightarrow \rangle$ is an implication structure, then for any A and B in S, $D(A, B) \Leftrightarrow D(B, A)$.*

Proof. By D_1, if $B \Rightarrow T$ and $A \Rightarrow T$, then $D(B, A) \Rightarrow T$. By Theorem 14.1, $B \Rightarrow D(A, B)$ and $A \Rightarrow D(A, B)$. Consequently, $D(B, A) \Rightarrow D(A, B)$. Similarly, $D(A, B) \Rightarrow D(B, A)$.

Theorem 14.3. *Let $I = \langle S, \Rightarrow \rangle$ be an implication structure. Then for any A in S, $D(A, A) \Leftrightarrow A$.*

Proof. By D_1, if $A \Rightarrow T$, then $D(A, A) \Rightarrow T$. Therefore $D(A, A) \Rightarrow A$, since $A \Rightarrow A$. And $A \Rightarrow D(A, A)$ follows from Theorem 14.1.

Theorem 14.4 (associativity). *Let $I = \langle S, \Rightarrow \rangle$ be an implication structure, and let A, B, and C be any members of S. Then $D(A, D(B, C)) \Leftrightarrow D(D(A, B), C)$.*

Proof. (1) $A \Rightarrow D(A, D(B, C))$, (2) $B \Rightarrow D(B, C) \Rightarrow D(A, D(B, C))$, and (3) $C \Rightarrow D(B, C) \Rightarrow D(A, D(B, C))$, by Theorem 14.1. (1) and (2) yield (4) $D(A, B) \Rightarrow D(A, D(B, C))$ (using D_1). Finally, (3) and (4), using D_1, yield $D(D(A, B), C) \Rightarrow D(A, D(B, C))$. The converse is proved similarly.

Exercise 14.1. If in some structure I, $A \Rightarrow A^*$, and $B \Rightarrow B^*$, then $D(A, B) \Rightarrow D(A^*, B^*)$.

Theorem 14.5. *Let $I = \langle S, \Rightarrow \rangle$ be any implication structure, and let C and D be the conjunction and disjunction operators on I. Then $C(A, B) \Rightarrow D(A, B)$ for all A and B in S.*

Proof. For any T in S, if $A \Rightarrow T$ and $B \Rightarrow T$, then $C(A, B) \Rightarrow T$. So $C(A, B)$ satisfies D_1. Since $D(A, B)$ is the weakest to do so, $C(A, B) \Rightarrow D(A, B)$.

Theorem 14.6 (disjunction is the dual of conjunction). *On any implication structure $I = \langle S, \Rightarrow \rangle$, $D(A, B) \Leftrightarrow C\hat{}(A, B)$ for all A and B in S.*

Proof. By condition (2) on $C\hat{}$ (at the end of Chapter 13), $C\hat{}(A, B)$ satisfies condition D_1. Therefore $C\hat{}(A, B) \Rightarrow D(A, B)$. By condition (1) at the end of Chapter 13, $A \Rightarrow C\hat{}(A, B)$ and $B \Rightarrow C\hat{}(A, B)$. Therefore $D(A, B) \Rightarrow C\hat{}(A, B)$ (by D_1).

Let $I = \langle S, \Rightarrow \rangle$ be any implication structure. $D\hat{}$, the dual of the disjunction operator D on I, is just the disjunction operator on $I\hat{}$. Therefore,

1. for any T in S, if $A \Rightarrow\hat{} T$ and $B \Rightarrow\hat{} T$, then $D\hat{}(A, B) \Rightarrow\hat{} T$, and
2. for any U, [if for all T in S, $A \Rightarrow\hat{} T$ and $B \Rightarrow\hat{} T$, then $U \Rightarrow\hat{} T$], then $U \Rightarrow D\hat{}(A, B)$.

Because $A \Rightarrow\hat{} B$ if and only if $B \Rightarrow A$, we have the more perspicuous formulation for $D\hat{}$:

(1) for any T in S, if $T \Rightarrow A$ and $T \Rightarrow B$, then $T \Rightarrow D^{\hat{}}(A, B)$, and
(2) for any U, [if for all T in S, $T \Rightarrow A$ and $T \Rightarrow B$, then $T \Rightarrow U$], then $D^{\hat{}}(A, B) \Rightarrow U$.

Theorem 14.7. *In any implication structure* $I = \langle S, \Rightarrow \rangle$, $D^{\hat{}}(A, B) \Leftrightarrow C(A, B)$ *for all* A *and* B *in* S.

Proof. Since $C(A, B)$ implies A as well as B, $C(A, B) \Rightarrow D^{\hat{}}(A, B)$, by (1). Moreover, by (2), taking U to be $C(A, B)$, if for all T in S, $T \Rightarrow A$ and $T \Rightarrow B$, then $T \Rightarrow C(A, B)$, then $D^{\hat{}}(A, B) \Rightarrow C(A, B)$. But the antecedent holds, by C_2 (from Chapter 13). So $D^{\hat{}}(A, B) \Rightarrow C(A, B)$.

Although the disjunction operator is a function of two arguments, we shall occasionally refer to the disjunction of more than two members of a structure. We shall mean, as in the case of conjunctions, by $D(A_1, \ldots, A_n)$ the member $D(D(\ldots D(D(A_1, A_2), A_3)\ldots), A_n)$ (if it exists).

Theorem 14.8. *Let* $I = \langle S, \Rightarrow \rangle$ *be an implication structure in which disjunctions always exist. Let* "$\Rightarrow^{\hat{}}$" *be the dual of the implication relation* "$\Rightarrow$." *Then for any* $A_1, \ldots, A_n$ *and* B *in* S, $A_1, \ldots, A_n \Rightarrow^{\hat{}} B$ *if and only if* $B \Rightarrow D(A_1, \ldots, A_n)$; *that is,* $B \Rightarrow (A_1 \vee \ldots \vee A_n)$.

Proof. If $A_1, \ldots, A_n \Rightarrow^{\hat{}} B$, then for any T in S, if all the A_i's imply T (using "$\Rightarrow$"), then $B \Rightarrow T$. Since $A_i \Rightarrow D(A_1, \ldots, A_n)$ for all A_i, $B \Rightarrow D(A_1, \ldots, A_n)$. Conversely, suppose that $B \Rightarrow D(A_1, \ldots, A_n)$. For any T in S, if each $A_i \Rightarrow T$, then $D(A_1, \ldots, A_n) \Rightarrow T$ (we leave this as an exercise, using D_1 $n - 1$ times). Therefore $B \Rightarrow T$. Consequently, $A_1, \ldots, A_n \Rightarrow^{\hat{}} B$.[2]

14.4 Exjunction

There is another logical operator that is closely related to disjunction. In fact, some writers, inspired by Latin, have claimed that the English particle "or" is ambiguous. There are two senses, it is sometimes urged, that correspond to the distinct Latin words *vel* and *aut*. The logical operator D comes closest to the former, and the latter can be thought of as a special kind of disjunction sometimes called exclusive disjunction. In English, it is argued, there is an ambiguity that is absent from Latin. Of course, these claims have not gone uncontested. Issues that concern the ambiguity of an English term, of the question of best overall fit of a piece of logical theory with natural language, are not matters that can be settled by appeals to usage, linguistic or logical. Usually there are old practices that have to be adjusted, and new practices that have to be accommodated. It is a subtle matter of trade-ins and trade-offs. But it is a reasonable hope that truth, accuracy, and theoretical interest will survive the outcome of such reflective deliberations.

We shall return to some of these problems later, but only to indicate the difficulty involved in their resolution, not to promote a "solution" one way or the other. However, it is clear that no steps can be taken to study the relative merits of these different notions if we do not have contrasting and corrresponding operators to study. This is, of course, not to suggest that it is one of these that will provide the best account of the English particle "or." For all we know, there might be something better than either. Nevertheless, here is a characterization of an operator that, in discussions of classical logical theory, corresponds to what is sometimes called exclusive disjunction. We shall call this operator *exjunction*.

Let $I = \langle S, \Rightarrow \rangle$ be an implication structure. For any A and B in S, the exjunction operator E is characterized by the following conditions:

E_1. (a) For any T in S, if $A \Rightarrow T$ and $B \Rightarrow T$, then $E(A, B) \Rightarrow T$.
  (b) $E(A, B), A, B \Rightarrow C$ for all C in S.
E_2. $E(A, B)$ is the weakest member of S to satisfy the two parts of condition E_1.

Condition E_1(a) is one that is shared with disjunction. That, of course, does not automatically guarantee that exjunction is a type of disjunction, for the condition holds for conjunction as well. E is a logical operator on I, since conditions (a) and (b) together constitute a filter condition, and E_2 assigns to the pair $\langle A, B \rangle$ the weakest members of the structure that satisfy the characterizing condition E_1.

14.5 Exjunction: existence and nonexistence

There are implication structures that indicate that exjunction is not a more basic operator than disjunction; in them, disjunction exists, but exjunction does not:

Theorem 14.9. *There is an implication structure $I = \langle S, \Rightarrow \rangle$, with A and B in S, such that $D(A, B)$ exists, but $E(A, B)$ does not.*

Proof. Consider the following structure:

Clearly, $D(A, B)$ exists, and is B. $E(A, B)$ does not exist, for there is no element U of the structure such that $U, A, B \Rightarrow C$ for all C in S. Clearly, neither A nor B will do, but if some A_n should satisfy the condition, then $A_n, A, B \Rightarrow C$ for all C in S. However, since A_n implies A as well as B, it follows that A_n implies all the members of S. But that is impossible, since A_n does not imply A_{n+1}.

Exercise 14.2. Show that the disjunction operator is not more basic than exjunction: Describe a structure in which the exjunction of two members exists, but their disjunction does not. (Suggestion: Use the following structure

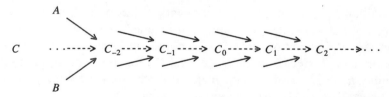

where there are infinitely many C_j's between C and C_i, and infinitely many that are implied by C_i, and A and B imply each of them.)

14.6 Exjunction: some simple consequences

Here are some immediate consequences of the characterization of exjunction:

Theorem 14.10. *Let $I = \langle S, \Rightarrow \rangle$ be any implication structure. For any A and B in S,*

(a) $E(A, A) \Rightarrow A$, and $E(A, A) \Rightarrow N(A)$,

(b) $E(A, B) \Rightarrow D(A, B)$,

(c) $E(A, B) \Rightarrow N(C(A, B))$,

(d) $E(A, B) \Rightarrow H(N(A), B)$.

Proof. (a) From E_1(a), if $A \Rightarrow T$, then $E(A, A) \Rightarrow T$ for all T in S. Since $A \Rightarrow A$, we have $E(A, A) \Rightarrow A$. From E_1(b), $E(A, A)$, $A \Rightarrow C$ for all C in S. By the second condition on negations, then, $E(A, A) \Rightarrow N(A)$.

(b) Since $A \Rightarrow D(A, B)$ and $B \Rightarrow D(A, B)$, by E_1(a), $E(A, B) \Rightarrow D(A, B)$.

(c) This follows immediately by E_1(b), since $E(A, B)$, $C(A, B)$ implies A, B, and $E(A, B)$.

(d) Since $A \Rightarrow NN(A)$, it follows that $D(A, B) \Rightarrow D(NN(A), B)$. Moreover, from $NN(A) \Rightarrow H(N(A), B)$ and $B \Rightarrow H(N(A), B)$, it follows that $D(NN(A), B) \Rightarrow H(N(A), B)$. So, by (b), $E(A, B) \Rightarrow H(N(A), B)$.

Exercise 14.3. Let $I = \langle S, \Rightarrow \rangle$ be an implication structure. Show that for any A and B in S, $E(A, B) \Leftrightarrow C(D(A, B), N(C(A, B)))$.

If either A or B implies the negation of the other, then there is no way of distinguishing (implicationally) their disjunction from their exjunction:

Theorem 14.11. *Let $I = \langle S, \Rightarrow \rangle$ be an implication structure. Then for any A and B in S, $E(A, B) \Leftrightarrow D(A, B)$ if and only if $A, B \Rightarrow C$ for all C in S.*

Proof. $E(A, B) \Rightarrow D(A, B)$, by Theorem 14.10(b). Now suppose that $A, B \Rightarrow C$ for all C in S. In that case, $D(A, B)$, $A, B \Rightarrow C$ for all C in S, so that $D(A, B)$ satisfies E_1(b). But $D(A, B)$ also satisfies E_1(a). Since $E(A, B)$ is the weakest to satisfy those conditions, $D(A, B) \Rightarrow E(A, B)$. Conversely, suppose that $D(A, B) \Leftrightarrow E(A, B)$. Then $A, B \Rightarrow C$ for all C in S, for $E(A, B)$, $A, B \Rightarrow C$ for all C in S, and $E(A, B)$ and $D(A, B)$ are equivalent, so that $D(A, B)$, $A, B \Rightarrow C$ for all C in S. But $A \Rightarrow D(A, B)$. Therefore, by Cut, $A, B \Rightarrow C$ for all C in S.

Lastly, it is worth noting that $E(A, B)$ is *antitransitive*. That is, for any A, B, and C, $E(A, B)$, $E(B, C)$, $E(A, C) \Rightarrow D$ for all D. However, that result seems to depend upon the parameterized account of negation (Chapter 15) and will be deferred for the present.

14.7   Disjunctive or exjunctive "or"

It is a difficult problem to determine whether some English statement "P or Q" is best construed as a disjunction or as an exjunction. There are difficulties aside from the major one of setting up the appropriate implication structure. Suppose that there were agreement on a structure, so that the relevant sentences that could be appealed to and the relevant implication relation were not in question. The requirement that $E(P, Q), P, Q \Rightarrow R$, for all R in the structure, and the result (Theorem 14.11) that $E(P, Q)$ is equivalent to $D(P, Q)$ if and only if $P, Q \Rightarrow R$ for all members of the structure both raise difficulties for one common way of discussing the status of "P or Q."

Suppose, to keep controversy at a minimum, that the relevant implication relation is truth-preserving and that the English statements in the structure are either true or false. We sometimes find arguments like this in the literature: "P" and "Q" are both true, and with a suitable background story T, we see that the sentence "P or Q" is false. Therefore, it is argued, we ought to paraphrase the sentence by $E(P, Q)$ rather than $D(P, Q)$.

Such an argument is far from conclusive. Even if we agreed that "P or Q" is false, and that "P" and "Q" are true, that would not suffice to favor $E(Q, Q)$ over $D(P, Q)$. If our characterization of $E(P, Q)$ is correct, then what has to be shown is that "P" together with "Q" *implies* that $E(P, Q)$ is false. It is not enough to show that $E(P, Q)$ is false; we need a demonstration that its falsity follows from the truth of "P" and "Q." Background stories, like T, make matters even worse. Either the narrative T is introduced to establish that "P or Q" is false, in which case we are still far from showing that the implication relation holds, or else the narrative T together with "P" and "Q" implies that "P or Q" is false. But in that case, all that will have been shown is that "P" and "Q," together with T, imply that "P or Q" is false. What is required, however, is that the falsity of the sentence follow from just "P" and "Q." Unless T can somehow be shown to be eliminable, such arguments that appeal to a background story do not help to favor a reading of "P or Q" as the exjunction of "P" with "Q," rather than their disjunction.

There may be another point to the telling of the story T, one that does not concern the truth of "P" and "Q" and the falsity of "P or Q." We know that there is no point in trying to distinguish between $E(P, Q)$ and $D(P, Q)$ for sentences "P" and "Q" for which $P, Q \Rightarrow R$ for all R in the structure, for the two are equivalent exactly under that condition

(Theorem 14.11). Thus, suppose that "P" together with "Q" does not imply all the members of the structure. In that case, since the exjunction and disjunction of "P" with "Q" are not equivalent, there is a point to asking which of the two (if any) is the way that "P or Q" behaves in the structure. Now, we know that if "P" together with "Q" does not imply all the members of the structure, then we always have $P \Rightarrow D(P, Q)$, but we do not have $P \Rightarrow E(P, Q)$ (otherwise, $P, Q \Rightarrow R$ for all R in the structure). And that is impossible. The story T is now supposed to have a special relation to "P," "Q," and the negation of "P or Q": Suppose, now, that T implies "P," implies "Q," and also implies the negation of "P or Q." In that case, the argument goes, if T does not imply all the members of the structure (assume that this is so), then "P" does not imply "P or Q." For suppose that "P" does imply "P or Q," then, since T implies "P," and the latter implies "P or Q," it follows that T implies "P or Q." But we have also assumed that T also implies the negation of "P or Q." Consequently, T implies all the members of the structure, and that is, by assumption, impossible. So, the argument continues, a background narrative T that implied "P," "Q," and the negation of "P or Q" would rule out the identification of "P or Q" with $D(P, Q)$. I agree that such a tale, T, satisfying the conditions described would rule out the $D(P, Q)$ option. But it would not further the claim that the statement is the exjunction of "P" with "Q." To show that, we would need an agrument to show that "P or Q" together with "P" and "Q" imply all the members of the structure. So we are back to the first argument, and that, as we have seen, is indecisive.

14.8 Stability of the disjunction operator

Just as in the case of the other logical operators, we are interested in those conditions under which something that is a disjunction in one implication structure will continue to be a disjunction in an extending structure.

Theorem 14.12 (stability). *Let $I^* = \langle S^*, \Rightarrow^* \rangle$ be a conservative extension of the structure $I = \langle S, \Rightarrow \rangle$. Let D and D^* be the disjunction operators on I and I^*, respectively. If S is closed under D^*, then $D(A, B) \Leftrightarrow^* D^*(A, B)$ for any A and B in S.*

Proof. Let A and B be in S. $A \Rightarrow^* D(A, B)$, $B \Rightarrow^* D(A, B)$, since $A \Rightarrow D(A, B)$ and $B \Rightarrow D(A, B)$, and I^* is an extension of I. Therefore $D^*(A, B) \Rightarrow^* D(A, B)$ (by D_1). Conversely, A

$\Rightarrow^* D^*(A, B)$, and $B \Rightarrow^* D^*(A, B)$. Since S is closed under D^*, there is some E in S such that $E \Leftrightarrow^* D^*(A, B)$. Therefore $A \Rightarrow^* E$ and $B \Rightarrow^* E$ for A, B, and E in S. Since I^* is a conservative extension of I, $A \Rightarrow E$ and $B \Rightarrow E$. Therefore $D(A, B) \Rightarrow E$. Since I^* extends I, $D(A, B) \Rightarrow^* E$. Consequently, $D(A, B) \Rightarrow^* D^*(A, B)$.

Exercise 14.4. Show that if the assumption that S is closed under disjunction is relaxed, then there is a structure I and a conservative extension I^* of it such that disjunction is not stable in the passage from I to I^*.

The next result is a simple one that tells us when something that is not a disjunction in one structure continues to fail to be a disjunction in another structure. That is,

Theorem 14.13. *If C is not a disjunction of A with B in an implication structure I, then C is not a disjunction of A with B in any implication structure I^* that is a conservative extension of I.*

Proof. The proof is essentially along the lines given for the preceding operators, and the details are left for the reader.

Exercise 14.5. Formulate and prove homomorphic stability for the disjunction operator.

15

The logical operators parameterized

15.1 Parametric conditions for the operators

The preceding chapters describe the various logical operators, each without reference to any of the others. The descriptions are uniform in format: the weakest to satisfy a certain condition that is characteristic for the operator under discussion. We now wish to supplement that account with an additional requirement, a "parametric" requirement. The description of each operator still will be independent of the others, and the uniform format will be preserved. However, without the additional condition, the system would be weaker than the system studied thus far; without parameterization, some of the logical operators would fail to have some of the familiar features we normally expect them to have. The need for the additional condition needs a bit of explanation.

When we described the conjunction operator, we required that $C(A, B)$ imply A as well as B and that it be the weakest member of the structure to imply A as well as B. It certainly seems as if that is the entire story to be told about conjunctions. Yet, surprisingly enough, that description will not guarantee that in all implication structures, A together with B implies their conjunction.

Let $I = \langle S, \Rightarrow \rangle$ be an implication structure. We shall require that the presence of an arbitrary finite number of antecedents in an implication makes no difference as far as the operator is concerned:

1. For any $P_1, \ldots, P_n$ in S, $P_1, \ldots, P_n, C(A, B) \Rightarrow A$, and $P_1, \ldots, P_n, C(A, B) \Rightarrow B$, and
2. $C(A, B)$ is the weakest to satisfy condition 1. That is, for any T in S, if $P_1, \ldots, P_n$ are any members of S, then if $P_1, \ldots, P_n, T \Rightarrow A$ and $P_1, \ldots, P_n, T \Rightarrow B$, then $P_1, \ldots, P_n, T \Rightarrow C(A, B)$.

The P_i's are what we shall call the "parameters" in the descriptions of the various logical operators. Fortunately there is a simple way of describing this additional requirement without so much indexing. We begin with the parametric form for the hypothetical operator:

Let $I = \langle S, \Rightarrow \rangle$ be an implication structure. Let Γ be any finite subset of S, and let "$\Rightarrow^\Gamma$" be the extension of "$\Rightarrow$" according to which $A_1, \ldots, A_n \Rightarrow^\Gamma B$ if and only if the A_i's together with all the members of Γ imply B [these are the (fixed) relativized implication relations of Section 9.4.1]. The hypothetical operator on I satisfies these two conditions:

(H) H_1. For all finite subsets Γ of S, $A, H(A, B) \Rightarrow^\Gamma B$, and
      H_2. $H(A, B)$ is the weakest to satisfy H_1: If T is any member of S, then for any finite subset Γ of S, if $A, T \Rightarrow^\Gamma B$, then $T \Rightarrow^\Gamma H(A, B)$.

The hypothetical operator in this official version is like the simple one of the preceding chapter. The only difference is that the simple account used a condition that involved only the implication relation "$\Rightarrow$" of the structure. The parametric account requires that the hypothetical not only satisfy the condition of the simple account with respect to "$\Rightarrow$" but also satisfy the condition with respect to all those (relativized) implication relations "$\Rightarrow^\Gamma$" that extend "$\Rightarrow$."

Of course, if $A, H(A, B) \Rightarrow B$, then $A, H(A, B) \Rightarrow^\Gamma B$ for all finite subsets Γ of S. Thus, any (simple) hypothetical will satisfy the first of the parameterized conditions on hypotheticals, but there is no guarantee that it will satisfy the second condition as well. On the other hand, it is clear that any member of S that satisfies the parametric conditions for hypotheticals also satisfies those for the nonparametric version of Chapter 11, for the simple, nonparametric account is just the special case in which Γ is the empty set (or consists only of theses of the structure). This holds true as well for the relations between the parametric and nonparametric accounts of the other logical operators.[1]

The parametric forms for the negation, conjunction, and disjunction operators follow the pattern given for the hypothetical. Let $I = \langle S, \Rightarrow \rangle$ be any implication structure, and let Γ be any finite subset of S.

For negation:

(N) N_1. For all finite subsets Γ of S, $A, N(A) \Rightarrow^\Gamma B$ for all B in S, and
      N_2. $N(A)$ is the weakest to satisfy N_1. That is, if T is any member of S, then for any finite subset Γ of S, if $A, T \Rightarrow^\Gamma B$ for all B in S, then $T \Rightarrow^\Gamma N(A)$.

For conjunction:

(C) C_1. For all finite subsets Γ of S, $C(A, B) \Rightarrow^\Gamma A$ and $C(A, B) \Rightarrow^\Gamma B$, and
      C_2. $C(A, B)$ is the weakest to satisfy C_1. That is, if T is any

member of S, then for all finite subsets Γ of S, if $T \Rightarrow^\Gamma A$ and $T \Rightarrow^\Gamma B$, then $T \Rightarrow^\Gamma C(A, B)$.

For disjunction:

(D) D_1. For any T in S, if Γ is any finite subset of S, then if $T \Rightarrow^\Gamma A$ and $T \Rightarrow^\Gamma B$, then $D(A, B) \Rightarrow^\Gamma T$, and

D_2. $D(A, B)$ is the weakest to satisfy D_1. That is, if U is any member of S, then for all finite subsets Γ of S, if [for all T in S, if $A \Rightarrow^\Gamma T$ and $B \Rightarrow^\Gamma T$, then $U \Rightarrow^\Gamma T$], then $U \Rightarrow^\Gamma D(A, B)$.

These, then, will be our official characterizations of the logical operators discussed thus far, and even if a nonparametric characterization is sometimes employed for other operators – such as exjunction, or the universal and existential quantifiers (Chapter 20) – it should be understood that it is the parametric version that is intended.

In certain implication structures there is nothing to be gained by distinguishing between the parametric and nonparametric conditions. In particular, if in an implication structure $I = \langle S, \Rightarrow \rangle$, $A, B \Rightarrow C(A, B)$ [and, by a simple inductive proof, $A_1, \ldots, A_n \Rightarrow C(C(\ldots C(C(A_1, A_2), A_3) \ldots), A_n)$], then any operator that satisfies the nonparametric conditions also satisfies the parametric conditions.

Consider the hypothetical operator, for example. Assume that (1) A, $H(A, B) \Rightarrow B$ and (2) $H(A, B)$ is the weakest to satisfy (1). Since "$\Rightarrow^\Gamma$" is an extension of "$\Rightarrow$," it follows from (1) that $A, H(A, B) \Rightarrow^\Gamma B$. Thus the first parametric condition on hypotheticals holds. As for the second of the parametric conditions, suppose that $A, T \Rightarrow^\Gamma B$ for any T in S. Let G be the conjunction of all the members $G_1, \ldots, G_n$ of Γ [if Γ is empty, then the second parametric condition is just (2)]. Then $A, C(T, G) \Rightarrow B$, so that $C(T, G) \Rightarrow H(A, B)$. Because $T, G_1, \ldots, G_n \Rightarrow C(T, G)$, it follows that $T \Rightarrow^\Gamma H(A, B)$. Thus the second parametric condition holds as well.

Obviously, no one would need bother with the use of parametric conditions on the operators if it were always true that $A, B \Rightarrow C(A, B)$. However, it can happen in some structures that even though $C(A, B)$ exists, $A, B \not\Rightarrow C(A, B)$. Here is a simple example:

Let S be a set whose only members are A, B, and C. Suppose that each implies itself and that $C \Rightarrow A$ (but not the converse), $C \Rightarrow B$ (but not the converse), and neither A nor B implies the other. This covers the case for all single-antecedent implications. Now extend the single-antecedent case by defining $A_1, \ldots, A_n \Rightarrow D$ (for any members of S) as holding if and only if some $A_j \Rightarrow D$. We retain the use of "$\Rightarrow$" for the single-antecedent as well as the multiple-antecedent implications. This is the type of implication relation we referred to as "Millean" (Section 8.2). In this structure, $C(A, B)$ is just C, since C implies A as well as B and is the weakest to do so. Since neither A nor B implies C, it follows that $A, B \not\Rightarrow C(A, B)$.

15.2 The parametric condition: further consequences

Theorem 15.1. *Let* $I = \langle S, \Rightarrow \rangle$ *be any implication structure. If* C *satisfies the parametric conditions for conjunction, then for any* A *and* B *in* S, $A, B \Rightarrow C(A, B)$.

Proof. Let $\Gamma = \{A, B\}$. Then for any T in S, $T \Rightarrow^\Gamma A$ and $T \Rightarrow^\Gamma B$. By the second parametric condition on conjunctions, $T \Rightarrow^\Gamma C(A, B)$. Thus, for any T in S, $T, A, B \Rightarrow C(A, B)$. Let T be A. Then $A, B \Rightarrow C(A, B)$.

Exercise 15.1. Describe an implication structure in which it is not true that for every A, B, and C, $H(C, A), H(C, B) \Rightarrow H(C, C(A, B))$. [If the implication holds, then an appropriate choice of C yields $A, B \Rightarrow C(A, B)$.]

In the remainder of this study we shall occasionally use "$A \rightarrow B$," "$A \lor B$," "$A \& B$," and "$\neg A$" instead of the functional notation "$H(A, B)$," "$D(A, B)$," "$C(A, B)$," and "$N(A)$." This familiar idiom is used only to make the results more perspicuous; no special reliance on syntactical devices is intended.

Theorem 15.2 (Interchange). *If* $I = \langle S, \Rightarrow \rangle$ *is an implication structure, then* $H(A, H(B, C)) \Rightarrow H(B, H(A, C))$ *[that is,* $A \rightarrow (B \rightarrow C) \Rightarrow B \rightarrow (A \rightarrow C)$*] for any* A, B, *and* C *in* S.

Proof. $A, B, H(A, H(B, C)) \Rightarrow C$. Therefore, by the second parametric condition on hypotheticals, $B, H(A, H(B, C)) \Rightarrow H(A, C)$. Therefore, $H(A, H(B, C)) \Rightarrow H(B, H(A, C))$, by the second parametric condition.

Theorem 15.3 (Exportation). *If* $I = \langle S, \Rightarrow \rangle$ *is an implication structure, then* $H(C(A, B), D) \Rightarrow H(A, H(B, D))$ *for any* A, B, *and* D *in* S *[that is,* $(A \& B) \rightarrow D \Rightarrow A \rightarrow (B \rightarrow D)$*]*.

Proof. $A, B \Rightarrow C(A, B)$ since we are now using parametric versions for all the operators (though, as noted earlier, the parametric condition on conjunctions will guarantee that the parametric conditions hold for the remaining logical operators). Now, $A, B, H(C(A, B), D)$ implies $C(A, B)$ as well as $H(C(A, B), D)$. Since D is implied by the latter two, $A, B, H(C(A, B), D) \Rightarrow D$. Consequently, by the second parametric condition on H, we have $A, H(C(A, B), D) \Rightarrow H(B, D)$, so that $H(C(A, B), D) \Rightarrow H(A, H(B, D))$.

Theorem 15.4 (Transitivity). *Let $I = \langle S, \Rightarrow \rangle$ be an implication structure, and let $A, B,$ and C be any members of S. Then $H(A, B), H(B, C) \Rightarrow H(A, C)$ [that is, $(A \rightarrow B), (B \rightarrow C) \Rightarrow (A \rightarrow C)$].*

Proof. $A, H(A, B), H(B, C) \Rightarrow C$, since $A, H(A, B), H(B, C)$ implies B as well as $H(B, C)$. By the second parametric condition on hypotheticals, $H(A, B), H(B, C) \Rightarrow H(A, C)$.

Exercise 15.2. For all $A, B,$ and C in the structure $I = \langle S, \Rightarrow \rangle$,

(a) $(A \rightarrow B) \Rightarrow [(B \rightarrow C) \rightarrow (A \rightarrow C)]$,
(b) $(A \rightarrow B) \Rightarrow [(C \rightarrow A) \rightarrow (C \rightarrow B)]$.

Theorem 15.5 (Contraposition). *If $I = \langle S, \Rightarrow \rangle$ is an implication structure, and A and B are any two members of S, then $H(A, B) \Rightarrow H(N(B), N(A))$ [that is, $(A \rightarrow B) \Rightarrow (\neg B \rightarrow \neg A)$].*

Proof. Since $A, N(B), H(A, B)$ implies B as well as $N(B)$, $A, N(B), H(A, B) \Rightarrow C$ for all C in S. Consequently, $N(B), H(A, B) \Rightarrow H(A, N(A))$. We need a small lemma:

Lemma 15.1. $H(A, N(A)) \Rightarrow N(A)$.

Proof. $A, H(A, N(A))$ implies A as well as $N(A)$. Therefore, $A, H(A, N(A)) \Rightarrow C$ for all C, so that $H(A, N(A)) \Rightarrow N(A)$.

Continuing the proof, $N(B), H(A, B) \Rightarrow N(A)$. Consequently, $H(A, B) \Rightarrow H(N(B), N(A))$.

Theorem 15.6 (Distribution). *Let $I = \langle S, \Rightarrow \rangle$ be an implication structure. Then for any $A, B,$ and E in S, $C(A, D(B, E))$*

$\Longleftrightarrow D(C(A, B), C(A, E)$ [*that is, A & $(B \vee E) \Longleftrightarrow (A$ & $B) \vee$ $(A$ & $E)$].

Proof. $C(A, B) \Longrightarrow A$, and $C(A, B) \Longrightarrow B \Longrightarrow D(B, E)$. Therefore $C(A, B) \Longrightarrow C(A, D(B, E))$. Similarly, $C(A, E) \Longrightarrow$ $C(A, D(B, E))$. By the first condition on disjunctions, $D(C(A, B), C(A, E)) \Longrightarrow C(A, D(B, E))$ [that is, $(A$ & $B) \vee (A$ & $E)$ $\Longrightarrow A$ & $(B \vee E)$]. It remains only to show the converse: $C(A, D(B, E)) \Longrightarrow D(C(A, B), C(A, E))$. From the first parametric condition on disjunctions, for all T in S, if $A, B \Longrightarrow T$ and A, E $\Longrightarrow T$, then $A, D(B, E) \Longrightarrow T$. Now $A, B \Longrightarrow C(A, B) \Longrightarrow$ $D(C(A, B), C(A, E))$, and $A, E \Longrightarrow C(A, E) \Longrightarrow D(C(A, B), C(A, E))$. Therefore $A, D(B, E) \Longrightarrow D(C(A, B), C(A, E))$. Since $C(A, D(B, E))$ implies A as well as $D(B, E)$, we have, by Cut, $C(A, D(B, E)) \Longrightarrow D(C(A, B), C(A, E))$.

Theorem 15.7. *If $I = \langle S, \Longrightarrow \rangle$ is an implication structure, and A, B, and E are any members of S, then $D(A, C(B, E)) \Longleftrightarrow C(D(A, B), D(A, E))$ [that is, $A \vee (B$ & $E) \Longleftrightarrow (A \vee B)$ & $(A \vee E)$].*

Proof. $A \Longrightarrow C(D(A, B), D(A, E))$, since $A \Longrightarrow D(A, B)$ [as well as $D(A, E)$]. Similarly, $C(B, E) \Longrightarrow C(D(A, B), D(A, E))$. Therefore $D(A, C(B, E)) \Longrightarrow C(D(A, B), D(A, E))$. That is the first half of the equivalence. Now for the second. By Theorem 15.7, $C(D(A, B), D(A, E)) \Longrightarrow D(C(D(A, B), A), C(D(A, B), E))$ {that is, $(A \vee B)$ & $(A \vee E) \Longrightarrow [(A \vee B)$ & $A]$ $\vee [(A \vee B)$ & $E]$}. Now $C(D(A, B), A) \Longrightarrow A$. Using Theorem 15.6, $C(D(A, B), E) \Longrightarrow D(C(A, E), C(B, E))$ [that is, $(A \vee B)$ & $E \Longrightarrow (A$ & $E) \vee (B$ & $E)$]. Consequently, $(A \vee B)$ & $E \Longrightarrow$ $A \vee (B$ & $E)$, since $(A$ & $E) \Longrightarrow A$ and $(B$ & $E) \Longrightarrow (B$ & $E)$. Therefore, $(A \vee B)$ & $(A \vee E) \Longrightarrow A \vee [A \vee (B$ & $E)]$. Thus, $(A \vee B)$ & $(A \vee E) \Longrightarrow A \vee (B$ & $E)$.

Theorem 15.8. *Let $I = \langle S, \Longrightarrow \rangle$ be an implication structure, and let A, B, and C be any members of S. Then for all D in S, $E(A, B), E(B, C), E(A, C) \Longrightarrow D$.*

Proof. $A, E(A, B), E(B, C), E(A, C) \Longrightarrow N(A)$, since A together with $E(A, B)$ implies $N(B)$, $N(B)$ together with $E(B, C)$ implies C [by Theorem 14.10(d)], and C together with $E(A, C)$ implies $N(A)$. Therefore, by the parametric conditions for the hypothetical, $E(A, B), E(B, C), E(A, C) \Longrightarrow$

$H(A, N(A))$. Therefore $E(A, B), E(B, C), E(A, C) \Rightarrow N(A)$ (by Lemma 15.1). Since $N(A)$ together with $E(A, B)$ implies B, and B together with $E(B, C)$ implies $N(C)$, and $N(C)$ together with $E(A, C)$ implies A, it follows that $E(A, B), E(B, C), E(A, C) \Rightarrow A$. Consequently, $E(A, B), E(B, C), E(A, C) \Rightarrow D$ for all D in S.

We have noted that to obtain the result that $A, B \Rightarrow C(A, B)$, the parametric conditions on conjunction are needed.

In a similar vein, it is easy to see that if $A, B \not\Rightarrow C(A, B)$ in some structure, then Exportation will fail for some members of that structure. Suppose that $A, B \not\Rightarrow C(A, B)$ for some A and B in the structure. If Exportation holds in the structure, then for all A, B, and D, $H(C(A, B), D) \Rightarrow H(A, H(B, D))$. Let D be $C(A, B)$. Then $H(A, H(B, C(A, B)))$ is a thesis of the structure. Consequently, $A \Rightarrow H(B, C(A, B))$. Therefore $A, B \Rightarrow C(A, B)$. But that is impossible.

It is an open question whether or not whenever Transitivity holds, so does $A, B \Rightarrow C(A, B)$ (provided, of course, that we are dealing with the interesting case in which all the relevant hypotheticals and conjunctions exist). And there are also open questions about the necessity of the parametric conditions for the Interchange feature of hypotheticals, the left-to-right part of the distribution theorem (15.6) and the right-to-left part of the distribution theorem (15.7).

Since the condition that $A, B \Rightarrow C(A, B)$ (or the equivalent requirement that the conjunction operator satisfy the parametric conditions) is sufficient to yield Exportation, Transitivity, Interchange, and Distribution, it is interesting to note that in various counterfactual logics the first three features do not hold for the hypothetical, and in various quantum logics, Distribution (left-to-right part of Theorem 15.6) fails to hold. We think that these differences can be traced to differences in whether or not parameterization holds in those cases. But an exact analysis of these variant operators will be postponed for another occasion.

16

Further features of the operators

Theorem 16.1 (expansion). *If $I = \langle S, \Rightarrow \rangle$ is an implication structure, and A and D are any elements of S, then $H(A, B) \Rightarrow H(C(A,D), B)$ [that is, $(A \rightarrow B) \Rightarrow ((A \& D) \rightarrow B)$].*

Proof. $C(A, D), H(A, B) \Rightarrow A$, since $C(A, D) \Rightarrow A$. By Projection, $C(A, D), H(A, B) \Rightarrow H(A, B)$. Therefore $C(A, D), H(A, B) \Rightarrow B$. Consequently, $H(A, B) \Rightarrow H(C(A, D), B)$.

Theorem 16.2 (importation). *If $I = \langle S, \Rightarrow \rangle$ is an implication structure, and A, B, and D are any members of S, then $H(A, H(B, D)) \Rightarrow H(C(A, B), D)$ [that is, $(A \rightarrow (B \rightarrow D)) \Rightarrow ((A \& B) \rightarrow D)$].*

Proof. $C(A, B), H(A, H(B, D)) \Rightarrow H(B, D)$, since $C(A, B), H(A, H(B, D)) \Rightarrow A$, as well as $H(A, H(B, D))$. Moreover, since $C(A, B) \Rightarrow B$, $C(A, B), H(A, H(B, D)) \Rightarrow D$. Consequently, by H_2, $H(A, H(B, D)) \Rightarrow H(C(A, B), D)$.

Theorem 16.3. *If $I = \langle S, \Rightarrow \rangle$ is an implication structure, and A and B are any members of S, then $D(N(A), B) \Rightarrow H(A, B)$ [that is, $(\neg A \lor B) \Rightarrow (A \rightarrow B)$].*

Proof. $B \Rightarrow H(A, B)$, and $N(A) \Rightarrow H(A, B)$. Consequently, by D_1, $D(N(A), B) \Rightarrow H(A, B)$.

Theorem 16.4. *It is not true that in every implication structure, for all A and B, $H(A, B) \Rightarrow D(N(A), B)$ [that is, $(A \rightarrow B) \Rightarrow (\neg A \lor B)$].*

Proof. To see that the converse of Theorem 16.3 fails, consider the following implication structure, where S is the set $\{A, B, C, D\}$ and the implication relation is indicated by the following diagram:

In this structure, $H(B, C) \not\Rightarrow D(N(B), C)$. $H(B, C)$ is the weakest member T or S, such that $B, T \Rightarrow C$. However, since B implies C, every member of S will satisfy this condition. So $H(B, C)$ is D, the weakest member of S. Moreover, $N(B)$ is A, since A is the weakest member T of S such that $B, T \Rightarrow E$ for all E in S. It remains only to compute the disjunction of $N(B)$ with C, that is, $D(A, C)$. From D_1 we know that for all T in S, if $A \Rightarrow T$ and $C \Rightarrow T$, then $D(A, C) \Rightarrow T$. The only members of S that satisfy this condition are A, B, and C. Since C is the weakest of these, by D_2, $D(A, C)$ is C. Therefore $H(B, C) \Rightarrow D(N(B), C)$ if and only if $D \Rightarrow C$. But that is impossible in this structure.

Theorem 16.5. *It is not true that in every implication structure, for all A and B, $H(N(A), N(B)) \Rightarrow H(B, A)$ [that is, $(\neg A \rightarrow \neg B) \Rightarrow (B \rightarrow A)$].*

Proof. To see that the converse of Contraposition fails, consider the set $S = \{A, B, C\}$, with the implication relation as follows:

In this structure, $H(N(B), N(C)) \not\Rightarrow H(C, B)$, for $N(B)$ is A, and so too is $N(C)$. Therefore $H(N(B), N(C))$ is $H(A, A)$, which is C. Moreover, $H(C, B)$ is B, and $C \not\Rightarrow B$.

Here is an example, discussed in Lemmon and Scott (1977),[1] of a schema that is not a theorem of the intuitionistic sentential calculus: (L): $(A \to B) \lor (B \to A)$. It also fails to be a thesis in every implication structure. That is,

Theorem 16.6. *It is not true in all implication structures that* $H(A, B) \lor H(B, A)$ *is a thesis.*

Proof. Consider the implication structure $I = \langle S, \Rightarrow \rangle$, *where* $S = \{A, B, C, D\}$, *and the implication is as follows:*

$H(A, B)$ is B, and $H(B, A)$ is A. Consequently, $H(A, B) \lor H(B, A)$ is $D(A, B)$, the disjunction of A with B. However, $D(A, B)$ is the weakest member U of S such that for every T in S, if $A \Rightarrow T$ and $B \Rightarrow T$, then $U \Rightarrow T$. The only members of S that satisfy this condition are A, B, and C, so that $D(A, B)$ is C. But C is not a thesis of this implication structure since it is not implied by D.

Theorem 16.7. *Let* $I = \langle S, \Rightarrow \rangle$. *For any A in S,* $D(A, N(A)) \Rightarrow H(NN(A), A)$ *[that is* $(A \lor N(A)) \Rightarrow NN(A) \to A$*].*

Proof. $D(A, N(A)) \Rightarrow D(NNN(A), A)$, since $D(A, N(A)) \Rightarrow D(N(A), A)$, and $N(A) \Rightarrow NNN(A)$. By Theorem 16.3, $D(NNN(A), B) \Rightarrow H(NN(A), B)$. The converse, however, does not hold in all implication structures; that is, $D(A, N(A))$ and $H(NN(A), A)$ are not equivalent in all structures:

Theorem 16.8. *There is an implication structure* $I = \langle S, \Rightarrow \rangle$ *for which there is some A in S such that* $H(NN(A), A) \not\Rightarrow D(A, N(A))$ *[that is,* $NN(A) \to A \not\Rightarrow A \lor N(A)$*].*

Proof. Let $I = \langle S, \Rightarrow \rangle$ *be an implication structure in which* $S = \{A, B, C, D, E\}$, *and the implication is as follows:*

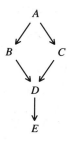

In this structure, $N(A) = E$, $N(B) = C$, $N(C) = B$, $N(D) = A$, and $N(E) = A$. Therefore, $NN(B)$ is B, so that $H(NN(B), B)$ is $H(B, B)$, which is E. The disjunction of B with C is just D. Consequently, $NN(B) \to B \Rightarrow (B \lor N(B))$ if and only if $E \Rightarrow D$. But that is impossible in this structure.

Although $D(A, N(A))$ and $H(NN(A), A)$ are not equivalent in all structures in which A is a member, nevertheless the situation is different when we consider the two conditions (1) $A \lor N(A)$ is a thesis for all A and (2) $NN(A) \Rightarrow A$ for all A. These two conditions are equivalent on any implication structure in which the appropriate disjunctions exist. Thus, if negation on a structure is classical [(2) holds], then (1) holds, and conversely. Thus, (1) could also be used as a condition for the classical character of the negation operator. The drawbacks to such use are those that we have already mentioned: the fact that (1) appeals to disjunction as well as negation, and the fact that there are implication structures (which fail to have the appropriate disjunctions) to which (2) is applicable, but (1) is not. In any case, we do have the following result:

Theorem 16.9. *Let $I = \langle S, \Rightarrow \rangle$ be an implication structure in which the disjunction of every member of S with its negation exists. Then $A \lor N(A)$ is a thesis for all A if and only if $NN(A) \Rightarrow A$ for all A.*

Proof. Suppose that for every A in S, $D(A, N(A))$ is a thesis of I – that is, it is implied by every member of S. Since $D(A, N(A)) \Rightarrow D(A, NNN(A))$, and by Theorem 16.3, $D(A, NNN(A)) \Rightarrow H(NN(A), A)$, $H(NN(A), A)$ is a thesis for all A in S. Consequently, $NN(A) \Rightarrow A$ for all A in S. Conversely suppose that $NN(A) \Rightarrow A$ for all A in S. To prove that the disjunction of every member of S with its negation is a thesis of I, we need a preliminary result:

Lemma 16.1. *For every A in the structure I, $NND(A, N(A))$ [that is, $NN(A \lor N(A))$] is a thesis.*

Proof. $A \Rightarrow D(A, N(A))$, and $N(A) \Rightarrow D(A, N(A))$. Therefore $ND(A, N(A)) \Rightarrow N(A)$, and $ND(A, N(A)) \Rightarrow NN(A)$. But $N(A)$, $NN(A) \Rightarrow C$ for all C in S. Consequently, $ND(A, N(A)) \Rightarrow C$ for all C in S, so that $N(C) \Rightarrow NND(A, N(A))$ for all C in S. Let B be any member of S. Then $NN(B) \Rightarrow NND(A, N(A))$ for all B in S. Since $B \Rightarrow NN(B)$, $B \Rightarrow NND(A, N(A))$ for all B in S. Therefore, $NND(A, N(A))$ [that is, $NN(A \lor N(A))$] is a thesis of I for every A in S. We can now continue the main proof:

By the preceding lemma, $NND(A, N(A))$ is a thesis for all A in S. But we assumed that every member of S is implied by its double negation. Therefore $NND(A, N(A)) \Rightarrow D(A, N(A))$. Since the antecedent is a thesis, so too is $D(A, N(A))$.

It is also clear that in a nonclassical implication structure, one does not, in general, have the result that $D(A, N(A))$ is a thesis, when A is taken to be the negation of some member of S:

Theorem 16.10. *There is an implication structure in which $D(N(A), NN(A))$ [that is, $N(A) \lor NN(A)$] is not a thesis.*

Proof. Let $I = \langle S, \Rightarrow \rangle$ be the implication structure described in the proof of Theorem 16.8. In this structure, $N(B)$ is C, and $N(C)$ is B. Therefore, the disjunction $D(N(B), NN(B))$ of $N(B)$ with $NN(B)$ is the disjunction of B with C, and that is just D. However, D is not a thesis of the structure, since E does not imply it.

Theorem 16.11. *Let $I = \langle S, \Rightarrow \rangle$ be an implication structure. Then for any A and B in S, $N(A)$, $D(A, B) \Rightarrow B$.*

Proof. $D(A, B) \Rightarrow D(NN(A), B)$, since $A \Rightarrow NN(A)$ and $B \Rightarrow B$. Since $D(NN(A), B) \Rightarrow H(N(A), B)$ (by Theorem 16.3), $D(A, B) \Rightarrow H(N(A), B)$. Therefore $N(A)$, $D(A, B) \Rightarrow N(A)$ [as well as $H(N(A), B)$]. Consequently, $N(A)$, $D(A, B) \Rightarrow B$.

Consider next some simple (DeMorgan) results about the relations among negation, conjunction, and disjunction.

Theorem 16.12. *Let* $I = \langle S, \Rightarrow \rangle$ *be an implication structure, with A and B any members of S. Then* $N(D(A, B)) \Leftrightarrow C(N(A), N(B))$ *[that is* $N(A \lor B) \Leftrightarrow N(A) \& N(B)$*].*

Proof. To see that $C(N(A), N(B)) \Rightarrow N(D(A, B))$, notice that since $C(N(A), N(B)) \Rightarrow N(A)$, it follows that $C(N(A), N(B))$, $D(A, B) \Rightarrow N(A)$ [as well as $D(A, B)$]. But $N(A)$, $D(A, B) \Rightarrow B$. Therefore $C(N(A), N(B))$, $D(A, B) \Rightarrow B$ [as well as $N(B)$]. Consequently, $C(N(A), N(B)) \Rightarrow N(D(A, B))$. That is one half of the equivalence. For the other half, notice that since $A \Rightarrow D(A, B)$, it follows that $N(D(A, B)) \Rightarrow N(A)$. Similarly, $N(D(A, B)) \Rightarrow N(B)$. Therefore $N(D(A, B)) \Rightarrow C(N(A), N(B))$.

The next two theorems show that we do not have the equivalence of $D(N(A), N(B))$ with $N(C(A, B))$ in all implication structures. Instead, $N(A) \lor N(B) \Rightarrow N(A \& B)$ holds in all structures, whereas the converse holds in all classical implication structures and fails in some nonclassical ones.

Theorem 16.13. *Let* $I = \langle S, \Rightarrow \rangle$ *be an implication structure, and let A and B be any members of S. Then* $D(N(A), N(B)) \Rightarrow N(C(A, B))$ *[that is,* $N(A) \lor N(B) \Rightarrow N(A \& B)$*].*

Proof. Note that $D(N(A), N(B))$, $C(A, B) \Rightarrow A$ [as well as B and $D(N(A), N(B))$]. But B together with $D(N(A), N(B))$ implies $N(A)$. Consequently, $D(N(A), N(B))$, $C(A, B) \Rightarrow E$ for all E in S, so that $D(N(A), N(B)) \Rightarrow N(C(A, B))$.

The converse does not hold in all structures. That is,

Theorem 16.14. *There is a (nonclassical) implication structure* $I = \langle S, \Rightarrow \rangle$*, with B and C in S, such that* $N(C(B, C)) \not\Rightarrow D(N(B), N(C))$ *[that is,* $N(B \& C) \not\Rightarrow N(B) \lor N(C)$*].*

Proof. Let $I = \langle S, \Rightarrow \rangle$ be the implication structure described in Theorem 16.8. The conjunction of B with C, $C(B, C)$, is A. The negation of A is E [since A implies all the members of S,

$N(A)$ is the weakest element of S]. We now have to compute $D(N(B), N(C))$. $N(B)$ is C, for only A and C are members of S that together with B imply all the rest – and C is the weakest. Similarly, $N(C)$ is B. Therefore $D(N(B), N(C))$ is $D(C, B)$, the disjunction of C with B. But $D(C, B)$ is D. Therefore, $N(B \ \& \ C) \Rightarrow N(B) \lor N(C)$ if and only if $E \Rightarrow D$. But that is impossible in this structure.

Exercise 16.1. Show that if $I = \langle S, \Rightarrow \rangle$ is a classical implication structure, then for all A and B in S, $N(A \ \& \ B) \Rightarrow N(A) \lor N(B)$. (Use Theorem 16.12.)

Finally, here is an example of a relation between disjunction and the hypothetical that does not hold in all implication structures, but does hold in all classical structures:

Theorem 16.15. *There is a nonclassical implication structure* $I = \langle S, \Rightarrow \rangle$ *with some members A, B, and C such that* $H(C, D(A, B)) \not\Rightarrow D(H(C, A), H(C, B))$ *[that is, $C \to (A \lor B) \not\Rightarrow (C \to A) \lor (C \to B)$].*

Proof. Let $S = \{A, B, C, D\}$, and let the implication relation "$\Rightarrow$" be the implication relation described in Theorem 16.6. In this structure, the disjunction $D(A, B)$ of A with B is C, so that the hypothetical $H(C, D(A, B))$ is $H(C, C)$, which is D. On the other hand, $H(C, A)$ is A. Similarly, $H(C, B)$ is B. So the disjunction $D(H(C, A), H(C, B))$ is $D(A, B)$, which is C. Consequently, $H(C, D(A, B)) \Rightarrow D(H(C, A), H(C, B))$ if and only if $D \Rightarrow C$. But that is impossible in this structure.

Theorem 16.16. *In any implication structure, $E(A, B) \Leftrightarrow C(D(A, B), N(C(A, B)))$. That is, the exjunction of A and B is equivalent to the conjunction of the disjunction of A and B, and the denial of their conjunction.*

Proof. $E(A, B)$ implies $D(A, B)$ and $N(C(A, B))$, by Theorem 14.10 (b) and (c), and so implies their conjunction. To see the converse, note that the conjunction of $D(A, B)$ with $N(C(A, B))$ satisfies the first condition on exjunction [Section 14.4, condition E_1(a)]. [Note that for any T in S, if $A \Rightarrow T$ and $B \Rightarrow T$, then $D(A, B) \Rightarrow T$, and therefore the conjunction of

$D(A, B)$ with $N(C(A, B))$ implies T.] As for the second condition E_1(b), note that the conjunction of $D(A, B)$ with $N(C(A, B))$, together with A and B, implies $C(A, B)$ as well as its denial. Since $E(A, B)$ is the weakest to satisfy both conditions, $C(D(A, B), N(C(A, B))) \Rightarrow E(A, B)$.

17

The dual of negation: Classical and nonclassical implication structures

The dual of the negation operator on a structure is just the negation operator on the dual of that structure. This characterization of the dual of negation yields some simple results, as we noted in Chapter 12: If $N^\wedge$ is the dual of N, then $N^\wedge N^\wedge(A) \Longrightarrow A$ for all A, but the converse does not hold in all structures; if $A \Longrightarrow B$, then $N^\wedge(B) \Longrightarrow N^\wedge(A)$ in all structures, but not conversely; even if $N(A)$ exists for some A, $N^\wedge(A)$ need not exist (if the structure is not classical); $N^\wedge$ is a logical operator. These simple consequences are part of the story about dual negation, but only a part. There is an interesting story about this little-studied operator that deserves telling.[1]

> **Theorem 17.1.** *Let $I = \langle S, \Longrightarrow \rangle$ be an implication structure for which disjunctions of its members always exist. Then $D(A, N^\wedge(A))$ [that is, $A \lor N^\wedge(A)$] is a thesis of I for all A in S.*
>
> *Proof.* For every A in S, $A, N^\wedge(A) \Longrightarrow^\wedge B$ for all B in S, since $N^\wedge$ is the negation operator on the dual of I. Since disjunctions always exist in the structure, it follows by Theorem 14.8 that $B \Longrightarrow D(A, N^\wedge(A))$ for all B in S. Consequently, $D(A, N^\wedge(A))$ is a thesis of I for all A in S.

Since N and $N^\wedge$ are logical operators on any structure, it is possible to compare N and $N^\wedge$ with respect to their implication strengths. The result is given by the following:

> **Theorem 17.2.** *Let $I = \langle S, \Longrightarrow \rangle$ be an implication structure in which disjunction of any two members always exists. Then $N(A) \Longrightarrow N^\wedge(A)$ for all A in S.*
>
> *Proof.* By the preceding theorem, $D(A, N^\wedge(A))$ is a thesis of I. Therefore $N(A) \Longrightarrow D(A, N^\wedge(A))$. Since $N(A), D(A, B) \Longrightarrow B$ for any A and B in S, it follows (by Cut) that $N(A) \Longrightarrow N^\wedge(A)$ for all A in S.

Theorem 17.3. *Let* $I = \langle S, \Rightarrow \rangle$ *be any implication structure in which the conjunction of any members of S always exists. Then* $(N^{\wedge})^{\wedge} = N$.

Proof. If conjunctions always exist in I, then "$\Rightarrow^{\wedge\wedge}$" is identical with "$\Rightarrow$" (Theorem 9.9). By the first condition on negations, $A, (N^{\wedge})^{\wedge}(A) \Rightarrow^{\wedge\wedge} B$ for all B in S. Since "$\Rightarrow^{\wedge\wedge}$" is identical with "$\Rightarrow$," $A, (N^{\wedge})^{\wedge}(A) \Rightarrow B$. Therefore $(N^{\wedge})^{\wedge}(A) \Rightarrow N(A)$. Moreover, $A, N(A) \Rightarrow^{\wedge\wedge} B$ for all B in S, since A, $N(A) \Rightarrow B$ for all B in S. Consequently, $N(A) \Rightarrow^{\wedge\wedge} (N^{\wedge})^{\wedge}(A)$ for all A in S. Thus, $N(A) \Rightarrow (N^{\wedge})^{\wedge}(A)$.

The negation operator is defined over a wide variety of structures, classical and otherwise. It is not true in every structure that A will be a thesis (implied by all the members of S) if and only if $N(A)$ is an antithesis (implies all the S's). It is true, of course, in every classical structure. Now the dual of N seems to pick up the slack. That is,

Theorem 17.4. *Let* $I = \langle S, \Rightarrow \rangle$ *be an implication relation for which disjunctions always exist. Then A is a thesis of I if and only if* $N^{\wedge}(A)$ *is an antithesis of I.*

Proof. If A is a thesis of I, then $B \Rightarrow A$ for all B in S. Consequently, by Theorem 12.9, $N^{\wedge}(A) \Rightarrow N^{\wedge}(B)$ for all B in S. Therefore, for $N^{\wedge}(C)$ (any C), we have $N^{\wedge}(A) \Rightarrow N^{\wedge}N^{\wedge}(C)$. By Theorem 12.8, $N^{\wedge}N^{\wedge}(C) \Rightarrow C$ for all C in S. Consequently, $N^{\wedge}(A) \Rightarrow C$ for all C in S. Conversely, suppose that $N^{\wedge}(A)$ is an antithesis of I. Then $N^{\wedge}(B) \Rightarrow N^{\wedge}N^{\wedge}(A)$ for all B, since $N^{\wedge}(A) \Rightarrow B$ for all B. Consequently, $N^{\wedge}(B) \Rightarrow A$ for all B in S. For $N(C)$ in particular (any C), $N^{\wedge}N(C) \Rightarrow A$. By Theorem 17.2, $N(E) \Rightarrow N^{\wedge}(E)$ for all E. Therefore $NN(C) \Rightarrow N^{\wedge}N(C)$ for all C. Consequently, $NN(C) \Rightarrow A$ for all C. But $C \Rightarrow NN(C)$, so that $C \Rightarrow A$ for all C in S.

There are implication structures that do not have disjunctions for distinct members, but that are classical. Consider the example that consists of just two elements, neither of which implies the other. The two members do not have a disjunction, since there is no member of the structure that is implied by each of them. Moreover, $NN(D) \Leftrightarrow D$ holds for each, since the negation of each one is the other – so that negation is classical. Thus the distinction between classical and nonclassical structures is available. Nevertheless, for those implication structures that always have disjunctions, there is a nice way of distinguishing between classical and nonclassical negation operators: The classical negation operators on these structures are those that are equivalent to their own duals – that is, $N(A) \Leftrightarrow N^{\wedge}(A)$ for all A. That is,

Theorem 17.5. *Let $I = \langle S, \Rightarrow \rangle$ be an implication structure in which disjunctions always exist. N is classical if and only if for all A in S, $N^{\wedge}(A) \Rightarrow N(A)$.*

Proof. Suppose that N is classical. By Theorem 17.1, $D(A, N(A))$ $[A \vee N(A)]$ is a thesis of I. Consequently, $B \Rightarrow D(A, N(A))$, so that $A, N(A) \Rightarrow^{\wedge} B$ for all B in S, by condition $N_2^{\wedge}$ (Section 12.6). Therefore $N(A) \Rightarrow^{\wedge} N^{\wedge}(A)$ – that is, $N^{\wedge}(A) \Rightarrow N(A)$ for all A. Conversely, suppose that for all A in S, $N^{\wedge}(A) \Rightarrow N(A)$. Then $NN(A) \Rightarrow NN^{\wedge}(A)$. By Theorem 17.2, $N(A) \Rightarrow N^{\wedge}(A)$ for all A. Consequently, $NN^{\wedge}(A) \Rightarrow N^{\wedge}N^{\wedge}(A)$. Therefore $NN(A) \Rightarrow N^{\wedge}N^{\wedge}(A)$. Since $N^{\wedge}N^{\wedge}(A) \Rightarrow A$, it follows that $NN(A) \Rightarrow A$.

Combining Theorems 17.2 and 17.5, N is classical on any structure in which disjunctions exist if and only if $N(A) \Leftrightarrow N^{\wedge}(A)$ for all A.

The following simple theorems are sometimes useful in carrying out computations, and they illustrate some of the systematic connections between N and $N^{\wedge}$:

Exercise 17.1. If $I = \langle S, \Rightarrow \rangle$ is an implication structure in which disjunctions always exist, then, for any A and B in S,

(a) if $N^{\wedge}(A) \Rightarrow B$, then $N(B) \Rightarrow A$,
(b) if $A \Rightarrow N(B)$, then $B \Rightarrow N^{\wedge}(A)$.

Exercise 17.2. Let $I = \langle S, \Rightarrow \rangle$ be any implication structure with disjunctions. Then

(a) if [for any A and B in S, if $N(B) \Rightarrow A$, then $N^{\wedge}(A) \Rightarrow B$], then N is classical on I (and conversely),
(b) if [for any A and B in S, if $B \Rightarrow N^{\wedge}(A)$, then $A \Rightarrow N(B)$], then N is classical on I (and conversely).

We saw (Theorem 12.8) that in any structure, $N^{\wedge}N^{\vee}(A) \Rightarrow A$. As one might expect, the converse holds if and only if negation is classical on the structure. That is indeed so, although the proof is a bit indirect:

Theorem 17.6. *Let* $I = \langle S, \Rightarrow \rangle$ *be an implication structure in which disjunctions and conjunctions always exist. Then* N *is classical on* I *if and only if* $A \Rightarrow N^{\wedge}N^{\vee}(A)$ *for all* A *in* S.

Proof. If N is classical, then since disjunctions exist in I, $N(A)$ is equivalent to $N^{\vee}(A)$ for all A in S. But $A \Rightarrow NN(A)$ holds in all structures. Therefore $A \Rightarrow N^{\wedge}N^{\vee}(A)$ for all A holds as well. The converse is not as direct. For this we need two preliminary results:

Lemma 17.1. *For any* A *in* I, $C(A, N^{\vee}(A)) \Rightarrow N^{\wedge}D(A, N^{\vee}(A))$ [*that is,* A & $N^{\vee}(A) \Rightarrow N^{\vee}(A \vee N^{\vee}(A))$].

Proof. (This is the only part of this proof where the presence of conjunctions as well as disjunctions is used.) We know that $C(A, N^{\vee}(A)) \Rightarrow A$, so that $N^{\vee}(A) \Rightarrow N^{\vee}C(A, N^{\vee}(A))$. Moreover, $C(A, N^{\vee}(A)) \Rightarrow N^{\vee}(A)$, so that $N^{\wedge}N^{\vee}(A) \Rightarrow N^{\wedge}C(A, N^{\vee}(A))$. By hypothesis, $A \Rightarrow N^{\wedge}N^{\vee}(A)$, so that $A \Rightarrow N^{\wedge}C(A, N^{\vee}(A))$. Therefore, since A and $N^{\vee}(A)$ each imply $N^{\wedge}C(A, N^{\vee}(A))$, we conclude that their disjunction implies $N^{\wedge}C(A, N^{\vee}(A))$ as well. That is, $D(A, N^{\vee}(A)) \Rightarrow N^{\wedge}C(A, N^{\vee}(A))$. Therefore $N^{\wedge}N^{\wedge}C(A, N^{\vee}(A)) \Rightarrow N^{\wedge}D(A, N^{\vee}(A))$. By hypothesis, $C(A, N^{\vee}(A)) \Rightarrow N^{\wedge}N^{\wedge}C(A, N^{\vee}(A))$. Consequently, $C(A, N^{\vee}(A)) \Rightarrow N^{\wedge}D(A, N^{\vee}(A))$.

Lemma 17.2. *For every* A *in* S, $N^{\wedge}D(A, N^{\vee}(A)) \Rightarrow T$ *for all* T *in* S [*that is,* $N^{\vee}(A \vee N^{\vee}(A))$ *is an antithesis of* I].

Proof. Since $D(A, N^{\vee}(A))$ is a thesis of I for all I in S, by Theorem 17.4, $N^{\wedge}D(A, N^{\vee}(A))$ is an antithesis of I.

We can now continue the proof. Since $C(A, N^{\vee}(A)) \Rightarrow N^{\wedge}D(A, N^{\vee}(A))$ (by Lemma 17.1), and $N^{\wedge}D(A, N^{\vee}(A)) \Rightarrow T$ for all T in S (by Lemma 17.2), we conclude that $C(A, N^{\vee}(A)) \Rightarrow T$ for all T in S. Since $A, N^{\vee}(A) \Rightarrow C(A, N^{\vee}(A))$, it follows that $A, N^{\vee}(A) \Rightarrow T$ for all T in S. Therefore $N^{\vee}(A) \Rightarrow N(A)$ for all A in S. By Theorem 17.5, N is classical on the structure I.

The following theorem is sometimes useful for computing with N and $N^{\wedge}$:

Theorem 17.7. *Let* $I = \langle S, \Rightarrow \rangle$ *be an implication structure with disjunctions for any of its members. Then* $NN^\wedge(A) \Rightarrow N^\wedge N^\wedge(A) \Rightarrow A \Rightarrow NN(A) \Rightarrow N^\wedge N(A)$ *for all* A *in* S.

Proof. We already have $A \Rightarrow NN(A)$ and $N^\wedge N^\wedge(A) \Rightarrow A$ from Theorems 12.1 and 12.8, respectively, without the use of the disjunctions assumption. With the use of the disjunctions assumption, we have the result that $N(A) \Rightarrow N^\wedge(A)$ for all A in S. Therefore $NN(A) \Rightarrow N^\wedge N(A)$ for all A in S, and $NN^\wedge(A) \Rightarrow N^\wedge N^\wedge(A)$ for all A in S.

There is the question whether or not the implications run in the opposite direction. Of course, on those classical structures (with disjunctions) they always do, for on those structures N is equivalent to $N^\wedge$.

Theorem 17.8. *There is always some nonclassical implication structure that shows the nonequivalence of any two of these implications:* $NN^\wedge(A) \Rightarrow N^\wedge N^\wedge(A) \Rightarrow A \Rightarrow NN(A) \Rightarrow N^\wedge N^\wedge(A)$.

Proof. One can just run through the various possibilities: (1) $NN(A) \Rightarrow A$, but then N is classical, so that one can find a structure on which this fails. (2) $A \Rightarrow N^\wedge N^\wedge(A)$. But we know that this implies that N is classical, so, as in (1), there are structures in which (2) fails. (3) $NN(A) \Rightarrow N^\wedge N^\wedge(A)$. But then $NN(A) \Rightarrow A$, which will fail in a nonclassical structure. (4) $NN(A) \Rightarrow NN^\wedge(A)$. In that case, $NN(A) \Rightarrow NN^\wedge(A) \Rightarrow N^\wedge N^\wedge(A) \Rightarrow A$, so that N would have to be classical. (5) $A \Rightarrow NN^\wedge(A)$, with the result $A \Rightarrow N^\wedge N^\wedge(A)$, and again N would be classical. This leaves five remaining cases: (6) $N^\wedge N^\wedge(A) \Rightarrow NN^\wedge(A)$. (7) $N^\wedge N(A) \Rightarrow NN(A)$. (8) $N^\wedge N(A) \Rightarrow A$. (9) $N^\wedge N(A) \Rightarrow N^\wedge N^\wedge(A)$. (10) $N^\wedge N(A) \Rightarrow NN^\wedge(A)$. In the case of (10), since we always have $NN^\wedge(A) \Rightarrow N^\wedge N(A)$, we have the situation in which $N^\wedge N = NN^\wedge$. Therefore N is classical [for then $NN(A) \Rightarrow N^\wedge N(A)$, so that $NN(A) \Rightarrow NN^\wedge(A) \Rightarrow A$]. Thus we are left with the four cases (6)–(9). From (6) we obtain, using the implications of the preceding theorem, that $NN^\wedge = N^\wedge N^\wedge$. Similar use of the preceding theorem yields, in the cases of (7)–(9), that $N^\wedge N = NN$. For each of these two equivalences, there is a nonclassical structure in which they fail. For $N^\wedge N(A) \Leftrightarrow NN(A)$ (all A), and $NN^\wedge(A) \Leftrightarrow N^\wedge N^\wedge(A)$ (all A), consider this structure:

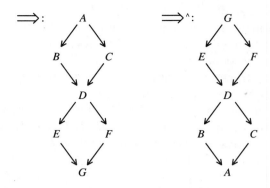

Notice that $N^{\wedge}N$ fails to be equivalent to NN for the element B, for $N(B) = C$, so that $N^{\wedge}N(B) = N^{\wedge}(C) = G$. On the other hand, $NN(B) = N(C) = B$. Now $N^{\wedge}N(B) \Longleftrightarrow NN(B)$ if and only if $G \Longleftrightarrow B$. But that is impossible in this structure. Furthermore, $NN^{\wedge}$ fails to be equivalent to $N^{\wedge}N^{\wedge}$ for the element E [for $N^{\wedge}(E) = F$, so that $NN^{\wedge}(E) = N(F) = A$. On the other hand, $N^{\wedge}N^{\wedge}(E) = N^{\wedge}(F) = E$. Thus, $NN^{\wedge}(E) \Longleftrightarrow N^{\wedge}N^{\wedge}(E)$ if and only if $A \Longleftrightarrow E$. But that is impossible.].

This provides a picture of the relations between the various ways of combining N and $N^{\wedge}$ two at a time. There is a relatively simple picture of the combinations of N and $N^{\wedge}$ taken three at a time:

Theorem 17.9. *Let $I = \langle S, \Longrightarrow \rangle$ be an implication structure with disjunctions. Then the following implications hold:*

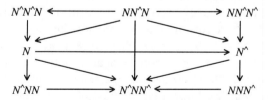

Proof. These implications indicated by the single arrows are easily established with the help of the implication relations of the preceding theorem. Moreover, none of the triples displayed is equivalent to any of NN, $NN^{\wedge}$, $N^{\wedge}N$, or $N^{\wedge}N^{\wedge}$. We can see this with the aid of an implication structure such as the one consisting of A, B, and C, where A implies B, and B implies C (and, of course, each implies itself). It is easy to see that in such a structure all of the six triples have the value of C on the element

A. However, all of NN, $NN^$, $N^N^$, and N^N have the value A on the element A. Consequently, none of the latter can be equivalent to any of the former. Moreover, none of the six triples is equivalent either to N or to $N^$. For example, the implication structure described above shows that none of the triples N^N^N, NN^N, and N^NN is equivalent to $N^$. The fact that none of them is equivalent to N can be shown by using an implication structure consisting of A, B, C, D, and E, where A implies B as well as C, each of B and C implies D, and D implies E. Similarly, none of the triples $NN^N^$, $N^NN^$, and $NNN^$ is equivalent to N (using the structure involving just A, B, and C, where $A \Rightarrow B \Rightarrow C$), and their nonequivalence with $N^$ can be shown by the use of an appropriate implication structure. Thus, all eight of the operators shown are nonequivalent, and none of them is equivalent to any of the binary combinations NN, N^N, $NN^$, and $N^N^$. Moreover, none of the six triples is equivalent to the identity operator (for each of those triples either implies N or implies $N^$).

We are left with an open question: Are there infinitely many or only finitely many nonequivalent combinations of N and $N^$?

We have indicated some of the systematic connections between N and $N^$. We have also mentioned that when N is nonclassical on a structure I, its dual, $N^$, seems to pick up some of the features of classical negation that N does not possess in I.

Thus, although classically we have $NN(A) \Leftrightarrow A$, in a nonclassical implication structure $I = \langle S, \Rightarrow \rangle$ we always have $A \Rightarrow NN(A)$ for all A in S, but we do not have $NN(A) \Rightarrow A$ for all A in S. However, we do have $N^N^(A) \Rightarrow A$ for all A in S, but not the converse.

Again, $D(A, N(A))$ [that is, $(A \lor N(A))$] is always a thesis of classical structures, but fails in some nonclassical structures. However, $A \lor N^N^(A)$ is a thesis in all structures, classical as well as nonclassical.

In the same vein, we know that in classical structures, A is a thesis if and only if $N(A)$ is an antithesis. In nonclassical structures, neither the "if" nor the "only if" holds for all members of the structure. However, for the dual of N, we always have the result that A is a thesis if and only if $N^(A)$ is an antithesis, for all members A, of the structure (when disjunctions always exist).

These examples suggest a "sandwiching" technique as a way of indicating the generalizations of classical results that are obtainable in nonclassical structures. Thus,

$$N^\wedge N^\wedge(A) \Rightarrow A \Rightarrow NN(A)$$

holds in all structures. In the case of classical structures (with disjunctions), the ends are equivalent to each other, and consequently equivalent to A.

Classically, we have $H(A, B) \Longleftrightarrow D(N(A), B)$ [that is, $N(A) \vee B$]. In nonclassical structures, $N(A) \vee B \Rightarrow H(A, B)$, but $H(A, B) \not\Rightarrow D(N(A), B)$. However, in nonclassical structures (with disjunctions and conjunctions) there is this result:

Theorem 17.10. *If* $I = \langle S, \Rightarrow \rangle$ *is an implication structure with disjunctions and conjunctions for any members, then* $D(N(A), NN^\wedge(B)) \Rightarrow H(A, B) \Rightarrow D(N^\wedge(A), N^\wedge N(B))$. *That is,* $N(A) \vee NN^\wedge(B) \Rightarrow H(A, B) \Rightarrow N^\wedge(A) \vee N^\wedge N(B)$.

Proof. To show that $N(A) \vee NN^\wedge(B) \Rightarrow H(A, B)$, notice that by Theorem 17.8, $NN^\wedge(A) \Rightarrow A$ for all A. Therefore $N(A) \vee NN^\wedge(B) \Rightarrow N(A) \vee B \Rightarrow H(A, B)$. To show that $H(A, B) \Rightarrow N^\wedge(A) \vee N^\wedge N(B)$, we need a preliminary result:

Lemma 17.3. *Let* $I = \langle S, \Rightarrow \rangle$ *be an implication structure with disjunctions and conjunctions. Then for any* A *and* B *in* S, $N^\wedge C(A, B) \Rightarrow D(N^\wedge(A), N^\wedge(B))$ [*that is,* $N^\wedge(A \& B) \Rightarrow N^\wedge(A) \vee N^\wedge(B)$].

Proof. Note that since $(A \vee N^\wedge(A))$ and $(B \vee N^\wedge(B))$ are theses, so too are $(A \vee N^\wedge(A) \vee N^\wedge(B))$ and $(B \vee N^\wedge(A) \vee N^\wedge(B))$. Since their conjunction is also a thesis, by the distribution theorem (15.8), $(A \& B) \vee (N^\wedge(A) \vee N^\wedge(B))$ is also a thesis of I. Therefore, for any T in S, $(A \& B), (N^\wedge(A) \vee N^\wedge(B)) \Rightarrow^\wedge T$ {since for any T in S, $T \Rightarrow [(A \& B) \vee (N^\wedge(A) \vee N^\wedge(B))]$}. Thus, $(N^\wedge(A) \vee N^\wedge(B)) \Rightarrow^\wedge N^\wedge(A \& B)$; that is, $N^\wedge(A \& B) \Rightarrow (N^\wedge(A) \vee N^\wedge(B))$.

Continuing the proof of the theorem, note that $H(A, B)$ together with $(A \& N(B))$ implies B as well as $N(B)$. Therefore $H(A, B) \Rightarrow N(A \& N(B)) \Rightarrow N^\wedge(A \& N(B))$, which, by the preceding lemma, implies $N^\wedge(A) \vee N^\wedge N(B)$. Thus the "sandwich" result that

$$N(A) \vee NN^\wedge(B) \Rightarrow H(A, B) \Rightarrow N^\wedge(A) \vee N^\wedge N(B).$$

It would be nice to have a simpler sandwich; perhaps $(N(A) \vee B) \Rightarrow H(A, B) \Rightarrow (N^\wedge(A) \vee B)$, or $(N^\wedge(A) \vee B) \Rightarrow H(A, B)$

$\Rightarrow (N^\frown(A) \lor B)$. But it is easy to see that $N^\frown(A) \lor B$ neither implies nor is implied by $H(A, B)$.

In the same vein, here is another sandwich with simple ends that become equivalent to each other and to H in the classical case:

Theorem 17.11. *Let $I = \langle S, \Rightarrow \rangle$ be an implication structure with disjunctions and conjunctions. Then $NC(A, N^\frown(B)) \Rightarrow H(A, B) \Rightarrow N^\frown C(A, N(B))$ [that is, $N(A \,\&\, N^\frown(B)) \Rightarrow H(A, B) \Rightarrow N^\frown(A \,\&\, N(B))$].*

Proof. To show that $H(A, B) \Rightarrow N^\frown(A \,\&\, N(B))$, notice that $H(A, B)$, $(A \,\&\, N(B))$ implies C for all C in S. Consequently, $H(A, B) \Rightarrow N(A \,\&\, N(B))$. Since $N(A) \Rightarrow N^\frown(A)$ for all A in S, $H(A, B) \Rightarrow N^\frown(A \,\&\, N(B))$. To show that $N(A \,\&\, N^\frown(B)) \Rightarrow H(A, B)$, notice that $N(A \,\&\, N^\frown(B))$, A, $N^\frown(B)$ implies $(A \,\&\, N^\frown(B))$ as well as $N(A \,\&\, N^\frown(B))$. Therefore $N(A \,\&\, N^\frown(B))$, $A \Rightarrow NN^\frown(B)$. Consequently, $N(A \,\&\, N^\frown(B))$, $A \Rightarrow B$, since $NN^\frown(B) \Rightarrow B$. Therefore $N(A \,\&\, N^\frown(B)) \Rightarrow H(A, B)$. Thus, for all A and B, we have

$$N(A \,\&\, N^\frown(B)) \Rightarrow H(A, B) \Rightarrow N^\frown(A \,\&\, N(B)).$$

Finally, we should note the DeMorgan "sandwich" that is available in nonclassical structures. By Theorem 16.13, $(N(A) \lor N(B)) \Rightarrow N(A \,\&\, B)$ for all A and B, and by Theorem 16.14 the converse fails in some structure. However, consider the following:

Theorem 17.12. *If $I = \langle S, \Rightarrow \rangle$ is an implication structure with disjunctions and conjunctions, then $(N(A) \lor N(B)) \Rightarrow N(A \,\&\, B) \Rightarrow (N^\frown(A) \lor N^\frown(B))$ for all A and B in S.*

Proof. By Theorem 16.13, $N(A) \lor N(B)$ implies $N(A \,\&\, B)$, and by Lemma 17.3, $N^\frown(A \,\&\, B)$ implies $N^\frown(A) \lor N^\frown(B)$, so $N(A \,\&\, B) \Rightarrow N^\frown(A) \lor N^\frown(B)$.

It should also be noted that there is no need for a sandwich generalization of the other DeMorgan law, $N(A \lor B) \Leftrightarrow N(A) \,\&\, N(B)$, since that holds in all structures, by Theorem 16.12.

18

The distinctness and relative power of the logical operators

18.1 The distinctness of the logical operators

In studying the formal languages of the classical or intuitionistic calculus, there is a concern that the notation ensure that there be "unique readability." If a sequence of expressions of the system is to count as a sentence of the system, then it should not happen that it counts as two sentences. Thus, where "$\lor$" is the sign for the disjunction connective, a sequence such as "$A \lor B \lor C$" is not counted as a sentence, because it could be thought of as "$(A \lor B) \lor C$" or as "$A \lor (B \lor C)$," and these sequences are intended to count as distinct sentences, no matter how closely related they are logically. One way of expressing the concern is to think of various operators associated with sentence-building. For example, let $E_\lor$ and $E_\to$ be the operators that assign to the sentences A and B the sentences "$(A \lor B)$" and "$(A \to B)$," respectively. Then the condition for unique readability can be expressed by the requirement that each of these E's be one-to-one functions and that no two of them have the same range. Thus, in particular, if $E_\lor(A, B) = E_\lor(C, D)$ for any sentences A, B, C, and D, then $A = C$, and $B = D$. And $E_\lor(A, B) \neq E_\to(C, D)$ for any A, B, C, and D.[1]

In this study, logical operators such as conjunction C and disjunction D do not yield unique readability results. This is to be expected, since in general the objects of a structure may not have any syntactic character, and even if they did, implication relations would not distinguish, for example, between $C(A, A)$ and $D(A, A)$, since both are equivalent to A.

Nevertheless, there is a related concept that brings out the differences between the various logical operators, even though they may, for some of their arguments, have equivalent values.

> **Definition 18.1.** Let O and O^* be operators (say both are functions of two arguments).
>
> (a) We shall say that O and O^* are *distinct from each other on the implication structure* $I = \langle S, \Rightarrow \rangle$ if and only if for *some* A and B in S, $O(A, B) \not\Leftrightarrow O^*(A, B)$.

(b) To compare an operator O^+ that (like negation) is a function of one argument with an operator O that is a function of two arguments, we shall say that O^+ is distinct from O on the implication structure I if and only if there are some A and B in S such that $O^+(A) \not\Leftrightarrow O(A, B)$.

Thus, two operators are distinct on a structure if and only if for some arguments their respective values fail to be equivalent. Concomitantly, we say that the operators are the same if and only if their values for all their arguments are equivalent.

We then have a necessary and sufficient condition for the distinctness of the logical operators:

Theorem 18.1. *The logical operators O and O^* are distinct from each other on an implication structure $I = \langle S, \Rightarrow \rangle$ if and only if I is not trivial.*

Proof. If I is trivial, then all the members of S are equivalent to each other. Consequently, for any A and B, the values of any operators O and O^* are equivalent to each other, and fail to be distinct.

The converse proceeds by cases, taking pairs of operators from among negation, disjunction, exjunction, the hypothetical, and, if one likes, the symmetric hypotheticals[2] and the Sheffer stroke. We shall consider only a few cases, leaving the rest for the reader.

Case 1: Disjunctions and conjunctions. Suppose that $I = \langle S, \Rightarrow \rangle$ is an implication structure and that for all A and B in S, $D(A, B) \Leftrightarrow C(A, B)$. Then, since $A \Rightarrow D(A, B)$, and $C(A, B) \Rightarrow B$, it follows that $A \Rightarrow D(A, B) \Rightarrow C(A, B) \Rightarrow B$. Since $A \Rightarrow B$ for all A and B in S, all the members of S are equivalent.

Case 2: Disjunctions and the hypothetical. If for all A and B in the structure I, $D(A, B) \Leftrightarrow H(A, B)$, it follows that $A \Rightarrow D(A, B) \Rightarrow H(A, B)$. Therefore A implies B for all A and B.

Case 3: Disjunction and negation. If for all A and B in I, $N(A) \Leftrightarrow D(A, B)$, then $N(A)$ implies B since it implies $D(A, B)$. Since this holds for any A and B, $NN(C) \Rightarrow B$ for any C. But $C \Rightarrow NN(C)$. Therefore $C \Rightarrow B$ for all B and C in S.

Case 4: Disjunction and exjunction. If $D(A, B) \Longleftrightarrow E(A, B)$ for all A and B in the structure I, then, since $A \Longrightarrow D(A, B) \Longrightarrow E(A, B)$, and $B \Longrightarrow D(A, B) \Longrightarrow E(A, B)$, it follows that $A \Longrightarrow E(A, B)$ and $B \Longrightarrow E(A, B)$. But $E(A, B), A, B \Longrightarrow C$ for all C in S. Consequently (by Cut), $A, B \Longrightarrow C$ for all A, B, and C in S. Therefore $A \Longrightarrow C$ for all A and C in S.

Case 5: Conjunction and the hypothetical. If $C(A, B) \Longleftrightarrow H(A, B)$ for all A and B in the structure I, then $B \Longrightarrow H(A, B) \Longrightarrow C(A, B) \Longrightarrow A$. Consequently, $B \Longrightarrow A$ for all A and B in S.

Case 6: Conjunction and negation. If $C(A, B) \Longleftrightarrow N(A)$ for all A and B in the structure I, then $N(A) \Longrightarrow B$ for all A and B. Consequently, for any C, $NN(C) \Longrightarrow B$, so that $C \Longrightarrow B$ for all B and C.

We leave for the reader the comparisons of the remaining combinations of the logical operators taken two at a time.

18.2 The relative power of the logical operators

We have from time to time called attention to the fact that there is no guarantee that hypotheticals, conjunctions, disjunctions, negations, and so forth will always exist for all the members in an implication structure. The question arises whether or not some logical operators are more basic than others, in the sense that whenever one operator has a value for certain members of a structure, so too does the other. We need some distinctions:

Definition 18.2. (a) Let O and O^* be two logical operators (each a function of two arguments). We shall say that O^* *is not more basic than* O if and only if there is some implication structure $I = \langle S, \Longrightarrow \rangle$ and some A and B in S such that $O(A, B)$ exists, but $O^*(A, B)$ does not.

(b) For comparisons of a logical operator such as negation (which is a function of one argument) with logical operators of two arguments, such as disjunction, we shall say, for example, that D is not more basic than N if and only if there is some implication structure $I = \langle S, \Longrightarrow \rangle$ and some A and B in S such that $N(A)$ and $N(B)$ exist, but $D(A, B)$ does not. And we shall say that N *is not more basic than* D if and only if there is some implication structure $I = \langle S, \Rightarrow \rangle$ and some A and B in S such that $D(A, B)$ exists, but $N(A)$ and $N(B)$ do not. Similar construals will hold for comparisons of negation with conjunction, the hypothetical, exjunction, and so forth.

Here, too, there are clear results that can be obtained by considering the various logical operators in pairs. We shall not run through all the possible combinations, but enough of them to indicate the general picture that emerges from pairwise comparison. The provision of implication structures for the remaining cases is left for the reader.

Theorem 18.2. *Neither disjunction nor conjunction is more basic than the other.*

Proof. The implication structure described in part (1) of the figure in Section 13.2 is one in which the conjunction of A with B exists, but their disjunction does not; the structure shown in part (2) is one in which the disjunction of A with B exists, but their conjunction does not.

Theorem 18.3. *Neither conjunction nor negation is more basic than the other.*

Proof. Here is a structure showing that negation is not more basic than conjunction:

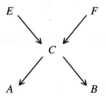

$C(A, B)$ in this structure is C, but neither $N(A)$ nor $N(B)$ exists. To see that conjunction is not more basic than negation, consider the structure consisting of

neither of which implies the other, for the negation of A is B, and the negation of B is A. However, the conjunction of the two does not exist.

Theorem 18.4. *Neither disjunction nor negation is more basic than the other.*

Proof. The implication structure of just *A* and *B*, neither implying the other, shows that disjunction is not more basic than negation. The following structure shows that negation is not more basic than disjunction, since the disjunction of *A* with *B* exists, but *N*(*A*) and *N*(*B*) do not:

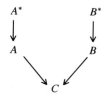

Theorem 18.5. *Neither the hypothetical nor conjunction is more basic than the other.*

Proof. The structure of just *A* and *B*, neither implying the other, is one in which the hypothetical *H*(*A*, *B*) exists, but their conjunction does not. That conjunction is not more basic than the hypothetical is shown by the structure in which *A* implies *B*, which implies B_1, which implies B_2, and so on, for all *n*, for the conjunction of *A* with *B* is *A*, but the hypothetical *H*(*A*, *B*) does not exist.

Theorem 18.6. *Neither the hypothetical nor disjunction is more basic than the other.*

Proof. The first implication structure of the preceding theorem is one in which the hypothetical *H*(*A*, *B*) exists (it is *B*), but *D*(*A*, *B*) does not. The second structure of that theorem is one in which *D*(*A*, *B*) exists (it is *B*), but *H*(*A*, *B*) does not.

Theorem 18.7. *Neither negation nor the hypothetical is more basic than the other.*

Proof. The second implication structure used in Theorem 18.5 is one in which $H(B, B_1)$ does not exist, but both *N*(*B*) and $N(B_1)$ exist (they are just *A*). The dual of the second structure used in Theorem 18.5 is one in which *N*(*B*) and $N(B_1)$ do not exist, but $H(B, B_1)$ does.

Theorem 18.8. *Neither disjunction nor exjunction is more basic than the other.*

Proof. To show that disjunction is not more basic than exjunction, we need an implication structure in which the exjunction of some members exists, but their disjunction does not. In the structure (I), $D(A, B)$ does not exist, but $E(A, B)$ is C. The structure (II) shows that exjunction is not more basic than disjunction, because in it, $D(A, B)$ is C, but $E(A, B)$ does not exist.

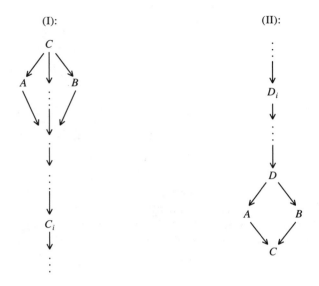

(I):   (II):

Before bringing these considerations on the relative power of the operators to an end, it is worth considering a logical operator that has been somewhat neglected in our considerations, the symmetric hypothetical, SH.

Theorem 18.9. *Neither the hypothetical nor the symmetric hypothetical is more basic than the other.*

Proof. Recall (note 2) that the symmetric hypothetical $SH(A, B)$ has the following features: (1) A, $SH(A, B) \Rightarrow B$, and B, $SH(A, B) \Rightarrow A$, and (2) $SH(A, B)$ is the weakest member of the structure to satisfy the first condition. The symmetric hypothetical is not more basic than the hypothetical since in structure (I) below, the hypothetical $H(C, D)$ exists (it is D), but $SH(C, D)$ does not. Moreover, the hypothetical is not more basic than SH, since the structure (II) below, $SH(A, B)$ exists (it is A), but $H(A, B)$ does not.

The outcome of the comparisons of the logical operators with each other is that none of them is more basic than any other. This is not an unexpected result, given the way in which each of the logical operators was characterized. Each of them was given a description that we called "pure" in that there was no reference to, or reliance upon, any other logical operator. That leaves open the possibility that there might be structures in which, for some members, one operator would have a value in the structure, but not another. And in fact, the notion of an implication structure allows for a sufficiently full range of examples so that structures exist that separate the operators from each other. It is the combination of the purity of the characterization of the logical operators together with the wide range of structures that count as implicational that lies behind the result that none of the logical operators considered is more basic than any of the others.

19

Extensionality

The logical operators have been defined over all implication structures. It is possible to develop a concept that is the generalization of the notion of a truth-value assignment that is also applicable in all structures,[1] despite the fact that most of them do not have truth-bearers as members. It is a notion that reduces to the familiar truth-value assignments on those structures that are associated with the usual logical systems, and it yields a general framework within which one can study the extensionality (or nonextensionality) of the logical operators on arbitrary structures.

19.1 Extensionality and bisection implications

Suppose that S is a nonempty set, and $T = \langle K, L \rangle$ is a bisection on it. Form the bisection implication relation "$\Rightarrow^T$" that is associated with T, and let $I_T = \langle S, \Rightarrow^T \rangle$. Since "$\Rightarrow^T$" is an implication relation, we can study the behavior of the logical operators with respect to it.

Consider the structure I_T. Since $C_T(A, B) \Rightarrow^T A$ and $C_T(A, B) \Rightarrow^T B$, and is the weakest to do so, it is possible to compute the distribution patterns for $C_T(A, B)$ in the sets K and L, given the distributions of A and B in K and L.

Conjunctions. Suppose that A is in K. Then, since $C_T(A, B) \Rightarrow^T A$, $C_T(A, B)$ cannot be in L. If it were, then since L is closed under "$\Rightarrow^T$," A would be in L. But that is impossible. Consequently, $C_T(A, B)$ is in K. Similarly, if B is in K, then $C_T(A, B)$ is in K. There is one remaining case to consider – when A and B both belong to L. In that case, since $A, B \Rightarrow^T C_T(A, B)$, and L is strongly closed under "$\Rightarrow^T$," $C_T(A, B)$ is in L (if A and B are in L). We can summarize this result as follows:

$C_T(A, B)$:	$A \backslash B$	L	K
	L	L	K
	K	K	K

Thus: (1) $C_T(A, B)$ is in L if and only if A is in L and B is in L.

Hypotheticals. For the structure $I = \langle S \Rightarrow^T \rangle$, (1) $A, H_T(A, B) \Rightarrow^T$ B, and (2) if $A, C \Rightarrow^T B$, then $C \Rightarrow^T H_T(A, B)$ for all C in S.

Suppose that A is in L and B is in K. Since $A, H_T(A, B) \Rightarrow^T B$, $H_T(A, B)$ is in K, for if it were in L, then both A and $H_T(A, B)$ would belong to L. Since L is strongly closed under "$\Rightarrow^T$," B would be in L. But that is impossible. Therefore $H_T(A, B)$ is in K (if A is in L and B is in K).

Suppose that A is in K. Since all members of K imply all members of S (by "$\Rightarrow^T$"), $A, C \Rightarrow^T B$ for all C in S. Therefore $C \Rightarrow^T H_T(A, B)$ for all C in S. Let C be in L. Consequently, $H_T(A, B)$ is in L. Therefore, if A is in K, then $H_T(A, B)$ is in L.

The remaining case is that for which B is in L. If B is in L, then every member of S implies ("$\Rightarrow^T$") it. Consequently, $A, C \Rightarrow^T B$ for all C in S, so that $C \Rightarrow^T H_T(A, B)$. Let C belong to L. Therefore $H_T(A, B)$ belongs to L. Thus, if B is in L, then $H_T(A, B)$ is also in L. These computations can be summarized as follows:

$H_T(A, B)$:	$A \backslash B$	L	K
	L	L	K
	K	L	L

Thus: (2) $H_T(A, B)$ is in K if and only if A is in L and B is in K.

Negations. For the special case of bisection implication relations "$\Rightarrow^T$," we have (1) $A, N_T(A) \Rightarrow^T B$ for all B in S, and (2) if $A, C \Rightarrow^T B$ for all B in S, then $C \Rightarrow^T N_T(A)$.

Suppose that A is in L. Since $A, N_T(A) \Rightarrow^T B$ for all B in S, let B be some member of K. Now, if $N_T(A)$ were in L, then B would be in L, since L is strongly closed under "$\Rightarrow^T$." Therefore, if A is in L, then $N_T(A)$ is in K.

Suppose that A is in K. Since every member of K implies ("$\Rightarrow^T$") every member of S, $A, C, \Rightarrow^T B$ for all B and C in S. Therefore $C \Rightarrow^T$ $N_T(A)$ for all C in S. Let C be in L. Consequently, $N_T(A)$ is in L. That is, if A is in L, so too is $N_T(A)$.

We can summarize these results as follows:

$N_T(A)$	A	$N_T(A)$
	L	K
	K	L

Thus: (3) $N_T(A)$ is in K if and only if A is in L.

Disjunction. The computation of the disjunction operator when it is relativized to bisection implications is a little more indirect than the computations for the other logical operators.

Suppose that A is in L. Since $A \Rightarrow^T D_T(A, B)$, and $B \Rightarrow^T D_T(A, B)$, and L is closed under "$\Rightarrow^T$," $D_T(A, B)$ is in L as well. Similarly, if B is in L, then $D_T(A, B)$ is in L. Therefore, if either A or B is in L, then $D_T(A, B)$ is in L.

There is only one remaining case: when both A and B are in K. Since A and B are in K, $A \Rightarrow^T C$ and $B \Rightarrow^T C$ for all C in S (since members of K imply, using "$\Rightarrow^T$," every member of S). Therefore $D_T(A, B) \Rightarrow^T C$ for all C in S. Let C be a member of K. Then $D_T(A, B)$ is in K (if it were in L, then C would have to be in L as well, since L is closed under "$\Rightarrow^T$"). Therefore, if A and B are in K, then so too is $D_T(A, B)$.

We can summarize the results for disjunction as follows:

$D_T(A, B)$:

$A\backslash B$	L	K
L	L	L
K	L	K

Thus: (4) $D_T(A, B)$ is in L if and only if A is in L or B is in L.

Thus, when the logical operators are relativized to a bisection implication, the result is that the logical operators yield the classical distribution patterns for L and K that one usually obtains for "truth" and "falsity" using the corresponding operators of the classical sentential or predicate calculus.

It is worth noting that this generalization of truth-value assignments uses certain sets (the K's and L's) instead of t's and f's (or 0's and 1's), according to which any bisection $T = \langle K, L \rangle$ on a structure assigns "L" ("K") to A if and only if A is in L (K).[2]

Exercise 19.1. Show that if S is a set of two elements $\{t, f\}$, and the implication relation is such that $t \Rightarrow f$ (but not conversely), and of course $t \Rightarrow t$ and $f \Rightarrow f$, then the logical operators on $I = \langle S, \Rightarrow \rangle$ are the classical truth functions.

19.2 Extensionality and the logical operators

We have seen that when the logical operators are relativized to a bisection implication there is a distributional pattern among the L's and K's associated with each operator that is strongly reminiscent of the familiar truth-table distribution for them. We want to study the general case in which an implication structure $I = \langle S, \Rightarrow \rangle$ is given, the logical operators are relativized to the relation "$\Rightarrow$" of that structure, and $T = \langle K, L \rangle$ is a strong bisection on the structure. The question is whether or not there are still distributional patterns among the L's and K's that can be associated with each of the operators on I. Do the same patterns prevail?

It is the strong bisections on an implication structure that are the generalizations of truth-value assignments, and we want to know under what conditions the patterns of conclusions (1)–(4) hold for the logical operators on a structure.

The short answer is this: The patterns of distribution among the L's and K's of a strong bisection are necessary and sufficient conditions for the *extensionality* of the various logical operators.[3] The notion of the extensionality of an operator on a structure has to be given a sufficiently general description if it is to be applicable to operators that act on implication structures generally.

Let us characterize the extensionality of an operator $O_\Rightarrow(A_1, \ldots, A_n)$ using strong bisections. If $I = \langle S, \Rightarrow \rangle$ is an implication structure, and $T = \langle K, L \rangle$ is any strong bisection on I (L is strongly closed under "$\Rightarrow$"), we shall say the following:

Definition 19.1 (extensionality)

(1) $O_\Rightarrow$ is *extensional with respect to T* if and only if whenever $A_1, \ldots, A_n$ and $A_1^*, \ldots, A_n^*$ are such that for each i, A_i and A_i^* both belong to the same member of T (K or L), then $O_\Rightarrow(A_1, \ldots, A_n)$ and $O_\Rightarrow(A_1^*, \ldots, A_n^*)$ belong to some one member of the bisection (K or L).

(2) $O_\Rightarrow$ is *weakly extensional over I* if and only if there is some strong bisection T of I such that $O_\Rightarrow$ is extensional with respect to T.

(3) $O_\Rightarrow$ is *extensional over I* if and only if $O_\Rightarrow$ is extensional with respect to every strong bisection T or I.

(4) $O_\Rightarrow$ is *extensional* if and only if $O_\Rightarrow$ is extensional over every implication structure I.

The connection between the extensionality of a logical operator and the distributional patterns of Definition 19.1(1)–(4) is direct. If we think of the operators of negation, disjunction, the hypothetical, and conjunction as relativized to the implication relation "$\Rightarrow$," then the following is provable:

Theorem 19.1. *Let* $I = \langle S, \Rightarrow \rangle$ *be an implication structure, and let* $T = \langle K, L \rangle$ *be any strong bisection on it. Then*

(1) The negation operator $N_\Rightarrow(A)$ *is extensional with respect to* T *if and only if* A *is in* L *if and only if* $N_\Rightarrow(A)$ *is in* K.

(2) The disjunction operator $D_\Rightarrow(A, B)$ *is extensional with respect to* T *if and only if* $D_\Rightarrow(A, B)$ *is in* L *if and only if* A *is in* L *or* B *is in* L.

(3) The hypothetical operator $H_\Rightarrow(A, B)$ *is extensional with respect to* T *if and only if* $H_\Rightarrow(A, B)$ *is in* K *if and only if* A *is in* L *and* B *is in* K.

(4) The conjunction operator $C_\Rightarrow(A, B)$ *is extensional with respect to* T *if and only if* $C_\Rightarrow(A, B)$ *is in* L *if and only if* A *is in* L *and* B *is in* L.

Proof. The proof is simple in each case. Here is the case for negation: If $N_\Rightarrow$ satisfies the distributional pattern of (1), then it is clearly extensional with respect to T. The converse: If A is in L, then $N_\Rightarrow(A)$ is in K. [Since $A, N_\Rightarrow(A) \Rightarrow$ (all) B, choose some B that is in K. If both A and $N_\Rightarrow(A)$ are in L, then B is in L, since L is strongly closed under "$\Rightarrow$." But that is impossible. Consequently, $N_\Rightarrow(A)$ is in K.] It remains only to prove that if A is in K, then $N_\Rightarrow(A)$ is in L. Suppose that for some A, both A and $N_\Rightarrow(A)$ are in K. Let B be any member of L. Consequently, $N_\Rightarrow(B)$ is in K. Since A and $N_\Rightarrow(B)$ are both in K, by extensionality, $N_\Rightarrow(A)$ and $N_\Rightarrow N_\Rightarrow(B)$ are both in the same member of the bisection T. That has to be K, since, by hypothesis, $N_\Rightarrow(A)$ is in K. However, $C \Rightarrow N_\Rightarrow N_\Rightarrow(C)$ for all C. Therefore $B \Rightarrow N_\Rightarrow N_\Rightarrow(B)$. Since the latter is in K, and L is closed under "$\Rightarrow$," B is in K. But that is impossible. Consequently, if A is in K, then $N_\Rightarrow(A)$ (for all A in S).

Exercise 19.2 Show that conditions (2)–(4) of Theorem 19.1 are necessary and sufficient conditions for the extensionality of the disjunction, hypothetical, and conjunction operators.

The patterns of L's and K's associated with the extensionality of each of the operators are familiar from the classical sentential calculus. In that special case, it is the distribution of t's and f's that is familiar. Given any truth-value assignment on the sentences of the classical sentential calculus, let L be all those sentences that are assigned "t," and let K be those assigned "*f*." It is clear that by using the rules for assignments, each pair $\langle K, L \rangle$ associated with a truth-value assignment is a strong bisection of the sentences of the calculus of the associated implication structure. In this sense the distribution of truth values on the classical sentential calculus is a particular case of strong bisections on an implication structure.

Extensionality gave way, we saw, to distributional patterns of the K's and L's of the strong bisections. But that does not answer the further question: Which, if any, of the logical operators are extensional?

Surprisingly enough, only the conjunction operator is extensional without any qualification. That is,

Theorem 19.2 (conjunction is extensional). *If I is any implication structure, then C is extensional over it.*

Proof. Let $T = \langle K, L \rangle$ be any strong bisection on I. Since A, B $\Rightarrow C(A, B)$ for any A and B in the structure, and L is strongly closed under "$\Rightarrow$," if A is in L and B is in L, then so too is $C(A, B)$. Moreover, since $C(A, B) \Rightarrow A$ (as well as B), it follows that if $C(A, B)$ is in L, then so too are A and B. Consequently, $C(A, B)$ is in L if and only if A is in L and B is in L, for any strong bisection.

The remaining logical operators on a structure are not unconditionally extensional with respect to the full class of strong bisections on that structure. However, this is not a defect in how the operators have been characterized, or the way extensionality has been relativized to strong bisections. Even for the classical sentential calculus it is known that the connectives "&," "¬," and "∨" do not satisfy the customary distributional patterns under all truth-value assignments. There are certain assignments (nonnormal truth-value interpretations) such that exactly all the tautologies have the same t value under them, the rules of inference are strongly t-preserving, and yet the disjunctions of sentences can be true when each disjunct is false, and the negations of false sentences can be false, despite the fact that the theorems are exactly those of the classical sentential calculus.[4]

Here, following Shoesmith and Smiley (1978, p. 3), is what the appropriate tables for a nonstandard assignment look like for negation and disjunction: There are four "values," t, f_1, f_2, f_3, with the f_i's thought of as kinds of f – so that any sentence that is assigned an f_i is then assigned "*f*."

¬:	p	$\neg p$		$\vee$:	$p\backslash q$	t	f_1	f_2	f_3
	t	f_3			t	t	t	t	t
	f_1	f_2			f_1	t	f_1	t	f_1
	f_2	f_1			f_2	t	t	f_2	f_2
	f_3	t			f_3	t	f_1	f_2	f_3

Thus, when p is assigned f_1 (and so f) and q is assigned f_2 (f), then "$p \vee q$" is assigned t. When p is assigned f_1 (and so f), then "$\neg p$" is assigned f_2 (and so f).

If these nonnormal assignments are excluded, then the operators for the classical sentential calculus all distribute in the usual way for the remaining (normal) assignments. This will be shown later. But before we do so we have to describe clearly the difference between the normal and the nonnormal assignments – or, in general, the difference between strong bisections that are normal and those that are not.

The particular example we just described, of a nonnormal assignment, can serve as an introduction to nonnormal bisections. The reason is that the tables given earlier describe exactly what happens in the following implication structure:

Let S be the set $\{p, q, r, s\}$, with an implication relation

$(K_3)p$

$(K_1)q$ $r(K_2)$

$(L)s$

This particular structure is classical – the law of double negation holds [$N(p)$ is s, $N(q)$ is r, $N(r)$ is q, and $N(s)$ is p]. Now let $T = \langle K, L \rangle$, where $K = \{p, q, r\}$, and $L = \{s\}$. L clearly is strongly closed under the implication relation. Moreover, let $K_1 = \{q\}$, $K_2 = \{r\}$, and $K_3 = \{p\}$. Then the negation operator on this structure distributes the K's and L as follows:

N:		
	L	K_3
	K_1	K_2
	K_2	K_1
	K_3	L

This is exactly the table we would get if we assigned the value $K_i (L)$ to an element of S if and only if it belonged to $K_i (L)$.

Other, similar computations show that the Church–Carnap–Bernstein nonnormal assignments for disjunction and the conditional are exactly what one obtains by using the particular structure given earlier, with the strong bisection as described. The fit is exact.[5]

We have just seen that even for the classical connectives, extensionality does not hold for negation, disjunction, and hypotheticals, as long as nonnormal assignments are permitted. In light of the foregoing example, we shall distinguish between normal and nonnormal (strong) bisections so that we can see how extensionality of the operators fares in a general setting, when the restriction to normal (strong) bisections is imposed.

> **Definition 19.5.** Let $I = \langle S, \Rightarrow \rangle$ be an implication structure, and let $T = \langle K, L \rangle$ be any bisection of I. We shall say that T is a *normal bisection* of I if and only if L is strongly closed under "$\Rightarrow$" (and so T is a strong bisection) and K is strongly closed under the dual implication relation "$\Rightarrow$^."

If T is a normal bisection, then if both A and B are in K, so too is $(A \lor B)$, since $A, B \Rightarrow^\wedge D(A, B)$, and K is strongly closed under "$\Rightarrow$^." Moreover, if T is a strong bisection that is not normal, then there are A, B such that A and B are in K, but $(A \lor B)$ is in L. The reason is that since the bisection is not normal, K is not strongly closed under "$\Rightarrow$^." Therefore, there are A and B and C such that A and B are in K, $A, B \Rightarrow^\wedge C$, but C is not in K. Consequently, $(A \lor B)$ is in L, since $C \Rightarrow (A \lor B)$ and C is in L.

Thus, there are "false" A and B, for which $(A \lor B)$ is "true." Consequently, for disjunction (as well as negation and hypotheticals), the Church–Carnap–Bernstein nonnormal interpretations are just those we obtain by using nonnormal bisections. These observations indicate why the notion of a nonnormal bisection is the appropriate generalization of the Carnap–Bernstein concept of a nonnormal interpretation.

> **Exercise 19.3.** Let I_{CSC} be the implication structure consisting of the set of sentences of the classical sentential calculus (CSC), with a deducibility relation on it. Let L be the set of all theorems of CSC, and K the rest. Then $T = \langle K, L \rangle$ is a strong bisection, but fails to be normal. [Show that for any atomic sentence p, both p and $\neg p$ are false (in K), though $(p \lor \neg p)$ is true (in L).] Show that some sentence and its negation are both false under this truth-value assignment.

We set out to answer the question of which of the logical operators was extensional, and we noted that extensionality with respect to a (strong) bisection $T = \langle K, L \rangle$ was, in the case of each of the logical operators, equivalent to a characteristic distribution pattern of K and L. Conjunction always qualified as extensional, but even the classical operators of negation, disjunction, and the hypothetical failed to be extensional when the bisection in question was taken to be nonnormal.

All is restored, however, once the restriction to normal bisections is imposed. *We wish to show that in structures in which negation is classical, all the logical operators are extensional with respect to all normal bisections.* In order to see this, we need to notice some simple ways in which the extensionality of negation, disjunction, and the hypothetical are related.

First, we note that for any bisection T, normal or not, the following relations hold:

Theorem 19.3. *Let $I = \langle S, \Rightarrow \rangle$ be an implication structure, and let $T = \langle K, L \rangle$ be any strong bisection of S. Then*

(1) Negation N is extensional with respect to T if and only if the hypothetical H is extensional with respect to T.

(2) If negation N is extensional with respect to T, then so too is disjunction D.

(3) If the hypothetical H is extensional with respect to T, then so too is D [this follows from (1) and (2)].

Let "$N(\text{ext}, T)$" hold if and only if N is extensional with respect to the bisection T (suppressing the reference to the implication relation under consideration), and similarly for "$H(\text{ext}, T)$" and "$D(\text{ext}, T)$." Thus, the following diagram holds for any strong bisection, normal or otherwise:

Proof. In order to prove (2), suppose that N is extensional with respect to T. If $D(A, B)$ is in K, then A (and B) is in K, since A (as well as B) implies $D(A, B)$. Thus, it remains only to show that if A and B are in K, then $D(A, B)$ is also in K. Suppose that A and B are in K. Since $A \Rightarrow NN(A)$ and $B \Rightarrow NN(B)$, it follows that $D(A, B) \Rightarrow D(NN(A), NN(B))$ [that is, $A \vee B$

$\Rightarrow NN(A) \vee NN(B)]$. However, by Theorem 16.13, $NN(A) \vee NN(B) \Rightarrow N(C(N(A), N(B)))$, so that $D(A, B) \Rightarrow N(N(A)$ & $N(B))$. Since A and B are in K, and N is assumed to be extensional with respect to T, it follows that $N(A)$ and $N(B)$ are both in L, and therefore so is their conjunction. Consequently, the negation of their conjunction, $N(C(N(A), N(B)))$, is in K. But $N(C(N(A), N(B)))$ is implied by the disjunction $D(A, B)$. Therefore $D(A, B)$ is in K if A and B are in K. Consequently, $D(A, B)$ is in K if and only if A and B are in K.

In order to prove (1), suppose that N is extensional with respect to T. Then $H(A, B)$ is in K if and only if A is in L and B is in K. Suppose that $H(A, B)$ is in K. Since $D(N(A), B) \Rightarrow H(A, B)$ [that is $N(A) \vee B \Rightarrow (A \to B)]$, $D(N(A), B)$ is in K. By (2), D is extensional, since N is extensional. Therefore $N(A)$ is in K, and B is in K. Since N is extensional, it follows that A is in L. Thus, if $H(A, B)$ is in K, then A is in L and B is in K. The converse is generally true: If A is in L and B is in K, then $H(A, B)$ is in K, for if $H(A, B)$ is in L, then, since $A, H(A, B) \Rightarrow B$, B is in L. But that is impossible. So $H(A, B)$ is in K if A is in L and B is in K. Consequently, H is extensional with respect to T if N is extensional with respect to T.

Conversely, if H is extensional with respect to T, then N is extensional with respect to T. Note first that if A is in L, then $N(A)$ is in K, for $A, N(A) \Rightarrow C$ for all C in the structure. If both A and $N(A)$ were in L, then C would be in L for all C. Thus, K would be empty, and that is impossible. Second, if $N(A)$ is in K, then A is in L: Assume that H is extensional with respect to T [that is, $H(A, B)$ is in K if and only if A is in L and B is in K]. In particular, $H(A, N(A))$ is in K if and only if A is in L and $N(A)$ is in K. So if $H(A, N(A))$ is in K, then A is in L. However, $N(A) \Leftrightarrow H(A, N(A))$. Therefore, if $N(A)$ is in K, then A is in L. Thus, $N(A)$ is in K if and only if A is in L.

In general, the extensionality of the operators runs according to the arrows in the diagram accompanying Theorem 19.3. Thus, it is not generally true that if disjunction is extensional with respect to a strong bisection T, then so too is negation.

Exercise 19.4. Let S be the set $\{p, q, r\}$, and let "$\Rightarrow$" be such that p implies q, and q implies r (of course, every member implies itself). Let T be a strong bisection $\{K, L\}$, where $K =$

$\{p, q\}$ and $L = \{r\}$. Show that D is extensional with respect to T, but N is not.

We have described the difference between normal and nonnormal bisections of an implication structure, and we have also described the situation in which an operator is extensional with respect to a bisection. In general, however, nonnormal bisections make trouble for extensionality: If a bisection is nonnormal, then negation is not extensional with respect to it. Neither is the hypothetical, nor disjunction. However, according to the following theorems, extensionality prevails if the bisections are normal and negation is classical.

Theorem 19.4. *Let* $I = \langle S, \Rightarrow \rangle$ *be an implication structure in which disjunctions exist. If* N *is extensional with respect to any strong bisection* T, *then* T *is normal.*

Proof. Suppose that N is extensional for some strong bisection $T = \langle K, L \rangle$, but that T is not normal. Since K is not strongly closed under "$\Rightarrow^{\wedge}$," there are some $A_1, \ldots, A_n$ and B such that the A_i's are in K, but B is in L. Assuming that the disjunction of the A_i's exists, it follows that $B \Rightarrow D(A_1, A_2, \ldots, A_n)$. By Theorem 19.3(2), since N is extensional with respect to T, so too is disjunction. That is, $D(A_1, \ldots, A_n)$ is in L if and only if some A_i is in L. But no A_i is in L. Consequently, $D(A_1, \ldots, A_n)$ is in K. Now B is in L. Moreover, $B \Rightarrow D(A_1, \ldots, A_n)$, so that $D(A_1, \ldots, A_n)$ is in L. But that is impossible.

Thus, we know that nonnormal bisections have to make trouble for the extensionality of negation [and therefore for the hypothetical as well, given Theorem 19.3(1)]. The next theorem tells us that nonnormal bisections also make trouble for the extensionality of the disjunction operator.

Theorem 19.5. D *is extensional with respect to any strong bisection* T *on a structure if and only if* T *is normal.*

Proof. First notice that if T is normal, then D is extensional with respect to it, for if either A or B is in L, then, since $A \Rightarrow D(A, B)$ [and $B \Rightarrow D(A, B)$], and L is closed under "$\Rightarrow$," $D(A, B)$ is in L. Conversely, suppose that $D(A, B)$ is in L, but both A and B are in K. Now $A, B \Rightarrow^{\wedge} D(A, B)$. Since T is normal, K is strongly closed under "$\Rightarrow$ˆ." Therefore $D(A, B)$ is in K. Conversely, suppose that D is extensional with respect to a strong bisection T. Then T is normal. For suppose that $A_1, \ldots, A_n$ are in K and that $A_1, \ldots, A_n \Rightarrow$ˆ B. By the extensionality of D, their disjunction $D(A_1, \ldots, A_n)$ is in K as well. Since $B \Rightarrow D(A_1, \ldots, A_n)$, B is in K.

We have seen that nonnormal bisections make trouble for the extensionality of negation (and so hypotheticals) and disjunction. Restriction to normal bisections restores extensionality for disjunction, but *not* for negation: There are normal bisections with respect to which N fails to be extensional. In such cases, as we shall see, N cannot be classical negation. Thus, normality alone does not guarantee the extensionality of negation.

Exercise 19.5. Verify that the bisection of the structure in Exercise 19.4 is normal (D is extensional with respect to it), but N is not [q and $N(q)$ both belong to K].

Trouble arose for extensionality in what one thinks of as the home case. Classical negation is not extensional on nonnormal bisections. By Theorem 19.4, no negation operator, classical or not, is extensional on nonnormal bisections. The situation for classical negation is restored if we restrict bisections to the normal ones. That is, if N is a classical negation operator, then N is extensional with respect to all normal bisections:

Theorem 19.6. *If N is a classical negation on an implication structure I (in which disjunctions exist), and T is any normal bisection of I, then N is extensional with respect to T.*

Proof. Suppose that N is classical, T is normal, and N fails to be extensional with respect to T. Since L is strongly closed under "$\Rightarrow$," if A is in L, then $N(A)$ is in K. Therefore, by the nonextensionality of N, there is some A such that $N(A)$ is in K but A is not in L (i.e., A is also in K). Since N is assumed to be classical, $B \Rightarrow D(A, N(A))$ for all B in S, or, equivalently, $A, N(A) \Rightarrow$ˆ B for all B in S. Now A and $N(A)$ both belong to K. Since T is normal, K is strongly closed under "$\Rightarrow$ˆ." Therefore B is in K for all B in S. Consequently, L is empty. But that is impossible.

This theorem also shows how to restore the parity among the negation, hypothetical, and disjunction operators with respect to extensionality. Recall that for N, H, and D, and any strong bisection T, N is extensional with respect to T if and only if H is extensional with respect to T. However, if N is extensional with respect to T, then so too is D, but not conversely (similarly for H and D). However, if we have a structure with classical negation, then any of the operators N, H, and D is extensional with respect to a strong bisection if and only if any of the others is extensional with respect to it. That is, *if N is classical*, then

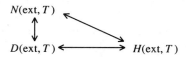

To see this, one need only show that if D is extensional with respect to T, then so is N. Suppose, then, that D is extensional with respect to T. By Theorem 19.5, T is normal. Therefore, since N is classical and T is normal, by Theorem 19.6, N is extensional with respect to T.

Thus, in the classical situation, all of the operators N, H, and D are extensional *if any one of them is*. But that does not settle whether or not any of them is extensional. However, since disjunctions are extensional with respect to a strong bisection T if and only if T is normal, we have the following:

Theorem 19.7. *In any implication structure for which negation is classical (and disjunctions exist), all the operators are extensional with respect to any normal bisection on the structure.*

There are two simple results that hold in the special case in which the negation operator is classical. They serve to identify those strong bisections on the structure that are normal. In effect, they tell us that the L's of strong bisections on classical structures are precisely the (proper) maximal subsets of the structure that are closed under the implication relation of the structure.

Definition 19.6. Let $I = \langle S, \Rightarrow \rangle$ be an implication structure, and let $T = \langle K, L \rangle$ be any strong bisection on I. Let us say that a subset L of S is *maximal* if and only if it is a proper subset of S that is closed under "$\Rightarrow$," and if L^* is any other proper subset of S that is closed under "$\Rightarrow$," and $L \subseteq L^*$, then $L = L^*$.

Then we have the following two theorems:

Theorem 19.8. *Let I be an implication structure for which negations, conjunctions, and disjunctions exist, and negation is classical, and let T = ⟨K, L⟩ be any strong bisection on I. If L is maximal, then T is normal.*

Proof. Assume that T is not normal. T is normal if and only if $D(A, B)$ is in K for any A and B in K. Suppose that A and B are in K, but $D(A, B)$ is not. Since L is assumed to be maximal, A is in K if and only if $N(A)$ is in L. [If $N(A)$ is in L, then A cannot be in L, because $A, N(A) \Rightarrow B$ for all B in S. Since L is strongly closed under "$\Rightarrow$," every element of B will be in L, and L will fail to be a proper subset of S. Conversely, suppose that A is in K, and $N(A)$ is not in L. Let L^* be the set of all C's that are implied by any finite number of elements of the set $L \cup \{N(A)\}$. L^* is strongly closed under "$\Rightarrow$." Moreover, L^* is a proper subset of S. For suppose that it is not. Then for some B, we have $A_1, \ldots, A_n, N(A) \Rightarrow B$, where the A_i's all belong to L. Similarly, $A_1', \ldots, A_m', N(A) \Rightarrow N(B)$. Therefore $A_1, \ldots, A_n, A_1', \ldots, A_m', N(A)$ implies B as well as $N(B)$. Consequently, all the A_i and A_i' together with $N(A)$ imply all the members of S. Therefore, all the A_i and A_i' together imply $NN(A)$. Since the negation operator is assumed to be classical, A is implied by all the A_i and A_i', all of which are in L. Since L is strongly closed under "$\Rightarrow$," A is in L. But that is impossible. Therefore L^* is a proper subset of S. Now, by construction, $L \subseteq L^*$. Since L is assumed to be maximal, $L = L^*$. But $N(A)$ is in L^* and, by hypothesis, not in L. That is impossible. Therefore, if A is in K, then $N(A)$ is in L.]

Continuing the main line of the proof, we have assumed that A and B are in K, but that $D(A, B)$ is not. Therefore $D(A, B)$ is in L. Since neither A nor B is in L, both $N(A)$ and $N(B)$ are in L, and so is their conjunction. Moreover, since N is classical, $N(A) \& N(B) \Rightarrow ND(A, B)$. Therefore $D(A, B)$ is in K, since $ND(A, B)$ is in L. But that is impossible. T is therefore normal.

Conversely, we have the following:

Theorem 19.9. *Let I be an implication structure for which negations, conjunctions, and disjunctions exist, and negation is classical, and let T = ⟨K, L⟩ be any strong bisection on I. If T is normal, then L is maximal.*

Proof. Suppose that $T = \langle K, L \rangle$ is normal. Since negation is classical, N is extensional with respect to T. Consequently, A is in K if and only if $N(A)$ is in L. Now, since T is a bisection, L is a proper subset of S (since K is nonempty). L is also strongly closed under "$\Rightarrow$" since T is normal. Suppose that L^* is a proper subset of S that is closed under "$\Rightarrow$" and that $L \subseteq L^*$. If there were some C in L^*, but not in L, then $N(C)$ would be in L (for N is extensional with respect to T) and therefore in L^*. Thus, C as well as $N(C)$, is in L^*. But that is impossible, since L^* is a proper subset of S that is strongly closed under "$\Rightarrow$." Therefore $L = L^*$.

Thus, combining the two preceding theorems, we know that if I is a structure that has negations, conjunctions, and disjunctions, and negation is classical, then for any strongly closed bisection $T = \langle K, L \rangle$, T is normal if and only if L is maximal.

There are several additional connections that are of some interest. The first concerns a connection between classical negation and extensionality: If the negation operator N is not classical on an implication structure I, then there is some strong bisection T of I such that N is not extensional with respect to T. Otherwise stated, we have the following:

Theorem 19.10. *If N is extensional with respect to all strong bisections T on the structure $I = \langle S, \Rightarrow \rangle$, then N is classical on I.*

Proof. Suppose that negation is extensional with respect to all strong bisections $T = \langle K, L \rangle$ on I and that N is not classical on I. Consequently, $NN(A) \not\Rightarrow A$ for some A in S. By the theorem of strong completeness (Theorem 8.11), there is some strong bisection $T^* = \langle K^*, L^* \rangle$ such that $NN(A) \not\Rightarrow^{T^*} A$. Consequently, $NN(A)$ is in L^*, and A is in K^*. N is extensional with respect to all strong bisections on I, and T^* in particular. Therefore A is in L^* if and only if $N(A)$ is in K^*, and $N(A)$ is in L^* if and only if $NN(A)$ is in K^*. Consequently, $N(A)$ is in K^* if and only if $NN(A)$ is in L^*. But $NN(A)$ is in L^*. Therefore $N(A)$ is in K^*. Consequently, A is in L^*. That, however, is impossible, since A is in K^*. Therefore $NN(A) \Rightarrow A$ for all A in S.

A second result also throws some light on the relation between classical negation and extensionality. We know that negation is not classical on all implication structures. Suppose that $I = \langle S, \Rightarrow \rangle$ is a structure on which N is nonclassical. Can we find another implication relation "$\Rightarrow$*" over the same set S such that although N (negation with respect to "$\Rightarrow$") is not classical, nevertheless N^* (negation with respect to "$\Rightarrow$*") is classical. A positive answer is given by the following:

Theorem 19.11. *Let $I = \langle S, \Rightarrow \rangle$ be an implication structure, and suppose that N is extensional with respect to at least one strong bisection T of I (N is weakly extensional over I). Then there is an implication relation "$\Rightarrow$*" such that*

(1) "$\Rightarrow$" is an extension of "$\Rightarrow$,"*
(2) N^* (negation relative to "$\Rightarrow$") is classical,*
(3) N^* is weaker than N (in I^*). That is, $N(A) \Rightarrow^* N^*(A)$ for all A in S.

Proof. Define $A_1, \ldots, A_n \Rightarrow^* B$ as holding if and only if $A_1, \ldots, A_n \Rightarrow^T B$ for all strong bisections T such that N is extensional with respect to T. By hypothesis, there is at least one. It is easy to verify that "$\Rightarrow$*" is an implication relation. Moreover, if $A_1, \ldots, A_n \Rightarrow B$, then $A_1, \ldots, A_n \Rightarrow^T B$ holds for all strong bisections T and so for all bisections T for which N is extensional. Therefore $A_1, \ldots, A_n \Rightarrow^* B$. Thus, (1) holds. Furthermore, $N(A) \Rightarrow^* N^*(A)$ for all A in S: Since "$\Rightarrow$*" extends "$\Rightarrow$," we have $A, N(A) \Rightarrow^* B$ for all B in S. Since $N^*(A)$ is the weakest element in S to satisfy this condition, $N(A) \Rightarrow^* N^*(A)$ for all A in S. Thus, (3) holds. Lastly, N^* is a classical negation operator with respect to "$\Rightarrow$*." For suppose it is not. Then, for some $T^* = \langle K^*, L^* \rangle$, $N^*N^*(A) \not\Rightarrow^{T^*} A$ for some A, where T^* is a strong bisection and N is extensional with respect to T^*. Therefore $N^*N^*(A)$ is in L^* and A is in K^*. Now N is extensional with respect to T^* (by the construction of "$\Rightarrow$*"). However, N^* is also extensional with respect to T^*. [Since L^* is strongly closed under "$\Rightarrow$*," $N^*(A)$ is in K^* if A is in L^*. So suppose that A is in K^*, and $N^*(A)$ is also in K^* for some A in S. Since $N(A) \Rightarrow^* N^*(A)$ and $N^*(A)$ is in K^*, it follows that $N(A)$ is in K^*. Thus, A and $N(A)$ are in K^*. But that is impossible, since N is extensional with respect to T^*.] Since N^* is extensional with respect to T^*, and $N^*N^*(A)$ is in L^*, we have that $N^*(A)$ is in K^*, and consequently A is in L^*. But that is impossible, since A is also in K^*. Therefore, $N^*N^*(A) \Rightarrow^* A$ for all A in S. Thus, (2) holds.

The preceding theorem leaves open an important question. If a structure $I = \langle S, \Rightarrow \rangle$ is nonclassical, then we can extend its implication structure "$\Rightarrow$" to "$\Rightarrow$*," one for which the negation operator N^* will be classical – provided that there is at least one strong bisection on I for which N is extensional. However, it is an open question whether on any nonclassical structure there is such a bisection.

Although the strong bisections are generalized truth-value assignments, these bisections can be of such various kinds that to say that negation or disjunction, for example, is extensional with respect to a strong bisection T can express very different things. Thus, the condition that N is extensional on a specific structure I is a bundle of conditions, one for each strong bisection of that structure. For some strong bisections of I the condition may be interesting; for other strong bisections it may be dull.

For example, suppose that $I = \langle S, \Rightarrow \rangle$ is an implication structure, and $T_0 = \langle K_0, L_0 \rangle$ is a bisection of I such that L_0 is the set of all theses of I (assuming that there are some), and $K_0 = S - L_0$. Assume also that I is nontrivial – so there are at least two members of S that are not equivalent. T_0 is clearly a strong bisection of T, since L_0 is strongly closed under "$\Rightarrow$." The condition that negation N is extensional with respect to the bisection T_0 is equivalent to a familiar condition in metalogic:

Theorem 19.12. *Let I be any implication relation, and let T_0 satisfy the conditions just described. Then N is extensional with respect to T_0 if and only if I is complete with respect to negation. [For every A, either A is a thesis or $N(A)$ is one.]*

Proof. Suppose that $N(\text{ext}, T_0)$. Then for any A in S, A is in L_0 if and only if $N(A)$ is in K_0. Therefore, if $N(A)$ is in K_0, then A is in L_0. Consequently, either $N(A)$ is in L_0 or A is in L_0. That is, either A is a thesis of L_0 or $N(A)$ is a thesis of L_0. The converse is obtained by noting that if A is in L_0, then $N(A)$ is in K_0 (since L_0 is strongly closed under "$\Rightarrow$"). So one only need show that if $N(A)$ is in K_0, then A is in L_0. But that follows from the assumption that for any A, either A is in L_0 or $N(A)$ is in L_0.

When we consider what extensionality of the other operators comes to with respect to certain bisections, we find that familiar distinctions and results emerge. There is a recharting of well-known territory that follows from the use of notions like extensionality in a general setting, where the set S of the structure not only is bisected into the truths and falsehoods (for this is possible in just some of the cases that are possible) but also is arbitrarily bisected in any way, so long as the set L of the bisection is strongly closed under the implication relation of the structure. Here is another simple example of some interest:

Using the bisection T_0 described earlier, we can ask whether or not the disjunction operator D on the structure is extensional with respect to T_0.

Definition 19.7. Let us say that an implication structure $I = \langle S, \Rightarrow \rangle$ has the *disjunctive property* if and only if the disjunction of any two members is a thesis of I if and only if at least one of them is a thesis of I.

Theorem 19.13. *Under the conditions stated above for T_0 the disjunction operator D on an implication structure I is extensional with respect to T_0 if and only if I has the disjunctive property.*

Proof. If either A is a thesis or B is a thesis, then so too is their disjunction, since each of A, B implies their disjunction. Suppose that D is extensional with respect to T_0. Therefore, for any A and B in S, $D(A, B)$ is in L_0 if and only if either A is in L_0 or B is in L_0. But L_0 is the set of all theses of I. Therefore I has the disjunctive property. Conversely, if I has the disjunctive property, then if $D(A, B)$ is a thesis of I, so too is A or B. Thus, if $D(A, B)$ is in L_0, then at least one of A, B is in L_0.

Exercise 19.6. Any implication structure I has the disjunctive property if and only if the strong bisection $T_0 = \langle K_0, L_0 \rangle$, with L_0 as the set of theses of I, is normal.

We know that for any implication structure, the conjunction operator is extensional with respect to all strong bisections on the structure. There does not seem to be a general answer for the other operators. We do not know, for example, whether or not negation operator on an arbitrary structure is extensional with respect to some strong bisection.

We do know, however, that if N is not classical on an implication structure, then there will be some strong bisection of that structure with respect to which N is not extensional (Theorem 19.10). And in the case in which N is a classical operator on a structure, then under certain conditions there will exist nonnormal strong bisections of the structure. That is,

Theorem 19.14. *If N is classical on an implication structure I, and I is incomplete with respect to negation, then there is a strong bisection T of I such that N is not extensional with respect to it.*

Proof. Let $T = \langle K, L \rangle$, where L is the set of all theses of I. L is nonempty (we assume that I has some theses), and K has at least one member, since I is incomplete with respect to negation (since there is some A such that neither it nor its negation is a thesis). L is strongly closed under "$\Rightarrow$," so T is a strong bisection. Since N is classical on I, A, $N(A) \Rightarrow^\wedge B$ for all B. Since neither A nor $N(A)$ is a thesis of I, both belong to K. If T were normal, K would be closed under "$\Rightarrow$," and then every B would belong to K. But that is impossible. Therefore T is nonnormal. It follows as well that N is not extensional with respect to T, for if T is nonnormal, then D is not extensional with respect to it (by Theorem 19.5). However, by Theorem 19.3(2), if N is extensional with respect to a bisection, so is D. Therefore N is not extensional with respect to T. Another simple result of the same type is this:

Theorem 19.15. *If N is classical on an implication structure I, and I fails to have the disjunctive property, then there is a strong bisection T on I that is nonnormal.*

Proof. As in the preceding theorem, let L_0 be the set of all theses of I, and let K_0 be $S - L_0$. K_0 is nonempty because I fails to have the disjunctive property, so that there are A and B such that $D(A, B)$ is a thesis, but neither A nor B is a thesis. Therefore K_0 and L_0 are nonempty. T_0 is a strong bisection of I. Moreover, since A and B are in K_0 but their disjunction $D(A, B)$ is in L_0, D is not extensional with respect to T_0, so that T_0 is nonnormal.

Thus, we have, in a general setting, the counterpart of the Church–Carnap–Bernstein result for the classical sentential calculus that is incomplete with respect to negation and fails to have the disjunctive property, for the strong bisection T_0 is nonnormal, and therefore a classical N cannot be extensional with respect to it (and, of course, the disjunction and the hypothetical also fail to be extensional with respect to T_0).

We can also see that for certain implication structures with nonclassical negation, there will be normal bisections with respect to which the negation operator is nonextensional. That is,

Theorem 19.16. *Let I be any implication structure on which N is nonclassical, I has the disjunctive property and is incomplete with respect to negation. Then there exists a normal bisection T or I such that N is not extensional with respect to T.*

Proof. Let L_0 be the set of all theses of I (we assume that there are some), so that it is nonempty. K_0 is the remainder of S. Since I is incomplete with respect to negation, there is some A such that neither it nor its negation is a thesis. So K_0 is nonempty. Since L_0 is strongly closed under "$\Rightarrow$," it follows that $T_0 = \langle K_0, L_0 \rangle$ is a strong bisection. Moreover, since I has the disjunctive property, D is extensional with respect to T_0. Therefore, by Theorem 19.5, T_0 is normal. It remains only to show that the negation operator N on I is not extensional with respect to the normal bisection T_0. Suppose that N is extensional with respect to T_0. Then A is in L_0 if and only if $N(A)$ is in K_0. Therefore, if $N(A)$ is in K_0, then A is in L_0. Consequently, $N(A)$ is in L_0 or A is in L_0. Thus, either A is a thesis or $N(A)$ is a thesis. But that is impossible.

It follows immediately that under the conditions of the preceding theorem, there is a normal bisection with respect to which the hypothetical fails to be extensional.

Exercise 19.7. Given a nonclassical implication structure that satisfies the conditions of the preceding theorem, provide a direct proof of the nonextensionality of the hypothetical with respect to some normal bisection T (without using the nonextensionality of negation with respect to T).

Using the normal bisection T_0 of the preceding theorem, another proof can be given to show that the extensionality of disjunction does not imply the extensionality of negation, for it does not do so on those implication structures that are incomplete with respect to negation and have the disjunctive property. That there are such implication structures can be seen from the following observations.

The preceding theorem also sheds some light on the question of the extensionality of the operators used in intuitionistic logic.

Recall from Chapter 7 that for any logical system $V = \langle S, \vdash_V \rangle$ consisting of a set of sentences and a deducibility relation "$\vdash_V$ on it (defined syntactically or semantically), there is an associated implication structure $I_V = \langle S, \Rightarrow^V \rangle$ consisting of the set of sentences of V and an implication relation defined by $A_1, \ldots, A_n \Rightarrow^V B$ if and only if $A_1, \ldots, A_n \vdash_V B$ for all sentences in S. If the system is sufficiently rich, as most known ones are, the implication relation can also be defined as holding if and only if $\vdash_V (A_1 \& \ldots \& A_n) \to B$, where it is assumed that there are some connectives in V that are equivalent to conjunction and the material conditional. It follows from Theorem 19.16 and the comment following it that for the intuitionistic sentential calculus (ISC), in particular, the negation and the hypothetical are nonextensional, and conjunction and disjunction are extensional. More precisely, let the logical operators $N_\neg$, $H_\to$, $C_\&$, and $D_\lor$ be those associated with the connectives "$\neg$," "$\to$," "$\&$," and "$\lor$" of ISC, and take them to act on the implication structure I_{ISC} associated with ISC as follows: $N_\neg$ is the operator on I_{ISC} that maps each sentence A of S to "$\neg A$," $H_\to$ maps each pair $\langle A, B \rangle$ of sentences of S to "$A \to B$," $C_\&$ maps every pair $\langle A, B \rangle$ to "$A \& B$," and $D_\lor$ maps $\langle A, B \rangle$ to "$A \lor B$." It is straightforward to confirm that these operators associated with the connectives of the ISC are, respectively, just the negation, hypothetical, conjunction, and disjunction operators on the structure I_{ISC} associated with the system ISC.

We can gather the necessary results together: Roughly, they say that the operators that correspond to the connectives for negation, the conditional, conjunction, and disjunction of the ISC are just the negation, hypothetical, conjunction, and disjunction operators on the implication structure that corresponds to or is associated with that calculus.

Theorem 19.17. *Let $I_{ISC} = \langle S, \Rightarrow^{ISC} \rangle$ be the implication structure associated with the ISC, and let $N_\neg$, $H_\to$, $C_\&$, and $D_\lor$ be the operators on I_{ISC} that are associated with the connectives "$\neg$," "$\to$," "$\&$," and "$\lor$," respectively, of ISC. Let N, H, C, and D be the negation, hypothetical, conjunction, and disjunction operators, respectively, on I_{ISC}. Then, for all sentences A, B of ISC,*

(a) $N(A) \Leftrightarrow^{ISC} N_\neg(A)$,
(b) $H(A, B) \Leftrightarrow^{ISC} H_\to(A, B)$,
(c) $C(A, B) \Leftrightarrow^{ISC} C_\&(A, B)$, and
(d) $D(A, B) \Leftrightarrow^{ISC} D_\lor(A, B)$.

Proof. We shall prove (a) and (c) and leave the remaining two cases as an exercise. The elementary theorems of ISC that are used in the following proofs can be found in the work of Kleene (1952), Heyting (1956), or Dummett (1977).

(a) It must be shown that $N(A) \Leftrightarrow^{ISC} N_\neg(A)$ for all A in S – that is, $N(A) \Leftrightarrow^{ISC} \neg A$ for all A in S. Since $N(A), A \Rightarrow^{ISC} \neg A$, $\vdash_{ISC}(N(A) \& A) \rightarrow \neg A$. Therefore, $\vdash_{ISC} N(A) \rightarrow (A \rightarrow \neg A)$. But $\vdash_{ISC}(A \rightarrow \neg A) \rightarrow \neg A$, so that $\vdash_{ISC} N(A) \rightarrow \neg A$. Consequently, $N(A) \Rightarrow^{ISC} \neg A$. Conversely, $\vdash_{ISC}(A \& \neg A) \rightarrow B$ for all B in S. Therefore $A, \neg A \Rightarrow^{ISC} B$ for all B in S. By definition of the negation operator, $\neg A \Rightarrow^{ISC} N(A)$. Therefore $N(A) \Leftrightarrow^{ISC} \neg A$, and so $N(A) \Leftrightarrow^{ISC} N_\neg(A)$.

(c) It must be shown that $C(A, B) \Leftrightarrow^{ISC} A \& B$. Since $C(A, B) \Rightarrow^{ISC} A$ (as well as B), it follows that $\vdash_{ISC} C(A, B) \rightarrow A$ and $\vdash_{ISC} C(A, B) \rightarrow B$. Therefore $\vdash_{ISC} C(A, B) \rightarrow A \& B$. Consequently, $C(A, B) \Rightarrow^{ISC} A \& B$. Conversely, because $\vdash_{ISC}(A \& B) \rightarrow A$ and $\vdash_{ISC}(A \& B) \rightarrow B$, it follows that $A \& B \Rightarrow^{ISC} A$, as well as B. Therefore, by our definition of conjunction, $A \& B \Rightarrow^{ISC} C(A, B)$. Consequently, $C_\&(A, B) \Leftrightarrow^{ISC} C(A, B)$.

Because the ISC is incomplete with respect to negation and has the disjunctive property, it follows that the implication structure I_{ISC} is also incomplete with respect to negation and has the disjunctive property. ISC is a structure that satisfies the conditions of Theorem 19.16. Consequently, both the negation and the hypothetical operator fail to be extensional on it. Conjunction, as we have noted, is extensional on all structures, and therefore on ISC in particular. Disjunction is extensional on all normal bisections (Theorem 19.5), and, by Exercise 19.6, ISC has normal bisections on it.

We have framed our account of extensionality in terms of how the operators on structures behave with respect to the strong bisections. We have noted that the conjunction operator is extensional with respect to all strong bisections. However, the strong bisections that are not normal create a certain amount of mischief, as noted by Carnap, Bernstein, and Church: Even for classical structures, the disjunction, negation, and hypothetical operators will fail to be extensional with respect to some nonnormal bisections, despite the fact that those bisections are strong. One could put an end to the mischief by narrowing the relevant bisections to only those that are normal. There is a nice symmetry to the normal bisections. L is strongly closed under the implication relation, and K is strongly closed under its dual. Moreover, the narrowing of scope is effective. As we have seen, if negation is classical, then all the operators will be extensional with respect to all normal bisections (Theorem 19.6 and the remarks following it).

On balance, it seems best to define extensionality as we have, using the entire class of strong bisections. In that case, conjunction is always extensional, and negation (even classical negation), the hypothetical, and disjunction fail to be extensional with respect to some strong bisections. Moving downward to the normal bisections, both conjunction and disjunction are extensional with respect all of those. If negation is classical, then it, as well as the hypothetical, will be extensional. But if negation is nonclassical, and the structure is incomplete with respect to negation and has the disjunctive property, as is the case for ISC, there will be some normal bisections with respect to which negation and the hypothetical will fail to be extensional.

20

Quantification

Quantification, universal or existential, concerns operators that act on implication structures. More precisely, they act on the predicates of what we shall call *extended implication structures*, as well as the members of what we have called implication structures. In order to see how these operators can be characterized as logical operators, we need first to introduce a somewhat more complex kind of implication structure than the kind we have employed thus far.

20.1 Extended implication structures

The extended implication structures are like the implication structures considered thus far, with two additions: (1) a set E of "objects," or "entities" (possibly empty), and (2) a set Pr (possibly empty) of special kinds of functions that we shall call "predicates." We shall indicate an extended implication structure by $I = \langle E, Pr, S, \Rightarrow \rangle$, where S is a nonempty set and "$\Rightarrow$" is an implication relation on S.

We think of a predicate P of the extended structure as a function that maps the infinite sequences of the set E to the set S. Thus, we shall let E^* be the set of all sequences $(s_1, s_2, \ldots)$, where the s_i belong to E, and a predicate P of the extended structure is a mapping of E^* to S.[1]

The idea of a predicate as a function on infinite sequences of objects may seem a bit strange, despite its central use in such classic studies as A. Tarski's work on truth and A. Mostowski's study of quantifiers. In part the oddity stems from the widespread use in standard logical systems of the idea that predicates come with different degrees, indicating places. There are one-place, two-place, and n-place predicates for each natural number n, and the notation used indicates the place (usually by a superscript) of the predicate. It is difficult to say whether this practice was inspired by the "observation" that a natural language such as English has verbs with a natural number of places or whether the influence is just the reverse, from logical practice to the analysis of English verbs and predicates. Whatever the etiology, the effect is the same: There is something very natural about the use of predicates that are sorted out with respect to places, or adicity. In fact, so natural is this view that even Mostowski made it a requirement on the notion of a propositional function (a mapping of E^* to truth values) that every propositional function have finite *support*. With the aid of the notion of the support of a predicate, it becomes possible to characterize predicates as functions of essentially one, two, or some finite number of arguments.

> **Definition 20.1.** Let P be any predicate of an extended implica-
> tion structure I. By the *support of P* we mean some subset $K(P)$
> of the natural numbers such that
>
> 1. if s and s' are sequences belonging to E^*, and $s_i = s_i'$ for all i
>   in $K(P)$, then $P(s) \Longleftrightarrow P(s')$, where s_i is a member of E and
>   is the ith member of the sequence s (similarly for s_i'), and
> 2. $K(P)$ is the smallest set to satisfy the first condition.[2]

Any predicate whose support is a unit set, say $\{i\}$, is essentially a function of one argument and is the counterpart of a monadic predicate. Similarly, predicates with a support of n natural numbers are functions of essentially n arguments and are the counterparts of n-place relations. Thus, among the predicates of the extended structure, one can distinguish those whose values depend essentially upon a finite number of arguments.

The theory of quantification would not have much value if we could not study how the quantifiers interact with logically complex predicates. Given our account of the logical operators, the task is to show how we can think of the logical operators as acting upon the predicates of an extended structure. However, in order to do so, we have to introduce an implication relation for predicates, since all the logical operators are relativized to implication relations.

20.2 Implication relations on predicates

Suppose that $P_1, P_2, \ldots, P_n$ and Q are predicates belonging to the set Pr of an extended implication structure $I = \langle E, Pr, S, \Longrightarrow \rangle$. We can introduce a relation "$\Longrightarrow$*" on predicates as follows:

> $P_1, \ldots, P_n \Longrightarrow^* Q$ if and only if $P_1(s), \ldots, P_n(s) \Longrightarrow Q(s)$
> for all s in E^*.

Notice that since we are dealing with predicates, the values $P_i(s)$ and $Q(s)$ all belong to S, so that the use of "$\Longrightarrow$," the implication relation on

S, is the appropriate one to use. We then have the following simple observation:

Theorem 20.1. *The relation "$\Rightarrow$*" on the set of predicates Pr of an extended implication structure is an implication relation on the set Pr.*

Proof. This is a simple computation that relies on the assumption that "$\Rightarrow$" is an implication relation on the set S.

We shall find it convenient to use an implication relation that will cover the cases in which predicates, as well as elements of S, are involved. Let $P_1, P_2, \ldots, P_n$, and Q be predicates of Pr, and let $A_1, A_2, \ldots, A_n$ and B be elements of S. Then define a relation "$\Rightarrow$*" (using the same notation as for the preceding relation, without too much resultant confusion, we hope) over the predicates and members of S as follows (allowing that the set of the A_i's can be empty, and the set of P_j's can be empty, but not simultaneously):

1. $P_1, \ldots, P_n, A_1, \ldots, A_n \Rightarrow^* Q$ if and only if for every s in E^*, $P_1(s)$, $\ldots, P_n(s)$, $A_1, \ldots, A_n \Rightarrow Q(s)$, and
2. $P_1, \ldots, P_n, A_1, \ldots, A_n \Rightarrow^* B$ if and only if for every s in E^*, $P_1(s)$, $\ldots, P_n(s)$, $A_1, \ldots, A_n \Rightarrow B$.[3]

The following are immediate consequences:

Theorem 20.2. *The relation "$\Rightarrow$*" is an implication relation on the set that is the union of S with Pr.*

Theorem 20.3. *The implication relation "$\Rightarrow$*" on the union of S with Pr is an extension of the implication relation "$\Rightarrow$" on S.*

With this implication relation in place, we can now study the behaviors of the logical operators on the predicates of extended implication structures.

20.3 The logical operators on predicates

We shall consider only conjunction, disjunction, the hypothetical, and negation on predicates. Consideration of the other logical operators is straightforward and yields exactly what one would expect.

20.4 Predicate conjunction

Predicate conjunction is just the conjunction operator acting on predicates of the structure. Let P and Q be predicates in Pr of an extended implication structure. Then, relative to the implication relation "$\Rightarrow$*," the conjunction operator on this structure, call it C^*, satisfies the following two conditions (the parametric form is, however, the official version):

1. $C^*(P, Q) \Rightarrow^* P$, and $C^*(P, Q) \Rightarrow^* Q$, and
2. $C^*(P, Q)$ is the weakest predicate (using "$\Rightarrow$*") of Pr to satisfy the first condition. That is, if R is any predicate in Pr, and $R \Rightarrow^* P$ and $R \Rightarrow^* Q$, then $R \Rightarrow^* C^*(P, Q)$.

Theorem 20.4. *Let $I = \langle E, Pr, S, \Rightarrow \rangle$ be an extended implication structure with the conjunction operator C^* on it, as characterized by the foregoing two conditions. Then, for all s in E^*, $C^*(P, Q)(s) \Leftrightarrow C(P(s), Q(s))$, where C is the conjunction operator relative to the implication relation "$\Rightarrow$" on S.*

Proof. Since $C^*(P, Q) \Rightarrow^* P$ and $C^*(P, Q) \Rightarrow^* Q$, $C^*(P, Q)(s) \Rightarrow P(s)$ and $C^*(P, Q)(s) \Rightarrow Q(s)$ for all s in E^*. Therefore, for all sequences s in E^*, $C^*(P, Q)(s) \Rightarrow C(P(s), Q(s))$, where C is the conjunction operator with respect to the implication relation "$\Rightarrow$" on S. Conversely, one has to show that for every s in E^*, $C(P(s), Q(s)) \Rightarrow C^*(P, Q)(s)$. Using the parameterized characterization of the conjunction operator (Chapter 15), $P, Q \Rightarrow^* C^*(P, Q)$. Therefore, for all s in E^*, $P(s), Q(s) \Rightarrow C^*(P, Q)(s)$. Consequently, $C(P(s), Q(s)) \Rightarrow C^*(P, Q)(s)$.

This shows that $C^*(P, Q)$ is in Pr of the structure if and only if the predicate U that maps s to $C(P(s), Q(s))$ for every s in E^* is in Pr.

20.5 Predicate disjunction

Predicate disjunction is the disjunction operator acting upon predicates in an extended implication structure. Thus, for any predicates P and Q of the structure, their disjunction $D^*(P, Q)$ is the disjunction operator relative to the implication relation "$\Rightarrow$*." Therefore, $D^*(P, Q)$ is characterized by the following conditions:

1. If $P \Rightarrow^* T$ and $Q \Rightarrow^* T$, then $D^*(P, Q) \Rightarrow^* T$ for all T (whether in Pr or in S, since "$\Rightarrow^*$" covers both cases), and

2. $D^*(P, Q)$ is the weakest member of the structure to satisfy the first condition. That is, for any U (whether in Pr or in S), if for all T, [if $P \Rightarrow^* T$ and $Q \Rightarrow^* T$, then $U \Rightarrow^* T$], then $U \Rightarrow^* D^*(P, Q)$.

We then have the result that the disjunction of any two predicates is a predicate whose value for any s in E^* is equivalent to the disjunction of the values of the predicates for s. We have to be a bit careful. If P and Q are two predicates in the set Pr of the structure, then there is a mapping U of E to S that can be defined by setting $U(s)$ as equivalent (using "$\Rightarrow$") to the disjunction $D(P(s), Q(s))$ of $P(s)$ and $Q(s)$, where the latter are members of S, and D is the disjunction operator with respect to the implication relation "$\Rightarrow$" on S. Thus, U is a predicate, since it maps E^* to S. However, there is no guarantee that U belongs to Pr, since there is no requirement that Pr contain all the functions that map E^* to S. However, if the predicate U described earlier is in the set Pr of the structure, then it is easy to see that there is a disjunction operator D^* on the predicates such that $D^*(P, Q)(s) \Leftrightarrow D(P(s), Q(s))$:

Theorem 20.5. *Let $I = \langle E, Pr, S, \Rightarrow \rangle$ be an extended implication structure. Let P and Q be any predicates of Pr, and assume that the predicate U for which $U(s) \Leftrightarrow D(P(s), Q(s))$ belongs to Pr (where D is the disjunction operator on S, with respect to the implication relation "$\Rightarrow$"). Then, for the disjunction operator D^* on I with respect to the implication relation "$\Rightarrow^*$," $D^*(P, Q)(s) \Leftrightarrow D(P(s), Q(s))$ for all s in E^*.*

Proof. Let U be defined as before. We want to show that U satisfies conditions 1 and 2. For condition 1, since $P(s) \Rightarrow T(s)$ and $Q(s) \Rightarrow T(s)$ (if T is in Pr), and $P(s) \Rightarrow T$ and $Q(s) \Rightarrow T$ (if T is in S), we have in either case the result that $D(P(s), Q(s)) \Rightarrow T$ for all s in E^*. Consequently, $U(s) \Rightarrow T$ for all s. Therefore $U \Rightarrow^* T$. Thus, condition 1 is satisfied. As for condition 2, suppose that for all T that are in either Pr or S, if $P \Rightarrow^* T$ and $Q \Rightarrow^* T$, then $V \Rightarrow^* T$ (for all T in S or Pr). For U in particular, if $P \Rightarrow^* U$ and $Q \Rightarrow^* U$, then $V \Rightarrow^* U$. But $P \Rightarrow^* U$ and $Q \Rightarrow^* U$. Consequently, $V \Rightarrow^* U$. So U also satisfies the second condition for $D^*(P, Q)$. Since conditions 1 and 2 characterize $D^*(P, Q)$ up to equivalence with respect to "$\Leftrightarrow^*$," we conclude that $U \Leftrightarrow^* D^*(P, Q)$ – that is, $D^*(P, Q)(s) \Leftrightarrow U(s) \Leftrightarrow D(P(s), Q(s))$ for all s in E^*.

20.6 Predicate hypotheticals

Again, a predicate hypothetical is the hypothetical operator acting on the predicates of an extended implication structure. Thus, the following two conditions are required:

1. $P, H^*(P, Q) \Longrightarrow^* Q$, and
2. $H^*(P, Q)$ is the weakest to satisfy the first condition. That is, for any V in Pr or S, if $P, V \Longrightarrow^* Q$, then, $V \Longrightarrow^* H^*(P, Q)$.

Assume that for predicates P and Q in Pr, the function U for which $U(s)$ is equivalent (by "$\Longrightarrow$") to $H(P(s), Q(s))$ is in Pr (where H is the hypothetical operator on S with respect to the implication relation "$\Longrightarrow$"). In that case, it follows that $H^*(P, Q)(s) \Longleftrightarrow H(P(s), Q(s))$ for all s in E^*. That is,

> **Theorem 20.6.** *Let $I = \langle E, Pr, S, \Longrightarrow \rangle$ be an extended implication structure. Let P and Q be any predicates of Pr, and assume that the predicate U described above belongs to Pr (where H is the hypothetical operator with respect to the implication relation "$\Longrightarrow$" on S). Then, for the hypothetical operator H^* on I with respect to the implication relation "$\Longrightarrow^*$," $H^*(P, Q)(s) \Longleftrightarrow H(P(s), Q(s))$.*
>
> *Proof.* $P, U \Longrightarrow^* Q$ holds – that is, $P(s), U(s), \Longrightarrow Q(s)$ for all s in E^* holds, since $U(s) \Longleftrightarrow H(P(s), Q(s))$. Therefore the first condition on $H^*(P, Q)$ is satisfied. Suppose that $P, V \Longrightarrow^* Q$ (where V is either in Pr or in S). If V is in Pr, then for all s in E^*, $P(s), V(s) \Longrightarrow Q(s)$. Consequently, $V(s) \Longrightarrow H(P(s), Q(s))$. However, since $U(s) \Longleftrightarrow H(P(s), Q(s))$, $V(s) \Longrightarrow U(s)$ for all s in E^*. Therefore $V \Longrightarrow^* U$. If V is in S, it also follows that $V \Longrightarrow^* U$ [for $P(s), V \Longrightarrow Q(s)$ for all s in E^*, so that $V \Longrightarrow H(P(s), Q(s))$ for all s in $E,^*$ and consequently $V \Longrightarrow^* U$]. So the second condition on $H^*(P, Q)$ is also satisfied. But any two predicates that satisfy the two conditions for $H^*(P, Q)$ are equivalent (by "$\Longleftrightarrow^*$"). Therefore $H^*(P, Q) \Longleftrightarrow^* U$ – that is, for all s in E^*, $H^*(P, Q)(s) \Longleftrightarrow H(P(s), Q(s))$.

20.7 Predicate negation

The negation operator on the predicates of an extended implication structure satisfies the following conditions:

1. $P, N^*(P) \Rightarrow^* R$ for all R (in either S or Pr), and
2. $N^*(P)$ is the weakest to satisfy the first condition. That is, if P, $V \Rightarrow^* R$ for all R (in either S or Pr), then $V \Rightarrow^* N^*(P)$.

Assume that for P in Pr there is a predicate U in Pr that has the following property: $U(s) \Leftrightarrow N(P(s))$ for all s in E^*, where N is the negation operator on S with respect to the implication relation "$\Rightarrow$." Then we have the following:

Theorem 20.7. *Let $I = \langle E, Pr, S, \Rightarrow \rangle$ be an extended implication structure. Let P be any predicate in Pr, and assume that the predicate U described above is in Pr. Then $N^*(P)(s) \Leftrightarrow N(P(s))$ for all s in E^*.*

Proof. U satisfies both conditions on N^*. The first condition requires that $P, U \Rightarrow^* R$ for all R (in either S or Pr). Now if R is in Pr, then $P(s), U(s) \Rightarrow R(s)$ for all s in E^*. $P(s), N(P(s))$ $\Rightarrow A$ for all A in S, since $U(s) \Leftrightarrow N(P(s))$. Now, for all predicates, $R, R(s)$ is in S, so that $P(s), U(s) \Rightarrow R(s)$ for all s. Therefore, if R is in Pr, $P, U \Rightarrow^* R$. On the other hand, if R is in S, then since $P(s), N(P(s)) \Rightarrow A$ for all A in S, we have, in particular, that $P(s), N(P(s)) \Rightarrow R$ for all s in E^*. Consequently, if R is in S, we have $P, U \Rightarrow^* R$. Therefore U satisfies the first condition on $N^*(P)$. For the second condition, suppose that $P, V \Rightarrow^* R$ for all R in S or Pr. Then $P, V \Rightarrow^* A$ for all A in S, so that for all s in E^*, $P(s), V(s) \Rightarrow A$ for all A in S. Consequently, $V(s) \Rightarrow N(P(s))$. But $U(s) \Leftrightarrow N(P(s))$. Therefore $V(s) \Rightarrow U(s)$ for all s in E^*, with the result that $V \Rightarrow^* U$. Thus, U also satisfies the second condition for $N^*(P)$. Since the two conditions on $N^*(P)$ determine $N^*(P)$ up to equivalence (by "$\Leftrightarrow^*$"), it follows that $N^*(P) \Leftrightarrow^* U$, so that $N^*(P)(s)$ $\Leftrightarrow N(P(s))$ for all s in E^*.

Exercise 20.1. In any extended implication structure, $P \Rightarrow^*$ $N^*N^*(P)$.

The point of introducing extended implication structures is to provide an account of universal and existential quantification. The quantifiers, universal and existential, will be thought of as logical operators that act on the predicates of extended implication structures. (Later, with Definition 20.2, we shall allow the quantifiers to be defined over the members of S as well as the predicates of a structure.) As with all logical operators, they are relative to an implication structure, and in this case the implication relation is the relation "$\Rightarrow$*," as characterized earlier.

20.8 Universal quantification

Let $I = \langle E, Pr, S, \Rightarrow \rangle$ be an extended implication structure. To each natural number i we shall associate an operator U_i, and we shall say that U_i is a universal operator on I if and only if it satisfies the following conditions:

1. If P is a predicate in Pr, then $U_i(P)$ is also in Pr.
2. U_i is support-reducing. That is, if the predicate P has support $K(P)$, then $U_i(P)$ has support $K(P) - \{i\}$.

For the remaining conditions, which are the heart of the matter for universal quantification, we need to introduce a type of function that maps E^* to E^* (sequences to sequences) as follows:

For any natural number i and any element e of E, let J_e^i be the mapping of E^* to E^* that satisfies the following condition:

> If s is any sequence in E^*, then $J_e^i(s)$ is a sequence s'
> of E^* such that $s_i' = e$ and $s_j' = s_j$ for all $j \neq i$.

We shall assume for the remainder of this chapter that if P is a predicate of the structure, so too is $(P \circ J_e^i)$ (the composition of the functions P and J_e^i) for every natural number i and any element e of E. The J-functions simply take any sequence s of E^* and transform it to a sequence s' of E^* that has e in its ith place, but is elsewhere identical with s. And the value that the predicate $(P \circ J_e^i)$ assigns to the sequence $(s_1, s_2, \ldots)$ is that member of S that the predicate P assigns to $(s_1, s_2, \ldots, s_{i-1}, e, s_{i+1}, \ldots)$, with e in the ith place.

With these observations in place, we can now state the remaining condition on the operators U_i:

U_1. For any predicate P in Pr, $U_i(P) \Rightarrow^* (P \circ J_e^i)$ for all e in E, and
U_2. $U_i(P)$ is the weakest (under "$\Rightarrow$*") to satisfy the first condition. That is, if $R \Rightarrow^* (P \circ J_e^i)$ for all e in E, then $R \Rightarrow^* U_i(P)$.

The conditions U_1 and U_2 make it clear that the various universal quantifier operators are logical operators, in that the first is a filter condition, and the second assigns as values those items that are the weakest of those that satisfy the filter condition. Before describing existential quantification, it is worthwhile considering some simple consequences of this characterization of universal quantification.

20.9 Universal quantifiers: Some simple features

Theorem 20.8 (instantiation). *Let $I = \langle E, Pr, S \Rightarrow \rangle$ be any extended implication structure, and let P be any predicate in Pr. Then for any universal quantifier U_i on the structure I, $U_i(P)$ $\Rightarrow^* P$.*

Proof. By the first condition U_1 on universal quantifiers, $U_i(p)$ $\Rightarrow^* (P \circ J_e^i)$ for all e in E. Let s be any sequence in E^*. Therefore $U_i(P)(s) \Rightarrow (P \circ J_e^i)(s)$. However, $(P \circ J_e^i)(s) \Leftrightarrow P(s')$, where $s_i' = e$ and $s_j' = s_j$ for all $j \neq i$. Since the implication holds for all e in E, let e be s_i, so that s' for this choice of e is just s itself. Consequently, $(P \circ J_e^i)(s) \Leftrightarrow P(s)$. Therefore, for all s in E^*, $U_i(P)(s) \Rightarrow P(s)$, so that $U_i(P) \Rightarrow^* P$.

Theorem 20.9. *Let I be an extended implication structure, and let P be any predicate of I with the support $K(P)$. If i is not in the support of P, then $U_i(P) \Leftrightarrow^* P$.*

Proof. By the preceding theorem, $U_i(P) \Rightarrow^* P$. To see that $P \Rightarrow^* U_i(P)$, let s be any sequence in E^*. Then, $P(s) \Rightarrow (P \circ J_e^i)(s)$ for all e in E, since $(P \circ J_e^i)(s) \Leftrightarrow P(s')$, where s' differs from s at most in the ith member, where s' has e. However, we assumed that i is not in the support $K(P)$ of P. Therefore, s and s' agree on the support of P. Consequently, $P(s) \Leftrightarrow P(s')$. Since $P(s) \Rightarrow (P \circ J_e^i)(s)$ for all e in E, $P \Rightarrow^* (P \circ J_e^i)$ for all e in E. However, by the first condition on universal quantifiers, $U_i(P) \Rightarrow^* (P \circ J_e^i)$, and by the second condition, $U_i(P)$ is the weakest (under "$\Rightarrow^*$") to do so. Since P satisfies the first condition, $U_i(P)$ is weaker than P. That is, $P \Rightarrow^* U_i(P)$.

Theorem 20.10. *If I is an extended implication structure, P is any predicate of I, and U_i is any universal quantifier on I, then $U_i(U_i(P)) \Leftrightarrow^* U_i(P)$.*

Proof. Since the support $K(U_i(P))$ of $U_i(P)$ is $K(P) - \{i\}$, it follows that i is not in the support of $U_i(P)$. By Theorem 20.9, it follow that $U_i U_i(P) \Leftrightarrow^* U_i(P)$.

We can now extend the domain of the function U_i to include the members of S and Pr.

Definition 20.2. Let $I = \langle E, Pr, S, \Rightarrow \rangle$ be an extended implication structure. A predicate P is a *constant predicate* of I if and only if $P(s) \Longleftrightarrow P(s')$ for all s and s' in E^*.

For any A in S, let P_A be the constant predicate (unique up to "$\Rightarrow^*$") such that $P_A(s) \Longleftrightarrow^* A$ for all s in E^*. Then, for any member A of S and any natural number i, define $U_i(A)$ to be $U_i(P_A)$.

Theorem 20.11. *If I is an extended implication structure and A is any member of S, then for any i, $U_i(A) \Longleftrightarrow^* A$.*

Proof. Note first that $K(P_A)$ is empty (we leave this as an exercise). Since i is not in $K(P_A)$, by Theorem 20.9, $U_i(P_A) \Longleftrightarrow^* P_A$. Consequently, $U_i(P_A)(s) \Longleftrightarrow P_A(s) \Longleftrightarrow A$. Therefore $U_i(P_A) \Longleftrightarrow^* A$.

Theorem 20.12 (distribution over implication). *Let $I = \langle E, Pr, S, \Rightarrow \rangle$ be an extended implication structure in which conjunctions (with respect to "$\Rightarrow^*$") always exist, and let $P_1, P_2, \ldots, P_n$ and Q be predicates of I. If $P_1, \ldots, P_n \Rightarrow^* Q$, then $U_i(P_1), \ldots, U_i(P_n) \Rightarrow^* U_i(Q)$.*[4]

Proof. Suppose that $P_1, \ldots, P_n \Rightarrow^* Q$. Since $U_i(P_j) \Rightarrow^* (P_j \circ J_e^i)$ for all e in E, $U_i(P_1), \ldots, U_i(P_n) \Rightarrow^* (P_1 \circ J_e^i)$ [as well as $(P_2 \circ J_e^i), \ldots, (P_n \circ J_e^i)$]. Let s^* be any sequence in E^*. Since $P_1, \ldots, P_n \Rightarrow^* Q$, it follows that $P_1(s), \ldots, P_n(s) \Rightarrow Q(s)$ for all s in E^*. Therefore, for s', in particular, where $s' = J_e^i(s^*)$, we have $P_1(s'), \ldots, P_n(s'), \Rightarrow Q(s')$. However, $P_1(s')$ is $(P_1 \circ J_e^i)(s^*)$ [similarly for $P_2(s'), \ldots, P_n(s')$], and $Q(s')$ is $(Q \circ J_e^i)(s^*)$. Therefore, $(P_1 \circ J_e^i)(s^*), \ldots, (P_n \circ J_e^i)(s^*) \Rightarrow (Q \circ J_e^i)(s^*)$ for all s^* in E^*. Consequently, $(P_1 \circ J_e^i), \ldots, (P_n \circ J_e^i) \Rightarrow^* (Q \circ J_e^i)$. Therefore $U_i(P_1), \ldots, U_i(P_n) \Rightarrow^* (Q \circ J_e^i)$ for all e in E. Therefore $C^*(U_i(P_1), \ldots, U_i(P_n)) \Rightarrow^* (Q \circ J_e^i)$ for all e in E. Now we know from the first condition on $U_i(Q)$ that $U_i(Q) \Rightarrow^* (Q \circ J_e^i)$ for all e in E, and we know by the second condition on $U_i(Q)$ that it is the weakest to imply (under "$\Rightarrow^*$") $(Q \circ J_e^i)$ for all e in E. Consequently, $C^*(U_i(P_1), \ldots, U_i(P_n)) \Rightarrow^* U_i(Q)$. Since $U_i(P_1), \ldots, U_i(P_n) \Rightarrow^* C^*(U_i(P_1), \ldots, U_i(P_n))$, we conclude that $U_i(P_1), \ldots, U_i(P_n) \Rightarrow^* U_i(Q)$.

Theorem 20.13 (full distribution over conjunction). *Let I be an extended implication structure, and let P and Q be predicates.*

Let C^* be the conjunction operator on I. Then for any universal quantifier U_i, it follows that $U_i(C^*(P, Q)) \Longleftrightarrow^* C^*(U_i(P), U_i(Q))$ [that is, using an unofficial notation, $U_i(P \& Q) \Longleftrightarrow^* U_i(P) \& U_i(Q)$].

Proof. Since $C^*(P, Q) \Longrightarrow^* P$ (as well as Q), by the preceding theorem, $U_i(C^*(P, Q)) \Longrightarrow^* U_i(P)$ [as well as $U_i(Q)$]. Consequently, $U_i(C^*(P, Q)) \Longrightarrow^* C^*(U_i(P), U_i(Q))$. To obtain the converse, notice that $U_i(P) \Longrightarrow^* (P \circ J_e^i)$ and $U_i(Q) \Longrightarrow^* (Q \circ J_e^i)$ for all e in E. Therefore $(P \circ J_e^i), (Q \circ J_e^i) \Longrightarrow^* (C^*(P, Q) \circ J_e^i)$ for all e in E (we leave the proof for the reader). Consequently, $U_i(P), U_i(Q) \Longrightarrow^* (C^*(P, Q) \circ J_e^i)$ for all e in E (using the parametric conditions for U_i – see note 4). However, $U_i(C^*(P, Q))$ is the weakest member of the structure to imply (under "$\Longrightarrow^*$") $(C^*(P, Q) \circ J_e^i)$ for all e in E. Consequently, $U_i(P), U_i(Q) \Longrightarrow^* U_i(C^*(P, Q))$. Therefore $C^*(U_i(P), U_i(Q)) \Longrightarrow^* U_i(C^*(P, Q))$.

Theorem 20.14 (distribution of universal quantification over the hypothetical). *Let $I = \langle E, Pr, S, \Longrightarrow \rangle$ be an extended implication structure. If P and Q are predicates of I, and H^* is the hypothetical operator with respect to "$\Longrightarrow^*$," then $U_i(H^*(P, Q)) \Longrightarrow^* H^*(U_i(P), U_i(Q))$ [that is, $U_i(P \to Q) \Longrightarrow^* U_i(P) \to U_i(Q)$].*

Proof. Since $P, H^*(P, Q) \Longrightarrow^* Q$, by Theorem 20.12 it follows that $U_i(P), U_i(H^*(P, Q)) \Longrightarrow^* U_i(Q)$. Since $H^*(U_i(P), U_i(Q))$ is the weakest R for which $U_i(P), R \Longrightarrow^* U_i(Q)$, it follows that $U_i(H^*(P, Q)) \Longrightarrow^* H^*(U_i(P), U_i(Q))$.

Theorem 20.15 (the order of universal quantifiers). *Let I be an extended implication structure, and let P be any predicate of I. If U_i and U_j are any universal quantifiers on I, then $U_i(U_j(P)) \Longleftrightarrow^* U_j(U_i(P))$.*

Proof. $U_i U_j(P) \Longrightarrow^* P$, since $U_i(U_j(P)) \Longrightarrow^* U_j(P) \Longrightarrow^* P$. By Theorem 20.12, we can distribute the universal quantifier U_i so as to obtain $U_i(U_i U_j(P)) \Longrightarrow^* U_i(P)$. By Theorem 20.10, $U_i(U_i(P)) \Longleftrightarrow^* U_i(P)$ for any predicate P, so that $U_i U_j(P) \Longrightarrow^* U_i(P)$. By Theorem 20.12, we can distribute the quantifier U_j over this implication, so that $U_j(U_i U_j(P)) \Longrightarrow^* U_j U_i(P)$. Since j is not in the support of $U_i U_j(P)$, by Theorem 20.9, $U_j U_i U_j(P) \Longleftrightarrow^* U_i U_j(P)$. Consequently, $U_i U_j(P) \Longrightarrow^* U_j U_i(P)$. The converse is proved similarly.

Before we turn to a consideration of the existential quantifiers on extended implication structures, it is worth observing two results about the universal quantifiers. Both concern implications that fail to hold in all structures. The first states that the universal quantification of a disjunction of predicates does not always imply the disjunction of their quantifications. The second concerns a result that holds in all classical structures, but fails to hold in some nonclassical ones.

Theorem 20.16. *There is an extended implication structure* $I = \langle E, Pr, S, \Rightarrow \rangle$, *with predicates P and Q, and a universal quantifier* U_i, *such that* $U_i(D^*(P, Q)) \not\Rightarrow^* D^*(U_i(P), U_i(Q))$ *[that is,* $U_i(P \vee Q) \not\Rightarrow^* U_i(P \vee U_i(Q))$].

Proof. Let E be a set consisting of three elements $\{e_1, e_2, e_3\}$, and let S be the set of four items $\{A, B, C, D\}$ with the following implication relation:

Let E^* be the set of infinite sequences of the members of E, and let Pr, the predicates of the structure, be any set that includes the predicates P, Q, and R and $D^*(P, Q)$, the disjunction of P with Q, as defined below. These predicates are essentially functions of one argument, intuitively described as follows: $P(e_1)$ and $P(e_2)$ are A, and $P(e_3)$ is B. $Q(e_1)$ and $Q(e_2)$ are B, and $Q(e_3)$ is A. $D^*(P, Q)$ is assigned the value for each member of E that is the disjunction of their values. That is, $D^*(P, Q)$ (e_1) is $D^*(P(e_1), Q(e_1))$, which is $D(A, B)$ – that is, C. Similarly, $D^*(P, Q)(e_2)$ is $D(A, B)$, which is C, and $D^*(P, Q)(e_3)$ is $D(B, A)$, which is C. Finally, R is assigned the value D for all the members of E. Now $U_1(D^*(P, Q))$ implies $D^*(P, Q)(e)$ for all e in E. Therefore it implies C and is the weakest to imply C. Thus, $U_1(D^*(P, Q))$ is C. On the other hand, since P is a function of one argument, $U_1(P)$ is a constant predicate, and implies $P(e)$ for all e in E. Consequently, it implies A as well as B and is the weakest to do so. Therefore $U_1(P)$ is R. Similarly, $U_1(Q)$ is also R. Therefore $U_1(D^*(P, Q)) \Rightarrow^* D^*(U_1(P), U_1(Q))$ if and only if C implies the disjunction of D with D, that is, if and only if $C \Rightarrow D$. But that is impossible in this particular structure.

This is the intuitive way to look at the structure. However, officially, predicates are mappings of E^* into S, so that this structure has to be described slightly differently to make it official. However, it is easy enough to redescribe the functions of E to S slightly differently so that they are mappings of E^* to S and are predicates of essentially one argument.[5]

The final theorem in this section is familiar from the study of the intuitionistic predicate calculus.

Theorem 20.17. *There is an extended implication structure $I =$ $\langle E, Pr, S, \Rightarrow \rangle$ such that for some predicate P of I and some member B of S and some universal quantifier U_i, $U_i(D^*(P, B))$ $\not\Rightarrow^* D^* (U_i(P), B)$ [that is, $U_i(P \vee B) \not\Rightarrow^* U_i(P) \vee B$].*

Proof. Let $S = \{A, B, B_1, B_2, C, C_1, C_2\}$, with the implication relation "$\Rightarrow$" as diagrammed. Let $E = \{e_1, e_2\}$, and let the predicate P be thought of as essentially a function of one argument in Pr, where $P(e_1)$ is B_1, $P(e_2)$ is B_2, and we assume that the predicates $D^*(P, B)$, P_A, P_B, and P_C (the constant predicates whose values are A, B, and C, respectively) are also in Pr. Then we have the following situation:

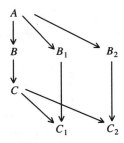

Since $U_1(P)$ is the weakest predicate that implies $P(e_1)$ as well as $P(e_2)$ (that is, B_1 as well as B_2), it follows that $U_1(P)$ is P_A. Therefore, for all s in E, $D^*(U_1(P), B)(s)$ is the disjunction $D(A, B)$ (in S) of A with B. Since A implies B, it follows that $D(A, B)$ is B. Consequently, $D^*(U_1(P), B)$ is P_B. On the other hand, in this structure, $D(P(e_1), B)$ is C_1, and $D(P(e_2), B)$ is C_2. Now $U_1(D^*(P, B))$ is the weakest to imply $D(P(e_1), B)$ as well as $D(P(e_2), B)$ – that is, it is the weakest to imply C_1

as well as C_2. Consequently, $U_1(D^*(P, B))$ is P_C. Therefore $U_1(D^*(P, B)) \Rightarrow^* D^*(U_1(P), B)$ if and only if $C \Rightarrow B$. But that is impossible in this structure.

Theorem 20.17 looks like a special case of Theorem 20.16, where a universal quantifier does not always distribute over a disjunction. The first case is something that holds for classical implication structures. There is a classical structure in which the quantifier will not distribute over the disjunction of some two of its predicates. This is a familiar but important result, because together with the fact already proved, that universal quantifiers distribute over implication, we have the basis for the claim that the universal quantifier is a modal operator on predicates (Section 31.1). On the other hand, where P is a predicate of nonempty support, and B is a member of S, $U_i(P \vee B)$ implies $U_i(P) \vee B$ in all classical structures. If there is a failure of implication, it can only be in some nonclassical structure. Indeed, the structure used in Theorem 20.17 is nonclassical.

Exercise 20.2. Show that the structure used in the proof of Theorem 20.17 is nonclassical (see Chapter 13, note 1).

We turn now to a brief study of the existential quantifiers on extended implication structures and some of their basic features.

20.10 Existential quantifiers

Let $I = \langle E, Pr, S, \Rightarrow \rangle$ be an extended implication structure. For each natural number i, we shall think of E_i as a special kind of operator that acts upon the predicates of I (and later we shall extend the domain to include members of S as well). Like the universal quantifiers, the E_i's are support-reducing.

The following two conditions characterize the existential quantifiers and differentiate them from the universal ones. Let $I = \langle E, Pr, S, \Rightarrow \rangle$ be an extended implication structure. Then we shall say that for each natural number i, E_i is an existential quantifier on the structure I if and only if

E_1. for any P in Pr, if T is in Pr or S, then if $(P \circ J_e^i) \Rightarrow^* T$ for all e in E, then $E_i(P) \Rightarrow^* T$, and

E_2. $E_i(P)$ is the weakest member of the structure to satisfy the first condition. That is, for any U, if for any T in Pr or S, if [if $(P \circ J_e^i) \Rightarrow^* T$ for all e in E, then $U \Rightarrow^* T$], then $U \Rightarrow^* E_i(P)$.

According to this characterization, the existential operators on extended implication structures are logical operators, for the first condition is a filter condition, and the second condition selects, as the values of the operator, those items that are the weakest among those that satisfy the filter condition. As with the universal quantifiers, this version should be stated in a parameterized form, which we shall forgo.

Exercise 20.3. For any predicate P in an extended implication structure, show that (1) $(P \circ J_e^i) \Rightarrow^* E_i(P)$ for all e in E and any i (compare the proof of Theorem 14.1) and (2) E_i is the strongest to satisfy the first condition. That is, for any T, if $(P \circ J_e^i) \Rightarrow^* T$ for all e in E, then $E_i(P) \Rightarrow^* T$.

We can now look at some simple consequences of this characterization of existential quantifiers on extended implication structures.

20.11 Existential quantifiers: some simple features

Theorem 20.18. *Let I be an extended implication structure, and let P be any predicate of I. Then $P \Rightarrow^* E_i(P)$ for any existential quantifier E_i on I.*

Proof. By the preceding exercise (1), $(P \circ J_e^i) \Rightarrow^* E_i(P)$ for all e in E. Let s be any member of E^*. Then $(P \circ J_e^i)(s) \Rightarrow (E_i(P))(s)$ for all e in E. Consequently, $P(J_e^i(s)) \Rightarrow (E_i(P))(s)$. In particular, take e to be s_i (the ith member of the sequence s). Since $J_{s_i}^i(s) = s$, it follows that $P(s) \Rightarrow^* (E_i(P))(s)$. This holds for every s in E^*. Therefore $P \Rightarrow^* E_i(P)$.

Theorem 20.19. *Let I be any extended implication structure, with P any predicate of I with support $K(P)$, and E_i any existential quantifier on I. If i is not a member of $K(P)$, then $E_i(P) \Leftrightarrow^* P$.*

Proof. By the preceding theorem, $P \Rightarrow^* E_i(P)$. To prove the converse, first note that if i is not in the support $K(P)$ of P, then $(P \circ J_e^i) \Rightarrow^* P$ for all e in E. For let s be any member of E^*, let e be any member of E, and let $J_e^i(s) = s'$. Consequently, $(P \circ J_e^i)(s) \Leftrightarrow P(J_e^i(s)) \Leftrightarrow P(s')$. Since s and s' agree on $K(P)$, $P(s) \Leftrightarrow P(s')$. Consequently, $(P \circ J_e^i)(s) \Rightarrow P(s)$ for all s and all e. Therefore $(P \circ J_e^i) \Rightarrow^* P$ for all e in E. Consequently, by E_1, it follows that $E_i(P) \Rightarrow^* P$.

We now extend the functions E_i so that they are mappings on S, as well as Pr, by setting $E_i(A)$ equal to $E_i(P_A)$, where P_A is the constant predicate such that $P_A(s) \Longleftrightarrow A$ for all s in E^*.

Theorem 20.20. *Let I be an extended implication structure, and E_i any existential quantifier on I. Then for any A in S, $E_i(A)$ $\Longleftrightarrow^* A$.*

Proof. Since the support $K(P_A)$ of P_A is empty, the result follows from Theorem 20.19.

Theorem 20.21. *Let I be an extended implication structure, and E_i any existential quantifier on I. Then for any predicate P, $E_iE_i(P) \Longleftrightarrow^* P$.*

Proof. Since the quantifiers are support-reducing, i is not in the support of $E_i(P)$. Therefore $E_iE_i(P) \Longleftrightarrow^* E_i(P)$, by Theorem 20.20.

Theorem 20.22 (distribution over implication). *Let I be an extended implication structure, E_i any existential quantifier on I, and P and Q predicates of I. If $P \Longrightarrow^* Q$, then $E_i(P) \Longrightarrow^* E_i(Q)$.*

Proof. Assume that $P \Longrightarrow^* Q$. It follows that $(P \circ J_e^i) \Longrightarrow^* (Q \circ J_e^i)$ for all i and all e in E. The reason is that for any s in E^*, $P(s) \Longrightarrow Q(s)$. So, in particular, for any e in E, and $s' = J_e^i(s)$, we have $P(s') \Longrightarrow Q(s')$. Consequently, $(P \circ J_e^i)(s) \Longrightarrow (Q \circ J_e^i)(s)$ for any s in E^* and e in E. Since $(Q \circ J_e^i) \Longrightarrow^* E_i(Q)$ for all i and all e in E, it follows that $(P \circ J_e^i) \Longrightarrow^* E_i(Q)$ for all e in E. However, by the first condition on $E_i(P)$, it follows that $E_i(P) \Longrightarrow^* E_i(Q)$.

This distribution theorem for existential quantifiers differs from the one proved for universal quantifiers (Theorem 20.12). The universal quantifiers will always distribute over several predicates that imply Q. In general, the existential quantifier will distribute when it is a case of one predicate implying Q, but not when there are several.

Exercise 20.4. There is an extended implication structure I in which there are predicates $P_1, \ldots, P_n$ and Q such that $P_1, \ldots, P_n \Longrightarrow^* Q$, but $E_i(P_1), \ldots, E_i(P_n) \not\Longrightarrow^* E_i(Q)$.

Theorem 20.23 (distribution over conjunctions). *Let I be an extended implication structure, P and Q any predicates of I, and E_i any existential quantifier on I. Then $E_i(C^*(P, Q)) \Rightarrow^* C^*(E_i(P), E_i(Q))$ [that is, $E_i(P \& Q) \Rightarrow^* E_i(P) \& E_i(Q)$].*

Proof. $C^*(P, Q) \Rightarrow^* P$ (as well as Q). By Theorem 20.22, $E_i(C^*(P, Q)) \Rightarrow^* E_i(P)$ [as well as $E_i(Q)$]. Therefore $E_i(C^*(P, Q)) \Rightarrow^* C^*(E_i(P), E_i(Q))$.

Theorem 20.24 (full distribution over disjunctions). *Let I be an extended implication structure, P and Q any predicates of I, and E_i any existential quantifier on I. Then $E_i(D^*(P, Q)) \Leftrightarrow^* D^*(E_i(P), E_i(Q))$ [that is, $E_i(P \vee Q) \Leftrightarrow^* E_i(P) \vee E_i(Q)$].*

Proof. Since $P \Rightarrow^* D^*(P, Q)$, by the distribution over implication, $E_i(P) \Rightarrow^* E_i(D^*(P, Q))$. Similarly, $E_i(Q) \Rightarrow^* E_i(D^*(P, Q))$. Consequently, by the first condition on disjunctions, $D^*(E_i(P), E_i(Q)) \Rightarrow^* E_i(D^*(P, Q))$ [that is, $E_i(P) \vee E_i(Q) \Rightarrow^* E_i(P \vee Q)$]. To prove the converse, note that $(P \circ J^i_e) \Rightarrow^* E_i(P) \Rightarrow^* D^*(E_i(P), E_i(Q))$. Similarly, $(Q \circ J^i_e) \Rightarrow^* D^*(E_i(P), E_i(Q))$. Consequently, by the first condition on disjunctions, the disjunction of $(P \circ J^i_e)$ with $(Q \circ J^i_e)$ implies (using "$\Rightarrow^*$") $D^*(E_i(P), E_i(Q))$. Therefore $D^*(P, Q) \circ J^i_e \Rightarrow^* D^*(E_i(P), E_i(Q))$. Consequently, by the first condition on existential quantifiers, $E_i(D^*(P, Q)) \Rightarrow^* D^*(E_i(P), E_i(Q))$ [that is, $E_i(P \vee Q) \Rightarrow^* E_i(P) \vee E_i(Q)$].

20.12 Universal and existential quantifiers

We now look at some typical examples of the interaction of universal and existential quantifiers.

Theorem 20.25. *Let I be an extended implication structure, and P any predicate of I. Then for any universal quantifier U_i and existential quantifier E_i, $U_i(P) \Rightarrow^* E_i(P)$.*

Proof. From the first condition on $U_i(P)$, $U_i(P) \Rightarrow^* (P \circ J^i_e)$ for all e in E. However, for all e in E, $(P \circ J^i_e) \Rightarrow^* E_i(P)$. Consequently, $U_i(P) \Rightarrow^* E_i(P)$.

Theorem 20.26. *Let I be an extended implication structure, U_i and E_i universal and existential quantifiers on I, and N^* the negation operator on I. Then for any predicate P on I, $U_i(P) \Rightarrow^* N^*(E_i(N^*(P)))$.*

Proof. $U_i(P) \Rightarrow^* (P \circ J_e^i)$ for all i and all e in E. Therefore $N^*(P \circ J_e^i) \Rightarrow^* N^*U_i(P)$. However, $N^*(P \circ J_e^i) \Leftrightarrow^* (N^*P) \circ J_e^i$. {For any s in E^*, $[N^*(P \circ J_e^i)](s) \Leftrightarrow^* N^*[(P \circ J_e^i)(s)] \Leftrightarrow^* N^*[P(J_e^i(s))] \Leftrightarrow^* (N^*P)(J_e^i(s)) \Leftrightarrow^* [(N^*P) \circ J_e^i](s).$} Consequently, $(N^*P) \circ J_e^i \Rightarrow^* N^*U_i(P)$. Therefore, by the first condition on existential quantifiers, $E_i(N^*P) \Rightarrow^* N^*U_i(P)$. Therefore $N^*N^*U_i(P) \Rightarrow^* N^*E_i(N^*P)$. Since $P \Rightarrow^* N^*N^*(P)$ for any predicate P of the structure (Exercise 20.1), $U_i(P) \Rightarrow N^*N^*U_i(P)$. Consequently, $U_i(P) \Rightarrow^* N^*E_iN^*(P)$.

Theorem 20.27. *Let I be an extended implication structure, U_i and E_i universal and existential quantifiers on I, and N^* the negation operator on I. Then for any predicate P on I, $E_i(P) \Rightarrow^* N^*(U_i(N^*(P)))$.*

Proof. For any predicate P, we know that $U_i(P) \Rightarrow^* (P \circ J_e^i)$ for all i and e in E. Therefore, for $N^*(P)$ in particular, we have $U_i(N^*P) \Rightarrow^* (N^*P) \circ J_e^i$. Consequently, $N^*[(N^*P) \circ J_e^i] \Rightarrow^* N^*U_i(N^*P)$. However, $(N^*N^*P) \circ J_e^i \Rightarrow^* N^*[(N^*P) \circ J_e^i]$. (The reason is similar to that given in the preceding theorem.) Therefore $(N^*N^*P) \circ J_e^i \Rightarrow^* N^*U_iN^*(P)$. However, since $P \Rightarrow^* N^*N^*(P)$, it follows that $(P \circ J_e^i) \Rightarrow^* (N^*N^*P) \circ J_e^i$. Consequently, $(P \circ J_e^i) \Rightarrow^* N^*U_iN^*(P)$. Therefore, by the first condition on existential quantifiers, $E_i(P) \Rightarrow^* N^*U_iN^*(P)$.

Theorems 20.26 and 20.27 hold in all structures, although their converses do not. However, those converses hold in all extended implication structures in which the negation operator N^* is classical. It is easy to describe extended implication structures in which the converses of these theorems fail. Of course, they will have to be nonclassical.

Exercise 20.5. There is an extended implication structure I, and a predicate P on I, such that $N^*E_iN^*(P) \not\Rightarrow^* U_i(P)$.

Exercise 20.6. There is an extended implication structure I, and a predicate P on I, such that $N^*U_iN^*(P) \not\Rightarrow^* E_i(P)$.

Theorem 20.28 (the order of existential quantifiers). *Let I be an extended implication structure, P any predicate on I, and E_i and E_j two existential quantifiers on I. Then $E_iE_j(P) \Leftrightarrow^* E_jE_i(P)$.*

Proof. By Theorem 20.18, $P \Rightarrow^* E_i(P)$. Using the distribution of E_j over this implication, $E_j(P) \Rightarrow^* E_jE_i(P)$. Distributing E_i over this implication in turn, $E_iE_j(P) \Rightarrow^* E_i(E_jE_i(P))$. Since the existential quantifier is support-reducing $[K(E_jE_i(P)) = K(E_i(P)) - \{j\}$, and $K(E_i(P)) = K(P) - \{i\}]$, neither i nor j is in the support of $E_jE_i(P)$. Therefore, by Theorem 20.19, $E_i(E_jE_i(P)) \Leftrightarrow^* E_jE_i(P)$. Consequently, $E_iE_j(P) \Rightarrow^* E_jE_i(P)$. The converse is proved similarly.

Theorem 20.29 (changing the order of quantifiers). *Let I be an extended implication structure. If U_i and E_j are any universal and any existential quantifiers on I, then $E_iU_j(P) \Rightarrow^* U_jE_i(P)$ for any predicate P on I.*

Proof. We need to prove a small lemma:

Lemma 20.1. $(U_jP) \circ J_e^i \Rightarrow^* U_j(E_iP)$.

Proof. Since $U_j(P) \Rightarrow^* P \circ J_{e'}^j$ for all e' in E, it follows that $(U_jP) \circ J_e^i \Rightarrow^* (P \circ J_{e'}^j) \circ J_e^i \Rightarrow^* P \circ (J_{e'}^j \circ J_e^i) \Rightarrow^* P \circ (J_e^i \circ J_{e'}^j) \Rightarrow^* (P \circ J_e^i) \circ J_{e'}^j$. Now $P \circ J_e^i \Rightarrow^* E_i(P)$. Therefore $(P \circ J_e^i) \circ J_{e'}^j \Rightarrow^* (E_iP) \circ J_{e'}^j$. Consequently, $(U_jP) \circ J_e^i \Rightarrow (E_iP) \circ J_{e'}^j$ for all e' in E. However, $U_j(E_iP) \Rightarrow^* (E_iP) \circ J_{e'}^j$ for all e' in E, and $U_j(E_iP)$ is the weakest to do so. Therefore $(U_jP) \circ J_e^i \Rightarrow^* U_j(E_iP)$ for all e in E. By the first condition on existential quantifiers, for any Q and F in an extended implication structure, if $Q \circ J_e^i \Rightarrow^* F$ for all e in E, then $E_i(Q) \Rightarrow^* F$. In particular [taking U_jP for Q, and $U_j(E_iP)$ for F], $E_iU_j(P) \Rightarrow^* U_jE_i(P)$.

We know that, in general, $U_i(P) \Rightarrow^* E_i(P)$ for all i. Here is a result about those conditions under which the converse holds:

Theorem 20.30. *Let I be an extended implication structure. If for some predicate P of I, $E_i(P) \Rightarrow U_i(P)$ for all i in $K(P)$, then P is a constant predicate of I.*

Proof. Suppose that $E_i(P) \Rightarrow^* U_i(P)$ for all i, and $K(P)$ is nonempty. Since $(P \circ J_e^i) \Rightarrow^* E_i(P)$ for all i and all e in E, and $U_i(P) \Rightarrow^* (P \circ J_{e'}^i)$ for all e' in E, it follows that for all e and e' in E, $(P \circ J_e^i) \Rightarrow^* (P \circ J_{e'}^i)$. Let $s = (s_1, s_2, \ldots)$ and $t = (t_1, t_2, \ldots)$ be any two sequences in E^*. Then $(P \circ J_e^i)(s) \Rightarrow (P \circ J_{e'}^i)(s)$. Let i be in $K(P)$. Let e be s_i. Since $J_{s_i}^i(s) = s$, $P(s) \Rightarrow (P \circ J_{e'}^i)(s)$. Let e' be t_i, and let t^i be the sequence $J_{t_i}^i(s) = (s_1, s_2, \ldots, t_i, s_{i+1}, \ldots)$. So $P(s) \Rightarrow P(t^i)$. Similarly, $P(t^i) \Rightarrow P(s)$, so that $P(s) \Leftrightarrow P(t^i)$. Consequently, if s and t

agree everywhere on $K(P) - \{i\}$, then $P(s) \Longleftrightarrow P(t)$. But $K(P)$ is the smallest set (the support of P) for which this holds. Therefore $K(P)$ is empty. Now note that if $K(P)$ is empty, then P is a constant predicate, and that concludes the proof.

Exercise 20.7. Let s and t be two sequences of E^*. Show that if $K(P)$ is empty for the predicate P, then P is a constant predicate [note that if $P(s) \not\Longleftrightarrow P(t)$, then for some i in $K(P)$, $s_i \neq t_i$].

Of course, it is true that if P is a constant predicate on an extended implication structure, then, whether or not the support of P is finite, $E_i(P) \Longrightarrow^* U_i(P)$ for all i. That is,

Theorem 20.31. *Let I be an extended implication structure, and P any constant predicate of I. Then $E_i(P) \Longrightarrow^* U_i(P)$ for all i.*

Proof. Since $K(P)$ is empty, $U_i(P) \Longleftrightarrow^* P$ (Theorem 20.9), and $E_i(P) \Longleftrightarrow^* P$ (Theorem 20.19).

It is important to note that a formalized theory L of first-order quantification can be used to provide an example of an extended implication structure in addition to the simple nonsyntactical ones that were used in Theorems 20.16 and 20.17.

Here is one way of seeing how the formulas of L can be taken as the members of an extended implication structure:

Suppose that Q is a formalized theory of quantification, with individual variables x_1, x_2, ..., and predicate letters P^j_k (the subscript marking the difference between various j-place predicate letters). To describe an extended implication structure, we have to provide E, S, "$\Longrightarrow$," and Pr. (1) Let E be the set of the individual variables of Q. (2) Let S be the set of all (well-formed) formulas of Q. (3) For any A_1, ..., A_n and B in S, define "$A_1, \ldots, A_n \Longrightarrow B$" as holding if and only if the corresponding conditional "$(A_1 \& \ldots \& A_n) \to B$" is a theorem of Q. If the formulation of Q does not permit formulas with free occurrences of variables to be theorems, we require instead that the closure of the corresponding conditional be a theorem of Q. In any case, take "$\Longrightarrow^*$" to be the relation that requires the closure of the corresponding conditional to be a theorem of Q. Both of these relations, "$\Longrightarrow$" and "$\Longrightarrow^*$," are implication relations on the formulas of Q – that is, the members of S. It remains only to specify the set Pr of predicates of the extended implication structure. (4) Recall that the predicates of an extended implication structure are mappings of E^* (the set of infinite sequences of E – the variables of Q) to S (the formulas of Q). To each predicate letter P_k^j of L we associate a mapping $[P_k^j]$ of E^* to S as follows: For each sequence $v = (v_1, v_2, \ldots)$ of E^*, let $[P_k^j](v) = P_k^j(v_1, v_2, \ldots, v_j)$. Thus, for the sequence of the individual variables of Q in their standard order, $[P_k^j](x_1, x_2, \ldots) = P_k^j(x_1, x_2, \ldots, x_j)$. We include all the functions $[P_k^j]$ in Pr. For any formula of the form "$P_k^n(x_{i_1}, x_{i_2}, \ldots, x_{i_n})$," let the associated predicate be the function of E^* to S given by $[P_k^n] \circ J^1 x_{i_1} \circ \ldots \circ J^n x_{i_n}$. In addition, if P^* and Q^* are any predicates of the structure I, then so too are $\neg P^*$ (the function that assigns to any sequence v the negation of the formula of Q that P^* assigns to v), their disjunction, $P^* \vee Q^*$ (the function that assigns to every sequence, v the disjunction of the formulas that P^* and Q^* assign to v), their conjunction, the hypothetical with either one as antecedent and the other as consequent, and so forth. Finally, for each i, let $(\forall x_i)P^*$ be the function that assigns to any sequence v the formula that P^* assigns to v, prefixed by the universal quantifier with respect to x_i [similarly for the function $(\exists x)P^*$]. Close off the set Pr by taking it as the smallest set of functions of E^* to S that satisfies the preceding conditions. Finally, introduce for each i the mapping U_i on the predicates of I as follows: For each P^* in Pr, let $U_i(P^*)$ be $\forall x_i(P^* \circ J_{x_i}^i)$ – that is, a function from E^* to S that for any sequence v of E^* assigns the formula of Q that consists of the formula of Q assigned by $(P^* \circ J_{x_i}^i)$ to v prefixed by the universal quantifier with respect to x_i. It is a long process, but straightforward, to show with this characterization of U_i [and the corresponding one for E_i, which defines $E_i(P^*)$ in this structure as $(\exists x_i)(P^* \circ J_{x_i}^i)$] that (1) $U_i(P^*) \Rightarrow^* (P \circ J_e^i)$ for every variable e in E and (2) $U_i(P^*)$ is the weakest to do so. Similarly, the characteristic conditions for $E_i(P^*)$ also hold. Thus, we have the following result:

Theorem 20.32. *There is an extended implication structure $I = \langle E, Pr, S, \Rightarrow \rangle$ in which S consists of the formulas of Q, a formulation of first-order quantification theory.*

It is worth noting in passing that as a consequence of the definition of "$\Rightarrow^*$" of the structure I, it follows that A is a thesis of I (for all B in S, $B \Rightarrow^* A$) if and only if the closure of A is a theorem of Q.

21

Identity

In the preceding chapter we introduced the notion of an extended implication structure $\langle E, Pr, S, \Rightarrow \rangle$ in order to study predication. The idea was to show how an account of predicates could be developed within the framework that we adopted for the logical operators. Once an account of predicates was in place, we then characterized the universal and existential quantifiers within the same framework. Predicates, it will be recalled, were taken to be mappings of E^* to S, where E^* consists of all the infinite sequences of the members of E. The theory of quantification was developed without singling out any predicates in particular.

There is one particular predicate, however, that is worth isolating for further study. The identity predicate has traditionally been regarded as a special predicate of logical theory, although it has sometimes been questioned that it is properly part of "logic." In any case, the identity relation or predicate usually is regarded as a predicate of two arguments that has a characteristic connection with the predicates of the structure under study. We shall see that in the characterization we give for it, it has strong affinities with the characterization of the other logical operators. And it will be shown how its reflexivity, symmetry, and transitivity follow from that characterization. There is, in addition, a traditional connection, due principally to Leibniz, between the identity of e and e' and the sharing of all the one-argument predicates of a structure (those whose support has only one element). It will be seen that on our account of identity, if e is identical with e', then e and e' share all the one-argument predicates of the structure. The converse, however, is not true in all extended implication structures.

Let $\langle E, Pr, S, \Rightarrow \rangle$ be an extended implication structure. We shall characterize an identity predicate I as a special function of essentially two arguments [its support $K(I)$ has just two members]. Let $K(I) = \{n, m\}$. Furthermore, for any e and e' in E, we can then introduce the new predicate $(I \circ J_e^n \circ J_{e'}^m)$, which is in the structure if I is in the structure. This predicate has the feature that it is, for any e and e' in E, a constant predicate:

Theorem 21.1. *If I is a predicate on an extended implication structure, with support $K(I) = \{n, m\}$, then for any sequences s and s' in E^*, $(I \circ J_e^n J_{e'}^m)(s') \Longleftrightarrow^* (I \circ J_e^n \circ J_{e'}^m)(s')$.*

Proof. For any s and s' in E^*, $(I \circ J_e^n \circ J_{e'}^m)(s) \Longleftrightarrow^* (I \circ J_e^n \circ J_{e'}^m)(s')$ if and only if $I(J_e^n \circ J_{e'}^m(s)) \Longleftrightarrow^* I(J_e^n \circ J_{e'}^m(s'))$. Now the sequences $J_e^n \circ J_{e'}^m(s)$ and $J_e^n \circ J_{e'}^m(s')$ agree on $\{n, m\}$, the support of I because the nth member of both sequences is e, and the mth member of both is e'. Therefore, by the definition of the support of a predicate, it follows that the predicate I is equivalent on them. Since the predicate $(I \circ J_e^n \circ J_{e'}^m)$ always has the same value (up to equivalence by "$\Longrightarrow$") on all the sequences of E^*, we shall indicate that constant predicate by "$I(e, e')$."

Definition 21.1. I is an identity predicate on an implication structure if and only if its support has two members and the following conditions are satisfied:

I_1. For any predicate P of the structure, any e and e' of E, and any natural number i, we have $(P \circ J_e^i)$, $I(e, e') \Longrightarrow^* (P \circ J_{e'}^i)$, as well as $(P \circ J_{e'}^i)$, $I(e, e') \Longrightarrow^* (P \circ J_e^i)$, and

I_2. $I(e, e')$ is the weakest predicate of the structure to satisfy the first condition. That is, if any predicate I' of the structure has a two-member support and satisfies the first condition, then $I' \Longrightarrow^* I$.

The first condition is the counterpart of the familiar requirement of substitutivity on the identity relation. It is the one that is used to distinguish the identity relation from the other equivalence relations. These conditions on the identity predicate are reminiscent of the usual ones that were imposed upon the logical operators, for the first condition on $I(e, e')$ is a filter condition, and the second condition selects out those items that are the weakest to satisfy the first condition. We have given the simple version, though the official version (given later) is the parametric one (the full parametric version, which is needed for a proof of the transitivity of identity).

There are several consequences of this characterization of the identity predicate. The first one is that the identity predicate is uniquely described, up to implication. That is,

Theorem 21.2. *If I and I^* are identity predicates on some extended implication structure, then for any e and e' in E, $I(e, e') \Longleftrightarrow^* I^*(e, e')$.*

Proof. The proof is straightforward. For all the predicates P of the structure, and for all i, and for all e and e' in E, $I(e, e')$ satisfies the first condition and is the weakest to do so. But, by hypothesis, $I^*(e, e')$ also satisfies the first condition. Consequently, $I^*(e, e') \Rightarrow^* I(e, e')$. Similarly, since I^* is assumed to be an identity predicate of the structure, it satisfies the first condition and is the weakest to do so. But $I(e, e')$ satisfies the first condition as well (since it is an identity predicate of the structure). Consequently, $I(e, e') \Rightarrow^* I(e, e')$. Therefore, for all e and e' in E, $I(e, e') \Leftrightarrow^* I^*(e, e')$.

The remaining results show that the identity predicate is reflexive, symmetric, and transitive.

Theorem 21.3 (reflexivity). *Let I be the identity predicate on an extended implication structure $\langle E, Pr, S, \Rightarrow \rangle$. Then for all e in E, $I(e, e)$ is a thesis of the structure.*

Proof. From the first condition on identity, for any predicate P of the structure, and any e in E, $(P \circ J_e^i)$, $I(e, e) \Rightarrow^* (P \circ j_e^i)$. However, every predicate (or member of S) of the structure satisfies this condition. Therefore, since $I(e, e)$ is the weakest of those that satisfy the condition, it follows that $Q \Rightarrow^* I(e, e)$ for all Q (predicate, or member of S). Therefore $I(e, e)$ is a thesis of the structure.

Theorem 21.4 (symmetry). *Let I be the identity predicate on an extended implication structure $\langle E, Pr, S. \Rightarrow \rangle$. Then for any e and e' in E, $I(e, e') \Leftrightarrow^* I(e', e)$.*

Proof. From the first condition on identity, $(P \circ J_{e'}^i)$, $I(e', e) \Rightarrow^* (P \circ J_e^i)$, and $(P \circ J_e^i)$, $I(e', e) \Rightarrow^* (P \circ J_{e'}^i)$. Therefore $I(e', e)$ satisfies the first condition on identity for $I(e, e')$. Consequently, $I(e, e')$ is weaker than $I(e', e)$. That is, $I(e', e) \Rightarrow^* I(e, e')$. On the other hand, $(P \circ J_e^i)$, $I(e, e') \Rightarrow^* (P \circ J_{e'}^i)$, and $(P \circ j_{e'}^i)$, $I(e, e') \Rightarrow^* (P \circ J_e^i)$. That is, $I(e, e')$ satisfies the first condition on identity for $I(e', e)$. Since $I(e', e)$ is the weakest to satisfy that condition, it follows that $I(e, e') \Rightarrow^* I(e', e)$. Consequently, $I(e, e') \Leftrightarrow^* I(e', e)$ for all e and e' in E.

In order to prove that the identity predicate is transitive, we shall need a parameterized characterization of it.

We shall say that a predicate I is an identity predicate on the extended implication structure $\langle E, Pr, S, \Rightarrow \rangle$ if and only if its support has two members, and the following parameterized conditions are satisfied:

I_{p1}. For any predicate P of the structure, any e and e' of E, any natural number i, and any finite subset Γ of predicates or members of S, we have $(P \circ J_e^i), I(e, e') \Rightarrow^{*\Gamma} (P \circ J_{e'}^i)$, as well as $(P \circ J_{e'}^i), I(e, e')$ $\Rightarrow^{*\Gamma} (P \circ J_e^i)$, and

I_{p2}. $I(e, e')$ is the weakest predicate to satisfy the first condition.

Theorem 21.5 (transitivity). *Let I be the identity predicate on an extended implication structure $\langle E, Pr, S, \Rightarrow \rangle$. Then for any e, e', and e'' in E, $I(e, e'), I(e', e'') \Rightarrow^* I(e, e'')$.*

Proof. From the parametric conditions for $I(e, e')$, we have (1) $(P \circ J_e^i), I(e, e') \Rightarrow^{*\Gamma} (P \circ J_{e'}^I)$ and (2) $(P \circ J_{e'}^i), I(e, e') \Rightarrow^{*\Gamma}$ $(P \circ J_e^i)$. The identity conditions for $I(e', e'')$ yield (3) $(P \circ J_{e'}^i)$, $I(e', e'') \Rightarrow^{*\Gamma} (P \circ J_{e''}^i)$ and (4) $(P \circ J_{e''}^i), I(e', e'') \Rightarrow^{*\Gamma} (P \circ J_{e'}^i)$. Consequently, $(P \circ J_e^i), I(e, e'), I(e', e'') \Rightarrow^{*1} (P \circ J_{e''}^i)$, and $(P \circ J_{e''}^i), I(e, e'), I(e', e'') \Rightarrow^{*\Gamma} (P \circ J_e^i)$. Let Γ be the singleton $\{I(e', e'')\}$. Then $(P \circ J_e^i), I(e, e') \Rightarrow^{*\Gamma} (P \circ J_{e''}^i)$, and $(P \circ J_{e''}^i)$, $I(e, e') \Rightarrow^{*\Gamma} (P \circ J_e^i)$. However, by the second parametric condition, $I(e, e'')$ is the weakest (under "$\Rightarrow^{*\Gamma}$") for which these two implications hold. Therefore $I(e, e') \Rightarrow^{*\Gamma} I(e, e'')$. Consequently, $I(e, e'), I(e', e'') \Rightarrow^* I(e, e'')$.

It is, of course, no surprise to have reflexivity, symmetry, and transitivity as consequences of a substitutivity condition. However, in the usual case this is shown for some extension of a formalized first-order theory of quantification. In this case, however, the same results can be obtained for a broad spectrum of extended implicational structures.

It is worth noting some connections between the identity operator and the one-argument predicates of the extended structure. If we have an extended implication structure $\langle E, Pr, S, \Rightarrow \rangle$, and P is any one-argument predicate of it, then for any e in E we can form the new predicate $(P \circ J_e^i)$ [where we assume that the support of P, $K(P)$, is the set $\{i\}$]. The predicate $(P \circ J_e^i)$ is a mapping of E^* to S, of course, but it is a constant predicate. That is,

Theorem 21.6. *If P is any predicate of $\langle E, Pr, S, \Rightarrow \rangle$ such that $K(P) = \{i\}$, then for all sequences s and s' in E^*, $(P \circ J_e^i)(s) \Leftrightarrow^* (P \circ J_e^i)(s')$.*

Proof. We know that $(P \circ J_e^i)(s) \Longleftrightarrow^* (P \circ J_e^i)(s')$ holds if and only if $P(J_e^i(s)) \Longleftrightarrow^* P(J_e^i(s'))$. Now the sequences $J_e^i(s)$ and $J_e^i(s')$ agree on the support of P (the ith members of both sequences are e). Therefore the values of P on those sequences are equivalent, according to the definition of the support of a predicate.

Since the predicate $(P \circ J_e^i)$ has the same value (up to equivalence under "$\Longrightarrow$") for all sequences in E^*, we shall denote that constant predicate by "$P(e)$." Similarly, "$P(e')$" denotes the constant predicate $(P \circ J_{e'}^i)$.

The first simple result we want to note is that if P is any one-argument predicate P of the structure, and $T = \langle K, L \rangle$ is any strong bisection of the structure (a truth-value assignment), and s is any sequence of E^*, and $I(e, e')(s)$ is true (belongs to L), then $P(e)(s)$ is true (is in L) if and only if $P(e')(s)$ is true (belongs to L) (i.e., e and e' share all the one-argument predicates of the structure). That is,

Theorem 21.7. *If $I = \langle E, Pr, S, \Longrightarrow \rangle$ is an extended implication structure, and $T = \langle K, L \rangle$ is any strong bisection on I, and e and e' are any members of E, and s is any sequence of E^*, and $I(e, e')(s)$ is in L, then for every one-argument predicate P of the structure, $P(e)(s)$ is in L if and only if $P(e')(s)$ is in L.*

Proof. From the first condition on identity, for any predicate P of the structure, $I(e, e'), (P \circ J_e^i) \Longrightarrow^* (P \circ J_{e'}^i)$ for any i and any e and e' in E. In particular, let P be any predicate whose support $K(P) = \{i\}$. Consequently, for any sequence s in E^*, we have $I(e, e')(s), (P \circ J_e^i) (s) \Longrightarrow (P \circ J_{e'}^i)(s)$. However, $(P \circ J_e^i)(s) \Longleftrightarrow P(e)(s)$, and $(P \circ J_{e'}^i)(s) \Longleftrightarrow P(e')(s)$ so that $I(e, e')(s), P(e)(s) \Longrightarrow P(e')(s)$. Thus, if $I(e, e')(s)$ is in L, then $P(e')(s)$ is in L if $P(e)(s)$ is in L. The converse is proved similarly.

We now wish to consider a converse to this observation. If in any extended structure e and e' share all the one-argument predicates of that structure, does it follow that e and e' are identical? The answer is negative. That is,

Theorem 21.8. *There is an extended implication structure $\langle E, Pr, S, \Longrightarrow \rangle$, a strong bisection $T = \langle K, L \rangle$, and some e and e' of E that share all the one-argument predicates of the structure, but "$I(e, e')(s)$" is false (is in K).*

Proof. Consider the extended implication structure in which E has only two members e and e', $S = \{A_1, A_2, A\}$, and the implication relation on S is as follows:

$$A_1$$
$$\downarrow$$
$$A_2$$
$$\downarrow$$
$$A$$

Furthermore, let $T = \langle K, L \rangle$ be the strong bisection on S that consists in taking K to be $\{A_1, A_2\}$, and taking L to be the remainder of S. T is a strong bisection of S. Let Pr, the predicates of this structure, contain all the one-argument predicates that are shared by e and e'. That is, if P is a mapping of E^* to S with unit support $[K(P) = \{i\}$ for some $i]$ such that for every s in E^*, $\{P(e)(s), P(e')(s)\}$ is either a subset of K or a subset of L, then P is among the predicates of the structure. We do not care whatever else may be included among the predicates of the structure, just so long as these predicates are included. Then, even though the predicates of the structure contain all those that are shared by e and e', nevertheless $I(e, e')(s)$ is in K. The reason is this: Let Q be the following mapping of E^* to S. For any sequence s in E^*, $Q(s)$ is A_1 if s_i is e' and A if S_i is e'. Since E has only these two members, the predicate Q is a well-defined one-argument function from E^* to S [its support $K(Q) = \{i\}$]. Consequently, it belongs to the predicates of the structure. We let $Q(e)$ be the predicate $(Q \circ J_e^i)$ (which, as we noted, is constant). Similarly for $Q(e')$. It follows that $I(e, e')(s)\ Q(e')(s) \Rightarrow Q(e)(s)$. However, $Q(e)(s)$ is A_1, since for any s in E^*, $(Q \circ J_e^i)(s)$ is $Q(J_e^i(s))$, and the ith member of the sequence $J_e^i(s)$ is e. Similarly, $Q(e')(s)$ is A_2. Consequently, $I(e, e')(s), A_2 \Rightarrow A_1$. However, in the structure just described, the hypothetical $H(A_2, A_1)$ exists. In fact, $H(A_2, A_1)$ is just the element A_1, since A_1 is the weakest member of the structure that together with A_2 implies (by "$\Rightarrow$") A_1. So $I(e, e')(s) \Rightarrow A_1$, since $I(e, e')(s) \Rightarrow H(A_2, A_1)$. However, A_1 is in K. Since L is closed under "$\Rightarrow$," $I(e, e')(s)$ is in K.

In the preceding example of a structure in which the identity of e and e' fails, even though all the one-argument predicates of the structure are shared by e and e', we used a nonclassical structure $[NN(A_2) \not\Rightarrow A_2]$.

The natural question is whether or not there are classical extended implication structures in which it turns out that "$I(e, e')$" is false, despite the fact that e and e' share all the one-argument predicates of the structure. Here is a simple example: Let E be $\{e, e'\}$, and let the set of predicates be the same as in the preceding example, but take S to be as follows:

Let us suppose, in addition, that A_0, A_1, and A_2 constitute K, and $\{A_3\}$ is L. The structure is classical, since $N(A_0) = A_3$, $N(A_1) = A_2$, $N(A_2) = A_1$, and $N(A_3) = A_0$. Although the bisection is strong, it is not normal (see Chapter 19).

The extended implication structure just described certainly is a classical structure of the kind that satisfies Theorem 21.8. Nevertheless, the nonnormal character of the truth assignment on the structure may lead one to think of the associated truth assignments as true, but tricky. It is an open question whether or not there is a classical structure satisfying the conditions of Theorem 21.8 on which the distribution of truth values is normal.

22

Special structures I: Logical operators on individuals: Mereology reconstituted

22.1 Introduction

It has been a recurrent theme in this study that the logical operators are functions on implication structures, simple or extended, and that these structures are so varied in their objects that the study of the logical operators is truly topic-neutral.

The conjunction and negation operators, for example, are defined over all implication structures, so that one can think of conjunctions of sets, statements, properties, individuals, and so forth. The subject in each case is only as interesting as the implication relations with respect to which the operators are relativized. Any set, and in particular a set of objects (or a set of names of those objects), can be thought of as having an implication relation on it. The question is whether or not there is an implication relation on a set of individuals, or the set of names of those individuals, that has theoretical interest. We shall call implication relations on individuals *objectual implication* relations (and implication on names of individuals, *nominal implication*).

It might be thought that the whole idea of an implication relation holding between individuals is incoherent, since implication is a relation between truth-bearers. On the more general view that we have advocated, the fact that individuals and names are not generally truth-bearers is no impediment to the development of a theory of the logical operators on them. All that is required, since all the logical operators are relativized to implication relations, is that an implication relation be specified for them.

We shall introduce an implication relation "$\Rightarrow^i$" on a set of individuals. We think of these objects as individuals because we regard them as subject to a certain relation, the whole–part relation, which will be explained below.

We shall see below that there is the striking but simple result that *with the choice of "$\Rightarrow^i$" the key concepts of the calculus of individuals are just the logical operators relativized to "$\Rightarrow^i$."* For example, disjunction (relative to "$\Rightarrow^i$") turns out to be the familiar notion of the sum of

individuals in the calculus of individuals. The details for disjunction and
the other logical operators will be studied in the following section. In a
sense, then, the calculus of individuals is just the study of the logical
operators with respect to a natural notion of implication on individuals.

Thus, even if we did not have the pioneering work of Lesniewski,
Leonard, and Goodman to lead us, the concepts that they introduced
for the study of individuals could be obtained by seeing what the logical
operators are with respect to a certain implication relation. And *the
theorems and nontheorems of the calculus of individuals turn out to be
just the familiar logical theses and nontheses of classical implication
structures*. This is the same kind of result that we saw when we noted
that the central algebraic operations of Tarski's calculus of systems were
just the logical operators with respect to a special implication relation on
Tarskian theories, and the theses of the calculus of systems turned out to
be the theses of a nonclassical implication structure.

In other words, just as with the Tarskian calculus of systems, the
Lesniewski–Leonard–Goodman calculus of individuals is a study of
the behavior of the logical operators with respect to specially chosen
implication relations.

In Section 9.3 we gave three axioms governing the whole–part relation ("$<$") and the definitions of the sum (SUM) and product (PRO) of
any two individuals, as well as the negate (NEG) of any individual.

Exercise 22.1. Show that if every individual that overlaps A
overlaps B, then A is a part of B.

There are several quite simple theorems that follow, though we leave
them as an exercise for the reader. They look like results that are special
to the calculus of individuals. But in fact, they are, as we shall see later,
merely the counterparts of some familiar theorems of the classical
sentential calculus.

Exercise 22.2

(a) $A < \mathrm{SUM}(A, B)$ and $B < \mathrm{SUM}(A, B)$ for any A and B in S.
(b) $\mathrm{PRO}(A, B) < A$ and $\mathrm{PRO}(A, B) < B$ for any A and B in S.
(c) $\mathrm{SUM}(A, \mathrm{SUM}(B, C)) = \mathrm{SUM}(\mathrm{SUM}(A, B), C)$ for any A,
    B, and C in S.
(d) If $A < C$ and $B < C$, then $\mathrm{SUM}(A, B) < C$ for any A, B,
    and C in S.
(e) $\mathrm{SUM}(A, B) < C$ if and only if $A < C$ and $B < C$.

(f) $C <$ PRO(A, B) if and only if $C < A$ and $C < B$. (This is just the characterization given for the product of individuals.)

It should be noted that neither "If PRO$(A, B) < C$, then $A < C$ and $B < C$" nor "If $C <$ SUM(A, B), then $C < A$ and $C < B$" is a theorem of the calculus of individuals. We wish to show that the operations of SUM, PRO, and NEG on individuals are just the logical operators in a special classical implication structure (that is, NEG is the negation operator on that structure and is classical). The results of Exercise 22.2 (a)–(f) are just the usual theses for the logical operators of disjunction and conjunction in that classical structure. We must first describe some objectual implication relations.

22.2 Objectual implication relations

Let S be any nonempty set, with a part–whole relation "$<$" on it, that satisfies the conditions for such a relation (Section 9.3). Thus, we think of the members of S as individuals. Recall that for individuals, we defined an objectual implication relation "$\Rightarrow^i$" as follows (Section 9.3.2): For any $A, A_1, \ldots, A_n$ and B in S,

1. $A \Rightarrow^i B$ if and only if $A < B$ and
2. $A_1, \ldots, A_n \Rightarrow^i B$ if and only if for every C in S, if $C \Rightarrow^i A_i$ for all A_i, then $C \Rightarrow^i B$.

We intend to study the logical operators when they are relativized to the implication relation "$\Rightarrow^i$." It should be noted that the dual of this implication relation is also an implication relation on individuals, with some interesting features of its own, which we shall not pursue here.

> **Exercise 22.3.** Let "$\Rightarrow^{i\wedge}$" be the dual of "$\Rightarrow^i$." Show that for any $A_1, \ldots, A_n$ and B in S, $A_1, \ldots, A_n \Rightarrow^{i\wedge} B$ holds if and only if $B \Rightarrow^i$ SUM$(A_1, \ldots, A_n)$. That is B is a part of the sum of all the A_i's.

22.3 The logical operators on an objectual structure

Let us, for the sake of brevity, refer to the implication structure $I = \langle S, \Rightarrow^i \rangle$ as an *objectual structure*, where S is a nonempty set with a part–whole relation "$<$" defined over it, and "$\Rightarrow^i$" is the objectual implication relation that was described above. We are now able to see that *the individual forming operations SUM, PRO, and NEG are just the logical operators of disjunction, conjunction, and negation on the objectual implication structure.*

22.3.1 The disjunction of individuals

Here the main result is given by the following:

Theorem 22.1 (disjunction is SUM). *Let $I = \langle S \Rightarrow^i \rangle$ be the objectual implication structure described above, and let D_i be the disjunction operator on I. Then for any two individuals A and B of S, $D_i(A, B) = SUM(A, B)$.*

Proof. For any disjunction operator on a structure, $A \Rightarrow D(A, B)$, and $B \Rightarrow D(A, B)$. Therefore, in the particular structure $I, A \Rightarrow^i D_i(A, B)$, and $B \Rightarrow^i D_i(A, B)$. Consequently, $A < D_i(A, B)$, and $B < D_i(A, B)$. Therefore, by Exercise 22.2(d), we know that $SUM(A, B) < D_i(A, B)$. The second condition on disjunctions requires, in this case, that if $A \Rightarrow^i T$ and $B \Rightarrow^i T$, then $D_i(A, B) \Rightarrow^i T$. Now we know, by Exercise 22.2(a), that $A \Rightarrow^i SUM(A, B)$, since $A < SUM(A, B)$. Similarly, $B \Rightarrow^i SUM(A, B)$. Therefore, by the second condition on disjunctions, $D_i(A, B) \Rightarrow^i SUM(A, B)$. Consequently, $D_i(A, B) < SUM(A, B)$. Since $D_i(A, B)$ is a part of $SUM(A, B)$, and $SUM(A, B)$ is a part of $D_i(A, B)$, it follows from the characterization of identity in the calculus of individuals that $D_i(A, B) = SUM(A, B)$.

22.3.2 The conjunction of individuals

Here the main result is that the conjunction of any two individuals is identical with their product. That is,

Theorem 22.2 (Conjunction is PRO). *Let $I = \langle S, \Rightarrow^i \rangle$ be the objectual implication structure described earlier, and let C_i be the conjunction operator on I. Then for any two individuals A and B in S, $C_i(A, B) = PRO(A, B)$.*

Proof. In any implication structure, $C(A, B) \Rightarrow A$, and $C(A, B) \Rightarrow B$. Therefore $C_i(A, B) \Rightarrow^i A$, and $C_i(A, B) \Rightarrow^i B$. Consequently, $C_i(A, B) < A$, and $C_i(A, B) < B$. Therefore, by Exercise 22.2(f), $C_i(A, B) < PRO(A, B)$. Moreover, by Exercise 22.2(b), $PRO(A, B) < A$, and $PRO(A, B) < B$.

Consequently, $PRO(A, B) \Rightarrow^i A$, and $PRO(A, B) \Rightarrow^i B$. However, by the second condition on conjunctions, $C_i(A, B)$ is the weakest member of S (using "$\Rightarrow^i$") of all those that imply A as well as B. Therefore $PRO(A, B) \Rightarrow^i C_i(A, B)$. Consequently, $PRO(A, B) < C_i(A, B)$. Since $PRO(A, B)$ is a part of $C_i(A, B)$, and $C_i(A, B)$ is a part of $PRO(A, B)$, $PRO(A, B) = C_i(A, B)$.

It is worth noting that the conjunction of two individuals exists if and only if they have a part in common.

22.3.3 The negation of individuals

The main result is that the negation of any individual A is exactly that individual which is called the negate of A in the calculus of individuals. That is,

Theorem 22.3 (negation is NEG). *Let* $I = \langle S, \Rightarrow^i \rangle$ *be the objectual structure described earlier, and let* N_i *be the negation operator on* I. *Then for all* A *in* S, $N_i(A) = NEG(A)$.

Proof. Notice first that for any A in S, A, $NEG(A) \Rightarrow^i B$ for all B in S, for there is no C for which $C < A$ and $C < NEG(A)$; the latter implies that C does not overlap A, and the former implies that C does overlap A. By the first condition on the negation operator, A, $N_i(A) \Rightarrow^i B$ for all B in S, and by the second condition, it is the weakest member in S to do so. Therefore $NEG(A) \Rightarrow^i N_i(A)$. Consequently, $NEG(A) < N_i(A)$. It remains only to be shown that $N_i(A) < NEG(A)$. Notice that if A, $T \Rightarrow^i B$ for all B in S, then $T \Rightarrow^i NEG(A)$. For suppose that A, $T \Rightarrow^i B$ for all B in S. Assume that T overlaps A. Then there is some C such that $C < T$ and $C < A$. Since A, $T \Rightarrow^i B$ for all B in S, $C < B$, for all B in S. In particular, $C < NEG(A)$. However, by the characterization of $NEG(A)$, $C < NEG(A)$ if and only if C does not overlap A. But that is impossible, since $C < A$. Therefore T does not overlap A. Consequently, $T < NEG(A)$, so that $T \Rightarrow^i NEG(A)$. By the first condition on negations, A, $N_i(A) \Rightarrow^i B$ for all B in S. Consequently, $N_i(A) \Rightarrow^i NEG(A)$. Thus, $N_i(A) = NEG(A)$.

Theorem 22.4 (NEG as classical negation). *Let I be the objectual implication structure described earlier. Then NEG is a classical negation operator on I.*

Proof. We see from the preceding theorem that $NEG(A) = N_i(A)$, where N_i is the negation operator on I. Since $A \Rightarrow NN(A)$ on any implication structure, we have, in particular, that $A \Rightarrow^i N_i N_i(A)$ for all A in S. To show that N_i is classical, we have to show that $N_i N_i(A) \Rightarrow^i A$ for all A in S. Let C be any element of S that overlaps $NEG(NEG(A))$, but does not overlap A. Then, since C overlaps $NEG(NEG(A))$, C is not a part of $NEG(A)$. However, if C does not overlap A, C is a part of $NEG(A)$. That is impossible. Therefore, if C overlaps $NEG(NEG(A))$, then C overlaps A. Consequently, by Exercise 22.3, $NEG(NEG(A)) < A$. Therefore $NEG(NEG(A)) \Rightarrow^i A$.

In the preceding two theorems, $NEG(A)$ is $N_i(A)$ for all A for which NEG is defined. However, in standard formulations of the calculus of individuals, NEG may not be defined for all individuals. In particular it is not defined for the universal individual U (if it exists) – that individual which has every individual as a part. In fact, if the universal individual exists [as it will if for any A the SUM of A and $NEG(A)$ exists], then $NEG(U)$ exists if and only if there is an individual that is a part of every individual. For suppose that $NEG(U)$ exists; then, since $B < U$ for all B, $NEG(U) < NEG(B)$ for all B. Since NEG is classical negation on this structure, for every A there is some A^* such that A is $NEG(A^*)$. Therefore $NEG(U) < A$ for all A. Conversely, if there is some V such that $V < A$ for all A, then V satisfies the two conditions for the negation of U. Therefore $V = NEG(U)$. We leave the proof as an exercise.

Thus, the special results in the calculus of individuals listed in Exercise 22.2 are just familiar theses of standard logic when the logical operators act on the objectual structure we have been studying: Exercise 22.2(a) says that A and B each imply the disjunction of A and B; 22.2(b) says that the conjunction of A and B implies A as well as B; 22.2(c) is just the associativity of disjunction; 22.2(d) is the familiar condition that if A (as well as B) implies C, then their disjunction implies C; 22.2(e) is the result that the disjunction of A and B implies C if and only if each disjunct implies C; 22.2(f) tells us that C implies the conjunction of A with B if and only if C implies A (as well as B).

There are simple but systematic connections between certain kinds of individuals and certain kinds of predicates that have a use in the calculus of individuals. Thus, if SUM(A, B) is the individual that is the sum of individuals A and B, then it is interesting to ask what kind of predicate Q it is that always yields the following: If Q(SUM(A, B)), then $Q(A)$ and $Q(B)$. Let us, following Goodman, call a predicate *dissective* if and only if, if $Q(C)$, and $D < C$, then $Q(D)$. As he notes, "is smaller than Utah" is dissective. Then we have the following result, whose proof we leave for the reader:

> **Exercise 22.4 (SUMs and dissective predicates).** On the objectual implication structure I, the predicate Q is dissective if and only if for every A and B in S, if Q(SUM(A, B)), then $Q(A)$ and $Q(B)$.

Again, following Goodman, a predicate is *expansive* if and only if whenever it holds for any individual C, it also holds for any individual that has C as a part. There is a systematic connection between products of individuals and expansive predicates:

> **Exercise 22.5 (PROs and expansive predicates).** On the objectual implication structure I, Q is an expansive predicate if and only if for all A and B in S, if Q(PRO(A, B)), then $Q(A)$ and $Q(B)$.

Following Goodman, a one-place predicate is called *nucleative* if and only if whenever $Q(A)$ and $Q(B)$, then Q(PRO(A, B)), and it is called *collective* if and only if whenever $Q(A)$ and $Q(B)$, then Q(SUM(A, B)). We leave it as an exercise to show the following:

> **Exercise 22.6.** On the objectual implication structure I, a one-place predicate Q is such that [Q(SUM(A, B)) if and only if $Q(A)$ and $Q(B)$ (for all A and B in S)] if and only if Q is collective and dissective. Similarly, [Q(PRO(A, B)) if and only if $Q(A)$ and $Q(B)$ (for all A and B in S)] if and only if Q is nucleative and expansive.

Sums and products of individuals play prominent roles in the calculus of individuals, and there is a growing literature that has tried to put these concepts to other philosophical work. Given any individuals A and B, we have the notion of an individual that is their sum and another that is their product. These are, as we saw, just the result of using the disjunction and conjunction operators with respect to the objectual implication relation.

With very little extra effort we can introduce a new implication relation on the names of individuals, rather than on the individuals themselves. If we consider, for example, the conjunction operator, or the negation operator with respect to this nominal implication relation, we obtain for any two names a name that is their conjunction, or a name that is the negation of some name. This is a handy thing to have for linguistics, since linguists do have a notion of phrasal conjunction, the conjunction of expressions each of which refers. Thus, they think of "Dick and Jane" as a conjunctive name, and on our account of conjunction this can be understood in exactly the same way that any conjunction is understood when it is relativized to an implication relation. The fact that neither "Dick" nor "Jane" has a truth value is no obstacle, on our account, of their having a conjunction. Whether or not there is a simple and fruitful use for such conjunctive names is an open question.

22.4 Nominal implication

Let S be a nonempty set of names of individuals. For any $A_1^*, \ldots, A_n^*$ and B^* in S, we shall say that $A_1^*, \ldots, A_n^* \Rightarrow^n B^*$ if and only if $A_1, \ldots, A_n \Rightarrow^i B$, where the starred items are the names of the respective unstarred ones. It is a straightforward check that "$\Rightarrow^n$" is an implication relation.

Although, as we have mentioned, the two implication relations, the objectual one and its corresponding nominal one, are not coextensional (since they are relations on different sets), nevertheless it is of course true that any two names are equivalent (using "$\Rightarrow^n$") if and only if the things they name are identical. That is,

> **Exercise 22.7.** If A and B are any individuals, and A^* and B^* are their respective names, then $A^* \Leftrightarrow^n B^*$ if and only if $A = B$.

The conjunction, disjunction, and negation of names follow the general pattern of those operators on individuals – as one might expect, given the close connection between the objectual and nominal implication relations.

The use of "$\Rightarrow^n$" on names of individuals requires that the conjunction operator acting on a pair of names yield a name as their conjunction. In a similar vein is the discussion between P. Geach and P. Strawson regarding whether or not predicates have negations, but names do not. Since the negation operator, relative to "$\Rightarrow^n$," yields a notion of the negation of a name, there is no question of the coherence of such a notion. Whether or not such notions will prove helpful, for example, in analyzing the implications of English statements to each other, is still an open question. It need not turn out that the notion of the conjunction of two names, "Bob" and "Margaret," is helpful in understanding the implicational differences between "Bob and Margaret are married" and "Bob and Margaret are philosophers." If the concept of a conjunctive name does not help bring out the differences between such sentences, perhaps a relativization to another implication relation will fare better. Of course, there is always the possibility that none of the battery of conjunctions of names will prove useful. However, our theory of the logical operators provides a number of possibilities that would otherwise be unavailable. Whether or not any of those possibilities will prove to be viable is an open question.

23

Special structures II: Interrogatives and implication relations

23.1 Elementary questions about interrogatives

There has been some penetrating work on the logic of interrogatives, but it is not the aim of this study to review those findings. It is well known that there are interestingly different kinds of questions that count as interrogatives, and it has also been suggested that an account of questions can profitably be seen as part of the study of a more general notion. That is, if, roughly speaking, the logic of questions (erotetic logic) is seen as the study of wanted answers, then the somewhat more general setting would consider the notion of a relevant answer. And still other, more general settings for the logic of questions have been suggested.[1] Perhaps the most complex issue that has to be faced is the typology of questions, since each study seems to use a different classification. No doubt this reflects, in part, the variety of theoretical devices that are brought to bear on the subject.

In this chapter we want to show how the use of a special implication relation among certain kinds of questions can be used to answer some elementary problems about questions. We shall not introduce a special typology to sort out different kinds of questions from each other. The problems that we shall consider lie at a rather elementary level and do not seem to need a more subtle classification for their discussion. A more detailed classification will eventually be necessary, because it is only with the aid of more refined structures that anything interesting can be proved and that anything accurate can be said about whether specific sentences in English are examples of one type of interrogative rather than another.

The simple problems that we wish to consider concern the logical character of questions: When is a question a hypothetical? When is it a conjunction, or a disjunction, and so forth? Given that our characterization of the logical operators relativizes them to implication relations, it is natural on our account of these operators to ask if there is an appropriate implication for interrogatives.

If we wish to inquire whether or not the statement "if you have disposable income, will you invest it?" is a hypothetical, then the question that has to be settled is whether or not it enters into the appropriate implications with "You have disposable income" and the interrogative "Will you spend your disposable income?" If a theory of hypotheticals requires them to act on truth-bearers then there is an obvious obstacle to regarding such a statement as a hypothetical. For such reasons, it is occasionally suggested that interrogatives can be "reduced" to or are "identical" with statements that have truth values. On our account, however, there is no restriction to truth-bearers. What is required, however, is an appropriate implication relation.

It is sometimes suggested that the logic of questions ought to be developed in analogy with the logic of statements. I think that it is not a case of an analogy. The logic in either case is given by the logical operators, but the relevant implication relation for interrogatives is different from those used for statements that have truth values. It is also sometimes suggested that it is simply wrong to think of the logic of questions as a deductive system. That would be to take the analogy too far. Thus, Belnap and Steel (1976, p. 1) assert that "absolutely the wrong thing is to think it [erotetic logic] is a logic in the sense of a deductive system, since one would thus be driven to the pointless task of inventing an inferential scheme in which questions or interrogatives could serve as premises and conclusions. This is to say that what one wants erotetic logic to imitate of the rest of logic is not its proof theory but rather its other two grand parts, grammar (syntax) and semantics."

I agree with the first part of their advice, but disagree with the second part. Although we shall introduce an implication relation for interrogatives, it is not a deducibility relation involving premises and conclusion. As for the second part of their advice, it should by now be obvious that the tasks of a logical theory of statements can be carried out without appeal to either syntax or semantics. There is therefore no need to imitate syntactic and semantic features in order to see how the logical operators behave with respect to interrogatives.

Following Prior and Prior (1955, pp. 43–59), Belnap and Steel distinguish among *hypothetical*, *conditional*, and *"given that"* questions and illustrate the difference by three examples:

(1) If you were to go, would you take an umbrella?
(2) If you are going, are you taking an umbrella?
(3) Given that you are going, are you taking an umbrella?

The first is an example of a hypothetical question. The second is a conditional question, and the third is a "given that" question. According to them, there are enormous differences between these kinds of questions. The distinctions among them are explained with the aid of the notion of a *direct answer* to a question, a notion that, as Belnap and Steel observe, is due originally to D. Harrah.[2]

We shall use the term "interrogative" to include any question that has a *direct answer*. The most important feature of the direct answers to a question is that they are statements that, whether they are true or false, tell the questioner exactly what he wants to know – neither more nor less. As Belnap and Steel put the matter, "a direct answer, then, is what counts as completely, but just completely, answering the question" (1976, p. 13). Or, again, "the crucial point is that a direct answer must provide an unarguably final resolution to the question" (1976, p. 13).

This is an intuitively rich idea, and it suggests that the direct answers to an interrogative are logically independent of each other. That is, no one of them implies or is implied by any other. We shall adopt this as an explicit assumption about direct answers. Thus, when "$\Rightarrow$" is an implication relation among the answers to an interrogative, we shall gloss their condition on complete direct answers this way:

(*I*) If A_i and A_j are any two nonequivalent direct answers to an interrogative, then $A_i \not\Rightarrow A_j$, and $A_j \not\Rightarrow A_i$.

Thus, the direct answers to an interrogative are maximal in this sense: If any one of them implies another, then they are equivalent. The plausibility of such an assumption about direct answers stems from the requirement that each direct answer constitute a complete answer to the question. If there were two direct answers, one of which implied the other, but not conversely, then how could both of them "completely, but just completely," answer the question? The stronger of the two would contain information that would be unnecessary for a complete answer. Condition (*I*) has, as we shall see, important consequences for the Belnap–Steel theory (e.g., Theorem 23.4).

The distinctions among the hypothetical, conditional, and "given that" questions use the notion of a direct answer and, according to Belnap and Steel, go something like this:

Let us use "$\langle G;\ U? \rangle$" as a notation for sentence (1). According to Belnap and Steel, a direct answer to the question $\langle G;\ U? \rangle$ has the form of "If G, then A," where A is a direct answer to the question U?. That is, direct answers to (1) seem to take the form "Yes, if I were to go, I would take an umbrella," or "No, if I were to go, I would not take an umbrella." Thus, the hypothetical interrogatives are distinguished from the other types this way:

If A is a direct answer to the question U?, then "If G, then A" is a direct answer to the complex question $\langle G; U? \rangle$. Conversely, a direct answer to the question $\langle G; U? \rangle$ has the form "If G, then A," where A is a direct answer to the question U? (where it is not assumed that the conditional is the material conditional).

On the other hand, interrogatives such as (2) take direct answers that are not direct answers to the component question U?, on the hypothesis G. That is, (2) may have direct answers that are not direct answers to $\langle G; U? \rangle$. If the person is going, a direct answer is called for. However, if the person is not going, then, according to Belnap and Steel, that information may be volunteered, but no direct answer is called for. Thus (2), unlike (1), may not have a direct answer, even though the component question U? does have a direct answer.

Direct answers to questions like (3) seem, according to Belnap and Steel, to imply the truth of the "given that" clause: "Yes, I am going, and I am taking an umbrella."; "No, I am going, but I am not taking an umbrella." Their suggestion, then, is that direct answers to "given that" interrogatives have the form "G and A," where A is any direct answer to the component question U?.

The tripartite distinction seems clear enough. The first and third kinds of interrogatives are distinguished by the form of their direct answers. The former use conditionals of sentences (however those conditionals are to be understood), and the latter use conjunctions. The interrogatives of the second kind, conditional questions, are a breed apart, according to Belnap and Steel, since they are of the sort that call for an answer if a condition is true, but do not call for an answer if the condition is false. A wholly new set of linguistic forms is added to their erotetic logic, to help account for their features. They are a special case of what Belnap and Steel (1976, p. 101) call "relativized questions."

These three kinds of complex questions arise from operations on statements, G, and questions, U?. There are other kinds of complex questions that arise from two or more questions. One such is what Belnap and Steel call a conjunction of interrogatives. Briefly, if U_1?, ... and U_n? are interrogatives, they call the expression "U_1? & ... & U_n?" a conjunction of interrogatives, and they *define* its answers to be just the conjunctions A_1 & ... & A_n of the direct answers A_i to U_i?. They have a nice example from English: "Have you ever been to Sweden, and have you ever been to Germany?" The reason they call such a question a conjunction of interrogatives is that its direct answers are (defined to be) conjunctions of the direct answers to the interrogatives that are ingredient in the conjunction. And, as they say, "it is the answers that count!"

However, it is possible to do a little better than that. Certainly it is plausible that a question whose direct answers are *defined* to be the conjunctions of the direct answers to some interrogatives should be called the conjunction of those interrogatives. But that is only to say that the choice of terminology is well motivated. However, with the aid of an implication relation for interrogatives it is possible to show that any question that is the conjunction of interrogatives (according to our account of the conjunction operator) must have the conjunctions of the direct answers to those interrogatives as its direct answers. And conversely, any question whose direct answers are the conjunctions of the direct answers to several interrogatives must be the conjunction of those interrogatives (again, on our account of the conjunction operator).

It is not a matter of a felicitous terminological choice, but rather a consequence of the characterization of the conjunction operator on interrogatives, that $C_q(U?, V?)$ has as its direct answers all statements $C(A, B)$, where A and B are direct answers to $U?$ and $V?$, respectively. And conversely, if $T?$ is a question whose direct answers are exactly the conjunctions $C(A, B)$, for any direct answers A and B to the questions $U?$ and $V?$, respectively, then T is equivalent (using the appropriate implication relation) to $C_q(U?, V?)$.

In addition, it is possible to show that the first kind of interrogative, $\langle G; U? \rangle$, is a hypothetical $H_q(G, U?)$ with antecedent G and consequent $U?$ (on our account of the hypothetical operator) if and only if its direct answers are exactly the statements $H(G, A)$, where A is any direct answer to the question $U?$. Thus, here, too, Belnap and Steel's terminology is felicitous. But more is involved than a happy terminological choice. The interrogatives that they pick out as their hypothetical interrogatives are exactly the ones that are the hypotheticals with antecedent G and consequent $U?$, once our theory of hypotheticals is relativized to a special implication relation for interrogatives.

One might wonder what our theory of the logical operators has to say about the disjunction of interrogatives. Here, the too-literal attempt to follow the logic of statements has misled Belnap and Steel. Whereas they think that "and" stands for a logical operation between interrogatives (because the "answers to the resultant interrogative are the conjunctions of answers to the ingredient interrogatives"), they do not seem to think that "or" stands for a logical operation between interrogatives. The reason seems to be that the answers to an English interrogative such as "How can one get from here to Detroit by plane, or how can one get there by automobile?" are not formed by taking disjunctions of the answers to each of the ingredient questions. As they quite rightly observe, "Either TWA has a flight leaving at 9:00 a.m. or Route 26 runs from here to there" is no answer. Instead, the answers are any of the answers to the ingredient questions. Thus, the set of direct answers is the union of the sets of direct answers to each question. The conclusion they draw from these perfectly correct observations is this: "We can now see why the English locutions 'and' and 'or' do not preserve the duality relationship which the analogy with assertoric logic would suggest" (Belnap and Steel, 1976, p. 90).

That is not the right conclusion to draw from those observations. We have seen that the conjunction and disjunction operators are duals of each other, no matter what implication structure they operate on. The case for interrogatives is no different. We shall see below that with the use of a particular implication relation for interrogatives, not only does the conjunction $C_q(U?, V?)$ have as its direct answers the conjunctions of the direct answers of $U?$ with those of $V?$, but also the disjunction $D_q(U?, V?)$ can be proved to have as its answers any of the direct answers of $U?$ as well as $V?$.

Lastly, we want to show that without assuming that questions are somehow to be "reduced to" or "identified with" the statements that are their answers, the remark that "it is the answers that count" is true in this sense: Two interrogatives are equivalent if and only if they have the same (that is, equivalent) direct answers. This does not follow by defining interrogatives as equivalent if their direct answers are the same; it follows from the implication relation that holds for interrogatives.

Let us turn, then, to a consideration of an appropriate implication relation for interrogatives, for with its aid, the resulting theorems to be proved below will provide a gloss on the elementary part of the theory of questions constructed by Belnap and Steel. The difference between this elementary part of erotetic logic and the familiar sentential or assertoric logic lies not in the logical operators but in the different implication relations that are used.

23.2 An implication relation for interrogatives

Let Q be a collection of interrogatives, each of which will be denoted by a capital letter followed by a question mark, and we shall let S be a set of sentences that includes all the (sentential) direct answers to the questions in Q. Let S^* be the union of S with Q. Suppose further that "$\Rightarrow$" is an implication relation on the sentences of S. We now wish to define an implication relation "$\Rightarrow^q$" on the set S^* that can involve only questions of Q, or combinations of questions in Q and statements in S. We do this using several conditions:

Let $M_1?, \ldots, M_n?$ and $R?$ be questions in Q, and let $F_1, \ldots, F_m$ and G be statements of S (the set of M's or the set of F's may be empty, but not both), and A_i is any direct answer to the question $M_i?$ (i ranging over 1 to n). Then

1. $F_1, \ldots, F_m, M_1?, \ldots, M_n? \Rightarrow^q R?$ if and only if there is some direct answer B to the question $R?$, such that $F_1, \ldots, F_m, A_1, \ldots, A_n \Rightarrow B$.

2. $F_1, \ldots, F_m, M_1?, \ldots, M_n? \Rightarrow^q G$ if and only if $F_1, \ldots, F_m, A_1, \ldots, A_n \Rightarrow G$.

The first condition is designed to cover the case in which some statements together with some questions imply a question. The second condition covers the case in which some statements together with some questions imply a statement. It follows from the first condition that one interrogative implies another if and only if every direct answer to the first implies (under "$\Rightarrow$") some direct answer to the second. It is a straightforward matter to check the following:

Theorem 23.1. *Let S^* and the relation "$\Rightarrow^q$" on S^* be defined as earlier. Then*

(a) *"$\Rightarrow^q$" is an implication relation on S^*, and*

(b) *the implication relation "$\Rightarrow^q$" on S^* is an extension of the implication relation "$\Rightarrow$" on S.*

We can now inquire into the behavior of the logical operators on the interrogative implication structure $I_q = \langle S^*, \Rightarrow^q \rangle$.

It should now be clear why it is that the direct answers to a conjunction of questions are equivalent to the conjunctions of their direct answers. That is,

Theorem 23.2. *Let $U?$ and $V?$ be any questions, let C be the conjunction operator on S, with respect to the implication relation "$\Rightarrow$," and let C_q be the conjunction operator on I_q. Then for any direct answer A to $C_q(U?, V?)$ there are direct answers B to $U?$ and C to $V?$ such that $A \Leftrightarrow C(B, C)$.*

Proof. Suppose that A is any direct answer to $C_q(U?, V?)$. Since $C_q(U?, V?) \Rightarrow^q U?$, $A \Rightarrow B$ for some direct answer B to $U?$. Similarly, since $C_q(U?, V?) \Rightarrow^q V?$, $A \Rightarrow C$ for some direct answer C to $V?$. Consequently, $A \Rightarrow C(B, C)$. More-over, since $U?, V? \Rightarrow^q C_q(U?, V?)$, for any B^* that is a direct answer to $U?$ and any C^* that is a direct answer to $V?$, there is some A^* that is a direct answer to $C_q(U?, V?)$, such that $B^*, C^* \Rightarrow A^*$. For B and C in particular, $B, C \Rightarrow A^*$. Assuming that conjunctions are available in this implication structure, we conclude that $C(B, C) \Rightarrow A^*$. Consequently, $A \Rightarrow C(B, C) \Rightarrow A^*$. Now A and A^* are direct answers to $C_q(U?, V?)$. However, by the assumption (I), $A \Leftrightarrow A^*$, since $A \Rightarrow A^*$. Consequently, $A \Leftrightarrow C(B, C)$.

The converse is also true:

Theorem 23.3. *If $T?$ is a question whose direct answers are equivalent to $C(B, C)$ for any direct answer B to the question $U?$ and any direct answer C to the question $V?$, then $T? \Leftrightarrow^q C_q(U?, V?)$.*

Proof. Note first that $T? \Rightarrow^q U?$, and $T? \Rightarrow^q V?$, for if A is any direct answer to $T?$, then $A \Leftrightarrow C(B, C)$ for some B that is a direct answer to $U?$ and some C that is a direct answer to $V?$. Consequently, $A \Rightarrow B$ – that is, any direct answer to $T?$ implies some direct answer to $U?$. Therefore, by condition 1, it follows that $T? \Rightarrow^q U?$. Similarly, $T \Rightarrow^q V?$. Thus, $T?$ satisfies the first condition for being a conjunction of $U?$ and $V?$. The second condition on conjunctions is also satisfied – that is, that $T?$ is the weakest question to imply (using "$\Rightarrow^q$") $U?$ as well as $V?$. For suppose that there is some question $W?$ such that $W? \Rightarrow^q U?$ and $W? \Rightarrow^q V?$. Let A be any direct answer to $W?$. Then there is some direct answer B to $U?$ such that $A \Rightarrow B$, and there is some direct answer C to $V?$ such that $A \Rightarrow C$. Therefore $A \Rightarrow C(B, C)$. But $C(B, C)$ is some direct answer to $T?$. Therefore $W? \Rightarrow^q T?$. Since $T?$ satisfies the conditions for being the conjunction $C_q(U?, V?)$, and any two items that satisfy those conditions are equivalent (using "$\Rightarrow^q$"), $T? \Leftrightarrow^q C_q(U?, V?)$.

The next theorem furnishes a gloss on the dictum of Belnap and Steel that "it is the answers that count." That is, two interrogatives are equivalent if and only if every direct answer to the one is equivalent to a direct answer to the second, and conversely. Thus, interrogatives are equivalent if and only if they have the same direct answers (up to equivalence). That is,

Theorem 23.4. *Let U? and V? be any interrogatives. Then U? $\Leftrightarrow^q$ V? if and only if every direct answer to U? is equivalent to some direct answer to V? and every direct answer to V? is equivalent to some direct answer to U?.*

Proof. If every direct answer to U? is equivalent to some direct answer to V?, and conversely, then, of course, U? and V? are equivalent (under "$\Rightarrow^q$"). Conversely, suppose that U? and V? are equivalent. Since U? $\Rightarrow^q$ V?, if A is any direct answer of U?, then there is some direct answer B of V? such that $A \Rightarrow B$. Similarly, since V? $\Rightarrow^q$ U?, then if B^* is any direct answer to V?, there is some direct answer to U? that is implied by B^*. So, for B in particular, there is some direct answer A^* to U? such that $B \Rightarrow A^*$. Therefore, $A \Rightarrow B \Rightarrow A^*$, where A and A^* are direct answers to U?. However, by (I), $A \Leftrightarrow A^*$. Therefore $A \Leftrightarrow B$. So every direct answer to U? is equivalent to some direct answer to V?. Similarly, every direct answer to V? is equivalent to some direct answer to U?.

There are comparable results that can be proved for the hypothetical and the disjunction operators on interrogatives. Consider the hypothetical case first.

Theorem 23.5. *Let U? be any interrogative, and let G be any statement. If there is an interrogative T? whose direct answers are equivalent to the statements H(G, B) for any direct answer to U?, then T? $\Leftrightarrow^q$ $H_q(G, U?)$.*

Proof. Note that the first condition on hypotheticals is satisfied by T?. That is, $G, T? \Rightarrow^q U?$. For let A be any direct answer to T?. Since it is equivalent to H(G, B) for some B that is a direct answer to U?, then $G, H(G, B) \Rightarrow B$. So G together with any direct answer to T? implies some direct answer to U? (namely, B). The second condition on hypotheticals holds as well. For suppose that for some interrogative W?, $G, W? \Rightarrow^q$ U?. Let A be any direct answer to W?. Then for some B that is a direct answer to U?, $G, A \Rightarrow B$. Therefore $A \Rightarrow H(G, B)$. But H(G, B) is a direct answer to T?. Since every direct answer to W? implies some direct answer to T?, $W? \Rightarrow^q T?$. Since T?

satisfies the two conditions for the hypothetical $H_q(G, U?)$, $T?$ $\Longleftrightarrow^q H_q (G, U?)$.

We can now see under what conditions the direct answers to the hypothetical $H_q(G, U?)$ are equivalent to the hypotheticals $H(G, A)$, where A is any direct answer to the question $U?$:

Theorem 23.6. *If there is some interrogative T? whose direct answers are the hypotheticals H(G, A), where A is any direct answer to the question U?, then the direct answers to the interrogative $H_q(G, U?)$ are the hypotheticals H(G, A), where A is any direct answer to U?.*

Proof. By the preceding theorem we know that $T? \Longleftrightarrow^q H_q(G, U?)$. However, by Theorem 23.4, $T?$ and $H_q(G, U?)$ have the same direct answers (up to equivalence), so that the direct answers to $H_q(G, U?)$ are just the hypotheticals $H(G, A)$, for any direct answer to $U?$.

We leave it for the reader to prove the following result of an export–import type for the antecedent of the hypothetical $H_q(G, U?)$:

Exercise 23.1. For any statements G and J, $H_q(C(G, J), U?)$ is equivalent to $H_q(G, H_q(J, U?))$.

Contrary to what one might think, the disjunction of two interrogatives $U?$ and $V?$ does not have the disjunctions of the direct answers to $U?$ and $V?$ as its direct answers. In fact, we can show that the disjunction operator $D_q(U?, V?)$ has as its direct answers exactly those statements that are the direct answers of $U?$ as well as those that are the direct answers of $V?$. That is,

Theorem 23.7. *If there is some interrogative T? whose direct answers are either the direct answers of U? or the direct answers of V?, then $T? \Longleftrightarrow^q D_q(U?, V?)$.*

Proof. Let $T?$ be some interrogative whose direct answers are either the direct answers to $U?$ or the direct answers of $V?$. Notice that $U? \Longrightarrow^q T?$ and that $V? \Longrightarrow^q T?$, for if A is any direct answer to $U?$, it is also a direct answer to $T?$. Since every direct answer to $U?$ implies some direct answer to $T?$, $U? \Longrightarrow^q T?$. Similarly, $V? \Longrightarrow^q T?$. Now, by the first condition on disjunctions, if $U? \Rightarrow^q T?$ and $V? \Rightarrow^q T?$, then $D_q(U?, V?)$ $\Rightarrow^q T?$. Therefore $D_q(U?, V?) \Rightarrow^q T?$. Moreover, $T? \Rightarrow^q D_q(U?, V?)$. For suppose that A is any direct answer to $T?$. There are two possibilities: Either A is a direct answer to $U?$ or it is a direct answer to $V?$. In the former case, since $U? \Rightarrow^q D_q(U?, V?)$, A implies some direct answer to $D_q(U?, V?)$. In the latter case, A implies some direct answer of $D_q(U?, V?)$, since A implies some direct answer of $V?$, and $V? \Rightarrow^q D_q(U?, V?)$. Thus, in either case, every direct answer to $T?$ implies some direct answer to $D_q(U?, V?)$. That is, $T? \Rightarrow^q D_q(U?, V?)$.

With the introduction of a special implication relation for interrogatives and the relativization of the logical operators to that relation, there results a simplification and a systematization of the elementary parts of a well-known theory of questions and answers. The dictum that "only the answers" count becomes a theorem on how the equivalence of questions is determined by their direct answers. With the use of the usual characterization of the conjunction, the hypothetical, and the disjunction operators, it can then be proved that (1) the direct answers to conjunctions of interrogatives are the conjunctions of their direct answers, (2) the hypothetical with antecedent G and interrogative $U?$ has as direct answers the hypotheticals with antecedent G and the direct answers of the interrogative as consequents, and (3) the direct answers to a disjunction of interrogatives are just the direct answers to the interrogatives (rather than the disjunctions of their direct answers).

There are some qualifications that should be added. The simplification and systematization achieved are for a particular theory of questions and answers – that due to Belnap and Steel. If that theory should turn out to be seriously deficient, then all that will have been achieved is the systematization of a flawed theory. What has been shown is that the operators of that theory are just the usual logical operators relativized to a special implication relation. Nothing has been said about the correctness of the theory. However, even if their theory should turn out to be unviable, that would not diminish the utility of our account of the operators on interrogatives, for it shows, contrary to what Belnap and Steel maintain, that the logical operators are shared common ground for erotetic and assertoric logic.

24

Completeness

24.1 Constant features of varied structures

Throughout the preceding chapters we have, from time to time, remarked that certain implications, $A_1, \ldots, A_n \Rightarrow B$, do not hold in all implication structures, and that other implications do. For example, we noted that in any structure $I = \langle S, \Rightarrow \rangle$ in which $NN(A)$ exists for A in S, one always has $A \Rightarrow NN(A)$. However, there are structures that have members that are not implied by their double negation. We also noted that there are certain quantificational implications, such as $U_i(P) \Rightarrow^* N^*(E_i N^*(P))$ [Theorem 20.26, the counterpart of "'$(\forall x)Px \rightarrow \neg(\exists x)\neg Px$' is a theorem"], that hold in all extended implication structures in which the relevant operators have values. On the other hand, we saw that $N^*(E_i N^*(P)) \Rightarrow^* U_i(P)$ [the counterpart of "'$\neg(\exists x)\neg Px \rightarrow (\forall x)Px$' is a theorem"] does not hold in all extended implication structures (Exercise 20.5).

Thus, some results hold in all implication structures (when the relevant negations, hypotheticals, and quantifications exist), and some do not. We noted in passing that, in general, it was the "intuitionistic" results that held in *all* implication structures, and it was the "classical" ones that held in all the classical structures.

We shall now provide a more precise description of this situation and sketch a proof of it. We do have to be careful in the description of what holds in all structures. We know that $A \Rightarrow A$ in all structures [or that $H(A, A)$ is a thesis in all structures in which it exists]. However, that is a natural but a loose way of speaking. Strictly speaking, since the structures are so varied, in regard to their sets as well as the implication relations on those sets, what is meant is this: If $I = \langle S, \Rightarrow \rangle$, $I^* = \langle S^*, \Rightarrow^* \rangle$, and so forth, are implication structures, then for every A in S, $A \Rightarrow A$, and for every A in S^*, $A \Rightarrow^* A$ – and so forth. In terms of theses, what is meant, strictly speaking, is that $H_I(A, A)$ (if it exists) is a thesis of I (where H_I is the hypothetical operator on the structure I). Similarly, $H_{I^*}(A, A)$ (if it exists) is a thesis of the structure I^* (where H_{I^*} is the hypothetical operator on the structure I^*).

In order to obtain a picture of those results that hold in all implication structures, we cannot focus on particular items in any particular structure, for an item can be in one structure, but not in another. Although a result such as "$P \vdash (Q \to P)$" of the classical propositional calculus will not always hold in all implication structures (since the items P and Q will not belong to most other structures), there is a corresponding result that does hold in any implication structure $I = \langle S, \Rightarrow \rangle$: $P_I \Rightarrow H_I(Q_I, P_I)$, where "$\Rightarrow$" is the implication relation of I, P_I and Q_I range over the members of S (or they can be taken to be schematic letters), and H_I is the hypothetical operator on the structure I.

Thus, we have a way of expressing the idea that the results that "correspond" to a formula of a formal propositional language L hold (or fail to hold) in all implication structures. Once we render these suggestions more precisely, we can then prove that all the formulas of L that are provable in the intuitionistic sentential calculus (ISC) are exactly those whose counterparts are theses in all implication structures (in which negations, conjunctions, disjunctions, and hypotheticals always exist). Similarly, those formulas of L that are provable in the classical sentential calculus (CSC) are exactly those whose counterparts are theses in all classical implication structures (in which negations, conjunctions, disjunctions, and hypotheticals always exist). These results can be extended to a formal first-order language QL and those extended implication structures in which universal and existential quantifications, as well as the other logical operators, always exist.

24.2 The formal language L and its structural counterparts

A formal language L is specified by its sentential letters $p, q, r, \ldots$, the logical connectives "$\vee$," "$\&$," "$\neg$," and "$\to$," and its parentheses: (1) Every sentential letter is a formula. (2) If A and B are formulas, then so too are $\neg A$, $(A \& B)$, $(A \vee B)$, and $(A \to B)$. (3) The usual closure condition, that is, that nothing is a formula unless it is so by (1) and (2). Let S_L be the set of all formulas of L.

To each formula X of L, and each implication structure $I = \langle S, \Rightarrow \rangle$, we define the notion of an *f-counterpart of X*, $I_f(X)$ (in I), where f is a mapping of the set of all the sentential letters of X into the set S, such that

(1) If X is a sentential letter, say p, then $I_f(X)$ is $f(p)$.
(2) If X is $\neg A$, then $I_f(X) = I_f(\neg A) = N_I(I_f(A))$, where N_I is the negation operator on I.
(3) If X is $(A \& B)$, then $I_f(X) = I_f(A \& B) = C_I(I_f(A), I_f(B))$, where C_I is the conjunction operator on I.

(4) If X is $(A \vee B)$, then $I_f(X) = I_f(A \vee B) = D_I(I_f(A), I_f(B))$, where D_I is the disjunction operator on I.

(5) If X is $(A \rightarrow B)$, then $I_f(X) = I_f(A \rightarrow B) = H_I(I_f(A), I_f(B))$, where H_I is the hypothetical operator on I.

(6) For any structure $I = \langle S, \Rightarrow \rangle$, the function f is the identity function on all the sentential letters of L that belong to S.

We shall say that $I(X)$ (no subscript) exists in the structure I if and only if for all f, $I_f(X)$ exists in I. And we shall say that $I(X)$ (no subscript) is a thesis of the structure I if and only if for every f, $I_f(X)$ exists and is a thesis of I.

24.3 Generality and the intuitionistic connection

We can now state two results for formulas of the propositional language L. Let ISC be an axiomatic formulation of the intuitionistic sentential calculus, with only modus ponens as its rule of inference.[1] Let "$\vdash_{ISC} X$" indicate that the formula X of L is a theorem of ISC.

For the remainder of this chapter we shall indicate by means of an asterisk notation for structures that negations, conjunctions, disjunctions, and hypotheticals always exist in those structures. If I^* is an extended implication structure, then it is required, in addition, that universal and existential quantifications always exist in it.

Theorem 24.1. *If X is any formula of L, then if $\vdash_{ISC} X$, then $I^*(X)$ is a thesis of every implication structure $I^* = \langle S, \Rightarrow \rangle$.*

Proof. Note that for any formula X of L, and any f, $I_f^*(X)$ always exists in I^*. [We leave the proof as an exercise, using induction on the length of X, conditions (1)–(6), and the fact that negations, conjunctions, disjunctions, and hypotheticals always exist in any structure I^*.] So, for any formula X of L and any I^*, $I^*(X)$ exists in I^*. Then proceed by a proof by induction on the length n of proofs. First check that for every axiom A_i of ISC, $I^*(A_i)$ is a thesis of every implication structure I^*. Suppose that $\vdash_{ISC} X$. If $n = 1$, then X is an axiom, and by the preceding remark, $I^*(X)$ is a thesis of any structure I^*. Suppose, next, that X is the last line of a proof of length $n + 1$, and assume that for all proofs of length less than or equal to n, the conclusion holds. Then either X is an axiom, and the conclusion holds, or else X follows by modus ponens from two formulas Y and $(Y \rightarrow X)$, occurring earlier in the proof. In that case, by the induction hypothesis, for any structure I^* and for any f, $I_f^*(Y)$ and $I_f^*(Y \to X)$ [that is, $H_{I^*}(I_f^*(Y), I_f^*(X))$] exist and are theses in I^*. Therefore, in any structure I^*, $C \Rightarrow I_f^*(Y)$ for all C, and $C \Rightarrow H_{I^*}(I_f^*(Y), I_f^*(X))$ for all C. By Cut, then, for all f, $C \Rightarrow I_f^*(X)$ for all C in the structure I^*. Consequently, $I^*(X)$ is a thesis of I^*.

We turn next to the converse, completeness result:

Theorem 24.2. *If X is any formula of L, then if $I^*(X)$ is a thesis of every implication structure $I^* = \langle S, \Rightarrow \rangle$, then $\vdash_{ISC} X$.*

Proof. Suppose that X is a formula of L, but that it is false that $\vdash_{ISC} X$. It will suffice to show that there is some implication structure I^* in which $I^*(X)$ exists, but is not a thesis.

Take $I_{ISC} = \langle S_L, \Leftrightarrow^{ISC} \rangle$, where for any formulas, $X_1, \ldots, X_n$ and Y of L, $X_1, \ldots, X_n \Rightarrow^{ISC} Y$ if and only if $\vdash_{ISC}(X_1 \& \ldots \& X_n) \to Y$. For the remainder of this proof we shall use "I^*" for the more cumbersome "I_{ISC}." Thus, I^* is an implication structure – the one that we have called the structure associated with the formal system ISC. Several observations are now in order. First, note that since the set S of the structure is the set of formulas of L itself, then by condition (6), f is just the identity function. Consequently, for all formulas X and Y of L, the conditions on counterparts in this case reduce to

(C) (a) $I_f^*(\neg X) = N_{I^*}(I_f^*(X))$,
 (b) $I_f^*(X \& Y) = C_{I^*}(I_f^*(X), I_f^*(Y))$,
 (c) $I_f^*(X \vee Y) = D_{I^*}(I_f^*(X), I_f^*(Y))$,
 (d) $I_f^*(X \to Y) = H_{I^*}(I_f^*(X), I_f^*(Y))$, and
 (e) $I_f^*(p) = f(p) = p$ (for all the sentential letters of L).

We now need to show that negations, conjunctions, disjunctions, and hypotheticals always exist in I^*:

Lemma 24.1. *For any formulas X and Y of L, and the structure I^* described above, the following hold in $I^*(I_{ISC})$:*

(a) $\neg X$ is the negation of X,
(b) $X \& Y$ is the conjunction of X with Y,
(c) $X \vee Y$ is the disjunction of X with Y, and
(d) $X \to Y$ is the hypothetical with antecedent X and consequent Y.

Proof. We shall consider only (a), and leave the remainder for the reader. Note that (1) $X, \neg X \Rightarrow^* Z$ (all Z), since $\vdash_{\text{ISC}} X$ & $\neg X \to Z$ for all Z, and (2) for any T, if $X, T \Rightarrow^* Z$ (all Z), then $T \Rightarrow^* \neg X$. For suppose that $\vdash_{\text{ISC}}(X$ & $T) \to Z$ for all Z. Then $\vdash_{\text{ISC}} T \to (X \to Z)$ for all Z. In particular, then, $\vdash_{\text{ISC}} T \to (X \to \neg X)$. However, $\vdash_{\text{ISC}}(X \to \neg X) \to \neg X$. Consequently, $\vdash_{\text{ISC}} T \to \neg X$. Therefore $T \Rightarrow^* \neg X$.

By $C(a)$–$C(d)$ and Lemma 24.1, it is a simple proof by induction on the length of formulas that for any X in L and any f, $I_f^*(X)$ exists in the structure I^*. Moreover, again by a simple inductive proof, we have the following:

Lemma 24.2. *For any X and Y in L, and any f,*

(a) $I_f^*(\neg X) \Leftrightarrow^* \neg I_f^*(X)$,
(b) $I_f^*(X$ & $Y) \Leftrightarrow^* I_f^*(X)$ & $I_f^*(Y)$,
(c) $I_f^*(X \lor Y) \Leftrightarrow^* I_f^*(X) \lor I_f^*(Y)$, and
(d) $I_f^*(X \to Y) \Leftrightarrow^* I_f^*(X) \to I_f^*(Y)$.

Lemma 24.3. *For any formula Z of L, and any f, $I_f^*(Z)$ exists in I^*.*

Proof. Use induction on the number of occurrences of logical connectives in Z. For $n = 0$, Z is some sentential letter, say p. Then $I_f^*(p) = f(p) = p$ [by condition (6)]. Suppose that Z has $n + 1$ occurrences of logical connectives and that the lemma holds for all formulas of L with n or fewer occurrences of connectives. If Z has the form "X & Y," then by the induction hypothesis, $I_f^*(x) \Leftrightarrow^* X$, and $I_f^*(Y) \Leftrightarrow^* Y$. By Lemma 24.2(b), $I_f^*(X$ & $Y) \Leftrightarrow^* I_f^*(X)$ & $I_f^*(Y)$, so that $I_f^*(X$ & $Y) \Leftrightarrow^*$ X & Y. So $I_f^*(X$ & $Y)$ exists in I^*. The remaining cases are proved similarly.

Lemma 24.4. *For any formula Z of L, and any f, $I_f^*(Z) \Leftrightarrow^* Z$.*

Proof. By induction on the number of occurrences of logical connectives. For $n = 0$, Z is a sentential letter, say p. But $I^*(p) = f(p) = p$. Suppose that Z has $n + 1$ occurrences of logical connectives, and assume that the lemma holds for all formulas of L with n or fewer such occurrences. If Z has the form $\neg X$, then by the induction hypothesis, for any f, $I_f^*(X) \Leftrightarrow^* X$. Then, by Lemma 24.2(a), $I_f^*(\neg X) \Leftrightarrow^* \neg I_f^*(X)$, so that

$I_f^*(\neg X) \Longleftrightarrow^* \neg X$. If Z has the form "$X \& Y$," then by the induction hypothesis, $I_f^*(X) \Longleftrightarrow^* X$, and $I_f^*(Y) \Longleftrightarrow^* Y$. Then, by Lemma 24.2(b), $I_f(X \& Y) \Longleftrightarrow^* X \& Y$. The remaining cases are similar.

We can now conclude the proof of Theorem 24.2. We supposed that for some formula X, it is false that $\vdash_{\mathrm{ISC}} X$. By Lemma 24.3, for any f, $I_f^*(X)$ exists in the structure I^*. Suppose that $I^*(X)$ is a thesis of I^*. Then $I_f^*(X)$ is a thesis of I^* for every f. Since $I_f^*(X) \Longleftrightarrow^* X$ (by Lemma 24.4), X is a thesis of I^*. Therefore, for all Z, $Z \Longrightarrow^* X$, so that $\vdash_{\mathrm{ISC}} Z \to X$. Let Z be any theorem of ISC ("$p \to p$" will serve). Then $\vdash_{\mathrm{ISC}} X$. But that is impossible. So there is some implication structure, namely I^*, in which $I^*(X)$ exists, but is not a thesis. And that completes the proof.

There are parallel results for the classical sentential calculus (CSC).

24.4 Less generality and the classical connection

Theorem 24.3. *If X is any formula of the propositional language L, then if $\vdash_{CSC} X$, then $I^*(X)$ is a thesis of every classical implication structure $I^* = \langle S, \Longrightarrow \rangle$.*

Proof. As in the proof of Theorem 24.1, an induction on the length of proofs will suffice. Select a formulation of the CSC that differs from that of ISC in that the axiom schema $\neg A \to (A \to B)$ of ISC is replaced by $\neg\neg A \to A$.[2] In this formulation of CSC, all the axiom schemata A_i except $\neg\neg A \to A$ are theorems of ISC. Consequently, by Theorem 24.1, $I^*(A_i)$ is a thesis in every implication structure. Therefore it is a thesis of every classical implication structure I^*. Now any formula of the form $\neg\neg X \to X$ is such that for any f, $I_f^*(\neg\neg X \to X)$ is a thesis in all classical structures, for $I_f^*(\neg\neg X \to X)$ is $H_{I^*}(N_{I^*} N_{I^*}(I_f^*(X)), I_f^*(X))$. Since I^* is classical, $N_{I^*}N_{I^*}(A) \Longrightarrow A$ for all A in S. Therefore $N_{I^*}N_{I^*}(I_f^*(X)) \Longrightarrow I_f^*(X)$. Consequently, $H_{I^*}(N_{I^*}N_{I^*}(I_f^*(X)), I_f^*(X))$ is a thesis of I^*. Thus, for every axiom of CSC, and any classical implication structure $I^* = \langle S, \Longrightarrow \rangle$, $I^*(A_i)$ is a thesis of I^*. The remainder of the proof proceeds exactly like the proof of Theorem 24.1, by an induction on the length of a proof of any X for which $\vdash_{CSC} X$.

There is the parallel completeness result with respect to classical implication structures:

Theorem 24.4. *For any formula X of L, if $I^*(X)$ is a thesis of every classical implication structure $I^* = \langle S, \Rightarrow \rangle$, then $\vdash_{CSC} X$.*

Proof. The argument is parallel to that given for Theorem 24.2. Suppose that X is a formula of L, but that it is false that $\vdash_{CSC} X$. It suffices to show that there is some classical implication structure I^* in which $I^*(X)$ exists, but fails to be a thesis. Let I_{CSC} be the implication structure associated with the formal system CSC, where for any formulas $X_1, \ldots, X_n$ and Y of L, $X_1, \ldots, X_n \Rightarrow^{CSC} Y$ if and only if $\vdash_{CSC}(X_1 \& \ldots \& X_n) \to Y$.

We need a preliminary observation in order to show that I_{CSC} is a classical structure:

Lemma 24.5. *For any formulas any X and Y of L, and the structure I_{CSC} described above,*

(a) $\neg X$ *is the negation of X,*
(b) $X \& Y$ *is the conjunction of X with Y,*
(c) $X \lor Y$ *is the disjunction of X with Y, and*
(d) $X \to Y$ *is the hypothetical with X as antecedent and Y as consequent.*

Proof. Exactly the same as for Theorem 24.2 (Lemma 24.1), using "$\vdash_{CSC}$" and "$\Rightarrow^{CSC}$" instead of "$\vdash_{ISC}$" and "$\Rightarrow^*$."

It follows from (a) that I_{CSC} is a classical implication structure: Since $\neg X$ is the negation (in I_{CSC}) of X, $N_{CSC}N_{CSC}(X) \Rightarrow^{CSC} X$ for all formulas X of L. The proof can now be continued, as in Theorem 24.2, using the counterpart mapping of the formulas of L to I_{CSC}, rather than the mapping of those formulas to I_{ISC}.

Thus, Theorems 24.1 and 24.2 together tell us that for any formula X of the language L, X is a theorem of the ISC if and only if $I^*(X)$ is a thesis of all implication structures I^*.

Theorems 24.3 and 24.4 together tell us that for any formula X of L, X is a theorem of the CSC if and only if $I^*(X)$ is a thesis of all classical implication structures I^*.

These results can be extended to include quantification theory in this sense: Let I^* range over those extended implication structures in which the universal and existential quantifiers, as well as negation, conjunction, disjunction, and hypotheticals, always exist.

If QL is a formal quantificational language extending L, then for any formula Z of QL, Z is a theorem of intuitionistic predicate calculus (IPC) if and only if $I^*(Z)$ is a thesis of all extended implication structures I^*. And Z is a theorem of the CPC if and only if $I^*(Z)$ is a thesis of all classical extended implication structures I^*.

PART IV

The modal operators

25

Introduction

25.1 Background

It is part of the lore of logical theory that sooner or later one comes to the study of implication. This study of the modal operators is a consequence of taking the old advice to heart by considering implication sooner rather than later. Modality, on our account, is a way of studying the question whether or not implication continues to be preserved when the elements related by implication are transformed by an operator. The basic idea is that a modal operator is any operator or function φ that transforms or maps the set S of an implication structure $I = \langle S, \Rightarrow \rangle$ to itself in such a way that if $A_1, \ldots, A_n \Rightarrow B$, then $\varphi(A_1), \varphi(A_2), \ldots, \varphi(A_n) \Rightarrow \varphi(B)$. There is a second condition concerning the relation of φ to the dual implication relation "$\Rightarrow^{\wedge}$," which we shall introduce shortly. The two conditions will then specify the kind of functions that count as having modal character.

If we are correct about this, then the study of modal operators is a natural continuation of the study of implication itself. Whatever reservations a philosopher might have about the philosophical merit of such concepts as "necessity" and "possibility," there is every reason for studying the modal operators, since they are among the operators that preserve implication. The key idea, then, is to think of a modal operator as modal relative to some implication relation. We shall see that most, if not all, of the operators associated with the box, $\Box$, of the various modal systems in the literature will count as modal, and so too will a host of other operators associated with a variety of implication structures.

Our aim is to provide a simple and fruitful way to think of the modal operators. Anyone who has had to provide an account of modal logic for beginners has eventually been confronted with this elementary question: Why, given the diversity of modal systems that are studied, do they all count as modal? Our proposal is, we hope, a satisfactory answer in the right direction. What gives an operator its modal character is its very special role with respect to an implication relation. Although we shall sometimes refer to modals with the reference to implication suppressed, we shall regard the official description as always including a reference to an implication relation.

Just as with the case for the logical operators, we want to study the concept of a modal operator in a general setting. The modal operators are capable of acting not only upon sentences but also upon propositions, predicates, sets, or any other elements of interest that can figure in implication relations. The intention is to have a theory of modals whose range is as extensive as the range of the implication relations.

Our aim of finding a general characterization of modals would be easier to fulfill if there were already at hand some general idea of what it is to be a modal operator for the wide variety of extensively studied examples of modal systems that have been investigated. However, if we look to those modal systems[1] that, up to recent times, have dominated the subject, two difficulties immediately become evident. The first arises from the variety to be found among even the best-known modal systems, such as (T), (K_4), (S_4), (S_5), (B), (D), and (G) [or $(G\text{-}L)$].[2] It was this proliferation of modal systems that prompted Lemmon (1959) to raise the question whether there was one "correct" modal system or whether each of the systems he surveyed isolated some special sense of "necessity" (or "possibility"). Thus, when considering a modal law such as $\Box A \to A$, and (reading $\Box A$, for the present, as "It is necessary that A"), should we, on our understanding of "necessity," adopt that law as correct? If we did so, then what about the other well-known theses, such as $\Box A \to \Diamond A$ (where $\Diamond A$ is read as "It is possible that A"), $\Box A \to \Box\Box A$, and $\Diamond A \to \Box\Diamond A$, to mention some of the best-known, most contested modal theses, as well the Brouwerian law, $A \to \Box\Diamond A$, which, even though no one now thinks that it says anything plausible about the modals, still counts as a modal thesis.

Lemmon attempted to find suitable interpretations for $\Box A$ as it occurs in certain well-known systems. The problem of finding why $\Box$ counts as modal in these various cases is also complicated somewhat by the consideration of the system (G) (or $(G\text{-}L)$, to refer to Gödel and Löb), in which $\Box A$ is understood as "It is provable in (first-order) Peano arithmetic that A," and the characteristic modal law for that system is given by $\Box(\Box A \to A) \to \Box A$. The difficulty arises once it is realized that there is no consistent normal modal system that includes both $\Box A \to A$ and $\Box(\Box A \to A) \to \Box A$ as theses. For such modal systems there is no reading of the box that would render both of these theses true. We agree with Lemmon that a uniform reading or interpretation for the box in all such modal systems is unlikely, and we do not have such a firm grasp of the various concepts of necessity as to warrant thinking that however different the readings of □ are, they are all types of, or special cases of, necessity.

Nevertheless, despite the variety of theses, we do seem to think of □ as representing a modal operator in each of these cases, although it may not be the same modal operator. Our question is this: What is a plausible way in which to characterize the modal operators so that most, if not all, of the commonly studied operators of the best-known modal systems will count as modal. The task is not that of trying to argue for some one modal system as the correct one, nor is it to argue that the various modal systems each isolate a special type of necessity. We shall be concerned with conditions under which the operators of these various systems qualify as modal operators, independently of whether or not a uniform reading can be given for them, or whether or not they are thought of as representing types of necessity. Consequently, the conditions for being a modal operator should not be formulated in a way that relies essentially upon one or even several concepts of necessity. We shall therefore not require that the box represent some kind of necessity in order for the operator associated with the box to count as modal. Although the range of the modal operators will be wide, we shall, later in this study, speculate on the way in which necessity-style modals might be distinguished within the broad class of modals.

The last suggestion might be considered as constituting too great a departure from traditional modal theory. The box is usually read as a necessity operator, and there has been a long tradition, dating back at least to Aristotle, of thinking of modal theory as concerned principally with the concepts of necessity and possibility. Why should not some concept of necessity play a central role in the formulation of a general notion of a modal operator? However, if we look to the historical sources of modal theory, as described, for example, by Kneale and Kneale (1962), the result is no less perplexing than that which arose from observing the diversity of contemporary modal systems. A cursory glance at the theories of Aristotle, the Stoics, and some medieval theorists reveals them to be concerned with modal notions, but there seems to be no common notion of necessity or possibility that they all share; the various theories do not appear to have a common subject. What seems to be shared is a modal square of opposition, involving four types of statements:

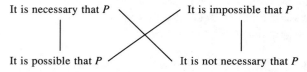

It is necessary that *P*   It is impossible that *P*

It is possible that *P*   It is not necessary that *P*

Statements appearing immediately above others imply those others, and the statements joined by a diagonal line are contradictories. Although the modal schema of opposition seems to have been common ground, the candidates for the entries in the square have varied markedly. What persists through much of the historical record is the modal schema of opposition, rather than any single concept of necessity or possibility.

Thus, the problem remains: Why, despite the diversity in formal as well as informal accounts, is the subject still modality? Appeals to some concern with necessity or possibility are unhelpful. Although various concepts of necessity and possibility may, on our account, qualify as modal operators, they do so (if they do) because they satisfy certain conditions to be described later. On the other hand, if one thought that, in good philosophical conscience, one could not use such concepts in one's investigations, then there would still be modal operators worth studying. Modal theory would not be left without a subject matter.

Once the conditions for being a modal operator are in place, we shall see that the modals are "topic-neutral": They are as wide-ranging as the concept of an implication relation – which, as we have seen, is quite general. Indeed, modals can operate on syntactical as well as nonsyntactical elements. Thus, some modals operate upon sentences, but there are others that can operate upon predicates (such as the universal and existential quantifiers), and some can act upon sets. The operator that to any set assigns its power set is a modal operator, and so too are the operators that in certain topological spaces yield the interior and the closure of a set. The operator that yields for any set of sentences the set of all its consequences (the Tarskian closure) is a (restricted) modal operator. Moreover, in the intuitionistic sentential calculus, operators corresponding to double negation, and to some conditionalizations of sentences, count as modal. It is also true that there are modal operators even for the classical sentential calculus.

There are other concepts, such as "knowledge," "belief," and "truth," that have sometimes been considered to be modal. I do not wish to settle the matter of their modal character. What I hope will become evident are the special conditions that these notions have to satisfy if the general conditions for their being modal are applied to knowledge, belief, and truth, as special cases. It is worthwhile noticing that if we are correct in thinking that the various operators mentioned earlier are modal, then the centrality of necessity in modal theory is somewhat misleading. If it is true that one or several concepts of necessity are modal, they are not the only modals. Furthermore, the modals that we have mentioned are not modal in virtue of some analogy with necessity. Universal quantifiers are modal operators on predicates not because they are analogous to some kind of necessity but for the simpler reason that they distribute over hypotheticals, but not over disjunctions. Although, as we shall see, they share these features with other modals, there is no need to think of them as representing a type of necessity. Similarly, when we noted that double negation is a modal in intuitionistic systems of logic, the reason relies upon what we know about intuitionistic double negation directly, not on some presumed analogy with necessity or possibility.

In fact, the attempt to think of necessity as the hallmark of modality becomes a hindrance if we wish to think of the Tarskian closure of sets of sentences as a modal operator, and the link to necessities almost vanishes altogether once we regard the topological interior or closure as modal operators. It is sometimes customary to regard these operators as modal because of some analogy with the ways in which necessity operators are believed to behave. But the reason for their modal character lies in the fact that they satisfy certain conditions that even the necessity operators have to satisfy if they are to count as modal. Thus, in light of the various operators other than necessity that count as modal, it is misleading to think of necessity or possibility as the very paradigm of modality, the touchstone to which the other operators must assimilate if their modal character is at stake. Necessity may be the most interesting modal of all, but it is one modal among others, having to meet the same conditions as the others – even though for some philosophers it may hold more interest than the others. Furthermore, the insistence that any modal operator must be analogous to some kind of necessity or possibility impedes our understanding of a modal operator such as intuitionistic double negation, for this double negation satisfies some modal laws that one might think of as possibility-style, and it satisfies others that have been thought of as characteristic of some type of necessity. In fact, intuitionistic double negation fits neither style exactly, and still has modal character.

In addition to these desiderata for the general characterization of modal operators, there is one further point that we should add: The characterization of modal operators should be given in such a way that there is a point to studying them. If the focus of modal theory is taken to be the study of the concept of necessity or possibility, then the point of such a study is obvious. However, once it is conceded that necessity and possibility, if they qualify, are only two of several different kinds of modal operators, then there is the risk that those who eschew the concept of necessity will find it pointless to pursue the subject of modal theory. After all, if the object of constructing modal theories were simply the systematic study of concepts like necessity and possibility, then the chief target of the theory would no longer be of concern. To retain an interest in modal theory, while eschewing necessity, would, on this account of the aim of modal theory, be intellectually quixotic. We should like to say that there is a point to studying the modal operators, in addition to the intrinsic interest that some of them, like necessity and possibility, may have, and that point is directly related to their characterization.

Why, then, should one study the modal operators? The short answer that we propose is this: If we consider any implication structure, then a modal operator over the structure is any mapping φ of the set S to itself that preserves the implication relation "$\Rightarrow$" but does not preserve the dual of that implication relation. Since implication relations are at the center of logic, and, as we have argued, they provide a basis upon which all the other logical operators can be defined, it is natural to inquire into those transformations that leave implications intact. What could be more natural than inquiring into those conditions under which implication is preserved? No matter what one's favorite system of logic may be, no matter how conservative one's interests in logic may be, there is always the natural problem of what sorts of transformations lead from implications to implications. And this problem, if we are correct, is the study of the modal operators for the particular theory. It is a problem that can be raised even if in the particular logical system under study there is no special sign like the box (or an equivalent) to be found. The use of a box does not automatically signify that modality is the topic. However, as we shall see, in the familiar modal systems that do have the box (or an equivalent) as part of their vocabulary, the corresponding operator that assigns to each sentence A of the system the sentence $\Box A$ is a modal operator. Thus, the usual modal systems concern modals in the sense that the operators that correspond to the box in those systems count as modal according to the conditions that we described. Consequently, despite the diversity of these systems, they are all, on our account, modal.

25.2 Notational remarks

Before we study the modal operators in detail, it is worth noticing that by characterizing certain *functions* or operators as modal, we have set to one side certain controversial matters of a technical nature. In thinking of the modals as operators, we have assumed a common ground between competing views regarding the way in which modals like necessity and possibility are to be registered in familiar logical idiom. The study of modals, however, can be advanced quite far independently of how those more refined issues are resolved.

Thus, there has been some controversy over whether a modal like necessity or possibility is best studied as a connective or as a predicate – that is, whether, in registering or recording a necessity, we write "It is necessary that A" or "Necessarily A" (where a sentence or statement is supposed to replace "A") or, instead, write "'A' is necessary" or "'A' is necessarily true." In the first way, "It is necessary that" is used as a (one-place) connective that prefixes the sentence, much as "$\neg$" in "$\neg A$" is a one-place connective prefixing the sentence, or "$\vee$" in "$A \vee B$" is a (two-place) connective infixed between sentences. The second option treats "necessarily" or "necessarily true" as a predicate, according to which something is being said of a sentence, and so the name of the sentence is preceded (or sometimes followed) by a predicate – that is, "necessarily A," or "A" is necessarily true.[3] As we noted, we take no stand on the connective versus predicate options. We regard "necessity" as an operator, taking the neutral ground between the two usual views.[4] Representing necessity by the box, $\square$, a predicate registers the necessity of A as $\square("A")$, using the name of the sentence rather than the sentence itself, which the connective account simply uses $\square A$. On either account, to any sentence there is associated another sentence, its necessity. We think of necessity as an operator or function, $\square$, that assigns to any item A another item $\square(A)$ (using functional notation to indicate the value that the function $\square$ assigns to A). We want to focus on the problem of what distinguishes a function like $\square$ as a modal operator. The more refined problem of whether the value of the function is to be thought of as $\square("A")$ (the predicate view) or as $\square A$ (the connective view) is not the issue before us. The modal character of the operator $\square$ does not depend upon how the values of the function are to be registered.[5]

26

Modality

26.1 The Conditions for Modal Character

Let $I = \langle S, \Rightarrow \rangle$ be an implication structure. We shall say that any function φ that maps S to S is a modal operator on I if and only if the following conditions are satisfied:

M_1. For any $A_1, \ldots, A_n$ and B in S, if $A_1, \ldots, A_n \Rightarrow B$, then $\varphi(A_1), \ldots, \varphi(A_n) \Rightarrow \varphi(B)$.

M_2. For some $A_1, \ldots, A_n$ and B in S, $A_1, \ldots, A_n \Rightarrow\hat{} B$, but $\varphi(A_1), \ldots, \varphi(A_n) \not\Rightarrow\hat{} \varphi(B)$.

Briefly expressed, the first condition for being a modal operator with respect to the implication relation "$\Rightarrow$" is that the operator distributes over the implication relation. The second condition states that the operator does not distribute over "$\Rightarrow\hat{}$," the dual of the implication relation. According to the first condition, the operator φ preserves all implications of the structure I. This in itself is a very natural "homomorphism-style" condition. But natural or not, the condition would be beside the point if most of the operators associated with familiar modal systems did not satisfy it. This, as we shall see later, they certainly do. In fact, for all so-called normal modal systems L, those for which a distribution axiom over conditionals holds [i.e., $\vdash_L \Box(A \rightarrow B) \rightarrow (\Box A \rightarrow \Box B)$] yield an associated operator that satisfies the first condition of modality. The difference is that a distribution axiom such as the one just described concerns the behavior of an operator with respect to conditionals, and neither of our conditions refers to any of the logical operators. They concern just the implication relation and its dual. However, once we characterize the various logical operators as we have done in Part III, the distribution condition for hypotheticals becomes a consequence of condition M_1 and our characterization of hypotheticals.[1]

The second condition is less familiar and requires some motivation. Part of the unfamiliarity can be traced to the use of the dual implication relation that was used in its formulation. Under certain conditions the second condition has some simpler formulations:

In the remainder of this part of the study we shall use "$\rightarrow$," "$\neg$," "&," and "$\vee$" instead of the official operators H, N, C, and D. This is, of course, not a shift to a syntactic mode, but only an adjustment so as not to have too many unfamiliar notations running together at the same time.

Theorem 26.1. *Let* $I = \langle S, \Rightarrow \rangle$ *be an implication structure in which disjunctions always exist. Let* φ *be a modal operator on* I. *Then* φ *distributes over the dual "*$\Rightarrow^{\wedge}$*" if and only if* $\varphi(A \vee B) \Rightarrow \varphi(A) \vee \varphi(B)$ *for all* A *and* B *in* S.

Proof. If φ distributes over "$\Rightarrow^{\wedge}$," $\varphi(A)$, $\varphi(B) \Rightarrow^{\wedge} \varphi(A \vee B)$ for any A and B in S, since A, $B \Rightarrow^{\wedge} (A \vee B)$. Consequently, $\varphi(A \vee B) \Rightarrow \varphi(A) \vee \varphi(B)$ (Theorem 14.8). Conversely, suppose that $\varphi(A \vee B) \Rightarrow \varphi(A) \vee \varphi(B)$ for all A and B in S. Suppose that $A_1, \ldots, A_n \Rightarrow^{\wedge} B$, so that $B \Rightarrow (A_1 \vee \ldots \vee A_n)$. By M_1, $\varphi(B) \Rightarrow \varphi(A_1 \vee \ldots \vee B)$. But $\varphi (A_1 \vee \ldots \vee A_n) \Rightarrow \varphi(A_1) \vee \ldots \vee \varphi (A_n)$ (by an inductive proof, using the assumption that φ distributes over the disjunction of any two members of S). Consequently, $\varphi(A_1), \ldots, \varphi(A_n) \Rightarrow^{\wedge} \varphi(B)$, since $\varphi(B) \Rightarrow \varphi(A_1) \vee \ldots \vee \varphi(A_n)$.

We shall say that φ distributes over disjunction if and only if for every A and B, $\varphi(A \vee B) \Rightarrow \varphi(A) \vee \varphi(B)$. Thus, from the preceding theorem we conclude that in structures with disjunctions always available, the second condition on modals is equivalent to this condition:

For some A and B, $\varphi(A \vee B) \not\Rightarrow \varphi(A) \vee \varphi(B)$.

There is another condition that is equivalent to (M_2) under certain conditions.

Definition 26.1. Let φ be a modal operator on I. We shall say that it is a *necessitation modal* if and only if $\varphi(A)$ is a thesis of I if A is a thesis of I.

Theorem 26.2. *Let* $I = \langle S, \Rightarrow \rangle$ *be a classical implication structure in which negations and disjunctions always exist. Let* φ *be a necessitation modal. Then for any* A *and* B *in* S, $\varphi(A \vee B) \Rightarrow \varphi(A) \vee \varphi(B)$ *if and only if* $\varphi(A \vee \neg A) \Rightarrow \varphi(A) \vee \varphi(\neg A)$.

Proof. If φ distributes over disjunction, then $\varphi (A \vee \neg A) \Rightarrow \varphi(A) \vee \varphi(\neg A)$. Conversely, suppose that φ distributes over $(A \vee \neg A)$. Since negation is assumed to be classical, $(A \vee B)$

$\Rightarrow (\neg A \to B)$. By M_1, then, $\varphi(A \vee B) \Rightarrow \varphi(\neg A \to B)$. Here we need a result that is proved in the next chapter – that the modal of a hypothetical implies the hypothetical of the modals. Then $\varphi(\neg A \to B) \Rightarrow \varphi(\neg A) \to \varphi(B)$. Since negation is classical, $\varphi(\neg A) \to \varphi(B) \Rightarrow \neg\varphi(\neg A) \vee \varphi(B)$, so that $\varphi(A \vee B) \Rightarrow \neg\varphi(\neg A) \vee \varphi(B)$. Moreover, $\varphi(A \vee \neg A)$ is a thesis, since φ is a necessitation modal and negation is classical. Consequently, $\varphi(A) \vee \varphi(\neg A)$ is a thesis. Therefore $\neg\varphi(\neg A) \Rightarrow \varphi(A)$. We then have the result that $\varphi(A \vee B) \Rightarrow \neg\varphi(\neg A) \vee \varphi(B) \Rightarrow \varphi(A) \vee \varphi(B)$ for all A and B in S.

Thus, for necessitation modals on classical structures, the second condition on modal operators is equivalent to this:

$$\varphi(A) \vee \varphi(\neg A) \text{ is not a thesis for some } A.$$

Exercise 26.1. Assume that an operator φ distributes over implication, that disjunctions and negations always exist, that negation is classical, and that the necessitation condition holds. Then if $\neg\varphi(\neg A) \not\Rightarrow \varphi(A)$ for some A, the second condition for modals is satisfied.

We are now in a better position to see the import of the condition M_2. If we required only the first condition, distribution over implication, then trivial mappings, such as the identity mapping, and conjunction with some fixed member of S would count as modal operators. This seems to us to be just wrong. However, there are, it might be thought, simpler ways to deal with such trivia. One could just directly rule them out – if we had an overall grasp of what it was we wanted to rule out as obviously nonmodal. But it is not clear that we do have such an understanding. The second condition will do the work for us.

Exercise 26.2. Show that if φ satisfies M_2, then (1) φ is not the identity mapping on S, and (2) $\varphi(A)$ cannot be equivalent to $(A \mathbin{\&} C)$ for some fixed C in S [note that $(A \vee B) \mathbin{\&} C \Rightarrow (A \mathbin{\&} C) \vee (B \mathbin{\&} C)$].

Exercise 26.3. Those cases in which the box of a modal system is such that $\Box A$ is equivalent to A for all A are described as "the collapse of the modal." Show that in those cases the associated operator fails to be modal.

In fact, the second condition does much more than this. If one surveys the modal operators associated with most, if not all, of the most familiar modal systems, such as T, K_4, S_4, S_5, B, D, and G-L, for example, it is clear that in each case the associated operators satisfy the second condition. This, it seems to us, is no "accident," and we have accordingly made this feature of our familiar modals explicit.

We can put the matter this way: Suppose that an operator distributed over an implication relation as well as its dual. Suppose further that the operator is a necessitation and that negation in the structure is classical. Then, by Theorem 26.2, $\varphi(A) \lor \varphi(\neg A)$ is a thesis for all A. We know that this is not so for the familiar modals mentioned above. Thus, the second condition simply makes explicit what everyone already knows about those modals.[2]

> **Exercise 26.4.** Assuming that I is a classical implication structure with negations and disjunctions always available, and that φ is a T modal [φ is a modal operator, and $\varphi(A) \Rightarrow A$ for all A], show that $\varphi(A) \lor \varphi(\neg A)$ is not a thesis for some A.

A further consequence of the second condition on modal operators is that every modal operator is nonextensional (in the sense used in chapter 19). This will be proved later. It is, of course, no news to be told that modals such as necessity and possibility, and the box, $\Box$, of familiar modal systems are nonextensional. No one really thinks otherwise, and no one really thinks that it just happens that all those modals are nonextensional. What is striking is that this feature follows from the characterization of modal operators – and it is the second condition that leads to this result.

Our characterization of modal operators did not rely upon the use of any of the logical operators in its formulation. Operators are modal because of the way that they behave with respect to implication relations. Nevertheless, there are systematic ways in which the hypotheticals, conjunctions, negations, disjunctions, and quantifiers interact with the modal operators on a structure. Even though the modals are characterized without the help of any of the logical operators, it is not surprising that there are systematic connections between them. That possibility arises when the various logical operators as well as the modal operators are relativized to the same implication relation.

26.2 Modals and hypotheticals

Modal operators always distribute over implication. However, when the hypothetical of any two members of a structure exists, modals distribute over hypotheticals:

Theorem 26.3 (distribution over hypotheticals). *Let $I =$ $\langle S, \Rightarrow \rangle$ be an implication structure in which hypotheticals always exists. If φ is any modal operator on I, then $\varphi(A \to B)$ $\Rightarrow \varphi(A) \to \varphi(B)$ for all A and B in S.*

Proof. Since $(A \to B)$ is a hypothetical, $A, (A \to B) \Rightarrow B$. Therefore, for any modal operator φ on I, $\varphi(A), \varphi(A \to B) \Rightarrow$ $\varphi(B)$. Moreover, $\varphi(A), \varphi(A) \to \varphi(B) \Rightarrow \varphi(B)$. By the second condition on hypotheticals, $\varphi(A) \to \varphi(B)$ is the weakest member of S that together with $\varphi(A)$ implies $\varphi(B)$. Consequently, $\varphi(A \to B) \Rightarrow \varphi(A) \to \varphi(B)$.

26.3 Modals and Conjunctions

Modal operators distribute over conjunctions in both directions:

Theorem 26.4. *Let $I = \langle S, \Rightarrow \rangle$ be an implication structure in which conjunctions always exist. Then for any A and B in S, and any modal operator φ on I,*

(a) $\varphi(A) \;\&\; \varphi(B) \Rightarrow \varphi(A \;\&\; B)$, and
(b) $\varphi(A \;\&\; B) \Rightarrow \varphi(A) \;\&\; \varphi(B)$.

Proof. For (a), note that since $A, B \Rightarrow (A \;\&\; B)$, and φ distributes over implication, $\varphi(A), \varphi(B) \Rightarrow \varphi(A \;\&\; B)$. Since the conjunction of $\varphi(A)$ with $\varphi(B)$ implies each of them, (a) follows by Cut. As for (b), we note that $(A \;\&\; B) \Rightarrow A$ (as well as B). Consequently, $\varphi(A \;\&\; B) \Rightarrow \varphi(A)$ [as well as $\varphi(B)$]. Therefore $\varphi(A \;\&\; B)$ implies their conjunction.

26.4 Is ◊, or possibility, a modal?

The preceding result may raise certain objections, for it seems too strong a result. Not every familiar modal distributes over implication. Some do, but it might be argued, some do not. For example, if we think of the box as some kind of necessity (modulo the reservations to which we alluded), then it does seem plausible that the necessity of A and the necessity of B together imply the necessity of their conjunction. However, when we consider the diamond, ◊, the dual of the box, as representing a kind of possibility, then it is implausible that the possibility of A and the possibility of B together imply the possibility of their conjunction. So possibility seems to be a clear (enough) example of a modal that, contrary to the preceding theorem, fails to distribute over conjunctions.

We agree. But there is no difficulty here. One has to be careful in keeping track of the implication relations with respect to which an operator is modal.

If the box, $\square$, is a modal operator with respect to "$\Rightarrow$," then the diamond, $\lozenge$ (taken as $\neg\square\neg$), is also a modal operator – only it is modal with respect to the dual implication relation "$\Rightarrow\hat{\ }$," provided that negation is classical. We shall prove that in classical structures, the box and the diamond are dual modal operators, and, as is only natural, it turns out that although they are modals, they are modals with respect to implication relations that are duals of each other. It will be shown that if a structure is classical, then $\square$ is a modal operator with respect to "$\Rightarrow$" if and only if $\lozenge$ ($\neg\square\neg$) is modal with respect to "$\Rightarrow\hat{\ }$," and it will be shown that the box and the diamond cannot be modal with respect to the same implication relation. These observations can be proved directly. But they also follow as special cases of a few theorems to be proved below. Our observations about $\square$ and $\lozenge$ are not especially about necessity and possibility; they hold in any classical structure in which disjunctions and conjunctions always exist for any modal operator φ and its dual $\neg\varphi\neg$.

Theorem 26.5. *Let $I = \langle S, \Rightarrow \rangle$ be a classical implication structure in which disjunctions and conjunctions always exist. Let φ be any mapping of S to S. Then*

(a) if φ is a modal operator on I, then $\neg\varphi\neg$ is a modal operator on the dual structure $I\hat{\ } = \langle S, \Rightarrow\hat{\ } \rangle$, and

(b) if $\neg\varphi\neg$ is a modal operator on $I\hat{\ }$, then φ is a modal operator on I.

Proof. We shall prove (a), and leave (b) for the reader. One has to show that $\neg\varphi\neg$ distributes over "$\Rightarrow\hat{\ }$," but does not distribute over "$\Rightarrow$" (since conjunctions always exist in I, by Theorem 9.9, $\Rightarrow\hat{\ }\hat{\ } = \Rightarrow$). Suppose, then, that $A_1, \ldots, A_n \Rightarrow\hat{\ } B$. Then $B \Rightarrow (A_1 \vee \ldots \vee A_n)$, since disjunctions always exist in I (Theorem 14.8), so that $\neg(A_1 \vee \ldots \vee A_n) \Rightarrow \neg B$. Since negation is classical, $\neg A_1 \ \& \ \ldots \ \& \ \neg A_n \Rightarrow \neg B$. Consequently, $\neg A_1, \ldots, \neg A_n \Rightarrow \neg B$. By hypothesis, φ is modal on I, so that $\varphi(\neg A_1), \ldots, \varphi(\neg A_n) \Rightarrow \varphi(\neg B)$. Therefore $\varphi(\neg A_1) \ \& \ \ldots \ \& \ \varphi(\neg A_n) \Rightarrow \varphi(\neg B)$, so that $\neg\varphi(\neg B) \Rightarrow \neg\varphi(\neg A_1) \vee \ldots \vee \neg\varphi(\neg A_n)$. Consequently, $\neg\varphi(\neg A_1)$,

..., $\neg\varphi(\neg A_n) \Rightarrow^\wedge \neg\varphi(\neg B)$. So $\neg\varphi\neg$ distributes over "$\Rightarrow^\wedge$." It remains only to be shown that $\neg\varphi\neg$ does not distribute over "$\Rightarrow$." Suppose that it did. Assume that A_1, ..., $A_n \Rightarrow^\wedge B$. Then $B \Rightarrow (A_1 \vee \ldots \vee A_n)$, so that $\neg A_1$ & ... & $\neg A_n \Rightarrow \neg B$. Consequently, $\neg A_1, \ldots, \neg A_n \Rightarrow \neg B$. By hypothesis, $\neg\varphi\neg$ distributes over "$\Rightarrow$." Therefore $\neg\varphi(\neg\neg A_1), \ldots, \neg\varphi(\neg\neg A_n) \Rightarrow \neg\varphi(\neg\neg B)$. Thus, $\neg\varphi(A_1)$, ..., $\neg\varphi(A_n) \Rightarrow \neg\varphi(B)$, so that $\varphi(B) \Rightarrow \varphi(A_1) \vee \ldots \vee \varphi(A_n)$. Therefore $\varphi(A_1), \ldots, \varphi(A_n) \Rightarrow^\wedge \varphi(B)$. Consequently, φ distributes over "$\Rightarrow^\wedge$." But that is impossible, since φ is a modal with respect to "$\Rightarrow$."

Exercise 26.5. Under the conditions of Theorem 26.5, show that if φ is a modal operator with respect to "$\Rightarrow^\wedge$," then $\neg\varphi\neg$ is a modal operator with respect to "$\Rightarrow$."

It follows immediately from Theorem 26.5 that although φ and $\neg\varphi\neg$ are both mappings on the same structure, they cannot both be modal operators on the same structure, for if φ is modal with respect to "$\Rightarrow$," then $\neg\varphi\neg$ is modal with respect to "$\Rightarrow^\wedge$" (assuming that the structure is classical and disjunctions and conjunctions always exist). Therefore $\neg\varphi\neg$ distributes over "$\Rightarrow^\wedge$," but fails to distribute over "$\Rightarrow$." So it is not modal with respect to "$\Rightarrow$." It is true, generally, that no operator can be modal with respect to both "$\Rightarrow$" and "$\Rightarrow^\wedge$," for being modal with respect to "$\Rightarrow$," it distributes over "$\Rightarrow$," and being modal with respect to "$\Rightarrow^\wedge$," it distributes over "$\Rightarrow^\wedge$," but fails to distribute over "$\Rightarrow$." But that is impossible. Therefore no modal on a structure can be equivalent to any modal on the dual structure. And, in particular, since the dual of a modal is some modal on the dual structure, it follows that no modal operator is self-dual (i.e., equivalent to its dual).

The difference between a modal operator and its dual, or (if the structure is classical) between φ and $\neg\varphi\neg$, shows up only when implications are considered that involve multiple antecedents. When only a single antecedent is involved, both φ and $\neg\varphi\neg$ distribute over "$\Rightarrow$" as well as the dual "$\Rightarrow^\wedge$." More generally:

Theorem 26.6. *Let $I = \langle S, \Rightarrow \rangle$ be an implication structure, and let φ be any modal operator on I. Let $I^\wedge = \langle S, \Rightarrow^\wedge \rangle$ be the dual structure, and let σ be any modal on $I^\wedge$. Then for any A and B in S,*

(a) if A $\Rightarrow^{\wedge}$ B, then $\varphi(A) \Rightarrow^{\wedge} \varphi(B)$, and
(b) if A $\Rightarrow$ B, then $\sigma(A) \Rightarrow \sigma(B)$.

Proof. (a) Suppose that $A \Rightarrow^{\wedge} B$. Then $B \Rightarrow A$. Since φ is modal with respect to "$\Rightarrow$," $\varphi(B) \Rightarrow \varphi(A)$. Therefore $\varphi(A) \Rightarrow^{\wedge} \varphi(B)$. (b) is proved similarly.

Thus, in the single-antecedent cases, a modal with respect to "$\Rightarrow$" will also distribute over "$\Rightarrow^{\wedge}$," and a modal with respect to "$\Rightarrow^{\wedge}$" will distribute over "$\Rightarrow$." In particular, the difference between a box and its corresponding diamond shows up only with implications that have several antecedents.

The fact that an operator like $\Diamond$, which is taken to be modal over "$\Rightarrow^{\wedge}$," distributes over single-antecedent implications explains why we do not have, for arbitrary A and B, that $\Diamond(A \to B) \Rightarrow \Diamond(A) \to \Diamond(B)$, for if the latter always held, then $\Diamond$ would distribute over "$\Rightarrow$," contradicting the requirement that it be modal with respect to "$\Rightarrow^{\wedge}$."

Exercise 26.6. Show that if σ is a modal with respect to "$\Rightarrow^{\wedge}$," but not with respect to "$\Rightarrow$," then for some A and B, $\sigma(A \to B) \not\Rightarrow \sigma(A) \to \sigma(B)$.

Exercise 26.7. Let $I = \langle S, \Rightarrow \rangle$ be an implication structure in which disjunctions and conjunctions always exist. Assume that σ is a modal operator with respect to "$\Rightarrow^{\wedge}$," and prove that for any A and B, $\sigma(A \vee B) \Leftrightarrow \sigma(A) \vee \sigma(B)$. [Use $A, B \Rightarrow^{\wedge} (A \vee B)$ to show that $\sigma(A \vee B) \Rightarrow \sigma(A) \vee \sigma(B)$ and, since σ distributes over single-antecedent implications in "$\Rightarrow$," and A (as well as B) $\Rightarrow (A \vee B)$, show that $\sigma(A) \vee \sigma(B) \Rightarrow \sigma(A \vee B)$.]

Exercise 26.8. Let I and $I^{\wedge}$ be as described in Exercise 26.7. Show that if σ is any modal on $I^{\wedge}$, then (a) there are some A and B in S such that $\sigma(A) \,\&\, \sigma(B) \not\Rightarrow \sigma(A \,\&\, B)$ and (b) for any A and B in S, $\sigma(A \,\&\, B) \Rightarrow (A) \,\&\, \sigma(B)$.

27

Modals: Existence and nonextensionality

27.1 Modals as functions

In our characterization of modal operators we stressed the idea that they are certain kinds of functions or mappings on implication structures, $I = \langle S, \Rightarrow \rangle$, mapping the set S of the structure to itself and preserving the implication relation "$\Rightarrow$," but not its dual.

There are several types of questions that arise naturally if we focus on the modals as operators: (1) Given any implication structure I, are there any modals on it? That is, do any modals exist? We shall show that there is a simple necessary and sufficient condition for their existence. (2) If several modal operators exist on a structure, how are they related? For example, will any two, such as φ and φ^*, have to be comparable in the sense that either $\varphi(A) \Rightarrow \varphi^*(A)$ for all A in S or else $\varphi^*(A) \Rightarrow \varphi(A)$ for all A in S. We shall see that the modals on some structures need not be comparable, but that there are interesting consequences when they are. (3) What about more refined descriptions of modals as special kinds of functions? That is, what can one say about those kinds of modals φ for which $\varphi(A) \Rightarrow A$ for all A in S? Under what conditions do they exist? Furthermore, if φ is a modal operator, is its functional product with itself, $\varphi\varphi$, always a modal operator as well? What can be said about those special modal operators that always map theses of the structure into theses? Can one give necessary and sufficient conditions for a modal operator being a function of these various types?

Those who know of the very dramatic systematization by Kripke (1963a,b) of these various kinds of modals, using a possible worlds semantics, will wonder if any systematization can be given on the basis of our account of the modal operators. We shall prove later that a Kripke-style systematization of these special modal operators can be provided, using accessibility relations that are defined not on possible worlds but on nonempty Tarskian theories (those subsets of S that are closed under the implication relation of the structure). Thus, to anticipate later results, it will turn out that $\varphi(A) \Rightarrow A$ for all A in a structure $I = \langle S, \Rightarrow \rangle$ if and only if a certain binary relation R^φ (depending upon the modal operator φ) is reflexive. That is, for all nonempty Tarskian theories U of the structure, $UR^\varphi U$. Similar results hold for the other familiar special modals. (4) Lastly, it is natural to ask of any function, and certainly of the modal operators in particular, whether they are mappings of S onto S or whether they are "not onto." There is a very simple and somewhat surprising answer to the last question, and we begin our discussion with it.

27.2 Modal operators: onto or not onto?

Recall that a mapping of S to S is called *onto* S if and only if every member of S is the image or value of S under the mapping. We shall use a slightly modified version of this standard notion: For every A in S there is some B in S such that $\varphi(B)$ is equivalent to A (under the implication relation of the structure). Otherwise, the mapping is not onto. In the latter case, there is some A in S such that no B of S ever gets mapped to A or to an equivalent of A. Thus, the onto/not onto distinction is now relativized to the implication relation of the structure.

We can now ask whether or not a modal operator on an implication structure $I = \langle S, \Rightarrow \rangle$ maps S onto itself. The following result indicates that there is a very interesting price that has to be paid if a modal operator is onto: At least one of two familiar modal theses will fail to hold. That is,

Definition 27.1. Let $I = \langle S, \Rightarrow \rangle$ be an implication structure, and let φ be a modal operator on I. We shall say that

(a) φ satisfies the *T condition* if and only if for all A in S, $\varphi(A) \Rightarrow A$, and

(b) φ satisfies the *K_4 condition* if and only if for all A in S, $\varphi(A) \Rightarrow \varphi\varphi(A)$.

(We shall say that if a modal operator satisfies an X condition, then it is an X-style modal operator.)

Theorem 27.1 (onto/not onto). *Let $I = \langle S, \Rightarrow \rangle$ be an implication structure, with a modal operator φ on I. If φ is a mapping of S onto S, then φ cannot satisfy both the T condition and the K_4 condition.*

Proof. Suppose that both modal theses hold, and assume that φ maps S onto S. Therefore, for any A in S, there is a B in S such that $A \Leftrightarrow \varphi(B)$. Therefore $\varphi(A) \Leftrightarrow \varphi\varphi(B)$, since φ distributes over "$\Rightarrow$." But $\varphi(B) \Leftrightarrow \varphi\varphi(B)$, since $\varphi(B) \Rightarrow B$, so that $\varphi\varphi(B) \Rightarrow \varphi(B)$, and $\varphi(B) \Rightarrow \varphi\varphi(B)$, by hypothesis. Consequently, $\varphi(A) \Leftrightarrow \varphi(B)$, so that $A \Leftrightarrow \varphi(A)$ for all A in S. This is what is usually called the "collapse" of the modal. It shows that φ is not a modal operator, because any operator that collapses cannot be modal, for with collapse, $\varphi(A \vee B) \Rightarrow \varphi(A) \vee \varphi(B)$ for all A and B.

There is a corollary that one can draw concerning certain attempts to construe some concepts modally. Intuitionists usually are believed to hold the view that a certain collection of mathematical propositions they consider have a necessary character. If one thought that and attempted to mark that necessary character with a special modal, $\square_i$, such that every proposition M in the collection was equivalent to $\square_i N$ for some N in the collection, then $\square_i$ would be a mapping of the collection onto itself. It could not therefore satisfy both of the T and K_4 conditions. That would constitute something of a problem for such intuitionists: how to express the necessary character of all the members of a special set of mathematical propositions and still retain the modal theses T and K_4 for the kind of necessity that they have in mind.[1]

There are some further observations worth making about the onto/not onto question for modals:

Definition 27.2. Let $I = \langle S, \Rightarrow \rangle$ be an implication structure. We shall say that a modal operator φ on I is a *necessitation modal* if and only if whenever A is a thesis of I, so too is $\varphi(A)$.

Theorem 27.2. *Let $I = \langle S, \Rightarrow \rangle$ be an implication structure, and suppose that φ is a modal – either with respect to "$\Rightarrow$" or with respect to the dual "$\Rightarrow\hat{\ }$." If φ is a mapping of S onto S (under "$\Rightarrow$"), then φ maps theses of I to theses of I.*

Proof. Suppose that φ is a modal on I. Let A be any thesis of I. Then $B \Rightarrow A$, and so $\varphi(B) \Rightarrow \varphi(A)$ for all B in S. Let C be any member of S. Since φ is onto, there is some C^* in S such that $C \Leftrightarrow \varphi(C^*)$. Therefore $C \Rightarrow \varphi(A)$ for all C in S. Consequently, $\varphi(A)$ is a thesis. If φ is a modal with respect to "$\Rightarrow\hat{\ }$" and maps S onto S, then φ also maps theses of I to theses of *I*. The proof is similar to the case when φ is modal with respect to "$\Rightarrow$."

Exercise 27.1. Let *I* be a classical implication structure, and let φ be a modal operator on *I*. Then φ is a mapping of *S* onto *S* if and only if $\neg\varphi\neg$ is also a mapping of *S* onto *S*.

Exercise 27.2. Let *I* be a classical implication structure that has a thesis, and let φ be a modal operator on *I* such that $\varphi(\varphi(A) \to A) \Rightarrow \varphi(A)$ (such modals are Gödel – Löb modals, and will be studied later). Assuming that for such modals $\neg\varphi\neg(A)$ is never a thesis, show that φ is not a mapping of *S* onto *S*. [Assume that φ maps *S* onto *S*, and use Exercise 27.1 and Theorem 27.2 to conclude that $\neg\varphi\neg(A)$ is a thesis for some member of the structure.]

27.3 The existence of modal operators

There is, in general, no assurance that there is some modal on an arbitrary implication structure. We shall give an example of a structure that has no modals on it. Neither is there any guarantee that if there are several modals on a structure, then of any two, one is weaker (implicationally) than the other. Nevertheless, there are some fairly weak conditions under which modal operators can be shown to exist.

27.3.1 Noncomparable modals

Here is an elementary example of a structure with two modals φ and φ* on it, neither being stronger (implicationally) than the other:

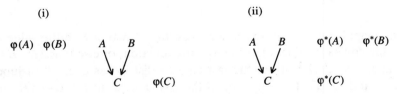

(i)   (ii)

Both φ and φ* are easily seen to be modals over the set {*A, B, C*} (to check that there is no distribution over the dual implication relation, note that the dual is obtained by reversing the arrows). The two modals, however, are not comparable, for $\varphi(T) \Rightarrow \varphi^*(T)$ fails to hold for all *T* in *S*, since φ(*A*) is *A*, and φ*(*A*) is *B*, and *A* does not imply *B* in this structure. Similarly, φ*(*A*) does not imply φ(*A*).

27.3.2 Nonnecessitation and noniterable modals

Consider the following implication structure, whose set $S = \{A, B, C, D\}$ and whose implication relation are as shown:

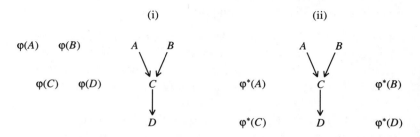

It is straightforward to verify that the mapping φ in (i) is a modal operator [note, for the failure to distribute over disjunctions, that $(A \vee B)$ is C, so that $\varphi(A \vee B)$ is C, but $\varphi(A) \vee \varphi(B)$ is A, and C does not imply A]. However, φ is not a necessitation modal, since D is a thesis of the structure, but $\varphi(D)$ (that is, C) is not, since D does not imply C.

The modal φ^* in (ii) is a necessitation modal, but $\varphi^*\varphi^*$, its iteration, is not, for $\varphi^*\varphi^*$ has the constant value D on S, and therefore is not modal (it distributes over the dual).

27.3.3 A structure with no modal

Consider this structure with just two members A and B:

Any mapping φ of S to S is either a constant function with the value A (or the constant value B) or the identity function, or else it assigns B to A and A to B. In all but the last case, φ distributes over all disjunctions, and so fails to be modal. In the last case, φ distributes over any disjunction of any member with itself. Since the disjunction of A with B is B, $\varphi(A \vee B) \Rightarrow \varphi(A) \vee \varphi(B)$ has to hold, since $\varphi(A \vee B)$ is A. In all cases, then, φ distributes over disjuction, and therefore fails to be modal.

There is a reason for this. In order for an implication structure I to have a modal operator on it, it is necessary that there be at least three members A, B, and C in S such that neither A nor B implies the other, and C implies neither A nor B. That is,

Theorem 27.3. *Let $I = \langle S, \Rightarrow \rangle$ be an implication structure, and let φ be a modal operator on I. Then there are A, B, and C in S such that $A \not\Rightarrow B$, $B \not\Rightarrow A$, $C \not\Rightarrow A$, and $C \not\Rightarrow B$.*

Proof. For some $A_1, \ldots, A_n$, and B in S, $A_1, \ldots, A_n \Rightarrow^\wedge B$, and $\varphi(A_1), \ldots, \varphi(A_n) \not\Rightarrow \varphi(B)$, since φ does not distribute over "$\Rightarrow^\wedge$." Without loss of generality we can assume that none of the A_i's imply each other, for if, say, $A_1 \Rightarrow A_2$ then $A_2 \Rightarrow^\wedge A_1$. Then, by Cut, $A_2, \ldots, A_n \Rightarrow^\wedge B$, and $\varphi(A_2), \ldots, \varphi(A_n) \not\Rightarrow^\wedge \varphi(B)$ [if "$\Rightarrow^\wedge$" held between $\varphi(A_2), \ldots, \varphi(A_n)$ and $\varphi(B)$, then it would also hold, by Dilution, if $\varphi(A_1)$ were added to the antecedents – and that is impossible]. Note also that there must be at least two antecedents, say A_1 and A_2, for if there were only one, then it would be impossible to have $A \Rightarrow^\wedge B$ and $\varphi(A) \not\Rightarrow^\wedge \varphi(B)$. We conclude, then, that $A_1 \not\Rightarrow A_2$ and $A_2 \not\Rightarrow A_1$. Moreover, $B \not\Rightarrow A_1$, for if $B \Rightarrow A_1$, then $A_1 \Rightarrow^\wedge B$, so that $\varphi(A_1) \not\Rightarrow^\wedge \varphi(B)$. Then $\varphi(A_1), \ldots, \varphi(A_n) \Rightarrow^\wedge \varphi(B)$. But that is impossible. Similarly, $B \not\Rightarrow A_2$. Thus, there are A_1, A_2, and B in S such that $A_1 \not\Rightarrow A_2$, $A_2 \not\Rightarrow A_1$, $B \not\Rightarrow A_1$, and $B \not\Rightarrow A_2$.

We have a simpler necessary and sufficient condition for the existence of modals if the implication structure always has disjunctions:

Theorem 27.4. *If $I = \langle S, \Rightarrow \rangle$ is an implication structure in which disjunctions always exist, then there is a modal operator on I if and only if there are two members of S neither of which implies the other.*

Proof. By the preceding theorem, if there is a modal on I, then there are two members of S neither of which implies the other. Conversely, let A and B be in S, neither implying the other, and let C be their disjunction. (Note, in passing, that C implies neither A nor B.) Define an operator φ on S as follows: For any E in S,

$$\varphi(E) = \begin{cases} C, \text{ if } C \Rightarrow E \\ \\ A, \text{ otherwise.} \end{cases}$$

Then φ is a modal operator on I. Note first that φ does not distribute over "$\Rightarrow^\wedge$," for $A, B \Rightarrow^\wedge C$, since C is the disjunction of A and B. However, $\varphi(A), \varphi(B) \not\Rightarrow^\wedge \varphi(C)$, for C implies neither A nor B, so that $\varphi(A)$ and $\varphi(B)$ are A, while $\varphi(C)$ is C. Thus, $\varphi(A), \varphi(B) \not\Rightarrow^\wedge \varphi(C)$ because $A \not\Rightarrow^\wedge C$ (i.e., $C \not\Rightarrow A$). That φ distributes over "$\Rightarrow$" is shown by cases: Suppose that $A_1, \ldots, A_n \Rightarrow D$. Case 1: For all A_i, $C \Rightarrow A_i$. Then $C \Rightarrow D$. Therefore all the φ (A_i) as well as $\varphi(D)$ are C, so that $\varphi(A_1), \ldots, \varphi(A_n) \Rightarrow \varphi(D)$. Case 2: For all A_i, $C \not\Rightarrow A_i$. Then all the $\varphi(A_i)$ are A. Now if $C \Rightarrow D$, then $\varphi(D)$ is C, so that $\varphi(A_1), \ldots, \varphi(A_n) \Rightarrow \varphi(D)$, since $A, \ldots, A \Rightarrow C$ $(A \vee B)$. If $C \not\Rightarrow D$, then $\varphi(D)$ is A, and $\varphi(A_1), \ldots, \varphi(A_n) \Rightarrow \varphi(D)$, since $A, \ldots, A \Rightarrow A$. Lastly, Case 3: Some A_i is implied by C, and some A_j is not implied by C (A_i and A_j different). Then $\varphi(A_i)$ is C, and $\varphi(A_j)$ is A. Now if $C \Rightarrow D$, then $\varphi(D)$ is C, and if $C \not\Rightarrow D$, then $\varphi(D)$ is A. In either case, $\varphi(A_1), \ldots, \varphi(A_i), \ldots, \varphi(A_j), \ldots, \varphi(A_n) \Rightarrow \varphi(D)$, because whether $\varphi(D)$ is C or A, $\varphi(A_1), \ldots, C, \ldots, A, \ldots, \varphi(A_n) \Rightarrow \varphi(D)$.

A simple consequence that follows from the preceding theorem concerns those structures that are incomplete with respect to negation:

Theorem 27.5. *If $I = \langle S, \Rightarrow \rangle$ is a classical implication structure in which disjunctions always exist, then I is incomplete with respect to negation if and only if there exists a modal operator on I that is also a necessitation modal.*

Proof. Suppose that I is incomplete with respect to negation. Then there is some A in S such that neither A nor $\neg A$ is a thesis of I. Neither A nor $\neg A$ implies the other, for if A implies $\neg A$, then since I is classical, $(A \vee \neg A)$ implies $\neg A$, so that $\neg A$ is a thesis. Similarly, if $\neg A$ implies A, then A is a thesis. But either case is impossible. By the preceding theorem, there is a modal operator φ on I such that if $(A \vee \neg A) \Rightarrow E$, then $\varphi(E)$ is $(A \vee \neg A)$. Thus, φ is also a necessitation modal. For the Converse, suppose that I is complete with respect to negation and that φ is a necessitation modal on I. Then for any A, either A is a thesis [in which case $\varphi(A)$ is a thesis] or else $\neg A$ is a thesis [so that $\varphi(\neg A)$ is a thesis]. Therefore $\varphi(A) \vee \varphi(\neg A)$ is a thesis for all A. Consequently, $\neg\varphi(\neg A) \Rightarrow \varphi(A)$. In that case, however, φ distributes over disjunctions, for negation is classical, so that $\varphi(A \lor B) \Rightarrow \varphi(\neg A \to B) \Rightarrow \varphi(\neg A) \to \varphi(B)$ $\Rightarrow \neg\varphi(\neg A) \lor \varphi(B) \Rightarrow \varphi(A) \lor \varphi(B)$. Thus, φ is not a modal on I. But that is impossible.

From Theorem 27.5 it follows that there are necessitation modal operators on the classical sentential calculus (CSC). Form the associated implication structure I_{CSC}, which is classical and incomplete with respect to negation. In it, disjunctions always exist, and A is a thesis of it if and only if $\vdash_{CSC} A$. In fact, there are infinitely many such modals on I_{CSC}, no two of which are comparable. Take any atomic sentence p of CSC. Let φ_p be the modal operator such that $\varphi_p(E)$ is $(p \lor \neg p)$ if $(p \lor \neg p) \Rightarrow E$, and p otherwise. Thus,

Theorem 27.6. *For each atomic sentence of the CSC, there is a necessitation modal operator on the implication structure associated with CSC.*

Exercise 27.3. Show that the modal operators of Theorem 27.6 that are associated with distinct atomic sentences are implicationally incomparable (neither implies the other for all sentences of CSC).

We have been considering those features of modal operators taken generally. Before discussing some of the special kinds of modal operators, let us consider one other feature that all modals possess: They are nonextensional. This is, of course, no great news. What is interesting is that it is a consequence of our characterization of the modals.

27.4 The nonextensionality of modal operators

Modal operators, like the logical operators, are defined over structures that need not consist of truth-bearers. In a general discussion of the extensionality of the modals we shall therefore use the strong bisections of the structure as providing the general notion of a "truth-value" assignment. However, as with the logical operators, it is helpful to see what the situation looks like in the special case in which the modals are defined over statements or truth-bearers. Here is a preliminary informal argument that such modal operators are nonextensional. It will be followed by a more rigorous general proof.

Let $I = \langle S \Rightarrow \rangle$ consist of a set of sentences or statements, and let "$\Rightarrow$" be an appropriate implication relation that satisfies the following conditions: There is a nonempty set C of truth-value assignments to the members of S such that the following hold: (1) For each assignment in C, "$\Rightarrow$" is truth-preserving. That is, if $A_1, \ldots, A_n \Rightarrow B$, and T_i belongs to C, and T_i assigns "truth" to all the A_i, then it assigns "truth" to B as well. (2) Disjunction is extensional for each T_i in C. It was proved in Chapter 19 that the requirement comes to this: T_i assigns "truth" to $(A \lor B)$ if and only if it assigns "truth" to at least one of A, B. (3) If $A \nRightarrow B$, then there is some truth-value assignment T_j in C such that T_j assigns "truth" to A, but not to B.

Suppose that φ is a modal operator on I. Then for some A and B in S, $\varphi(A \lor B) \nRightarrow \varphi(A) \lor \varphi(B)$. By (3), there is some truth-value assignment in C that assigns "truth" to $\varphi(A \lor B)$, but "false" (does not assign "true") to $\varphi(A) \lor \varphi(B)$. By (2), it follows that $\varphi(A)$ is "false," and so too for $\varphi(B)$. The situation then is this: There is some assignment in C (say T^*) under which $\varphi(A \lor B)$ is true and $\varphi(A)$ and $\varphi(B)$ are false. What about the extensionality of the modal?

We shall say that φ is extensional if and only if (for any assignment belonging to C) whenever A and B have the same truth value, then so too do $\varphi(A)$ and $\varphi(B)$.

It follows that φ is not extensional. Consider the assignment T^*. There are two cases to consider: when both A and B are true, and when they are both false. (1) Suppose that A and B are both true (under T^*). Since the implication relation on S preserves truth, and $A \Rightarrow (A \lor B)$, it follows that $(A \lor B)$ is also true (under T^*). Thus, A and $(A \lor B)$ are both true (under T^*), but $\varphi(A \lor B)$ is true (under T^*), while $\varphi(A)$ is false (under T^*). (2) Suppose that A and B are both false (under T^*). Then $(A \lor B)$ is false. Thus, both A and $(A \lor B)$ are false (under T^*), but $\varphi(A \lor B)$ is true, and $\varphi(A)$ is false (under T^*). (3) Suppose that A is true and B is false (under T^*). Then both A and $(A \lor B)$ are true, while $\varphi(A \lor B)$ is true and $\varphi(A)$ is false (under T^*). (4) Suppose that A is false but B is true (under T^*). Then B and $(A \lor B)$ are both true (under T^*), but $\varphi(A \lor B)$ is true and $\varphi(B)$ is false (under T^*). Therefore, no matter what the truth-value distribution is over A and B, there is always a case in which two statements have the same truth value, but φ of them do not.

The argument just given informally for statements can be proved for the general case. We shall use the general definition for the extensionality of a mapping of S to S (Definition 19.1), according to which a mapping φ of S to S is extensional with respect to a strong bisection $T = \langle K, L \rangle$ on $I = \langle S, \Rightarrow \rangle$ if and only if whenever A and B in S have the same truth value (either they both belong to K or they both belong

L), then $\varphi(A)$ and $\varphi(B)$ have the same truth value (they are either both in K or both in L).

Theorem 27.7. *Let $I \langle S, \Rightarrow \rangle$ be an implication structure, with φ any modal operator on it. Suppose that for any E and F in S, if $E \not\Rightarrow F$, there is a normal bisection $T = \langle K, L \rangle$ on I such that $E \not\Rightarrow^T F$. Then φ is not extensional with respect to the bisection T.*

Proof. Since φ is a modal on I, there are two members A_0 and B_0 of S such that $\varphi(A_0 \vee B_0) \not\Rightarrow \varphi(A_0) \vee \varphi(B_0)$. By hypothesis there is a normal bisection $T = \langle K, L \rangle$ of I such that $\varphi(A_0 \vee B_0)$ is in L and $\varphi(A_0) \vee \varphi(B_0)$ is in K. Now both $\varphi(A_0)$ and $\varphi(B_0)$ are in K, for if either of them were in L, then $\varphi(A_0) \vee \varphi(B_0)$ would be in L, and that is impossible. Thus, $\varphi(A_0)$ and $\varphi(B_0)$ are in K, and $\varphi(A_0 \vee B_0)$ is in L. There are four cases to consider: (1) Both A_0 and B_0 are in L. Then A_0 and $(A_0 \vee B_0)$ are in L, but then $\varphi(A_0 \vee B_0)$ is in L, while $\varphi(A_0)$ is in K. (2) A_0 is in L, and B_0 is in K. Then both A_0 and $(A_0 \vee B_0)$ are in L, but $\varphi(A_0)$ is in K, while $\varphi(A_0 \vee B_0)$ is in L. (3) A_0 is in K, and B_0 is in L. Then both B_0 and $(A_0 \vee B_0)$ are in L, but $\varphi(B_0)$ is in K, while $\varphi(A_0 \vee B_0)$ is in L. (4) Both A_0 and B_0 are in K. Then, since T is a normal bisection, $(A_0 \vee B_0)$ is in K. Thus, A_0 and $(A_0 \vee B_0)$ are in K, while $\varphi(A_0)$ is in K and $\varphi(A_0 \vee B_0)$ is in L. In every case, then, φ fails to be extensional with respect to the normal bisection T.

One might be concerned that normal bisections are a bit special, as bisections go, and thus the result for nonextensionality of the modal operators is less general than it seems. But normality is precisely the condition that one wants. If nonnormal bisections were used to evaluate the extensionality of the modals, then even the operators of negation, hypotheticals, and disjunctions would be nonextensional (see the observations of Bernstein, Carnap, and Church in chapter 19). So the use of normal bisections is precisely to the point, and the modals are nonextensional on those bisections, where the extensionality of the logical operators is not in question.[2]

We have thus far been concerned with only the most general features of modal operators – their existence or nonexistence, their distribution over hypotheticals and conjunctions, their onto/not onto character as functions, and their nonextensionality.

Early on we also noted that there are special modal theses, certain conditions that modals may or may not satisfy. We do not think of any of these special modal theses as characterizing what is truly modal. All of these conditions are, as it were, above and beyond the call of modality. We do not think of the satisfaction of the T condition, or the S_4, S_5, and other conditions, as the core of modality. There is no special point to thinking of the various conditions for the special modals yielding a special fund of operators, among which only certain ones have true modal character. Just as one can study particular functions in mathematical analysis, so one can study particular modal operators. It is the subject, in any given case, that determines whether or not a certain operator on a structure is modal. And it is to the subject that we also look in determining whether or not the modal has characteristic features that distinguish it from other modal operators. We should no more look to the particular modal theses for a clue to true modal character than we should try to decide between continuous and discontinuous functions for the true character of what it is to be a function. With this little homily behind us, it is time to have a look at some of the particular modal operators, most of which are more or less familiar.

28

Special modals

28.1 D modals

Definition 28.1. Let $I = \langle S, \Rightarrow \rangle$ be an implication structure. We shall say that a modal operator φ on I satisfies the D *condition* if and only if for all A in S, $\varphi(A) \Rightarrow \neg\varphi(\neg A)$.

One reason for studying modals that satisfy this special condition can be traced to the interest in what is obligatory and what is permissible. We shall not worry, for the moment, whether it is acts, or sentences, or statements upon which the corresponding operators O and P are defined. It is suggested that "$P(A)$" ("it is permissible that A") conveys that it is not obligatory that "not A" (or it is not obligatory that you do "not A"), and conversely. Thus it looks as if "P" might be defined simply as "$\neg O\neg$," and it is then argued that the condition $O(A) \Rightarrow P(A)$ holds: It is obligatory that A implies that it is permissible that A. Nothing can be both obligatory and not permissible. Together with the definition of "P," we have the particular condition $O(A) \Rightarrow \neg O(\neg A)$ for all A's in the relevant structure. This is, then, if one is persuaded, a particular case of a D modal.[1]

There is another way of looking at the D condition that is more logical in flavor and in turn sheds some light on the plausibility of the D condition holding for obligation.

Consider a structure I, with a modal operator φ on it. For any A and its negation, $A, \neg A \Rightarrow B$ for all B in the structure. Since φ is a modal operator, it distributes over all implications, so that, in general, $\varphi(A)$, $\varphi(\neg A) \Rightarrow \varphi(B)$ for all B. This is not, in general, equivalent to the condition that $\varphi(A)$ and $\varphi(\neg A)$ are contradictory.

Definition 28.2. Let $I = \langle S, \Rightarrow \rangle$ be an implication structure. We shall say that a modal φ on I *preserves negation* if and only if whenever $A_1, \ldots, A_n \Rightarrow B$ for all B in S, then $\varphi(A_1), \ldots, \varphi(A_n) \Rightarrow B$ for all B in S.

We then have the following equivalent for the D condition:

Theorem 28.1. *For any modal operator φ on a structure I, φ satisfies the D condition if and only if it preserves negation.*

Proof. Suppose that φ preserves negation. Then $\varphi(A)$, $\varphi(\neg A)$ $\Rightarrow B$ for all B. By negation, $\varphi(\neg A) \Rightarrow \neg\varphi(A)$, so that $\varphi(A)$ $\Rightarrow \neg\varphi(\neg A)$. Conversely, suppose that φ satisfies the D condition and that $A_1, \ldots, A_n \Rightarrow B$ for all B. Then $A_1, \ldots, A_{n-1}$ $\Rightarrow \neg A_n$. Consequently, $\varphi(A_1), \ldots, \varphi(A_{n-1}) \Rightarrow \varphi(\neg A_n)$ $\Rightarrow \neg\varphi(A_n)$. Then $\varphi(A_1), \ldots, \varphi(A_n) \Rightarrow B$ for all B.

There are modal operators that fail to preserve negation. As we shall see later, all Gödel–Löb modals are important examples. Preservation of negation is a special condition. Usually, in the study of modal systems, possibility, $\Diamond$, is defined as $\neg\Box\neg$, so that the D condition requires that $\Box(A) \Rightarrow \Diamond(A)$ (all A in S). However, even if $\Diamond$ is defined as $\neg\Box\neg$, the condition is equivalent to the requirement that $\Box(A)$ and $\Box(\neg A)$ be inconsistent – and that is something special. The requirement usually assumed in the deontic situation is likewise special. It is not obvious that $O(A) \Rightarrow P(A)$ even if "$P(A)$" is defined as "$\neg O(\neg A)$," for the characteristic deontic thesis $O(A) \Rightarrow \neg O(\neg A)$ holds if and only if it is inconsistent for both A and $\neg A$ to be obligatory. This is a moot point concerning obligation. Some have held that it is possible that it is obligatory that A, and obligatory that B, even when A and B are incompatible. Indeed, that is one kind of serious moral predicament. We have no case for one side rather than the other. However, it is important to note that whether or not the D condition holds for obligation turns exactly on this issue about incompatible obligations.[2]

Exercise 28.1 (deontic dominance). Let $I = \langle S, \Rightarrow \rangle$ be an implication structure with a modal φ on it. Say that φ *dominates* S if and only if for every A in S there is some B in S such that $\varphi(B) \Rightarrow A$. Show that φ satisfies the D condition if and only if φ dominates S. In the deontic case, this means that every statement is implied by some obligation. Is this plausible for obligation?

Theorem 28.2. *Let $I = \langle S, \Rightarrow \rangle$ be an implication structure, and let φ and ψ be modal on I. If $\psi(A) \Rightarrow \varphi(A)$ for all A, and φ is a D modal, then so too is ψ.*

Proof. Since $\psi(A) \Rightarrow \varphi(A)$ for all A, $\psi(\neg A) \Rightarrow \varphi(\neg A)$. Therefore $\neg\varphi(\neg A) \Rightarrow \neg\psi(\neg A)$. Then $\psi(A) \Rightarrow \varphi(A) \Rightarrow \neg\varphi(\neg A)$ (since φ is a D modal). Therefore $\psi(A) \Rightarrow \neg\psi(\neg A)$, so that ψ is a D modal.

Definition 28.3. Modal operators φ and ψ are *Comparable* on the implication structure $I = \langle S, \Rightarrow \rangle$ if and only if either $\varphi(A) \Rightarrow \psi(A)$ for all A in S or $\psi(A) \Rightarrow \varphi(A)$ for all A in S.

Theorem 28.3. *If φ and ψ are comparable modals on the structure $I = \langle S, \Rightarrow \rangle$, and φ is a D modal, but ψ is not, then $\varphi(A) \Rightarrow \psi(A)$ for all A in S.*

Proof. If $\psi(A) \Rightarrow \varphi(A)$, then by Theorem 28.2, ψ is a D modal. But that is impossible. Therefore $\varphi(A) \Rightarrow \psi(A)$ for all A in S.

Exercise 28.2. Let $I = \langle S, \Rightarrow \rangle$ be an implication structure, and φ a modal operator on I. Show that φ is a D modal if and only if $\neg\varphi(\neg A)$ is a thesis of I for some A in S.[3]

28.2 T modals

This kind of modal operator, for which $\varphi(A) \Rightarrow A$ for all A, seems most familiar, since "necessarily true" is the notion usually used to introduce modal theory itself. In general, modal operators need not satisfy the T condition, although the modal systems (T) [or (M)], (S_4), (B), (S_5), and even Prior's radical system Q (Hughes and Cresswell, 1968, p. 303) make use of it. The Gödel–Löb modal system, on the other hand, is the most prominent (aside from (D)) for which it does not hold. Consequently, we have not made, and do not wish to make, the T condition the sine qua non of modality. To do so would seem to be just another way of insisting that no operator is modal unless it is a type of necessity.

There are implication structures with modals on them that fail to satisfy the T condition [cf. the structures (i) and (ii) in Section 27.3.1]. However, there are conditions under which there has to be at least one T-style modal on a structure:

Theorem 28.4. *Let $I = \langle S, \Rightarrow \rangle$ be a classical implication structure in which conjunctions and disjunctions always exist, and let φ be a necessitation modal on I. If φ is not a T-style* *modal, then there exists a T-style modal operator on I that is definitely stronger (implicationally) than φ.*

Proof. If φ is not T-style, then for some C in S, $\varphi(C) \not\Rightarrow C$. Let φ*(A) be defined as φ(A) & A (for all A in S). Note first that φ* is a modal operator on I. It distributes over "$\Rightarrow$." In addition, φ* fails to distribute over the dual implication. Suppose that it does so distribute. Then for every A and B in S, φ*(A ∨ B) $\Rightarrow$ φ*(A) ∨ φ*(B). In particular, φ*(A ∨ ¬A) $\Rightarrow$ φ*(A) ∨ φ*(¬A), so that φ(A ∨ ¬A) & (A ∨ ¬A) $\Rightarrow$ φ(A) & A ∨ φ(¬A) & ¬A. Since negation is classical, φ(A ∨ ¬A) $\Rightarrow$ φ(A) ∨ φ(¬A). But this condition, together with the assumption that φ is a necessitation, implies that φ distributes over all disjunctions (Theorem 26.2). That is impossible, since φ is modal on I. Consequently, φ* is a modal on I. It is obviously a T-style modal that is at least as strong as φ, since φ*(A) $\Rightarrow$ φ(A) & A $\Rightarrow$ φ(A) (as well as A) for all A in S. Moreover, φ* is definitely stronger than φ, for φ*(C) implies C, but φ(C) does not, so that $\varphi(C) \not\Rightarrow \varphi^*(C)$.[4]

28.3 Necessitation modals, I

We have already used the necessitation condition in some of the preceding theorems, but it is a special condition that is not satisfied by all modals [cf. the modal of structure (i) in Section 27.3.2].

Necessitation modals enjoy a prominent role in contemporary modal theory, since the best-understood parts of that theory concern normal modal systems, for which it is required (in part) not only that the modal distribute over hypotheticals but also that a rule of necessitation, the counterpart of our necessitation condition, hold.

There are several different equivalent descriptions of the necessitation condition. The one with which we began will count as the "official" version. Here are some others:

Theorem 28.5. *Let I $\langle S, \Rightarrow \rangle$ be an implication structure that has at least one thesis. Let φ be a modal operator on I. The following are equivalent:*

(1) (Official): If A is a thesis of I, so too is φ(A).
(2) $\varphi(A_0)$ is a thesis of I for some thesis A_0.
(3) φ(B) is a thesis for some B in S.

(4) S is dominated by φ. That is, for any A in S, there is some B such that $A \Rightarrow \varphi(B)$.

Proof. Because I has at least one thesis, (1) implies (2). (2) implies (3), for assume that $\varphi(A_0)$ is a thesis for some thesis A_0; then A_0 can serve for the B required by (3). (3) implies (4), for let A be any member of S; then by (3), $\varphi(B)$ is a thesis for some B. Thus $A \Rightarrow \varphi(B)$. Lastly, (4) implies (1): Suppose that A is a thesis of I. Then $C \Rightarrow A$ for all C in S. Since φ is modal on I, $\varphi(C) \Rightarrow \varphi(A)$ for all C in S. Let E be any member of S. By (4), there is some E^* in S such that $E \Rightarrow \varphi(E^*)$. But $\varphi(E^*) \Rightarrow \varphi(A)$. Consequently, $E \Rightarrow \varphi(A)$ (for all E in S). So $\varphi(A)$ is a thesis of I.[5]

Exercise 28.3. Let $I = \langle S, \Rightarrow \rangle$ be a classical implication structure in which disjunctions and conjunctions always exist. Show that φ is a necessitation modal on I if and only if $\neg\varphi\neg$ is a necessitation modal on the dual structure $I^{\wedge}$.

With the introduction of some additional notions it becomes possible to study the necessitation modals in ways that reveal their connection with the Kripke-style systematization of various kinds of modal operators. We shall need a few definitions:

Definition 28.4. Let $I = \langle S, \Rightarrow \rangle$ be an implication structure. By a *(weak) Tarskian theory U* of the structure I we mean any subset of S that is (weakly) closed under "$\Rightarrow$". That is, if A is in U and $A \Rightarrow B$, then B is in U. If U is (strongly) closed under "$\Rightarrow$" [that is, if $A_1, \ldots, A_n \Rightarrow B$, and all the A_i's are in U, then so too is B], then U is a (strong) Tarskian theory.

Except in Chapter 36, we shall be concerned mainly with weak Tarskian theories and shall refer to them simply as "theories."

When an implication structure has a modal operator on it, we shall also need the notion of an accessibility relation for that modal:

Definition 28.5. Let $I = \langle S, \Rightarrow \rangle$ be an implication structure, and φ a modal operator on I. An *accessibility relation* (for φ), R^{φ}, is a binary relation defined over the set T of all theories $U, V, \ldots$ of I, such that for all U and V, $UR^{\varphi}V$ if and only if $\varphi^{-1}U \subseteq V$.[6]

By $\varphi^{-1}U$, the inverse image of U under φ, we mean the set of all those A's in S for which $\varphi(A)$ is in U. We have left open the possibility that a theory of I may be empty. Even if U is a nonempty theory of a structure, there is no assurance that $\varphi^{-1}U$ is also nonempty. Aside from the issue of whether or not a theory is empty, a matter that is important for the study of necessitation modals, it is generally true that $\varphi^{-1}U$ is a theory provided that U is a theory and φ is a modal on I. That is,

Theorem 28.6. *Let $I = \langle S, \Rightarrow \rangle$ be an implication structure, and φ a modal operator on I. If U is a theory of I, then so too is $\varphi^{-1}U$.*

Proof. One has to show that $\varphi^{-1}U$ is (weakly) closed under "$\Rightarrow$." Suppose that A is in $\varphi^{-1}U$ and that $A \Rightarrow B$. Since A is in $\varphi^{-1}U$, $\varphi(A)$ is in U. And $\varphi(A) \Rightarrow \varphi(B)$, since φ is modal on I. Moreover, U is closed, so that $\varphi(B)$ is in U. Consequently, B is in $\varphi^{-1}U$.

Exercise 28.4. Let σ be any modal operator with respect to the dual implication relation "$\Rightarrow^\wedge$," where $I = \langle S, \Rightarrow \rangle$. Show that if U is (weakly) closed with respect to "$\Rightarrow$," then so too is $\sigma^{-1}U$. (Recall that even if an operator is modal on the dual of I, it still distributes over single-antecedent implications involving "$\Rightarrow$.") The result does not hold if strong rather than weak closure is used.

We can now describe two further conditions, each necessary and sufficient for a modal's being a necessitation modal:

Theorem 28.7. *Let $I = \langle S, \Rightarrow \rangle$ be an implication structure that has some theses, and let φ be a modal on I. Then φ is a necessitation modal if and only if $\varphi^{-1}U$ is nonempty for every nonempty theory U of I.*

Proof. Suppose that φ is a necessitation modal on I, and let U be any nonempty theory of I. Let A be any member of U. By Theorem 28.5(4), there is some B in S such that $A \Rightarrow \varphi(B)$. Since U is closed, $\varphi(B)$ is in U, so that B is in $\varphi^{-1}U$, which is therefore nonempty. Conversely, suppose that $\varphi^{-1}U$ is nonempty for every nonempty U. Let A be a thesis of I. If U is nonempty, then A is a member of U, since it is implied by every member of S, and therefore by any member of U. Therefore

$\varphi^{-1}U$ is nonempty. Let B be some member of it. Then $\varphi(B)$ is in U. Now $B \Rightarrow A$, since A is a thesis. Therefore $\varphi(B) \Rightarrow \varphi(A)$. Consequently, $\varphi(A)$ is in U. Thus, $\varphi(A)$ is a member of every nonempty theory U. Consequently, $\varphi(A)$ is a thesis, for if A is a thesis, then it is in every nonempty weakly closed theory, since it is implied by some member of U. (Conversely, suppose that A is not a thesis. Then there is a nonempty theory in which it fails to belong: Let U^* be the set of all C such that $C \nRightarrow A$.)

The second necessary and sufficient condition involves the use of accessibility relations on the nonempty theories of a structure:

Theorem 28.8. *Let $I = \langle S, \Rightarrow \rangle$ be an implication structure, and φ a modal operator on I. Let R^φ be the accessibility relation defined earlier. Then φ is a necessitation modal on I if and only if [for every A in S, and every nonempty theory U of I, $\varphi(A) \in U$ if and only if for all nonempty theories $(V)(UR^\varphi V \to A \in V)$].*

Proof. In one direction the result is generally true, independent of whether or not the modal is a necessitation:

Lemma 28.1. *If φ is any modal operator on an implication structure I, and U, V, ... range over nonempty theories of the structure I, then for any A in S, $\varphi(A) \in U \to (V)(UR^\varphi V \to A \in V)$.*

Proof. Suppose that $\varphi(A)$ is in U, and $UR^\varphi V$. Then $A \in \varphi^{-1}U$, and $\varphi^{-1}U \subseteq V$. Consequently, $A \in V$.

Proof of Theorem 28.8 (continued). We now have to show only that φ is a necessitation modal if and only if for all nonempty theories U, if $(UR^\varphi V \to A \in V)$ for all nonempty theories V, then $\varphi(A) \in U$. Suppose that φ is a necessitation modal. Then by Theorem 28.7, $\varphi^{-1}U$ is a nonempty theory, since U is nonempty and φ is a necessitation modal. Suppose that for all nonempty theories V, $(UR^\varphi V \to A \in V)$. Then for $\varphi^{-1}U$, in particular, $UR^\varphi(\varphi^{-1}U) \to A \in (\varphi^{-1}U)$. It is evident that $UR^\varphi(\varphi^{-1}U)$, since U and $\varphi^{-1}U$ are nonempty theories of I, and $\varphi^{-1}U \subseteq \varphi^{-1}U$. Therefore $A \in \varphi^{-1}U$. That is, $\varphi(A) \in U$. Thus, for all nonempty V, $(UR^\varphi V \to A \in V) \to \varphi(A) \in U$, if φ is a necessitation modal. Conversely, suppose that $(UR^\varphi V \to A \in V) \to \varphi(A) \in U$, for all nonempty V, and that A is a thesis of I.

Then A belongs to every nonempty theory of I. Thus, $A \in V$ for all nonempty theories V, and consequently $(UR^\varphi V \to A \in V)$ holds for all nonempty V. Therefore $\varphi(A) \in U$ for all nonempty theories U. Consequently, $\varphi(A)$ is a thesis of I. Therefore φ is a necessitation modal.

Thus, φ is a necessitation modal if and only if [$\varphi(A)$ belongs to any nonempty weak theory U if and only if A belongs to all nonempty theories that are accessible from U]. This condition has a ring to it for those who are already acquainted with the canonical models of normal modal systems. Familiar though it may appear, the role of this condition is somewhat different from the usual one, principally because the theories used here are much weaker than the maximal consistent sets usually used. Every maximal consistent set is, of course, a theory in the sense used in the preceding theorem, but not conversely. We also noted that the accessibility relation is here defined over weakly closed Tarskian theories, rather than maximal consistent subsets of S. In fact, in some cases, some of the theories having the form $\varphi^{-1}U$ cannot be maximal consistent sets:

Exercise 28.5. Let $I = \langle S, \Rightarrow \rangle$ be a classical implication structure in which disjunctions and conjunctions always exist. Let φ be a necessitation modal on I. Show that there is some (weak) theory U such that $\varphi^{-1}U$ is not a maximal consistent (proper) subset of S. [Show that if $\varphi^{-1}U$ is maximal consistent (proper) for all nonempty theories, then $\varphi(A) \vee \varphi(\neg A)$ is a thesis for all A. In that case, φ distributes over disjunction and is not a modal operator.]

In the preceding theorem we also made use of an accessibility relation R^φ that, we said, depended upon the particular modal operator (as well as the structure). Some features of that dependence can be found in the following exercise:

Exercise 28.6. If φ and ψ are modal operators on I, and φ is a necessitation modal, then (a) $\varphi(A) \Rightarrow \psi(A)$ for all A if and only if $R^\psi \subseteq R^\psi$ and (b) if $\varphi\psi$ is a modal on I, then $R^{\varphi\psi}$ is the relational product of R^φ and R^ψ (that is, for all U and V, $UR^{\varphi\psi}V$ if and only if there is some W such that $UR^\varphi W$ and $WR^\psi V$).

Before we consider other topics, it may have occurred to the reader that the use of the particular relation R^φ is a special but fortunate choice of a relation on theories — let us call this particular accessibility relation *canonical*. What other binary relations, if any, would do as well? How much slack is there in the choice of R^φ?

Let U, V, ... range over the nonempty weak Tarskian theories of a structure. Let $\Sigma_\varphi(R)$ be the condition that for all U and A, $(V)\,(URV \rightarrow A \in V) \rightarrow \varphi(A) \in U$, and let $\Pi_\varphi(R)$ be the condition that for all U and A, $\varphi(A) \in U \rightarrow (V)(URV \rightarrow A \in V)$. We have just seen that $\Sigma_\varphi(R^\varphi)$ holds if and only if φ is a necessitation modal and that $\Pi_\varphi(R\varphi)$ is provable without any constraints on the modal operator φ. The situation is different for $\Sigma_\varphi(R)$ and $\Pi_\varphi(R)$ when relations other than the canonical R^φ are considered. $\Pi_\varphi(R)$ is no longer provable without any constraints on φ. What is provable is this:

Theorem 28.9. *$\Pi_\varphi(R)$ if and only if $R \subseteq R^\varphi$.*

We leave the proof for the reader. Since $R^\varphi \subseteq R^\varphi$, $\Pi_\varphi(R^\varphi)$ is provable without any constraints on φ, so that the old result is recovered. According to the theorem, the canonical accessibility relation R^φ is the weakest binary relation that satisfies the condition that $\Pi_\varphi(R)$.

The situation for $\Sigma_\varphi(R)$ is not as clear (as far as we know). If the condition $\Sigma_\varphi(R)$ holds for any arbitrary binary relation R at all, then φ is a necessitation modal. The converse, for arbitrary R, is another matter. We do not seem to have the following: It φ is a necessitation modal, then $\Sigma_\varphi(R)$ for any binary relation R. Instead, we have this qualified version:

Theorem 28.10. *If φ is a necessitation modal, and for all nonempty theories U, $UR(\varphi^{-1}U)$, then $\Sigma_\varphi(R)$.*

The proof is left for the reader. Once again, the old result is recoverable from this one, for if φ is a necessitation modal, then for any nonempty theory U, $\varphi^{-1}U$ is a nonempty theory. Since $UR^\varphi(\varphi^{-1}U)$ holds, so too does $\Sigma_\varphi(R^\varphi)$.

It is sometimes handy to have several different ways of thinking about the necessitation condition on modal operators. The condition of necessitation may look plausible on some versions, but not on others.

Consider, for example, the case of an operator like K, which associates to each statement A the statement $K(A)$: "It is known that A." We assume, for the sake of the example, that there is an appropriate implication structure available and that K behaves as a modal operator on it. We have already noted that this is a moot assumption. The second condition on modality requires that there be at least two members A and B such that $K(A \lor B) \not\Rightarrow K(A) \lor K(B)$. This is the plausible part of the claim that K is modal. However, the first condition for modality requires that K distribute over implication, and that is far from plausible, for it has as a consequence that knowledge of anything at all implies knowledge of all the theses of the structure. This has seemed to some to be an unrealistic requirement – at least if implication is taken to be some standard deductive relation rather than some epistemic notion. The necessitation condition, however, is an additional requirement beyond modality. In order for K to be a necessitation modal, $K(A)$ would have to be a thesis for any thesis A. That looks even more unrealistic than what the first condition for modality requires. One might think it more plausible to require only that $K(A_0)$ be a thesis for some thesis A_0, or even that $K(B)$ be a thesis for some statement B (where B may not even be a thesis, but perhaps records a state that one could not fail to know). But all these variants come, as we have seen, to the same thing.

The idea that φ is a necessitation modal if and only if $\varphi^{-1}U$ is nonempty for every nonempty theory U provides another idea of the strength of the requirement that K be a necessitation modal. In the case of K it comes to this: Some knowledge is available or is scattered throughout every nonempty theory U. That is, no matter what nonempty set of statements U we choose, if it is (weakly) closed under implication, then there will always be some statement $K(B)$ that belongs to U (it can be different B's for different U's). Every theory contains some knowledge statement. This theoretical ubiquity of knowledge is another way of assessing the power of the assumption that K satisfies the necessitation condition.

28.4 Necessitation modals, II

There are some interesting features of necessitation modals as a group. It is clear that, in general, if there are several modals φ, ψ on an implication structure, they need not be comparable (implicationally) with each other. In fact, restricting the modals to the necessitation variety does not improve the situation: There still can be several necessitation modals on a structure, without comparability (cf. the necessitation modals in Section 27.3.1).

However, if two modals are comparable, then necessitation modals are always weaker than nonnecessitation modals:

Theorem 28.11. *Let $I = \langle S, \Rightarrow \rangle$ be an implication structure that has theses. Let φ and ψ be modals on I. If φ and ψ are* *comparable, and φ is a necessitation modal, but ψ is not, then ψ (A)* $\Rightarrow$ $\varphi(A)$ *for all A in S.*

Proof. Suppose that either $\varphi(A) \Rightarrow \psi(A)$ (all A) or $\psi(A) \Rightarrow \varphi(A)$ (all A). If the former holds, then let B be any thesis of I. Therefore $\varphi(B) \Rightarrow \psi(B)$. Since φ is a necessitation modal, $\varphi(B)$ is a thesis. Therefore $\psi(B)$ is a thesis. Thus, ψ is a necessitation modal. But that is impossible. Therefore $\psi(A) \Rightarrow \varphi(A)$ for all A in S.

There are structures, as we have seen, with noncomparable necessitation modal operators on them. In such cases there always exists a necessitation modal that is definitely stronger than either:

Theorem 28.12. *Let $I = \langle S, \Rightarrow \rangle$ be a classical implication structure in which disjunctions and conjunctions always exist. Let φ and φ^* be two necessitation modals on I that are not comparable. Then there is a necessitation modal φ^c on I that is definitely stronger than either.*

Proof. Let φ^c be the operator that assigns $\varphi(A) \& \varphi^*(A)$ to A. Then it distributes over implication, since φ and φ^* do. Moreover, it does not distribute over disjunctions. If it did, then $\varphi^c(A \lor \neg A) \Rightarrow \varphi^c(A) \lor \varphi^c(\neg A)$. The two modals are necessitations. Consequently, $\varphi^c(A) \lor \varphi^c(\neg A)$ is a thesis. Since $\varphi^c(A) \Rightarrow \varphi(A)$ for all A, therefore $\varphi(A) \lor \varphi (\neg A)$ is a thesis for all A. But that is impossible, since φ is a necessitation modal (Theorem 26.2). Lastly, φ^c is definitely stronger than either of the two modals if and only if they are not comparable, for if there are B and C such that $\varphi(B) \not\Rightarrow \varphi^*(B)$ and $\varphi^*(C) \not\Rightarrow \varphi(C)$, then $\varphi(B)$ fails to imply $\varphi^c(B)$, and $\varphi^*(C)$ fails to imply $\varphi^c(C)$. The converse is left for the reader.

Exercise 28.7

(a) Any modal that is implied by a necessitation modal operator is a necessitation modal.
(b) If the functional product of any two necessitation modals is a modal operator, then it is also a necessitation modal operator.

Exercise 28.8. Let $I = \langle S, \Rightarrow \rangle$ be an implication structure with modals φ and ψ on it. If φ is a necessitation and a D modal, and ψ is neither a necessitation nor a D modal, then they are not comparable.

There is another type of modal operator closely related to D modals, but a bit stronger. It is the kind of modal that is a D modal under certain widely used conditions, but it is worth isolating because there is at least one important example of a modal that is a D modal but is not of this type.

Definition 28.6. Let $I = \langle S, \not\Rightarrow \rangle$ be an implication structure. We call a modal on I a *core modal* on I if and only if

(1) $\varphi(A) \Rightarrow \neg\varphi(\neg A)$ for all A in S, and
(2) for some B in S, $\neg\varphi(\neg B) \not\Rightarrow \varphi(B)$.

Exercise 28.9

(a) If φ and ψ are modals on $I = \langle S, \Rightarrow \rangle$, and $\psi(A) \Rightarrow \varphi(A)$ for all A in S, then if φ is a core modal, so too is ψ.
(b) If φ and ψ are modals on I, and φ is a core modal, but ψ is not, then if φ and ψ are comparable, $\varphi(A) \Rightarrow \psi(A)$ for all A in S.

Every core modal is a D modal, and under certain familiar conditions the converse is also true:

Theorem 28.13. *If $I = \langle S, \Rightarrow \rangle$ is a classical implication structure in which disjunctions and hypotheticals always exit, then any D modal is also a core modal.*

Proof. Suppose that φ is a D modal, but not a core modal. Then for all A in S, $\neg\varphi(\neg A) \Rightarrow \varphi(A)$. Since I is classical, for any A and B in S, $\varphi(A \lor B) \Rightarrow \varphi (\neg A \to B) \Rightarrow \varphi(\neg A) \to \varphi(B) \Rightarrow \neg\varphi(\neg A) \lor \varphi(B) \Rightarrow \varphi(A) \lor \varphi(B)$. Thus φ distributes over disjunction. But that is impossible, since it is a modal operator.

Another way of putting the matter is this: Any modal that is a D modal but not a core modal can exist only on a nonclassical structure. There is an important example of this kind that we shall study later (intuitionistic modals), namely, double negation.

28.5 Gödel–Löb modals

We have been considering various types of modal operators without assuming that there is anything special about the kinds of implication structures on which they act. We shall see below that there are numerous modal operators that are associated with the boxes of various modal systems, once those modal systems are recast as implication structures. Here we wish to consider one modal system in particular, because it is probably the best example we have at present of a modal system for which it is clear that the intended interpretation of "$\Box A$" is that "A" is provable in first-order Peano arithmetic (PA). Indeed, the fact that one can study the syntactic concept of provability in PA by means of the modal system (G-L) is an impressive reason for taking modals seriously. However, our present interest in (G-L) is the much simpler one of showing that the operator associated with the box of (G-L) counts as modal, so that an important operator falls inside rather than outside the fold of modal operators as we have characterized them. Some writers seem to have different views about this operator. Some think of it as obviously modal, even though no modal operator can satisfy the condition for being a Gödel–Löb modal as well as the condition that $\Box A \Rightarrow A$ (all A). The (G-L) box does share some features with more familiar modal operators, so there is some formal kinship, and it is regarded as a modal, but a strange one, since its dual $\Diamond$ is such that no sentence of the form $\Diamond A$ is a theorem of the system (G-L). Still others deny that it is even modal.

We have been at pains to indicate that modality is one thing, and the special modal laws another. An operator does not miss out on modal character if it is not a T modal. And as for strangeness, how strange can the concept of provability in PA be? The denial of modal character to the (G-L) box might rest on a tacit requirement that some type of necessity has to be present. But such a dictum has no support, either from current theory or from the historical record. It is a virtue of our description of the modal operators that the box of (G-L) counts as modal for exactly the same reasons that the operators associated with the boxes of the more familiar modal systems count as modal.

The modal system (G-L) can be thought of as an extension of the classical propositional calculus, together with the rules of modus ponens, necessitation, and substitution, the distribution axiom $\Box(p \rightarrow q) \rightarrow (\Box p \rightarrow \Box q)$ thus far, a normal modal system), and a characteristic axiom $\Box(\Box p \rightarrow p) \rightarrow \Box p$ distinguishing it from the other normal modal systems. The system thus obtained does express the intended meaning of $\Box A$, as Solovay's completeness theorem shows.[7]

As we shall see later, one can think of the normal modal system (G-L) as an implication structure $I_G = \langle S_G, \Rightarrow^G \rangle$, where S_G is the set of sentences of the system, and $A_1, \ldots, A_n \Rightarrow^G B$ if and only if

$(A_1 \& \ldots \& A_n \to B)$ is a theorem of $(G\text{-}L)$. To the box of $(G\text{-}L)$ associate the operator φ_G, which maps any sentence A of S_G to $\Box A$. The result is a particular syntactic implication structure with the modal operator φ_G on it. From the distribution axiom it is clear that the operator φ_G distributes over "$\Rightarrow^G$" because it will also be a necessitation modal. The second condition on modals also holds: φ_G will not distribute over disjunctions, since there are sentences A and B of $(G\text{-}L)$ such that $\Box(A \lor B) \to (\Box A \lor \Box B)$ is not a theorem. The reason is that if it were a theorem for all A and B, then, in particular, $\Box(A \lor \neg A) \to \Box A \lor \Box\neg A$ is a theorem. Since the antecedent is a theorem (by necessitation), $\Box A \lor \Box\neg A$ is a theorem for every A. But it is known (Boolos, 1979, p. 105) that in that case, either A is a theorem of $(G\text{-}L)$ or $\neg A$ is. However, $(G\text{-}L)$ is not complete with respect to negation. Thus, φ_G is a modal operator.

> **Exercise 28.10.** If $\Box$ of $(G\text{-}L)$ distributes over all disjunctions, then $\Box\Box A$ is a theorem of $(G\text{-}L)$ for all A. [Note that $\Box A \lor \neg\Box A$ is a theorem, distribute $\Box$ over the disjunction, and use the fact that $\Box\neg\Box A \to \Box(\Box A \to A)$, $\Box(\Box A \to A) \to \Box A$, and $\Box A \to \Box\Box A$ are theorems of $(G\text{-}L)$.]

These remarks yield a particular operator on a particular syntactic structure. That, given our interest in the concept of provability in PA, may represent the heart of the matter. But it is possible to regard this particular operator as an example of a type of operator that can act on implication structures, syntactic or not. We propose in the following remarks to develop the notion of a $G\text{-}L$-type modal operator for implication structures generally, rather than limit the study to a particular operator on a particular syntactic structure.

The choice of characterization seems straightforward. Just take the $G\text{-}L$ modals to be those φ's for which $\varphi(\varphi(A) \to A) \Rightarrow \varphi(A)$ for all A in the structure. However, that would make the characterization of the modal operator depend upon the existence of specific logical operators on the structures. It would restrict the structures to those in which the hypothetical always exists, and that would represent a departure from the way in which we characterized the other modal operators.

There is another way of characterizing such modals that yields the same result for those structures in which hypotheticals exist.

> **Definition 28.7.** Let $I = \langle S, \Rightarrow \rangle$ be an implication structure, with a modal operator φ on it. φ is a *Gödel–Löb G-L modal*

on I if and only if for all A and H in S, if $\varphi(A)$, $H \Rightarrow A$, then $\varphi(H) \Rightarrow \varphi(A)$.

It should be noted that we have not required that a $G\text{-}L^8$ modal be a necessitation modal as well, though this is true of the box of the system $(G\text{-}L)$, since that system is normal. Some features of $G\text{-}L$ modals can be proved without necessitation, but where necessitation is needed we shall make explicit mention of that fact.

Theorem 28.14. *Let* $I = \langle S, \Rightarrow \rangle$ *be an implication structure in which the hypothetical always exists, and let* φ *be a modal operator on* I. *Then* φ *is a G-L modal if and only if* $\varphi(\varphi(A) \to A) \Rightarrow \varphi(A)$.

Proof. Suppose that $\varphi(\varphi(A) \to A) \Rightarrow \varphi(A)$. Assume that $\varphi(A)$, $H \Rightarrow A$. Then $H \Rightarrow \varphi(A) \to A$. Since φ is modal, $\varphi(H) \Rightarrow \varphi(\varphi(A) \to A) \Rightarrow \varphi(A)$. Conversely, since $\varphi(A)$, $(\varphi(A) \to A) \Rightarrow A$, it follows that $\varphi(\varphi(A) \to A) \Rightarrow \varphi(A)$.

In fact, the characterization of $G\text{-}L$-type modal operators yields some familiar results fairly easily. One of these is that no $G\text{-}L$ modal can be a T modal:

Theorem 28.15. *If* φ *is a G-L modal on a structure* I, *then it cannot be that* $\varphi(A) \Rightarrow A$ *for all* A.

Proof. Suppose that $\varphi(A) \Rightarrow A$ for all A. Then $\varphi(A)$, $H \Rightarrow A$ for any A and H. Therefore $\varphi(H) \Rightarrow \varphi(A)$ for all A and H. Thus, for any A and B, $\varphi(A) \Leftrightarrow \varphi(B)$. As a result, $\varphi(A \vee B) \Rightarrow \varphi(A) \vee \varphi(B)$, since they are all equivalent to each other. Since φ distributes over disjunctions, it is not a modal operator. But that is impossible.

It is a fact about the modal system $(G\text{-}L)$ that no sentence of the form $\Diamond A$ (roughly, the intended meaning is that A is consistent with PA) is a theorem. The corresponding result for structures is as follows:

Theorem 28.16. *If* $I = \langle S, \Rightarrow \rangle$ *is a classical implication structure, and* φ *is a G-L modal on* I, *then* $\neg\varphi(\neg A)$ *fails to be a thesis of* I, *for each* A.

Proof. Suppose that $\neg\varphi(\neg A)$ is a thesis for some A in S. Then $B \Rightarrow \neg\varphi(\neg A)$ for all B. Consequently, $\varphi(\neg A) \Rightarrow \neg B$, and since I is classical, $\varphi(\neg A) \Rightarrow C$ for all C. In particular, $\varphi(\neg A)$ $\Rightarrow \neg A$, so that for any H, $\varphi(\neg A)$, $H \Rightarrow \neg A$. Since φ is a G-L modal, $\varphi(H) \Rightarrow \varphi(\neg A)$ for all H. Therefore $\varphi(H) \Rightarrow$ $\varphi(\neg A) \Rightarrow \varphi(H)$; that is, for any H, $\varphi(H)$ is equivalent to $\varphi(\neg A)$. Consequently, for any C and D in S, $\varphi(C) \Leftrightarrow \varphi(D)$, so that φ distributes over all disjunctions, and therefore fails to be modal. But that is impossible.

Exercise 28.11. If φ is a G-L modal and a necessitation modal on I, then for some A_0, $\varphi(A_0) \not\Rightarrow \neg\varphi(\neg A_0)$. That is, it fails to be a D modal.

There is a theorem about the modal system G-L, due independently to S. Kripke, D. de Jongh, and G. Sambin, that $\Box p \to \Box\Box p$ is a theorem (Boolos, 1979, p. 130). The counterpart for structures is as follows:

Theorem 28.17. *If φ is a G-L modal on the structure I, then for all A, $\varphi(A) \Rightarrow \varphi\varphi(A)$.*

Proof. Note that $\varphi(A \,\&\, \varphi(A)) \Rightarrow \varphi(A)$, since $(A \,\&\, \varphi\,(A)) \Rightarrow A$. Therefore $\varphi(A \,\&\, \varphi(A))$, $A \Rightarrow A \,\&\, \varphi(A)$. So $\varphi(A) \Rightarrow$ $\varphi(A \,\&\, \varphi\,(A))$. However, $\varphi(A \,\&\, \varphi\,(A)) \Rightarrow \varphi\varphi(A)$. since $(A \,\&\, \varphi\,(A)) \Rightarrow \varphi(A)$. Therefore $\varphi(A) \Rightarrow \varphi\varphi(A)$.

Theorem 28.18. *Let I be an implication structure that has a thesis, and let φ be a G-L modal operator on I that is also a necessitation modal. Then $\varphi(A) \Rightarrow A$ if and only if A is a thesis.*

Proof. If A is a thesis of I, then $C \Rightarrow A$ for all C, and so $\varphi(A)$ $\Rightarrow A$. Conversely, suppose that $\varphi(A) \Rightarrow A$ for some A. Then for any H, $\varphi(H) \Rightarrow \varphi(A)$. Let H be some thesis of I. Since φ is a necessitation modal, $\varphi(H)$ is a thesis. Therefore A is a thesis.

Consider next the "set-strengthening" version of the Löb theorem (Boolos, 1979, p. 59):

Theorem 28.19. *If φ is a G-L modal on I, then $\varphi(\varphi(A) \,\&\, \varphi(A')$ $\to A) \Rightarrow \varphi(\varphi(A') \to A)$ [the counterpart of $\vdash_{G\text{-}L}\Box((\Box A \,\&\, \Box A') \to A) \to \Box(\Box A' \to A)]$.*

Proof. Note that $\varphi(\varphi(A') \to A)$, $(\varphi(A) \,\&\, \varphi(A')) \to A \Rightarrow$ $\varphi(A') \to A$, for $\varphi(\varphi(A') \to A) \Rightarrow \varphi\varphi(A') \to \varphi(A) \Rightarrow \varphi(A') \to$ $\varphi(A)$ (by Theorem 28.17), and $\varphi(A) \,\&\, \varphi(A') \to A \Rightarrow \varphi(A') \to$

($\varphi(A) \rightarrow A$). So the two antecedents together imply $\varphi(A') \rightarrow A$. Therefore, by the condition on G-L modals, $\varphi(\varphi(A)$ & $\varphi(A') \rightarrow A)$ $\Rightarrow$ $\varphi(\varphi(A') \rightarrow A)$.

Theorem 28.20. *Let φ be a G-L modal on the implication structure I. If $\varphi(A)$, $\varphi(A')$ $\Rightarrow A$, then $\varphi(A')$ $\Rightarrow A$.*

Proof. Since $\varphi(A)$, $\varphi(A')$ $\Rightarrow A$, $\varphi\varphi(A')$ $\Rightarrow \varphi(A)$ (φ is a G-L modal). Therefore $\varphi(A')$ $\Rightarrow \varphi(A)$ (by Theorem 28.17). By Cut, then, $\varphi(A')$ $\Rightarrow A$.

The characterization of a G-L modal operator on structures that need not consist of syntactical or semantical object is a development that goes off in a direction other than the one that motivated the study of the modal system $(G$-$L)$ in the first place. The original aim was to study the concept of provability in PA. The object of the study, then, was highly syntactical, and the idea behind translating "$\square A$" as "it is provable in PA that A" was to study the modal laws of such a box and to use the resultant modal system to shed light back upon PA. It is a little odd, then, to frame a characterization of a G-L-type modal for implication structures in which, in effect, the syntactical character of the elements of the structure (if they have any) is ignored. Nevertheless, there are some benefits from doing so. As we have seen, the counterparts of some theorems of the modal system $(G$-$L)$ can be proved without assuming that the items on which the operator acts have any syntactical structure. It is always nice to know whether or not a theorem has exploited the syntactical structure, and this is one way of finding out. Moreover, there cannot be any question that the operator associated with the box of the system $(G$-$L)$ is genuinely modal. Lastly, we should emphasize again that the more general characterization of G-L modal operators does not disturb any of the results of the particular system $(G$-$L)$. Those remain intact as the study of a particular G-L modal operator acting on a particular syntactical structure $I_{G\text{-}L}$.[9] Are there other structures that have G-L modals on them, and are there interesting conditions on implication structures in general – not just those that are syntactical – under which the existence of a G-L-type modal exists? The following two results are a start in the direction of an answer.

The first result concerns the classical sentential calculus (CSC). CSC (more exactly, the associated implication structure I_{CSC}) is an example of an implication structure that has a G-L modal operator on it. The second result generalizes the first so as to yield a necessary and sufficient condition under which a structure has a G-L modal on it.

We have already seen that there are modal operators on CSC (Theorem 27.6). Those modals φ_p for each sentence letter p are necessitation modals, but they fail to be T-modals, and they fail to be G-L modals as well (see Exercises 28.12 and 28.13). What we want to describe is a G-L modal on the structure I_{CSC} associated with CSC.

Exercise 28.12. Show that each of the modals on CSC described in the proof of Theorem 27.6 is a K_4 modal $[\varphi(A) \Rightarrow \varphi\varphi(A)$ for all sentences of CSC], but fails to be a T modal. [For the latter, suppose that $\varphi_p(A) \Rightarrow^{CSC} A$ for all sentences A of CSC. Let q be any sentential letter other than p. Then $\varphi_p(q) \Rightarrow^{CSC} q$. But the latter holds if and only if $p \rightarrow q$ is a theorem of CSC. But that is impossible, for then (substituting a theorem for p) q would be a theorem of CSC, so that CSC would be inconsistent. But that is impossible.]

Exercise 28.13. Show that none of the modals φ_p of CSC described in the proof of Theorem 27.6 is a G-L modal – that is, suppose that $\varphi_p(\varphi_p(p) \rightarrow p) \Rightarrow \varphi_p(p)$. However, since $\varphi_p(p)$ is p, then $\varphi_p(\varphi_p(p) \rightarrow p)$ is $\varphi_p(p \rightarrow p)$, which by definition is $(p \vee \neg p)$. So the G-L condition is satisfied if and only if $(p \vee \neg p) \rightarrow p$ is a theorem of CSC. But that is impossible.

Let p be any sentential letter of CSC, and Let $Cn(p)$ be the set of all the consequences of p. That is, A is in $Cn(p)$ if and only if $\vdash_{CSC}(p \rightarrow A)$, or, equivalently, $p \Rightarrow^{CSC} A$. Then define an operator φ_p (not to be confused with the operators φ_p of Theorem 27.6) on the sentences of CSC this way:

$$\varphi_p(A) = \begin{cases} (p \vee \neg p), \text{ if } A \text{ is in } Cn(p) \\ \\ p, \text{ otherwise.} \end{cases}$$

Note first that φ_p is a modal operator on $I_{CSC} = \langle S_{CSC}, \Rightarrow^{CSC} \rangle$. The first condition, distribution over implication, holds: Suppose that A_1, ..., $A_n \Rightarrow^{CSC} B$. There are two cases: (1) B is in $Cn(p)$. In that case, $\varphi_p(B)$ is $(p \vee \neg p)$, so that $\varphi_p(A_1), \ldots, \varphi_p(A_n) \Rightarrow^{CSC} \varphi_p(B)$. (2) B is not in $Cn(p)$. In that case, $\varphi_p(B)$ is p. Moreover, not all of the A_i's are in $Cn(p)$. Otherwise B would be in $Cn(p)$. Therefore, some A_j is not in $Cn(p)$, so that $\varphi_p(A_j)$ is p. Therefore $\varphi_p(A_1), \ldots, \varphi_p(A_n) \Rightarrow^{CSC} \varphi_p(B)$. The second condition for modality also holds: Note that $Cn(p)$ is incomplete with respect to negation [for example, neither q nor $\neg q$ is in

$Cn(p)$, since neither $p \rightarrow q$ nor $p \rightarrow \neg q$ is a theorem of CSC]. Let A be any sentence of CSC such that neither it nor its negation belongs to $Cn(p)$. Then $\varphi_p(A \vee \neg A)$ is $(p \vee \neg p)$, since every theorem of CSC is in $Cn(p)$. However, $\varphi_p(A)$ and $\varphi_p(\neg A)$ are each p, since neither one belongs to $Cn(p)$. Therefore $\varphi_p(A \vee \neg A) \not\Rightarrow \varphi_p(A) \vee \varphi_p(\neg A)$.

It remains only to show that $\varphi_p(\varphi_p(A) \rightarrow A) \Rightarrow^{\text{CSC}} \varphi_p(A)$ for all A in CSC. There are two cases: (1) Suppose that A is in $Cn(p)$. Then $\varphi_p(A)$ is $(p \vee \neg p)$, so that the implication holds. (2) Suppose that A is not in $Cn(p)$. Then $\varphi_p(A)$ is p. Therefore $\varphi_p(A) \rightarrow A$ is $(p \rightarrow A)$. It cannot be in $Cn(p)$, for then $\vdash_{\text{CSC}} (p \rightarrow (p \rightarrow A))$, that is, $\vdash_{\text{CSC}} (p \rightarrow A)$, and A is thereby in $Cn(p)$, which is impossible. Therefore $\varphi_p(\varphi_p(A) \rightarrow A)$ is p. Since $\varphi_p(A)$ is also p, it follows that $\varphi_p(\varphi_p(A) \rightarrow A) \Rightarrow^{\text{CSC}} \varphi_p(A)$.

Exercise 28.14. Show that φ_p is a necessitation modal.

Exercise 28.15. Show that no two of the infinite number of G-L modals φ_p, φ_q, ... (for every sentential letter) are comparable.

With a slight modification of the preceding construction of a G-L modal on I_{CSC} we obtain a necessary and sufficient condition for the existence of a G-L modal that is also a necessitation modal on an implication structure.

Theorem 28.21. *Let $I = \langle S, \Rightarrow \rangle$ be a classical implication structure in which disjunctions and hypotheticals always exist. Suppose, in addition, that there is some W in S that is not a thesis of I, such that $Cn(W)$ is incomplete with respect to negation. Then there is a G-L modal operator on I that is also a necessitation modal.*

Proof. Define the operator χ as follows: For all A in S,

$$\chi(A) = \begin{cases} (W \vee \neg W), & \text{if } A \text{ is in } Cn(W) \\ W, & \text{otherwise.} \end{cases}$$

Although the proof is similar to that just given for φ_p, it is worthwhile seeing it in the more general setting. We first verify that the operator distributes over implication. Suppose that A_1, ..., $A_n \Rightarrow B$. There are two cases: (1) Suppose that B is in $Cn(W)$. Then $\chi(A)$ is $(W \vee \neg W)$, so that $\chi(A_1), \ldots, \chi(A_n) \Rightarrow \chi(B)$. (2) Suppose that B is not in $Cn(W)$. Then $\chi(B)$ is W. Then there is at least one A_j that is not in $Cn(W)$ [otherwise

they would all belong to $Cn(W)$, and then so would B]. There-
fore $\chi(A_j)$ is W, so that, again, $\chi(A_1), \ldots, \chi(A_n) \Rightarrow X(B)$. The
operator also fails to distribute over disjunctions: Since $Cn(W)$
is incomplete with respect to negation, there is some Z in
S such that neither it nor its negation is in $Cn(W)$. Therefore
$\chi(Z \vee \neg Z) \not\Rightarrow \chi(Z) \vee \chi(\neg Z)$.

There remains only the condition that χ is a G-L modal that
has to be checked. There are two cases: (1) A is in $Cn(W)$.
Then $\chi(A)$ is $(W \vee \neg W)$, so that $\chi(\chi(A) \to A) \Rightarrow \chi(A)$. (2)
A is not in $Cn(W)$. In that case, $\chi(A)$ is W. Then $\chi(A) \to A$
is $(W \to A)$, and it is not in $Cn(W)$, for if it were, then since
W is in $Cn(W)$, so too is A, and that is impossible. Therefore
$\chi(\chi(A) \to A)$ is W, so that $\chi(\chi(A) \to A) \Rightarrow \chi(A)$. χ is also a
necessitation (see Exercise 28.17).

Exercise 28.16. Avoid the use of hypotheticals in showing that
χ, as described above, is a G-L modal, by showing that for all A
and H, if $\chi(A), H \Rightarrow A$, then $\chi(H) \Rightarrow \chi(A)$.

Exercise 28.17. Show that χ, as described earlier, is a necessitation modal.

There is also the converse to Theorem 28.21:

Theorem 28.22. *Let $I = \langle S, \Rightarrow \rangle$ be a classical implication
structure in which disjunctions and hypotheticals always exist. If
there is a modal operator on I that is a G-L modal as well as a
necessitation modal, then there is a member W of S such that W is
not a thesis of I, and $Cn(W)$ is incomplete with respect to
negation.*

Proof. Suppose that φ is a modal on I that is both a G-L modal
and a necessitation modal. Suppose further that the conclusion
is false. Thus, for every nonthesis A of I, $Cn(A)$ is complete
with respect to negation. Since φ is a necessitation modal on a
classical structure, there is some A^* such that $\varphi(A^* \vee \neg A^*)$
$\not\Rightarrow \varphi(A^*) \vee \varphi(\neg A^*)$ (Theorem 26.2). Therefore $\varphi(A^*) \vee$
$\varphi(\neg A^*)$ is not a thesis, and as a consequence, none of $\varphi(A^*)$,
$\varphi(\neg A^*)$, A^*, and $\neg A^*$ are theses either.

Consider $\varphi(A^*) \to A^*$. It is not a thesis of I, for if it were, then since φ is
a necessitation modal, $\varphi(\varphi(A^*) \to A^*)$ would also be a thesis. Therefore, $\varphi(A^*)$ would also be a thesis, since φ is also a G-L modal. That

is impossible. So, by hypothesis, $Cn(\varphi(A^*) \to A^*)$ is complete with respect to negation. Then either A^* belongs to it or $\neg A^*$ does. Now $\neg A^*$ is not in it, for if it were, then $\varphi(A^*) \to A^* \Rightarrow \neg A^*$. But in that case $A^* \Rightarrow \neg A^*$, and $\neg A^*$ would be a thesis. That is impossible. So A^* is in $Cn(\varphi(A^*) \to A^*)$. In that case, $\varphi(A^*) \to A^* \Rightarrow A^*$. Then $\neg\varphi(A^*) \Rightarrow A^*$, so that $\neg A^* \Rightarrow \varphi(A^*)$.

Now consider $\varphi(\neg A^*) \to \neg A^*$. By an argument parallel to the preceding one, it is not a thesis of I [for then $\varphi(\neg A^*)$ would be a thesis, and that is impossible]. By hypothesis, then, $Cn(\varphi(\neg A^*) \to A^*)$ is complete with respect to negation. Then either A^* is in it or $\neg A^*$ is in it. In the former case, $\varphi(\neg A^*) \to \neg A^* \Rightarrow A^*$, so that $\neg A^* \Rightarrow A^*$. Then A^* is a thesis, and that is impossible. In the latter case, $\varphi(\neg A^*) \to \neg A^* \Rightarrow \neg A^*$, so that $\neg\varphi(\neg A^*) \Rightarrow \neg A^*$. In that case, $A^* \Rightarrow \varphi(\neg A^*)$.

Thus, $\neg A^* \Rightarrow \varphi(A^*)$, and $A^* \Rightarrow \varphi(\neg A^*)$. Since the structure is classical, it follows that $\varphi(A^*) \vee \varphi(\neg A^*)$ is a thesis. But that is impossible. Therefore there is some W in S that is not a thesis, such that $Cn(W)$ is incomplete with respect to negation.

Theorems 28.21 and 28.22 together tell us that if I is any classical implication structure in which disjunctions and hypotheticals always exist, then a necessary and sufficient condition for there to exist a modal operator on I that is both a G-L modal and a necessitation modal is that there be some nonthesis of I whose consequence set is incomplete with respect to negation.

It is worth emphasizing that in a general setting there may be several G-L modals on a structure, just as there may be several T modals on a structure. Some of them may be of interest, and some not. The types of G-L modals that may be available when the structure has a sufficiently rich syntax simply will not be available if that kind of structure is not provided for the set S or for the implication relation of a structure. Nevertheless, what the two preceding theorems show is that certain minimal conditions on an implication structure are necessary and sufficient for there to be *some* G-L modal on it. But to obtain theoretically interesting G-L modals, more structure has to be provided, beyond the fact that there is some nonthesis whose consequence set is incomplete. The implication structure associated with a first-order theory of PA is a case in point.

28.6 Duals of modals

Duals of modal operators are special operators that come as pairs; one modal is or is not the dual of another. When $I = \langle S, \Rightarrow \rangle$ is an implication structure, and φ is a modal with respect to "$\Rightarrow$," and σ is a modal with respect to the dual, "$\Rightarrow$^," we shall write "$[\varphi, \sigma]$" to indicate that σ is the dual of φ.

Perhaps the most familiar of such pairs are the box, $\Box$, and the diamond, $\Diamond$, that are used to formulate various classical modal systems. Usually one does not find an independent characterization of what it is for one modal to be the dual of another; only the standard pair is given. Sometimes, when the box is taken as the primitive modal of a system, the operator $\neg \Box \neg$ that, as we have seen, is a modal operator on the dual structure is called its dual and is denoted by the diamond. Sometimes the box and the diamond are both taken as primitive and described as duals, and then a law is laid down to the effect that $\Diamond$ is $\neg \Box \neg$, and, equivalently, $\Box$ is $\neg \Diamond \neg$. Let us call this the *not-not relation*. All this is straightforward and unproblematic. We have seen that, in general, on classical structures, φ is modal with respect to "$\Rightarrow$" if and only if $\neg \Box \neg$ is modal with respect to "$\Rightarrow$^." In a syntactical setting, it is usual to obtain the dual of an *expression* by replacing all atomic sentences by their negations and interchanging all occurrences of "$\bot$" and "$\top$," "$\lor$" and "&," and "$\Box$" and "$\Diamond$" throughout. More care is needed if other connectives occur in the expression.[10] However, in the more general structures that we have been studying, the members may not be syntactical, so that the idea of replacing occurrences of expressions that are embedded within others is not always applicable. It is possible, however, to carry over some of the ideas that lie behind the syntactical description of duality to the more general situation.

It is clear that the basic ideas about duality presuppose, in their usual treatment, that negation is classical. In our account of the duality of the various logical operators, we used a notion of dual implication, as well as the dual of a logical operator that was not restricted to classical structures, but that yielded the standard results anyway. In the case of modal operators, there is even greater difficulty in finding an account of duality that will cover the classical as well as the nonclassical cases and that will also yield the customary results when the structures are classical. In what follows, we shall try to provide such an account. But first, it is instructive to say a few things that hold for duals in the classical case. Let $I = \langle S, \Rightarrow \rangle$ be a classical implication structure. Then

(1) If φ is a modal with respect to "$\Rightarrow$," and σ is a modal with respect to the dual implication relation "$\Rightarrow$^," and σ is the dual of φ (i.e., $[\varphi, \sigma]$), then $\varphi(A) \Leftrightarrow N\sigma(N(A))$, and, equivalently, $\sigma(A) \Leftrightarrow N\varphi(N(A))$ for all A in S. (In order to avoid too much notational clutter, we have here reverted to the official use of "N" for negation on I.)

(2) If φ is the weakest modal with respect to "$\Rightarrow$," and σ is the weakest modal with respect to "$\Rightarrow\hat{\ }$," then they stand in the not-not relation to each other. The same holds with "strongest" replacing "weakest" (we leave the proof for the reader). There is, however, no assurance that even if I has a modal that it also has a weakest or a strongest one.

Exercise 28.18. If φ is modal with respect to "$\Rightarrow$," and σ is modal with respect to "$\Rightarrow\hat{\ }$," and they stand in the not-not relation, then φ is the weakest (strongest) modal with respect to "$\Rightarrow$" if and only if σ is the weakest (strongest) modal with respect to "$\Rightarrow\hat{\ }$."

(3) If φ and φ^* are modals with respect to "$\Rightarrow$," and σ and σ^* are modals with respect to "$\Rightarrow\hat{\ }$," and $[\varphi, \sigma]$ and $[\varphi^*, \sigma^*]$, then $\varphi \Rightarrow \varphi^*$ if and only if $\sigma \Rightarrow\hat{\ } \sigma^*$ (the proof is left for the reader).

(4) If φ and σ are dual modal operators, then $N\varphi N \Rightarrow \sigma$, where σ is the weakest modal on $I\hat{\ }$ for which this holds. (That is, if ψ is any modal on $I\hat{\ }$ such that $N\varphi N \Rightarrow \psi$, then $\psi \Rightarrow\hat{\ } \sigma$.) And $\sigma \Rightarrow N\varphi N$, where φ is the weakest modal on I for which this holds. (That is, if ψ is a modal on I, and $\sigma \Rightarrow N\psi N$, then $\psi \Rightarrow \varphi$.)

If the implication structure is not classical, then it is no longer true generally that if φ is modal with respect to "$\Rightarrow$," then $N\varphi N$ will be modal with respect to "$\Rightarrow\hat{\ }$," nor will it be true that if σ is modal with respect to "$\Rightarrow\hat{\ }$," then $N\sigma N$ will be modal with respect to "$\Rightarrow$." Therefore, the usual relations for classical structures, $\varphi \Leftrightarrow N\sigma N$ and $\sigma \Leftrightarrow N\varphi N$, will fail to hold between a modal and its dual. Some different connection is called for.

Definition 28.8. Let $I = \langle S, \Rightarrow \rangle$ be an implication structure, where N is negation with respect to "$\Rightarrow$," and $N\hat{\ }$ is negation with respect to the dual "$\Rightarrow\hat{\ }$." Let φ be a modal operator on I, and let σ be a modal operator on $I\hat{\ }$. Then $[\varphi, \sigma]$; that is, σ *is the dual of* φ if and only if for all A in S,

(1) $N\varphi N\hat{\ }(A) \Rightarrow \sigma(A) \Rightarrow N\hat{\ }\varphi N(A)$,
(2) $N\sigma N\hat{\ }(A) \Rightarrow \varphi(A) \Rightarrow N\hat{\ }\varphi N(A)$,
(3) σ is the weakest modal on $I\hat{\ }$ for which $N\varphi N\hat{\ }(A) \Rightarrow \sigma(A)$ for all A in S, and
(4) φ is the weakest modal on I for which $\varphi(A) \Rightarrow N\hat{\ }\sigma N(A)$ for all A in S.

Thus, by (3), if $N\varphi N\hat{\ }(A) \Rightarrow \psi(A)$ (all A) for any modal ψ on $I\hat{\ }$, it follows that $\sigma \Rightarrow \psi$ (i.e., $\psi \Rightarrow\hat{\ } \sigma$). And by (4), if for any modal ψ on I, $\psi(A) \Rightarrow N\hat{\ }\sigma N(A)$ (all A), then $\psi(A) \Rightarrow \varphi(A)$.

The four implications contained in (1) and (2) have an equivalent formulation:

Theorem 28.23. *Conditions (1) and (2) of the definition of dual modals are equivalent to the following four:*

(1) $N\varphi(A) \Rightarrow \sigma N\hat{\ }(A)$,
(2) $N\sigma(A) \Rightarrow \varphi N\hat{\ }(A)$,
(3) $\varphi N(A) \Rightarrow N\hat{\ }\sigma(A)$,
(4) $\sigma N(A) \Rightarrow N\hat{\ }\varphi(A)$.

Proof. The proof proceeds by showing that (1) is equivalent to the condition that $N\varphi N\hat{\ }(A) \Rightarrow \sigma(A)$, that (2) is equivalent to $N\sigma N\hat{\ }(A) \Rightarrow \varphi(A)$, that (3) is equivalent to $\varphi(A) \Rightarrow N\hat{\ }\sigma N(A)$, and that (4) is equivalent to $\sigma(A) \Rightarrow N\hat{\ }\varphi N(A)$. Consider just the second case; the remaining cases are similar. Suppose that $N\sigma N\hat{\ }(A) \Rightarrow \varphi(A)$ for all A. Therefore $N\sigma N\hat{\ }N\hat{\ }(A) \Rightarrow \varphi N\hat{\ }(A)$. Since $N\hat{\ }N\hat{\ }(A) \Rightarrow A$, $\sigma N\hat{\ }N\hat{\ }(A) \Rightarrow \sigma(A)$. Consequently, $N\sigma(A) \Rightarrow N\sigma N\hat{\ }N\hat{\ }(A)$. Therefore $N\sigma(A) \Rightarrow \varphi N\hat{\ }(A)$. Conversely, suppose that $N\sigma(A) \Rightarrow \varphi N\hat{\ }(A)$. Then $N\sigma N\hat{\ }(A) \Rightarrow \varphi N\hat{\ }N\hat{\ }(A)$. But $N\hat{\ }N\hat{\ }(A) \Rightarrow A$, so that $\varphi N\hat{\ }N\hat{\ }(A) \Rightarrow \varphi(A)$. Consequently, $N\sigma N\hat{\ }(A) \Rightarrow \varphi(A)$.

It also follows from the definition that either one of a pair of dual modals determines the other (up to equivalence):

Theorem 28.24. *Let $I = \langle S, \Rightarrow \rangle$ be an implication structure, and let φ and φ^* be modals on I, and let σ and σ^* be modals with respect to "$\Rightarrow\hat{\ }$." Then*

(a) if $[\varphi, \sigma]$ and $[\varphi, \sigma^*]$, then $\sigma \Leftrightarrow \sigma^*$, and
(b) if $[\varphi, \sigma]$ and $[\varphi^*, \sigma]$, then $\varphi \Leftrightarrow \varphi^*$.

Proof. The proof of (a) is straightforward, and we leave (b) for the reader. From $[\varphi, \sigma]$ we have $N\varphi N\hat{\ }(A) \Rightarrow \sigma(A)$, and σ is the weakest modal on $I\hat{\ }$ to satisfy this condition. And from $[\varphi, \sigma^*]$ we have that σ^* is a modal with respect to "$\Rightarrow\hat{\ }$," and $N\varphi N\hat{\ }(A) \Rightarrow \sigma^*(A)$. Since σ^* is the weakest modal on $I\hat{\ }$ to satisfy this condition, $\sigma(A) \Rightarrow^{\wedge} \sigma^*(A)$. That is, $\sigma^*(A) \Rightarrow$ $\sigma(A)$. Similarly, if follows that $\sigma(A) \Rightarrow \sigma^*(A)$.

The next result is, in a way, the hallmark of duality for duals of modal operators: The implicational relation between modals on a structure I is exactly the same as the implicational relation between their duals on the dual structure $I^{\wedge}$:

Theorem 28.25. *Let $I = \langle S, \Rightarrow \rangle$ be an implication structure, and let φ and φ^* be modals on I, and let σ and σ^* be modals with respect to "$\Rightarrow^{\wedge}$." If $[\varphi, \sigma]$ and $[\varphi^*, \sigma^*]$, then $\varphi(A) \Rightarrow \varphi^*(A)$ if and only if $\sigma(A) \Rightarrow^{\wedge} \sigma^*(A)$ for all A in S.*

Proof. Suppose that $\varphi(A) \Rightarrow \varphi^*(A)$. Then $\varphi N^{\wedge}(A) \Rightarrow$ $\varphi^* N^{\wedge}(A)$. Therefore $N\varphi^* N^{\wedge}(A) \Rightarrow N\varphi N^{\wedge}(A) \Rightarrow \sigma(A)$. Since $(\varphi^*, \sigma^*]$, σ^* is the weakest modal on $I^{\wedge}$ such that $N\varphi^* N^{\wedge}$ implies it. But σ is implied by $N\varphi^* N^{\wedge}$. Therefore $\sigma(A) \Rightarrow^{\wedge} \sigma^*(A)$. Conversely, suppose that $\sigma(A) \Rightarrow^{\wedge} \sigma^*(A)$ for all A in S; that is, $\sigma^*(A) \Rightarrow \sigma(A)$. Therefore $\sigma^* N(A) \Rightarrow \sigma N(A)$, so that $N^{\wedge}\sigma N(A) \Rightarrow N^{\wedge}\sigma^* N(A)$. Since $[\varphi, \sigma]$, $\varphi(A) \Rightarrow N^{\wedge}\sigma^* N(A)$. But $[\varphi^*, \sigma^*]$, so that φ^* is the weakest modal on I that implies $N^{\wedge}\sigma^* N$. Thus, $\varphi(A) \Rightarrow \varphi^*(A)$.

Lastly, the general account of modal duality reduces to the usual result when the structures are classical. More precisely,

Theorem 28.26. *Let $I = \langle S, \Rightarrow \rangle$ be a classical implication structure in which disjunctions always exist. If φ and σ are modals on I and on the dual $I^{\wedge}$, respectively, such that $[\varphi, \sigma]$, then $\varphi(A) \Leftrightarrow N\sigma N(A)$, and $\sigma(A) \Leftrightarrow N\varphi N(A)$ for all A in S.*

Proof. If a structure always has disjunctions, the negation operator is classical if and only if $N(A) \Leftrightarrow N^{\wedge}(A)$ (for all A) (Theorem 17.5). From conditions (1) and (2) of the definition of modal duality it follows that $N\varphi N(A) \Rightarrow \sigma(A) \Rightarrow N\varphi N(A)$ and $N\sigma N(A) \Rightarrow \varphi(A) \Rightarrow N\sigma N(A)$ for all A in S. Therefore $\sigma(A) \Leftrightarrow N\varphi N(A)$ and $\varphi(A) \Leftrightarrow N\varphi N(A)$ for all A in S.

We shall have occasion to return to these results when we consider intuitionistic modals.

29

The possibility of necessity-style modals

29.1 The Montague lesson

Before we consider a host of examples of modal operators that draw upon traditional as well as nontraditional sources, we should say something about a bundle of theorems due to Montague (1963). The import of his results seems to be that syntactic treatments of modality for sufficiently rich languages are in deep trouble. It is true, of course, that our characterization of modality is not syntactical and is not restricted to structures that are syntactical. Nevertheless, it is worth looking at his results, for it might happen that there will be analogues to them that could create trouble for the more general account that we have been developing. It might just be that even when modals are taken as operators (so that modals of sentences are just certain kinds of functions that map sentences to sentences), analogues or counterparts to Montague's theorems might still hold.

By a syntactical characterization of modality Montague seems to have had in mind the idea that "□" or "N" (his notation) is predicated of sentences [i.e., $N(\ulcorner A \urcorner)$, rather than prefixed to the sentence itself as NA, as it would be were "N" regarded as a connective].

Consider one of Montague's theorems.[1] It is the counterpart of the Tarski result that certain kinds of formal languages are inconsistent if they contain their own truth predicate and the diagonalization lemma is provable for the predicates of that language. Assume that T is some formal language for which a diagonalization lemma or a principle of self-reference is provable. That is, if ψ is any formula (with one free variable) of T, then there is some sentence A_0 of T such that $A_0 \leftrightarrow \psi(\ulcorner A \urcorner)$ is a theorem of T. Assume that N is a formula of T for which (1) $N(\ulcorner A \urcorner) \to A$ is a theorem of T for all sentences A of T (where a sentence in "corners" is the Gödel number of the sentence cornered) and (2) (necessitation) if A is a logical axiom of T, then so too is $N(\ulcorner A \urcorner)$. A contradiction follows. Since "$\neg N$" (and "$N \neg$") is a formula of T, by the principle of self-reference there is a sentence A_0 of T such that (3) $A_0 \leftrightarrow \neg N(\ulcorner A_0 \urcorner)$ is a theorem of T. Consequently, $N(\ulcorner A_0 \urcorner) \to$

$\neg A_0$ is a theorem of T. So too is $N(\ulcorner A_0 \urcorner) \rightarrow A_0$. Therefore $N(\ulcorner A_0 \urcorner) \rightarrow A_0 \,\&\, \neg A_0$ is a theorem, and so too then is $\neg N(\ulcorner A_0 \urcorner)$. By (3), then, A_0 is a theorem, and therefore, by (2), so too is $N(\ulcorner A_0 \urcorner)$. Therefore $\neg A_0$ is a theorem of T, so that T is inconsistent.

Exercise 29.1. Show that T is inconsistent, using (1), (2), and the predicate "$N\neg$" rather than "$\neg N$."

All this is familiar. How much of it carries over to an account of modals, where "N" is not a formula of T, but an operator that assigns to each sentence A *of* T the sentence "$N(A)$" of T? The principle of self-reference does not guarantee that there is a fixed point A^* of the operator N such that $A^* \Longleftrightarrow N(A^*)$. The situation is like that discussed by Feferman (1984) for the truth operator, rather than the truth predicate [where a truth operator T assigns to each sentence A of the theory a sentence $T(A)$: "It is true that A"].

In fact, it is difficult to see what the proper operator counterpart is for the principle of self-reference. It cannot be the requirement that for every implication structure $I = \langle S, \Longrightarrow \rangle$, every operator on I has a fixed point, for negation is an operator on I, and negation cannot have a fixed point unless the structure is trivial. So the requirement that every operator on I have a fixed point is too strong. On the other hand, every necessitation operator on a structure will have any thesis of the structure as a fixed point. The problem, then, is to find a "reasonable" class of operators φ for which it is provable that $\varphi\neg$ and $\neg\varphi$ have fixed points. However, it is provable that this cannot hold for any operator that is a modal on I of the type considered by Montague (and that is a "lesson" to be learned from Montague). That is,

Theorem 29.1. *Let $I = \langle S, \Longrightarrow \rangle$ be an implication structure, and let φ be any modal operator on I that is a necessitation and for which $\varphi(A) \Longrightarrow A$ for all A in S. Then neither $\varphi\neg$ nor $\neg\varphi$ has fixed points in S.*

Proof. Suppose that the operator $\neg\varphi$ has some fixed A^* in S. Then $A^* \Longleftrightarrow \neg\varphi(A^*)$. So $\varphi(A^*) \Longrightarrow \neg A^*$. Since $\varphi(A^*) \Longrightarrow A^*$, it follows that $\varphi(A^*) \Longrightarrow B$ for all B in S. Therefore $\neg B \Longrightarrow \neg\varphi(A^*)$ for all B. Then for any C in S, $C \Longrightarrow \neg(\neg C) \Longrightarrow \neg\varphi(A^*) \Longrightarrow A^*$. Thus, A^* is a thesis, and so, by necessitation, $\varphi(A^*)$ is a thesis. Moreover, $\neg\varphi(A^*)$ is also a thesis, since A^*

$\Rightarrow \neg\varphi(A^*)$. Since $\varphi(A^*)$, $\neg\varphi(A^*) \Rightarrow C$ for all C, it follows that all C's are theses. Therefore all the members are equivalent to each other. Consequently, φ is not a modal operator (for φ will distribute over the dual implication relation "$\Rightarrow\hat{}$," or, if there are disjunctions in the structure, it will always distribute over them). But that is impossible.

Exercise 29.2. Show that under the conditions of Theorem 29.1, $\varphi\neg$ does not have any fixed points in S.

It might be thought that the preceding result is vacuous because the conditions of Theorem 29.1 are inconsistent. But that is not so. The situation is more complicated that that for a truth operator. The consistency for the truth operator condition, $T(A) \Leftrightarrow A$, follows from the fact that the identity operator satisfies it, as noted by Feferman (1984). In the case of modal operators, there is the further condition that $\varphi(A \vee B) \not\Rightarrow \varphi(A) \vee \varphi(B)$. Thus, an example more complicated than the identity operator is needed. Here are two simple examples of necessitation modal operators on a structure $I = \langle S, \Rightarrow \rangle$, for which $\varphi(A) \Rightarrow A$ (all A):

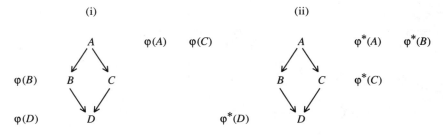

Exercise 29.3. For the modal operators φ and φ^* described above, show that

(a) negation is classical on the structure,
(b) $\varphi(A) \Rightarrow A$ for all A in S (same for φ^*),
(c) both φ and φ^* are necessitation modals, and
(d) φ and φ^* are not comparable. [The modal of (i) does not always imply the modal of (ii); it fails to do so for B. Similarly, the modal of (ii) does not always imply the modal of (i); it fails to do so for C.]

The two modals have an additional interest that we shall note now, but discuss later. They are noncomparable [by (d)]. Moreover, each is a K_4

modal, but fails to be an S_5 modal $[\neg\varphi\neg(A) \Rightarrow \varphi\neg\varphi(\neg A)$ for all A, the counterpart of the familiar condition on modal systems that $\Diamond A \Rightarrow \Box\Diamond A)]$ and fails to be a B modal $[A \Rightarrow \varphi(\neg\varphi(\neg A))$ for all A, the counterpart of the condition on modal systems that $A \Rightarrow \Box\Diamond A]$. For the modal in (i), it is easy to check that $\neg\varphi(\neg C)$ is just C, since $\neg C$ is B, $\varphi(B)$ is B, and $\neg B$ is C. On the other hand, $\varphi(\neg\varphi(\neg C))$ is $\varphi(C)$, which is A. Since C does not imply A, it follows that φ is not an S_5 modal. The same element C also serves to show that φ is not a B modal either. Thus, there are examples of modal operators that satisfy the conditions of the modal systems (T), (K_4), and (S_4) [but not (B) and (S_5)], but fail to be comparable. This will be of some interest when we consider the problem of evaluating the relative strengths of the various modal operators.

29.2 A necessity-style modal

The lesson that we drew from Montague's argument was drawn for any modal of a certain kind – although Montague's argument was originally constructed with necessity in mind. So far we have not said much about necessity, except to say that if there is a necessity modal, then it is one among others, and it is not the very paradigm of modality. It is not true that if necessity is not a modal, then nothing is. But, one might ask, is there a kind of modal operator that is a reasonable candidate as a necessity modal? We think that there is. It is a type of operator that is always available on classical implication structures that are incomplete with respect to negation.

The kind of operator that we have in mind is closely tied to the implication relation of the structure. If the structure $I = \langle S, \Rightarrow \rangle$ is classical and has at least one thesis A^* (and thus at least one antithesis Z^*), then consider the operator φ_n defined as follows:

$$\varphi_n(A) = \begin{cases} A^*, \text{ if } A \text{ is a thesis of } I \\ \\ Z^*, \text{ otherwise.} \end{cases}$$

Two immediate questions are whether or not φ_n is a modal operator and what its special features are. The modal character is settled by the following observation:

Theorem 29.2. *Let* $I = \langle S, \Rightarrow \rangle$ *be a classical implication structure that is incomplete with respect to negation and in which disjunctions always exist. Then* φ_n *is a modal operator on* I.

Proof. φ_n distributes over implication. Suppose that $A_1, \ldots,$ $A_n \Rightarrow B$. If B is a thesis, then since $\varphi_n(B)$ is A^*, it too is a thesis. Consequently, $\varphi_n(A_1), \ldots, \varphi_n(A_n) \Rightarrow \varphi_n(B)$. If B is not a thesis, then at least one of the A_i's, say A_1, is not a thesis. Then $\varphi_n(B)$ and $\varphi_n(A_1)$ are both Z^*. Therefore $\varphi_n(A_1), \ldots,$ $\varphi_n(A_n) \Rightarrow \varphi_n(B)$, since $Z^*, \ldots, \varphi_n(A_n) \Rightarrow Z^*$. Moreover, φ_n does not distribute over all disjunctions. Since I is incomplete with respect to negation, there is some W in S such that neither W nor $\neg W$ is a thesis of I. Consequently, $\varphi_n(W \vee \neg W) \not\Rightarrow$ $\varphi_n(W) \vee \varphi_n(\neg W)$, for $(W \vee \neg W)$ is a thesis of I, so that $\varphi_n(W \vee \neg W)$ is A^*. However, $\varphi_n(W)$ and $\varphi_n(\neg W)$ are both Z^*, since neither W not $\neg W$ is a thesis. But $A^* \not\Rightarrow Z^*$. (Otherwise, since A^* is a thesis, Z^* would be a thesis as well as an antithesis, and as a result every member of S would be equivalent to Z^*. Then every member of S would be a thesis, and I would not be incomplete with respect to negation. But that is impossible.)

What are the special features that make φ_n a strong candidate for being a necessity-style modal? Here are some. First we note that the dual of φ_n, call it σ_n, is given by

$$\sigma_n(A) = \begin{cases} Z^*, \text{ if } \neg A \text{ is a thesis of } I \\ \\ A^*, \text{ otherwise.} \end{cases}$$

Theorem 29.3. *Let $I = \langle S, \Rightarrow \rangle$ be a classical implication structure that is incomplete with respect to negation and in which disjunctions always exist. Let φ_n and σ_n be defined as above. Then for all A in S,*

(a) φ_n is a necessitation modal,
(b) $\varphi_n(A) \Leftrightarrow \neg\sigma_n(\neg A)$,
(c) φ_n is a T modal,
(d) φ_n is a D modal,
(e) φ_n is a K_4 modal,
(f) φ_n is a B modal, and
(g) φ_n is an S_5 modal.

Proof. (a) If A is a thesis, then $\varphi_n(A)$ is A^*, and therefore a thesis. (b) If A is a thesis, then by (a), so too is $\varphi_n(A)$. $\sigma_n(\neg A)$ is Z^*, because $\neg\neg A$ is a thesis. Therefore $\neg\sigma_n(\neg A)$ is $\neg Z^*$, which is equivalent to A^*, and thus it is a thesis. Thus, $\varphi_n(A)$

$\Longleftrightarrow \neg\sigma_n(\neg A)$, since both are theses. On the other hand, if A is not a thesis, then $\varphi_n(A)$ is Z^*. But $\sigma_n(\neg A)$ is A^*, since $\neg\neg A$ is not a thesis. Therefore $\neg\sigma_n(\neg A)$ is $\neg A^*$, and since $\neg A^*$ and Z^* are equivalent, (b) holds. (c) To show that $\varphi_n(A) \Longrightarrow A$, suppose first that A is a thesis. Then so too is $\varphi_n(A)$, and since any two theses are equivalent, the implication holds. Suppose, on the other hand, that A is not a thesis; then $\varphi_n(A)$ is Z^*, an antithesis that implies all the members of S, and so the implication holds. Then (d) follows immediately from (b), noting that negation is classical. (e) $\varphi_n(A) \Longrightarrow \varphi_n\varphi_n(A)$, for if A is a thesis, then by two uses of (a), $\varphi_n\varphi_n(A)$ is a thesis and is implied by everything, including $\varphi_n(A)$. If A is not a thesis, then $\varphi_n(A)$ is Z^*, which implies everything, including $\varphi_n\varphi_n(A)$. (f) $A \Longrightarrow \varphi_n\sigma_n(A)$. If $\neg A$ is a thesis, then A implies everything, including $\varphi_n\sigma_n(A)$. If $\neg A$ is not a thesis, $\sigma_n(A)$ is A^*, a thesis, which is implied by everything, including A. (g) We need to show that $\sigma_n(A) \Longrightarrow \varphi_n\sigma_n(A)$. If $\neg A$ is a thesis, then $\sigma_n(A)$ is Z^*, which implies everything. If $\neg A$ is not a thesis, $\sigma_n(A)$ is A^*, so that $\varphi_n\sigma_n(A)$ is A^*. And that is implied by everything.

Exercise 29.4. Let I be an implication structure satisfying the conditions of Theorem 29.3, and let φ_n and σ_n be defined as before. Then $\varphi_n(\varphi_n(\neg A) \vee \varphi_n\sigma_n(A))$ is a thesis of I for all A.

Exercise 29.5. There are nonnormal modal systems for which the box fails to be a necessitation modal, or fails to distribute over hypotheticals. Show that for such systems the operator associated with the box will not be a necessity-style operator.

The fact that φ_n has all the features listed in the preceding theorem goes a long way toward its credibility as a necessity-style modal. However, there are several additional reasons that are also persuasive, perhaps more so. It is natural to think of necessity as a strong kind of modal, and of its dual, possibility, as weak. The question is how to make evident the strength of an operator such as φ_n with respect to the other modals. Here are some results in that direction. The necessity modal φ_n is the strongest modal of all the necessitation modals on the structure. More precisely:

Theorem 29.4. *Let I be a classical implication structure that is incomplete with respect to negation, and let φ be any modal operator on I. Then*

(a) $\varphi_n(A) \Rightarrow \varphi(A)$ for all A if and only if φ is a necessitation with respect to "$\Rightarrow$."

(b) $\varphi(A) \Rightarrow \sigma_n(A)$ for all A if and only if $\neg\varphi\neg(A)$ is a thesis of I, if A is a thesis of I.

Proof. (a) Suppose that φ is a necessitation modal on I. If A is a thesis, then $\varphi(A)$ is a thesis and is therefore implied by $\varphi_n(A)$. If A is not a thesis, then $\varphi_n(A)$ is Z^*, which implies all the members of I, and $\varphi(A)$ in particular. Conversely, if $\varphi_n(A) \Rightarrow \varphi(A)$, and A is a thesis, then so too is $\varphi(A)$, since $\varphi_n(A)$ is a thesis. (b) Suppose that $\varphi(A) \Rightarrow \sigma_n(A)$ for all A. Then $\varphi(\neg A) \Rightarrow \sigma_n(\neg A)$, and so $\neg\sigma_n(\neg A) \Rightarrow \neg\varphi(\neg A)$. Therefore $\varphi_n(A) \Rightarrow \neg\varphi(\neg A)$ [by Theorem 29.3(b)]. Thus, if A is a thesis of I, so too is $\neg\varphi(\neg A)$. Conversely, suppose that $\neg\varphi(\neg A)$ is a thesis of I, if A is one. In that case, $\varphi_n(A) \Rightarrow \neg\varphi(\neg A)$ for all A. [If A is a thesis, then both $\varphi_n(A)$ and $\neg\varphi(\neg A)$ are theses, and so the implication holds. And if A is not a thesis, then $\varphi_n(A)$ is Z^*, which implies all the members of the structure, and $\neg\varphi(\neg A)$ in particular.] Consequently, $\varphi_n(\neg A) \Rightarrow \neg\varphi(A)$, so that $\varphi(A) \Rightarrow \neg\varphi_n(\neg A)$. That is [by Theorem 29.3(b)], $\varphi(A) \Rightarrow \sigma_n(A)$ for all A.

Thus, for any classical implication structure that is incomplete with respect to negation, the neccesity-style modal φ_n and its dual, the possibility-style modal σ_n, constitute the upper and lower bounds, respectively, of a large class of modal operators. For any modal φ on I, $\varphi_n(A) \Rightarrow \varphi(A) \Rightarrow \sigma_n(A)$ for all A if and only if φ and $\neg\varphi\neg$ are necessitations on I (i.e., they map theses of I to theses of I).

Equivalently, φ lies between φ_n and σ_n if and only if $\varphi(A)$ is a thesis of I for some A, and $\neg\varphi(\neg A)$ is a thesis for some A. In order for a modal φ to fall outside the spectrum provided by φ_n and σ_n, it would have to be such that either (1) $\varphi(A)$ is never a thesis or (2) $\neg\varphi(\neg A)$ is never a thesis.

There are known modals that do fall outside the proposed necessity–possibility band. Three are nonstandard. The first is a modal studied by Lemmon in which $\Box A$ has the intended interpretation "it is scientifically but not logically certain that A." In these systems, although it is true that $\Box A$ is never a thesis, it is also true that the intended interpretation does not fit the systems described. A. Prior's system Q and C. Lukasiewicz's system L also fail to have any $\Box A$ as a thesis. The former is a system in which "$\Box$" and "$\Diamond$" are not interdefinable, even though negation is classical. The latter is a system that is strange by any yardstick of comparison, so strange that Hughes and Cresswell (1968, p. 310) think of it as a system that "takes us to the limit of what we should regard as a modal logic at all." Even those writers who think that the diamond should always be interpreted as a kind of possibility seem to have difficulty, because that would require of the Lukasiewicz diamond that if any sentence and its negation are possible, then all sentences are possible, and any two sentences that are possible are consistent with each other.[2] It is on all counts an extreme case, perhaps *the* extreme case. It should be noted, however, that since it has $(\Diamond\ A\ \&\ \Diamond\ B) \to \Diamond$ $(A\ \&\ B)$ as a theorem, $\Box$ distributes over all disjunctions. It does not, therefore, count (for us) as a modal operator.

There is, however, one clearly modal operator that is not entirely in the necessity–possibility spectrum. The Gödel–Löb-type modal was described earlier in a way that did not require it to be a necessitation. However, those $G\text{-}L$ modals that are necessitations are bounded from above by φ_n. However, $\neg\varphi(\neg A)$ is never a thesis for any $G\text{-}L$ modal (Theorem 28.16). And so no $G\text{-}L$ modal is ever bounded from below by σ_n. In fact, no $G\text{-}L$ modal is weaker than σ_n. [Suppose that $\sigma_n(A) \Rightarrow$ $\varphi(A)$ for some $G\text{-}L$ modal φ. Since the structure is incomplete with respect to negation, let R be some member such that neither R nor $\neg R$ is a thesis. Then $\sigma_n(R)$ and $\sigma_n(\neg R)$ are A^* (a thesis). Consequently, $\varphi(R)$ and $\varphi(\neg R)$ are theses. Since $R, \neg R \Rightarrow C$ for all C, it follows that $\varphi(R),\ \varphi(\neg R)\ \Rightarrow\ \varphi(C)$. Thus, $\varphi(C)$ is a thesis for all C. Then φ distributes over all disjunctions, so that φ is not a modal operator. But that is impossible.] So no $G\text{-}L$ modal operator (on a classical implication structure that is incomplete with respect to negation) is even comparable with the possibility-style operator σ_n.

The particular construction of φ_n is closely tied to the implication structure of classical implication structures that are incomplete with respect to negation. It is essentially a characteristic function whose value on the theses of the structure is some constant thesis, and whose value on nontheses is some constant antithesis. It is equivalent to the operator that is the identity function on theses, and it has some constant antithesis as its value on all nontheses. The dual, possibility-style operator then is the operator whose value on A is $\neg A$ if $\neg A$ is a thesis, and A^* (some constant thesis) otherwise:

Exercise 29.6. Let I be a classical implication structure that is incomplete with respect to negation. Define an operator $\varphi^*(A)$ to be A if A is a thesis, and Z^* (some fixed antithesis) otherwise. And define $\sigma^*(A)$ to be A if $\neg A$ is a thesis, and A^* (some fixed thesis) otherwise. Show that $\varphi_n(A) \Longleftrightarrow \varphi^*(A)$ and $\sigma_n(A) \Longleftrightarrow \sigma^*(A)$ for all A.

In the case in which there are two implication relations on the same set, one being definitely stronger than the other, then the necessity operator associated with the stronger implication is definitely stronger than that associated with the weaker:

Theorem 29.5 (shifting necessity). *Let $I = \langle S, \Longrightarrow \rangle$ be a classical implication structure that is incomplete with respect to negation, and let $I^* = \langle S, \Longrightarrow^* \rangle$ be a structure, subject to the same conditions, in which "$\Longrightarrow^*$" is an extension of "$\Longrightarrow$" such that there is some thesis of I^* that is not a thesis of I. Let φ_n be a necessity-style modal on I, and let φ_n^* be one on I^*. Then*

(a) $\varphi_n(A) \Longrightarrow^* \varphi_n^*(A)$ for all A in S, and
(b) there is a B in S such that $\varphi_n^*(B) \not\Longrightarrow^* \varphi_n(B)$.

Proof. (a) Two cases: (1) Suppose that A is a thesis of I. Then it is also a thesis of I^*. Therefore $\varphi_n^*(A)$ is A_0^* (some fixed thesis of I^*). So $\varphi_n(A) \Longrightarrow^* \varphi_n^*(A)$. (2) Suppose that A is not a thesis of I. Then $\varphi_n(A)$ is Z_0 (some fixed antithesis of I). Therefore $\varphi_n(A) \Longrightarrow C$ for all C in S. Consequently, $\varphi_n(A) \Longrightarrow \varphi_n^*(A)$. Since "$\Longrightarrow^*$" extends "$\Longrightarrow$," $\varphi_n(A) \Longrightarrow^* \varphi_n^*(A)$.

   (b) Let B be some member of S that is a thesis of I^*, but not a thesis of I. Then $\varphi_n^*(B)$ is A_0^* (some fixed thesis of I^*), and $\varphi_n(B)$ is Z_0, since B is not a thesis of I. If $\varphi_n^*(B) \Longrightarrow^* \varphi_n(B)$, then $A_0^* \Longrightarrow^* Z_0$. Then, since $Z_0 \Longrightarrow C$ (all C) (it is an antithesis of I), $Z_0 \Longrightarrow^* C$ (all C) (since "$\Longrightarrow^*$" is an extension of "$\Longrightarrow$"). Consequently, $A_0^* \Longrightarrow^* C$ (all C), so that every member of S is a thesis of I^*. But that is impossible, since I^* is incomplete with respect to negation.

The comparison of the necessity-style modals for I and I^* was made with respect to the implication relation of I^*. However, the same results hold if the comparison is made with respect to the implication relation of I:

Exercise 29.7. Show that (a) and (b) of Theorem 29.5 hold for the implication relation "$\Longrightarrow$" of I as well as for "$\Longrightarrow^*$" of I^*. (The proof is straightfoward if the description of the necessity-style modal in Exercise 29.6 is used.)

There is a special case worth noting: the change in necessity-style modals when there is a shift from one implication relation on a set to another that is a proper extension of it. It concerns a case of relativized modals.

Suppose we begin with an implication structure $I = \langle S, \Rightarrow \rangle$. Assume, in addition, that there is some T that belongs to S; perhaps it is a theory of some sort, perhaps a physical theory, that belongs to the structure but is not a thesis of it. We can then form the relativized implication relation "$\Rightarrow^T$" (Section 9.4). The implication relativized to T is an extension of "$\Rightarrow$," and since T is not a thesis of I, it is a proper extension. Let I^T be the implication structure $\langle S, \Rightarrow^T \rangle$. To apply the preceding theorem, we require, in addition, that the structure I^T be incomplete with respect to negation. That will hold if and only if $Cn(T)$, the set of all consequences of T (in I), is itself incomplete with respect to negation.[3]

We can then try to identify the necessity-style and possibility-style modal operators on I^T. Let $\Box$ be the necessity operator on I, and $\Box^T$ be the *relative necessity* on I, that is, the necessity operator on I^T. It follows from the preceding theorem that plain necessity is always definitely stronger than relative necessity (since T is a thesis of I^T, but not a thesis of I). That is, for all A is S, $\Box(A) \Rightarrow \Box^T(A)$, but not conversely. When T is some physical theory, it is natural to think of $\Box^T$ as expressing a physical necessity. The naturalness of this expression is reinforced by the fact that it is provable that $\Box^T(A)$ is a thesis of I^T if and only if $T \Rightarrow A$ (we leave the proof as an exercise). Moreover, with "$\Diamond^T$" as the possibility-style dual of $\Box^T$ (the possibility modal on I^T), it can also be proved that $\Diamond^T(A)$ is a thesis of I^T if and only if $T \nRightarrow \neg A$, that is, if and only if A is consistent with T (in I).

Exercise 29.8. Let $I = \langle S, \Rightarrow \rangle$ be a classical implication structure that is incomplete with respect to negation. Let T be some member of S that is not a thesis of I, such that $Cn(T)$ is incomplete with respect to negation. Let $\Box$, $\Box^T$, and $\Diamond^T$ be as described above. Then

(a) $\Box^T(A)$ is a thesis of I^T if and only if $T \Rightarrow A$, and
(b) $\Diamond^T(A)$ is a thesis of I^T if and only if $T \nRightarrow \neg A$.

Of course, this is one possible way of understanding the concept of physical necessity and possibility, relative to some theory T. It does not speak to any notion of physical necessity and possibility one might have that goes unrelativized to any theory at all. However, this proposal accords well with the idea that an item is physically necessary if and only if it is a consequence of the relevant physical theory, and it is physically possible if it is consistent with that theory. These considerations go some way toward indicating that the necessity and possibility-style modals, tied as they are to the theses of structures, are not far off the mark, for when relativized, they yield the kinds of relative necessity and possibility commonly proposed.

Necessity-style modals are not for every structure. They were taken to be operators that assigned a fixed thesis to theses, and a fixed antithesis to nontheses, provided the structure was classical and incomplete with respect to negation. Nonclassical structures, as we shall see, have modal operators on them. However, if one wanted to provide them with something like a necessity modal, that would have to be done some other way. For example, the implication structure associated with the intuitionistic sentential calculus (ISC) does not have a necessity-style modal on it. Suppose that we introduce an operator $\Box_i$ on the implication structure I_{ISC} associated with ISC, such that $\Box_i(A)$ is some fixed thesis if A is a thesis of I_{ISC}, and is some fixed antithesis otherwise. Then $\Box_i$ fails to be a modal operator on the structure, because it distributes over all disjunctions. [Two cases: (1) Suppose that $(A \vee B)$ is a thesis. That happens if and only if $(A \vee B)$ is a theorem of ISC. But the latter holds if and only if either A is a theorem or B is a theorem of ISC. So either A is a thesis or B is a thesis of I_{ISC}. Then either $\Box_i(A)$ is a thesis or $\Box_i(B)$ is a thesis. Therefore $\Box_i(A) \vee \Box_i(B)$ is a thesis. So if $(\Box_i A) \vee \Box_i(B)$ is a thesis, then every member of S implies it, and, in particular, $\Box_i(A \vee B) \Rightarrow^{\text{ISC}} \Box_i(A) \vee \Box_i(B)$. (2) Suppose that $(A \vee B)$ is not a thesis. Then $\Box_i(A \vee B)$ is some antithesis that implies all members, and $\Box_i(A) \vee \Box_i(B)$ in particular.]

30

Modals revisited I

We have characterized the modal operators as a special type of function that maps the set of an implication structure to itself. Certainly there are such operators, as the various examples show. It is also true that these operators behave in ways that modals are supposed to. They appear, then, to be familiar, not foreign. They count as modal. One question remains: How do some of the familiar kinds of modals figure in this scheme of things? One of our aims is to capture most, if not all, of what has usually been regarded as modal. Have we done so? Are there any blatant omissions? We turn now to a review of some traditional and nontraditional sources for modal operators.

30.1 Modal Operators of Normal Modal Systems

Normal modal systems consist of the language of the classical sentential calculus, with the addition of the box, $\Box$, to its vocabulary, and appropriate formation rules. In addition to the distribution axiom $\Box(p \to q)$ $\to (\Box p \to \Box q)$, they have the rules modus ponens, necessitation, and, in some formulations, substitution. These systems differ from each other in the addition (beyond the distribution axiom) of axioms involving the box. The simplest normal system is (K), which has only the distribution axiom. (The usual normal systems were described in Chapter 25, notes 1 and 2.)

Let (L) be a normal modal system. Given the box, $\Box$, of the system, let us say that the mapping φ_L of the language of (L) to itself is the operator corresponding to "$\Box$" if and only if to each sentence A of the language of (L), φ_L has the value "$\Box A$". We want to show that for each normal modal system (L) the operator φ_L is a modal operator.

Of course, to do so we have to construe the mapping associated with $\Box$ as a mapping of a structure to itself. The structure to use is the one that is associated with the normal modal system (L): $I_L = \langle S_L, \Rightarrow^L \rangle$, where S_L is the set of formulas of the normal modal system (L), and A_1, $\ldots$, $A_n \Rightarrow^L B$ if and only if $\vdash_L (A_1 \& \ldots \& A_n) \to B$.

Consider the case for the normal modal system (T).

Theorem 30.1. *If I_T is the implication structure corresponding to the normal modal system (T), then the associated operator φ_T is a modal operator on I_T and is a necessitation modal, and $\varphi_T(A) \Rightarrow^T A$ for all A in S_T.*

Proof. To show that φ_T is modal, we have to show (1) that it distributes over "$\Rightarrow T$" and (2) that there are two sentences of (T) such that φ_T does not distribute over their disjunction. For (1), suppose that $A_1, \ldots, A_n \Rightarrow^T B$. Then $(A_1 \& \ldots \& A_n) \to B$ is a theorem of (T). By the rule of necessitation, $\Box(A_1 \& \ldots \& A_n \to B)$ is also a theorem of (T). It is relatively straightforward, then, to show that $\Box A_1 \& \ldots \& \Box A_n \to \Box B$ is also a theorem of (T). Therefore $\Box A_1, \ldots, \Box A_n \Rightarrow^T \Box B$. By the definition of φ_T, $\varphi_T(A_1), \ldots, \varphi_T(A_n) \Rightarrow^T \varphi_T(B)$. Thus, φ_T distributes over "$\Rightarrow^T$." In order to show (2), suppose, on the contrary, that $\varphi_T(A \lor B) \Rightarrow^T \varphi_T(A) \lor \varphi_T(B)$ for all disjunctions of members of the structure. In that case, $\Box(A \lor B) \to \Box A \lor \Box B$ is a theorem of (T) for all A and B in the language of (T). In particular, $\Box(A \lor \neg A) \to \Box A \lor \neg A$ is a theorem of (T). Since negation is classical, $(A \lor \neg A)$ is a theorem, and by the rule of necessitation, $\Box(A \lor \neg A)$ is also a theorem of (T). Consequently, $\Box A \lor \Box \neg A$ is a theorem, and then so too is $\neg \Box \neg A \to \Box A$. Moreover, since $\Box A \to A$ is a theorem of (T) for all A, it follows that $\neg \neg A \to \neg \Box \neg A$ (since $\Box \neg A \to \neg A$). Therefore $A \to \Box A$. Since $\Box A \to A$, it follows that for every A, $\Box A \leftrightarrow A$ is a theorem of (T). This is what is usually called the "collapse" of the modal. Now it is well known that the modal does not collapse in (T) (Hughes and Cresswell, 1968, p. 71). Consequently, φ_T fails to distribute over disjunctions. Thus, φ_T is a modal operator on the structure I^T associated with (T).

Moreover, $\varphi_T(A) \Rightarrow^T A$ for all A, since $\Box A \to A$ is a theorem of (T), and we leave it for the reader to check that φ_T is a necessitation modal.

In showing that the operator φ_T is a modal operator, we made essential use of the distribution axiom and the fact that $\Box A \to A$ is a theorem of (T) for all A. The proof carries over to any normal modal system that extends (T). Thus the operators associated with the box in the system (B), (S_4), and (S_5) all qualify as modal operators on the implication structures associated with those respective modal systems.

When it is a case of modal systems like (K) and (K_4), which do not extend (T), the preceding proof is of no help. Nevertheless, their associated operators are also modal. Here is a simple result that helps in case the normal modal system (L) is extended by some normal modal system (L^*) that extends both (L) and (T).

Theorem 30.2. *Let (L) be a normal modal system, I_L its associated implication structure, and φ_L the operator associated with the box of (L). If (L^*) is a normal modal system that extends (L) and (T), and the box of (L^*) does not collapse $[B \leftrightarrow \Box B$ fails to be a theorem of (L^*) for some $B]$, then φ_L is a modal operator on I_L.*

Proof. (1) φ_L distributes over "$\Rightarrow^L$." The proof is the same as that used in Theorem 30.1(1). (2) φ_L does not distribute over disjunctions. Suppose, on the contrary, that for every A and B in S_L, $\varphi_L(A \vee B) \Rightarrow^L \varphi_L(A) \vee \varphi_L(B)$. In particular, $\varphi_L(A \vee \neg A) \Rightarrow^L \varphi_L(A) \vee \varphi_L(\neg A)$. Therefore $\Box(A \vee \neg A) \rightarrow (\Box A \vee \Box \neg A)$ is a theorem of (L), and therefore a theorem of (L^*), since (L^*) extends (L). Since (L^*) is normal, $\Box(A \vee \neg A)$ is a theorem, so that $\Box A \vee \Box \neg A$ is a theorem of (L^*). Moreover, since (L^*) extends (T), $\Box A \rightarrow A$ is a theorem of (L^*) as well. Using the same proof as given for Theorem 30.1(2), $\Box A \leftrightarrow A$ is a theorem of (L^*). But that is impossible, since there is no modal collapse in (L^*). Therefore φ_L is a modal operator on the structure I_L.

Thus, the operators that are associated with the modal systems (K) and (K_4) are modal operators on their respective associated structures, since the normal modal system (S_5), for example, is a normal modal system that extends (K) and (T) and also extends (K_4) and (T) (and, of course, does not have modal collapse).

Of course, this theorem does not apply to the Gödel–Löb system, since there is no normal modal system that extends it as well as (T) (Boolos, 1979, p. 30); see Theorem 28.15. However, it is known that in the system $(G\text{-}L)$, $\Box$ does not distribute over disjunction. Otherwise the Gödel–Löb system would be complete with respect to negation (Section 28.5).

30.2 Intuitionistic modals

We have already seen that there are modal operators available on implication structures in which negation is classical. The simplest example of interest was the structure associated with the classical sentential calculus. Those modal operators were not associated with any connective in the structure. In the preceding section we were concerned with the normal modal systems (and therefore classical) in which the operator associated with the box proved to be modal. In all those cases the proof of modal character relied upon the classical character of negation in the structure. The question we now wish to consider is whether or not one can be assured of the existence of modal operators on nonclassical implication structures. Such structures include the one that is associated with an axiomatized formulation of the intuitionistic sentential calculus (ISC).

What we wish to show is that there are modal operators on nonclassical structures, and, in particular, there are at least two of interest on ISC. In a general way it is known that ISC has to have modal character. We know from the results of Tarski and McKinsey (1984), Gödel (1933), and others that there is a close connection between ISC and the modal system (S_4). There are various schemes of translation T that provide mappings of the sentences A of ISC to sentences $T(A)$ of (S_4), such that A is a theorem of (ISC) if an only if $T(A)$ is a theorem of (S_4). What we have in mind is something different from those results. The translation functions of ISC to (S_4) are mappings between different structures. For implication structures that are nonclassical, and for ISC in particular, we seek a mapping of the structure to itself that is modal. Here are two examples:

30.2.1 Double negation

It is not true that double negation is a modal operator in every nonclassical structure, for the nonclassical condition requires only that $\neg\neg A \not\Rightarrow A$, for some A in the structure. Something more is needed. That is,

Theorem 30.3. *Let $I = \langle S, \Rightarrow \rangle$ be a nonclassical implication structure in which hypotheticals, disjunctions, and negations always exist, and for which $\neg A_0 \vee \neg\neg A_0$ fails to be a thesis for some A_0 in S. Then the operator φ_{NN} that assigns $\neg\neg A$ to A is a modal operator on I.*

Proof. Note first that double negation distributes over implication. Suppose that $A_1, \ldots, A_n \Rightarrow B$. Then $A_1, \ldots, A_{n-1} \Rightarrow A_n \to B$. Consequently, since $A_n \to B \Rightarrow \neg B \to \neg A_n \Rightarrow \neg\neg A_n \to \neg\neg B$, we obtain $A_1, \ldots, A_{n-1}, \neg\neg A_n \Rightarrow \neg\neg B$. By a similar argument for $A_{n-1} \to \neg\neg B$, and all the remaining antecedents in turn, it follows that $\neg\neg A_1, \ldots, \neg\neg A_n \Rightarrow \neg\neg B$. Thus, double negation distributes over "$\Rightarrow$." It remains only to be shown that double negation fails to distribute over some disjunction. Now, by hypothesis, $\neg A_0 \vee \neg\neg A_0$ fails to be a thesis of I. Therefore $\neg\neg(A_0 \vee \neg A_0) \not\Rightarrow \neg\neg A_0 \vee \neg\neg\neg A_0$. [If the implication held, then since $\neg\neg(A_0 \vee \neg A_0)$ is a thesis in the structure, so too would $\neg\neg A_0 \vee \neg\neg\neg A_0$, but the latter is equivalent to $\neg\neg A_0 \vee \neg A_0$, which fails to be a thesis.]

The implication structure associated with the ISC satisfies the conditions of the preceding theorem, so that φ_{NN} is a modal operator on ISC. Unlike the modal operators exhibited for the classical sentential calculus, the double-negation modal in ISC is the operator associated with a connective of ISC.

There is also a result that goes in the other direction:

Theorem 30.4. *If the operator φ_{NN} is a modal operator on an implication structure I in which disjunctions and negations exist, then I is nonclassical.*

Proof. If I is classical, then $\neg\neg A \Leftrightarrow A$ for all A. Consequently, for any A and B, $\neg\neg(A \vee B) \Rightarrow \neg\neg(A) \neg\neg \vee (B)$, so that double negation distributes over disjunction. Therefore it is not modal, and that is impossible.

Exercise 30.1. Show that the condition that disjunctions exist in the preceding theorem can be relaxed. Note that if $A_1, \ldots, A_n \Rightarrow^{\wedge} B$, and $\neg\neg(A) \Leftrightarrow A$ for all A, then $\neg\neg(A) \Leftrightarrow^{\wedge} A$ for all A, so that $\neg\neg(A_1), \ldots, \neg\neg(A_n) \Rightarrow^{\wedge} \neg\neg(B)$. Thus, double negation distributes over the dual implication "$\Rightarrow^{\wedge}$," and therefore fails to be modal (with respect to "$\Rightarrow$").

When φ_{NN} is modal, it is natural to ask about the modal laws that it satisfies. How do its theses compare with those of other modal operators? We have a delicate problem before us. From the preceding theorem it is clear that double negation is modal only on nonclassical structures. However, a full comparison of the modal laws of double negation requires some knowledge of its dual, and the study of the duals of modal operators on such structures is not, as we noted, well understood. The usual computational machinery that makes such computations relatively easy in the classical case is not always available in the nonclassical situation. The calculations tend to be a bit messy, and the results are sometimes incomplete. Nevertheless, we should like to say something about the type of modal we have in nonclassical double negation.

The combination of modal theses characteristic of nonclassical double negation is rather unusual. First, some observations about its dual.

Theorem 30.5. *Let $I = \langle S, \Rightarrow \rangle$ be a nonclassical implication structure in which hypotheticals, disjunctions, and conjunctions always exist, and for which $\neg A_0 \vee \neg\neg A_0$ fails to be a thesis for some A_0 in S. Then the dual of φ_{NN} is the operator $\varphi_{N^\wedge N^\wedge}$, such that $\varphi_{N^\wedge N^\wedge}(A)$ is $N^\wedge N^\wedge(A)$ for all A in S.*

Proof. (We shall revert, to avoid notational clutter, to our official use of "N" for negation on I, and "$N^\wedge$" for its dual.) If φ is a modal on I, and σ is its dual, then $N\varphi N^\wedge(A) \Rightarrow \sigma(A)$, where σ is the weakest modal on $I^\wedge$ to satisfy this condition (cf. Definition 28.8). For the modal φ_{NN} in particular, $N(NN)N^\wedge(A) \Rightarrow \sigma(A)$. That is, $NN^\wedge(A) \Rightarrow \sigma(A)$. Since σ is the weakest modal operator on $I^\wedge$ to satisfy this condition, $N^\wedge N^\wedge(A) \Rightarrow^\wedge \sigma(A)$ for all A in S, because $NN^\wedge(A) \Rightarrow N^\wedge N^\wedge(A)$ (all A), and $N^\wedge N^\wedge$ is a modal on $I^\wedge$.[1] That is, $\sigma(A) \Rightarrow N^\wedge N^\wedge(A)$. We need to show that this is indeed an equivalence, that is, that $N^\wedge N^\wedge(A) \Rightarrow \sigma(A)$ also holds. For that, we need a lemma:

Lemma 30.1. *Let I be a structure as described in the theorem, and let σ be the dual of φ_{NN}. Then for any C in S there is a C^* in S such that $C \Rightarrow \sigma(C^*)$.*

Proof. If σ is the dual of φ_{NN}, then $NN^\wedge(A) \Rightarrow \sigma(A)$ [Definition 28.8(1)]. Now $C \Rightarrow NN(C)$ for all C. Since $N^\wedge N^\wedge N(C) \Rightarrow N(C)$, $NN(C) \Rightarrow NN^\wedge N^\wedge N(C)$. Therefore $C \Rightarrow NN^\wedge N^\wedge N(C)$. Let C^* be $N^\wedge N(C)$. Then $C \Rightarrow NN^\wedge(C^*)$. Consequently, $C \Rightarrow \sigma(C^*)$. [Note that this is the best possible result, since if $\sigma(A) = N^\wedge N^\wedge(A)$, then for every C there is a C^* such that $C \Rightarrow N^\wedge N^\wedge(C^*)$, for by Theorem 17.8, $C \Rightarrow N^\wedge N(C) \Rightarrow N^\wedge N^\wedge N^\wedge N(C)$, and let C^* be $N^\wedge N(C)$.]

Continuing with the proof of Theorem 30.5, note that since A, $N^\wedge(A) \Rightarrow^\wedge B$ for all B, and σ is a modal with respect to "$\Rightarrow^\wedge$," then $\sigma(A)$, $\sigma(N^\wedge(A)) \Rightarrow^\wedge \sigma(B)$ for all B in S. By Lemma 30.1, for any C there is a C^* such that $\sigma(C^*) \Rightarrow^\wedge C$. For C^* in particular, $\sigma(A)$, $\sigma(N^\wedge(A)) \Rightarrow^\wedge \sigma(C^*)$, so that we obtain $\sigma(A)$, $\sigma(N^\wedge(A)) \Rightarrow^\wedge C$ for all C in S.

Therefore $\sigma(N^\wedge(A)) \Rightarrow^\wedge N^\wedge(\sigma(A))$. That is, $N^\wedge(\sigma(A)) \Rightarrow \sigma(N^\wedge(A))$ for all A in S. Moreover, since $\sigma(A) \Rightarrow N^\wedge N^\wedge(A) \Rightarrow A$, $\sigma(N^\wedge(A)) \Rightarrow N^\wedge(A)$. Therefore $N^\wedge(\sigma(A)) \Rightarrow \sigma(N^\wedge(A)) \Rightarrow N^\wedge(A)$. Consequently, $N^\wedge N^\wedge(A) \Rightarrow N^\wedge N^\wedge(\sigma(A)) \Rightarrow \sigma(A)$. That is, $N^\wedge N^\wedge(A) \Rightarrow \sigma(A)$, and that completes the proof.

We can now say something about the modal laws for φ_{NN}:

Theorem 30.6. *Let $I = \langle S, \Rightarrow \rangle$ be a nonclassical implication structure in which hypotheticals, disjunctions, and conjunctions always exist, and for which $\neg A_0 \vee \neg\neg A_0$ fails to be a thesis for some A_0 in S. Then φ_{NN} is a modal operator on I such that*

(a) φ_{NN} is a necessitation modal,

(b) φ_{NN} is not a T modal,

(c) φ_{NN} is a K_4 modal,

(d) φ_{NN} is not a D modal,

(d) φ_{NN} is not a B modal, and

(f) φ_{NN} is an S_5 modal.

Proof. (a) If A is any thesis of I, then since $A \Rightarrow NN(A)$, $\varphi_{NN}(A)$ is also a thesis.

(b) Since I is nonclassical, $NN(A) \not\Rightarrow A$ for some A in S, so $\varphi_{NN}(A) \not\Rightarrow A$ for some A. Of course, $A \Rightarrow \varphi_{NN}(A)$.

(c) $\varphi_{NN}(\varphi_{NN}(A)) \Rightarrow \varphi_{NN}(A)$. In fact, the equivalence also holds, since $NNNN(A) \Leftrightarrow NN(A)$.

(d) φ_{NN} does not imply its dual, for $NN(A)$ does not imply $N^\wedge N^\wedge(A)$ for all A; otherwise $NN(A) \Rightarrow A$ for all A, and negation would be classical.

(e) To see why the B condition fails, note that, in general, A does not imply $NN(N^\wedge N^\wedge(A))$. Consider the simple nonclassical structure in which P implies Q, and Q implies R. In the dual structure, the implications are reversed. $N^\wedge(Q)$ is R, and $N^\wedge(R)$ is P, so that $N^\wedge N^\wedge(Q)$ is P. Moreover, $N(P)$ is R, and $N(R)$ is P. Therefore $NNN^\wedge N^\wedge(Q)$ is P. Therefore $Q \Rightarrow NNN^\wedge N^\wedge(Q)$ if and only if $Q \Rightarrow P$. But that is impossible in this structure. In addition, the converse of the characteristic B condition also fails. Consider the element E in the implication structure for "$\Rightarrow$" (Theorem 17.8). In that structure, $NNN^\wedge N^\wedge(E)$ is G, and $G \not\Rightarrow E$.

(f) Recall that the S_5 condition is the counterpart of the condition that $\Diamond A \Rightarrow \Box \Diamond A$. It holds for φ_{NN} if and only if $N^\wedge N^\wedge(A) \Rightarrow NNN^\wedge N^\wedge(A)$ for all A. But of course $C \Rightarrow NN(C)$ holds for all C, and for $N^\wedge N^\wedge(A)$ in particular. Note that the structure used in (e) suffices to show that the converse fails, since $N^{\char94}N^{\char94}(E)$ is E, $NN(E)$ is G, and $G \not\Rightarrow E$.

Double negation is a modal operator on certain nonclassical structures (those for which $\neg A \lor \neg\neg A$ fails to be a thesis for some (A). A more refined picture reveals that double negation on such structures satisfies a combination of modal laws that are not associated with any of the more familiar modal systems. It is a type of modal not usually studied, but modal nonetheless.

There is a subtle and interesting issue that is raised by the comparison of double negation with other modal operators. Some of the modal laws involved in that comparison used the duals of operators on the nonclassical structure. Thus, $N^{\char94}$ was taken as an operator on the structure that has N as its negation operator. That seemed alright, since $N^{\char94}$, like N, acts on the same set; it is just that $N^{\char94}$ is the negation with respect to the dual implication relation. Now, the discussion of double negation was restricted to nonclassical structures, and the particular implication structure that is associated with the ISC is, of course, nonclassical. Moreover, to the intuitionistic connective "$\neg$", we have the associated negation operator "N." However, we also made use of the dual $N^{\char94}$ as an operator on the structure I_{ISC}, and one might ask if $N^{\char94}$ is an operator that corresponds to some connective of ISC. That is not so. In light of the absence of such a connective in ISC, the next step might be to extend ISC by adding such a connective (say "$\vdash$") to it, together with axioms or rules governing its use. The question that immediately arises is whether or not "$\vdash$" is an *intuitionistic* connective or, more generally, whether or not the dual of any intuitionistic connective is also intuitionistic. An answer would add to our understanding of what makes a connective intuitionistic.[2]

There are other modals of theoretical interest on nonclassical structures, and on I_{ISC} in particular, that differ from double negation. Here is an example that uses hypotheticals rather than double negation. Let us call such modal operators "conditionalization modals."

30.2.2 Conditionalization modals

What we have in mind by this kind of modal operator is a mapping of the structure that takes any element and makes it conditional upon some element, say P. Thus, let P be any member of a nonclassical structure. Let $\varphi_p(A)$ be the hypothetical $(P \to A)$ for each A in the structure. Are such φ_p's modal operators?

One thing is clear. If φ_P is a modal operator on a structure for some member P, then the structure is nonclassical.

Theorem 30.7. *Let* $I = \langle S, \Rightarrow \rangle$ *be an implication structure, and let* φ_P *be a modal operator on* I *such that* $\varphi_P(A)$ *is* $(P \rightarrow A)$. *Then* I *is nonclassical.*

Proof. Suppose, on the contrary, that I is classical. Then $(P \rightarrow A)$ is equivalent to $(\neg P \vee A)$. Now φ_P does distribute over the implication relation. However, it also distributes over arbitrary disjunctions. The reason is that $\varphi_P(A \vee B) \Rightarrow (P \rightarrow (A \vee B)) \Rightarrow (\neg P \vee (A \vee B)) \Rightarrow (\neg P \vee A) \vee (\neg P \vee B) \Rightarrow \varphi_P(A) \vee \varphi_P(B)$. Therefore φ_P fails to be modal on I, and that is impossible.

The converse is not true. Even if the structure I is nonclassical, there may not be any P in it such that φ_P is modal. Here is a counterexample. Suppose that $S = \{A, B, C\}$, and that A implies B, which in turn implies C. This structure is nonclassical, and all three operators φ_A, φ_B, and φ_C fail to be modal – they all distribute over disjunctions.

However, there is a qualified converse to the preceding theorem that yields conditionalization modals. Let us call a structure *strongly nonclassical* if and only if for some A_0 and B_0 in it, $[(A_0 \rightarrow B_0) \vee (B_0 \rightarrow A_0)]$ fails to be a thesis. The implication structure described at the beginning of this section is nonclassical, but fails to be strongly nonclassical. The structure that consists of $\{A, B, C, D, E\}$, where A implies each of B and C, B (as well as C) implies D, and D implies E, is a strongly nonclassical structure, for $[(B \rightarrow C) \vee (C \rightarrow B)]$ fails to be a thesis.

If a structure is strongly nonclassical, then there will be some conditionalization modal on it:

Theorem 30.8 (conditionalization modals). *Let* $I = \langle S, \Rightarrow \rangle$ *be any strongly nonclassical implication structure. Let* A_0 *and* B_0 *be elements of* S *such that* $[(A_0 \rightarrow B_0) \vee (B_0 \rightarrow A_0)]$ *fails to be a thesis of* I. *Let* P *be* $(A_0 \vee B_0)$. *Then* $\varphi_P(C) = (P \rightarrow C)$ *is a modal operator on* I.

Proof. (1) φ_P distributes over implication. Suppose that $A_1, \ldots, A_n \Rightarrow B$. Then $P, \varphi_P(A_1), \ldots, \varphi_P(A_n) \Rightarrow B$, so that $\varphi_P(A_1), \ldots, \varphi_P(A_n) \Rightarrow (P \rightarrow B)$ [i.e., $\varphi_P(B)$]. (Notice that distribution holds, no matter what P in S is used.) (2) φ_P, where P is $(A_0 \vee B_0)$, fails to distribute over disjunctions. Suppose, on the contrary, that φ_P distributes over all disjunctions. Then $\varphi_P(A_0 \vee B_0) \Rightarrow \varphi_P(A_0) \vee \varphi_P(B_0)$. Note that $\varphi_P(A_0 \vee B_0)$ is a thesis, since $(A_0 \vee B_0) \rightarrow (A_0 \vee B_0)$ is a thesis. Consequently, $[(A_0 \vee B_0) \rightarrow A_0] \vee [(A_0 \vee B_0) \rightarrow B_0]$ is a thesis. But the first disjunct implies $(B_0 \to A_0)$, and the second implies $(A_0 \to B_0)$. Therefore $[(A_0 \to B_0) \vee (B_0 \to A_0)]$ is a thesis. But that is impossible.

It can happen in some nonclassical structures that even though $(A^* \vee \neg A^*)$ is not thesis for some A^*, the conditionalization with it as antecedent will fail to be modal. However, there is a condition under which a disjunction $(A \vee \neg A)$ will yield a conditionalization modal:

Theorem 30.9. *If I is a nonclassical implication structure, and $(\neg A \vee \neg\neg A)$ fails to be a thesis, then $\varphi_{(A \vee \neg A)}$ is a conditionalization modal on I.*

Proof. Note that $(\neg A \vee \neg\neg A) \Leftrightarrow [(A \to \neg A) \vee (\neg A \to A)]$. Therefore $[(A \to \neg A) \vee (\neg A \to A)]$ fails to be a thesis. Consequently, by Theorem 30.8, conditionalization with respect to $(A \vee \neg A)$ is a modal on the structure.

There is a natural question about the modals of double negation and conditionalization: Are they just different descriptions of equivalent operators? In fact, there are strongly nonclassical structures in which the two kinds of modals are not equivalent. That is,

Theorem 30.10. *There is a strongly nonclassical structure I, with elements A^* and B^* in it, such that the conditionalization modal with respect to $(A^* \vee B^*)$ and the double-negation modal are not equivalent.*

Proof. Let $I = \langle S, \Rightarrow \rangle$ be given as follows: $S = \{A, B, B', C, C', D, D', E\}$, with the implication relation

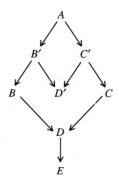

Take B' and C' to be A^* and B^*, respectively. Since $\neg B'$ is C', and $\neg C'$ is $\neg B'$, $(\neg B' \lor \neg\neg B')$ is D', which is not a thesis. By Theorem 30.9, the mapping $\varphi_{D'}$ is modal on I. It remains only to show that $\varphi_{D'}$ and φ_{NN} are not equivalent in this structure. Suppose that they are. Then for all A in S, $\neg\neg A \Leftrightarrow (D' \to A)$. For D in particular, $\neg\neg D \Leftrightarrow (D' \to D)$. Now $\neg\neg D$ is E, and $(D' \to D)$ is D. Therefore the equivalence holds if and only if $E \Leftrightarrow D$, which is impossible.

Exercise 30.2. If for A^* in some structure I, $(\neg A^* \lor \neg\neg A^*)$ fails to be be a thesis, then for all A, $\varphi_{(A^* \lor \neg A^*)} (A) \Rightarrow \varphi_{NN} (A)$.

Exercise 30.3. Show that there may be nonequivalent conditionalization modals on a structure ($\varphi_{D'}$ and φ_D are two such on the structure used in Theorem 30.10).

We turn next to a description of the universal and existential quantifiers as modal operators, and a discussion of how some modal operators and the quantifiers interact. The main idea is to see how the Barcan formula and its converse fare on our account of the modals.

31

Quantification and modality

31.1 Quantifiers as modals

It is a familiar observation that the universal quantifier of, say, standard first-order theory behaves in a way that is very similar to the necessity operator or box in most standard modal systems. The universal quantifier acts on predicates, open sentences, or formulas in such a way that the quantification of a conjunction implies the conjunction of the conjuncts, $\forall x(Px)$ implies Px, and several other familiar truths of quantification all combine to suggest strongly that the quantifier "$\forall x$" has modal character.[1]

Similar observations have been noted for the relation of the existential quantifier "Ex" and the corresponding modal, the diamond. Thus, it seems natural to think that "$\forall x$" corresponds to some kind of $\square$, and "Ex" corresponds to its dual, $\lozenge$. The network of correspondences becomes even more compelling when it is observed that (at least classically), "Ex" can be defined as "$\neg \forall x \neg$."

It seems to be no accident that the quantifiers look very much like modals. We need not try to force our understanding of quantification to make it appear as if quantification is a type of necessity (or possibility).[2] The reason that universal and existential quantifiers count as modal operators is the same as in all the other cases that we have considered: There is a certain implication structure containing the items that are quantified, and quantification over those items is modal when the corresponding operator distributes over the implication relation, but fails to distribute over its dual.

What we would like to show is how universal quantifiers are associated with operators that distribute over the implication relation of certain structures, and how the existential quantifiers are associated with operators that distribute over the dual of that implication relation. In the following section we shall consider the Barcan formula and its converse as an example of how the universal and existential modals interact with other modal operators that may be defined on the structure.

It will be recalled that we introduced (Chapter 20) the notion of an extended implication structure in order to characterize the universal quantifiers U_i and the existential quantifiers E_i on those structures. An extended implication structure, it will be recalled, is given by $I^* = \langle E, Pr, S, \Rightarrow \rangle$, where $\langle S, \Rightarrow \rangle$ is an implication structure, E is a (possibly empty) set of entities, Pr is a (possible empty) set of predicates, and an implication relation "$\Rightarrow^*$" is defined, in terms of "$\Rightarrow$," to extend "$\Rightarrow$" and cover the cases of implication that involve the predicates as well as the members of S. The restriction of "$\Rightarrow^*$" to S is equivalent to "$\Rightarrow$." We also noted that in the special case in which the extended implication structure is one that is associated with a formal language of first-order quantification, with variables $x_1, x_2, \ldots$, then the universal quantifiers U_i are operators associated with the quantification expressions "$\forall x_i$," and the existential operators E_i are operators associated with the expression "Ex_i." We then have the following result:

Theorem 31.1. *Let* $I^* = \langle E, Pr, S, \Rightarrow \rangle$ *be an extended implication structure in which disjunctions and conjunctions (with respect to* "$\Rightarrow^*$"*) always exist. Then every universal quantifier operator* U_i *is a modal operator (with respect to* "$\Rightarrow^*$"*).*

Proof. According to Theorem 20.12, for any $P_1, P_2, \ldots, P_n$ and Q (which may be either predicates or members of S), if $P_1, \ldots, P_n \Rightarrow^* Q$, then for any universal quantifier U_i, $U_i(P_1), \ldots, U_i(P_n) \Rightarrow^* U_i(Q)$. Thus, U_i distributes over implication. Moreover, U_i does not distribute over disjunctions. The reason is that if the structure has at least three members $e_1, e_2,$ and e_3 in E, and at least two members A and B in S such that neither implies the other, and their conjunction and disjunction exist, then the construction used in the proof of Theorem 20.16 yields two predicates P and Q and a quantifier U_i such that $U_i(P \lor Q)$ $\not\Rightarrow^* U_i(P) \lor U_i(Q)$.

Thus, the universal quantifier operators are modal on extended structures. In the familiar case in which the extended structure is the one that is associated with a formulation of first-order quantification, then the universal operators on the structure are those that correspond for each quantifier expression "$\forall x$" (for example) to the mapping that assigns to each formula G of the first-order theory the formula "$\forall x G$." And $A_1, \ldots, A_n \Rightarrow^* B$ holds if and only if the closure of "$(A_1 \ \& \ \ldots \ \& \ A_n)$

$\rightarrow B$" is a theorem of the first-order theory. What makes universal quantification in this case a modal operator is the fact that, in general, "$\forall x(Px \rightarrow Qx) \rightarrow [\forall x(Px) \rightarrow \forall x(Qx)]$" is a theorem, but for some Px and Qx, "$\forall x(Px \vee Qx) \rightarrow [\forall x(Px) \vee \forall x(Qx)]$" is not.

Similar considerations show that the existential quantification operators E_i on extended implication structures are modals with respect to the dual implication relation. Theorem 20.24 shows that existential quantifiers distribute over disjunction, and Exercise 20.4 shows that existential quantifiers do not distribute over the implication relation of an extended structure. Thus, given an extended structure I^*, the existential quantifiers will distribute over the implication relation of the dual $(I^{*\wedge})$, but will not distribute over the implication relation of I^*.

It should be noted that the modal character of quantification does not appear if quantification is restricted to S, the "sentences" of the extended structure, or to their associated constant predicates (Definition 20.2), for in that case, universal quantification distributes over any disjunction of constant predicates, and so quantification has no modal character to speak of. The modal character of quantification comes into play once there are nonconstant predicates in the structure, predicates for which at least $P(e)$ and $P(e')$ are not equivalent for some e and e'.

31.2 Quantification and modalities: Barcan formulas and their converses

The problem we now wish to consider concerns the ways in which the quantifier modals interact with other modal operators that may exist on the structure. It is part of the larger question of how any two modal operators on a structure are related to each other. One touchstone here is the pair of formulas of quantified modal logic, known as the *Barcan formula* (BF), $\forall x \Box Px \Rightarrow \Box \forall x Px$, and the *converse Barcan formula* (CBF), $\Box \forall x Px \Rightarrow \forall x \Box Px$, each of which is expressed here as an implication.

We want to show first that the converse Barcan formula holds for a certain kind of modal operator. Let $I^* = \langle E, Pr, S, \Rightarrow \rangle$ be an extended implication structure, with the implication relation "$\Rightarrow^*$" defined in the usual way (Chapter 20). Let φ be a modal operator on I^*. It is a mapping of the union $(Pr \cup S)$ to itself, which distributes over "$\Rightarrow^*$" (but not over its dual). In particular, then, to each predicate P, φ assigns the value $\varphi(P)$. As in Chapter 20, E^* is the set of all infinite sequences of members of E, and for any predicate P, and any s in E^*, $P(s)$ is the value in S that the predicate assigns to the sequence s.

To render the following discussion a bit more perspicuous, we shall use "$\forall$" to denote a particular universal quantifier operator U_i and shall describe the two formulas this way: If φ is a modal operator on I^*, then

(BF) $\quad \forall(\varphi(P)) \Rightarrow^* \varphi(\forall(P))$ and
(CBF) $\varphi(\forall(P)) \Rightarrow^* \forall(\varphi(P))$

will be called the Barcan formula for φ and the converse Barcan formula for φ respectively.

Definition 31.1. Given a modal φ on I^* (as before), we shall say that it is a *DRDD modal* (DeReDeDicto) if and only if for any s in E^*, and any predicate P in Pr, $(\varphi(P))(s) \Leftrightarrow^* \varphi(P(s))$.[3]

That is, the value that $\varphi(P)$ assigns to s is equivalent to the value that φ assigns to $P(s)$. We then have

Theorem 31.2. *Let* $I^* = \langle E, Pr, S, \Rightarrow \rangle$ *be an extended implication structure, and let* φ *be any modal on* I^* *that satisfies the DRDD condition. Then the converse Barcan formula holds.*

Proof. For any predicate P, $\forall(P) \Rightarrow^* P(s)$ for all s in E^*. Since φ is a modal on I^*, $\varphi(\forall(P)) \Rightarrow^* \varphi(P(s))$. By the DRDD condition, then, $\varphi(\forall(P)) \Rightarrow^* (\varphi(P))(s)$. Now $\varphi(P)$ is also a predicate of the structure, so that $\forall(\varphi(P)) \Rightarrow^* (\varphi(P))(s)$, and $\forall(\varphi(P))$ is the weakest member to imply $(\varphi(P))(s)$ for all s in E^*. Therefore $\varphi(\forall(P)) \Rightarrow^* \forall(\varphi(P))$.[4]

We consider next the Barcan formula itself. In its familiar form, the question is whether or not $\forall x \Box Px \to \Box \forall x Px$ is provable in some particular quantified modal system. In the present setting, there is a corresponding question: If φ is a modal operator on some extended implication structure I^*, does it follow that $\forall(\varphi(P)) \Rightarrow^* \varphi(\forall(P))$? Does BF hold for all modals φ, for some, or for none? (Here, "$\forall$" stands for a universal quantifier operator on the structure.) The answer depends upon the particular type of structure, as well as the particular modal under study.

A simple case in which BF will hold for φ: Let the modal in question by any universal quantifier modal. Then

Theorem 31.3 (Barcan and universal quantification). *If* I^* *is an extended implication structure, and P is any predicate of* I^*, *and*

U_j is any universal quantifier of I^*, then both BF and CBF hold for U_j.

Proof. The converse Barcan formula for U_j is given by $U_j(\forall P)$ $\Rightarrow^* \forall(U_j(P))$. Now "$\forall$" is any universal quantifier modal – say U_i. Therefore CBF holds for U_j if and only if $U_j U_i(P) \Rightarrow^*$ $U_i U_j(P)$. But this is the familiar result about the interchange of the order of universal quantifiers (Theorem 20.15). The result for BF is proved similarly.

There are, as we noted, modal quantificational systems for which BF for the box of such a system fails to be a theorem. However, that fact seems to originate in the particular formulations of the quantificational bases of those theories.[5] There are, however, some particular modal operators for which BF holds, and some for which it fails (and the same for CBF). We turn now to those particular cases. Since double negation is a modal on nonclassical implication structures (that satisfy the conditions of Theorem 30.3), we have this observation:

Theorem 31.4 (Barcan and double negation). *If I^* is a nonclassical extended implication structure (in which disjunctions and hypotheticals always exist, and $\neg A^* \vee \neg\neg A^*$ fails to be a thesis for some A^*), then BF with respect to double negation (NN) fails, but CBF holds.*

Proof. Under these conditions, φ_{NN} is a modal operator on I^*. When the modal of double negation is used, BF becomes $\forall(\varphi_{NN}(P)) \Rightarrow^* \varphi_{NN}(\forall(P))$. However, it is known that in nonclassical systems, "$\forall x(\neg\neg Px) \to \neg\neg\forall x(Px)$" fails to be a theorem, and the counterpart of it in the associated structure fails as well.[6] However, CBF, $\varphi_{NN}(\forall(P)) \Rightarrow^* \forall(\varphi_{NN}(P))$, holds. We leave the proof for the reader.

Theorem 31.5 (Barcan and conditionalization). *If $I^* = \langle E, Pr, S, \Rightarrow \rangle$ is a strongly nonclassical extended implication structure in which φ_Q is a conditionalization modal for some Q in S, then BF and CBF hold with respect to φ_Q.*

Proof. BF with respect to φ_Q states that $\forall(\varphi_Q(P)) \Rightarrow^*$ $\varphi_Q(\forall(P))$. It is straightforward to show that in any extended structure, $\forall(A \to P) \Leftrightarrow^* (A \to \forall(P))$ for any A in S and any predicate P. But $\varphi_Q(\forall(P)) \Leftrightarrow^* (Q \to \forall(P))$, and $\forall(\varphi_Q(P))$ $\Leftrightarrow^* \forall(Q \to P)$. Similar remarks hold for CBF.

Theorem 31.6 (Barcan and necessity-style modals). *If I^* is an extended implication structure that is incomplete with respect to negation, and $\square$ is a necessity-style modal operator on I^*, then BF and CBF hold with respect to $\square$.*

Proof. Note that for any predicate P of I^*, P is a thesis of I^* if and only if $\forall(P)$ is a thesis. Now BF with respect to $\square$ states that $\forall(\square(P)) \Rightarrow^* \square(\forall(P))$ for any predicate P of I^*. Let "$\square$" be defined as a necessity-style modal (Section 29.2), so that if P is a thesis, then $\square(P)$ is P; otherwise $\square(P)$ is, say, Z for some fixed antithesis Z. Suppose that P is a thesis of I^*. Then $\square(P)$ is P, so that $\forall(\square(P))$ is $\forall(P)$. BF with respect to $\square$ then becomes $\forall(P) \Rightarrow^* \forall(P)$. On the other hand, suppose that P is not a thesis. Then $\square(P)$ is Z, and since $\forall(Z) \Rightarrow^* Z$, and Z implies ("$\Rightarrow^*$") every member of the structure, $\forall(\square(Z)) \Rightarrow^* \square(\forall(P))$. The proof for CBF is similar.

Exercise 31.1 (Barcan and (S_5)). In any extended implication structure, φ is any (S_5) modal [where σ is the dual of φ, $\varphi(A) \Rightarrow^* A$, $A \Rightarrow^* \sigma(A)$, $\sigma(A) \Rightarrow^* \varphi\sigma(A)$, and $\sigma\varphi(A) \Rightarrow^* \varphi(A)$], and φ is a DRDD-modal, then BF with respect to φ holds. It would also hold if the third and fourth conditions listed were replaced by the B condition: $A \Rightarrow^* \varphi\sigma(A)$ and $\sigma\varphi(A) \Rightarrow^* A$.

Exercise 31.2 (Barcan and finite domains). If $I^* = \langle E, Pr, S, \Rightarrow \rangle$ is an extended implication structure for which E is nonempty and finite, then for any modal that satisfies the DRDD condition, BF and CBF hold.

32

Modals revisited II

Our aim has been to study the modal operators as functions on implication structures. There is nothing mysterious or arcane about the kind of functions that they are, and there is nothing recherché about the particular examples that qualify as modal. It should come as no surprise, then, that some of the operators commonly studied in elementary logic and mathematics should turn out to have modal character. This should help reinforce the idea that some modals are quite familiar, ordinary, and uncontroversial. With this in mind, we turn to some elementary examples.

32.1 Power sets

The power set of a set A is the set of all the subsets of A. Suppose S is a set of sets (1) that is closed under finite intersections and unions of its members, and (2) for any set A in S, $P(A)$ is in S, and (3) there are at least two members, A^* and B^*, of S such that neither is a subset of the other.

Let $I = \langle S, \Rightarrow \rangle$ be an implication structure, where S is as described above, and for any sets $A_1, \ldots, A_n$ and B in S, $A_1, \ldots, A_n \Rightarrow B$ if and only if $A_1 \cap \ldots \cap A_n \subseteq B$. Then there is a simple result:

Theorem 32.1. *Let $I = \langle S, \Rightarrow \rangle$ be the implication structure described above. Let P be the mapping of S to S that assigns the power set of A to A, for each A in S. Then P is a modal operator on I.*

Proof. To see why, note first that P distributes over implication: If $A_1, \ldots, A_n \Rightarrow B$, then $A_1 \cap \ldots \cap A_n \subseteq B$. Consequently, $P(A_1) \cap \ldots \cap P(A_n) \subseteq P(B)$, so that $P(A_1), \ldots, P(A_n) \Rightarrow P(B)$. Moreover, P fails to distribute over disjunctions. Now, as we noted, the disjunction of A and B in S is (relative to this implication relation) just their union. So it remains only to show that P does not distribute over unions. Suppose, in particular, that $P(A^* \cup B^*) \subseteq P(A^*) \cup P(B^*)$. By

(3), there is some a in A^* that is not in B^*, and some b in B^* that is not in A^*. The set $\{a, b\}$ is a subset of $A^* \cup B^*$, and so a member of $P(A^* \cup B^*)$. Consequently, it is either a member of $P(A^*)$ or a member of $P(B^*)$. But if $\{a, b\}$ is a member of $P(A^*)$, then it is a subset of A^*, so that b is a member of A^*. That is impossible. Similarly, if it is a member of $P(B^*)$, then a is a member of B^*. And that is impossible.

There are some elementary results that hold for the power-set modal.

Theorem 32.2. *Let $I = \langle S, \Rightarrow \rangle$ be an implication structure satisfying the same conditions as in the preceding theorem. Let P be the power-set modal on I. Then*

(a) *P fails to be a T modal if there is some member of S that is not a member of itself,*

(b) *$A \Rightarrow P(A)$ holds if and only if A is transitive (every member of A is a subset of A), and*

(c) *P is a K_4 modal if and only if all the members of S are transitive.*

Proof. (a) Suppose that A is not a member of itself. If $P(A) \Rightarrow A$, then since A is a member of $P(A)$, it is also a member of A. But that is impossible.

(b) If A is transitive, then since every member of A is a subset of A, $A \subseteq P(A)$ – that is, $A \Rightarrow P(A)$. Conversely, if $A \Rightarrow P(A)$, then every member of A is a member of $P(A)$ and therefore a subset of A.

(c) Note that $P(A) \subseteq P(B)$ if and only if $A \subseteq B$. Therefore $P(A) \Rightarrow P(P(A))$ if and only if $A \Rightarrow P(A)$. The result then follows from (b).

Exercise 32.1. Add the following to the conditions on S: that the members of S are all subsets of some set D. It follows that $P^{\wedge}$, the dual of P, is given by cPc, where $c(A)$ is the relative complement $(D - A)$ of A. Then

(a) P is not a D modal. That is, $P(A) \not\Rightarrow cPc(A)$ for some A in S.

(b) Define $P^+(A)$, the positive power set of A, as the set of all nonempty subsets of A, and show that P^+ is a modal operator that is stronger than P, that it satisfies (a)–(c) of the preceding theorem, and that it is a D modal.

That the power-set operator is a modal operator on certain set-theoretical structures is no deep truth. It tells us nothing that we did not already know, and certainly nothing that was not mathematically quite simple and ordinary. That is a virtue of the example. Modal operators need not be thought of as arcane or overly subtle. In addition, there is nothing about necessity or possibility that has to be invoked in order to see that this particular operator is modal. It has its modal character not by some unseen connection with necessity or possibility, but directly.

In fact, there are certain mathematical operators, such as the closure and the interior operators on topological spaces, whose behavior is similar to those of the box and the diamond of some modal systems. But that in itself does not make such operators modal. Any topological space can be described with the aid of these operators, but it is only for certain kinds of topological spaces that the closure and interior operators will be modal. This ties in well with the fact that a modal system such as (S_4) is related to special kinds of topological spaces, namely, those that are normal, separable, and discrete-in-themselves.

Let us consider some simple reasons why it turns out that despite the similarity of the conditions for closure and interior operators to certain modal laws, those topological operators are modal only for some topological spaces.

32.2 Topological closure and interior operators

Topological spaces are sometimes characterized by means of a closure operator K, and sometimes by the use of an interior operator I. In the former case, a topological space is a set S and a closure mapping K on S that maps subsets of S to subsets of S such that (1) $A \subseteq K(A)$, (2) $K(A \cup B) = K(A) \cup K(B)$, (3) $K(K(A)) = K(A)$, and (4) $K(\varnothing) = \varnothing$. The monotonicity condition, (5) if $A \subseteq B$, then $K(A) \subseteq K(B)$, follows from the preceding four.[1]

The formulation that uses the interior operator requires (1) $I(A) \subseteq A$, (2) $I(A \cap B) = I(A) \cap I(B)$, (3) $I(A) = I(I(A))$, and (4) $I(S) = S$. The monotonicity condition, (5) if $A \subseteq B$, then $I(A) \subseteq I(B)$, follows from the preceding four.

We can take any topological space S with interior operator I and form an implication structure $\langle S, \Rightarrow \rangle$, where for any subsets $A_1, \ldots, A_n$ and B of S, $A_1, \ldots, A_n \Rightarrow B$ if and only if the intersection of all the A_i's is a subset of B. The question is whether or not the operator I on the structure is modal. If we were guided solely by formal considerations, then the resemblance of some of these conditions to familiar modal laws would suggest a positive answer. In general, however, the interior operator, for example, is not modal, though it will be modal for special topological spaces.

To see why, in general, I is not modal, notice first that the problem is not with distribution over the implication relation, for if $A_1, \ldots, A_n \Rightarrow B$, then $A_1 \cap \ldots \cap A_n \subseteq B$. Consequently, $I(A_1 \cap \ldots \cap A_n) \subseteq I(B)$ [by (5)]. By (2), then, $I(A_1) \cap \ldots \cap I(A_n) \subseteq I(B)$, so that $I(A_1), \ldots, I(A_n) \Rightarrow I(B)$. The failure to be modal lies in the fact that I will distribute over unions in some topological spaces (in the discrete topology, I is the identity operator). Similar remarks hold for the closure operator K.

However, there are simple but important topological spaces that do guarantee the modal character of the interior operator. Consider the example of a Euclidean line

0	P	1

where the interval A contains 0 and all points between 0 and P, and B contains P and all points between P and 1. Then $(A \cup B)$ is the entire interval, and its interior is the set of points between, but not including, the endpoints. $I(A)$ is the set of points between 0 and P, but not including either 0 or P, and $I(B)$ is the set of all points between, but not including, P and 1. Since P is in $I(A \cup B)$, but in neither $I(A)$ nor $I(B)$, $I(A \cup B) \nsubseteq I(A) \cup I(B)$. In this case, as in its generalization to a normal, separable, dense-in-itself topological space, I and K are modal operators. That is,

Theorem 32.3. *If S is a normal, separable, dense-in-itself topological space, then the closure operator K and the interior operator I are modal operators on the associated implication structure.*[2]

32.3 Tarskian theories

Thus far we have been examining examples of operators that are fully modal in that they distribute over all cases of implication of the structure (and, of course, fail to distribute over the dual implication relation). One way of relaxing the condition of modality is to weaken the requirement that the operator distribute over all cases of implication, and require instead that the operator distribute only over $A_1, \ldots, A_n \Rightarrow B$, when it belongs to a special subset of such implicational statements. We shall call such modals *restricted modals*. An interesting case of a restricted modal consists of the mapping Cn of the subsets A of a structure of their consequence sets $Cn(A)$ [where $Cn(A)$ is the set of all elements of the structure that are implied by finitely many members of A]. Let us see how this happens.

Let X be any subset of some implication structure. The consequence operator Cn satisfies the following conditions:

(1) $X \subseteq Cn(X)$,
(2) $CnCn(X) \subseteq Cn(X)$, and
(3) if $X \subseteq Y$, then $Cn(X) \subseteq Cn(Y)$.

These conditions have a formal similarity to the topological closure K of the preceding section, except for the important difference that (unlike K), $Cn(X \cup Y)$, in general, is not a subset of $Cn(X) \cup Cn(Y)$. There usually are consequences of some set $(X \cup Y)$ that fail to be either consequences of X or consequences of Y. However, it does follow from these conditions that

(4) for any X and Y, $Cn(X \cup Y) = Cn(Cn(X) \cup Cn(Y))$.

For any set X, $Cn(X)$ is called the *closure* of X, and a set is called *closed* if and only if it is equal to its own closure. Closed sets are also called *Tarskian theories* (sometimes *Tarskian systems*). Thus, every set $Cn(X)$ is a Tarskian theory.

32.3.1 Tarskian theories and restricted modals

We can now see how the consequence operator on certain structures is a restricted modal. Let $I = \langle S, \Rightarrow \rangle$ be an implication structure, and let $I^* = \langle P(S), \Rightarrow^* \rangle$ be an implication structure, where $P(S)$ is the set of all subsets of S, and for any subsets $X_1, \ldots, X_n$ and Y of S, $X_1, \ldots, X_n \Rightarrow^* Y$ if and only if $Y \subseteq (X_1 \cup \ldots \cup X_n)$. The implication relation "$\Rightarrow^*$" is just the dual of the implication "$\Rightarrow$" used in the preceding section.

Now, it is not generally true that whenever $X_1, \ldots, X_n \Rightarrow^* Y$, then $Cn(X_1), \ldots, Cn(X_n) \Rightarrow^* Cn(Y)$, but it is true if $(X_1 \cup \ldots \cup X_n)$ is closed (i.e., whenever the union of the antecedents is a Tarskian theory). That is,

Theorem 32.4. *Let* $I = \langle S, \Rightarrow \rangle$ *and* $I^* = \langle P(S), \Rightarrow^* \rangle$ *be implication structures as described above. Let Cn be the mapping on P(S) that assigns to any member X of P(S) the Tarskian theory Cn(X). Then Cn is a restricted modal operator on* I^*.

Proof. If $X_1, \ldots, X_n \Rightarrow^* Y$, and $(X_1 \cup \ldots \cup X_n)$ is a Tarskian theory, then $Cn(X_1), \ldots, Cn(X_n) \Rightarrow^* Cn(Y)$, for then $Y \subseteq (X_1 \cup \ldots \cup X_n)$, so that $Cn(Y) \subseteq Cn(X_1 \cup \ldots \cup X_n)$. Since $(X_1 \cup \ldots \cup X_n)$ is assumed to be closed, $Cn(Y) \subseteq (X_1 \cup \ldots \cup X_n)$, so that $Cn(Y) \subseteq Cn(X_1) \cup \ldots \cup Cn(X_n)$. Consequently, $Cn(X_1), \ldots, Cn(X_n) \Rightarrow^* Cn(Y)$. It remains only to show that Cn does not distribute over the dual of "$\Rightarrow^*$." But the dual of "$\Rightarrow^*$" is the implication relation "$\Rightarrow$," according to which $X_1, \ldots, X_n \Rightarrow Y$ if and only if the intersection of the X_i's is a subset of Y. If Cn distributed over "$\Rightarrow$," then since $X, Y \Rightarrow (X \cap Y)$ for all X and Y, $Cn(X) \cap Cn(Y) \subseteq Cn(X \cap Y)$ for all subsets X and Y of S. But clearly that is not so.[3] Consequently, Cn is a restricted modal on the structure I^*.

Exercise 32.2. For the structure I^* of Theorem 32.4, (a) $Cn(X) \Rightarrow^* X$ and (b) $CnCn(X) \Rightarrow^* Cn(X)$ for all subsets X of S.

32.3.2 Tarskian theories and nonmonotonicity

There is another way of describing the behavior of the consequence operator so that it distributes over a relation in an unrestricted way (and does not distribute over the dual of that relation). It involves making the conditions under which Cn distributes over "$\Rightarrow^*$" a part of the conditions of a new relation. However, the relation for which this happens is not the standard kind of implication relation that we have used throughout this study. It is a relation of the kind that is called *nonmonotonic*, since the Dilution conditon fails.

Let us begin with the implication relation "$\Rightarrow^*$" of the preceding section and define a new relation "$\Rightarrow^\circ$" (this is, strictly speaking, a temporary abuse of our usual double-arrow notation for implication relations only) that is a subrelation of "$\Rightarrow^*$." For any subsets $X_1, \ldots, X_n$ and Y of S, $X_1, \ldots, X_n \Rightarrow^\circ Y$ if and only if $(X_1 \cup \ldots \cup X_n)$ is a Tarskian theory (multiple-antecedent case), and for any X and Y, $X \Rightarrow^\circ Y$ if and only if $X \Rightarrow^* Y$ (note that the single-antecedent case does not require X to be a Tarskian theory). Then we have the following:

Theorem 32.5. *Let $I = \langle S, \Rightarrow \rangle$ and $I^* = \langle P(S), \Rightarrow^* \rangle$ be implication structures as in Theorems 32.2 and 32.4, let Cn be the mapping of subsets A of S to the Tarskian theory Cn(A) and let "$\Rightarrow^\circ$" be as defined earlier. Then Cn distributes over "$\Rightarrow^\circ$" and fails to distribute over its dual.*

Proof. (1) *Cn* distributes over "$\Rightarrow°$." The single-antecedent case is obvious. Suppose that $X_1, \ldots, X_n \Rightarrow° Y$. Then $X_1, \ldots, X_n \Rightarrow^* Y$, and $(X_1 \cup \ldots \cup X_n)$ is closed. By Theorem 32.4, $Cn(X_1), \ldots, Cn(X_n) \Rightarrow^* Cn(Y)$. To show that *Cn* distributes over "$\Rightarrow°$," we have to show in addition that $Cn(X_1) \cup \ldots \cup Cn(X_n)$ is closed. However, by (4) in Section 32.3, $Cn(Cn(X_1) \cup \ldots \cup Cn(X_n)) = Cn(X_1 \cup \ldots \cup X_n) = (X_1 \cup \ldots \cup X_n)$ [since $(X_1 \cup \ldots \cup X_n)$ is closed]. Moreover, since $X_i \subseteq Cn(X_i)$, $Cn(Cn(X_1) \cup \ldots \cup Cn(X_n)) \subseteq (Cn(X_1) \cup \ldots \cup Cn(X_n))$. By (1) in Section 32.3, the right-hand side is a subset of the left-hand side. So the equality holds between the two, and $Cn(X_1) \cup \ldots \cup Cn(X_n)$ is closed.

It remains only to be shown that *Cn* does not distribute over the dual of "$\Rightarrow°$." In those cases for which $X_1 \cup \ldots \cup X_n$ is a Tarskian theory, "$\Rightarrow°$" and "$\Rightarrow^*$" are equivalent. Therefore, in those cases, the dual of "$\Rightarrow°$" is the dual of "$\Rightarrow^*$," which is just "$\Rightarrow$" (where the intersection of the antecedents is a subset of the consequent). Consequently, if *Cn* distributed over the dual of "$\Rightarrow°$," we would then have that $Cn(X) \cap Cn(Y) \subseteq Cn(X \cap Y)$, since $X, Y, \Rightarrow (X \cap Y)$. However, that is not generally true, even when, as restricted here, the union of X and Y is taken to be closed.

Although the consequence operator *Cn* behaves with respect to the relation "$\Rightarrow°$" exactly as modal operators are required to behave, the relation "$\Rightarrow°$" is a a relation that is, strictly speaking, not implicational. Dilution and Projection no longer hold generally, though Permutation and simplification do. Also, the Cut condition no longer holds, though there is another version of it, originally due to P. Hertz, that one could use instead, and thereby salvage most of the original conditions for implication relations, but not, of course, Dilution or Projection.[4]

The consequence operator can be thought of either as a restricted modal or as a full modal with respect to a nonmonotonic "implication" relation. In either case, the attempt to describe the modal character of *Cn* leads to some notions that are worthy of further study.[5]

32.3.3 Tarskian theories and theoretical operators

There is yet a third way of studying the consequence operator. It retains the standard conditions for implication relations, but it modifies the conditions for being a logical operator (such as conjunction and disjunction), as well as the conditions for being a modal operator. I am not recommending that one make such modifications, but rather speculating how those changes might be introduced. The effect is then that Cn is a modal operator (modulo the changes).

Let $I = \langle S, \Rightarrow \rangle$ and $I^* = \langle P(S), \Rightarrow^* \rangle$ be implication structures as in Theorem 32.4. There is first the matter of modifying the definitions of the logical operators on I^*. Instead of describing the conjunction of the sets X and Y in $P(S)$ (subsets of S) as the weakest subset of S that implies X as well as Y, we shall say that the *theoretical conjunction* $C_T(X, Y)$ of X with Y is the weakest theory in $P(S)$ that implies ("$\Rightarrow^*$") X as well as Y. Similar modifications can then be introduced for *theoretical disjunction* (D_T), *theoretical negation* (N_T), and so forth. Theoretical logical operators do not, of course, have the generality of the logical operators. They are defined only for those special implication structures whose members belong to $P(S)$, and that, of course, is a very special circumstance. Next, there is the matter of modifying the conditions for modality. Instead of having a modal operator distribute over implication, but not over the dual, we require instead that the modals distribute over conjunctions, but not over disjunctions of the structure. This modification also seriously reduces the scope of those implication structures for which it is applicable.

It is straightforward to check that for the structure I^*, the theoretical conjunction of X and Y, $C_T(X, Y)$, is $Cn(X \cup Y)$, and the theoretical disjunction of X and Y, $D_T(X,Y)$, is $Cn(X \cap Y)$.

With these modifications in place, it follows that Cn is a modal operator on I^*, for it now follows that (1) Cn distributes over conjunctions and (2) Cn does not distribute over disjunctions.

Condition (1) holds if and only if for every X and Y, $C_T(Cn(X), Cn(Y)) \Rightarrow^* Cn(C_T(X, Y))$, that is, if and only if $Cn(C_T(X, Y))$ is a subset of $C_T(Cn(X), Cn(Y))$. But the former is just $CnCn(X \cup Y)$ – that is, $Cn(X \cup Y)$ – and the latter is just $Cn(Cn(X) \cup Cn(Y))$. But this holds, since $(X \cup Y) \subseteq Cn(X) \cup Cn(Y)$, and so $Cn(X \cup Y) \subseteq CnCn(X) \cup Cn(Y))$.

Condition (2) holds if and only if there are X and Y such that $Cn(D_T(X, Y)) \not\Rightarrow^* D_T Cn(X), Cn(Y))$ – that is, if and only if $D_T(Cn(X), Cn(Y))$ is not a subset of $Cn(D_T(X, Y))$ for some X and Y. But the former is $Cn(Cn(X) \cap Cn(Y))$, which is $Cn(X) \cap Cn(Y)$ (since the intersection of any two closed sets is closed), and the latter is $CnCn(X \cap Y)$ [i.e., $Cn(X \cap Y)$]. However, it is not generally true that $Cn(X) \cap Cn(Y) \subseteq Cn(X \cap Y)$ (see note 2).

Some comment is in order about the implication relation "$\Rightarrow^*$" that was used to relate theories. It is the dual of the implication "$\Rightarrow$" that is usually used to relate sets implicationally. Although there can, of course, be various implication relations on a set, we usually have not advocated any particular one over the other in the course of our study of them. Nevertheless, it might be thought that the use of "$\Rightarrow$*" is a bit strange for theories, so perhaps a word or two on why that is not so, or at least not obviously so.

If X and Y are theories, then $X \Rightarrow^* Y$ if and only if Y is a subset of X. Thus, X implies Y if and only if all the consequences of Y are also consequences of X, and that is not an inappropriate way of marking off X's strength against that of Y. Moreover, since "$\Rightarrow$*" is the dual of the usual relation on sets, the conjunction of two sets is not their intersection, but rather their union. When it is theories that are under discussion, this is not so inappropriate as it might seem at first. After all, the conjunction of two theories usually is not thought of as their common part or intersection. Usually it is thought of as the result of amalgamating the two theories, something larger than either, rather than some subtheory or fragment of both. This usage is not uniform, but it is common enough in discussions of scientific and logical theories. Moreover, if there are two consistent theories such that one has, say, A in it, and the other has its denial, then their conjunction usually will be thought of as inconsistent. However, if the conjunction of these theories is taken to be their intersection, then it is consistent. Even worse, on the intersection view, the conjuction of a consistent theory with any other theory whatever will be consistent (it will be a subset, indeed, a subtheory, of a consistent theory). In contrast, the conjunction of theories based upon "$\Rightarrow$*" requires that the conjunction of the theories (one of which has A and the other $\neg A$ as consequences) be inconsistent, and the conjunction of a consistent theory with any other theory is not automatically consistent. On the whole, then, if these views about the consistency and inconsistency of theories are granted, then it seems that the use of the implication relation "$\Rightarrow$*" yields results that are in close accord with these views.[6]

33

Knowledge, truth, and modality

We have been considering various kinds of operators, some familiar and some foreign, as examples of modal operators. We now wish to consider the possible modal character of the concepts of knowledge and truth, to take two central philosophical notions. Our aim is not to establish either that they have or that they fail to have modal character. Our purpose is to reinforce the idea that although many familiar concepts are modal on our account, the claim that a particular concept is modal can be a strong one that may not be consonant with what we believe to hold for those concepts. Knowledge and truth provide a case in point. The claim for their modality places some very strong constraints upon them. These requirements go beyond the simple matter of attending to certain formal analogies with necessity or possibility operators of familiar modal systems. That alone will not settle the matter of the modal character of a concept.

33.1 Knowledge

In the few passing remarks we made in Sections 25.1 and 28.3 concerning knowledge, we were concerned with eliciting the conditions under which the operator "K" [$K(A)$: "It is known that A"] is modal.[1] Whether or not these conditions hold is not at issue. Similar remarks hold for the truth operator "T" [$T(A)$: "It is true that A"], which we shall study in the following section.

In order that K should count as a modal operator, we have to specify an implication structure $I = \langle S, \Rightarrow \rangle$, where S is a set of statements (or whatever it is that one knows), and K maps S to S. The implication relation usually is taken as a standard deducibility relation of some logical system. For our purposes, however, that does not matter much. What is required is an implication relation, and that might be some epistemic relation, so long as it satisfies the conditions for being an implication relation.

The first condition on modality requires that whenever $A_1, \ldots, A_n \Rightarrow B$, then $K(A_1), \ldots, K(A_n) \Rightarrow K(B)$ holds as well. Many writers have found this condition to be implausible. A consequence of it is that if one knows any A at all, then one knows all the B's that are implied by A. In particular, it follows that one's knowing anything at all implies that one knows all the theses of the structure.[2] Perhaps the use of an epistemic, rather than a notion of implication based upon some standard logical system, would make the first requirement more plausible.[3]

The second condition on modal operators requires that there be statements A and B in the structure such that $K(A \lor B) \not\Rightarrow K(A) \lor K(B)$. This condition seems very plausible for all that is known about what we know. All that is required is that there be two statements such that it is known that one or the other, but neither one is known.

If one were to deny the second condition, then, in particular, $K(A \lor \neg A)$ implies that $K(A)$ or $K(\neg A)$. So all it would take would be knowledge of $(A \lor \neg A)$, and either A would be known or else its denial would be known. Matters would seem even worse if one assumed that negation was classical and that the first condition held but the second did not, for then $K(C) \Rightarrow K(A \lor \neg A) \Rightarrow K(A) \lor K(\neg A)$ for all A and C. Thus, if any statement C were known, that would imply that every statement A was known or else its negation was known.

According to an earlier result (Theorem 27.1), if (1) K is a mapping of S onto S and (2) K is modal, then either (3) $K(A) \Rightarrow A$ fails for some A or (4) $K(A) \Rightarrow KK(A)$ fails for some A.[4] If we assume that K is a modal operator and that $K(A) \Rightarrow A$ is a characteristic condition for the knowledge operator, then either K is not a mapping of S onto S or the KK thesis fails. We shall not pursue the matter any further; it goes beyond considerations of mere modality.

> **Exercise 33.1.** Say that a statement A of S is *epistemic* if and only if there is some B in S such that $A \Leftrightarrow K(B)$. Suppose that K is modal, that $K(A) \Rightarrow A$, and that $K(A) \Rightarrow KK(A)$ for all A in S. Let A^* be any statement such that $A^* \not\Rightarrow K(A^*)$. Show that the statement "$A^* \ \& \ \neg K(A^*)$" is not epistemic.

33.2 Truth and modality

We do not want to assume at the outset that truth is modal or not. That matter is, as we shall see, intimately connected with the ways in which the principle of bivalence (PB) and the law of excluded middle (LEM) are formulated and how they are related to each other.

We shall assume that we have an implication structure $I = \langle S, \Rightarrow \rangle$ in which the members of S are statements. We want a truth operator to be some function that maps S to S, such that for any A, $T(A)$, the value of the function, is some member of S that records or registers the truth of A. The idea that truth is a function is a middle ground between two views that echo a similar issue in discussions of modality. There are those who think of truth as a connective. ("It is true that A," with a prefix preceding the sentence. This is to take truth as a connective, on a par with negation.) On that construal, one would write "TA." Others regard truth as a predicate ("A" is true), and on this construal, one would write "$T(\ulcorner A \urcorner)$," using the name of the sentence, rather than the sentence itself. On our account, we use the functional notation $T(A)$, disregarding how the truth of the sentence is registered or recorded.

Settling a canonical notation does not bring out what is special about truth. What does, then? As in the case with modality, the character is in the kind of operator that it is. And in the case of truth, one wants to determine its special character. Here, unlike the situation for modals, the answer may appear totally disappointing, though to some it will appear just right.

Before we present the basic axioms for a truth operator, essentially the counterparts of Tarski's convention T, it is worth noting a well-known problem facing those who take truth to be a predicate. Given certain sufficiently rich languages, it is possible to prove a diagonalization lemma or principle of self-reference for them. According to these principles, for every (one-place) predicate P of the language, there is some sentence C (a *fixed point* of "P") such that $P(\ulcorner C \urcorner) \leftrightarrow C$ is a theorem. The basic axioms for a theory of truth in which truth is a predicate are given by $T(\ulcorner A \urcorner) \leftrightarrow A$ for each sentence A of the language. Since "$\neg P$" is also a predicate of the language, there is some sentence C^* such that $\neg P(\ulcorner C^* \urcorner) \leftrightarrow C^*$ is a theorem. For such theories we have the following for the truth predicate:

$\vdash T(\ulcorner A \urcorner) \leftrightarrow A$ for every sentence of the language,
$\vdash \neg T(\ulcorner C^* \urcorner) \leftrightarrow C^*$ by the diagonalization lemma for the predicate "$\neg T$."
$\vdash T(\ulcorner C^* \urcorner) \leftrightarrow C^*$, and so
$\vdash C^* \leftrightarrow \neg C^*$, and from this it follows that
$\vdash C^*$ as well as $\vdash \neg C^*$.

Thus the theory is inconsistent, and the proof that it is would hold good even in intuitionistic logic.

S. Feferman[5] remarked that if one used an operator account of truth, then the basic axioms would be (following Tarski) $T(A) \Leftrightarrow A$ for all instances A. He noted that the principle of self-reference (the diagonalization lemma) gives no way to construct some sentence A^* such that $\neg T(A^*) \Leftrightarrow A^*$.

There is no doubt that the basic conditions for the operator account are the counterparts of the basic axioms used in the theory with truth as a predicate. And there is also no doubt that the condition that $T(A) \Leftrightarrow A$ for all A in the structure looks skimpy when compared with its predicate-style counterparts. We do not know what the reason for this appearance might be. Perhaps it has something to do with the mere fact that in the one case a predicate is used, and there must be something substantive about the equivalence of "$T(\ulcorner A \urcorner)$" with A, unlike the equivalence of "$T(A)$" with A. But this is not a view that is widely shared, so it cannot be all that obvious. J. Etchemendy, for example, thinks that the instances of the T condition are logical truths, consequences of stipulative definitions, even on Tarski's own theory.[6] And, of course, there are the views attributed to F. P. Ramsey and perhaps L. Wittgenstein, among others, to the effect that the equivalence is one of meaning.

I am inclined to think that the equivalences of the T condition are equivalences relative to some theory, not "logical" equivalences. There is parity with the operator view, for it is not true that whenever $A \Leftrightarrow B$ holds for some structure, then the equivalence is in some special sense "logical." An implication relation on a structure can be of the sort that is relativized to a body of fixed sentences R, so that $A \Rightarrow^R B$ if and only if $R, A \Rightarrow B$. In that case, the relativized relation "$\Rightarrow^R$" is an implication relation as well as "$\Rightarrow$," and equivalence with respect to the implication "$\Rightarrow^R$" will depend upon the statements in R, and need not be a "logical" equivalence, but an equivalence that is a consequence of R. The equivalence in Tarski's instances of the T condition, it seems to me, is something of that sort.

Nevertheless, the operator version looks empty, for, after all, the identity operator satisfies the condition that $T(A) \Leftrightarrow A$, and so it might be thought that nothing much has been said. However, this observation is not quite right. If an implication structure I^* were an extension of the structure I, there could be many functions differing from each other, and from the identity, that would map the structure I^* to itself and would be truth operators on the substructure I. As far as I can see, there is nothing that determines the truth operator uniquely, although if there were two such truth operators T and T^* on I, then for all A, $T^*(A) \Leftrightarrow T(A)$ (where T and T^* would be the restrictions of operators on I^* to I). All "instances" would be equivalent. Moreover, the inference from

$T(A) \Leftrightarrow A$ (all A) to the conclusion that T is the identity function is too hasty. Suppose that T is a truth operator on $I = \langle S, \Rightarrow \rangle$. If we shift to another implication "$\Rightarrow'$" on S, it does not follow that T will be a truth operator on $I' = \langle S, \Rightarrow' \rangle$, for it would not follow that $T(A) \Leftrightarrow' A$, even though $T(A) \Leftrightarrow A$. Two statements that are equivalent under one implication relation need not be equivalent under another. Equivalence under an implication relation holds in general between statements that may not be identical. Similarly, even for Tarski's theory, the uniqueness of the truth predicate is not a consequence of that theory.[7]

Let us say that T is a *Tarski truth operator* on an implication structure $I = \langle S, \Rightarrow \rangle$ if and only if $T(A) \Leftrightarrow A$ for all A in S.[8] The Tarski operators will be distinguished from other operators that we shall call simply *truth operators*. They have a crucial role to play when considering the possibility of the failure of bivalence.

The notions of bivalence and the law of excluded middle that we shall use are closely related to some versions found in the literature. But, of course, there are so many variations in the literature that it is impossible to square with them all. We shall follow Tarski on bivalence. On his version of the principle, it has a semantic cast, expressed with the aid of "truth." Bivalence, it will be recalled, is one of the conditions of adequacy (the other being the T convention), according to which all instances of "$T(\ulcorner A \urcorner) \lor T(\ulcorner \neg A \urcorner)$" are consequences of the theory of truth. Accordingly, we adopt this version of the principle of bivalence:

(PB) For any implication structure $I = \langle S, \Rightarrow \rangle$ and truth operator T on I, $T(A \lor \neg A)$ is a thesis of I for all A in S.

The law of excluded middle is another matter. Some writers, indeed most writers, think of the principle as formal, concerning provability. In that regard, LEM is the requirement of any formal system that every instance of "$A \lor \neg A$" is a theorem. Dummet (1978, p. xix) takes it to be the requirement that every instance of "$A \lor \neg A$" is true. Our version is actually a combination of the two ideas, combining both provability and truth:

(LEM) For any implication structure $I = \langle S, \Rightarrow \rangle$ and truth operator T on I, $T(A \lor \neg A)$ is a thesis of I for all A in S.

It should already be apparent that it is not a stigma to be a modal operator on a structure. Far from it. It is possible that truth might be a modal on certain kinds of structures. So it is worthwhile, I think, to try to find some sufficient conditions under which truth will be modal and to study the consequences of truth being modal, if it is.

We should like to know when LEM holds and PB does not. But these problems are nonsense if we regard all truth operators as Tarski operators.[9] It is easy to see that no truth operator that is Tarskian is modal. And if a truth operator were required to be Tarskian, then all sufficient conditions for modal truth operators would be inconsistent.

In order to study these problems, something less than the Tarskian conditions must be used as a characterization, however provisional, of a truth operator. To many, the Tarskian convention T is already minimal. However, unless it is relaxed, there is no way of inquiring about the conditions under which truth can be modal, or those under which standard connections between LEM and PB are severed. We suggest the following, though there are other possibilities as well.

Let $I = \langle S, \Rightarrow \rangle$ be an implication structure. We shall say that T is a *truth operator* on I if and only if the following conditions are satisfied (a fourth condition, CON*, will be added once we have motivated it):

(1) T distributes over the implication relation "$\Rightarrow$,"
(2) T is a necessitation operator on I; that is, if A is any thesis of I, so too is $T(A)$, and
(3) $T(A) \Rightarrow A$ for all A in S.

Some brief comments are in order.

(1) The first condition is stronger than the requirement that if $A_1, \ldots, A_n \Rightarrow B$, then B will be true if all the A_i's are true. It requires that $T(A_1), \ldots, T(A_n)$ *imply* $T(B)$. Any Tarskian operator distributes over implication. The distribution condition itself is weaker than the full equivalence of A with $T(A)$. Moreover, it is a condition that seems acceptable even to those who hold that truth has modal character.[10]

(2) The requirement that T be a necessitation is, I believe, widely shared. It is a difficult condition to assess in terms of power. There are several equivalent formulations (assuming that T distributes over implication): (a) $T(B)$ is a thesis for some B (whether B is a thesis or not) and (b) for every nonempty theory U of the structure, $T^{-1}(U)$ is nonempty. According to the latter, those statements that register the truth of statements are widespread. Every nonempty theory of the structure has some statement $T(B)$ in it, for some B.

(3) The condition that $T(A) \Rightarrow A$ is a plausible candidate if one seeks some condition that is weaker than the full Tarski condition. I have never seen an argument for it, however, and consequently it is difficult to gauge how plausible it is or how preferable it may be over certain alternatives – such as $A \Rightarrow T(A)$, or some others. I am inclined not to use $A \Rightarrow T(A)$ on the grounds that it does not

generalize well if we are interested in characterizing truth operators that are defined over classical as well as nonclassical structures. In the latter case, although not much is known about modal operators on nonclassical structures, it would turn out that two modals (double negation and conditionalization) would count as modal truth operators on nonclassical structures. And neither of these seems plausible as a candidate for truth in the nonclassical case.

There is one condition that one might think to add to (1)–(3), still trying to keep to an operator that is weaker than Tarskian:

(CON) For any A in S, if $T(A) \Rightarrow C$ (all C in S), then $A \Rightarrow C$ (all C in S).

This condition is satisfied by any operator that satisfies the Tarskian condition. In relaxing the T condition, it seems important to try to retain the idea that if a statement A is consistent, so too is $T(A)$. That is, a truth operator will not make you inconsistent, unless you already are so. Truth may make you free, but it won't make you that free. Combined with the third condition, it follows that *T(A) is consistent if and only if A is consistent.*

It is helpful in assessing the condition CON to see that it is equivalent [given the conditions that T distributes over implication, and that $T(A) \Rightarrow A$ for all A in the structure] to the following principle of *truth deletion*:

(TD) For any A and B in S, if $T(A) \Rightarrow T(B)$, then $A \Rightarrow B$.

Thus, if A does not imply B, then neither does the truth of A imply the truth of B. There is the following theorem:

Theorem 33.1. *Let $I = \langle S, \Rightarrow \rangle$ be an implication structure, and assume that $T(A) \Rightarrow A$ for all A in S and that T distributes over the implication relation "$\Rightarrow$." Then CON holds if and only if TD holds.*

Proof. Assume that TD holds. If for some A, $T(A) \Rightarrow C$ for all C in S, then $T(A) \Rightarrow T(B)$ for all B in S. By TD, $A \Rightarrow B$ for all B in S. Therefore CON holds. Conversely, suppose that CON holds and that $T(A) \Rightarrow T(B)$. Then $T(A), \neg T(B) \Rightarrow C$ for all C in S. However, since $T(C) \Rightarrow C$ for all C, $T(B)$, $T(\neg B) \Rightarrow E$ for all E in S. Consequently, $T(\neg B) \Rightarrow \neg T(B)$. Therefore $T(A), T(\neg B) \Rightarrow C$ for all C. Now $T(A \& \neg B) \Rightarrow T(A) \& T(\neg B)$, since T distributes over implication. Therefore

$T(A \& \neg B) \Rightarrow C$ for all C in S. By CON, then, $A \& \neg B \Rightarrow C$ for all C. Since negation is assumed to be classical, $A \Rightarrow B$.

However, CON is too strong if the aim is to have a truth operator that is weaker than Tarskian truth: In the presence of conditions (1) and (3), it has the consequence of restoring the full Tarskian condition. That is,

Theorem 33.2. *If T is a truth operator on a classical structure $I = \langle S, \Rightarrow \rangle$, and CON holds, then T is Tarskian $[T(A) \Leftrightarrow A$ for all A in $S]$.*

Proof. Consider the sentence $(A \& \neg T(A))$ for any A. Let us call these "Moorean sentences." $(A \& \neg T(A))$ implies A, so that by (1), $T(A \& \neg T(A)) \Rightarrow T(A)$. However, by (3), $T(A \& \neg T(A)) \Rightarrow (A \& \neg T(A)) \Rightarrow \neg T(A)$. Therefore $T(A \& \neg T(A)) \Rightarrow C$ for all C in S. By CON, then, $(A \& \neg T(A)) \Rightarrow C$ for all C in S. Since negation is assumed to be classical, it follows that $A \Rightarrow T(A)$ for all A in S. But that, together with (3), restores the Tarskian condition.

Exercise 33.2. Using a Moorean sentence "$A \& \neg T(A)$," and TD, show that $T(A) \Leftrightarrow A$.

This result shows how difficult it is to avoid the Tarski equivalence. Even so plausible a condition as CON will restore $T(A) \Leftrightarrow A$ in the presence of conditions considerably weaker than the equivalence. If the aim is to leave the possibility open that truth is modal, then some qualification is needed. The point of the condition CON was, roughly, that if A is a consistent statement that does not involve[11] some statement $T(B)$, then $T(A)$ is also consistent. Thus, we might qualify CON along the following lines and include it, along with the other three, as characterizing a truth operator on a structure:

(CON*) If $T(A) \Rightarrow C$ (all C in S), then $A \Rightarrow C$ (all C in S) for any A in S that does not involve some $T(B)$ in its construction.

With this restriction, the argument showing that $T(A) \Leftrightarrow A$ for all A in S is now blocked. The truth operator T applied to the Moorean sentence "$A \& \neg T(A)$" is inconsistent, but the inference that "$A \& \neg T(A)$" is also inconsistent is blocked, since "$A \& \neg T(A)$" involves some $T(B)$ [i.e., $T(A)$] in its construction.

The conditions (1)–(3) and CON* for being a truth operator are weaker than the requirement that the operator be Tarskian. There are operators that satisfy the former but not the latter. Without the CON* condition, there are operators that satisfy (1)–(3) and still fail to be Tarskian. The two following theorems provide examples:

Definition 33.1. Let I be any implication structure that has some theses and antitheses, and let i be any truth-value assignment on I. We shall say that T_i is a *truth operator associated with* i if and only if $T_i(A)$ is A if $i(A) = t$, and it is Z (some fixed antithesis of I) otherwise.

Theorem 33.3. *Let* $I = \langle S, \Rightarrow \rangle$ *be a classical implication structure that has at least one thesis and one antithesis. Let i be any truth-value assignment on I that assigns f to some member of I that is neither a thesis nor an antithesis of I. Let T_i be the truth operator associated with i. Then*

(a) T_i satisfies conditions (1)–(3), and
(b) T_i is not a Tarskian truth operator.

Proof. (a) Condition (1) (distribution over implication): If $A_1, \ldots, A_n \Rightarrow B$, then $T_i(A_1), \ldots, T_i(A_n) \Rightarrow T_i(B)$: Suppose that $i(A_j) = t$ for all $j = 1, \ldots, n$. Then $T_i(A_j)$ is A_j. Since the A_i's imply B and all the A_i's are true under i, B is true under i. Therefore $T_i(B)$ is B. If, on the other hand, for some j (take it to be 1, without loss of generality), $i(A_j) = f$, then $T_i(A_1) = Z$ (some fixed antithesis of I). Then since Z implies every member of I, $T_i(A_1), \ldots, T_i(A_n) \Rightarrow T_i(B)$. As for condition (2) (necessitation), note that if A is a thesis of I, then $i(A)$ is t. Then $T_i(A)$ is just A, which is a thesis of I. Condition (3) $[T_i(A) \Rightarrow A$ for all $A]$ holds: Suppose that A is a thesis. Then it is implied by all members, including $T_i(A)$. And if A is not a thesis, then $T_i(A)$ is Z, which implies every member of I, and A in particular.

(b) T_i is not Tarskian. Let A be some member of I such that it is neither a thesis nor an antithesis of I, and $i(A) = f$. In that case, if $T_i(A) \Leftrightarrow A$, then $Z \Leftrightarrow A$, so that A is an antithesis of I. But that is impossible.

Exercise 33.3. Let $\Box_n$ be a necessity-style modal, where I is a structure that is incomplete with respect to negation (some member is not a thesis, nor is its negation a thesis), and $\Box_n(A)$ is A, if A is a thesis, and is some fixed antithesis otherwise. Then $\Box_n$ satisfies conditions (1)–(3) for truth operators and fails to be Tarskian.

Exercise 33.4. The operators T_i and $\Box_n$ described in Theorem 33.3 and Exercise 33.3 fail to satisfy CON*.

Several simple observations are now possible. The first two indicate the consequences of truth being modal. The first holds whether the structure is classical or not; the second holds for classical structures.

Theorem 33.4. *No Tarski operator T on a structure I is modal on I.*

Proof. Suppose that T is modal on I. Then there are A and B such that $T(A \lor B) \not\Rightarrow T(B)$. Since T is a Tarski operator, $T(A) \Leftrightarrow A$ for all A. Therefore $(A \lor B) \not\Rightarrow A \lor B$. But that is impossible.

One price that has to be paid for truth as a modal is the rejection of the Tarski condition.

Theorem 33.5. *If I is a classical implication structure, and T is a modal operator on I, then PB fails on I.*

Proof. I is classical, so $(A \lor B) \Rightarrow \neg A \to B$. Since T is modal, $T(A \lor B) \Rightarrow T(\neg A \to B)$. Now $T(\neg A \to B) \Rightarrow T(\neg A) \to T(B)$ (as we noted for modals generally). Since negation is classical, $T(\neg A) \to T(B) \Rightarrow \neg T(\neg A) \lor T(B)$. Assume that PB holds for I. Then $T(A) \lor T(\neg A)$ is a thesis for all A. Therefore $\neg T(\neg A) \Rightarrow T(A)$. Consequently, $\neg T(\neg A) \lor T(B) \Rightarrow T(A) \lor T(B)$. Therefore, for all A and B, $T(A \lor B) \Rightarrow T(A) \lor T(B)$. But that is impossible, since T is a modal on I. Therefore PB fails.

The next observation shows the reason that if, like van Fraassen (1971), one accepts LEM but rejects PB, then there is no choice but that truth will be modal. The result holds whether the implication structure is classical or not.

Theorem 33.6. *If I is an implication structure (classical or not), and T is a truth operator on it, and LEM holds, but PB does not, then T is a modal operator on I.*

Proof. Since PB fails, there is some B such that $T(B) \lor T(\neg B)$ is not a thesis of I. Since LEM holds, $T(B \lor \neg B)$ is a thesis. Consequently, $T(B \lor \neg B) \not\Rightarrow T(B) \lor T(\neg B)$. Otherwise the right-hand side would be a thesis. Thus, T fails to distribute over disjunctions. Since T is a truth operator, it distributes over implication. Consequently, T is a modal operator on I.

This explains why someone who holds the view that van Fraassen does on LEM and PB must also require that truth be modal; it is not an option.

There is a sharpening of the result of the preceding theorem if the structure is classical, for the dependence on LEM can be dropped:

Theorem 33.7. *If I is a classical implication structure, and T is a truth operator on it, and PB fails on I, then T is a modal operator.*

Proof. Since T is a truth operator, it distributes over implication. Suppose that it fails to be modal. Then T distributes over disjunctions. In particular, $T(A \lor \neg A) \Rightarrow T(A) \lor T(\neg A)$. The structure is classical, so that $(A \lor \neg A)$ is a thesis, and since T is a truth operator, by necessitation, $T(A \lor \neg A)$ is a thesis as well. Therefore $T(A) \lor T(\neg A)$ is a thesis. That is, PB holds for I. But that is impossible.

Theorems 33.6 and 33.7 combined tell us that for any classical structure and any truth operator T on it, T is modal if and only if PB fails.

Theorem 33.8. *If I is an implication structure (classical or not), then if PB holds, so too does LEM.*

Proof. $A \Rightarrow (A \lor \neg A)$, and $\neg A \Rightarrow (A \lor \neg A)$. Since T distributes over implication, $T(A) \Rightarrow T(A \lor \neg A)$, and $T(\neg A) \Rightarrow T(A \lor \neg A)$. Therefore $T(A) \lor T(\neg A) \Rightarrow T(A \lor \neg A)$. Since PB holds, the antecedent is a thesis. Therefore $T(A \lor \neg A)$ is a thesis as well.

In some classical structures, if LEM holds, then so too does PB:

Theorem 33.9. *If I is a classical implication structure, and T is a truth operator that is not modal, then if LEM holds, so too does PB.*

Proof. Since T is a truth operator, but not modal, it distributes over all disjunctions. In particular, $T(A \lor \neg A) \Rightarrow T(A) \lor T(\neg A)$. So if LEM holds, so too does PB.

We have seen (Theorem 33.4) that if a truth operator is Tarskian, then it is not modal. That is true whether the structure is classical or not. Although truth operators are, in general, weaker than Tarskian ones, there are conditions under which truth operators are Tarskian. Here is a kind of converse to Theorem 33.4.

Theorem 33.10 (the recovery of Tarski). *If I is a classical implication structure, and T is a truth operator that is not modal, then T is Tarskian.*

Proof. Since T is a truth operator that is not modal, it distributes over all disjunctions. Therefore $T(A \lor \neg A) \Rightarrow T(A) \lor T(\neg A)$. The structure is classical, so $A \lor \neg A$ is a thesis, and therefore so too is $T(A \lor \neg A)$. Therefore $T(A) \lor T(\neg A)$ is a thesis, so that $\neg T(\neg A) \Rightarrow T(A)$. Moreover, since $T(\neg A) \Rightarrow \neg A$, we have $T(A) \Rightarrow A \Rightarrow \neg \neg A \Rightarrow \neg(T \neg A)$, that is, $T(A) \Rightarrow \neg T(\neg A)$. Therefore $T(A) \Leftrightarrow \neg T(\neg A)$. Now since $T(A) \Rightarrow A$, we have $\neg A \Rightarrow \neg T(A) \Rightarrow \neg \neg T(\neg A) \Rightarrow T(\neg A)$ (since the structure is classical). Consequently, $\neg \neg A \Rightarrow T(\neg \neg A)$. Since the structure is classical, $A \Rightarrow T(A)$. Therefore $T(A) \Leftrightarrow A$.

Theorems 33.4 and 33.10 combined tell us that on any classical structure, any truth operator T is Tarskian if and only if T is not modal.

Theorem 33.11. *If I is an implication structure, and T is a modal truth operator on it, then for some B in S, $B \not\Rightarrow T(B)$.*

Proof. If $A \Rightarrow T(A)$ for all A, then $T(A) \Leftrightarrow A$ for all A. Therefore $T(A \lor B) \Rightarrow T(A) \lor T(B)$ for all A and B, so that T is not modal. But that is impossible.

Theorem 33.12. *If T is a modal operator on I, then T is nonextensional on I.*

Proof. If the truth operator is modal on some structure, then, since it is modal, it is nonextensional (Theorem 27.7), and there will be members A and B of it such that A and B will have the same truth value under some truth-value assignment, but $T(A)$ and $T(B)$ will not.

This is one consequence of truth being a modal that is not well understood, certainly not discussed and probably the most telling consequence of all. By condition (1), it follows that if A and B are both assigned the value "f," then both $T(A)$ and $T(B)$ have the value "f." But if they are both assigned the value "t," the values of $T(A)$ and $T(B)$ will differ.

Exercise 33.5. If T is any truth operator on a classical implication structure I, then T is a Tarskian operator on I if and only if T is extensional on I. [If T is extensional, then T is not modal (Theorem 27.7), and so T is Tarskian (Theorem 33.10).]

We began these brief observations with a Tarskian operator, thought to be weak, and proceeded to weaken the condition still further so as to accommodate a coherent investigation of those conditions under which the familiar connections between LEM and PB are relaxed and modality enters the scene. Thus the truth operators, as we termed them. The condition thus weakened may prove no barrier to there being a multitude of operators on a structure, claiming truth. That is so, and many of them may be incomparable with each other. But the situation is not all that different from the one that Tarski gave us. For there, too, it seems to us, and it seemed to Tarski as well, that his theory did not determine a unique truth predicate.

It is possible, of course, to make things look a little better by requiring that the truth operator be the weakest operator to satisfy all four conditions. That would ensure that the truth operator would be unique up to the equivalence relation "$\Leftrightarrow$" on the structure. But I think it is premature to close the books in this way. We do not yet know under what conditions there will be such a weakest operator on the structure, nor do we have a clear idea of the various kinds of operators that qualify as truth operators. It is certainly worth reminding ourselves that some of our best theories, in logic and elsewhere, countenance a certain non-categorical slack when central theoretical terms fail to be even implicitly defined. The truth of the matter may be just this: When it comes to ideological slack, our best theories of truth are like the best theories we have everywhere else.

In any case, the present point is not to advocate that the connections between LEM and PB be severed, or that truth is a modal operator. It is to frame suitably clear descriptions of these concepts and principles so that the matter can be given a coherent discussion and the problems for developing a modal concept of truth can at least be studied.

34

The comparative strength of modals

There is a question that naturally arises when modal operators are thought of as operators on implication structures. Suppose that there are several modals on a structure. How are they related, if at all? What are their comparative strengths?

> **Definition 34.1.** Let $I = \langle S, \Rightarrow \rangle$ be an implication structure, and let φ and φ^* be two modal operators on I. Then φ *is stronger than* φ^* if and only if $\varphi(A) \Rightarrow \varphi^*(A)$ for all A in S. We shall say that φ *is definitely stronger than* φ^* if and only if φ is stronger than φ^* and there is some A^* in S such that $\varphi^*(A^*) \not\Rightarrow \varphi(A^*)$.

If φ and φ^* are modal operators on some structure $I = \langle S, \Rightarrow \rangle$, then φ and φ^* are *comparable* (on I) (Definition 28.3) if and only if at least one of them is stronger than the other.

We have already observed (Section 27.3.1) that there are implication structures on which there are noncomparable modals. Thus, the comparability of modal operators is not to be expected in general, not even for very simple structures. Nevertheless, there are a few results available concerning the comparative strengths of modal operators, provided they are comparable.

We have already noted two results on the strength of modals that are comparable. The first concerned necessitation modals: If there are two comparable modals on a structure, one of which is a necessitation modal, and the other not, then the necessitation modal is the weaker of the two (Theorem 28.11). The second result concerned D modals: If there are two comparable modals on a structure, one of which is a D modal, and the other not, then the D modal is the stronger of the two (Theorem 28.3).

Here is another result in the same vein that concerns T modals:

> **Theorem 34.1.** Let $I = \langle S, \Rightarrow \rangle$ be an implication structure, and let φ and φ^* be comparable modals on I, where φ is a T modal and φ^* is not. Then φ is definitely stronger than φ^*.

Proof. Since φ^* is not a T modal, $\varphi^*(B) \not\Rightarrow B$ for some B in S. Suppose that $\varphi^*(A) \Rightarrow \varphi(A)$ for all A in S. Then $\varphi^*(B) \Rightarrow \varphi(B)$. Since φ is a T modal, $\varphi(B) \Rightarrow B$, so that $\varphi^*(B) \Rightarrow B$. But that is impossible. Since the two modals are comparable, $\varphi(A) \Rightarrow \varphi^*(A)$ for all A in S. Moreover, φ is definitely stronger than φ^*. Suppose that $\varphi^*(A) \Rightarrow \varphi(A)$ for all A. Since φ is a T modal, it follows that $\varphi^*(A) \Rightarrow A$. But that is impossible.

Since no Gödel–Löb modal is a T modal (Theorem 28.15), it follows that any T modal is definitely stronger than any G-L modal with which it is comparable.

Comparison of other types of modals seems to require a more elaborate type of argument. Recall that a K_4 modal, φ, is one for which $\varphi(A) \Rightarrow \varphi\varphi(A)$ for all A in the structure. Let us say that some element B of the structure is a *witness against φ being a K_4 modal* (or a *witness for φ failing to be a K_4 modal*) if and only if $\varphi(B) \not\Rightarrow \varphi\varphi(B)$. Similar terminology is intended to cover the cases of other kinds of modal operators as well.

In addition, we shall say that if φ is a modal on a structure $I = \langle S, \Rightarrow \rangle$, then the element B in S is *in the range of φ* if and only if there is some B^* in S such that $B \Leftrightarrow \varphi(B^*)$.

Theorem 34.2. *Let $I = \langle S, \Rightarrow \rangle$ be an implication structure, and let φ and φ^* be comparable modal operators on I such that φ^* is a K_4 modal, but φ is not. Assume that there is some B in the range of φ^* that is a witness against φ being a K_4 modal. Then φ, the non-K_4 modal is definitely stronger than φ^*, the K_4 modal.*

Proof. We know that for some B in S, $\varphi(B) \not\Rightarrow \varphi\varphi(B)$, and that $B \Leftrightarrow \varphi^*(B^*)$ for some B^* in S. From the latter it follows that $\varphi^*(B) \Leftrightarrow \varphi^*\varphi^*(B^*)$. Then $\varphi^*(B^*) \Rightarrow \varphi^*\varphi^*(B^*) \Rightarrow \varphi^*(B)$, since φ^* is a K_4 modal. Thus, $B \Rightarrow \varphi^*(B)$. Now φ and φ^* are comparable. Suppose that $\varphi^*(A) \Rightarrow \varphi(A)$" for all A. Then $\varphi^*(B) \Rightarrow \varphi(B)$. Consequently, $B \Rightarrow \varphi(B)$. Therefore $\varphi(B) \Rightarrow \varphi\varphi(B)$. But that is impossible. Therefore $\varphi(A) \Rightarrow \varphi^*(A)$ for all A in S. Clearly, φ^* cannot be stronger than φ; φ is definitely stronger than φ^*.

Thus, non-K_4 modals are always weaker that K_4 modals with which they are comparable, provided that the witness for the failure of the non-K_4 modal is in the range of the K_4 modal.

The reader will have noticed that for modals that are comparable, sometimes modals that are of one type are stronger than modals that are not of that type, and, depending on the type, sometimes they are weaker. There is a simple reason why certain types of modals are always stronger than comparable modals not of that type, and modals of other types are always the weaker.

Let us say that a condition Σ on the modal operators of a structure I is a *filter condition* (on modal operators) if and only if for any modals φ and φ^* on I, if whenever $\Sigma(\varphi)$ holds, and φ^* is stronger than φ, then $\Sigma(\varphi^*)$ holds as well. T modals and D modals are characterized by filter conditions. We shall say that a condition Σ on the modals of I is an *ideal condition* if and only if for any modals φ and φ^* on I if $\Sigma(\varphi)$ holds and φ^* is weaker than φ, then $\Sigma(\varphi^*)$ holds as well. Necessitation modals are characterized by an ideal condition.

Theorem 34.3. *Let $I = \langle S \Rightarrow \rangle$ be an implication structure. Let φ and φ^* be any two comparable modals on I. Then*

(a) *if Σ is a filter condition such that $\Sigma(\varphi)$, but not $\Sigma(\varphi^*)$, then φ is stronger than φ^*, and*

(b) *if Σ is an ideal condition such that $\Sigma(\varphi)$, but not $\Sigma(\varphi^*)$, then φ^* is stronger than φ.*

Proof. (a) Suppose that φ^* is stronger than φ. Since $\Sigma(\varphi)$ holds, and is a filter condition, $\Sigma(\varphi^*)$ also holds. But that is impossible. By comparability, then, φ is stronger than φ^*.

(b) Suppose that φ is stronger than φ^*. Since $\Sigma(\varphi)$ holds, and is an ideal condition, $\Sigma(\varphi^*)$ holds as well. But that is impossible. By comparability, then, φ^* is stronger than φ.

Exercise 34.1. Show that the "stronger than" clauses in (a) and (b) of the preceding theorem can be strengthened to "definitely stronger than."

The next two results are concerned with the comparative strengths of modal operators that are associated with the familiar modal systems (T), (S_4), and (S_5). A brief reminder of the relevant conditions may be helpful. Consider the three conditions (1) $\varphi(A) \Rightarrow A$, (2) $\varphi(A) \Rightarrow \varphi\varphi(A)$, and (3) $\neg\varphi\neg\varphi(A) \Rightarrow \varphi(A)$. The first is the T condition, the second the K_4 condition, and the third the S_5 condition (the counterpart of $\neg\Box\neg\Box A \Rightarrow \Box A$). We shall say that φ is a (T) modal if and only if it satisfies (1), an (S_4) modal if and only if it satisfies (1) and (2), and an (S_5) modal if and only if it satisfies (1), (2), and (3).

We want to say something about the strength of (T) modals compared with modals that are (S_4), as well as to compare (S_4) modals with those that are (S_5). Finally we shall comment on how these results about relative strength square with some informal interpretations that Lemmon (1959) proposed for the modal systems (S_4) and (S_5).

Theorem 34.4. *Let $I = \langle S, \Rightarrow \rangle$ be an implication structure such that φ and φ^* are comparable modals on it, where φ is a (T) modal, but not an (S_4) modal, and φ^* is an (S_4) modal. In addition, suppose that there is some B in the range of φ^* that is a witness against φ being a K_4 modal. Then φ is definitely stronger than φ^*.*

Proof. This is an easy consequence of Theorem 34.2. Since φ is a (T) modal, but not an (S_4) modal, it must fail to be a K_4 modal. Moreover, φ^* is a K_4 modal since it is an (S_4) modal. In addition, the element B of S is a witness against φ being a K_4 modal and is in the range of φ^*. By Theorem 34.2, then, φ is definitely stronger than φ^*.

Consider, next, the situation in which there are two comparable modals on a structure, where one is an (S_4) modal, [but not (S_5)], and the other is an (S_5) modal. Then, subject to a witness condition, the modal that is (S_4) [but not (S_5)] is stronger than the (S_5) modal. That is,

Theorem 34.5. *Let $I = \langle S, \Rightarrow \rangle$ be an implication structure such that φ and φ^* are comparable modals on it, where φ is an (S_4) modal, but not (S_5), φ^* is an (S_5) modal, and there is some B in the range of φ^* that is a witness against φ being an (S_5) modal. Then φ is definitely stronger than φ^*.*

Proof. There is a B such that $\neg\varphi\neg(B) \not\Rightarrow \varphi(B)$, and $B \Leftrightarrow \varphi^*(B^*)$ for some B^* in S. From the latter we have $\varphi^*\varphi^*(B^*) \Rightarrow \varphi^*(B)$, so that $\varphi^*(B^*) \Rightarrow \varphi^*(B)$ (φ^* is a K_4 modal). Thus, $B \Rightarrow \varphi^*(B)$. However, since φ^* is an (S_5) modal, it is also a (T) modal. So $\varphi^*(B) \Rightarrow B$. Consequently, $B \Leftrightarrow \varphi^*(B)$. Assume that φ^* is stronger than φ. Then $\varphi^*(B) \Rightarrow \varphi(B)$. Therefore $B \Rightarrow \varphi(B)$. But φ is a (T) modal [it is an (S_4) modal], so that $\varphi(B) \Rightarrow (B)$. Consequently, $B \Leftrightarrow \varphi(B)$. Therefore $\varphi^*(B) \Leftrightarrow \varphi(B)$. Now $\neg\varphi\neg\varphi^*(A) \Rightarrow \varphi^*(A)$ for all A in S [φ^* is an (S_5) modal]. So $\neg\varphi^*\neg\varphi^*(B) \Rightarrow \varphi^*(B)$. Consequently, $\neg\varphi^*\neg\varphi^*(B) \Rightarrow \varphi(B)$ [using the equivalence of $\varphi(B)$ and $\varphi^*(B)$]. More-

over, by the assumption that φ^* is stronger than φ, we have
$\varphi^*(A) \Rightarrow \varphi(A)$ for all A. Therefore $\neg\varphi(A) \Rightarrow \neg\varphi^*(A)$ for all
A in S. In particular, $\neg\varphi(\neg\varphi(B)) \Rightarrow \neg\varphi^*(\neg\varphi(B))$. Using the
equivalence of $\varphi(B)$ with $\varphi^*(B)$, $\neg\varphi(\neg\varphi(B)) \Rightarrow \neg\varphi^*(\neg\varphi^*B))$.
But $\neg\varphi^*(\neg\varphi^*(B)) \Rightarrow \varphi(B)$. Therefore $\neg\varphi(\neg\varphi(B)) \Rightarrow \varphi(B)$.
That is impossible. By comparability, then, φ is stronger than
φ^*, and it is definitely stronger, since φ^* is not stronger than φ.

The preceding theorem, which compares those modals that are (S_4)
[but not (S_5)] with those that are (S_5) bears on some observations of
Lemmon (1959). In his discussion of some possible interpretations for
the box of the modal systems (S_4) and (S_5), Lemmon tentatively
suggested that "$\Box A$" for (S_4) be read as "It is a logical law that A" and
that it might also be read as "It is informally provable in mathematics
that A." He noted that neither of these readings is sharply formulated
and that there is some reason for being tentative about whether or not
the modal laws of the system (S_4) are satisfied on either of them.
Nevertheless, there is a good deal that is plausible about those readings
as interpretations of a modal that is (S_4) but not (S_5). For the system
(S_5), Lemmon suggested the admittedly controversial reading "It is
analytically the case that A."

Although one might have some qualms about the cogency of the
readings that Lemmon offered for the (S_4) [but not (S_5)] modals and the
(S_5) modals, it is clear that the order of strength of those readings is just
what one would expect on the basis of the preceding theorem. Thus, "It
is a logical law that A" seems to imply "It is analytically the case that
A" (but not conversely), and similarly, "It is informally provable in
mathematics that A" seems to imply "It is analytically the case that A" (but
not conversely). We say "seems in both cases," for despite the fact
that those readings have seemed correct to some, to others they appear
to rest on confusion and untenable presuppositions. Nevertheless, despite those misgivings, it is still possible, I think, modulo those demur-
rers, to see that even if there is much that is moot about such informal
interpretations, nevertheless they are of the right strength with respect
to each other. Even if we decided to modify or to reject them
altogether, their replacements still would have to stand in the same
implication relations to each other (assuming, of course, that they are
comparable).

35

Kripke-style systematization of the modals without possible worlds

35.1 Accessibility relations and the diversity of modals

We have already observed (Section 28.3) how the nonempty theories of an implication structure can be used to provide a necessary and sufficient condition for an operator to be a necessitation modal. There we introduced the idea of an accessibility relation R^φ for each modal operator on the implication structure I (and, where σ is the dual of φ, R^σ is the appropriate accessibility relation). They are binary relations on the theories of the structure such that for all theories U, V, $\ldots$,

(1) $UR^\varphi V$ if and only if $\varphi^{-1}U \subseteq V$ [where A is in $\varphi^{-1}U$ if and only if $\varphi(A)$ is in U], and

(2) $UR^\sigma V$ if and only if $V \subseteq \sigma^{-1}U$ (where σ is the dual of φ).

Each accessibility relation is, according to these two conditions, tailored to the particular modal operator under study. The tightness of the relation between a modal and its accessibility relation was discussed, and need not be repeated here. The theories, as used in this chapter, are those subsets of the structure that are (weakly) closed under implication in this sense: If A is in U, and $A \Rightarrow B$, then B is in U as well.

Anyone who is even remotely aware of S. Kripke's ground-breaking work on the semantics of modal logic knows how the idea of accessibility relations and the possible worlds that they relate were used with startling effect to provide a series of completeness proofs of familiar modal systems and to distinguish the variety of modal laws from each other in a very simple and coherent manner. The idea of a Kripke frame $\langle W, R \rangle$ consisting of a set of possible worlds, with an accessibility relation R on them, probably is the major landmark of the whole semantic modal landscape. There are modal systems that do not yield to this kind of semantic theory, and there are variations on it that use maximal consistent sets as the items that are related by R, as well as variations that do not. Then, too, there are other methods for proving completeness results. But the striking result, that the different kinds of modal laws correspond to simple and, in most cases, familiar properties of the accessibility relation (reflexivity, symmetry, transitivity, and density, to name a few), gave an overall coherence to the study of the diversity of modal systems.

Indeed, perhaps the first big step toward distinguishing modal concepts from other logical concepts was the modal square of opposition (Section 25.1), with its placement of modals and their duals in a schema involving implications. However, that did not shed any light on the differences among modals. One cannot help but think that in one way or another the association of T modals with reflexive R, K_4 modals with transitive R, B modals with symmetric R, and S_5 modals with Euclidean R, as well as many other correspondences, has now become a hallmark of those modal operators. Because of this dramatic systematization, we have come to think of the various modal systems as a coherent family with different, but related, members. The pressure to think of any one of them as "the correct one," dispensing with all the others, has dissipated. The whole tableau has itself become an object of study. If we did not think of them as a group, what would have been systematized? And if modal theory consisted of the study of just one system, what would be the point of that dramatic and powerful systematization?

Nevertheless, there has been controversy over the items on which those accessibility relations are supposed to be defined. "Possible worlds" have been taken by some to be at least as problematic as the intensional modals that they serve to organize. They introduce into logical theory, so it is thought, a suspect metaphysical notion that has no explanatory value. Others have tried to explain the use of possible worlds as no metaphysical adventure, but simply akin to the use of quite respectable concepts that are used in ordinary and scientific reasoning.[1]

It seems clear, however, that something powerful and systematic has been achieved, despite the controversies that have gathered around it. And it also seems clear that what has been achieved should not be made to depend upon, for example, whether or not one is a realist about possible worlds. Without advocating one position over another on the status and philosophical credibility of the concept of possible worlds, we want to see if the Kripkean systematization of modal laws can be achieved with the use of concepts that are less controversial for logical theory. In fact, we think that the systematization can be attained by using only the theories of implication structures, with accessibility relations defined over them.

We now wish to show the way in which the various different but familiar modal operators can be characterized systematically with the aid of accessibility relations that are defined over the theories of implication structures.

35.2 *T* modals and reflexivity

Suppose that φ is a *T* modal on the implication structure $I = \langle S, \Rightarrow \rangle$, and the theories of I are just those closed subsets of S as described earlier. Let the accessibility relation R^φ be the relation between theories given by the foregoing condition (1):

Theorem 35.1 (reflexivity). *Let $I = \langle S, \Rightarrow \rangle$ be an implication structure, with φ a modal operator on I. Then φ is a T modal on I if and only if R^φ is reflexive.*

Proof. Any binary relation is reflexive if and only if xRx holds. Suppose that $\varphi(A) \Rightarrow A$ for all A in S. Then for any theory U of I, if $\varphi(A)$ is in U, so too is A. However, $\varphi(A)$ is in U if and only if A is in $\varphi^{-1}U$. Thus, for any A, if A is in $\varphi^{-1}U$, then A is in U. That is, $\varphi^{-1}U \subseteq U$. Therefore $UR^\varphi U$ for all theories U, so R^φ is reflexive. Conversely, suppose that $UR^\varphi U$ for all theories U of I. Then $\varphi^{-1}U \subseteq U$. Therefore, if any A is in $\varphi^{-1}U$, then it is in U. Thus, for all A, if $\varphi(A)$ is in U, then A is in U. But this holds for all theories U. Therefore, by Theorem 8.12 (weak completeness), it follows that $\varphi(A) \Rightarrow A$.[2]

This result is the counterpart of the result obtained using Kripkean semantics, when the box of a modal system is a *T* modal – that is, all instances of "$\Box A \to A$" are axioms of that system. Sometimes the *T* condition for modal systems is expressed using the dual: "$A \to \Diamond A$." On our account, the dual version is expressed by the condition that $A \Rightarrow \sigma(A)$ for all A in the structure, where σ is the dual of φ. Now if φ is a modal operator on I, then, as noted earlier, σ, its dual, is not a modal on I, but a modal on the dual structure $I\hat{\,}$, so that φ is a modal with respect to "$\Rightarrow$" (of I), and σ, is a modal with respect to "$\Rightarrow\hat{\,}$" (of $I\hat{\,}$). The corresponding accessibility relation R^σ for the dual modal is given by condition (2). There is the corresponding result:

Theorem 35.2. *Let $I = \langle S, \Rightarrow \rangle$ be an implication structure, and let $I\hat{\,} = \langle S, \Rightarrow\hat{\,} \rangle$ be its dual. Let φ be a modal operator on I, and let σ be its dual. Then $A \Rightarrow \sigma(A)$ for all A in S if and only if R^σ is reflexive on the theories of I. (We leave the proof, which is essentially the same as that for Theorem 35.1, for the reader.)*

The usual condition of reflexivity on one accessibility relation has here been separated into the reflexivity of two relations: R^φ is reflexive if and only if $\varphi(A) \Rightarrow A$ for all A, and R^σ is reflexive if and only if the dual law, $A \Rightarrow \sigma(A)$, holds. Why this separation? Although $(U)UR^\varphi U$ and $(U)UR^\sigma U$ are equivalent if negation is assumed to be classical on the structure, it is not generally true that $UR^\varphi V$ and $UR^\varphi V$ are equivalent under those conditions. The use of theories $U, V, \ldots$ is too weak to yield the equivalence of R^φ and R^σ. With only the use of theories, the usual accessibility relation splits into two: one for the modal and the other for its dual. However, if $U, V, \ldots$ were assumed to be maximal consistent sets (a strong assumption that we do not make), then only one accessibility relation would be needed to cover the case of a modal φ and its dual σ. That is,

Theorem 35.3. *Let $I = \langle S, \Rightarrow \rangle$ be a classical implication structure. Let φ be a modal operator on I, so that its dual, σ, is given by $\sigma(A) \Leftrightarrow \neg\varphi\neg(A)$. Let $U, V, \ldots$ be maximal consistent subsets of S. Then $UR^\varphi V$ holds if and only if $UR^\varphi V$.*

Proof. The consistent theories of I are the closed proper subsets of S. So no element and its negation belong to the consistent theories. The maximal consistent theories are those that are not proper subsets of any consistent theory. Suppose that U and V are maximal consistent theories of I. Then for every A in S, exactly one of A, $\neg A$ belongs to U (similarly for V). Suppose that $UR^\varphi V$ holds. Then $\varphi^{-1}U \subseteq V$. Now if A is in V but not in $\sigma^{-1}U$, the $\sigma(A)$ is not in U. Therefore $\neg\sigma(A)$ is in U, by the maximal consistency of U. Since $\sigma(A) \Leftrightarrow \neg\varphi\neg(A)$, $\neg\neg\varphi(\neg A)$ is in U. Since negation is classical, $\varphi(\neg A)$ is in U. Consequently, $\neg A$ is in $\varphi^{-1}U$. But $\varphi^{-1}U \subseteq V$. Therefore $\neg A$ is in V. Therefore both A and $\neg A$ are in V, and that is impossible. Thus, every member of V is a member of $\sigma^{-1}U$. That is $V \subseteq \sigma^{-1}U$, so that $UR^\sigma V$. Thus, if $UR^\varphi V$, then $UR^\sigma V$. The converse is proved similarly.

Exercise 35.1. Let (RR) be the relation that holds between theories U and V if and only if $UR^\varphi V$ and $UR^\sigma V$, where φ is a modal on I, and σ is its dual. Then $\varphi(A) \Rightarrow A$ and $A \Rightarrow \sigma(A)$ if and only if (RR) is reflexive.

35.3 K_4 modals and transitivity

We consider next the K_4 modals, for which $\varphi(A) \Rightarrow \varphi\varphi(A)$, and the dual version, for which $\sigma\sigma(A) \Rightarrow \sigma(A)$, for all A in the structure. Here we have the familiar result:

Theorem 35.4. *If $I = \langle S, \Rightarrow \rangle$ is an implication structure, and φ is a modal operator on I, then φ is a K_4 modal if and only if R^φ is transitive.*

Proof. The transitivity condition is the one for which xRz holds if xRy and yRz hold. We need two lemmas:

Lemma 35.1. *φ is a K_4 modal on I if and only if $\varphi^{-1}U \subseteq \varphi^{-1}\varphi^{-1}U$ for all theories U of I.*

Proof. Suppose that $\varphi(A) \Rightarrow \varphi\varphi(A)$ for all A in S. Then if $\varphi(A)$ is in U (i.e., A is in $\varphi^{-1}U$), so too is $\varphi\varphi(A)$. Therefore $\varphi(A)$ is in $\varphi^{-1}U$, and so A is in $\varphi^{-1}\varphi^{-1}U$. Thus, $\varphi^{-1}U \subseteq \varphi^{-1}\varphi^{-1}U$. The converse is obtained by tracing the steps backward.

Lemma 35.2. *R^φ is transitive if and only if for all theories U of I, $\varphi^{-1}U \subseteq \varphi^{-1}\varphi^{-1}U$.*

Proof. Suppose that $\varphi^{-1}U \subseteq \varphi^{-1}\varphi^{-1}U$ for all theories U of the structure and that $UR^\varphi V$ and $VR^\varphi W$. Then $\varphi^{-1}U \subseteq V$, and $\varphi^{-1}V \subseteq W$. From the former we have $\varphi^{-1}\varphi^{-1}U \subseteq \varphi^{-1}V$. Therefore $\varphi^{-1}U \subseteq \varphi^{-1}\varphi^{-1}U \subseteq \varphi^{-1}V \subseteq W$. That is, $\varphi^{-1}U \subseteq W$, or $UR^\varphi W$. Thus, if $UR^\varphi V$ and $VR^\varphi W$, then $UR^\varphi W$ (i.e., R^φ is transitive). To see the converse, let V be $\varphi^{-1}U$, and let W be $\varphi^{-1}\varphi^{-1}U$. (Remember from Theorem 28.6 that since φ is a modal, then if U is a theory, so is $\varphi^{-1}U$.) Now $UR^\varphi(\varphi^{-1}U)$, and $(\varphi^{-1}U)R^\varphi(\varphi^{-1}\varphi^{-1}U)$. By the transitivity of R^φ, we have $UR^\varphi(\varphi^{-1}\varphi^{-1}U)$. That is, $\varphi^{-1}U \subseteq \varphi^{-1}\varphi^{-1}U$.

From Lemmas 35.1 and 35.2 it follows that φ is a K_4 modal if and only if R^φ is transitive.

Exercise 35.2. If φ is a K_4 modal, and σ is its dual, then $\sigma\sigma(A) \Rightarrow \sigma(A)$ if and only if R^σ is transitive.

Exercise 35.3. Let $U(RR)V$ hold if and only if $UR^\varphi V$ and $UR^\sigma V$, where φ is a modal on a structure, and σ is its dual. Then (RR) is transitive if and only if $\varphi(A) \Rightarrow \varphi\varphi(A)$ and $\sigma\sigma(A) \Rightarrow \sigma(A)$.

35.4 Y modals and density

Thus far we have considered modal laws that do not use both a modal and its dual in their formulation. Before we turn to the study of some of those familiar modal laws, perhaps a look at a less familiar modal law will be of some interest.

Let us say that φ is a *Y modal* on a structure $I = \langle S, \Rightarrow \rangle$ if and only if $\varphi\varphi(A) \Rightarrow \varphi(A)$ for all A in S. Standardly, $\Box$ is a Y modal of some modal system if and only if the accessibility relation is *dense*: For any x and y, such that xRy, there is some z such that xRz and zRy. In our case, we have the following result:

Theorem 35.5. *Let $I = \langle S, \Rightarrow \rangle$ be an implication structure. Let φ be a modal operator on I. Then φ is a Y modal on I if and only if R^φ is dense.*

Proof. Suppose that φ is a Y modal. Then $\varphi\varphi(A) \Rightarrow \varphi(A)$ for all A in S. Consequently, for every A, if A is in $\varphi^{-1}\varphi^{-1}U$, then A is in $\varphi^{-1}U$. Therefore $\varphi^{-1}\varphi^{-1}U \subseteq \varphi^{-1}U$ for all theories U of I. Suppose that $UR^\varphi V$. Then $\varphi^{-1}U \subseteq V$. Take W to be $\varphi^{-1}U$. Then $UR^\varphi W$ (since $\varphi^{-1}U \subseteq^{-1} U$), and $WR^\varphi V$ (since $\varphi^{-1}\varphi^{-1}U \subseteq \varphi^{-1}U$). Therefore R^φ is dense. Conversely, suppose that R^φ is dense. Then for any U and V such that $UR^\varphi V$, there is a W such that $UR^\varphi W$ and $WR^\varphi V$. Let V be $\varphi^{-1}U$. So $UR^\varphi V$. Then for some W, $\varphi^{-1}U \subseteq W$, and $\varphi^{-1}W \subseteq \varphi^{-1}U$. Consequently, $\varphi^{-1}\varphi^{-1}U \subseteq \varphi^{-1}U$. Thus, for any A in S, if $\varphi\varphi(A)$ is in U, then $\varphi(A)$ is in U (for all theories U of I). Therefore $\varphi\varphi(A) \Rightarrow \varphi(A)$.

Exercise 35.4. If φ is a modal on the structure I, and σ is its dual, then $\sigma(A) \Rightarrow \sigma\sigma(A)$ for every A if and only if R^σ is dense.

35.5 D modals and seriality

Thus far we have not considered modal laws that use both a modal and its dual in their formulation. The simplest modal of this type is the D modal operator, which corresponds to the condition on modal systems that $\Box A \Rightarrow \Diamond A$. In this case, the standard result is that the accessibility relation associated with the box is *serial* – that is, for every x there is a y such that xRy. However, for the reasons mentioned earlier, we do not have one accessibility relation; we have two: one for the modal, and the other for its dual. The result that follows is a generalization of the seriality condition that reduces to the familiar condition when R^φ and R^σ are equivalent.

Definition 35.1. Let φ be a modal on I, and let σ be its dual. We shall say that R^φ is *serial* if and only if for every theory U there is some theory V such that $UR^\varphi V$ and $UR^\sigma V$.

Theorem 35.6. *Let* $I = \langle S, \Rightarrow \rangle$ *be an implication structure, and let* φ *be a modal operator on* I, *with* σ *its dual. Then* $\varphi(A)$ $\Rightarrow \sigma(A)$ *for all* A *in* S *if and only if* R^φ *is serial.*

Proof. Suppose that $\varphi(A) \Rightarrow \sigma(A)$ for all A in S. Then if $\varphi(A)$ is in U, so too is $\sigma(A)$. Therefore $\varphi^{-1}U \subseteq \sigma^{-1}U$ for all theories U of I. Since $\varphi^{-1}U \subseteq \sigma^{-1}U$, and $\sigma^{-1}U \subseteq \sigma^{-1}U$, we have $UR^\varphi(\sigma^{-1}U)$ and $UR^\sigma(\sigma^{-1}U)$. Thus, for any U there is a V (namely, $\sigma^{-1}U$) such that $UR^\varphi V$ and $UR^\sigma V$. (Note that since U is a theory, not only is $\varphi^{-1}U$ a theory, as we have already observed, but so too is $\sigma^{-1}U$.)[3] Conversely, suppose that for every U there is some V such that $UR^\varphi V$ and $UR^\sigma V$. Then $\varphi^{-1}U \subseteq V$, and $V \subseteq \sigma^{-1}U$. Consequently, $\varphi^{-1}U \subseteq \sigma^{-1}U$ for all U. Thus, for any theory U, if $\varphi(A)$ is in U, then so too is $\sigma(A)$. Therefore $\varphi(A) \Rightarrow \sigma(A)$.

35.6 Brouwerian modals and symmetry

Brouwerian modal operators, or B modals, are the counterparts of those conditions on modal systems that require that all instances of "$A \rightarrow \Box\Diamond A$" are theorems. We consider B modal operators on the structure $I = \langle S, \Rightarrow \rangle$ to be those modals φ on I for which $A \Rightarrow \varphi\sigma(A)$ for all A in the structure, where σ is the dual of φ. The standard result in this case is that the accessibility relation R is symmetric: For any x and y, if xRy, then yRx. On our account, we use a generalization of the standard notion of symmetry that reduces to the usual condition if $UR^\varphi V$ and $UR^\sigma V$ are equivalent.

Definition 35.2. Let φ be a modal on I, and let σ be its dual. We shall say that R is *symmetric* if and only if for all theories U and V of I, if $UR^\varphi V$, then $VR^\sigma U$.

Theorem 35.7. *Let* $I = \langle S, \Rightarrow \rangle$ *be an implication structure, and let* φ *be a modal operator on* I, *with* σ *its dual. Then* $A \Rightarrow \varphi\sigma(A)$ *for all* A *in* S *if and only if for all* U *and* V, *if* $UR^\varphi V$, *then* $VR^\sigma U$.

Proof. Suppose that $A \Rightarrow \varphi\sigma(A)$ for all A in S. Then for all U, if A is in U, then $\varphi\sigma(A)$ is in U. Then $\sigma(A)$ is in $\varphi^{-1}U$, and consequently A is in $\sigma^{-1}\varphi^{-1}U$. *Thus,* $U \subseteq \sigma^{-1}\varphi^{-1}U$ for all U. Now suppose that $UR^\varphi V$. Then $\varphi^{-1}U \subseteq V$. Therefore $\sigma^{-1}\varphi^{-1}U \subseteq \sigma^{-1}V$. Therefore $U \subseteq \sigma^{-1}V$ – that is, $VR^\sigma U$. Conversely, suppose that for every theory U and V, if $UR^\varphi V$, then $VR^\sigma U$. Let V be $\varphi^{-1}U$. Then $UR^\varphi V$. Consequently, $VR^\sigma U$ – that is, $U \subseteq \sigma^{-1}\varphi^{-1}U$. Therefore if A is in U, then $\varphi\sigma(A)$ is in U for all U. Consequently, $A \Longrightarrow \varphi\sigma(A)$ for all A.

In a similar way, using the dual version $\sigma\varphi(A) \Longrightarrow A$ for all A in S, it follows that $\sigma\varphi(A) \Longrightarrow A$ (for all A in S) if and only if for all U and V, if $UR^\sigma V$, then $VR^\varphi U$.

Exercise 35.5. If $I = \langle S, \Longrightarrow \rangle$ is a classical implication structure and φ is a modal on I, and σ is its dual $(\neg\varphi\neg)$, then $A \Longrightarrow \varphi\sigma(A)$ if and only if $\sigma\varphi(A) \Longrightarrow A$. Thus, $A \Longrightarrow \varphi\sigma(A)$ if and only if $[UR^\varphi V$ if and only if $VR^\sigma U]$ for all U and V.

Exercise 35.6. Let $U(RR)V$ hold if and only if $UR^\varphi V$ and $UR^\sigma V$. If φ is a B modal on I, then (RR) is symmetric.

35.7 Q modals and incestuousness

Before we consider the condition for being an S_5 modal operator, consider a somewhat unfamiliar modal operator for which there is a standard-style accessibility relation. Although the modal law corresponding to Q ("$\Diamond\Box A \to \Box\Diamond A$") does not seem to have much theoretical importance at the present time, the standard result is clear enough. The corresponding accessibility relation is called *incestuous* if and only if [if xRy and xRz, then there is a w such that yRw and zRw] (it is as if the offspring of some parent have an offspring).[4] We shall use a generalized version of this condition that uses both the modal and its dual, but that reduces to the usual condition when R^φ and R^σ are equivalent: If $UR^\varphi V$ and $UR^\sigma W$, then there is some X such that $VR^\sigma X$ and $WR^\varphi X$. The simple result is as follows:

Theorem 35.8. *If $I = \langle S, \Longrightarrow \rangle$ is an implication structure, and φ is a modal operator on I, and σ is its dual, then $\sigma\varphi(A) \Longrightarrow \varphi\sigma(A)$ for every A in S if and only if for every theory U, V, and W such that $UR^\varphi V$ and $UR^\sigma W$, there is a theory X such that $VR^\sigma X$ and $WR^\varphi X$.*

Proof. Actually, the splitting of accessibility into two relations R^φ and R^σ renders the original name of the condition less appropriate. Anyway, suppose that $\sigma\varphi(A) \Longrightarrow \varphi\sigma(A)$ for all A in S. It follows that $\varphi^{-1}\sigma^{-1}U \subseteq \sigma^{-1}\varphi^{-1}U$ for all U. Suppose that $UR^\varphi V$ and $UR^\sigma W$. From the former we have $\varphi^{-1}U \subseteq V$, and the latter yields $W \subseteq \sigma^{-1}U$. Therefore $\sigma^{-1}\varphi^{-1}U \subseteq \sigma^{-1}V$, and $\varphi^{-1}W \subseteq \varphi^{-1}\sigma^{-1}U$. Thus, $\varphi^{-1}W \subseteq \sigma^{-1}V$. Take X to be $\sigma^{-1}V$. Then $VR^\sigma X$ (since $\sigma^{-1}V \subseteq \sigma^{-1}V$), and $WR^\varphi X$ (since $\varphi^{-1}W \subseteq \sigma^{-1}V$). As for the converse, suppose that if $UR^\varphi V$ and $UR^\sigma W$, then there is some X such that $VR^\sigma X$ and $WR^\varphi X$. Therefore, if $\varphi^{-1}U \subseteq V$ and $W \subseteq \sigma^{-1}U$, then for some X, $\varphi^{-1}W \subseteq X$, and $X \subseteq \sigma^{-1}V$. In particular, take V to be $\varphi^{-1}U$, and W to be $\sigma^{-1}U$. Then $\varphi^{-1}\sigma^{-1}U \subseteq X \subseteq \sigma^{-1}\varphi^{-1}U$ for some X. Therefore $\varphi^{-1}\sigma^{-1}U \subseteq \sigma^{-1}\varphi^{-1}U$ for all U. Unpacking this in the usual way, we have that if A is in $\varphi^{-1}\sigma^{-1}U$, then A is in $\sigma^{-1}\varphi^{-1}U$. Thus, if $\varphi(A)$ is in $\sigma^{-1}U$, then $\sigma(A)$ is in $\varphi^{-1}U$. Therefore, if $\sigma\varphi(A)$ is in U, then $\varphi\sigma(A)$ is in U for all theories U of I. Therefore $\sigma\varphi(A) \Longrightarrow \varphi\sigma(A)$ for all A in S.

35.8 S_5 modal operators and the Euclidean condition

The S_5 modal operators are those modal operators φ (whose dual is σ) such that for all A in S, $\sigma(A) \Longrightarrow \varphi\sigma(A)$. This condition corresponds to the requirement that all instances of "$\Diamond A \to \Box\Diamond A$" are theorems. It is the condition that is added to the modal system (S_4) to obtain the system (S_5). The dual in the usual case is given by the requirement that all instances of "$\Diamond\Box A \to \Box A$" be theorems, and in the general setting we use the modal law that $\sigma\varphi(A) \Longrightarrow \varphi(A)$ for all A. The standard result concerning the accessibility relation is the requirement that it be *Euclidean*: For any x, y, and z, if xRy and xRz, then yRz. We shall use, as usual, a generalized condition that reduces to the standard one when R^φ and R^σ are equivalent: For any theories U, V, and W, if $UR^\varphi V$ and $UR^\sigma W$, then $VR^\sigma W$.

Theorem 35.9. *Let $I = \langle S, \Longrightarrow \rangle$ be an implication structure, and let φ be a modal operator on I, with σ its dual. Then for all A $\sigma(A) \Longrightarrow \varphi\sigma(A)$ if and only if for all U, V, and W, if $UR^\varphi V$ and $UR^\sigma W$, then $VR^\sigma W$.*

Proof. Suppose that $\sigma(A) \Longrightarrow \varphi\sigma(A)$ for all A in S. Then $\sigma^{-1}U \subseteq \sigma^{-1}\varphi^{-1}U$ for all theories U. Suppose that $UR^\varphi V$ and

354 IV THE MODAL OPERATORS

$UR^\sigma W$. From the former, we have $\varphi^{-1}u \subseteq V$, and the latter yields $W \subseteq \sigma^{-1}U$. Therefore $\sigma^{-1}\varphi^{-1}U \subseteq \sigma^{-1}V$. Consequently, $\sigma^{-1}U \subseteq \sigma^{-1}V$. Therefore $W \subseteq \sigma^{-1}V$. That is, $VR^\sigma W$. Conversely, suppose that for any U, V, and W, if $UR^\varphi V$ and $UR^\sigma W$, then $VR^\sigma W$. Take V to be $\varphi^{-1}U$, and W to be $\sigma^{-1}U$. Then $UR^\varphi V$ and $UR^\sigma W$ both hold. Consequently, $VR^\sigma W$. That is, $\sigma^{-1}U \subseteq \sigma^{-1}\varphi^{-1}U$. Unpacking this condition in the usual way, we then have, for every A in S, that if $\sigma(A)$ is in U, then so too is $\varphi\sigma(A)$. That is $\sigma(A) \Longrightarrow \varphi\sigma(A)$ for all A in S.

If the dual form of the S_5 condition, $\sigma\varphi(A) \Longrightarrow \varphi(A)$, is used, then there is a parallel result, whose proof we leave for the reader:

Theorem 35.10. *If $I = \langle S, \Longrightarrow \rangle$ is an implication structure, φ is a modal operator on I, and σ is its dual, then $\sigma\varphi(A) \Longrightarrow \varphi(A)$ if and only if for all U, V, and W, if $UR^\sigma V$ and $UR^\varphi W$, then $VR^\varphi W$.*

Exercise 35.7. Let $U(RR)V$ hold if and only if $UR^\varphi V$ and $UR^\sigma V$. Then $[\sigma(A) \Longrightarrow \varphi\sigma(A)$ and $\sigma\varphi(A) \Longrightarrow \varphi(A)]$ hold for all A in S if and only if for all U, V and W, if $U(RR)V$ and $U(RR)W$ then $V(RR)W$.

To each modal φ on an implication structure we have associated an accessibility relation R^φ, a binary relation defined on the theories U, V, ... of that structure. The dual σ, if it exists, is a modal on the dual structure. It can, however, be assigned an accessibility relation R^σ as well. There are, as we observed, conditions under which the two relations are equivalent, though in general that will not be the case given the wide variety of structures that are possible. There are some distinct advantages to this way of using accessibility relations to study the specific modal character of various modal operators. Nothing suspect or controversial is involved in the use of those theories that are related by accessibility relations. There is no need to assume that there are possible worlds whose special character has to be explained or whose use has to be justified. The controversies that surround the use of a semantic theory based upon possible worlds have been put to one side. Those controversies are irrelevant to the systematization of the various modals. The usual results obtained with their aid can be obtained without their use. Moreover, the theories used in their stead are a standard part of logical theory, already in use for the study of familiar nonmodal theories of logic. The use of accessibility relations, when they are available, provides one way of studying the specific modal character of a modal and of explaining the differences in modal character in a very perspicuous, sometimes compelling, manner.

One of the prices paid for using theories, rather than some controversial notion of possible world, is that the accessibility relation will now divide into two such relations: one for the modal on the structure, and the other for its dual. This in itself is not surprising. Since each modal has an accessibility relation associated with it, this is just a case of two modals whose accessibility relations are, in general, different. As we observed, although no modal operator is ever equivalent to its dual, nevertheless there are conditions under which their accessibility relations are equivalent.

The familiar landmarks remain, even with the simple resources used. Let us summarize the results thus far. I is an implication structure, φ is a modal operator on I, and σ is its dual. Let U, V, ... be the theories of I. The accessibility relation R^φ associated with φ is $UR^\varphi V$: $\varphi^{-1}U \subseteq V$. The accessibility relation R^σ associated with σ is $UR^\sigma V$: $V \subseteq \sigma^{-1}U$. We then have the following definitions:

1. (a) R^φ is *reflexive* if and only if $UR^\varphi U$ holds for all U.
   (b) R^σ is *reflexive* if and only if $UR^\sigma U$ holds for all U.
2. (a) R^φ is *transitive* if and only if for all U, V, and W, $UR^\varphi V$ & $VR^\varphi W$ $\rightarrow$ $UR^\varphi W$.
   (b) R^σ is *transitive* if and only if for all U, V, and W, $UR^\sigma V$ & $VR^\sigma W$ $\rightarrow$ $UR^\sigma W$.
3. (a) R^φ is *serial* if and only if for every U there is some V such that $UR^\sigma V$ & $UR^\varphi V$.
   (b) R^σ is *serial* if and only if for every U there is some V such that $UR^\varphi V$ & $UR^\sigma V$.
4. (a) R^φ is *symmetric* if and only if for all U and V, $UR^\varphi V \rightarrow VR^\sigma U$.
   (b) R^σ is *symmetric* if and only if for all U and V, $UR^\sigma V \rightarrow VR^\varphi U$.
5. (a) R^φ is *Euclidean* if and only if for all U, V, and W, $UR^\varphi V$ & $UR^\sigma W$ $\rightarrow$ $VR^\sigma W$.
   (b) R^σ is *Euclidean* if and only if for all U, V, and W, $UR^\sigma V$ & $UR^\varphi W$ $\rightarrow$ $VR^\varphi W$.

We then have the following results (omitting the less familiar):

T modals

1. $\varphi(A) \Longrightarrow A$ for every A if and only if R^φ is *reflexive*.
2. $A \Longrightarrow \sigma(A)$ for every A if and only if R^σ is *reflexive*.

K₄ modals

1. $\varphi(A) \Rightarrow \varphi\varphi(A)$ for every A if and only if R^φ is *transitive*.
2. $\sigma\sigma(A) \Rightarrow \sigma(A)$ for every A if and only if R^σ is *transitive*.

D modals

1. $\varphi(A) \Rightarrow \sigma(A)$ for every A if and only if R^φ is *serial*.
2. $\varphi(A) \Rightarrow \sigma(A)$ for every A (this modal law is the same as the dual version) if and only if R^σ is *serial*.

B modals

1. $A \Rightarrow \varphi\sigma(A)$ for every A if and only if R^φ is *symmetric*.
2. $\sigma\varphi(A) \Rightarrow A$ for every A if and only if R^σ is *symmetric*.

S₅ modals

1. $\sigma(A) \Rightarrow \varphi\sigma(A)$ for every A if and only if R^φ is *Euclidean*.
2. $\sigma\varphi(A) \Rightarrow \varphi(A)$ for every A if and only if R^σ is *Euclidean*.

We have seen how the systematization of the familiar modal systems has remained intact, using the uncontroversial set-theoretical concept of a closed theory of an implication structure. It is also of some interest that much of familiar and nonfamiliar modal theory can be developed without assuming that the items under study are syntactical, or have some special semantic value. Modal systems, of course, usually are presented syntactically. The familiar theorems of those systems and the characterization of their modals can nevertheless be obtained without the assumption that the structures have either syntactical or semantical members. As in the case of the logical operators such as negation, the hypothetical, disjunction, conjunction, and quantification, we see how much of logical theory remains without the imposition of syntactical or semantical constraints upon the items over which those operators are defined. We can now see that a substantial part of the systematization of various modal operators can also be obtained without any reliance upon a possible world semantics.[5]

35.9 Gödel–Löb modals revisited

Thus far the idea has been to study the specific modal character of a modal on an implication structure by using the structure to specify its theories, as well as an accessibility relation R^φ on those theories that makes specific use of the modal operator φ. Special problems emerge with the consideration of the Gödel–Löb modal operators. In the particular case, when the implication structure is $I_{G\text{-}L}$, the one that is associated with the modal system $(G\text{-}L)$, it is known that the accessibility relation cannot be taken as the usual canonical one ($UR^\varphi V$ if and only if $\varphi^{-1}U \subseteq V$).[6] It is clear, then, that the kind of accessibility relation used thus far will not be suitable for $G\text{-}L$ modal operators on structures in general, because of the failure in the case of $I_{G\text{-}L}$.

In the special case of $I_{G\text{-}L}$ there are accessibility relations that are transitive subrelations of the canonical accessibility relation that do work – for example, "well-capped" binary relations.[7] It is not known whether or not they work for arbitrary structures with $G\text{-}L$ modal operators on them. However, in the next chapter we shall see how it is possible to recover the standard result by strengthening the requirements on the theories of implication structures.

Nevertheless, it is of some interest that even with the weak notion of theory that we have used, there is a binary relation R that plays a role with respect to the $G\text{-}L$ modals like the one that the canonical accessibility relation has to the more familiar modals we considered earlier.

Definition 35.3. Let $I = \langle S, \Rightarrow \rangle$ be an implication structure in which hypotheticals always exist, and let φ be a modal operator on I. For any theory U of the structure I, we shall say that U is a *Löb theory*, $L(U)$, of I if and only if for every A in S, if $\varphi(A) \to A$ is in U, then A is in U.

Let R be a binary relation defined on the theories of the structure as follows: URV if and only if $UR^\varphi V$ and $L(V)$.

Exercise 35.8. Let φ be a $G\text{-}L$ modal operator on a structure I. Then (a) the relation R, defined above, is a subrelation of R^φ, and (b) it is transitive. (Use the fact proved in Theorem 28.17 that every $G\text{-}L$ modal is a K_4 modal, so that R^φ is transitive and consequently so too is R.)

The following theorem for $G\text{-}L$ modal operators (which are also necessitation modals) is analogous to the one proved for necessitation modals.

Theorem 35.11. *Let $I = \langle S, \Rightarrow \rangle$ be an implication structure. Let R be a binary relation on the theories of I, as defined above.*

*Then φ is a G-L modal operator on I if and only if for all U,
$[\varphi(A) \in U$ if and only if for all V, $(URV \to A \in V)]$.*

Proof. Assume that φ is a *G-L* modal on *I*. If $\varphi(A)$ is in *U*, and
URV, then *A* is in $\varphi^{-1}U$, and $UR^\varphi V$ and $L(V)$ hold. Since
$UR^\varphi V$, and *A* is in $\varphi^{-1}U$, *A* is in *V*. Therefore, for any *A* and *U*,
if $\varphi(A)$ is in *U*, then for any *V*, $URV \to A \in V$. For this much,
the *G-L* character of φ is not needed. To prove the converse,
suppose that for all *V*, $URV \to A \in V$ [and then show that $\varphi(A)$
$\in U$]. In particular, $UR(\varphi^{-1}U) \to A \in \varphi^{-1}U$. We want to use
the fact that for any *U*, $UR(\varphi^{-1}U)$, for which we need a lemma.

Lemma 35.3. *If φ is a G-L modal operator on a structure I, then
for every theory U of I, $UR(\varphi^{-1}U)$.*

Proof. If *U* is a theory, and φ is a modal, then, as we have seen,
$\varphi^{-1}U$ *is also a theory. Therefore* $UR^\varphi(\varphi^{-1}U)$, since $\varphi^{-1}U \subseteq$
$\varphi^{-1}U)$. It remains only to check that $L(\varphi^{-1}U)$ (i.e., $\varphi^{-1}U$ is a
Löb theory). That, however, is guaranteed by the fact that φ is a
Gödel–Löb modal: Suppose that $\varphi(A) \to A$ is in $\varphi^{-1}U$. Then
$\varphi(\varphi(A) \to A)$ is in *U*. Since φ is a *G-L* modal on *I*, $\varphi(\varphi(A) \Rightarrow A)$
$\Rightarrow \varphi(A)$. Therefore $\varphi(A)$ is in *U*. Consequently, *A* is in $\varphi^{-1}U$, so
that $\varphi^{-1}U$ is a Löb theory. Since $UR^\varphi(\varphi^{-1}U)$ and $L(\varphi^{-1}U)$, it
follows that $UR(\varphi^{-1}U)$.

Returning to the proof, then, since $UR(\varphi^{-1}U)$ for all theories
U of *I*, *A* is in $\varphi^{-1}U$; that is $\varphi(A)$ is in *U*. So if φ is a *G–L* modal,
then for all *U*, $\varphi(A) \in U \leftrightarrow$ for all *V*, $[URV \to A \in V]$.
Conversely, we need to show that if for all *U*, $\varphi(A) \in U \leftrightarrow$ for
all *V*, $[URV \to A \in V]$, then φ is a Gödel–Löb modal on *I*.
Suppose that the antecedent holds. Suppose that $\varphi(\varphi(A) \to A)$
is in *U*. Then $URV \to (\varphi(A) \to A) \in V$. Therefore, if *URV*,
then $L(V)$, and $(\varphi(A) \to A) \in V$. Consequently, $A \in V$. Thus,
assuming that $\varphi(\varphi(A) \to A)$ is in *U*, it follows that for all *V*,
$URV \to A \in V$. But from the latter it follows that $\varphi(A) \in U$.
Therefore, for any *U*, if $\varphi(\varphi(A) \to A)$ is in *U*, then so too is
$\varphi(A)$. Consequently, $\varphi(\varphi(A) \to A) \Rightarrow \varphi(A)$. That is φ is a *G-L*
modal operator on *I*. And that completes the proof.

We noted earlier that the modal system *(G-L)* was designed to study the
syntactical notion of provability in Peano arithmetic. Therefore, the
G-L-style modal operator that was defined over arbitrary implication
structures may not have immediate theoretical interest. Why should one

be interested in abstracting away the syntactical structure in such a case? If it should turn out that the accessibility relation used for the syntactical system $(G\text{-}L)$ cannot be generalized to cover all cases of structures that have $G\text{-}L$ modals on them, that might not be so serious, given the reasons for studying the $G\text{-}L$ modals in the first place.

Nevertheless, it is of some interest that this might be a case, unlike the situation for the modal systems (T), (K_4), (D), (S_4), (B), and (S_5), for example, where syntax cannot be neglected in systematizing the modals by accessibility relations. The problem of determining where syntax is really needed must be qualified somewhat by the observations of the next chapter. There, as we shall see, with the use of *strong theories* of implication structures and binary relations defined over them, a notion of a *model* can be provided for implication structures, whether syntactical or not, that will enable one to recover all the customary pairings between the familiar modals and certain kinds of accessibility relations – including the case of $G\text{-}L$ modals. We turn to a sketch of how that can be done.

36

Model functions, accessibility relations, and theories

36.1 Models for structures

Let $I = \langle S, \Rightarrow \rangle$ be an implication structure. Let T be the set of all *strongly closed* subsets of S – that is, those subsets U of S for which whenever $A_1, \ldots, A_n \Rightarrow B$, and all the A_i's belong to U, then B belongs to U. In this section, when we speak of theories, it will be these strong theories that are intended. Let R be any binary relation on the set T of all theories of the structure I. Under these conditions we shall say that $F = \langle T, R \rangle$ is a *frame* for the implication structure I.

We now wish to introduce the notion of a *model* of (or for) the structure I. Essentially this is given by specifying a function f, the *model function*, that associates to each A in S a collection $f(A)$ of theories of I, that is, some subset of T, and satisfies certain additional conditions.

We do not always have connectives available in an implication structure. Consequently, the usual way of providing conditions for a model are not generally available. The use of "$\vee$," for example, in indicating disjunction, was a convenience for indicating the elements in the structure that are assigned by the disjunction operator (if it assigns an element at all). Similar remarks hold for our use of the other connective signs. Thus, the usual method of exploiting the syntax to define the notion of a model by saying what the model assigns to "$A \vee B$," "$A \to B$," "$A \& B$," "$\neg A$," and so forth, is not available generally.

What we shall do instead is to exploit the most prominent feature of implication structures, their implication relations. We shall see that with enough conditions placed upon these model functions, their behavior on disjunctions, conjunctions, and the other logical operators (when they exist) is just what one would wish it to be. The notion of a model will be defined in such a way that it does not require the existence of any particular connective sign, say "$\vee$," nor does it even require that disjunctions (understood nonsyntactically) on our operator view always exist. We shall see later how the behavior of model functions on the logical operators follows from the conditions on f, even though there is, in general, no syntax for the model functions to exploit.

Definition 36.1. Let $I = \langle S, \Rightarrow \rangle$ be an implication structure, and let φ be a modal operator on I, with σ its dual. Let $F = \langle T, R \rangle$ be a frame for I. Then M_f is *a model of I*, based on the frame F, if and only if

(1) for each A in S, $f(A) \subseteq T$.

That is, f is a function that maps each A in S to a collection of theories of the implication structure I.

(2) If $A_1, \ldots, A_n \Rightarrow B$, then $f(A_1) \cap \ldots \cap f(A_n) \subseteq f(B)$.

Thus, in particular, if $A \Rightarrow B$, then $f(A) \subseteq f(B)$. And if $A \Rightarrow^{\wedge} B$, then $f(B) \subseteq f(A)$.

(3) The dual of (2): If $A_1, \ldots, A_n \Rightarrow^{\wedge} B$, then $f(B) \subseteq f(A_1) \cup \ldots \cup f(A_n)$.

(4) $f(\varphi(A)) = \{U \mid (V)(URV \to V \in f(A))\}$.

Condition (4) tells us about the value of f, when the element in question is $\varphi(A)$. Thus, f assigns a collection of theories to $\varphi(A)$ such that if a theory belongs to that collection, then all theories that are accessible from it belong to the collection of theories that f assigns to A. So U is a member of $f(\varphi(A))$ if and only if $(V)(URV \to V \in f(A))$.

(5) $f(\sigma(A)) = \{U \mid (\exists V)(URV \ \& \ V \in f(A))\}$.

Thus, for any theory U, U is in $f(\sigma(A))$ if and only if there is some theory V such that URV and V is in $f(A)$.

(6) There is a C in S such that $f(C) = \varnothing$.

Usually it is assumed that there is some special sentence in a modal system that figures as a *falsum*. There generally will not be some one item that has this role in all implication structures. However, condition (6) requires that there be, in any structure for which M_f is a model, some member that has that role.

(7) There is a C^* in S such that $f(C^*) = T$.

Similarly, there is no one item that will function as a *verum* in all structures. This condition assumes that each structure for which M_f is a model will have such an item in it.

Assume that I is an implication structure and that M_f is a model for I based on the frame F. Then the following consequences hold for the logical operators:

Theorem 36.1

(a) $f(A \ \& \ B) = f(A) \cap f(B)$.
(b) $f(A \lor B) = f(A) \cup f(B)$.
(c) $f(A) \cap f(\neg A) = \varnothing$.
(d) If the structure I is classical, then $f(A) \cup f(\neg A) = T$.

Proof. (a) Since $(A \ \& \ B)$ implies A as well as B, we have, by (2), that $f(A \ \& \ B) \subseteq f(A)$ [and $f(B)$]. Therefore $f(A \ \& \ B) \subseteq f(A) \cap f(B)$. Moreover, since $A, B \Rightarrow (A \ \& \ B)$, then, by (2), $f(A) \cap f(B) \subseteq f(A \ \& \ B)$.

(b) Since A (as well as B) implies $(A \lor B)$, then, by (2), $f(A) \subseteq f(A \lor B)$, and $f(B) \subseteq f(A \lor B)$. Therefore $f(A) \cup f(B) \subseteq f(A \lor B)$. Moreover, $A, B \Rightarrow^{\wedge} (A \lor B)$, so, by (3), $f(A) \lor B \subseteq f(A) \cup f(B)$.

(c) $A, \neg A \Rightarrow B$ for all B in S. By (2), $f(A) \cap f(\neg A) \subseteq f(B)$ for all B in S. By (6), there is a C in S such that $f(C) = \varnothing$. Therefore $f(A) \cap f(\neg A) \subseteq f(C) = \varnothing$.

(d) Since negation is classical, $(A \lor \neg A)$ is a thesis of the structure. Therefore $B \Rightarrow (A \lor \neg A)$ for all B in S. By (2), then, $f(B) \subseteq f(A \lor \neg A)$. By part (b) of this proof, $f(B) \subseteq f(A) \cup f(\neg A)$ for all B in S. By (7), there is some C^* in S such that $f(C^*) = T$. Therefore $T = f(C^*) \subseteq f(A) \cup f(\neg A)$. Since the right-hand side is a subset of T, $T = f(A) \cup f(\neg A)$.

Theorem 36.2. *Under the same conditions as for the preceding theorem, and with I a classical structure, for all theories U, $U \in f(A \to B)$ if and only if $U \in f(A) \to U \in f(B)$.*

Proof. Since $A, A \to B \Rightarrow B$, then, by (2), $f(A) \cap f(A \to B) \subseteq f(B)$. Therefore, if U is in $f(A \to B)$, then if it is in $f(A)$, it is also in $f(B)$. Conversely, suppose that either (1) U is not in $f(A)$ or (2) U is in $f(B)$. (1) If U is not in $f(A)$, then since $f(A) \cup f(\neg A) = T$, U is in $f(\neg A)$. But $\neg A \Rightarrow A \to B$, so that $f(\neg A) \subseteq f(A \to B)$. Therefore U is in $f(A \to B)$. (2) If U is in $f(B)$, then since $B \Rightarrow (A \to B)$, $f(B \subseteq f(A \to B)$. Therefore U is in $f(A \to B)$.

Exercise 36.1. If I is a classical implication structure, and φ is a modal operator on I, and $\sigma \ (\neg \varphi \neg)$ is its dual, and M_f is a model for I with respect to the frame $F = \langle T, R \rangle$, then (4) and (5) are equivalent.

We can now see how to recapture our earlier Kripke-style systematization of familiar modals, this time including the standard result for *G-L*
modals (Boolos, 1979). We shall give the proofs for *T*, K_4, and *G-L*
modals. The reader who is familiar with the standard proofs in the
literature will see that those proofs can be taken over, almost line for
line.

Definition 36.2. Let $I = \langle S, \Rightarrow \rangle$ be a classical implication
structure, with modal φ on it. Let M be a collection of models
M_f of I based upon the frame $F = \langle T, R \rangle$. Then

(a) *M is a full collection of models of I based upon the frame F*
    if and only if

(8) for every subset T^* of T there is some function f^* such that
    (1) M_{f^*} is a member of M and (2) there is some B^* in S such
    that $f^*(B^*) = T^*$.[1]

(b) *M is a complete collection of models of I based upon the*
    frame F if and only if M is a full collection of models of I
    and

(9) for every A in S, if $f(A) = T$ for all M_f in M, then A is a
    thesis of I.

Exercise 36.2. If I is a classical structure, and M is a complete
collection of models of I, then $A \Rightarrow B$ if and only if
for all M_f in M, $f(A) \subseteq f(B)$. [By Theorem 36.2, for every f,
every member of T is in $f(A \rightarrow B)$, so that $A \rightarrow B$ is a thesis of
I.]

36.2 *T* modals and reflexivity

Here the basic result is given by the following two theorems:

Theorem 36.3. *Let $I = \langle S, \Rightarrow \rangle$ be an implication structure,*
with φ a T modal on I. If M is a full set of models of I based on
the frame $F = \langle T, R \rangle$, then R is reflexive.

Proof. Suppose that $\varphi(A) \Rightarrow A$ for all A in S. Let M_f be in M.
Then f satisfies conditions (1)–(8). By (2), $f(\varphi(A)) \subseteq f(A)$ for all
A in S. Consequently, for any U in T, if U is in $f(\varphi(A))$, then U
is in $f(A)$. Let U_0 be any member of T. By (5), U_0 is in $f(\varphi(A))$ if

and only if (V) $(U_0RV \to V \in f(A))$ for all A in S. Therefore, for all A, if (V) $(U_0RV \to V \in f(A))$, then $U_0 \in f(A)$. Now let T^* be the set $\{X \mid U_0RX\}$. By Definition 36.2, there is an M_{f^*} in M and a B^* in S such that $f^*(B^*) = T^*$. So, for f^*, T^*, and B^*, in particular, if (V) $(U_0RV \to V \in T^*)$, then $U_0 \in T^*$. But for any X in T, X is in T^* if and only if U_0RX. Therefore, if (V) $(U_0RV \to U_0RV)$, then U_0RU_0. Since the antecedent holds, U_0RU_0 also holds for all theories U_0 of I (i.e., R is reflexive).[2]

The preceding theorem did not require that the structure be classical. However, classical negation is needed for the converse:

Theorem 36.4. *Let $I = \langle S, \Rightarrow \rangle$ be a classical implication structure, with a modal operator φ on it. If M is a complete collection of models for I based upon the frame $F = \langle T, R \rangle$, where R is a reflexive relation on T, then φ is a T modal.*

Proof. Suppose that U is in $f(\varphi(A))$. Then, by (4), $(V)(URV \to V \in f(A))$, from which it follows that $URU \to U \in f(A)$. Since R is reflexive, U is in $f(A)$. Consequently, for all A in S, $f(\varphi(A)) \subseteq f(A)$ for all f. By Exercise 36.2, $\varphi(A) \Rightarrow A$.

36.3 K_4 modals and transitivity

The standard result for K_4 modals is that all the models for a modal system in which $\varphi(A) \to \varphi\varphi(A)$ is a theorem (for all A) are based on frames $\langle T, R \rangle$ for which R is transitive.

Theorem 36.5. *Let $I = \langle S, \Rightarrow \rangle$ be an implication structure, with φ a K_4 modal on it. If M is a full collection of models of I based on $F = \langle T, R \rangle$, then R is transitive.*

Proof. Suppose that $\varphi(A) \Rightarrow \varphi\varphi(A)$ for all A in S, and let M be any full collection of models of I based upon the frame $F = \langle T, R \rangle$. For any M_f in M, $f(\varphi(A)) \subseteq f(\varphi\varphi(A))$, by (2). Therefore, by (4), for any U, $(V)(URV \to V \in f(A)) \to (V)(URV \to V \in f(\varphi(A)))$. Thus, $(V)(URV \to V \in f(A)) \to (V)(URV \to (X)(VRX \to X \in f(A)))$ for all A in S. Let T^* be the set $\{Y \mid URY\}$. By Definition 36.2 there is an M_{f^*} in M and some B^* in S such that $f^*(B^*) = T^*$. In particular, then, using f^* and B^*, and since $f^*(B^*) = T^*$, $(V)(URV \to V \in T^*) \to (V)(URV \to (X)(VRX \to X \in T^*))$. Therefore, since Y is in T^*

if and only if URY, $(V)(URV \rightarrow URV) \rightarrow (V)(URV \rightarrow (X)(VRX \rightarrow URX))$. Now the antecedent holds. Consequently, $(V)(URV \rightarrow (X)(VRX \rightarrow URX))$. But this implies that R is transitive: Suppose that URV and VRX. Then $(X)(VRX \rightarrow URX)$, since URV. Therefore $(X)(VRX \rightarrow (URX))$. Since VRX, it follows that URX. So R is transitive.

Theorem 36.6. *Let $I = \langle S, \Rightarrow \rangle$ be a classical implication structure, with a modal operator φ on it. If M is a complete collection of models for I based upon the frame $F = \langle T, R \rangle$, where R is a transitive relation on T, then φ is a K_4 modal.*

Proof. Suppose that R is transitive and M is a complete collection of models of I based on the frame $\langle T, R \rangle$. Let U be any theory of I, and M_f any member of M. Suppose that U is in $f(\varphi(A))$. Then $(V)(URV \rightarrow V \in f(A))$. Assume that URV and VRX. By transitivity, URX. However, $URX \rightarrow X \in f(A)$. Therefore $X \in f(A)$. Consequently, if $(V)(URV \rightarrow V \in f(A))$ and URV, then $(X)(VRX \rightarrow X \in f(A))$. By (4), the latter is equivalent to $V \in f(\varphi(A))$. Thus, if $(V)(URV \rightarrow V \in f(A))$, then $(V)(URV \rightarrow V \in f(\varphi(A)))$. By (4), then, if U is in $f(A)$, then U is in $f(\varphi\varphi(A))$. That is, for any A in S, $f(A) \subseteq f(\varphi\varphi(A))$ holds for all f. By Exercise 36.2, $\varphi(A) \Rightarrow \varphi\varphi(A)$. That is, φ is a K_4 modal operator on I.

36.4 *G-L* modals, transitivity, and well cappedness

It may be helpful to reconsider one last example, the case of implication structures with *G-L* modal operators on them.

Theorem 36.7. *Let $I = \langle S, \Rightarrow \rangle$ be an implication structure, and let φ be a G-L modal on it. If M is a full collection of models of I based on $F = \langle T, R \rangle$ then R is transitive and well capped.*

Proof. Since φ is a *G-L* modal, $\varphi(\varphi(A) \rightarrow A) \Rightarrow \varphi(A)$ for all A in S. Let M_f be any member of M. Therefore $f(\varphi(\varphi(A) \rightarrow A)) \subseteq f(\varphi(A))$. Consequently, for any U in T if $(V)(URV \rightarrow V \in f(\varphi(A) \rightarrow A))$, then $(X)(URX \rightarrow X \in f(A))$. By Theorem 36.2, V is in $f(\varphi(A) \rightarrow A)$ if and only if $V \in f(\varphi(A)) \rightarrow V \in f(A)$. Therefore,

(1) if $(V)(URV \rightarrow ((Y)(VRY \rightarrow Y \in f(A)) \rightarrow V \in f(A)))$, then $(X)(URX \rightarrow X \in f(A))$ for all A in S and all M_f in M.

Let T^* be a subset of T given by $\{Z \mid (W)(ZRW \rightarrow URW)\} \cap \{Z \mid URZ\}$. Since M is a full set of models, there is some M_{f^*} in M such that $f^*(B^*) = T^*$ for some B^* in S. Therefore, for f^* and B^*, in particular,

(2) $(V)(URV \rightarrow ((Y)(VRY \rightarrow Y \in T^*) \rightarrow V \in T^*)) \rightarrow (X)(URX \rightarrow X \in T^*)$.

Now the antecedent of (2) holds: Suppose that URV, and $(Y)(VRY \rightarrow Y \in T^*)$. If VRW, then $W \in T^*$, and so URW. Therefore $(W)(VRW \rightarrow URW)$. Since URV, it follows that $V \in T^*$. Consequently, $(X)(URX \rightarrow X \in T^*)$. But from this it follows that R is transitive: Suppose that URV, and VRW. From the former we get $V \in T^*$. Therefore $(Z)(VRZ \rightarrow URZ)$. Since VRW, we obtain URW. Thus, R is transitive.

It still must be shown that R is well capped. That is, for any nonempty subset T' of T there is a member of T' that does not bear R to any member of T'. Suppose now that R is not well capped. Then there is some nonempty subset $T^\#$ of T such that every member of $T^\#$ bears R to some member of $T^\#$. Let $S^\# = T - T^\#$ (the set whose members belong to T but not to $T^\#$). Now $S^\#$ is a subset of T, so there is some model $M_{f\#}$ in M and a $B^\#$ in S such that $f^\#(B^\#) = S^\#$. Therefore, since (1) holds for all model functions f and all A in S, for $f^\#$ and $B^\#$, in particular, we have

(3) $((V)(URV \rightarrow ((Y)(VRY \rightarrow Y \in S^\#) \rightarrow V \in S^\#))) \rightarrow (X)(URX \rightarrow X \in S^\#)$.

Notice that $(Y)(VRY \rightarrow Y \in S^\#) \rightarrow V \in S^\#$ holds for any V. The reason is that if $(Y)(VRY \rightarrow Y \in S^\#)$ holds, but V is not in $S^\#$, then V is in $T^\#$. Since every member of $T^\#$ bears R to some member of $T^\#$, there is some W in $T^\#$ such that VRW. Then W is in $S^\#$ (since it was assumed that if V bears R to Y, then Y is in $S^\#$). But then W is in $T^\#$ as well as $S^\#$, and that is impossible. Since the antecedent of (3) holds, we have $(X)(URX \rightarrow X \in S^\#)$. Suppose that there is some U_0 in $T^\#$. Then there is some W in $T^\#$ such that U_0RW. Consequently, W is in $S^\#$. That is, W is in $T^\#$ as well as $S^\#$, and that is impossible. Therefore $T^\#$ is empty. But that is impossible. Therefore R is well capped. And that completes the proof.

Theorem 36.8. *Let* $I = \langle S, \Rightarrow \rangle$ *be a classical implication structure, with a modal operator* φ *on it. If* M *is a complete collection of models for* I *based upon the frame* $F = \langle T, R \rangle$, *where* R *is a transitive, well-capped relation on* T, *then* φ *is a G-L modal.*

Proof. We want to show, first, that for any M_f in M, $f(\varphi(\varphi(A) \rightarrow A)) \subseteq f(\varphi(A))$; that is, for any U in T, if $(V)(URV \rightarrow V \in f(\varphi(A) \rightarrow A))$, then $(V)(URV \rightarrow V \in f(A))$. Unpacking this condition, if $(V)(URV \rightarrow ((X)(VRX \rightarrow X \in f(A)) \rightarrow V \in f(A)))$, then $(V)(URV \rightarrow V \in f(A))$.

Now suppose that the consequent fails. Then there is some V_0 such that URV_0, and V_0 is not in $f(A)$. Let S' be the set of all Y in T such that URY, and Y is not in $f(A)$. Since V_0 is in it, S' is not empty. Moreover, since R is assumed to be well capped, there is some Z in S' such that Z does not bear R to any member of S'. For this special Z, URZ, and Z is not a member of $f(A)$, since Z is in S'. Suppose now that $(V)(URV \rightarrow ((X)(VRX \rightarrow X \in f(A)) \rightarrow V \in f(A)))$. Since URZ holds, $(X)(ZRX \rightarrow X \in f(A)) \rightarrow Z \in f(A)$. But Z is not in $f(A)$. Therefore $(X)(ZRX \rightarrow X \in f(A))$ fails. Consequently, for some X_0, ZRX_0, and X_0 is not in $f(A)$. Thus, X_0 is in S'. Since ZRX_0, and Z does not bear R to any member of S', X_0 is not in S'. But that is impossible. Therefore $f(\varphi(\varphi(A) \rightarrow A)) \subseteq f(\varphi(A))$ for all M_f in M. By Exercise 36.2, it follows that for any A in S, $\varphi(\varphi(A) \rightarrow A) \Rightarrow \varphi(A)$. So φ is a *G-L* modal.

Exercise 36.3. If I is an implication structure, with a modal φ on it, and M is a complete collection of models of I based on any frame $F = \langle T, R \rangle$, then φ is a necessitation modal.

These results, enabling one to pass from types of modals to types of frames and back again, are useful in those cases in which full collections and complete collections of models are available for implication structures and their modals. For some structures – those associated with well-studied modal systems – those collections of models are available. However, the general problem of distinguishing those structures with modals that have complete collections of models from those that do not is an open question.

37

Migrant modals

37.1 The loss of modal character

On our account, one may sometimes come across operators that seem to have modal character, but do not distribute over implication. Indeed, one may, to take a parallel example, come across hypotheticals that do not seem to satisfy the condition that corresponds to modus ponens. How is this possible? It is one of our conditions on the modals that they distribute over implication, and it is part of our conditions on hypothetical operators that A, $A \to B \Rightarrow B$.

The answer lies in the recognition that modal operators as well as the logical operators are relativized to implication relations. That feature is an integral part of our account, and one of its deepest resources. A structure consists of a base set S, with an implication relation on it. There can, as we have seen, be various implication relations on a given set. However, with, say, two implication relations on a given set, the possibility arises that an operator may be modal with respect to one implication relation, but fail to be modal with respect to the other. Similarly, an operator may be a hypothetical with respect to one implication relation, but not with respect to another over the very same set. The result of this shift from one implication relation to another can be dramatic: Modus ponens will seem to fail in the case of hypotheticals,[1] and modals will seem to violate the conditions even of *monotonicity* [if $A \Rightarrow B$, then $\varphi(A) \Rightarrow \varphi(B)$],[2] or even seem to fail to be *classical*[3] [if $A \Leftrightarrow B$, then $\varphi(A) \Leftrightarrow \varphi(B)$]. Moreover, if an operator is called *normal*[4] if and only if it is a necessitation and distributes over hypotheticals, then the failure of monotonicity implies a failure of the modal to be normal.

However, these apparent failures do not mean that the hypothetical is an operator that violates modus ponens, nor that certain operators that appear to be modal nevertheless fail to meet our standards of modality. The latter may be cases of what I shall call *migrant modals*. They occur when an operator is modal with respect to an implication relation "$\Rightarrow$," but fails to be modal with respect to another implication relation

"$\Rightarrow$*" on the same set. It has "wandered" or migrated, as it were, from its home relation, the source of its modality in the first place.

Some examples may prove helpful. Let $I = \langle S, \Rightarrow \rangle$ be an implication structure, with a modal operator φ on it:

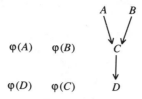

$$\varphi(A) \quad \varphi(B)$$

$$\varphi(D) \quad \varphi(C)$$

Now relativize the implication relation "$\Rightarrow$" with respect to B, obtaining the relativized implication relation "$\Rightarrow^B$" on S (Section 9.4.1). Thus, for any $E_1, \ldots, E_n$ and F in S, $E_1, \ldots, E_n \Rightarrow^B F$ if and only if $B, E_1, \ldots, E_n \Rightarrow F$. Note that (1) even though φ is modal with respect to "$\Rightarrow$," nevertheless φ is nonmonotonic with respect to "$\Rightarrow^B$." The reason is that although $C \Rightarrow^B B$, $\varphi(C) \not\Rightarrow^B \varphi(B)$. [If $\varphi(C) \Rightarrow^B \varphi(B)$, then $D \Rightarrow^B A$; that is, $B, D \Rightarrow A$. But in that case, $B \Rightarrow A$, since $B \Rightarrow D$. But that is impossible.] Note also that (2) φ is not classical with respect to "$\Rightarrow^B$." The reason is that $B \Leftrightarrow^B C$. If $\varphi(B) \Leftrightarrow^B \varphi(C)$, then $A \Leftrightarrow^B D$. But $D \not\Rightarrow^B A$, as noted in (1).

This is a case, then, in which there are two implication relations on a set, and an operator is modal with respect to one but not the other. There are cases, unlike the one just described, in which the operator is modal with respect to both implication relations:

> **Exercise 37.1.** Let $I = \langle S, \Rightarrow \rangle$ and $I_C = \langle S, \Rightarrow^C \rangle$ be two implication structures, where C is a member of S, and let φ be a necessitation operator on I that distributes over "$\Rightarrow$." Then φ distributes over "$\Rightarrow^C$" if and only if $C \Rightarrow \varphi(C)$. Verify that the reason the operator in the preceding example does not distribute over "$\Rightarrow^B$" is that $B \not\Rightarrow \varphi(B)$.

Example of a migrant modal though it is, φ is not strikingly modal in character. It is a modal that is devised for the occasion, but it does not seem to be the kind of modal operator that will unsettle anyone's theory of modals. There is, however, another example whose modal character is more obvious. It also uses a relativized implication relation, and when it migrates from an implication relation for which it is modal to a relativized cousin, it seems, as an operator, to lose its modal character:

Let $I = \langle S, \Rightarrow \rangle$ be a classical implication structure (with at least one thesis) that is incomplete with respect to negation. Then the operator φ_n that we called a necessity-style modal on I exists. Recall that $\varphi_n(A)$ is A^* (a fixed thesis of I) if A is a thesis of I, and is Z^* (a fixed antithesis of I) otherwise. As we saw (Theorem 29.3), this modal is an S_5 modal that has as strong a claim for being a necessity as does any modal. At any rate, it is clearly modal.

Since I is incomplete with respect to negation, let C be some member of S such that neither C nor $\neg C$ is a thesis of I. Then φ_n fails to be a modal operator with respect to "$\Rightarrow^C$" in a serious way: (1) φ_n is not monotonic with respect to "$\Rightarrow^C$," and (2) φ_n is not even classical with respect to "$\Rightarrow^C$."

Consider (1). Since $A \Rightarrow^C C$ for all A in S, if φ_n were monotonic with respect to "$\Rightarrow^C$," then $\varphi_n(A) \Rightarrow^C \varphi_n(C)$ for all A. Consequently, $C, \varphi_n(A) \Rightarrow \varphi_n(C)$ for all A. Let A be a thesis of I. Then $C \Rightarrow \varphi_n(C)$. Now $\varphi_n(C)$ is Z^*, since C is not a thesis. Therefore $C \Rightarrow Z^*$, so that $\neg C$ is an antithesis. But that is impossible. So φ_n is not monotonic with respect to "$\Rightarrow^C$."

As for (2), let A be any thesis of I. Since $C \Rightarrow A$, $C \Rightarrow^C A$. In addition, $A \Rightarrow^C C$. Therefore $A \Leftrightarrow^C C$. If φ_n were classical, then $\varphi_n(A) \Leftrightarrow^C \varphi_n(C)$. Consequently, $A^* \Leftrightarrow^C Z^*$. So $C, A^* \Rightarrow Z^*$. Since A^* is a thesis of I, $C \Rightarrow Z^*$. Since Z^* is an antithesis, $\neg C$ is a thesis of I. But that is impossible.

Exercise 37.2. Although φ_n is a necessitation modal on the structure $I = \langle S, \Rightarrow \rangle$ described earlier, it ceases to be a necessitation modal on the structure $I = \langle S, \Rightarrow^C \rangle$.

Clearly, then, we have a simple case of a necessity-style modal operator that suffers a loss of modal character with a shift away from the implication relation that gave it modal status in the first place. The moral is that one has to keep in mind that the logical operators as well as the modals are characterized relative to implication relations, and one cannot assume that the dependence on the relation can be suppressed. It is simply a mistake to take a perfectly good modal like φ_n and then note that when referred to the relativized structure, the modal no longer has the characteristic properties of modality. In the new setting, the old modal is an operator, but may not be modal any longer. It is simply not true that once a modal, always a modal.[5]

If one thinks of logical theory as ongoing and continually developing, as we do, then there is no denying the possibility that for good theoretical reasons changes might be made in the conditions for modality as we presently find them. In that case, the modal character of operators will need rethinking. But that, as we see it, is the typical situation in the history of logical theory, when "settled" theory meets "unsettled" examples. That is the source for much of the development of logical theory, and in principle it is no different for our theory of modal character than it is for logical theory generally.

APPENDIXES

A

An implication relation for the integers in the programming language BASIC

The discovery of the following underlying implication relation is due to D. T. Langendoen (private communication).

A.1 BASIC implication

In the BASIC programming language available on IBM personal computers (*BASIC Compiler 2.00, Fundamentals*, Boca Raton, Florida, 1985) there are many numeric functions called "logical operators." These functions are defined over a finite set of integers that are encoded in binary notation as strings of sixteen bits of 0's and 1's. The first bit is 0 if the integer is positive, and 1 if negative. That leaves fifteen bits for encoding, so that the range of these functions consists of all the integers from -32768 to $+32767$ (-2^{15} to $+2^{15}$). The representing string for any integer in this range, therefore, consists of an initial 0 or 1 according as it is positive or negative, and a tail end that depends on the binary representation of the integer. If the integer is positive, then the tail end consists of its binary representation; if the integer is negative, then the tail end is determined as follows: If the negative integer is $-m$, and the binary encoding of m has n digits, then calculate what integer together with $-2^{(n-1)}$ would sum to $-m$, and let its binary representation be at the tail end on the sixteen-bit string. Thus, 3, being positive, would be represented as 0000000000000011, the initial bit representing the positive character, and the tail end (11) being the binary representation of 3. The intermediate thirteen 0's bring the string to the standard sequence of sixteen, but they can, for convenience, be omitted, so that we think of the encoding as just 011. The integer -3, on the other hand, is represented as 101 [the initial 1 indicating the negative character, and the tail, 01, is the binary representation of the number that when added to $-2^{(3-1)}$ yields -3 (namely, 1)]. Thus, restricting ourselves for the moment to strings of length three (including the positive–negative head), the numbers -4, -3, -2, -1, 0, 1, 2, 3 will be encoded as 100, 101, 110, 111 ($= T$), 000 ($= F$), 001, 010, 011.

Let A and B be sequences of 0's and 1's. The operators of BASIC, the functions on one or more strings that encode some finite set of integers, are AND, OR, NEG, HYP (which is called "IMP" in the programming language), and EXOR and EQV (which we shall omit). These can be described as follows:

1. AND: $(A \text{ AND } B)_j = \min\{A_j, B_j\}$. That is, the jth member of the sequence $(A \text{ AND } B)$ is the minimum of the jth member of A and the jth member of B (0 is taken to be less than 1).
2. OR: $(A \text{ OR } B)_j = \max\{A_j, B_j\}$. That is, the jth member of the sequence $(A \text{ OR } B)$ is the maximum of the two items A_j and B_j.
3. NEG: $\text{NEG}(A_j) = 1 - A_j$.
4. HYP: $\text{HYP}(A, B)_j = \max\{1 - A_j, B_j\}$.

Thus, for example, using the encodings of -4 to 3 given earlier (1 AND 2) (that is, 001 AND 010) is 000 (that is, 3), whereas (1 OR 2) is 3.

These operations on strings have suggestive-sounding names for them, but it is not obvious why the string $(A \text{ AND } B)$ should be regarded as even analogous to conjunction, and it is even less obvious what NEG has to do with negation.

On our account of the logical operators, each is an operator relativized to an implication relation. There is no implication relation provided for the strings that encode integers; one has to be provided. The set S of strings of 0's and 1's of length sixteen (or of any uniform length) can be provided with an implication relation due to D. T. Langendoen, as follows:

Let $A_1, A_2, \ldots, A_n$ and B members of S. Then

(L) $A_1, \ldots, A_n \Rightarrow^L B$ holds if and only if (for all j) $B_j = 1$ if the jth members of all the A_i's are 1 (that is, for every j, either $B_j = 1$ or the jth member of some A_i is 0).

Exercise A.1. "$\Rightarrow^L$" is an implication relation on S.

What do the logical operators yield when they are applied to the implication structure $I_L = \langle S, \Rightarrow^L \rangle$? On our account, the conjunction, disjunction, negation, and hypothetical operators, when computed for this particular structure with the Langendoen implication relation, yield exactly the AND, OR, NEG, and HYP operations, respectively.

Thus, (1) $(A \text{ AND } B) \Rightarrow^L A$ (as well as B), and $(A \text{ AND } B)$ is the weakest (using "$\Rightarrow^L$") string to imply both A and B. That is, (2) if $T \Rightarrow^L A$ and $T \Rightarrow^L B$, then $T \Rightarrow^L (A \text{ AND } B)$ for every string of 0's and 1's of length sixteen that is in S. Thus, on this particular structure, AND is the conjunction operator. That is, $C(A, B) = (A \text{ AND } B)$.

Exercise A.2. Show that $N(A)$ = NEG (A). That is, (1) A, NEG$(A) \Rightarrow^L B$ for all B in S, and (2) NEG(A) is the weakest member of S (using "$\Rightarrow^L$") to satisfy (1). That is, for any T in S, if A, $T \Rightarrow^L B$ for all B in S, then $T \Rightarrow^L$ NEG(A). Similarly for OR and HYP.

Thus, for the implication structure $I_L = \langle S, \Rightarrow^L \rangle$, the negation operator N_L with respect to "$\Rightarrow^L$" is identical with the numeric function NEG. It is straightforward to check that the negation operator is classical, since for every string A in S, NEG(NEG(A)) = A. However, if the Langendoen implication relation $\Rightarrow^L$ is considered on a subset S^* of S, then it may turn out that the negation operator N_L is nonclassical on the structure $I^* = \langle S^*, \Rightarrow^L \rangle$ (see Exercise A.3), while NEG is not everywhere defined. Thus, NEG will not always be a negation operator on sets of strings of uniform length. However, it will be a negation operator so long as the set S consists of all strings of some uniform length.

Exercise A.3. Let S be the set of all three-digit sequences of 0's and 1's, and let S^* be the subset whose members are on the list 000, 010, 110, 111. Show that "$\Rightarrow^L$" holds between any members of the sequence if and only if they are identical or the first is to the left of the second in the sequence listed. Show that the negation operator on 010 yields 000, and on 000 it is 111. Thus, $NN(010) \not\Rightarrow^L 010$, since $111 \not\Rightarrow^L 010$, so that N is nonclassical on S^*. NEG (010), however, is 101, which is not in S^*, so that NEG is not everywhere defined on the structure $I^* = \langle S^*, \Rightarrow^L \rangle$.

Symmetric sequents as products of implication relations and their duals

Before we prove the various results, we need to state the conditions that are characteristic of the Gentzen symmetric relation used in his symmetric sequents. Here we shall use a formulation of the conditions that is based on the rules provided by Takeuti (1975).

Let us suppose that we have some nonempty set S. Let us employ, in this section only, the useful notation whereby A^*, B^*, C^*, ... indicate any finite (possibly empty) sequences of members of S, and continue to use the unasterisked A, B, C, ... to indicate the members of S.

We shall say that "$\Rightarrow^G$" is a *symmetric Gentzen relation on S* if and only if the following conditions hold (where A^*, B^* indicates the sequence of members of S that consists of the sequence A^* followed by the sequence B^*):

1. Weakening, or Dilution, comes in two parts:
   Left: If $A^* \Rightarrow^G B^*$, then $D, A^* \Rightarrow^G B^*$.
   Right: If $A^* \Rightarrow^G B^*$, then $A^* \Rightarrow^G B^*, D$.
2. Contraction, or Simplification, also in two parts:
   Left: If $D, D, A^* \Rightarrow^G B^*$, then $D, A^* \Rightarrow^G B^*$.
   Right: If $A^* \Rightarrow^G B^*, D, D$, then $A^* \Rightarrow^G B^*, D$.
3. Exchange, or Permutation, also in two parts:
   Left: If $A^*, C, D, E^* \Rightarrow^G F^*$, then $A^*, D, C, E^* \Rightarrow^G F^*$.
   Right: If $F^* \Rightarrow^G A^*, C, D, B^*$, then $F^* \Rightarrow^G A^*, D, C, B^*$.
4. Cut: If $A^* \Rightarrow^G B^*, D$ and $D, C^* \Rightarrow^G E^*$, then $A^*, C^* \Rightarrow^G B^*, E^*$.

Let us consider, first, the result that a symmetric Gentzen relation can be defined using an implication relation and its dual. Let $I = \langle S, \Rightarrow \rangle$ be an implication relation and let A^* and B^* be any (nonempty) finite sequences of members of S. We define a relation "$\Rightarrow^P$" as a relational product:

$$A^* \Rightarrow^P B^* \text{ if and only if for some } C \text{ in } S,$$
$$A^* \Rightarrow C \text{ and } B^* \Rightarrow^\wedge C.$$

Then we have the following result:

Theorem B.1. *Let $I = \langle S, \Rightarrow \rangle$ be an implication structure for which negation is classical, and the disjunction and conjunction are available of any members of S. Then the relational product "$\Rightarrow^P$," of "$\Rightarrow$" with its dual "$\Rightarrow^\wedge$" is a symmetric Gentzen relation on S.*

Proof. We need to check that "$\Rightarrow^P$" satisfies the conditions of Weakening, Contraction, Exchange, and Cut. Weakening is easy. For left weakening we need to show that if $A^* \Rightarrow^P B^*$, then $A^*, D \Rightarrow^P B^*$. Suppose the former. Then for some C in S, $A^* \Rightarrow C$, and $B^* \Rightarrow^\wedge C$. Since "$\Rightarrow$" is an implication relation, $D, A^* \Rightarrow C$. Since we have $B^* \Rightarrow^\wedge C$, we therefore have $D, A^* \Rightarrow^P B^*$. All the remaining conditions, other than Cut, are straightforward.

As for Cut, assume that (1) $A^* \Rightarrow^P D, B^*$ and (2) $D, C^* \Rightarrow^P E^*$. It remains only to show that $A^*, C^* \Rightarrow^P B^*, E^*$. Suppose that (1) and (2). From (1), we have $A^* \Rightarrow T$, and $D, B^* \Rightarrow^\wedge T$ for some T in S. Therefore $A^* \Rightarrow T$, and $T \Rightarrow [D \vee \text{Disj}(B^*)]$, since disjunctions are available in the structure. [Note that we used "$\vee$" to indicate the disjunction operator simply to avoid unnecessary notational complexity in the proof, and we let $\text{Disj}(B^*)$ be the disjunction of the members of the sequence B^*.] Consequently, $A^* \Rightarrow [D \vee \text{Disj}(B^*)]$. Moreover, from (2) we conclude that $D, C^* \Rightarrow U$ and $E^* \Rightarrow^\wedge U$ for some U in S. Therefore $U \Rightarrow \text{Disj}(E^*)$, with the result that $D, C^* \Rightarrow \text{Disj}(E^*)$. By using the assumption that negation is classical on the structure and that conjunctions and disjunctions always exist, it follows that $C^* \Rightarrow [N(D) \vee \text{Disj}(E^*)]$. Since we have $A^* \Rightarrow [D \vee \text{Disj}(B^*)]$, and the implication structure is classical, we conclude that $A^*, C^* \Rightarrow [\text{Disj}(B^*) \vee \text{Disj}(E^*)]$.

The preceding theorem tells us how to generate symmetric Gentzen relations from the appropriate implication relations on a structure.

The next theorem tells us that if there is a symmetric Gentzen relation on some nonempty set S, then under certain weak conditions it is equivalent to the relational product of some implication relation on the structure and its dual. That is,

Theorem B.2. *Suppose that we have a symmetric Gentzen relation "$\Rightarrow^G$" on a nonempty set S. Then there is an implication relation "$\Rightarrow^L$" defined on the set S (the restriction of "$\Rightarrow^G$" to*

the cases of single consequents). We assume that conjunctions and disjunctions of members of S with respect to the implication relation "$\Rightarrow^L$" always exist. Then it follows that $A^* \Rightarrow^G B^*$ holds if and only if $A^* \Rightarrow^L C$, and $B^* (\Rightarrow^L)^\wedge C$ for some C in S.

Proof. Suppose that "$\Rightarrow^G$" is a symmetric Gentzen relation on S. Then define a relation "$\Rightarrow^L$" as follows: $A^* \Rightarrow^L B$ if and only if $A^* \Rightarrow^G B$ ("L" is for "left"). It is easy to check, using the four conditions for symmetric Gentzen relations, that "$\Rightarrow^L$" *is an implication relation on S.* We want to show that for any A^* and B^*, $A^* \Rightarrow^G B^*$ if and only if for some C in S, $A^* \Rightarrow^L C$ and $B^* \Rightarrow^{L^\wedge} C$ [where "$\Rightarrow^{L^\wedge}$" is the dual of "$\Rightarrow^L$" – that is , "$(\Rightarrow^L)^\wedge$"]. Suppose, first, that $A^* \Rightarrow^G B^*$. We want to show that there is some C in S such that $A^* \Rightarrow^L C$ and $B^* \Rightarrow^{L^\wedge} C$. It is relatively easy to show that if conjunctions and disjunctions are characterized with respect to the implication relation "$\Rightarrow^L$," then $A^* \Rightarrow^G B^*$ if and only if $\text{Conj}(A^*) \Rightarrow^G B^*$ if and only if $A^* \Rightarrow^G \text{Disj}(B^*)$ [and, hence, if and only if $\text{Conj}(A^*) \Rightarrow^G \text{Disj}(B^*)$, where $\text{Conj}(A^*)$ is the conjunction of all the members of the sequence A^*, and $\text{Disj}(B^*)$ is the disjunction of all the members of the sequence B^*]. Therefore, if $A^* \Rightarrow^G B^*$, then $A^* \Rightarrow^G \text{Disj}(B^*)$. Consequently, $A^* \Rightarrow^L \text{Disj}(B^*)$, so that $A^* \Rightarrow^L [\text{Disj}(B^*) \vee \text{Conj}(A^*)]$. We would like to show that $B^* \Rightarrow^{L^\wedge} [\text{Disj}(B^*) \vee \text{Conj}(A^*)]$. That holds because $\text{Conj}(A^*) \Rightarrow^G \text{Disj}(B^*)$ (since $A^* \Rightarrow^G B^*$). Consequently, $\text{Conj}(A^*) \Rightarrow^L \text{Disj}(B^*)$. Therefore $[\text{Disj}(B^*) \vee \text{Conj}(A^*)] \Rightarrow^L \text{Disj}(B^*)$. Consequently, $B^* \Rightarrow^{L^\wedge} [\text{Disj}(B^*) \vee \text{Conj}(A^*)]$. [Recall that for any implication relation "$\Rightarrow$," $B^* \Rightarrow^\wedge A$ if and only if $A \Rightarrow \text{Disj}(B^*)$, provided disjunctions are available in the structure.] Thus, there is some C in S, namely, $[\text{Disj}(B^*) \vee \text{Conj}(A^*)]$, such that if $A^* \Rightarrow^G B^*$, then $A^* \Rightarrow^L C$ and $B^* \Rightarrow^{L^\wedge} C$. Conversely, suppose that $A^* \Rightarrow^L C$ and that $B^* \Rightarrow^{L^\wedge} C$ for some C in the structure. Then $C \Rightarrow^L \text{Disj}(B^*)$. Therefore $A^* \Rightarrow^L \text{Disj}(B^*)$. Consequently, $A^* \Rightarrow^G \text{Disj}(B^*)$. But the latter holds if and only if $A^* \Rightarrow^G B^*$. And that concludes the proof.

Symmetric Gentzen relations are not implication relations, because Transitivity fails when multiple consequents are present. That is, if B^* is not a single-member sequence, then there are cases in which $A^* \Rightarrow^G$

B^* and $B^* \Longrightarrow^G C^*$, but not $A^* \Longrightarrow^G C^*$. Nevertheless, it is possible to define the notion of the dual "$\Longrightarrow^{G^\wedge}$" of a symmetric Gentzen relation in a way that generalizes the notion of the dual of an implication relation:

Definition B.1. We define "$(\Longrightarrow^G)^\wedge$," the *dual of the Gentzen symmetric sequence relation* "$\Longrightarrow^G$," as follows: $A^* \Longrightarrow^{G^\wedge} B^*$ holds if and only if (1) for every T in S, if $T \Longrightarrow^G B_i$ (for all members B_i of the sequence B^*), then $T \Longrightarrow^G A^*$, and (2) for every T in S, if $A_i \Longrightarrow^G T$ (for every member A_i of the sequence A^*), then $B^* \Longrightarrow^G T$. Then we have the following:

Theorem B.3. *Let* "$\Longrightarrow^G$" *be a symmetric Gentzen relation on a nonempty set S (so that the relation* "$\Longrightarrow^L$," *which is just* "$\Longrightarrow^G$" *restricted to single consequents, is an implication relation on S). Assume, in addition, that conjunctions and disjunctions (with respect to the implication relation* "$\Longrightarrow^L$") *always exist. Then the dual of a symmetric Gentzen relation is just the converse relation. That is, $A^* \Longrightarrow^{G^\wedge} B^*$ if and only if $B^* \Longrightarrow^G A^*$.*

Proof. Suppose that $A^* \Longrightarrow^{G^\wedge} B^*$. We know that $\mathrm{Conj}(B^*) \Longrightarrow^G B_i$ (for all the members of the sequence B^*). Therefore, by (1), $\mathrm{Conj}(B^*) \Longrightarrow^G A^*$. Now we know that $B^* \Longrightarrow^G \mathrm{Conj}(B^*)$, so that, by Cut, we obtain the result that $B^* \Longrightarrow^G A^*$. Conversely, suppose that $B^* \Longrightarrow^G A^*$. If $T \Longrightarrow^G B_i$ (all B_i of B^*), then $T \Longrightarrow^L \mathrm{Conj}(B^*)$. Since $\mathrm{Con}(B^*) \Longrightarrow^L \mathrm{Disj}(A^*)$, $T \Longrightarrow^L \mathrm{Disj}(A^*)$. Therefore $T \Longrightarrow^G A^*$. Consequently, B.1(1) holds. Moreover, B.1(2) holds: Suppose that $A_i \Longrightarrow^G T$ (all A_i of A^*). Then $\mathrm{Disj}(A^*) \Longrightarrow^L T$. But $\mathrm{Con}(B^*) \Longrightarrow^L \mathrm{Disj}(A^*)$. So $\mathrm{Con}(B^*) \Longrightarrow^L T$. Therefore $B^* \Longrightarrow^G T$. Consequently $A^* \Longrightarrow^{G^\wedge} B^*$.

C

Component-style logical operators and relevance

Consider the logical operators when they are relativized to component implication. Let us call these operators *component conjunctions*, *component hypotheticals*, and so forth, when the implication relation is componential.

C.1 Component-style logical operators

Basically, the general picture of component-style logical operators is this: The logical operator O_c (the component-style version of the logical operator O) acts upon the elements $A, B, C, \ldots$, all of which belong to the same component of the implication structure, and assigns those elements of that component that the operator O assigns – if it assigns anything at all. If $A, B, C, \ldots$ do not all belong to the same component, then there is no member of S that O_c assigns to them. In other words, the component-style logical operators stay in the component of the elements that it acts upon; they are not component-hopping. Later we shall see what the situation is for each of the operators when they act on elements of S that may not all be in the same component.

C.2 Component-style conjunctions

In our preliminary (unparameterized) description of the conjunction operator, $C(A, B)$ was taken to be the weakest member of the structure that implied A as well as B. Implication is now taken to be component implication, "$\Rightarrow^c$," and conjunction is now taken to be the variant, *component conjunction*, $C_c(A, B)$:

1. $C_c(A, B) \Rightarrow^c A$, and $C_c(A, B) \Rightarrow^c B$, and
2. $C_c(A, B)$ is the weakest member (using "$\Rightarrow^c$") of the component containing A and B that implies (using "$\Rightarrow^c$") A as well as B.

It follows that if the conjunction $C_c(A, B)$ exists, then A and B belong to the same component of the implication structure [along with $C_c(A, B)$].

C.3 Component-style disjunctions

The relativization of the disjunction operator $D(A, B)$ to component implication satisfies these conditions:

1. $A \Rightarrow^c D_c(A, B)$, and $B \Rightarrow^c D_c(A, B)$, and
2. $D_c(A, B)$ is the strongest member (using "$\Rightarrow^c$") of the component containing A and B that is implied (using "$\Rightarrow^c$") by A as well as B.

Thus, as with conjunctions, if A and B belong to different components, then their component-style disjunction does not exist.

C.4 Component-style hypotheticals

Hypotheticals, relativized to component implication, satisfy the following conditions:

1. $A, H_c(A, B) \Rightarrow^c B$, and
2. $H_c(A, B)$ is the weakest member of the component containing A and B (using "$\Rightarrow^c$") for which (1) is satisfied.

Again, it is true that if A and B belong to different components, then their component-style hypothetical does not exist.

C.5 Component-style negations

The negation operator, by its very description, presents some problems for the formulation of a negation operator that is relativized to component implication. Recall that, in general, the negation of A, $N(A)$, is such that

1. $A, N(A) \Rightarrow B$ for all B in the structure, and
2. $N(A)$ is the weakest element in the structure (using "$\Rightarrow$") for which condition (1) is satisfied.

We cannot simply require that $A, N_c(A) \Rightarrow^c B$ for all B in the structure, since that would imply that all the members of the structure belong to one component. Thus, we adopt the following conditions for component-style negations:

1. $A, N_c(A) \Rightarrow^c B$ for all B in the component that contains both A and $N_c(A)$, and
2. $N_c(A)$ is the weakest member of the component containing A that satisfies condition (1).

Thus, there is a noticeable difference between our usual negation operator and this particular type of negation: An element together with its component-style negation does not "imply" ("$\Rightarrow^c$") all the members of the structure; it "implies" only all the members of the component to which A belongs.

Thus far we have experimented in two directions: We have been considering a modification of an implication relation on a structure when that structure has components. The resultant relation, component implication, fails to be an implication relation, for it does not satisfy the conditions of Dilution and Projection. Nevertheless, it is an example of the sort of relation sometimes called nonmonotonic implication. In addition, we adjusted the usual characterizations of the logical operators so that they can be regarded as relativized to component implication. The question that naturally arises concerns the implications that hold or fail to hold for component implication and component-style logical operators.

One starting place is a paper by Church (1951) on the weak implication relation. In it, a system is developed using four axioms expressed with the aid of a single connective "$\rightarrow$": (1) $A \rightarrow A$ (identity), (2) $A \rightarrow B \rightarrow .C \rightarrow A \rightarrow .C \rightarrow B$ (Transitivity), (3) $(A \rightarrow .B \rightarrow C) \rightarrow .B \rightarrow .A \rightarrow C$ (Permutation), and (4) $(A \rightarrow .A \rightarrow B) \rightarrow .A \rightarrow B$ (Contraction). Church's idea is that A is relevant to B if there is a deduction of a special sort from A to B, where the relevant kind of deduction is carefully described. As a result, it turns out that none of the following is a theorem:

1. $p \rightarrow (q \rightarrow p)$,
2. $p \rightarrow (q \rightarrow q)$,
3. $-p \rightarrow (p \rightarrow q)$, and
4. $-(p \rightarrow p) \rightarrow q$.

For component implication and the component-style logical operators, the counterparts are, in this special case:

(1') $p \Rightarrow^c H_c(q, p)$,
(2') $p \Rightarrow^c H_c (q, q)$,
(3') $N_c(p) \Rightarrow^c H_c(p, q)$, and
(4') $N_c(H_c(p, p)) \Rightarrow^c q$.

We can now see that all of (1')–(4') fail. Consider a structure with two components:

$$C_1: \quad A \qquad\qquad C_2: \quad B$$
$$\downarrow \qquad\qquad\qquad\qquad \downarrow$$
$$A^* \qquad\qquad\qquad\qquad B^*$$

(2') fails since $A \not\Rightarrow^c H_c(B, B)$. The reason is that $H_c(B, B)$ is the weakest member, D, of the second component, such that $B, D \Rightarrow^c B$. But $B, B^* \Rightarrow^c B$, so that $H_c(B, B)$ is just B^*. However, $A \not\Rightarrow^c B^*$ (for A and B^* are not in the same component; they are not relevant).

Condition (4') fails as well, since $N_c(H_c(B, B)) \not\Rightarrow^c A$. The reason is that $H_c(B, B)$ is just B^*. Now $N_c(B^*)$ is the weakest member, D, of the second component, such that $B^*, D \Rightarrow^c E$ for all E in C_2. So $N_c(B^*)$ is just B. But $B \not\Rightarrow^c A$, since A and B are in different components.

The failure of (1') and (3') is a more delicate matter. We know that if $H_c(A, B)$ exists, then $A, H_c(A, B) \Rightarrow^c B$. From the latter it follows that A and B are in the same component. But that is impossible. Therefore there is no hypothetical $H_c(A, B)$ in this particular structure. Can we say that (1') fails? The failure of implication is not like that of $A \not\Rightarrow B$, where A and B are elements in the structure, and the relation "$\Rightarrow^c$" does not hold between them. In the case of A and $H_c(B, A)$, there are no two elements that fail to be related by "$\Rightarrow^c$"; there is only one. However, the logical operators yield sets of elements that satisfy certain conditions, so that it can be shown that (1') and (3') fail. All that is needed is to recall that, officially, $H(A, B)$, in an implication structure $I = \langle S, \Rightarrow \rangle$, is the set of all C in S such that (1) $A, C \Rightarrow B$ and (2) for all T in S, if $A, T \Rightarrow B$, then $T \Rightarrow C$. To this characterization we then add some conditions that explain the use of the set $H(A, B)$ in implications, rather than its members. Thus, $A\, H(A, B) \Rightarrow B$ holds if and only if there is some D in $H(A, B)$ such that $A, D \Rightarrow B$ (any two such are equivalent). Similarly, $B \Rightarrow H(A, B)$ if and only if there is some D in $H(A, B)$ such that $B \Rightarrow D$ (any two such are equivalent). Thus, in the structure described earlier, (1') is false, for $A \Rightarrow^c H_c(B, A)$ if and only if there is some D in $H_c(A, B)$ such that $A \Rightarrow^c D$. But $H_c(B, A)$ is the empty set. Similarly, (3') fails as well: Suppose that $N_c(p) \Rightarrow^c H_c(p, q)$ for all p and q. Then for A and B, in particular, $N_c(A) \Rightarrow^c H_c(A, B)$. Now $N_c(A)$ is A^*, so that there is some D in $H_c(A, B)$ such that $A^* \Rightarrow^c D$. But $H_c(A, B)$ is the empty set, since A and B are in different components. Consequently, (3') fails.

Thus, (1')–(4') are all false, and there is much agreement with

Church's account of relevance. There are other interesting rejections as well:

(5') $H_c(p, p) \not\Rightarrow^c H_c(q, q)$,
(6') $C_c(p, N_c (p)) \not\Rightarrow^c q$, and
(7') $p, H_c(p, q) \not\Rightarrow^c q$

Thus, not all hypotheticals $H_c(p, p)$ imply each other, the conjunction of any p with its negation does not imply all q, and the condition that corresponds to modus ponens also fails.

These are familiar negative claims that can be found in many studies of relevance logic. From our observation that if component-style conjunction and disjunction of p with q exist, then p and q belong to the same component, we have the following consequences:

(8') $p \Rightarrow^c D_c (p, q)$ and
(9') $C_c(p, q) \Rightarrow^c p$

both fail. However, most systems of relevance logic that have conjunction and disjunction also have the axioms $p \rightarrow (p \lor q)$ and $(p \& q) \rightarrow p$, corresponding to (8') and (9') (Anderson and Belnap, 1975, p. 453). But the failure of (8') and (9') would not exclude component implication and component operators from the subject of relevance. After all, there are systems, as developed by W. Parry and J. Hintikka, that explore issues of relevance for which "$p \rightarrow (p \lor q)$" fails to be a theorem. So the matter of (8') and its dual (9') is somewhat moot.

Our concern has not been the advocacy of one notion of relevance over another, or one system of relevance logic over another. There are too few clear intuitions on what relevance requires, and too many systems of relevance logic that violate or compromise some of those intuitions. Our aim has been to indicate some resources that are available on our account of the logical operators that bear on these issues.

If we have an implication structure that has components, then one plausible account of relevance can be provided: A and B are relevant if and only if they belong to the same component. This is a nonsyntactical notion. The relation "$\Rightarrow^c$" (component implication) is a nonmonotonic relation. By adjusting the characterization of the logical operators with respect to such a relation, we obtain component-style logical operators. The interaction between these operators and component implication yields results that match up with some familiar results of relevance logic, but diverge from others. It is characteristic of this particular notion of relevance that *within* each component, it is logic as usual (classical or nonclassical). Only when the operators act on elements of different components do the familiar consequences of relevance logic emerge.

Notes

Chapter 1

1. Consequently, the account of each operator will not refer to or make use of any of the other operators.

2. In Part II, *Implication Relations*, we shall consider certain variations that concern additions or deletions from these six. The reference to "$\Rightarrow$" as a relation is a more general sense of that term than is usual, because the six conditions make it evident that it is finitary, but has no fixed adicity or degree. It is a subset of the union of all finite cartesian products of S with itself $(n > 1)$. It is important to note that those cases of implication associated with noncompact theories can be accommodated by recasting the implication relation as a binary relation $X \Rightarrow A$, where X is a subset and A is any member of S, and making the appropriate notational adjustments in the six conditions. Of course, conditions 3 and 4 will then become unnecessary, because X is a set.

3. A variety of examples and eloquent arguments for an abstract concept of implication can be found in Scott (1971). Further references and a discussion of the historical roots of this idea in the early works of P. Hertz and G. Gentzen can be found in Chapter 2.

4. There is a certain abuse of notation here. $C_{\Rightarrow}(A, B)$, on the official view, is a subset of S, not one of its members. However, we shall, for convenience, use "$C_{\Rightarrow}(A, B)$" to denote one of its members (if there are any). Because any two of its members are equivalent (by $\Rightarrow$), there is no harm done. When several implication relations on S are involved, more care is needed. The official characterization will say that an element K of S is in the set $C_{\Rightarrow}(A, B)$ if and only if C_1': $K \Rightarrow A$ and $K \Rightarrow B$. C_2': For any T in S, if $T \Rightarrow A$ and $T \Rightarrow B$, then $T \Rightarrow K$. Thus, the members of $C_{\Rightarrow}(A, B)$ are the weakest members of S to satisfy the condition C_1'.

5. In Section 9.2, note 3, it is observed that the various logical operators on an implication structure consisting of these Tarskian theories or systems turn out to be precisely the algebraic operations that Tarski introduced to study them, and the basic algebraic results that he demonstrated are familiar relations that hold between the logical operators. Thus, if we did not have Tarski to discover what the appropriate algebraic operations are on these sets of systems, we might come to them merely by considering the logical operators in this particular setting.

6. In Chapter 22 we introduce implication relations that are definable over individuals, and some that are suitable for names of individuals. They employ the calculus of individuals, and the basic idea is that one individual a implies

another, b, it and only if every part of a is a part of b, and $a_1, a_2, \ldots, a_n$ implies b if and only if every part of all the a_i's is a part of b. It is shown that the basic mereological operations are just the logical operators relativized to such an implication relation. There is also a brief discussion of the use of logical operators on names of individuals. For an interesting discussion of the issues involved in the possible negation of names, see Geach (1981). For an account of the calculus of individuals, or the whole–part calculus, see Goodman (1966), Lewis and Hodges (1968), and Hellman (1969).

7. In Chapter 23 it is shown how to provide an implication relation for interrogatives. This implication relation, together with a theory about what count as direct answers to certain kinds of interrogatives, yields a straightforward account of those interrogatives that are also hypotheticals. It should be noted that certain writers such as Belnap and Steele (1976) have remarked that it is mistaken to try to construct a logic of questions by providing rules of inference that will codify valid reasoning in this area. This observation seems to me to be correct. No one would try to give rules under which it would be valid to argue from "You are free" and "If you are free, will you marry me?" to the interrogative conclusion "Will you marry me?" Clearly, the implication relation here is not to be confused with a rule of inference. There are, as we shall see in the next chapter, many implication relations that cannot be construed as rules of inference – at least in the sense that when so construed they are not truth-preserving. Think of the implication relation of set inclusion between sets. No one is suggesting that sets occur as premises or conclusions in arguments. Implication relations, whether they are "inferential" or not, permit the sorting out of the various items in the structure into various logical types. Thus, on our view, there is a point to thinking about implication relations between interrogatives: it is not that of constructing sound arguments between interrogatives – there may not be any. The point of introducing implication relations for interrogatives is to enable interrogatives to be sorted into various logical types.

8. These stability results can be used to prove a general "homomorphic" stability result. Essentially, if one structure I is mapped by the function φ to another I', so that the elements in I are implicationally related with respect to I if and only if their corresponding images are implicationally related with respect to I', then the image of the conjunction (in I) of elements of I is equivalent (in I') to the conjunction (in I') of the images of those elements. Similar results hold for the other logical operators. Homomorphic stability of the operators can be obtained by applying the stability theorems to the set $\varphi[S]$, the set of all $\varphi(A)$, for A in S. I owe this nice observation to a referee for the press.

Chapter 2

1. There is an ambiguity in this way of stating the matter that is worth noting. Consider the conjunction operator as an example. On the one hand, for each implication structure I, there is the operator C_I, which we have described as the conjunction operator on I. On the other hand, there is the global operator, which assigns to each I, *the conjunction operator C_I*, which we

denote by C. Then $C(I) = C_I$. We shall call this global operator "conjunction" (no subscripting). It can be used to tell us the properties of conjunction over all the implication structures, whereas C_I tells us only about conjunction on I.

2. The abstract notion of an implication relation, in the sense that such relations can hold between sentential elements, as well as holding between classes, propositions, and events, was already suggested in the Hertz–Gentzen notion of a sentence*. The algebraic emphasis, in current studies of implication, comes from Tarski's study of the algebraic properties of the consequence relation. Both of these sources have been stressed by Scott (1971, 1974) and Gabbay (1981), among others.

3. See Gentzen (1934). There has been some very careful work on how this insight might be given a sharper formulation, whether it can be justified, and whether it can be generalized in such a way so that the case for the connectives becomes a special case of a general theory of meaning. See especially Prawitz (1977, 1980), Zucker and Tragesser (1978), and Dummett (1973).

4. One needs to show that the conditions that correspond to Gentzen's Introduction and Elimination rules can be formulated as statements that use an appropriate implication relation. However, it is easy to show that an implication relation can be defined over the set of expressions of this example in such a way that in all of Gentzen's Introduction and Elimination rules the items that are above the bar are related to the item below the bar by the defined implication relation.

5. As we noted in our discussion of conjunctions, there is a certain abuse of notation in this description. Officially, $H(A, B)$ will be taken as the set of all those members of the structure that are the weakest to satisfy H_1. Because they are all equivalent, there is no harm in using $H(A, B)$ as if it were some particular element of the structure.

6. There are other ways as well. Some writers have argued that the truth conditions for "$p \supset q$" show that it is a hypothetical. Such a proposal may be satisfactory in the end, but it is all too clear that the connection between hypotheticals and expressions like "$p \supset q$" is one that requires elaborate discussion. Cf. Grice (1989). On the other hand, the reply that the expression "$p \supset q$" is just the kind of expression that we *call* a hypothetical seems to me to miss the point entirely.

7. See Gentzen (1934).

Chapter 3

1. Gentzen (1934).

2. For example, Prawitz (1977, 1980) has provided a clear study of these issues and a perspicuous account of what is required of a theory of meaning in order to vindicate some of Gentzen's insights and give them a more general significance. The writings of M. Dummett, cited in Prawitz's articles and elsewhere, are devoted to a wider range of cases than mathematical or logical propositions, and Zucker and Tragesser (1978) have provided a clear discussion in which it is proposed that the meaning of a logical constant is given by the set of all its Introduction rules.

3. When the schema (I) for conjunctions is stated in its official form, using parameters $p_1, p_2, \ldots, p_n$, it looks like this:

   1. For any $p_1, p_2, \ldots, p_n$ in S, $C(p_1 \ldots, p_n, T)$ (i.e., for all $p_1, p_2, \ldots, p_n$ in S, $p_1, \ldots, p_n, T \Rightarrow A$, and $p_1, \ldots, p_n, T \Rightarrow B$), and
   2. If E is in S, then for any $p_1, p_2, \ldots, p_n$ in S if $C(p_1, \ldots, p_n, E)$, then $p_1, \ldots, p_n, E \Rightarrow T$.

   If we think of "A & B" as the conjunction of A with B, then condition 1 corresponds to Gentzen's Elimination rule for "&," and condition 2 reduces to the claim that $A, B \Rightarrow A$ & B, which corresponds to Gentzen's Introduction rule for "&."

4. These remarks about implicit definition are intended informally. Strictly speaking, in order to establish implicit definability one would have to provide a theory in which (1) the Introduction and Elimination conditions could be expressed. This means at the very least, that one has some notation available to express the relevant implication relation, and (2) it has to be *proved* that "$I(R)$ & $I^*(R) \to (U)[E(U) \leftrightarrow E^*(U)]$" is a consequence of the theory. Alternatively, the notion of implicit definability in a model can be used Enderton, 1972. Without such detail, the proof remains informal.

5. For penetrating studies of the relation between Introduction and Elimination rules, one should consult Prawitz (1965, 1977, 1980) and the works of M. Dummett cited in the latter two works for a fuller account of how a theory of meaning is supposed to be linked with those rules.

Chapter 4

1. The relevant papers are by Prior (1960) and Belnap (1962), followed by Prior's reply (1964).

2. Disjunction ("or"), however, seems to be a proposition-forming operator for Mill, unlike "and," whereas "P or Q," for Mill, means that Q is inferable from the denial of P. In addition, the hypothetical "If P, then Q" means for him that Q is inferable from P. These unusual accounts of the English logical particles do not seem to have contemporary interest. Yet is it worth noting that Mill's views on conjunction, disjunction, and the hypothetical can be reconstructed on our account of the logical operators. On our theory, the logical operators are relativized to implication relations. Let us say that an implication relation "$\Rightarrow^M$" is Millean if and only if $A_1, \ldots, A_n \Rightarrow^M B$ if and only if some $A_j \Rightarrow^M B$. [Equivalently, if T is any set of sentences, and $Cn(T)$ is the set of all consequences of finitely many T's then $Cn(T)$ is the union of all $Cn(U)$, for all members U.] This special kind of implication relation, together with the customary definitions of conjunction, disjunction, and the hypothetical, leads to the three views held by Mill. The same implication relation sheds some light on Mill's rather strange view of the syllogism. These remarks are intended only to illustrate the resources that are availabble for a theory that relativizes the logical operators to implication relations. It is possible to provide a uniform motivation and theory for his views. We do not claim to have "uncovered" Mill's motivation or theory of the three operators. On our account, which is not restricted to the Millean implication relation, it sometimes may happen that for items P and Q there is

no conjunction of them in a structure; on Mill's account it always happens. In this connection it also should be noted that Johnson (1964) thought that there is a special sense of "and" – the enumerative sense – that is like the sense that Mill gave to that particle: It is a way of listing items. However, Johnson did not argue that "and" always has this enumerative sense.

3. Both Belnap and Prior consider only the situation where the connective sign is embedded in sentences. Thus, the cases they discuss are limited to those kinds of items that can have signs embedded in them. The structures that we discuss are not limited to these. However, in the remainder of this section, we shall consider what our account of conjunction looks like when restricted to such items.

4. These are essentially the ones that we have listed, with these differences: The first condition we list is taken by Gentzen and Belnap as an axiom, and the remainder are taken as rules of inference. We, on the other hand, have taken the whole ensemble as conditions for a relation to be an implication relation, and we do not distinguish between those that are axioms and those that are rules. Belnap uses "⊢" where we use the double arrow, ("⟹"). Belnap is careful to indicate that by this use of "⊢" he allows us to understand either a syntactic notion of deducibility or some semantic concept of logical consequence. In either case, of course, some care is needed so that the connectives to be defined will not occur in the characterization of "⊢," whichever way that concept is understood. On our account, as we have noted, the double arrow is not restricted to deducibility relations.

5. There is potential trouble lurking here for Belnap's deducibility relation "⊢*" that extends "⊢." The extending relation has to be different from "⊢" because it relates sentences that "⊢" does not. And it also has to satisfy the structural rules. However, the extending deducibility relation has to be characterized without the help of the expressions "P & Q." Otherwise it would not be structural, because it would depend for its characterization on the composition of some of the sentences. What assurance, then, is there that such a structural extending relation exists? Of course, "and" (or "&") is defined by its role in inference, but the deducibility relation in question is not "⊢," but "⊢*." Because the latter has not been shown to be a structural relation, it is not clear that the connective "&" has been properly defined, even by Belnap's own requirements for such a definition.

6. The conservativeness shows, according to Belnap, that the connective exists. In fact, given the background theory of inference, it can also be shown that there is only one such connective satisfying the Introduction and Elimination conditions that he has laid down for "&." If "#" is another connective satisfying the matching conditions for "&," then it can be proved that P & Q ⊢* P # Q, and conversely. Thus, the results of forming the sentences "P & Q" and "P # Q" are equivalent by the deducibility relation in the extended structure. Some subtlety is required in establishing the uniqueness of the connective, for one has to consider an extension of S that contains the expressions "P # Q" as well as "P & Q," with matching Introduction and Elimination rules for each connective. The question is whether or not it makes a difference if one extends the original structure in stages: first from S to $S_\&$ (extending the deducibility relation also), and then extending this

extension again, to $(S_\&)_\#$ (again extending the extended deducibility relation). Or does one use the reverse order, extending to $S_\#$ in the first stage, or does one just extend S to a structure that simultaneously contains both connectives? At any rate, this is a secondary issue when compared with the problem whether or not there is such a connective as "&" in the first place.

7. "Shape" is a little too strong a word here, because it obviously does not matter whether "&" or "#" or some other sign is used as the connective. What is important about the connective is that it have some shape, though it does not matter what shape that may be.

8. This assumes that the "tonk" operator is totally defined on a structure, an assumption that Prior and Belnap share. If that assumption is relaxed, then "tonk" will be a partially defined function on the structure, having a value on a pair (A, B) if and only if A and B are equivalent.

Chapter 5

1. There are versions of Cut, other than that presented here, that yield the transitivity of implication. Not all of them are equivalent; see Shoesmith and Smiley (1978).

2. This is a nice observation brought to my attention by Professor Jody Azzouni, even though it may not be decisive. Those who think of using sets of items rather than sequences take "$\Rightarrow$" to be a binary relation, thus restoring the fixed degree. Nevertheless, it is still taken as a relation. On the other hand, Anderson and Belnap (1975) think of the sign "$\vdash$" in Gentzen-style sequents $A, B \vdash C$ (they call them "consequtions") as a connective. Just as "$A \& B$" is a conjunction of A and B, so they regard "$A \vdash B$" as a conseqution of A and B. They get around the problem of thinking of "$\vdash$" as a connective of finite but no fixed degree by thinking of $A, B \vdash C$ as a nesting of entailments: A entails that (B entails that C), thus construing the many-term sequent by nestings of the binary connective "$A \vdash B$" (that A entails that B).

3. It is true, as Smiley (1978) has noted, that Hertz, at least in his first paper (1922), did say that he thought of his "sentences" as "nothing but formal 'implications'" in the sense of Russell. He might have meant only that the arrow had the formal properties of Russell's strict implication. The arrow could not have been literally Russell's notion, because strict implication appeals to quantification, and quantification is not introduced by Hertz in this part of his theory.

4. Gentzen (1934) uses the single arrow to form *sequents* $A_1, \ldots, A_n \rightarrow B_1, \ldots,$ B_m, where the A_i's and B_j's are now formulas of a logical language with various logical connectives. For the single consequent case $A_1, \ldots, A_n \rightarrow B$, we understand him to mean what he had one year earlier called Hertzian sentences.

Chapter 6

1. The proof of this for each system L is usually called the elimination theorem for L. Elimination theorems provide a powerful means for proving significant

metamathematical results – beginning with Gentzen's *Hauptsatz*. But as Scott (1974) has noted, it is not true that the Cut rule is always eliminable.

Chapter 7

1. Somewhat more generally, if F is any set (finite or infinite) of sentences of the theory, one says that $F \vdash B$ if and only if there is a finite sequence of sentences $C_1, \ldots, C_m$ such that each C_i is either an axiom or a member of F, and $C_1, \ldots, C_m \vdash B$. See Mendelson (1987).
2. Again, one can consider any set (finite or infinite) of sentences of the theory and say that $F \Vdash B$ if and only if every interpretation under which all the sentences of F are assigned the value "true" also assigns "true" to B.
3. The relevant papers are by Tarski (1935, 1936), Scott (1971, 1974), and Gabbay (1981).
4. See Appendix B concerning dual implication relations and the relational product of an implication relation with its dual.

Chapter 8

1. This concept was more or less suggested in Gentzen's first paper (1933).
2. The bisection implication relation that is based upon such a partition could appropriately be called a *material implication relation*. It is an implication relation, but it is not to be confused with the material conditional, which is not a relation between sentences. These differences will emerge more sharply when we consider what the logical operators are on implication structures with bisection implications. As we shall see, there is a clear difference between "$A \Rightarrow^T B$" and the hypothetical "$H_T(A, B)$" relative to that implication relation. It is the latter that corresponds to the material conditional.
3. See Smorynski (1977, p. 854).
4. This result is also proved by Scott (1974) in a general setting, which, like this one, requires no reference to connectives or logical operators. Scott has aptly identified the theorem as Lindenbaum's.

Chapter 9

1. The operation of taking the power set of any set is not one of these logical operators; it is, as we shall see, a modal operator on sets (see Section 32.1).
2. Tarski (1935, 1936).
3. Tarski was surely aware of the logical character of his algebraic operations. He referred to those operations as "logical" when he wrote of the logical sum and the logical complement. Even more indicative is his description of the condition that the closure of the union of X with its complement is S, as the law of excluded middle for the theory X. Tarski's Theorem 17 proved (Corcoran, 1983) that the law of excluded middle holds of X if and only if X is finitely axiomatizable (X is the set of consequences of a single member of S), so that the law of excluded middle will fail exactly when the theory X is

not finitely axiomatizable. He recognized, therefore, that there is a close connection between Heyting's "intuitionistic sentential calculus" and his "calculus of systems." But he thought of the two structures as correlates and as analogous, rather than as a case of the logical operators operating on two different structures.

4. Associated with each implication relation "$\Rightarrow^i$" on individuals there is another, "$\Rightarrow^n$," which is an implication relation on the names of individuals. The implication relation "$\Rightarrow^n$" holds between names of individuals if and only if the implication relation "$\Rightarrow^i$" holds between the corresponding individuals who are named. The two implication relations "$\Rightarrow^i$" and "$\Rightarrow^n$" are closely related, but they are not coextensional. The implication relation "$\Rightarrow^i$" on individuals yields the interesting result that the logical operators with respect to them are just the mereological operations of the calculus of individuals. The operators with respect to implications on names yield interesting but much more speculative results that concern the problem of phrasal conjunction in English.

5. See Goodman (1966, pp. 46–61) and the references cited there to the work of Lesniewski, presented in a streamlined account by Tarski (1937) and by Leonard (1940, pp. 45–55). Also of interest are Lewis and Hodges (1968) and Hellman (1968).

6. Moreover, the theorems and nontheorems of the calculus of individuals turn out to be just the familiar logical theses and nontheses of classical implication structures. This is the same kind of result we saw when we noted that the central algebraic operations of Tarski's calculus of systems are just the logical operators with respect to a special implication relation on Tarskian theories, and the theses of the calculus of systems turn out to be the theses of a nonclassical implication structure.

7. The useful but somewhat unfamiliar feature of the sum of individuals is that the sum of individuals is an individual even though its parts may not be contiguous. For a spirited defense of the idea, the reader should consult the classic discussion by Goodman (1966).

8. The discovery of the implication relation that underlies the numerical computations for BASIC is due to D. T. Langendoen (private communication). Those results are described in Appendix A.

9. See Section 29.2.

10. For a subtle discussion of just how the dual of an implication relation might be related to arguments, one should study the discussion of Shoesmith and Smiley (1978, pp. 1–6).

11. The best source for studying relevance logics is Anderson and Belnap (1975).

12. But for those who do not, it is possible to refine the notion of a component to take possible nontransitivity into account by introducing a sequence of refinements within each component of the structure.

For any A in S, let the first-order *span* of A, $S_1(A)$, be the set of all C such that either $A \Rightarrow C$ or $C \Rightarrow A$. The $(n + 1)$-order span of A, $S_{n+1}(A)$, is the set of all C for which there is some C^* in $S_n(A)$ such that either $C \Rightarrow C^*$ or $C^* \Rightarrow C$.

Exercise 1. Show that for any A, (1) the sequence of $S_n(A)$'s is a nondecreasing sequence of sets, (2) for any n, A, and B, A is a member of $S_n(B)$ if and only if B is a member of $S_n(A)$, and (3) the union of all the spans of A is the component $C(A)$ that contains A.

Exercise 2. Say that A and B are relevant to the nth degree $A R_n B$, if and only if A is in $S_n(B)$, where n is the smallest natural number for which this is so. Then, for all n, R_n is reflexive and symmetric, but not necessarily transitive (for this case, note that in a structure in which A implies B and C, but neither of them implies the other, then $B R_1 A$ and $A R_1 C$, but not $A R_1 C$).

13. The Projection condition also fails for "$\Rightarrow^c$." However, it and the Dilution condition are equivalent, given the remaining conditions on implication relations. And "$\Rightarrow^c$" satisfies all the conditions other than Dilution and Projection.

Chapter 11

1. The conditions for being a hypothetical that take seriously the idea that $H_\Rightarrow(A, B)$ is a special set of elements of S can be described this way: Let $H_\Rightarrow(A, B)$ be the set of all members of S that are hypotheticals with antecedent A and consequent B. Then for any member of C of S, C is a member of $H_\Rightarrow$ if and only if (1) $A, C \Rightarrow B$ and (2) for any T in S, if $A, T \Rightarrow B$, then $T \Rightarrow C$.
2. In his discussion of probabilistic entailment (Adams, 1975, pp. 56–68).
3. See Lewis (1973, pp. 26–8) for the case of counterfactuals with true antecedents.
4. One might wonder how there can be any interaction between the various operators, given their "purity." In particular, how can a change in the features of one operator sometimes bring about a change in the features of another? The changes wrought by intuitionistic negation upon the features of disjunction provide a case in point. However, in a general way one can see how it can happen. For example, a change in the negation operator N, such that $H(NN(A,) A)$ was no longer a thesis, but Theorem 11.1 was left intact (as is the case for intuitionism), would imply that there was a change in the implication relation. And a shift in the implication relation could, of course, affect the features that the other operators have.
5. Church (1956, ex. 12.6, p. 84).
6. By far the most subtle of the defenses has been given by Grice (1989). One should not overlook how widespread the adherence to a material conditional account is. It certainly dominates the textbook literature, where it is defended, sometimes with qualification. Usually it is proposed as the best account of English conditionals available and is coupled with the admission that there are cases in which it does not do well at all. This is not Grice's view; he admits no untoward cases. On the other hand, the literature from F. Ramsey and N. Goodman onward certainly shows what an uphill battle is involved in the defense of a material conditional account of English con-

ditionals. Moreover, the work of D. Lewis and R. Stalnaker, to name but two from an extensive literature, indicates how deep the intuition is that English may contain many different kinds of conditionals, each requiring a subtle semantic theory much beyond the simple one usually provided for the material conditional.

7. Grice certainly has some effective replies. Moreover, if it is granted that there is some operator that yields some true conditionals with false antecedents, and some false ones, then clearly that operator is not extensional on the structure under study. However, the single arrow or horseshoe of the classical sentential calculus is not guaranteed to be extensional unless one rules out the nonnormal truth-value assignments (see Chapter 19). So to compare the truth values of the relevant conditionals of English with their material conditional versions, we would have to guarantee that truth and falsity were ascribed to the English conditionals by what one could think of as a normal truth-value assignment. Otherwise, if nonnormal assignments are being used, then even the material conditional will fail to be extensional. Now I do not have any clear idea for deciding such an issue. But it is an issue that should not be begged by too quick a use of the so-called mismatch of truth values.

Chapter 12

1. Officially, because $N(A)$ is a possibly empty subset of S, we should say that for every A in S, C is in $N(A)$ if and only if (1) $A, C \Rightarrow B$ for all B in S and (2) for any T in S, if $A, T \Rightarrow B$ for all B in S, then $T \Rightarrow C$.

2. On the official view of the negation operator, $N(A)$ is a subset of equivalent members of S. So, officially, $N[S]$ is the union of all the sets $N(A)$ for all A in S. This takes care of the cases in which $N(A)$ may be empty.

Chapter 13

1. Recall (Chapter 1) that when we write officially that $C(A, B) \Rightarrow D$, when $C(A, B)$ exists, we assume that $C(A, B)$ is a nonempty subset of S and that $E \Rightarrow D$ for every E in $C(A, B)$. If for some D, $C(A, B) \Rightarrow D$, then $C(A, B) \neq \varnothing$. If $C(A, B)$ is empty, then $C(A, B) \not\Rightarrow D$ for every D. Similar remarks hold for $D \Rightarrow C(A, B)$. Parallel remarks hold for all the other operators.

2. It is possible, in the particular case of conjunction (but not, as far as I am aware, for the other logical operators) to improve on this result by relaxing the assumption that S is closed under C^*. The simplification depends upon the assumption that $A, B \Rightarrow C(A, B)$, which is available if one uses the parameterized account of conjunction. In this chapter, however, only the simple unparameterized account of the operators is under study.

   On the assumption that $A, B \Rightarrow C(A, B)$, we have $A, B \Rightarrow^* C(A, B)$. Because $C^*(A, B) \Rightarrow^* A$ (and B), we obtain $C^*(A, B) \Rightarrow^* C(A, B)$. Conversely, $C(A, B) \Rightarrow^* A$ (and B), because $C(A, B) \Rightarrow A$ (and B). Therefore, $C(A, B) \Rightarrow^* C^*(A, B)$, by C_2.

Chapter 14

1. I do not know of any discussion of the dual of the hypothetical for classical logical systems. There is a study that we alluded to earlier, by Lopez–Escobar (1981), of the dual of the hypothetical for intuitionistic sentential and predicate logics. He discussed the intriguing problem whether or not the addition to the intuitionistic predicate logic of the dual of the hypothetical, with appropriate axioms, should count as an intuitionistic connective (such an addition yields a nonconservative extension of intuitionistic predicate calculus).
2. Alternatively, define $D(A_1, \ldots, A_n)$ as follows: (1) For any T in S, if $A_i \Rightarrow T$ $(1 \leq i \leq n)$, then $D(A_1, \ldots, A_n) \Rightarrow T$, and (2) $D(A_1, \ldots, A_n)$ is the weakest to satisfy condition (1). It follows immediately from (1) that $A_i \Rightarrow D(A_i \ldots, A_n)$ for all A_i (same proof as for Theorem 14.1), and from (2) it follows that if $A_i \Rightarrow B$ for each A_i, then $D(A_1 \ldots, A_n) \Rightarrow B$.

Chapter 15

1. Instead of thinking of the parametric and nonparametric conditions as different conditions on the hypothetical, we could have introduced two different logical operators – the parametric and the nonparametric (simple) hypotheticals – and studied how they are related (e.g., it is easy to see that if they both exist on any structure, then they are equivalent, as well as that in some structures the nonparametric operator can exist but not the parametric one; as we noted earlier, if the parametric operator exists in a structure, so does the nonparametric one).

Chapter 16

1. This corresponds to the schema K of Lemmon and Scott (1977). It is not a theorem of the intuitionistic sentential calculus.

Chapter 17

1. The reader should consult a paper by Lopez–Escobar (1981) for a discussion of this operator in connection with intuitionistic connectives.

Chapter 18

1. This nice formulation of the problem can be found in Enderton (1972, pp. 39–44).
2. By "symmetric hypothetical" we mean a logical operator that captures the character of "if and only if." Thus, it is a function $SH(A, B)$, that satisfies two conditions: (1) A, $SH(A, B) \Rightarrow B$ and B, $SH(A, B) \Rightarrow A$, and (2) $SH(A, B)$ is the weakest member of the structure to satisfy the first condition. That is, if for any U in S, A, $U \Rightarrow B$, and $U \Rightarrow A$, then $U \Rightarrow SH(A, B)$.

Chapter 19

1. With the exclusion of those structures that have only one element, for the notion we shall use is based upon bisections on the structure.
2. The use of sets or properties instead of abstract values like "t" and "f" is an insight due to Scott (1974).
3. Thus, we do not see that the truth tables for an operator determine its meaning or individuate it from the other logical operators. Given the characterization of the operators, it is a provable result that each of the operators has its associated distribution pattern if and only if it is extensional.
4. See Church (1956, ex. 19.10, fn. 199) for an account of nonnormal interpretations and references to the earlier work of Carnap and Bernstein. Shoesmith and Smiley (1978, p. 3) have some perceptive comments about the exclusion of these nonstandard interpretations.
5. It is suggestive not only to think of K and L of a strong bisection as truth values but also to extend this way of looking at truth values to the case of multiple truth values such as t, f_1, f_2, and f_3, as corresponding to the partition L, K_1, K_2, and K_3, and, in general, to think of multiple truth values as associated with the multiply membered partitions of an implication structure. The distribution patterns of those multiple values will then be determined by the logical operators on those structures. Unfortunately, the few results from such an approach are not sufficiently systematic to yield a general account.

Chapter 20

1. This is a modification of the Tarski–Mostowski description of a propositional function, which is a mapping of E^* to a truth value (t or f). To avoid confusion with that notion, we use "predicate" for the mappings from E^* to S (rather than to $\{t, f\}$), although the use of "predicate" has its problems, because usually it is used for linguistic expressions (or sets of linguistic expressions) rather than, as here, for functions. The use of "property" would be worse, for it would raise too many philosophical issues that are not relevant. See Corcoran (1983, p. 191), Mostowski (1979), and Halmos (1962).
2. Tarski and Mostowski require that the predicates of formal languages have finite support. That is, of course, standard practice. We have left the matter open for the predicates of extended structures, because there might be some use for them.
3. Another way of getting the benefit of this definition consists in requiring that for every member A of the set S there be a constant predicate P_A in Pr such that for every s in E^*, $P_A(s) \Longleftrightarrow A$. We can then cover the cases in which predicates as well as members of S are present, by replacing each of the members of S by its corresponding constant predicate, and using the implication relation "$\Longrightarrow^*$" for predicates of Theorem 20.1.
4. The requirement for existence of conjunctions can be relaxed by using the parametric conditions for U_i. Note, in the following proof, that from the step $U_i(P_1), \ldots, U_i(P_n) \Longrightarrow^* Q \circ J_e^i$ it follows that $U_i(P_1) \Longrightarrow^{*\Gamma} Q \circ J_e^i$ (for all e in E), where $\Gamma = \{U_i(P_2), \ldots, U_i(P_n)\}$. Consequently, by parameterized

universal quantification, $U_i(P_1) \Rightarrow^{*\Gamma} U_i(Q)$. Therefore $U_i(P_1), \ldots, U_i(P_n)$ $\Rightarrow^* U_i(Q)$.

5. Let E, S, and "$\Rightarrow$" be as described earlier. Define the predicates as follows: For any s in E^* (infinite sequences of members of E), let $P(s)$ be A if s_1 is either e_1 or e_2, and let $P(s)$ be B if s_1 is e_3. Let $Q(s)$ be A if s_1 is e_3, and let $Q(s)$ be B if s_1 is either e_1 or e_2. And the disjunction mapping $D^*(P, Q)$ that assigns to each s in E^* the value $D(P(s), Q(s))$ in S, as well as P, Q, and R, is assumed to be in Pr. It is easy to check that these predicates all have support $\{1\}$, and by essentially the same computations as used earlier it follows that $U_1(D^*(P, Q))$ is C, and $U_1(P)$ and $U_1(Q)$ are both R. Therefore $U_1(D^*(P, Q)) \not\Rightarrow^* D^*(U_1(P), U_1(Q))$, because $C \not\Rightarrow D$.

Chapter 23

1. I have relied heavily on Belnap and Steel (1976); there is an enormous literature that is admirably surveyed in that volume (by Urs Egli and Hubert Schleichert). In our discussion we assume that the answers to questions are sentential, but we do not assume that there is any reduction of questions to answers. Furthermore, we do use a concept of implication for questions. These issues are controversial, and the literature on them is well represented in the Bibliography. Of special interest on these issues are the writings of C. L. Hamblyn, D. Harrah, A. N. Prior, and J. J. Katz (1977).
2. The three examples are from Belnap and Steel (1976, pp. 95–9). The fact that the hypothetical question (1) is put in English with the use of the subjunctive is not an essential feature of hypothetical questions. As they note, hypothetical questions can also be put in English by using future-tense conditions.

Chapter 24

1. See Mendelson (1987, pp. 37–9).
2. As in Mendelson (1987, pp. 39–40).

Chapter 25

1. By a modal *system M*, following the usage of Segerberg (1971), we shall mean roughly a set of sentences some of which are the "axioms," including the usual logical connectives, as well as the box, $\Box$, and rules of inference including modus ponens, necessitation (If A is a theorem, then so too is $\Box A$.) and a rule of substitution. Also, there may be certain axioms in addition to those of, say, first-order logic: (1) $\Box(p \rightarrow q) \rightarrow (\Box p \rightarrow \Box q)$, (2) $\Box(p \ \& \ q) \leftrightarrow \Box p \ \& \ \Box q$ (3) $\Box p \rightarrow p$, (4) $\Box p \rightarrow \Box\Box p$, and (5) $\Box(\Box p \rightarrow p) \rightarrow \Box p$ provide a small sample. Usually, a dual operator, diamond, $\Diamond$ (where "$\Diamond$" is sometimes defined as "$\neg\Box\neg$"), is included, and the list can be extended to include (6) $\Diamond p \rightarrow \Box\Diamond p$, (7) $p \rightarrow \Box\Diamond p$, and (8) $\Box p \rightarrow \Diamond p$.
2. These correspond to the use of the distribution axioms (1) and (2), with the addition of (3), (4), (3) and (4), (3) and (6), (3) and (7), (3) and (8), and (5). In general, we use parentheses to indicate modal *systems*. Thus, "(T)"

indicates the familiar modal system, whereas "T" indicates condition (3), and "S_5" indicates condition (6), whereas "(S_5)" refers to the familiar modal *system.*

3. Similar options arise in the way that truths are registered – i.e., as "It is true that A" (connective style), or "'A' is true" (predicate style). Here, too, there is common ground afforded by thinking of truth as an operator rather than as a connective or as a predicate.

4. There are some real difficulties in trying to think of necessity as a predicate, in certain logical systems (Montague, 1963). We shall see that these difficulties do not carry over to an operator account of modals. There are parallel difficulties for "truth" as a predicate in systems in which the diagonalization lemma is provable. A truth operator is not vulnerable to diagonalization arguments, since "truth" is not a predicate of the language.

5. If one chose to use $\Box_c$ (connective style) or $\Box_p$ (predicate style), the values assigned by the associated operator might not be equivalent. We do not assume that there is a systematic reduction one way or the other. If the values are different, so too are the associated modal operators. Our point is that in that case we would then have two operators, and the modal character of each would have to be determined separately.

Chapter 26

1. Readers familiar with the study of normal modal systems might think, in light of the last observation, that the operators characterized by our two conditions are just the normal modals. However, the two conditions are weaker than those for normality. One reason is that normal systems usually require a rule of substitution. That rule makes sense only if the items in the structure are syntactical. The more important difference is this: Normal systems always assume a rule of necessitation ($\Box T$ is a theorem if T is). On our account, not every modal operator will be a necessitation modal [$\varphi(T)$ is a thesis if T is]. Necessitation modals are special types of modal operators, and later we shall provide a number of necessary and sufficient conditions for them. We shall show that not every operator that satisfies our two conditions is a necessitation modal. Thus, modal operators, according to the two conditions, are, appearances to the contrary, weaker than normal modals.

2. There are those (van Fraassen, 1971; Kneale and Kneale, 1962) who have held that "truth" is a modal. Kneale and Kneale's reason for doing so seems quite weak to me. Essentially, it is that if "necessarily true" is modal, then so too is "true." If truth is taken as an operator T (Feferman, 1984), and the relevant axiom is $T(A) \Leftrightarrow A$, then T cannot be a modal, since it would distribute over the implication relation as well as its dual. On our account of modals, for T to be modal (assuming that negation is classical), one would have to maintain that $T(A \lor \neg A) \not\Rightarrow T(A) \lor T(\neg A)$, and also reject the relevant axiom given above. This is exactly what van Fraassen does: He holds to the law of excluded middle [$T(A \lor \neg A)$] and rejects bivalence [$T(A) \lor T(\neg A)$]. This is exactly what one has to do to maintain that the truth operator is modal, on our account of modal operators. For a more detailed discussion of the truth operators, see Chapter 33.

Chapter 27

1. I want to thank Charles Parsons for raising this as a possible problem for the articulation of an intuitionist view of mathematical propositions.

2. The nonextensionality of a modal is proved for those structures in which whenever $E \not\Rightarrow F$, there is a normal bisection $T = \langle K, L \rangle$ for which E is in L ("true") and F is in K ("false"). Here is a sketch of how to obtain such a bisection (for denumerable structures): Suppose that $E \not\Rightarrow F$, and let A_1, A_2, ... be an enumeration of the members of the structure. Let $U_0 = \{E\}$; let $U_1 = U_0 \cup \{A_1\}$ if $U_0 \cup \{A_1\} \not\Rightarrow F$, and U_0 otherwise; and let $U_{n+1} = U_n \cup \{A_n\}$ if $U_n \cup \{A_n\} \not\Rightarrow F$, and U_n otherwise ($n = 1, 2, \ldots$). Note that $U_0 \subseteq U_1 \subseteq U_2 \subseteq \ldots$. Let U be the union of all the U_i's, and let U^* be the strong closure (under "$\Rightarrow$") of U. The claim is that the bisection $T = \langle K, L \rangle$, where $L = U^*$ and $K = S - U^*$, is a normal bisection of the structure $I = \langle S \Rightarrow \rangle$, for which E is in L and F is in K. Note that L is a proper subset of S: Since F is not a consequence of any U_i, and the U_i form a nondecreasing sequence, it cannot be a consequence of U (their union). Therefore F is not a member of U^* (i.e., L). So L and K are nonempty subsets of S, mutually disjoint, whose union is S. L is strongly closed (under "$\Rightarrow$"), so that T is a strong bisection. E is in L, since E is in U_0, and F is in K. [F is not a consequence of any U_i, so it cannot be a consequence of U – that is, it is not in L (U^*). So F is in K.] Finally, T is a normal bisection: If $(A \vee B)$ is in L, then either A is in L or B is in L (the converse always holds). Suppose now that $(A \vee B)$ is in L, but that A is not in L and B is not in L. Since A is not in L, A is not in any U_i. A is identical with some A_m of the enumeration. Therefore A_m is not in U_{m+1}. Consequently, U_{m+1} is not the union of U_m with $\{A_m\}$, so that $U_m \cup \{A_m\} \Rightarrow F$. Similarly, for B (which is A_n, for some n), $(U_n \cup \{A_n\}) \Rightarrow F$. Let r be the maximum of m and n. Then $U_r \cup \{A\} \Rightarrow F$, and $U_r \cup \{B\} \Rightarrow F$. Consequently, $U_r \cup \{(A \vee B)\} \Rightarrow F$. Since $(A \vee B)$ is a consequence of L, it is a consequence of some U_j. Let k be the maximum of r and j. Then F is a consequence of U_k together with $(A \vee B)$, and $(A \vee B)$ is a consequence of U_k. Therefore F is a consequence of U_k. But that is impossible. So $T = \langle K, L \rangle$ is a normal bisection.

Chapter 28

1. We do not wish to take sides on the question whether or not "O" is a modal operator. What we do want to say is that it will count as one if the two conditions are satisfied. In this case, if some A_i's imply B, then all the A_i's being obligatory will imply that it is obligatory that B, and there are A and B such that it is obligatory that $A \vee B$ does not imply that it is obligatory that A or that it is obligatory that B.

2. Even more serious is the doubt that $O(A), O(B) \Rightarrow O(A \,\&\, B)$ – that is, that O distributes over implication, for that would rule out obligation as a modal operator. See Chellas (1980, pp. 200–2).

3. This is the counterpart of what holds in modal systems that extend the modal system K – so that $\square$ distributes over conditionals: $\lozenge T$ (i.e., $\neg\square\neg T$) is a thesis if and only if $\square A \Rightarrow \lozenge A$ for all A (where T is a special member of

the system, called "truth"). This result was first noted, I believe, by Fitting (1983, p. 138). The exercise shows that the result is a special case for what holds if $\Diamond C$ is a thesis for any member of the system, not just for T.

4. In any modal system in which there are sentences of the form "$\Box A$," and conjunction, one can always form the sentence "$\Box A \ \& \ A$." The proof just given needs to be more elaborate because it has to be shown that the corresponding operator that assigns "$\Box A \ \& \ A$" to A is a modal operator. In particular, the operator φ associated with the box of the Gödel–Löb modal system satisfies the conditions of the theorem, and therefore the operator φ^* associated with the box of the Gregorcyzk–Solovay modal system G^* (in which "$\Box A$" has the intended meaning that A is provable in first-order Peano arithmetic, and is true) is also a modal operator.

5. There would seem to be a conflict between (2) and the claim that necessitation fails for C. I. Lewis's systems S_1. In that system, Lewis required that $\Box A_0$ be a thesis only when A_0 is a thesis of the propositional calculus (PC) (Hughes and Cresswell, 1968, p. 216). On our result, it is impossible to have φ of some thesis (say of the PC) be a thesis, but not have as well that φ of every thesis is a thesis. There is, in fact, no conflict. Lewis permits the distribution of $\Box$ over an implication only if the formulas involved belong to the PC; our first condition on modal operators permits distribution over all formulas (modalized as well as unmodalized formulas of PC).

6. Thus, the accessibility relation is defined for the implication relation and the modal on it. The history of these relations and their interpretation is not clear. See K. Segerberg's comments in Lemmon and Scott (1977, p. 25, fn. 16).

7. See Boolos (1979) for an elegant and lucid account of $(G\text{-}L)$'s properties and significance.

8. We continue the convention of Chapter 25, note 2, by referring to the box of the modal *system* $(G\text{-}L)$ as a $(G\text{-}L)$ modal and by referring to any modal that satisfies Definition 28.7 as a $G\text{-}L$ modal.

9. Of course, we know a good deal more about the structure $I_{G\text{-}L}$ with φ_G acting on it than we know if we are dealing only with some unspecified structure with a $G\text{-}L$-type modal on it. Think of the information that can be obtained from the syntax of $I_{G\text{-}L}$ by using, for example, the fact that every sentence of it has a finite number of subformulas. As far as I know, there is no counterpart, in a general setting, of the notion of a subformula, though it seems to me that it may be possible to frame one.

10. See Chellas (1980, p. 30) for a precise account of what is required.

Chapter 29

1. See Montague (1963) and Prior (1967).

2. See Hughes and Cresswell (1968, pp. 302–3) for an account of these Lemmon systems and the observation that the interpretation does not satisfy the systems studied (fn. 355).

3. Negation is, of course, always relativized to an implication relation. Here, "negation" refers to the negation operator N with respect to the implication relation "$\Rightarrow$" of I. The negation operator N_T with respect to "$\Rightarrow^T$" is

another matter. It is easy to lose sight of their difference because, in I^T, they are equivalent, i.e., $N(A) \Longleftrightarrow^T N_T(A)$ for all A in S. We leave the proof for the reader.

Chapter 30

1. (1) $N^\wedge N^\wedge$ distributes over "$\Longrightarrow$"" [the proof is similar to that of Theorem 30.3, using the dual $H^\wedge(A, B)$ of the hypothetical $H(A, B)$]. (2) $N^\wedge N^\wedge$ does not distribute over "$\Longrightarrow$^^" – which, under the conditions of the theorem, is just "$\Longrightarrow$" [note that if $N^\wedge N^\wedge(A)$, $N^\wedge N^\wedge(B) \Longrightarrow N^\wedge N^\wedge(A \& B)$ for all A and B, then $N^\wedge N^\wedge(A)$, $N^\wedge N^\wedge(B) \Longrightarrow A \& B$ (all A and B). Then $N^\wedge N^\wedge(B)$, $N^\wedge N^\wedge N(B)$ $\Longrightarrow B \& N(B) \Longrightarrow C$ (all C). Therefore, for all B, $N^\wedge N^\wedge N(B) \Longrightarrow NN^\wedge N^\wedge(B)$. But that is impossible, by Theorem 17.9, for then negation would be classical.].

2. There is some reason to think that the answer will not be easy. Lopez-Escobar (1981) has given an interesting argument to show that the dual of the intuitionistic conditional ("$\underline{\ \ }$") may not be intuitionistic. The reason is that when "$\underline{\ \ }$" and appropriate axioms or rules are added to the Heyting formulation of ISC (HSC) to obtain the Heyting–Brouwer sentential calculus H-BSC, the result is a conservative extension of the former: Roughly, no statement that is formulatable in the language of HSC is provable in H-BSC without also being provable in HSC in the first place. That is some reason for thinking that the dual of the conditional is an intuitionistic connective. However, when the Heyting formulation of the intuitionistic predicate calculus (IPC) is extended in a parallel way to yield H-BPC, the extension is not conservative with respect to HPC. That is some reason to think that the dual of the conditional is not an intuitionistic connective after all. These results have a bearing on the question whether or not the dual of intuitionistic negation is itself an intuitionistic connective, because of the interdefinability in H-BPC of the dual of negation and the dual of the conditional. Thus, there is also the question whether or not a connective corresponding to the dual of intuitionistic negation is also intuitionistic.

    Nevertheless, even if it should turn out that $N^\wedge$ is not an intuitionistic operator, even though N is, that would not affect the result that NN is a modal operator on any nonclassical structure (subject to the conditions in Theorem 30.3) and therefore on the implication structure I_{ISC} (which satisfies the conditions of that theorem) in particular.

Chapter 31

1. Care must be taken in listing the truths of quantification. For example, in some formulations of the predicate calculus, it is not true that $\forall x(Px)$ implies Px, since in those formulations no open sentence is allowed to be an intermediate step or conclusion in any proof. Thus, no open sentence is ever a theorem in those formulations.

2. Sometimes, however, there need be no forcing at all. There is ample historical evidence to indicate that when what is quantified is an item that has a temporal index, then various quantifications with respect to that index often have been thought of as necessities, possibilities, and contingencies.

3. The distinction between $(\varphi(P))(s)$ and $\varphi(P(s))$ is, I believe, closely connected to a suggestion in Hughes and Cresswell (1968, fn. 131).
4. This result does not conflict with the result due to S. Kripke, that for a certain modal predicate calculus, CBF fails to be a theorem. The reason is that the particular basis for quantification theory that is used in Kripke's formulation of classical predicate calculus (CPC) does not permit open sentences to be theorems. In the corresponding extended implication structure, therefore, certain predicates (functions) corresponding to an open sentence like "$Px \lor \neg Px$" would not count as a thesis. However, the implication relation "$\Rightarrow$*" that was used in the preceding theorem does count the corresponding predicate "$P \lor \neg P$" as a thesis, since $Q \Rightarrow^* P(s) \lor \neg P(s)$ (for all s in E^*). Thus, the implication structure that was used in the preceding theorem corresponds to the formulation of CPC in which open sentences can count as theorems, since the type of implication relation that it uses ("$\Rightarrow$*") allows that if $\forall (P)$ is a thesis, then so too is P. To describe what happens to CBF in implication structures that are associated with systems of quantification that do not permit open sentences as theorems, a different implication relation on the structure is needed.
5. See Hughes and Cresswell (1968, p. 180).
6. See Heyting (1956, p. 104).

Chapter 32

1. See Kuratowski (1966).
2. For a general account of this and related matters, see Rasiowa and Sikorski (1970, pp. 477ff.), as well as Appendix A by A. Mostowski in Kuratowski (1966), and see Mostowski (1966a, b) for reference to the early work of Tarski, McKinsey, and others.
2. Let $I = \langle S, \Rightarrow \rangle$ be an implication structure for which A and B are nonequivalent members of S such that $(A \lor B)$ is not a thesis of I. Let $X = \{A\}$ and $Y = \{B\}$. Then $Cn(X) \cap Cn(Y)$ is not a subset of $Cn(X \cap Y)$, for $Cn(X \cap Y)$ is the set of theses of I (we assume that I has some). Moreover, since $(A \lor B)$ is a consequence of X as well as Y, it is in the intersection of $Cn(X)$ and $Cn(Y)$. However, it is not in $Cn(X \cap Y)$, since $(A \lor B)$ is not a thesis.
4. See the discussion of P. Hertz's program (Section 2.1). Hertz's work was the basis for Gentzen's notion of the structural rules for implication relations. Gentzen's version of Cut was intended to replace Hertz's version, which the latter called the "Syllogism" and which required as a generalization of transitivity that if $X_1, \ldots, X_n \Rightarrow Y_i$ (1 to m), and $Y_1, \ldots, Y_m \Rightarrow Z$, then $X_1, \ldots, X_n \Rightarrow Z$.
5. In fact, in Part II, we have already considered, in passing, a variant on implication relations, *component implication*, which is also nonmonotonic. Once Dilution and Cut are dropped or weakened, it is no longer clear what the status is for certain implications like $Q \Rightarrow (P \to Q)$, Exportation, Importation, and Transitivity, for the proofs of such features seem to depend upon Dilution and Cut.

6. Of course, there are ways of thinking about theories other than as closed sets. One way would be to identify a theory with the set of its axioms, rather than with the full set of axioms and its consequences. Another way, if the theory is finitely axiomatizable, is to take the theory as just the conjunction of its axioms. In this case the conjunction of theories would have to be taken as $(A \& B)$. There are serious problems about the identity of theories in any case. Each account has its points and its problems.

Chapter 33

1. The earliest source familiar to me for taking "K" as an epistemic operator, rather than as a connective, is Hintikka (1962).
2. This is not to be confused with the claim that K is a necessitation operator: that $K(T)$ is a thesis, if T is one.
3. See Hintikka (1962) for a description and discussion of a variety of epistemic and virtual implication relations. According to the latter, A and B (virtually) imply C if and only if the set consisting of A, B, and $\neg C$ is inconsistent in the sense that its members cannot belong to any member of the model system that Hintikka develops. It seems to follow that if $A_1, \ldots,$ A_n virtually imply B, then $K(A_1), \ldots, K(A_n)$ virtually imply $K(B)$. Thus, the first condition holds if the implication is virtual.
4. See Hintikka (1962) for a defense of the KK thesis.
5. Feferman (1984, pp. 75–111).
6. Etchemendy (1988).
7. As noted by Tarski about his own theory, as a possible shortcoming (Corcoran, 1983, pp. 257–62).
8. The locus classicus is, of course, Tarski (Corcoran, 1983, essay VIII).
9. Not everyone agrees on this. Bas van Fraassen (1969) employs a notion of semantic entailment ("⊩") defined with the aid of supervaluations. Thus, something that looks like the Tarski equivalence is adopted by van Fraassen [$A⊩T(A)$ and $T(A)⊩A$], while the equivalence of LEM with PB fails. This is for the reason that in van Fraassen's system LEM is valid, but PB is not. However, this sort of comparison is misleading. The logical system one obtains using van Fraassen's semantic entailment is substantially weaker than standard logic. For example, there is no deduction theorem, conditionals do not imply their contrapositives, and the rule that from $A⊩C$ and $B⊩C$ one can infer $(A \lor B) ⊩C$ fails. I do not think that much of the standard theory remains, and that would call into question some elementary things: Is LEM, with its use of disjunction, the same principle for Tarski as for van Fraassen? Given the failure of the elementary rule that disjunction usually satisfies, but that is rejected by him, it seems doubtful. Again, given the failure of the deduction theorem for "⊩," is it plausible to think of the equivalence of A with $T(A)$ as even close to the Tarski condition? Given the failure of a conditional to imply its contrapositive (even intuitionism keeps that much), it seems to us that the conditional in his system is not quite what we usually take it to be.
10. Bas van Fraassen (1971) seems to accept it, and probably Michael Dummett

(1978) as well, though in Dummett's case, the texts are not determinate on this point.

11. If the elements of S were the sentences of some formal language, then "involvement" would be easily expressed by requiring that there be no occurrence of "$T(B)$" in A, for any B, thus allowing that there could be an occurrence of "$T(B)$" that would not be an occurrence of "B." If there is no syntax to fall back on, as is generally the case for structures, the formulation of an appropriate notion of involvement becomes more complicated.

The idea that A involves $T(B)$ in its construction can be sharpened this way: First define the notion of "$T(B)$" being *ingredient* in A. Let $R^1[T(B)]$ be the set that includes the negation of $T(B)$, any disjunction of $T(B)$ with any member of the structure, any conjunction of $T(B)$ with any member of the structure, and any hypothetical with $T(B)$ as either antecedent or consequent. Let $R^2[T(B)]$ be the union of all $R^1[A]$ for all A in $R^1[T(B)]$, and let $R^{n+1}[T(B)]$ be the union of all $R^1[A]$ for all A in $R^n[T(B)]$. Finally, let $R[T(B)]$ be the union of all $R^i[T(B)]$, $i = 1, 2, \ldots$. We shall then say that (1) $T(B)$ is *ingredient in* A if and only if A is equivalent to some member of $R[T(B)]$, and (2) $T(B)$ is *involved in the construction of* A if and only if $T(B)$ <⊧> B and $T(B)$ is ingredient in A. The proof of Theorem 33.2 is now blocked. For either $T(A)$ is equivalent to A, in which case CON* holds, because A & $\neg T(A)$ implies all C, or else $T(A)$ <⊧> A. However, since $T(A)$ is ingredient in A & $\neg T(A)$, then $T(A)$ is involved in A & $\neg T(A)$, and CON* is not applicable.

Note that if the truth operator were Tarskian, then no $T(B)$ would be involved in any A, so that CON* would hold for every member. The three conditions, together with CON*, are compatible with truth being Tarskian; they do not ensure that it is.

Chapter 35

1. See Kripke (1980, pp. 15–20) on the uses of sample spaces in probability theory, as well as Stalnaker (1984, ch. 3).

2. For convenience, recall that if for all theories, U, if A is in U then B is in U, then $A \Rightarrow B$. Just consider the theory U^* that is the set of all C's that are implied by A. Since A is in U^*, so too is B. Therefore A implies B.

3. This is essentially because theories are here used in a weak sense. All that is required is that if $A \Rightarrow B$ for some A in U, then B is in U. If theories are used in a stronger sense (as in the next chapter for models), so that if there are multiple antecedents $A_1, \ldots, A_n$ that imply B, and all the A_i's are in U, then so too is B, then in this strong sense of closure, if U is a theory and φ is a modal whose dual is σ, then $\varphi^{-1}U$ will, in general, be a theory in this strong sense, but $\sigma^{-1}U$ will not.

4. Chellas (1980, p. 81).

5. Indeed, Tarski and Jónsson (1951–2) showed that for any Boolean algebra $\langle B \cap, 0, U \rangle$, where B is a set field and U is the universal set of B, then when A is the set of all subsets of U, the normal and completely additive functions on A to A can be represented by relations R on U such that, for example, $X \subseteq F(X)$ (all X in A) holds if and only if R is reflexive, $FF(X) \subseteq F(X)$ (all X

in A) holds if and only if R is transitive, F is self-conjugate if and only if R is symmetric, and so forth. Similar results hold for normal, additive functions of B to itself. By taking the theories of an implication structure as the members of B, and by taking the complement $-V$ of any theory V as the smallest theory whose intersection with V is the set of theses of the structure, we can think of B as a set field. The functions φ^{-1} are normal and additive, so that we see in this algebraic setting the possibility of representing modal laws by relations on B, the set of theories.

I am indebted to E. Mendelson for calling my attention to these results of Tarski and Jónsson (1951–2). See Lemmon and Scott (1977, p. 25) for an important note by K. Segerberg on possible precursors for the use of possible worlds for semantic theory.

6. See Boolos (1979) for a proof that the accessibility relation for Gödel–Löb modals is not the canonical accessibility relation. The construction of an accessibility relation that does work was originally due to Segerberg (1971); a simpler proof has been provided by Boolos (1979), and a still more stream-lined proof is given by Boolos and Jeffrey (1989).

7. More precisely, in the case of the modal system $(G\text{-}L)$, it can be shown (see note 6) that there is a frame $\langle W, R \rangle$ such that $\Box(\Box A \to A) \to \Box A$ is a theorem if and only if it is valid in all models based upon the frame $\langle W, R \rangle$, where W is a set of possible worlds, and R is a binary relation on W that is "well-capped" – that is, there is no infinite sequence of worlds $w_1, w_2, \ldots$ such that $w_1 R w_2 R w_3 \ldots$, or, equivalently, every nonempty set S of possible worlds has a member that does not bear R to any member of S.

[handwritten margin note: very strange comment: $\Box(\Box A \to A) \to \Box A$ is ALWAYS a theorem of GL]

Chapter 36

1. The condition of being a full set of models corresponds to the result proved by Boolos (1979) for models of modal systems – that there is a one-to-one correspondence between the subsets of the set of possible worlds W and the evaluators P of the model (functions that assign truth values to the atomic sentences for each world in W). Models in that sense are given by $\langle W, R, P \rangle$. We use (essentially $\langle T, R, f \rangle$ for our models, since, in general, we may not have atomic sentences, or indeed any sentences, available in an implication structure. The conditions on the functions f do the work of evaluators when syntactic structure is available.

2. The resemblance, for example, between the condition that $(V)(URV \to V \in T^*) \to U \in T^*$, as used above, and the similar condition used by Boolos (1979, p. 79) is clear. The only difference is in what the $U, V, \ldots$ and T^* range over. Standardly, $U, V, \ldots$ range over members of the set W of possible worlds, and T^* is an arbitrary subset of W. Here, $U, V, \ldots$ range over the members of the set T of theories of I, and T^* is an arbitrary subset of T.

Chapter 37

1. Chellas (1980, p. 269) discusses a certain conditional that he describes as failing to satisfy modus ponens.

2. It is worth noting, and straightforward to prove, that if an operator is nonmonotonic, failing to distribute over implication, then either it is not a necessitation operator or it fails to distribute over hypotheticals.
3. Chellas (1980, pp. 231–4).
4. Thus, modals in our sense include some operators that are nonnormal, since some of them are not necessitations, though, of course, they do distribute over hypotheticals. We follow the usage of Boolos (1979) without requiring a rule of substitution. Segerberg (1971) requires necessitation and distribution over conjunctions for normal modals, and Chellas (1980) uses a rule that requires both necessitation and distribution over hypotheticals.

   It is worth noting that if an operator fails to distribute over implication, then either it is nonmonotonic or it fails to distribute over hypotheticals. By the result noted in note 2, nonmonotonic operators are nonnormal. It follows that any operator that fails to distribute over implication will also fail to be normal. Segerberg (1971), Chellas (1980), and Fitting (1983) are good sources for studying the nonnormal operators.
5. What makes it relatively easy to lose track of the different implication relations on the same set, in the examples given, is the fact that the hypothetical relative to "$\Rightarrow$" and the hypothetical relative to "$\Rightarrow^C$" are equivalent (under "$\Rightarrow^C$"). The same holds for all the logical operators, relativized and unrelativized.

Bibliography

Ackermann, W. 1956. "Begründung einer strengen Implikation," *Journal of Symbolic Logic*, 21:113–28.

Adams, E. 1975. *The Logic of Conditionals: An Application of Probability to Deductive Logic*. Dordrecht: Reidel.

Anderson, A. R., and Belnap, N. D., Jr. 1975. *Entailment, the Logic of Relevance and Necessity*. Princeton University Press.

Barwise, J., ed. 1977. *Handbook of Mathematical Logic*. Amsterdam: North Holland.

Belnap, N. D., Jr., 1962. "Tonk, Plonk and Plink." *Analysis*, 22(6):130–4.

Belnap, N. D., Jr., and Steel, T. B., Jr., 1976. *The Logic of Questions and Answers*. New Haven: Yale University Press.

Boolos, G. S. 1979. *The Unprovability of Consistency, an Essay in Modal Logic*. Cambridge University Press.

Boolos, G. S., and Jeffrey, R. C. 1989. *Computability and Logic*, 3rd ed. Cambridge University Press.

Chellas, B. F. 1980. *Modal Logic: An Introduction*. Cambridge University Press.

Church, A. 1951. "The Weak Theory of Implication," in *Kontrolliertes Denken, Untersuchungen zum Logikkalkül und der Logik der Einzelwissenschaften*, Menne-Wilhelmy-Angsil (ed.), pp. 22–37. Munich: Komissions-verlag Karl Alber.

1956. *Introduction to Mathematical Logic, Vol. I*, Princeton University Press.

Corcoran, J., ed. 1983. *Logic, Semantics, Mathematics: Papers from 1923 to 1938 by A. Tarski*, 2nd ed., J. H. Woodger (tr.). Indianapolis: Hackett.

Dummett, M. 1975. "The Philosophical Basis of Intuitionistic Logic," in *Logic Colloquium, Bristol, July 1973*, H. E. Rose and J. C. Shepherdson (eds.), pp. 5–40; reprinted (1978) in *Truth and Other Enigmas*, pp. 215–47. London: Duckworth; reprinted (1983) in *Philosophy of Mathematics*, 2nd ed., P. Benacerraf and H. Putnam (eds.), pp. 97–129. Cambridge University Press.

1977. *Elements of Intuitionism*. Oxford University Press.

Enderton, H. B. 1972. *A Mathematical Introduction to Logic*. New York: Academic Press.

1977. *Elements of Set Theory*. New York: Academic Press.

1972. *A Mathematical Introduction to Logic*. New York: Academic Press.

Etchemendy, J. 1988. "Tarski on Truth and Logical Consequence." *Journal of Symbolic Logic*, 53:51–79.

Feferman, S. 1984. "Toward Useful Type-Free Theories, I." *Journal of Symbolic Logic*, 49:75–111 (submitted 1982); reprinted (1984) in *Recent Essays on Truth and the Liar Paradox*, R. L. Martin (ed.), pp. 237–87. Oxford University Press.

Fitting, M. 1983. *Proof Methods for Modal and Intuitionistic Logics*. Dordrecht: Reidel.

Gabbay, D. M. 1981. *Semantical Investigations in Heyting's Intuitionistic Logic*. Dordrecht: Reidel.

Geach, P. T. 1981. *Logic Matters*. Oxford: Blackwell.

Gentzen, G. 1933. "Ueber die Existenz unabhängiger Axiomensysteme zu unendlichen Satzssystemen," *Mathematische Annalen*, 107:329–50; reprinted (1969) as "On the Existence of Independent Axiom Systems for Infinite Sentence Systems." in *The Collected Papers of Gerhard Gentzen*, M. E. Szabo (ed.), pp. 29–52. Amsterdam: North Holland.

⎯⎯⎯ 1934. "Untersuchungen über das logische Schliessen," *Mathematische Zeitschrift*, 39:176–210, 405–31; reprinted (1969) as "Investigations into Logical Deduction," in *The Collected Papers of Gerhard Gentzen*, M. E. Szabo (ed.), pp. 68–131. Amsterdam: North Holland.

Gödel, K. 1933. "Eine Interpretation des intuitionistischen Aussagen Kalküls." *Ergebnisse eines Mathematischen Kolloquiums* 4:39–40; English translation (1969) in *The Philosophy of Mathematics*, J. Hintikka (ed.). Oxford University Press.

Goodman, N. 1966. *The Structure of Appearance*, 2nd ed. Indianapolis: Bobbs-Merrill.

Grice, H. P. 1989. *Studies in the Way of Words. Part I: Logic and Conversation*. Cambridge: Harvard University Press.

Haack, S. 1974. *Deviant Logic: Some Philosophical Issues*. Cambridge University Press.

Hacking, I. 1979. "What Is Logic?" *Journal of Philosophy*, 76:285–319.

Halmos, P. R. 1962. *Algebraic Logic*. New York: Chelsea.

Harman, G. 1975. *If and Modus Ponens*, pp. 1–12. Bloomington: Indiana University Linguistics Publications.

Hellman, G. 1969. "Finitude, Infinitude, and Isomorphism of Interpretations in some Nominalistic Calculi." *Nous*, 3:413–25.

Hertz, P. 1922. "Ueber Axiomensysteme für beliebige Satzsysteme. I. *Mathematische Annalen*, 87:246–69.

⎯⎯⎯ 1923. "Ueber Axiomensysteme für beliebige Satzsysteme. II. *Mathematische Annalen*, 89:76–102.

⎯⎯⎯ 1929. "Ueber Axiomensysteme für beliebige Satzsysteme." *Mathematische Annalen*, 101:457–514.

Heyting, A. 1956. *Intuitionism: An Introduction*. Amsterdam: North Holland.

Hintikka, J. 1962. *Knowledge and Belief*. Ithaca: Cornell University Press.

Hughes, G. E., and Cresswell, M. J. 1968. *An Introduction to Modal Logic*. London: Methuen.

Johnson, W. E. 1964. *Logic*, 3 vols. New York: Dover; originally published (1921–4), Cambridge University Press.

Katz, J. J. 1977. *Propositional Structure and Illocutionary Force*. New York: Crowell.

Kleene, S. C. 1952. *Introduction to Metamathematics*. New York: Van Nostrand.

Kneale, W., and Kneale, M. 1962. *The Development of Logic*. Oxford University Press.

Kripke, S. 1963a. "Semantical Considerations on Modal Logic." *Acta Philosophica Fennica*, 16:83–94.

⎯⎯⎯ 1963b. "Semantical Analysis of Modal Logic. I. Normal Modal Propositional Calculi." *Zeitschrift für mathematische Logik und Grundlagen der Mathematik*, 9:67–96.

⎯⎯⎯ 1965. "Semantical Analysis of Modal Logic. II. Non-normal Modal Propositional Calculi." in *The Theory of Models*. J. W. Addison, L. Henkin, and A. Tarski (eds.), pp. 206–20. Amsterdam: North Holland.

1980. *Naming and Necessity*. Cambridge: Harvard University Press.

Kuratowski, K. 1966. *Topology, Vol. I*, New York: Academic Press; translated from French (1958), *Topologie Vol. I*, Warsaw: PWN (Polish Scientific Publishers).

Lemmon, E. J. 1959. "Is There Only One Correct System of Modal Logic?" *Proceedings of the Aristotelian Society (Supplement 23)*, pp. 23–40.

Lemmon, E. J., and Scott, D. 1977. *The Lemmon Notes: An Introduction to Modal Logic*, American Philosophical Quarterly Monograph Series, No. 11, K. Segerberg (ed.). Oxford: Blackwell.

Leonard, H. 1940. "The Calculus of Individuals and Its Uses." *Journal of Symbolic Logic*, 5:45–55.

Lewis, C. I., and Langford, C. H. 1959. *Symbolic Logic*. New York: Dover; Reprint of original edition (1932), with the addition of Appendix III by C. I. Lewis.

Lewis, D. 1973. *Counterfactuals*. Cambridge: Harvard University Press.

Lewis, D., and Hodges, W. 1968. "Finitude and Infinitude in the Atomic Calculus of Individuals." *Nous*, 2:405–10.

Lopez-Escobar, E. G. K. 1981. "Intuitionistic Connectives." Unpublished manuscript.

McGee, V. 1985. "A Counterexample to Modus Ponens," *Journal of Philosophy*, 462–71

Martin, R. L. 1984. *Recent Essays on Truth and the Liar Paradox*. Oxford University Press.

Mendelson, E. 1987. *Introduction to Mathematical Logic*, 3rd ed. Monterey: Brooks/Cole.

Montague, R. 1963. "Syntactical Treatments of Modality with Corollaries on Reflection Principles and Finite Axiomatizability." *Acta Philosophica Fennica*, 16:153–67; reprinted (1974) in *Formal Philosophy: Selected Papers of R. Montague*, R. H. Thomason, (ed.). New Haven: Yale University Press.

Mostowski, A. 1979. "On a Generalization of Quantifiers," in Mostowski, *Foundational Studies, Selected Works, Vol. II*. Amsterdam: North Holland.

1966a. *Thirty Years of Foundational Studies*. Oxford: Blackwell.

1966b. "Some Applications of Topology to Mathematical Logic," Appendix A in K. Kuratowski, *Topology, Vol. I*. New York: Academic Press.

Peacocke, C. 1976. "What Is a Logical Constant?" *Journal of Philosophy*, 73:221–40.

1981. "Hacking on Logic: Two Comments." *Journal of Philosophy*, 78:168–75.

Prawitz, D. 1965. *Natural Deduction*. Uppsala: Almqvist & Wiksell.

1977. "Meaning and Proofs: On the Conflict between Classical and Intuitionistic Logic." *Theoria*, 43(Part 1):2–40.

1980. "Intuitionistic Logic: A Philosophical Challenge," in *Logic and Philosophy*, G. H. von Wright (ed.), pp. 1–10. The Hague: Nijhoff.

Prior, A. N. 1960. "The Runabout Inference-Ticket." *Analysis*, 21(2):38–9.

1964. "Conjunction and Contonktion Revisited." *Analysis*, 24(6):191–5.

1967. "Modal Logic," in *The Encyclopedia of Philosophy*, Vol. 5–6, P. Edwards (ed.), pp. 5–12. New York: Macmillan.

Prior, A. N., and Prior, M. 1955. "Erotetic Logic." *Philosophical Review*, 64:43–59.

Rasiowa, H., and Sikorski, R. 1970. *The Mathematics of Metamathematics*, 3rd ed. revised Warsaw: PWN (Polish Scientific Publishers).

Scott, D. 1971. "On Engendering an Illusion of Understanding." *Journal of Philosophy*, 68:787–807.

——— 1974. "Completeness and Axiomatizability in Many-Valued Logic." in *Proceedings of the Tarski Symposium*, L. Henkin et al. (eds.), pp. 411–35. Providence: American Mathematical Society.

Segerberg, K. 1971. *An Essay in Classical Modal Logic*, 3 vols. Uppsala: Filosofiska Studier Nr. 13.

——— 1982. *Classical Propositional Operators, an Exercise in the Foundations of Logic*. Oxford: Clarendon Press.

Shoesmith, D. J., and Smiley, T. J. 1978. *Multiple-conclusion Logic*. Cambridge University Press.

Smorynski, C. 1977. "The Incompleteness Theorems." in *Handbook of Mathematical Logic*, J. Barwise (ed.), pp. 821–65. Amsterdam: North Holland.

Stalnaker, R. C. 1984. *Inquiry*. Cambridge: MIT Press.

Takeuti, G. 1975. *Proof Theory*. Amsterdam: North Holland.

Tarski, A. 1933. "The Concept of Truth in Formalized Languages," in *Logic, Semantics, Mathematics: Papers from 1923 to 1938 by A. Tarski*, J. Corcoran (ed.), pp. 152–278 (Essay VIII). Indianapolis: Hackett. This is a translation of "Der Wahrheitsbegriff in den formalisierten Sprachen," *Studia Philosophica*, 1(1935):261–405. It is a translation of the original Polish "Projęcie prawdy w językach nauk dedukcyjnych. Prace Towarzystwa Naukowego Warszawskiego, Wydzial III matematyczno-fizycznych," N. 34, Warsaw 1933.

——— 1935. "Foundations of the Calculus of Systems," in *Logic, Semantics, Mathematics: Papers from 1923 to 1938 by A. Tarski*, J. Corcoran (ed.), pp. 343–83 (Essay XII). Indianapolis: Hackett. Originally appeared in two parts as "Grundzüge des Systemenkalkül, Erster Teil," *Fundamenta Mathematicae*, 25(1935):503–26, and "Grundzüge des Systemenkalkül, Zweiter Teil," ibid., 26(1936):283–301.

——— 1937. "Appendix," in J. H. Woodger, *Axiomatic Method in Biology*. Cambridge University Press.

——— 1938. "Sentential Calculus and Topology," in *Logic, Semantics, Mathematics: Papers from 1923 to 1938 by A. Tarski*, J. Corcoran (ed.), pp. 421–54 (Essay XVII). Indianapolis: Hackett. Originally published as "Der Aussagenkalkül und die Topologie," *Fundamenta Mathematicae*, 31(1938): 103–34.

Tarski, A., and Jónsson, B. 1951–2. "Boolean Algebras with Operators. I and II." *American Journal of Mathematics*, 73:891–939; 74:127–62.

Tarski, A., and McKinsey, J. C. C. 1948. "Some Theorems about the Sentential Calculi of Lewis and Heyting." *Journal of Symbolic Logic*, 13:1–15.

van Fraassen, B. 1969. "Presuppositions, Supervaluations, and Free Logic," in *The Logical Way of Doing Things*, K. Lambert (ed.), pp. 67–91. New Haven: Yale University Press.

——— 1971. *Formal Semantics and Logic*. New York: Macmillan.

von Wright, G. H. 1951. *An Essay in Modal Logic*. Amsterdam: North Holland.

Zucker, J. I., and Tragesser, R. S. 1978. "The Adequacy Problem for Inferential Logic." *Journal of Philosophical Logic*, 7:501–16.

Index

elimination rules, 14 ff
  and the existence of operators, 16 ff
  and meaning, 18
Enderton, H. B., 151n1
equivalence relation, 5
Etchemendy, J., 330n6
exjunction, 121
  antitransitivity, 123, 132
  and disjunction, 124–5
  existence, 121–1
  stability, 125–6
expansion, 134
extended implication structure, 181 ff
extensionality, 158 ff

Feferman, S., 249n2, 291–2, 329, 329n5
f-counterpart, 231–2
filter condition
  on modals, 342
  on operators, 16
Fitting, M., 266n2, 368n4
fixed point, 329
frame, 360

Gabbay, D. M., 13n2, 43n3
Geach, P. T., 8n6
Gentzen, G., 6, 6n3, 12 ff, 17n6–7, 19n1,
  37n4
  sentences*, 13
Goodman, N., 57, 57n5, 58n7, 87n6, 210
Grice, H. P., 112–13, 87n6, 88n7

Halmos, P. R., 181n1, 182n2
Harman, G., 78
Hellman, G., 57n5
Hertz, P., 3n3, 12 ff, 17n7, 19n1, 37n3–4,
  324n4
Heyting, A., 316n6
Hintikka, J., 327n1, 328n3–4
Hodges, W., 57n5
homomorphic stability, 10n8
Hughes, G. E. and Creswell, M. J.,
  269n5, 297, 316n5
hypotheticals, 77–8
  closure under, 85
  contraposition, 131
  in English, 87 ff
  existence, 80
  exportation, 130–1
  extensionality, 172
  first-order, 80, 89
  homomorphic stability, 86
  interchange, 130
  of interrogatives, 226–7
  material, 79–80
  nonextensionality, 177
  nonsyntactic, nonsemantic, 82
  parameterization, 128

purity, 83
stability, 84–5
subjunctive, 79
symmetric, 152n2
transitivity, 131
uniqueness, 82

ideal conditions on modals, 342
identity, 203
  and logical operators, 202
  and Leibniz principle, 206–7
  reflexivity, symmetry, and transitivity,
  204
implication relation, 5
  abstract, 13n2
  bisection, 45 ff
  conditions for, 35 ff
  conservative extensions of, 28, 50
  components of, 67, 324n5
  deducicibility, 42 ff
  dual of, 60 ff
  extensions of, 28
  extensions to double duals, 65
  fixed, 59
  and inference, 9n7
  logical consequence, 42 ff
  material, 49n2
  minimal, 41
  nominal, 216
  objectual, 56, 57n4, 211
  on predicates, 182–3
  projective, 45
  relational, 5n2, 36 ff
  Rockefeller, 71
  on sets, 53 ff
  and syntactic completeness, 51
  on Tarskian theories, 55
  variable, 59
implication structure, 5
  almost trivial, 63
  and completeness, 52
  classical, 91
  components of, 68
  conservative extension of, 28, 150
  extension of, 28
  homomorphic conservative extension of,
  86
  trivial, 10
implicit definition, 24n4
importation, 134
individuals, 57
  calculus of, 57
  whole–part relation, 58
introduction conditions, 22 ff
  as definitions, 23
introduction rules, 14 ff, 15n4
  and existence of operators, 16 ff
  and meaning, 18

418 INDEX